P9-AGH-630

CORRELATION OF INTASC STANDARDS WITH CHAPTER OBJECTIVES (CON'T)

INTASC Standard	Description of Teacher Performance	Chapter Objective	Description of Teacher Performance
Principle 5	Creates a learning environment that encourages positive social interaction, active engagement in learning, and self-motivation	Ch. 3 (Obj. 1–3)	Develops planning skills
		Ch. 4 (Obj. 1–7)	Uses strategies to engage students in learning
		Ch. 5 (Obj. 1–5)	Uses effective questioning strategies
		Ch. 6 (Obj. 1–6)	Implements strategies for differentiating instruction
		Ch. 7 (Obj. 1–2, 4)	Understands and uses culturally responsive teaching strategies
		Ch. 8 (Obj. 1–3)	Implements effective classroom management strategies
		Ch. 9 (Obj. 2–7)	Uses cooperative learning strategies
Principle 6	Uses knowledge of communication techniques to foster active inquiry, collaboration, and supportive interaction.	Ch. 4 (Obj. 1–7)	Implements strategies for involving students in learning
		Ch. 5 (Obj. 1–5)	Uses effective questioning strategies
		Ch. 6 (Obj. 3–4)	Implements strategies for responsive instruction
		Ch. 7 (Obj. 3)	Uses strategies to make teaching more culturally responsive
		Ch. 9 (Obj. 1–7)	Uses cooperative learning strategies
Principle 7	Plans instruction based on knowledge of subject matter, students, the community, and curriculum goals	Ch. 2 (Obj. 1–3)	Write and uses instructional objectives
		Ch. 3 (Obj. 1–3)	Identifies key characteristics of effective planning
		Ch. 5 (Obj. 1–5)	Asks questions related to content
		Ch. 6 (Obj. 4–6)	Differentiates instruction based on student readiness, interest, and learning profile
		Ch. 7 (Obj. 1–4)	Uses strategies to make teaching more culturally responsive

(continued)

CORRELATION OF INTASC STANDARDS WITH CHAPTER OBJECTIVES (CON'T)

INTASC Standard	Description of Teacher Performance	Chapter Objective	Description of Teacher Performance
Principle 8	Understands and uses formal and informal assessment strategies	Ch. 3 (Obj. 3)	Incorporates assessment as part of the planning process
		Ch. 4 (Obj. 6–7)	Implements strategies for ending lessons effectively
		Ch. 5 (Obj. 1–5)	Implements questioning strategies to assess student learning
		Ch. 6 (Obj. 3–4)	Develops understanding of student needs through informal assessment strategies
		Ch. 9 (Obj. 3–7)	Assesses student mastery through cooperative learning activities
		Ch. 10 (Obj. 1–8)	Implements effective assessment strategies
Principle 9	Reflects on teaching	Ch. 1 (Obj. 1–4)	Identifies the teacher as a reflective decision maker
		Ch. 3 (Obj. 2–3)	Revises planning based on feedback
		Ch. 6 (Obj. 5–6)	Reflects on how to make students active learners
		Ch. 7 (Obj. 1–5)	Reflects on how to make classrooms culturally responsive
		Ch. 8 (Obj. 3)	Reflects on how to improve classroom management tasks and decisions
		Ch. 10 (Obj. 1–8)	Uses a variety of ways to collect information to form judgments in order to make teaching decisions
Principle 10	Fosters relationships with colleagues, parents, and agencies in the larger community	Ch. 3 (Obj. 2–3)	Use colleagues and community members as part of planning
		Ch. 6 (Obj. 6)	Works with and seeks advice from colleagues in solving particular situations
		Ch. 7 (Obj. 5)	Connects with community to understand better students' cultures
		Ch. 8 (Obj. 3)	Establishes productive relationships with parents
		Ch. 9 (Obj. 6–7)	Gains support for cooperative learning strategies from colleagues, administrators, and parents

Classroom Teaching Skills

Gift of
Pam Root
March 2014

WITHDRAWN
From Heritage University Library

Heritage University Library
3240 Fort Road
Toppenish, WA 98948

Classroom Teaching Skills

NINTH EDITION

JAMES M. COOPER *General Editor*
Professor Emeritus, University of Virginia

Jason G. Irizarry
Assistant Professor, University of Connecticut

Mary S. Leighton
Network Charter School, Eugene, Oregon

Greta G. Morine-Dershimer
Professor Emerita, University of Virginia

David Sadker
Professor Emeritus, The American University

Myra Sadker
The American University

Robert Shostak
Florida International University

Terry D. TenBrink
Kirksville College of Osteopathic Medicine

Carol Ann Tomlinson
University of Virginia

Wilford A. Weber
University of Houston

Carol S. Weinstein
Professor Emerita, Rutgers University

Karen R. Zittleman
Educational Consultant and Author

WADSWORTH
CENGAGE Learning

Australia • Brazil • Japan • Korea • Mexico • Singapore • Spain • United Kingdom • United States

Classroom Teaching Skills, Ninth Edition
James M. Cooper, Jason G. Irizarry,
Mary S. Leighton, Greta G. Morine-Dershimer,
David Sadker, Myra Sadker, Robert Shostak,
Terry D. TenBrink, Carol Ann Tomlinson,
Wilford A. Weber, Carol S. Weinstein,
Karen R. Zittleman

Senior Publisher: Linda Schreiber-Ganster

Assistant Editor: Caitlin Cox

Editorial Assistant: Linda Stewart

Associate Media Editor: Ashley Cronin

Marketing Manager: Kara Kindstrom

Executive Advertising Project Manager:
Brian Chaffee

Marketing Communications Manager:
Martha Pfeiffer

Content Project Management: Pre-PressPMG

Creative Director: Rob Hugel

Art Director: Maria Epes

Print Buyer: Rebecca Cross

Rights Acquisitions Account Manager, Text: Bob
Kauser

Rights Acquisitions Account Manager, Image:
Leitha Etheridge-Sims

Production Service: Pre-PressPMG

Photo Researcher: Pre-PressPMG

Copy Editor: Daniel Nighting

Cover Designer: Gia Giasullo

Cover Image: Illustration Works

Compositor: Pre-PressPMG

© 2011, 2006 Wadsworth, Cengage Learning

ALL RIGHTS RESERVED. No part of this work covered by the copyright herein may be reproduced, transmitted, stored, or used in any form or by any means graphic, electronic, or mechanical, including but not limited to photocopying, recording, scanning, digitizing, taping, Web distribution, information networks, or information storage and retrieval systems, except as permitted under Section 107 or 108 of the 1976 United States Copyright Act, without the prior written permission of the publisher.

For product information and technology assistance, contact us at
Cengage Learning Customer & Sales Support, 1-800-354-9706.
For permission to use material from this text or product,
submit all requests online at **www.cengage.com/permissions.**
Further permissions questions can be e-mailed to
permissionrequest@cengage.com

Library of Congress Control Number: 2009940487

ISBN-13: 978-0-495-81243-2

ISBN-10: 0-495-81243-9

Wadsworth, Cengage Learning
20 Davis Drive
Belmont, CA 94002-3098
USA

Cengage Learning is a leading provider of customized learning solutions with office locations around the globe, including Singapore, the United Kingdom, Australia, Mexico, Brazil, and Japan. Locate your local office at **www.cengage.com/global.**

Cengage Learning products are represented in Canada by Nelson Education, Ltd.

To learn more about Wadsworth, Cengage Learning, visit **www.cengage.com/ Wadsworth.**

Purchase any of our products at your local college store or at our preferred online store **www.ichapters.com.**

Printed in the United States of America
1 2 3 4 5 6 7 13 12 11 10 09

Table of Contents

1 The Effective Teacher

JAMES M. COOPER

2 Instructional Objectives

TERRY D. TENBRINK

3 Instructional Planning

GRETA MORINE-DERSHIMER

7 Culturally Responsive Teaching

JASON G. IRIZARRY

8 Classroom Management

CAROL S. WEINSTEIN AND WILFORD A. WEBER

9 Cooperative Learning

MARY S. LEIGHTON

10 Assessment

TERRY D. TENBRINK

Preface

Purposes of This Text

The ninth edition of *Classroom Teaching Skills* will help beginning teachers meld theory with practice. The book conceptualizes the effective teacher as a reflective decision maker, one who makes planning, implementing, evaluation, and management decisions as part of the instructional role. To make and carry out these decisions the teacher needs certain teaching skills. The conceptual framework of the teacher as a reflective decision maker is presented in Chapter 1. Each subsequent chapter addresses a particular skill by first discussing the theory behind the skill and then giving the reader practice situations in which knowledge about the skill can be applied and feedback received. Because each chapter presents specific learning objectives as well as mastery tests, the reader receives immediate feedback on this learning.

After students have completed the chapters, the instructor may want to set up experiences that will enable the students to practice the skills with actual learners. Ultimate acquisition of the skill must, of course, take place in actual classroom situations with expertise developing over time.

From the outset, our goal was to produce instructional materials that are (1) important, (2) flexible, (3) readable, and (4) scholarly.

First, the teaching skills contained in this book have been identified by many research studies and by best-practices literature as being *important* to the success of teachers. Studies of expert teachers demonstrate that these skills are essential to effective teaching. Furthermore, our experience indicates that prospective teachers emphatically want to master practical teaching skills that will enable them to cope successfully with their classroom responsibilities. It is our belief that these instructional materials, dedicated as they are to the mastery of basic teaching skills, will be retained and used by most students as an ongoing self-evaluation tool—to be referred to both during and after their field experiences.

Our second goal, to produce a highly *flexible* text, has been met in two ways. First, the content itself is ubiquitous; the skills reach into virtually every course in the teacher education curriculum. Second, we designed the book as a self-contained teacher education learning package that can be used in a variety of capacities in many parts of the curriculum. Some instructors may choose to use particular chapters for one course, while other instructors may use different chapters for another course, thus permitting students to use *Classroom Teaching Skills* for more than one course. How the book is used will depend on the structure and organization of a given teacher education program. In addition, the book has often been used for professional development courses and workshops with experienced teachers.

Our third goal, *readability*, is achieved by our commitment to communicating clearly and directly with our audience: teachers. Although this is a multi-authored book, all of its chapters are edited to retain the book's ease and utility. While each author's unique writing style is consciously preserved, the level and structure of writing is adjusted for accessibility to readers. Moreover, each chapter presents a consistent five-step, self-teaching format: (1) a statement of objectives, (2) a presentation of written information, (3) practice exercises with answers, (4) a mastery test with an answer key, and (5) observation worksheets.

Our fourth goal, developing materials representative of the best current *scholarship*, has been met by experienced authors, all recognized authorities on the particular skill about which they have written. Further information on each author is presented in the "About the Authors" section following this preface.

Response to Changes in the Field

At one time in the not-too-distant past, teacher education consisted of a few courses on education theory, some courses on methods, and a topping of student teaching. Except for the student teaching, and maybe a little observation experience, the program consisted of campus-based courses.

Teacher education today differs considerably from the preceding description. Programs are much more field-oriented than ever before, requiring prospective teachers to spend more time onsite working with students in schools. The present emphasis on practical experience with students should not be interpreted as a movement away from theory. Rather, educational theory is being integrated with practice. This integration recognizes that theory, to be internalized, must be learned in the context in which it is to be applied. In the past, prospective teachers were expected to translate theory into practice with little help. Often they were unsuccessful. Today, with the help of newly developed curriculum materials, including case studies, teacher educators help prospective teachers apply the theory in situated contexts and give them feedback on their efforts.

The standards movement has also changed teacher education just as it has changed elementary and secondary education. In 1987, the National Board for Professional Teaching Standards (NBPTS) began developing standards for accomplished performance for experienced teachers in a number of different content areas and age levels. The Interstate New Teacher Assessment and Support Consortium (INTASC), created in 1987 as a project of the Council of Chief State School Officers (CCSSO), has been developing teaching standards for beginning teachers that are modeled after those developed by the NBPTS. INTASC's primary constituency is state education agencies responsible for teacher licensing and professional development. Its work is guided by one basic premise: An effective teacher must be able to integrate content knowledge with pedagogical understanding to ensure that all students learn and perform at high levels.

Toward this end, INTASC has created model core standards for licensing teachers, which reflect those principles that should be present in all teaching, regardless of the subject or grade level taught, and serve as a framework for the systemic reform of teacher preparation and professional development. These core standards are currently being translated into standards for discipline-specific teaching. Many state departments of education are requiring teacher educators to demonstrate that the core INTASC standards are reflected in their teacher education programs, and requiring prospective teachers to provide evidence that they have met those standards. An important attribute of these core standards—and the content-specific standards being developed—is that they define the knowledge, performances, and dispositions that teachers are expected to demonstrate; that is, they describe what teachers should know and be able to do rather than listing courses that teachers should take in order to be awarded a license.

Because of the growing emphasis on standards for teacher education, *Classroom Teaching Skills* identifies the particular core INTASC standards that are addressed in each chapter and matches them with each chapter's objectives. A correlation table can be found in the inside front cover of this book. We have done this both to show how each chapter in the book addresses particular teaching standards and to facilitate each teacher education program's documentation of where and how INTASC standards are addressed in the program. The core standards are listed in the appendix on pages 373–378. Readers who would like to understand the rationale for these standards and assumptions underlying them are urged to visit the INTASC web site at http://www.ccsso.org/Projects/Interstate_New_Teacher_Assessment_and_Support_Consortium/.

Key Features of the Revision

Before revising *Classroom Teaching Skills*, questionnaires were mailed both to professors who had used the book in their classes and to nonusers, asking them to evaluate the various chapters and to suggest changes for improvement. These evaluations and comments were mailed to each author, along with my suggestions for revision. The resulting product is a ninth edition that addresses the reviewers' specific concerns and suggestions. Besides general updating such as new research citations and new recommended web sites, the ninth edition includes these significant changes:

- Every chapter now includes *video cases* which provide students with real-life teaching examples of problems, methodologies, and teaching styles in online video clips that add another layer of richness to the realistic case studies offered by the book.
- *A new chapter* on "Culturally Responsive Teaching" has replaced the former chapter on technology. Because teachers have students from many different ethnicities and cultures, learning how to work with and appreciate the diversity of experiences these students bring to the classroom is a crucial skill for effective teaching. While we still believe that effective technology use is crucial for new teachers, our reviewers told us that the use of technology was most often taught in courses other than the ones using our book.
- *Chapter 1* on the effective teacher features a new case study of a first-year teacher as an example of the teacher as a reflective decision maker.
- *Chapter 8* on classroom management includes new coverage of culturally responsive classroom management and identifies the ongoing tasks involved in classroom management. The chapter also includes new material on involving parents in behavior issues.
- *An attractive new two-color design* organizes information more clearly for students.
- *New marginal notations* identify the INTASC principles being addressed in the main text.

Ancillaries

For students:

Premium Website The ninth edition of *Classroom Teaching Skills* is accompanied by a web site that offers access to the TeachSource Video Cases including exercises, transcripts, classroom artifacts, and bonus videos. Other study tools and resources include: practice tests, interactive flashcards for vocabulary study and review, tutorials on major topics, and web links for further exploration. Log in at www.cengage.com/login using the access code packaged with your new text, or purchase access at www.iChapters.com.

For instructors:

Premium Website Materials for instructors on the premium website include the Instructor's Manual and PowerPoint slides. Go to www.cengage.com/login.

Instructor's Manual An Instructor's Resource Manual with Test Bank is available in electronic form. The IRM contains additional activities, discussion questions, resources, and assessment ideas for instructors.

PowerLecture with ExamView This one-stop digital library and presentation tool includes preassembled Microsoft® PowerPoint® lecture slides, an image library with graphics from the text, and videos. It also includes a full Instructor's Manual and Test Bank and ExamView® testing software with all the test items from the printed Test Bank in electronic format, enabling you to create customized tests in print or online.

WebTutor for WebCT™ or Blackboard® Jumpstart your course with customizable, rich, text-specific content within your Course Management System. Whether you want to web-enable your class or put an entire course online, WebTutor offers a wide array of resources including media resources, quizzes, and web links.

Acknowledgments

We appreciate the assistance offered in the revision of this text and web site by the following reviewers:

Valeri R. Helterbran, Indiana University of Pennsylvania
Dr. Ted B. Cox, University of Wisconsin-Superior
Tom V. Savage, Santa Clara University
Christine Baron, Principal, Baron Consulting
Alicia Mendoza, Florida International University
Michelle Hughes, James Madison University
Dr. Mary Ellen Bardsley, Niagara University
Linda M. Maguire, Penn State University
Olufunmilayo A. Amobi, Arizona State University West Campus
James P. Valle, Millersville University of Pennsylvania
Marylin Moore, Illinois State University
Kazi Hossain, Millersville University of Pennsylvania
Bea Baaden, Long Island University
Cindi Nicotera, Harrisburg Area Community College
Helene Robins, St. Thomas Aquinas College

I would also like to thank the editorial staff at Cengage Learning Company for all their support and help in bringing this edition of *Classroom Teaching Skills* to fruition. I am especially thankful to Caitlin Cox, development editor, for her careful and sensitive oversight of this revision and for answering my many questions; Chris Shortt, Acquisitions Editor, for his encouragement as Cengage brought the higher-education division of Houghton Mifflin under its fold; Ashley Cronin, Media Editor, for her oversight of the web page related to this book; and Janice Bockelman, Editorial Assistant, for securing the reviews that guided us in the revision of the book. I also want to thank Mary Stone, our production editor, for bringing home the final product and wrapping up all the loose ends. On behalf of all the authors, I offer my deep thanks and appreciation for all their important contributions to this ninth edition.

James M. Cooper, Professor Emeritus
University of Virginia

Using This Book

The Book's Design

The purpose of *Classroom Teaching Skills* is to help you develop competence in selected teaching skills that are basic to implementing the reflective decision-making model. Each chapter in the book focuses on a particular teaching skill. Within each chapter, a cognitive map of the skill you are to acquire is provided. This cognitive map includes the purpose of the skill, its various elements and their sequencing, and the nature of the final performance.

Each chapter consists of self-contained materials that require practice and provide you with feedback on your efforts. If circumstances permit it, your instructor may also provide you with opportunities to practice these skills in classroom contexts.

To develop smoothness and a high level of competence in teaching skills, far more practice is necessary than can be provided in this book. If you are an elementary school teacher, many of these skills must be practiced within the context of different subject matter areas. Your competence in questioning skills, for example, is greatly a product of your knowledge of the subject about which you are asking questions.

Format of Each Chapter

Each chapter is written with a common format that contains (1) objectives, (2) a rationale, (3) learning materials and activities, (4) mastery tests, and (5) observation worksheets.

1. **Objectives.** The objectives, stated in terms of learner outcomes, specify the competency or competencies you will be expected to demonstrate. Wherever it is appropriate, the objectives will be arranged in a learning hierarchy, leading you from relatively simple objectives to more complex ones.
2. **Rationale.** The rationale describes the purpose and importance of the objectives within the chapter. It attempts to explain why you should want to spend your time acquiring the competencies the chapter is designed to produce. The rationale is considered important because if you are not convinced that the particular skill you are being asked to develop is important to effective teaching, then it is unlikely that you will be willing to spend the time and effort needed to acquire competence in that skill.
3. **Learning Materials and Activities.** Each objective has an accompanying set of reading materials written specifically for that objective. In addition, some of the authors have provided backup activities for those who want additional work on a particular objective. The nature of the reading materials and activities varies depending on the specific objective for which they were constructed.
4. **Mastery Tests.** Each chapter contains mastery tests with answer keys to enable you to assess whether or not you have achieved the objectives. These mastery tests assess your learning after you have completed the reading and backup activities related to each objective.

This technique allows you to discover immediately after completing each section whether you have met the objective satisfactorily. In addition, at the end of some of the chapters there are final mastery tests that serve as a last check on your achievement.

5. **Observation Worksheets.** Observation worksheets have been included to help guide you in observing and analyzing the skills taught in this book when you are observing in schools. Watching experienced classroom teachers and analyzing their implementation of these skills will provide you with insights as to how the skills can be used with students in classrooms. You can also compare in what ways the teacher does or does not use the skills in the same ways as advocated in the book.

This format (objectives, rationale, learning activities, mastery tests, and observation worksheets) has been successfully tested in hundreds of teacher education programs. It is an efficient design because all the materials are geared to help students achieve the stated objectives. Extraneous and inconsequential materials are eliminated, allowing students to make best use of their time. If used properly, the format increases the probability that you will be able to acquire a beginning level of competency in these basic teaching skills.

Description of the Skills

Skills were included in this book on the basis of their importance in implementing the reflective decision-making model of teaching. Although other skills may have been included, those that were selected are among the most crucial to the model.

The three basic elements of the reflective decision-making model are to plan, to implement, and to evaluate. Each skill is important in carrying out at least one of these three functions. Some skills are useful for more than one function. The nine skills that make up this book are:

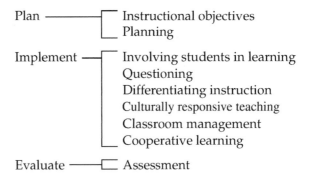

Instructional Objectives. Writing instructional objectives is a basic planning skill. By specifying instructional objectives, teachers define their purposes in terms that are clear and understandable. In Chapter 2, Terry TenBrink makes the distinction between well-written and poorly written objectives. Opportunities are provided within the chapter to (1) write well-defined instructional objectives, (2) use instructional objectives in planning, and (3) use objectives in implementing instruction. Well-written instructional objectives enable teachers to plan and implement their instructional strategies. The success of teachers' implementation skills greatly depends on the thoughtfulness and clarity of their instructional objectives.

Planning. Planning is perhaps the most important function a teacher performs—the whole decision-making model is based on this skill. In Chapter 3, Greta Morine-Dershimer emphasizes the key characteristics of productive planning. On the basis of research studies, Morine-Dershimer examines the differences in how novice and expert teachers plan. Expert teachers establish and effectively use routines such as collecting homework, distributing materials, and calling on students. They also have repertoires of alternative routines and procedures to use for different situations. Instead of having only one way of accomplishing an objective, expert teachers plan for and execute different procedures as needed. Morine-Dershimer also examines characteristics of effective lesson and unit plans by comparing teacher planning to dramatic productions, including the use of scripts, scenes, and improvisation.

Involving Students in Learning. In Chapter 4, Robert Shostak presents three basic skills for involving students in learning—planned beginnings, planned discussions, and planned endings—that research studies have demonstrated to be important components of engaging students in learning. *Planned beginnings* refers to teacher-initiated actions or statements that are designed to establish a communicative link between the experiences of students and the objectives of the lesson. Planned discussions encourage students to acquire new knowledge, reflect on ideas different from their own, and to share personal opinions. *Planned endings* refers to actions or statements designed to bring a lesson to an appropriate conclusion and to consolidate student learning. The effective use of these three skills will help establish and maintain student interest in the lesson, and will ensure that the main part of the lesson has been learned.

Questioning. Probably no teaching behavior has been studied as much as questioning. This is not surprising because most educators agree that questioning strategies and techniques are key tools in the teacher's repertoire of interactive teaching skills. In Chapter 5, David and Myra Sadker and Karen Zittleman chose Bloom's *Taxonomy of Educational Objectives: Cognitive Domain* as their system for classifying questions because it is the most widely used cognitive classification system in education. They provide opportunities to classify and construct questions according to the six levels of Bloom's *Taxonomy*; to identify the seven habits of effective questioners; to explore the related areas of wait time, probing, scaffolding, and feedback that can enhance questioning skills; and to explore how the growing diversity and multicultural nature of America's students affect questioning strategies. If the skills presented in this chapter are utilized in teaching, the net effect will be students who are more active participants in the learning process.

Differentiating Instruction. A given in classrooms is that students learn what the teacher has planned in different ways, at different times, and at different levels of sophistication. To teach all students in a class effectively, a teacher must take into account the variety of ways in which students differ from one another, and offer instruction that responds to this variety. Differentiated instruction is teaching with student variance in mind. As Carol Ann Tomlinson, the author of Chapter 6, writes, ". . . differentiated instruction is 'responsive' teaching rather than 'one-size-fits-all' teaching."

In this highly interactive chapter, Tomlinson helps the reader develop a personal rationale for teaching to address learner needs; provides specific ways to differentiate content, activities, and products in response to student readiness, interest, and learning profile; and helps the reader think about practical ways to become a responsive teacher.

Culturally Responsive Teaching. As America's classrooms continue to become more and more diverse, teachers are challenged to work effectively with students from ethnicities, cultures, and socioeconomic levels different from their own. Effective teachers can work with students of diverse backgrounds to affirm their identities and build upon who the students are and what they bring with them to school. Jason Irizarry provides a conceptual basis for why culturally responsive teaching is so important, as well as providing general strategies to make teaching more culturally responsive. He also emphasizes the need for teachers to become more in touch with their own cultural identities before they can appreciate and work with the cultural identities of their students.

Classroom Management. No problem concerns beginning teachers more than the problem of classroom management. Most new teachers are worried about not being able to control their students and are aware that lack of control will impede effective instruction. Few areas in teacher education curricula have been neglected as much as classroom management. The major reason for this neglect has been that educators formerly had a poor systematic understanding of classroom dynamics; however, our knowledge in this area has expanded to the point where systematic instruction in classroom management is now possible.

In Chapter 8, Carol Weinstein and Will Weber emphasize that teachers need to establish and maintain proper learning environments. While the purpose of teaching is to stimulate desired student learning, the purpose of classroom management is to establish the conditions that best promote student learning. Classroom management skills are necessary for effective teaching to occur, but they do not guarantee such behavior. Weinstein and Weber examine three different philosophical positions regarding classroom management—authoritative, authoritarian, and permissive approaches—and provide numerous opportunities for diagnosing classroom situations according to each of these three viewpoints. They also address the issue of culturally responsive classroom management, and identify the ongoing tasks needed for effective classroom management.

Cooperative Learning. One of the elements in the hidden curriculum of our schools is the emphasis on competition. Children learn how to compete with one another in numerous ways. Recently, the value of cooperation among learners to increase achievement levels has been recognized by educators. In Chapter 9, Mary Leighton examines various research-based cooperative learning strategies to help students significantly improve their academic achievement as well as developing social skills.

Cooperative learning strategies are organized around systematic methods that usually involve presentations of information, student practice and coaching in learning teams, individual assessment of mastery, and public recognition of team success. The three key characteristics of cooperative learning strategies are group goals, individual accountability, and equal opportunities for success. In this chapter, several of the most widely used cooperative learning strategies are described in some detail.

Assessment. Assessment (evaluation) and knowledge of results are essential if teachers are to improve their teaching effectiveness. The critical nature of assessment is rarely disputed; nevertheless, few teachers receive adequate training in assessment concepts and procedures. Terry TenBrink's chapter on assessment focuses on critical components of the evaluation process. His basic position is that educational assessment is useful only if it helps educators make decisions.

TenBrink perceives assessment as a four-stage process: (1) preparing for evaluation, (2) obtaining needed information, (3) forming judgments, and (4) using judgments in making decisions and preparing reports. Throughout the chapter, examples of problems and decisions that teachers are likely to face are used. Developing test items, checklists, and rating scales for evaluating student knowledge, products, and performance is a major focus of the chapter. This practical emphasis should make assessment concepts and procedures for making better instructional decisions easier to understand and apply.

About the Authors

James M. Cooper is Professor Emeritus in the Curry School of Education at the University of Virginia, where he also served as Dean from 1984 to 1994. He received four degrees from Stanford University—two in history and two in education, including his Ph.D. in 1967. He taught junior and senior high school social studies for four years in Palo Alto, California. Dr. Cooper authored, co-authored, or edited numerous publications, including *Those Who Can, Teach* and *Kaleidoscope: Contemporary and Classic Readings in Education*, both in their twelfth editions. His books and articles address the areas of teacher education, supervision of teachers, case studies in teacher education, and technology and teacher education. He was recognized as one of the nation's 70 Leaders in Teacher Education in 1990 by the Association of Teacher Educators, and as the Outstanding Professor in the Curry School of Education for 2001. He has been listed in *Who's Who in America* and *Who's Who in American Education* since 1990.

Jason G. Irizarry is an Assistant Professor in the Department of Curriculum and Instruction in the Neag School of Education at the University of Connecticut. Prior to his arrival at UConn, he was the Director of Project SPIRIT (Springfield Partnership to Improve the Recruitment of Inspiring Minority Teachers), a college-community collaboration aimed at increasing the number of teachers of color in urban schools. He received his doctorate from the University of Massachusetts Amherst and has taught undergraduate and graduate courses in multicultural education, philosophy of education, culturally responsive curriculum development, and urban education. A former middle school teacher in New York City, his research focuses on urban teacher recruitment, preparation, and retention with an emphasis on increasing the number of teachers of color, culturally responsive pedagogy, and youth participatory action research. A central focus of his work involves promoting the academic achievement of Latino and African American youth in urban schools by addressing issues associated with teacher education. Manuscripts documenting the findings of his research have been published or accepted for publication in a variety of journals in the field including *Education and Urban Society*, *Multicultural Perspectives*, *Race, Ethnicity and Education*, and the *Centro Journal of Puerto Rican Studies*, with others appearing as chapters in various books, including the *Handbook of Latinos and Education: Research, Theory & Practice* (Murillo, 2010) and *Race, Ethnicity and Education: The Influences of Racial and Ethnic Identity in Education* (Milner & Ross, 2006). Recognition of and support for Dr. Irizarry's scholarly endeavors and community involvement are evidenced, too, by his selection as a recipient of the Cultivating New Voices among Scholars of Color Fellowship from the National Council of Teachers of English (NCTE) and the UConn Neag School of Education Outstanding Early Career Researcher Award.

Mary S. Leighton is Executive Director of the Network Charter School in Eugene, Oregon. Since beginning her career as a teacher in Chicago public schools, she has taught grades pre-K–12 in urban, suburban, and rural schools and served as an administrator in public and parochial schools. She has also worked as a teacher educator in several institutions and settings. Dr. Leighton served on the Success for All development and dissemination team at Johns Hopkins University as well as on the staff of a private research firm where she reported on effective programs and practices for students at risk of school failure. As an independent consultant, she has helped many secondary and postsecondary faculties adapt cooperative learning strategies to their particular circumstances. She graduated from the University of Chicago and earned a doctorate in curriculum and instruction from the University of Oregon.

Greta G. Morine-Dershimer is Professor Emerita, Curry School of Education, University of Virginia, where she served as Director of Teacher Education and Senior Researcher in the Commonwealth Center for the Education of Teachers. She received her Ed.D. from Teachers College, Columbia University, in 1965 after teaching in elementary and junior high schools for ten years. She served as a teacher educator in universities in New York and California, and developed and tested teacher-training materials at the Far West Laboratory for Educational Research and Development in San Francisco. She was Vice President of Division K (Teaching and Teacher Education) of the American Educational Research Association and Editor of *Teaching and Teacher Education: An International Journal of Research and Studies*. Her research has focused on teacher and pupil thinking and learning in interactive classroom settings. Her publications include six books, more than twenty book chapters, and articles in a wide range of journals. Currently she volunteers with two local nonprofit groups dedicated to improving educational opportunities for low-income and minority students.

Myra Sadker was a Professor and Dean at American University (Washington, D.C.) until her death in 1995. **David Sadker** is Professor Emeritus at American University (Washington, D.C.), and now teaches and writes in Tucson, Arizona. Along with his late wife Myra Sadker, he gained a national reputation for work in confronting gender bias and sexual harassment. The Sadkers' book, *Failing at Fairness: How Our Schools Cheat Girls*, was published by Charles Scribner in 1994, and with Karen Zittleman, he updated that book in 2009, now entitled *Still Failing at Fairness: How Gender Bias Cheats Girls and Boys and What We Can Do About It*. David Sadker co-edited *Gender in the Classroom: Foundations, Skills, Methods and Strategies Across the Curriculum* (Lawrence Erlbaum, 2007), and a best-selling introductory textbook, *Teachers, Schools and Society*, (McGraw Hill, 2010, 9e; McGraw Hill, 2009, brief, 2e). David Sadker has directed more than a dozen federal education grants, authored seven books, and published more than seventy-five articles in journals such as *Phi Delta Kappan*, *Harvard Educational Review*, and *Psychology Today*. The Sadkers' work has been reported in hundreds of newspapers and magazines including *USA Today*, *USA Weekend*, *Parade Magazine*, *Business Week*, *The Washington Post*, *The London Times*, *The New York Times*, *Time*, and *Newsweek*. They appeared on local and national television and radio shows such as *The Today Show*, *Good Morning America*, *The Oprah Winfrey Show*, Phil Donahue's *The Human Animal*, National Public Radio's *All Things Considered*, and twice on *Dateline: NBC* with Jane Pauley. The American

Educational Research Association (AERA) honored the Sadkers for the best review of research published in the United States in 1991, for their professional service in 1995, and for "scholarship, activism, and community building on behalf of women and education" in 2004. The American Association of University Women awarded the Sadkers their Eleanor Roosevelt Award in 1995, and the American Association of Colleges of Teacher Education recognized their work with the Gender Architect Award in 2001. David Sadker has received two honorary doctorates and was selected as a Torchbearer by the U.S. Olympic Committee in 2002. He is interested in *Courage to Teach* work and exploring new frontiers of teaching.

Robert Shostak was formerly Coordinator of the English Education program and Administrative Director of the International Institute for Creative Communication at Florida International University. He received his bachelor's degree in humanities from Colgate University, an M.S. in teaching English from the State University of New York at Albany, and a Ph.D. in curriculum and instruction from the University of Connecticut. He taught high school English for six years before focusing his career on higher education and teacher training. Author of textbooks, monographs, and numerous articles, he has devoted his most recent publishing efforts to writing about computers and the teaching of English. Dr. Shostak's most current educational projects are in the field of telecommunications. Presently he is a full-time educational consultant.

Terry D. TenBrink is retired from administrative duties at the Kirksville College of Osteopathic Medicine in Kirksville, Missouri. Formerly on the faculty at the University of Missouri at Columbia, Dr. TenBrink received his Ph.D. in educational psychology from Michigan State University in 1969. His graduate studies emphasized learning theory, evaluation, measurement, and research design. His teaching experience spans elementary, junior high school, high school, and college students, and he has been principal of an elementary school. He stays in touch with the classroom through numerous consulting activities in public schools and in adult education and by teaching seminars and workshops to classroom teachers. While at the University of Missouri, Dr. TenBrink taught courses in evaluation, learning, human development, and general educational psychology. He has published numerous journal articles and is engaged in continuing research on the conditions under which learning occurs efficiently. He is the author of a textbook, *Evaluation: A Practical Guide for Teachers*.

Carol Ann Tomlinson is William Clay Parrish, Jr. Professor and Chair of Educational Leadership, Foundations, and Policy at the University of Virginia's Curry School of Education where she is also Co-Director of the University's Institutes on Academic Diversity. Prior to joining the faculty at UVa, she was a public school teacher for 21 years. During that time, she taught students in high school, preschool, and middle school and also administered programs for struggling and advanced learners. She was Virginia's Teacher of the Year in 1974. Carol is author of over 200 books, book chapters, articles, and other educational materials including *How to Differentiate Instruction in Mixed Ability Classrooms*, *The Differentiated Classroom: Responding to the Needs of All Learners*, *Fulfilling the Promise of the Differentiated Classroom: Strategies and Tools for Responsive Teaching*, (with Jay McTighe) *Differentiating Instruction and Understanding by*

Design: Connecting Content and Kids, and (with Kay Brimijoin and Lane Narvaez) *The Differentiated School: Making Revolutionary Changes in Teaching and Learning*. Her books have been translated into 12 languages. Carol was named Outstanding Professor at Curry in 2004 and received an All-University Teaching Award in 2008. She works throughout the United States and internationally with educators who seek to create classrooms that are more effective with academically diverse student populations.

Wilford A. Weber was Professor of Education in the Department of Curriculum and Instruction, College of Education, University of Houston, where he taught from 1971 until his death in 2007.

Carol S. Weinstein is Professor Emerita in the Department of Learning and Teaching at Rutgers Graduate School of Education. She received her bachelor's degree in psychology from Clark University in Worcester, Massachusetts, and her master's and doctoral degrees from Harvard Graduate School of Education. She is the author of *Secondary Classroom Management: Lessons From Research and Practice* (with Ingrid Novodvorsky), *Elementary Classroom Management: Lessons From Research and Practice* (with Molly Romano and Andrew J. Mignano), and numerous chapters and articles on classroom management. She is also the co-editor of the *Handbook of Classroom Management: Research, Practice, and Contemporary Issues* (with Carolyn Evertson).

Karen R. Zittleman (Ph.D.) is an education author and teacher. Her research and teaching interests focus on educational equity, foundations of education, teacher preparation, and contemplative practices in education. She is co-author of *Teachers, Schools, and Society* (McGraw-Hill), a leading education textbook, and *Still Failing at Fairness*, a trade book exploring gender bias in schools. Her articles have appeared in the *Journal of Teacher Education, Educational Leadership, Phi Delta Kappan, Principal* and other professional journals. Karen also is a contributing author to *Gender in the Classroom: Foundations, Skills, Methods and Strategies Across the Curriculum* and wrote *Making Public Schools Great for Every Girl and Boy*, a guide for promoting equity in math and science instruction (National Educational Association). She has taught in the School of Education, Teaching, and Health at American University in Washington, D.C. and in Milwaukee public schools. She has also taught several courses online through the Women's Educational Equity Act, and is foundation manager for the Myra Sadker Foundation. Dr. Zittleman lives in Tucson, Arizona.

1

The Effective Teacher

James M. Cooper

■ **INTASC Standards**

● **Principle 9:** The teacher is a reflective practitioner who continually evaluates the effects of his/her choices and actions on others (students, parents, and other professionals in the learning community) and who actively seeks out opportunities to grow professionally.

David Young-Wolff/PhotoEdit

teacher's desk

■ **OBJECTIVES**

1. To describe the characteristics of an effective teacher

2. To explain why reflection on teaching is so important for teacher growth

3. To describe the reflective decision making model of teaching

4. To identify important factors that affect instructional decision making

Effective Teaching

Before we talk about effective teaching, let's ask the question "What is a teacher?" At first glance such a question seems obvious. A teacher is a person charged with the responsibility of helping others to learn and to behave in new and different ways. But who is excluded from this definition? Parents? Band directors? Drill sergeants? Boy Scout leaders? At some time or another we all teach and, in turn, are taught.

We generally reserve the term *teacher*, however, for persons whose primary professional or occupational function is to help others learn and develop in new ways. While education, learning, and teaching can and do take place in many different settings, most societies realize that education is too important to be left to chance. Consequently, they establish schools to facilitate learning and to help people live better and happier lives. Schools are created to provide a certain type of educational experience, which can be called the *curriculum*. Teachers are trained and hired by societies to help fulfill the purposes of the curriculum. Teachers, in the formal educative process of schooling, are social agents hired by society to help facilitate the intellectual, personal, and social development of those members of society who attend schools.

Compared to the teachers of the 19th and much of the 20th century, today's teachers are better educated, earn more money, and are more highly respected members of society than their earlier counterparts. Society requires its teachers to obtain a college education and specific training as teachers. This increase in the educational level of teachers is recognition that, if teachers are to facilitate the intellectual, personal, and social development of their students, then they must be much better educated than ever before.

What Makes a Teacher Effective?

States require teachers to have a college degree, but possession of a college degree does not in any way ensure that teachers will be effective. What is it that makes a teacher effective? *The* **effective teacher** *is one who is able to bring about intended learning outcomes.* The nature of the learning is still most important, but two different teachers may strive for and achieve different outcomes and each be judged effective. The two critical dimensions of effective teaching are *intent* and *achievement*. Without intent, student achievement becomes random and accidental; however, intent is not enough by itself. If students do not achieve their intended learning goals (even if the failure is due to variables beyond the control of their teacher), the teacher cannot truly have been effective. More and more systems for evaluating teacher performance use student achievement data as a measure of teacher effectiveness.

A number of studies have concluded that the single most important factor determining the quality of the education a child receives is the quality of the teacher, and that effective teachers can produce significantly greater student learning gains than less effective teachers.[1] While effective teachers are defined as teachers who can demonstrate the ability to bring about intended learning outcomes, what enables them to achieve desired results with students? What should effective, professional teachers know, believe, or be able to do, that distinguishes them from other comparably educated people?

Importance of personality? ▸

Some people will state that the crucial dimension is the teacher's personality. Teachers, they will say, should be friendly, cheerful, sympathetic, morally virtuous, enthusiastic, and humorous. In a massive study, David Ryans concluded that effective teachers are fair, democratic, responsive, understanding, kindly, stimulating, original, alert, attractive, responsible, steady, poised, and confident. Ineffective teachers were described as partial, autocratic, aloof, restricted, harsh, dull, stereotyped, apathetic, unimpressive, evasive, erratic, excitable, and uncertain.[2] But as two educational researchers once remarked, ". . . what conceivable human interaction is not the better if the people involved are friendly, cheerful, sympathetic, and virtuous rather than the opposite?"[3] These characteristics, then, while desirable in teachers, are not uniquely desirable to that group alone.

Need special knowledge and skills ▸

It might be difficult to reach a consensus on exactly what knowledge and skills are unique to the teaching profession, but most educators would agree that special skills and knowledge are necessary and do exist. Certainly teachers must be familiar with children and their developmental stages. They must know something about events outside the classroom and school. They must possess enough command of the subject they are going to teach to be able to differentiate what is important and central from what is incidental and peripheral. They must have a philosophy of education to help guide them in their role as teachers. They must know how human beings learn and how to create environments that facilitate learning.

In recent years, several groups have attempted to identify what effective teachers should know and be able to do. The Interstate New Teachers Assessment and Support Consortium (INTASC) has identified the knowledge, dispositions, and performances that a beginning teacher should possess. These principles or standards are listed at the end of this book, and each chapter in the book identifies the INTASC principles that are addressed in that chapter. The INTASC standards are based on the standards that the National Board for Professional Teaching Standards has developed for experienced, accomplished teachers. Many states are working with INTASC to implement the standards as part of the states' own teacher licensing requirements.

General Areas of Teacher Competence

B. O. Smith has suggested that a well-educated teacher should be prepared in four areas of teacher competence to be effective in bringing about intended learning outcomes.[4]

1. Command of theoretical knowledge about learning and human behavior
2. Display of attitudes that foster learning and genuine human relationships
3. Command of knowledge in the subject matter to be taught
4. Repertoire of teaching skills that facilitate student learning

A fifth area of teacher competence, personal practical knowledge, will also be considered in addition to the four areas identified by Smith.

1. Command of Theoretical Knowledge About Learning and Human Behavior

For years education has been criticized for its "folkways" practices. Educational recipes and standardized procedures were formally and informally passed on to new teachers to help them survive in classrooms. While this practice still exists, many scientific concepts from psychology, anthropology, sociology, linguistics, cognitive sciences, and related disciplines are now available to help teachers interpret the complex reality of their classrooms. These make up the **theoretical knowledge** of teaching. Those teachers who lack the theoretical background and understanding provided by such scientifically derived concepts can only interpret the events of their classrooms according to popularly held beliefs or common sense. Although common sense often serves us well, there is ample evidence that teachers who habitually rely on it will too often misinterpret the events in their classrooms.

Common sense not enough

Beginning teachers frequently face the difficult situation of receiving different, contradictory messages from their professors and from the teachers with whom they work. While their professors are apt to focus on theoretical knowledge, the experienced teacher may often advise them, "Forget the fancy theoretical stuff and listen to me. I'll tell you what works in real life." This folkways approach to education may be in conflict with what the new teacher has learned and may create a dilemma about how to handle a situation.

Theories sometimes not internalized

The problem confronting new teachers is not that the theories put before them are unworkable, but that they simply haven't internalized those theories to the point where they can be used to interpret and solve practical problems. They have not been provided with sufficient opportunities to apply the knowledge, to translate it from theory into practice, and thereby to master it.

An example of a theoretical concept that is derived from psychology and that has enormous implications for teachers is the concept of reinforcement. From their educational psychology courses, most teachers know that a behavior that is reinforced will be strengthened and is likely to be repeated. Nevertheless, these same teachers often respond to a disruptive pupil by calling his or her actions to the attention of the class. If the pupil is misbehaving because of a need to be recognized, the teacher, by publicly acknowledging the misbehavior, may be reinforcing it. When the pupil continues to act up periodically, the teacher doesn't understand why. Although the teacher may have intellectually grasped the meaning of reinforcement, this understanding is not synonymous with internalizing or mastering the concept. Mastery requires practical application to concrete situations.

Because theoretical knowledge can be used to interpret situations and solve problems, many classroom events that might otherwise go unnoticed or remain inexplicable can be recognized and resolved by applying theories and concepts of human behavior. This is not an easy task. It requires understanding, insight, practice, and feedback from colleagues and professors. Proficiency will not be achieved as a result of formal training alone; it is a lifelong process involving both formal training and an unending program of on-the-job self-improvement.

2. Display of Attitudes That Foster Learning and Genuine Human Relationships

The second area of competence identified as essential for effective teaching has to do with attitudes. An **attitude** is a predisposition to act in a positive or negative way toward persons, ideas, or events. Virtually all educators are convinced that teacher attitudes are an important dimension in the teaching process. Attitudes have a direct effect on our behavior; they determine how we view ourselves and interact with others.

The major categories of attitudes that affect teaching behavior are (a) teachers' attitudes toward themselves, (b) teachers' attitudes toward children, (c) teachers' attitudes toward peers and parents, and (d) teachers' attitudes toward the subject matter.

Attitudes affect behavior; need for self-knowledge ▷

(a) *Teachers' Attitudes Toward Themselves.* There is evidence from psychology that persons who deny or cannot cope with their own emotions are likely to be incapable of respecting and coping with the feelings of others. If teachers are to understand and sympathize with their students' feelings, they must recognize and understand their own feelings. Many colleges are responding to this need by including counseling sessions, reflective thinking, and awareness experiences as part of their teacher education programs. These experiences emphasize introspection, self-evaluation, and feedback from other participants. The goal is to help prospective teachers learn more about themselves, their attitudes, and how others perceive them.

(b) *Teachers' Attitudes Toward Children.* Most teachers occasionally harbor attitudes or feelings toward students that are detrimental to their teaching effectiveness. Strong likes and dislikes of particular pupils, biases toward or against particular ethnic groups, low learning expectations for poverty-level children, and biases in favor of or against certain kinds of student behavior—all can reduce teaching effectiveness. Self-awareness of such attitudes toward individual pupils or classes of children is necessary if teachers are to cope with their own feelings and beliefs. If teachers possess empathy for their students and value them as unique individuals, they will be more effective and will derive more satisfaction from their teaching.

Teacher expectations important ▷

Considerable research on teacher expectations indicates that when teachers hold low expectations for students and, consciously or unconsciously, communicate these low expectations to the students by how they behave toward those students, a self-fulfilling prophecy may occur.[5] That is, the students may conform to the teacher's low expectations, thus confirming the teacher's original expectations. Conversely, when teachers hold high expectations for students and communicate these high expectations, students will often act in ways to live up to the teacher's expectations. A teacher's attitude toward and expectation of students are powerful influences on whether or not students learn.

(c) *Teachers' Attitudes Toward Peers and Parents.* Teachers do not exist in isolated classrooms. They interact with fellow teachers and administrators and often have sensitive dealings with parents. Sometimes they can be effective in dealing with children, but because of negative attitudes toward the adults they encounter, their professional life is unsuccessful. For example, some teachers may resent persons in authority positions, resisting their suggestions for improvement. Other teachers may yield too easily to suggestions from persons in authority, only to later feel guilty about complying instead of sticking up for their own convictions. Or some teachers may feel the need to compete with other teachers for administrative or student approval. Many of the comments already made regarding teachers' attitudes toward themselves and children also apply to their attitudes toward peers and parents.

(d) *Teachers' Attitudes Toward the Subject Matter.* The message, in one word, is ENTHUSIASM! Just as students are perceptive in discovering the teacher's attitude toward them, they are also sensitive to the teacher's attitude toward the subject matter. Teachers who are not enthusiastic about what they teach can hardly hope to instill enthusiastic responses in their pupils. After all, if you don't care about the subject matter, how can you ever hope to motivate your students into learning about it?

3. Command of Knowledge in the Subject Matter to Be Taught

Command of the subject matter to be taught is an obvious necessity for any teacher. But taking courses in biology or history or mathematics is not sufficient. A teacher's subject-matter preparation really has two aspects: (1) a study of the subject matter itself and (2) a judicious selection of the material that can be transmitted successfully to the student.

Content knowledge + pedagogy

College courses taken in disciplines such as mathematics or English help teachers acquire an understanding of the disciplines, their basic concepts, and their modes of inquiry; however, college courses are not directed toward what should be taught to elementary or secondary school students. What should be taught is obviously much less extensive and advanced than the content of the college courses and requires that teachers know the school curriculum as well.

Knowledge of the school curriculum is related to **pedagogical content knowledge**—that is, knowledge that bridges **content knowledge** and pedagogy. Pedagogical content knowledge represents the "blending of content and pedagogy into an understanding of how particular topics, problems, or issues are organized, represented, and adapted to the diverse interests and abilities of learners and presented for instruction."[6] Teachers who possess pedagogical content knowledge can translate the content knowledge they possess into forms that have great teaching power and that meet the needs and abilities of students. Such teachers understand the central topics in each subject, those aspects that are most difficult for students to learn, and what student preconceptions are likely to get in the way of learning. These teachers draw on powerful examples, illustrations, analogies, demonstrations, and explanations to represent and transform the subject so that students can understand it. For example, using the analogy of water flowing through a pipe to explain how electricity flows through a circuit might be useful initially. However, a teacher with pedagogical content knowledge would also understand the limitations of such an analogy and how it might later interfere with student understanding of other properties of electricity.

Teachers must therefore rethink much of the content of a particular discipline as it relates to the lives of their pupils. To be effective communicators, teachers need an understanding of both children and subject matter and, beyond that, special training in linking the two.

4. Repertoire of Teaching Skills That Facilitate Student Learning

The fourth area of competence required of effective teachers is possession of a repertoire of **teaching skills**, which are the specific sets of identifiable behaviors needed to perform teaching functions. Such a repertoire is necessary if teachers are to be effective with students who have varied backgrounds and learning aptitudes. Teacher education programs must therefore include a training component focusing on the acquisition of specific teaching skills, such as the ability to ask questions that require students to think more deeply, to write good assessments, or to manage classrooms to facilitate student learning. No program can afford to concentrate so exclusively on the acquisition of knowledge that it ignores or slights the practice dimension of teaching. Whereas the knowledge components involved in teacher preparation focus on the contexts or situations that confront teachers, the skills component focuses directly on the trainees—on the observation, analysis, and modification of their teaching behavior.

5. Personal Practical Knowledge

Personal practical knowledge is the set of understandings teachers have of the practical circumstances in which they work.[7] These understandings include teachers' beliefs, insights, and habits that enable them to do their jobs in schools. This personal practical knowledge tends to be time bound and situation specific, personally compelling, and oriented toward action. For years, researchers denigrated teachers' personal practical knowledge because they placed greater value on scientifically derived knowledge than on practical and personal knowledge. In more recent years, however, researchers have accorded much more importance to teachers' personal practical knowledge. Teachers use their personal practical knowledge to solve dilemmas, resolve tensions, and simplify the complexities of their work.

Unique to each teacher ▶ Because teachers' personal practical knowledge is so closely tied to them as individuals, research on this type of knowledge has not added up to a codified body of teaching knowledge.[8] However, case studies of teachers have provided rich pictures of how teachers use their knowledge to make sense of complex, ill-structured classrooms. These case studies provide evidence that teachers' personal practical knowledge provides an important dimension to a teacher's competence. The Video Case *Teaching as a Profession: What Defines Effective Teaching?* illustrates different dimensions of effective teaching.

▼ **TeachSource Video Case**   **Teaching as a Profession: What Defines Effective Teaching?**

In this video, you'll see vivid examples of various dimensions of teaching excellence—from command of one's subject matter to setting up an effective learning environment. As you watch the clips and study the artifacts in the case, reflect on the following questions. To access the video, go to www.cengage.com/login.

Questions

1. What aspects of effective teaching that are mentioned in this chapter are also mentioned in the video case?
2. Which aspects of effective teaching that are mentioned in the video seem particularly important to you? Why?

◼ Danielson's Framework for Professional Practice

Road map for teacher competency ▶

We have briefly examined five general areas of competence in which teachers must develop proficiency to be effective. While this examination is useful for obtaining an overview of the basic components of a well-designed teacher education program, it does not provide any guidelines on what a teacher does when teaching. To better understand the responsibilities of teachers, a framework for professional practice will be examined.

Charlotte Danielson has developed a framework for teaching that identifies aspects of a teacher's responsibilities that empirical studies have demonstrated as promoting improved student learning.[9] Because teaching is an extremely complex activity, this framework is useful in laying out the various areas of competence in which professional teachers need to develop expertise. Danielson divides the complex activity of teaching into twenty-two components clustered into four domains of teaching responsibility: (1) *planning and preparation*, (2) *the classroom environment*, (3) *instruction*, and (4) *professional responsibilities*. (These domains and their components are shown in Figure 1.1.[*]) A brief review of each of these domains will provide a road map of the skills and competencies new teachers need to develop. The chapters in this book specifically address many of these competencies.

Domain 1: Planning and Preparation

The components in Domain 1 outline how a teacher organizes the content of what students are expected to learn—in other words, how the teacher designs instruction. These include *demonstrating knowledge of content and pedagogy, demonstrating knowledge of the students, selecting instructional goals, demonstrating knowledge of resources, designing coherent instruction,* and *assessing student learning.*

The chapters in this book that address these components are Chapter 2: Instructional Objectives; Chapter 3: Instructional Planning; Chapter 7: Culturally Responsive Teaching; and Chapter 10: Assessment.

Domain 2: The Classroom Environment

The components in Domain 2 consist of the noninstructional interactions that occur in a classroom. These consist of *creating an environment of respect and rapport among the students and with the teacher, establishing a culture for learning, managing classroom procedures, managing student behavior,* and *organizing the physical space.* The chapters that address these components are Chapter 7: Culturally Responsive Teaching and Chapter 8: Classroom Management.

Domain 3: Instruction

The components in Domain 3 are what constitute the core of teaching— the engagement of students in learning content. These include *communicating clearly and accurately, using questioning and discussion techniques,*

---

*From Charlotte Danielson, "Enhancing Professional Practice: A Framework for Teaching, Second Edition" Association for Supervision and Curriculum Development, 2007, pp. 3–4. Reprinted with permission.

Components of Professional Practice

Domain 1: Planning and Preparation

Component 1a: Demonstrating Knowledge of Content and Pedagogy
  Knowledge of content and the structure of the discipline
  Knowledge of prerequisite relationships
  Knowledge of content-related pedagogy
Component 1b: Demonstrating Knowledge of Students
  Knowledge of child and adolescent development
  Knowledge of the learning process
  Knowledge of students' skills, knowledge, and language proficiency
  Knowledge of students' interests and cultural heritage
  Knowledge of students' special needs
Component 1c: Selecting Instructional Goals
  Value, sequence, and alignment
  Clarity
  Balance
  Suitability for diverse learners
Component 1d: Demonstrating Knowledge of Resources
  Resources for classroom use
  Resources to extend content knowledge and pedagogy
  Resources for students
Component 1e: Designing Coherent Instruction
  Learning activities
  Instructional materials and resources
  Instructional groups
  Lesson and unit structure
Component 1f: Designing Student Assessments
  Congruence with instructional outcomes
  Criteria and standards
  Design of formative assessments
  Use for planning

Domain 2: The Classroom Environment

Component 2a: Creating an Environment of Respect and Rapport
  Teacher interaction with students
  Student interaction with other students
Component 2b: Establishing a Culture for Learning
  Importance of the content
  Expectations for learning and achievement
  Student pride in work
Component 2c: Managing Classroom Procedures
  Management of instructional groups
  Management of transitions
  Management of materials and supplies
  Performance of noninstructional duties
  Supervision of volunteers and paraprofessionals
Component 2d: Managing Student Behavior
  Expectations
  Monitoring of student behavior
  Response to student misbehavior
Component 2e: Organizing Physical Space
  Safety and accessibility
  Arrangement of furniture and use of physical resources

■ Figure 1.1   (continued)
A framework for teaching

Components of Professional Practice (*continued*)

Domain 3: Instruction

Component 3a: Communicating with Students
Expectations for learning
Directions and procedures
Explanations of content
Use of oral and written language

Component 3b: Using Questioning and Discussion Techniques
Quality of questions
Discussion techniques
Student participation

Component 3c: Engaging Students in Learning
Activities and assignments
Grouping of students
Instructional materials and resources
Structure and pacing

Component 3d: Using Assessment in Instruction
Assessment criteria
Monitoring of student learning
Feedback to students
Student self-assessment and monitoring of progress

Component 3e: Demonstrating Flexibility and Responsiveness
Lesson adjustment
Response to students
Persistence

Domain 4: Professional Responsibilities

Component 4a: Reflecting on Teaching
Accuracy
Use in future teaching

Component 4b: Maintaining Accurate Records
Student completion of assignments
Student progress in learning
Noninstructional records

Component 4c: Communicating with Families
Information about the instructional program
Information about individual students
Engagement of families in the instructional program

Component 4d: Participating in a Professional Community
Relationships with colleagues
Involvement in a culture of professional inquiry
Service to the school
Participation in school and district projects

Component 4e: Growing and Developing Professionally
Enhancement of content knowledge and pedagogical skill
Receptivity to feedback from colleagues
Service to the profession

Component 4f: Showing Professionalism
Integrity and ethical conduct
Service to students
Advocacy
Decision making
Compliance with school and district regulations

■ Figure 1.1
A framework for teaching

engaging students in learning, providing feedback to students, and *demonstrating flexibility and responsiveness.* The chapters that address these components are Chapter 4: Involving Students in Learning; Chapter 5: Questioning Skills; Chapter 6: Differentiating Instruction for Academic Diversity; Chapter 7: Culturally Responsive Teaching; and Chapter 9: Cooperative Learning.

Domain 4: Professional Responsibilities

The components in Domain 4 represent the wide range of a teacher's responsibilities outside the classroom. These include *reflecting on teaching, maintaining accurate records, communicating with families, contributing to the school and district, growing and developing professionally,* and *showing professionalism.* Teachers who demonstrate these competencies are highly valued by their colleagues and administrators, as well as being seen as true professionals. Because of its focus on classroom teaching skills, this book does not cover many of the components in this domain. However, this chapter treats *reflecting on teaching,* and some aspects of *maintaining accurate records* are addressed in Chapter 10: Assessment.

Provides a shared vocabulary ▶

The benefits of having a framework for professional practice, as Danielson notes, are several. First, a framework offers the profession of teaching a shared vocabulary as a way to communicate about excellence. For novice teachers, a framework provides a pathway to excellence by laying out the twenty-two important components that constitute professional practice. A framework for teaching provides a structure for discussion among teachers and serves to sharpen the focus for professional development. A framework also serves to communicate to the larger community the array of competencies needed to be an effective teacher.

◼ A Reflective Decision-Making Model of Teaching

The hallmark of a professional ▶

There are many different models depicting the teacher's role. Each is based on different assumptions about effective teaching and the nature of teachers' work. The model of the teacher as a **reflective decision maker** was selected as the organizing rubric of this book because of the model's simplicity and its power to capture the essence of what teachers do in the instructional process. Teachers are professionals who are educated and trained to make and implement decisions. Admittedly, this conceptualization is a simplification of what occurs in teaching, but that is why models are useful. They allow us to see the forest without being confused by the trees.

This particular model represents a theory of teaching and makes several basic assumptions. First, the model assumes that teaching is goal directed; that is, some change in the students' thinking or behavior is sought. Second, the model assumes that teachers are active shapers of their own actions. They make plans, implement them, and continually adjust to new information concerning the effects of their actions. Third, the model assumes that teaching is basically a rational and reflective process that can be improved by examining its components in an analytical manner. Analytic decision making is particularly important because teachers often have to make their decisions quickly and under uncertain conditions.

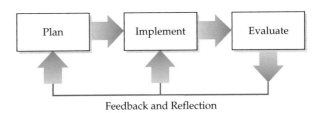

■ Figure 1.2

Model of the teacher as reflective decision maker

Reflecting on the decisions they have made will help teachers over time to develop personal practical knowledge. Fourth, the model assumes that teachers, by their actions, can influence students to change their own thinking or behavior in desired ways. Stated another way, the model assumes that teachers can affect student learning. The various steps of this decision-making model are depicted in Figure 1.2. Within the instructional role, teachers must make decisions related to the three basic teaching functions shown in Figure 1.2: (1) planning, (2) implementation, and (3) evaluation.

Planning ▸ The *planning* function requires that teachers make decisions about:

- their students' needs
- the most appropriate goals and objectives to help meet those needs
- the content to be taught
- the motivation necessary to attain their goals and objectives and
- the instructional modes and teaching strategies most suited to the attainment of those goals and objectives.

The planning function usually occurs when teachers are alone and have time to reflect and consider long- and short-range plans, the students' progress toward achieving objectives, the availability of materials, the time requirements of particular activities, and other such issues. Some teaching skills that support the planning function include observing pupil behavior, diagnosing pupil needs, setting goals and objectives, sequencing goals and objectives, and determining appropriate learning activities related to the objectives.

Implementing ▸ The *implementation* function requires that teachers implement the decisions that were made in the planning stage, particularly those related to instructional modes, teaching strategies, and learning activities. While much of the planning function is accomplished when teachers are alone, the implementation function occurs when teachers are interacting with students. Research indicates that teachers make an average of one interactive decision every two to six minutes.[10] These decisions frequently must be made rapidly in response to classroom situations. Often, teachers have to make adjustments in their plans based on student questions and how the teachers perceive the lesson to be going. Teaching skills that support the implementation function include presenting and explaining, questioning, listening, introducing, demonstrating, eliciting student responses, and achieving closure.

Evaluating ▸ The *evaluation* function requires decisions about the suitability of chosen objectives as well as the teaching strategies keyed to those objectives and, ultimately, whether or not the students are achieving what the teacher intended. To make the necessary decisions, teachers must determine what kind of information they need and then gather it. Teaching skills that support the evaluation function include specifying the learning objectives to be evaluated; describing the information needed to make such evaluation; obtaining, analyzing, and recording that information; and forming judgments.

The **feedback and reflection** dimension of the decision-making model simply means that you examine the results of your teaching, consider their meaning, and then decide how adequately you handled each of these three teaching functions. On the basis of this examination, you determine whether you have succeeded in attaining your objectives or whether you need to make new plans or try different implementation strategies. Feedback and your reflection on the feedback, then, is the new information you process into your decision making to adjust your planning, implementation, or evaluation functions—or to continue as before. It is the decision-making system's way of correcting itself.

Importance of Reflective Teaching

Developing the habit of reflection ▶

Principle 9: The teacher is a reflective practitioner who continually evaluates the effects of his/her choices and actions on others (students, parents, and other professionals in the learning community) and who actively seeks out opportunities to grow professionally.

Involves both logic and emotion ▶

Reflective teaching is a teacher's habit of examining and evaluating his or her teaching on a regular basis. Using the skills related to observation, analysis, interpretation, and decision making, reflective practitioners are able to inquire into teaching and to think critically about their work. Reflection typically includes reconstructing an experience, making connections to prior knowledge or skills, examining the thoughts and understandings that undergird our teaching, and making decisions about how to apply the knowledge or skills in a new situation. Walter Doyle identifies the knowledge base for reflective practitioners as including personal knowledge, craft knowledge of skilled practitioners, and propositional knowledge from classroom research and from the social and behavioral sciences.[11] According to Doyle, theoretical and empirical knowledge, along with teaching skills, are embedded in a conceptual framework that permits the teacher to deliberate about teaching problems and practices. Instead of blindly following rules and prescriptions that are derived from research, reflective practitioners use this theoretical and empirical knowledge, along with knowledge about themselves and craft knowledge derived from skilled teachers, to arrive at decisions that make sense to them given the particularities related to their students and their learning environment. Reflection is the process by which teachers continue to learn and improve their teaching.

What distinguishes reflective teaching from unreflective teaching? John Dewey, America's most famous and influential philosopher, described teachers who are unreflective about their teaching as accepting, without critical examination, the everyday reality of their schools. They tend to concentrate on the most effective and efficient ways to practice their craft and to solve problems without questioning the commonly accepted view of the problem. They do not consider that other views of problems and reality may exist.[12] Dewey recognized that teachers cannot reflect about everything that happens in a school day, but must balance reflection with routine.

Dewey goes on to say that reflection is not a series of steps or procedures; it is a holistic approach of examining and responding to problems. Nor is reflective teaching just a logical, rational problem-solving process. Rather, reflection also involves the affect—emotion, feelings, and intuition. As two writers describe the process, "In reflective action, in contrast to routine action, reason and emotion are engaged."[13]

Donald Schön, a professor at the Massachusetts Institute of Technology, described the reflective process as occurring in two phases: *reflection-on-action* and *reflection-in-action*.[14] *Reflection-on-action* occurs when planning for a lesson or in thinking about a lesson that has already been taught. This type of reflection tends to be more leisurely and less demanding of an immediate response. *Reflection-in-action* occurs during the teaching of a lesson, often requiring an immediate response. For example, if the teacher asks a question, and the student responds with a totally unexpected answer, the teacher must decide quickly how to react to the student's answer. In doing so, the teacher will likely consider the ability of the student, previous interactions with the student, and the range of reactions she might make in response.

Consider underlying assumptions ▶

Schön argues that practitioners make assumptions that undergird their actions. Through reflection on their actions, teachers can bring to the surface some of these assumptions that often go unrecognized and, in doing so, can criticize, examine, and improve these tacit understandings. Schön urges practitioners to engage in the process of framing and reframing problems in light of their experiences and what they learn in their settings. To do this effectively, teachers need to understand their own beliefs and values. Often, through the process of reflection, teachers come to achieve greater self-understanding.

Consider moral and ethical issues ▶

Reflection on the moral and ethical issues in the decision-making process is strongly urged and supported by many teacher educators. Teachers make moral and ethical decisions every day in the personal examples they set, in the classroom climate they create, and in their interactions with students, parents, and colleagues. These everyday ethics of teaching influence everyone with whom teachers come into contact. When teachers decide how they treat students and others, they make ethical decisions. When they elect to create a classroom climate that fosters safety, trust, and cooperation, they make ethical decisions. When they choose particular examples from history or literature for students to study, they make ethical decisions. In other words, you cannot teach without making ethical decisions.

In addition to the everyday ethics of teaching, teachers are often confronted with ethical dilemmas that demand action but involve competing values. For example, a normally uninterested student has spent hours and hours on a term paper, but its quality is quite poor. He expresses his hope that you will take effort into account when grading the paper. You want to encourage his new engagement in schoolwork, but you also feel the need to be fair to the other students. What do you do? Teaching is filled with many such ethical dilemmas. For further reading on the moral and ethical aspects of teaching, see the Strike and Soltis book listed at the end of the chapter.

Maria Dominguez: A Case of Reflective Decision Making

Maria Dominguez, a first-year third-grade teacher at Willow Oaks Elementary School, had spent the weekend prior to school opening setting up her classroom just the way she wanted it. The bulletin boards were lively and reflected the first theme she planned on teaching to her third graders. She had placed the desks in straight rows and had textbooks sitting on each of the desks, saving herself time trying to organize the class. Within the first two hours of class, things had begun to go wrong. Several of the boys had started a game of seeing how loud a noise they could make by pushing the textbooks off the desks onto the floor. After warning the boys a couple of times, Maria yelled at Bobby Chapel, something she never thought she would have to do to gain control. By the time recess rolled around, the neat rows of desks looked like serpentine walls, and students were wandering

*Ways to reflect on
problems of practice*

Tools for Reflective Teachers

Reflection on the practice of teaching can take many forms.

- *Teaching journal.* Many teachers keep a journal to record their thoughts and reactions to each day's events. Writing about and describing the events that occur in your classroom gives you the opportunity to reexamine these events in a calmer and less distracting setting (at home after school, for example) and to propose solutions to problems that may have arisen. A journal can also provide you, as a new teacher, with a potentially rewarding record of growth in your thinking and problem-solving ability.

- *Video recordings.* Videos provide a visual and aural reminder of what happened in the classroom and act as triggers for recalling feelings, events, and intentions. They also seem to objectify the teaching, allowing teachers to feel less defensive and more willing to consider alternatives. Viewing a video of your own teaching nearly always reveals patterns of behavior that you didn't know existed. Reflecting on the effects of these behavioral patterns on student learning provides motivation either to continue or to change these patterns.

- *Teaching portfolios.* **Teaching portfolios** consist of artifacts (videos, tests, lesson plans, student work, and other teacher-created materials) that provide a record of a teacher's professional growth and development. You can choose what items you want to include in your portfolio, justifying to yourself why you want to include particular items and what they say about you and your teaching. Reviewing their portfolios enables teachers to reflect on their teaching practices, see where they need to make changes, and recognize areas in which they are performing well. Teaching portfolios can be digitized or in hard copy.

- *Colleagues.* Reflection is easier when you work with a mentor or a colleague to obtain another's perspective and to get new ideas. By revealing your teaching to another teacher, you make your ideas explicit and open for examination. Observe your colleagues, too, if you can. Watching others can provide insights about your own practices, as well as giving you new ideas.

around the class to sharpen pencils or come to her desk to ask her questions. By the end of the day, she had emptied her bottle of Advil and was wondering if she had made a good career choice.

Before leaving to go home, Maria took 20 minutes to write in the journal she had been keeping since the beginning of her teacher education program. After she had finished writing, Maria realized that she had made at least six major mistakes during her class, and probably missed some others. Next to each of the mistakes that she had identified, she left space to comment after she thought about the incidents.

When Maria got home to her apartment, she put on her jogging outfit and took a 45-minute run. After showering and fixing a light dinner, Maria returned to look at her journal and reread what she had written. Next to each mistake that she had identified, she jotted down ideas of how she could correct the mistake or avoid it entirely in the future. For example, instead of having rows of desks, she decided she would try to group the desks in squares, four desks to a square. She also regretted yelling at Bobby and vowed to catch him doing something good tomorrow. By the time she went to sleep, she was feeling better about teaching, but she knew she had lots to learn.

We present Maria's case to illustrate that the teacher's role can be described as one of a *reflective decision maker*. Maria had made a number of planning decisions that turned out not to work so well—desks in a row and lack of instructions on how to get permission to leave desks, to name a couple. Her implementation decisions were also wanting, as she allowed the boys to play their "noise" game without stepping in to stop it at the first instance. However, what she really excelled at was her deliberate and active reflection on the day's events. By writing in her journal immediately after school had ended, she captured the day's events while they were fresh in her memory. She was also honest with herself by identifying her mistakes and not trying to blame the day's events on external factors such as bad kids. By taking each mistake and considering how the mistakes could be corrected or avoided in the future, Maria learned from the day's experience. A pattern of such reflective behavior over her teaching career will provide a great path to effective teaching.

Factors Influencing Instructional Decisions

Teachers do not make instructional decisions in a vacuum; many factors influence the decision-making process. For example, knowing and understanding your students and their backgrounds is imperative if you are to plan and implement instruction effectively. Your students will represent many kinds of diversity that will affect how they learn. They will differ from one another in terms of racial, ethnic, and cultural backgrounds. These differences influence their perspectives on many issues and often their preferred ways of learning and behaving. Some will speak a primary language other than English, which poses a particular challenge to teachers as they plan and implement their lessons.

Poverty ▶ Some students will come from backgrounds in poverty, which may influence their readiness to learn certain concepts and principles. Many studies have demonstrated the deleterious effects of poverty on student achievement. For example, children from poverty backgrounds are much more likely to suffer from the effects of inadequate health care, shelter, clothing, and nutrition. These negative conditions affect the children's abilities to attend school regularly, concentrate on learning, and do homework. Children from poverty backgrounds pose a particular challenge to schools, partly because schools tend to be more oriented toward serving middle-class children. Many more school dropouts come from poverty backgrounds than from middle-class backgrounds. Making the curriculum and instructional experiences relevant to poor children constitutes a major challenge that schools and teachers must meet.

Racial, Ethnic, and Cultural Diversity ▶ Our schools today have greater racial, ethnic, linguistic, and cultural diversity than at any time in our history. About 43 percent of school-age children are minorities—a figure that will continue to increase in coming years.[15] As might be expected with increased cultural diversity, teachers will have more students whose native language is not English and whose ethnic and cultural backgrounds reflect a Hispanic or Asian heritage. Chapter 7, "Culturally Responsive Teaching," is aimed toward helping prospective teachers succeed with students whose ethnic and cultural backgrounds may differ from their own.

Gender ▶ Students' gender also influences how we think of them and what we often expect of them. Treating boys and girls equitably as individuals rather than as gender stereotypes is a challenge for both male and female teachers.

Other factors ▶ Students also differ in terms of their needs for belonging, safety, and self-esteem. Children from stable, secure homes may have different needs from children who have not had this kind of security. Recognizing diverse needs will help you to better understand students and why they behave the way they do. Students will also come to your classroom with different abilities, achievements, and learning styles. A huge challenge for you as a teacher will be to provide a variety of learning experiences to accommodate your students' diverse backgrounds, needs, learning styles, and abilities.

Personal practical knowledge ▶ The teacher's personal practical knowledge also influences decision making. Richard Kindsvatter and colleagues argue that a well-informed belief system is the most credible basis for rational teacher decisions.[16] They assert that teachers should become aware of the assumptions and values that compose their belief systems. Then, as they develop attitudes and habits of practice (for instance, patterns of decision making), they should examine them carefully to ensure conformity to accepted educational principles. As teachers plan instruction, interact in classrooms, and evaluate instructional outcomes, these attitudes and habits of practice—tested against sound educational principles—will become a safeguard against poor educational decision making.

The five general areas of teacher competence discussed earlier represent the broad categories of preparation that teachers need to make intelligent, effective decisions. Thus, competence in theoretical knowledge about learning, attitudes that foster learning and positive human relationships, knowledge of the subject matter to be taught, a repertoire of teaching skills, and personal practical knowledge developed over time and with classroom experience provide teachers with the tools necessary to make and implement professional judgments and decisions. Figure 1.3 depicts this relationship.

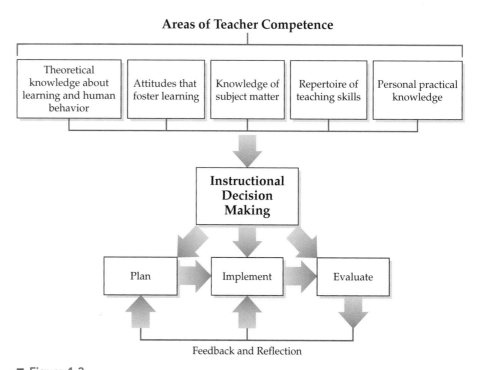

■ Figure 1.3

Relationship of teacher-competence areas to process of instructional decision making

As you think about Figure 1.3, it should become obvious to you that people may strive toward mastery of the reflective decision-making model without ever achieving it. To achieve mastery would require total command of the four general areas of competence and the ability to apply expertly the knowledge, attitudes, and skills acquired in each instructional decision. Even if decision making cannot be perfectly mastered, *through reflection* teachers can become increasingly competent at it and consequently become increasingly effective with their students. The use of cases, simulation activities, action research, and reflection are powerful means by which teacher decision making can be developed and fostered within the context of teacher education programs.

▼ TeachSource Video Case — Becoming a Teacher: Voices and Advice from the Field

In this video, you'll hear both novice and experienced teachers reflecting on why they became a teacher, the joys and challenges of the profession, and the many dimensions of being there for children to help them develop and learn. Throughout the segment, teachers offer advice culled from their own experiences to new teachers just entering the profession. As you watch the clips and study the artifacts in the case, reflect on the following questions. To access the video, go to www.cengage.com/login.

Questions

1. Of the advice given by the teachers in this video, what resonated most with you?
2. View the bonus video, "Essential Qualities That Teachers Must Possess." What essential qualities would you add to the qualities mentioned by the teachers in the video?

☀ Mastery Test for Objectives 1, 2, 3, and 4

OBJECTIVE 1   Describe characteristics of an effective teacher.

OBJECTIVE 2   Explain why reflection on teaching is so important for teacher growth.

OBJECTIVE 3   Describe the reflective decision-making model of teaching.

OBJECTIVE 4   Identify important factors that affect instructional decision making.

_____ 1. Identify five or six characteristics of an effective teacher that you believe are most important and explain why you think they are so important. What other characteristics of lesser importance would you add?

_____ 2. Why is reflective decision making such an important part of effective teaching?

_____ 3. Name some techniques or processes that teachers can use to promote reflective teaching.

_____ 4. Identify the stages of the reflective decision-making model of teaching and their relationship to one another.

_____ 5. What societal factors and characteristics of students affect instructional decision making? Give an example of each factor and how a teacher's decision making might be affected.

ADDITIONAL RESOURCES

Readings

Arends, Richard I. *Learning to Teach,* 8th ed. New York: McGraw-Hill, 2009. This text provides comprehensive coverage of general teaching methods and models.

Borich, Gary D. *Effective Teaching Methods,* 6th ed. Upper Saddle River, N.J.: Pearson/Merrill/Prentice Hall, 2007. This book presents effective teaching practices derived from empirical research.

Danielson, Charlotte. *Enhancing Professional Practice: A Framework for Teaching,* Second Edition. Alexandria, Va.: Association for Supervision and Curriculum Development, 2007. A useful book, organized around a framework of professional practice and based on the PRAXIS III criteria, including planning and preparation, classroom environment, instruction, and professional responsibilities.

Fenstermacher, Gary D., and Jonas F. Soltis with Matthew N. Sanger. *Approaches to Teaching,* 5th ed. New York: Teachers College Press, 2009. Using a number of case studies, this book explores the strengths and weaknesses of three different approaches to teaching—the Executive, the Facilitator, and the Liberationist.

Good, Thomas L., and Jere E. Brophy. *Looking in Classrooms,* 10th ed. New York: Longman, 2008. This excellent book provides teachers with skills that will enable them to observe and interpret the classroom behavior of both teachers and students.

Strike, Kenneth A., and Jonas F. Soltis. *The Ethics of Teaching,* 5th ed. New York: Teachers College Press, 2009. This book uses realistic case studies to explore day-to-day ethical dilemmas facing teachers.

Ryan, Kevin, Cooper, James M., and Susan Tauer. *Teaching for Student Learning: Becoming a Master Teacher.* Boston, MA: Houghton Mifflin Co., 2008. A comprehensive book of modules on various aspects of teaching, including working with diverse learners, teaching methods, assessment for learning, and professional teaching issues.

Zeichner, Kenneth M., and Daniel P. Liston. *Reflective Teaching: An Introduction.* Mahwah, N.J.: Lawrence Erlbaum Associates, 1996. An excellent introduction to the concept and practice of teacher reflection.

 ### Websites

Teacher's Edition Online: http://www.teachnet.com
A versatile site for teachers that includes lesson plans, educational news, and opportunities to share ideas and problems.

Teacher Information Network: http://www.teacher.com/
Contains web connections to educational organizations, resources, teacher sites, the USDOE, and state DOEs.

Teacher Education: http://educ-reality.com/
An Australian site for student teachers that deals with methodologies, theories, and learning concepts, including Bloom's taxonomy, behavior management, multiple intelligences, Piaget, multiculturalism, special needs, lesson ideas, classroom resources, discussions, web polls, and much more.

Mid-Continent Research for Education and Learning: http://www.mcrel.org/
A regional educational laboratory funded by the U.S. Department of Education, the site contains resources on content standards, school improvement, assessment, curriculum, technology, and much more.

Northwest Regional Educational Laboratory: http://www.nwrel.org/comm/index.php
A regional educational laboratory, the site contains services and products addressing classroom teaching and learning, research and evaluation, and school improvement, and family and community resources.

For these links and additional resources, please visit the Premium Website at **www.cengage.com/login.**

NOTES

1. Robert J. Marzano, *The Art and Science of Teaching* (Alexandria, VA: Association for Supervision and Curriculum Development, 2007), pp. 1–2.

2. David Ryans, *Characteristics of Teachers* (Washington, D.C.: American Council on Education, 1960).

3. J. W. Getzels and P. W. Jackson, "The Teacher's Personality and Characteristics," in *Handbook of Research on Teaching,* ed. N. L. Gage (Chicago: Rand McNally, 1963), p. 574.

4. B. O. Smith, *Teachers for the Real World* (Washington, D.C.: American Association of Colleges for Teacher Education, 1969), p. 122.

5. Thomas L. Good and Jere E. Brophy, *Looking in Classrooms,* 10th ed. (New York: Longman, 2008), pp. 49–51.

6. Lee S. Shulman, "Knowledge and Teaching: Foundations of the New Reform," *Harvard Educational Review* 57 (February 1987): 8.

7. Kathy Carter and Walter Doyle, "Personal Narrative and Life History in Learning to Teach," in *Handbook of Research on Teacher Education,* 2nd ed., ed. John Sikula (New York: Macmillan, 1996), pp. 124–125.

8. Kathy Carter, "Teachers' Knowledge and Learning to Teach," in *Handbook of Research on Teacher*

Education, ed. W. Robert Houston (New York: Macmillan, 1990), pp. 299–302.

9. Charlotte Danielson, *Enhancing Professional Practice: A Framework for Teaching*, Second Edition (Alexandria, Va.: Association for Supervision and Curriculum Development, 2007).

10. Christopher Clark and Penelope Peterson, "Teacher Stimulated Recall of Interactive Decisions" (Paper presented at the annual meeting of the American Educational Research Association, San Francisco, 1986); Richard Shavelson, "Review of Research on Teachers' Pedagogical Judgments, Plans, and Decisions," *Elementary School Journal* 83, no. 4 (1983): 392–413.

11. Walter Doyle, "Themes in Teacher Education Research," in *Handbook of Research on Teacher Education,* ed. W. R. Houston (New York: Macmillan, 1990), p. 6.

12. John Dewey, *How We Think* (Chicago: Henry Regnery, 1933).

13. Kenneth M. Zeichner and Daniel P. Liston, *Reflective Teaching: An Introduction* (Mahwah, N.J.: Lawrence Earlbaum Associates, 1996), p. 10.

14. Donald A. Schön, *Educating the Reflective Practitioner* (San Francisco: Jossey-Bass, 1987), p. 26.

15. U.S. Bureau of the Census, *Annual Estimates of the Population by Sex, Race, and Hispanic or Latino Origin for the United States: July 1, 2006.* Available at: http://www.census.gov/popest/national/asrh/NC-EST2006.xls; *The Condition of Education 2006* (Washington, D.C.: U.S. Department of Education, National Center for Education Statistics, 2006), p. 116.

16. Richard Kindsvatter, William Wilen, and Margaret Ishler, *Dynamics of Effective Teaching* (White Plains, N.Y.: Longman, 1996), pp. 2–3.

2

Instructional Objectives

Terry D. Tenbrink

□ **INTASC Standards**

● **INTASC Principle 1:** Understands the central concepts, tools of inquiry, and structure of the disciplines taught; creates learning experiences to make them meaningful to students.

● **INTASC Principle 2:** Understands how children learn and develop; provides learning opportunities that support their development.

● **INTASC Principle 4:** Understands and uses a variety of instructional strategies.

● **INTASC Principle 7:** Plans instruction based on knowledge of subject matter, students, the community, and curriculum goals.

Paul Conklin/PhotoEdit

□ **OBJECTIVES**

1. To recognize well-defined instructional objectives

2. To write well-defined instructional objectives

3. To use instructional objectives in instructional planning

4. To use objectives in implementing instruction

T hink for a moment about what teachers do. Sit back and try to remember the *one* teacher whom you felt had the most influence on you. Write down the characteristics of that teacher as well as you can remember them. Chances are that among the characteristics of your favorite teacher was the fact that the teacher knew you as an individual and knew what he or she wanted for you. This favorite teacher probably had a significant influence on your life, playing a part in the development of your attitudes, the formation of your habits, and the acquisition of information that was new and exciting to you. This teacher may have guided you subtly or may have directly "pushed" you towards these goals. The teacher may have used a great many visual aids or none at all, or may have given multiple-choice tests, essay tests, or no tests at all. What effective teachers have in common is *not* their techniques, their teaching styles, or the kinds of tests they use. It is *what* they accomplish, not how they accomplish it, that makes the difference.

☐ INTASC Principles 1, 7, 4

If teachers are going to make a significant difference in the lives of their students, they must know what they want their students to accomplish. Having formulated such goals, or **instructional objectives**, teachers can share them with their students so that the students will also know where they are going and what is expected of them.

There is considerable evidence to support the contention that when teachers have clearly defined instructional objectives and have shared them with their students, a number of things happen:[1]

1. Better instruction occurs.
2. More efficient learning results.
3. Better evaluation occurs.
4. The students become better self-evaluators.

Teachers need to define instructional objectives so that they will be clear, valid statements of what they want their students to know or be able to do. Then they must learn to use those objectives in ways that will improve their teaching and their testing. The rest of this chapter is designed to help you do just that.

☐ Sources of Instructional Objectives

Instructional objectives can come from numerous sources. These sources may provide you with the objectives that you can use exactly as they are, or you may wish to modify the objectives slightly before using them.

Textbooks and syllabi ▷ Textbooks and teacher's manuals frequently include well-written instructional objectives; check them to make certain they meet the criteria for useful instructional objectives. Another important source for objectives is the school-provided curriculum syllabus for the course you teach. These syllabi are most commonly supplied by the school system for middle school, junior high, and high school subjects.

Internet ▷ A more recent and rapidly growing source for instructional objectives is the Internet. There are several very good World Wide Web sites that provide curricular materials, including objectives and teaching strategies. At the end of the chapter is an annotated list of some of these web sites. Check them out and use the various search engines to search for other sites because new sites are being added regularly.

State and national standards ▷ As you begin the process of defining and/or identifying objectives for your classroom, it would be wise to develop objectives that consider the state and national educational standards that form the basis for much of today's educational reform movement (see Additional Resources at the end of this chapter for references). Note that there is currently an ongoing discussion on how local needs can be met while at the same time adhering to state and national standards.[2,3] This discussion will become especially relevant to you when you find yourself in your classroom trying to meet the needs of your individual students as you prepare them to function in a truly global society.

> **OBJECTIVE 1**   To recognize well-defined instructional objectives

■ Criteria for Useful Instructional Objectives

☐ INTASC Principle 7

Learning Activity 3.1

Instructional objectives that are useful in the classroom must meet certain criteria. We have outlined these criteria[*] below. Look them over carefully, and then we will discuss each of them in turn.

A useful instructional objective must be (1) student-oriented, (2) descriptive of an appropriate learning outcome, (3) clear and understandable, and (4) observable.

1. Student-Oriented

An instructional objective that is student-oriented places the emphasis on what the *student* is expected to do, not on what the teacher will do. Look at the following examples; notice that they all describe student behavior, not teacher behavior.

> ### Examples of Student-Oriented Objectives
>
> 1. Students should be able to solve long-division problems using at least two different methods.
> 2. Students should be able to name the notes on the treble clef lines.
> 3. Students should be able to write down their observations of a simple experiment, stating what was done and what happened.
> 4. When given the description of a form of government, students should be able to classify that form of government and list its probable strengths and weaknesses.

Sometimes teachers use instructional goals that emphasize what they themselves are expected to do rather than what they expect of their students. Such teacher-oriented objectives only have value if they direct the teacher to do something that ultimately leads to student learning. A teacher attempting to help students attain the goal of solving long-division problems may work out some of the problems on the chalkboard, explaining each of the steps involved. A teacher-oriented objective associated with this goal might read: "To explain the steps in long division on the blackboard." Notice that this might be a helpful teacher activity, but it is only *one* of many possible activities that could help students reach the goal of solving long division.

*List excerpted from *Evaluation: A Practical Guide for Teachers,* by T. D. TenBrink. Copyright © 1974 by McGraw-Hill Book Company. Reprinted with the permission of The McGraw-Hill Companies.

> **YOUR TURN** | **Recognizing Student-Oriented Objectives**

The following exercise will give you practice in distinguishing between student-oriented and teacher-oriented objectives. Place an *S* before each student-oriented and a *T* before each teacher-oriented objective.

_____ 1. To read at least 250 words per minute with no less than 80 percent comprehension

_____ 2. To discuss each student's individualized education plan with them and their parents

_____ 3. To outline my lecture on the board before class begins

_____ 4. When given the description of a complex machine, to identify the simple machines contained within it

_____ 5. To help the students appreciate classical music

_____ 6. To lecture on the basic steps in the scientific method

_____ 7. To carry out an investigation using the scientific method

_____ 8. To maintain discipline in my class

_____ 9. To draw a picture of a scene using a vanishing point

_____ 10. To evaluate a poem on the basis of the criteria for good poetry as discussed in class

Now check your answers against the Answer Key. If you missed more than three, you may wish to reread this section before going on.

2. Descriptive of Appropriate Learning Outcomes

The first thing to keep in mind here is that we are interested in what the students will learn to do. In other words, it is the learning *outcome* that is important, not the learning activities that lead to that outcome. To say that students will practice long-division problems using two different methods is not to specify a learning outcome. It specifies an activity designed to help the students reach some outcome. As such, it is a student-oriented activity, *not* an outcome.

Second, keep in mind that useful objectives are appropriate. To begin with, they must occur in an appropriate place in the instructional sequence (sequentially appropriate). They must also be developmentally appropriate; that is, they should be appropriate for the developmental level of the students.

Sequentially appropriate ▷ For an objective to be sequentially appropriate, all prerequisite objectives must already have been attained. Always make certain the prerequisite skills have been attained before starting to work on a new objective. It is particularly important when teaching special children (whether challenged or gifted) to make certain that prerequisite objectives have been met. Do not assume that a challenged child has not met the prerequisites or that a gifted child has.

As indicated earlier in the book, Model Standards for Beginning Teacher Licensing and Development have been developed by the Interstate New Teacher Assessment and Support Consortium (INTASC). You should read these standards carefully, since they represent the most current thinking about the competencies needed by beginning teachers (see the full listing of these standards beginning on p. 372). One of the knowledge standards reads as follows: "The teacher is aware of expected development progressions and ranges of individual variation within each domain (physical, social, emotional, moral, and cognitive), can identify levels of readiness in learning, and understands how development in any one domain may affect performance in others."

Developmentally
appropriate ▶

☐ **INTASC Principle 2**

Can be mental,
emotional, or ▶
movement-oriented

Elementary school teachers, especially, must be aware of the developmental stages of their students. No author or researcher has more clearly defined the stages of intellectual development than Jean Piaget.[4] Do take the time to study Piaget's work carefully. It would be a good idea to take a child development course and learn about other child development theories as well (such as Vygotsky's language development,[5] Erikson's social development,[6] and Kohlberg's moral development[7]).

Not all instructional objectives are cognitive in nature. There is widespread agreement among educators that instructional objectives fall into three categories or domains: cognitive, affective, and psychomotor. *Cognitive objectives* refer to outcomes that focus on what the mind is able to accomplish (including memorizing knowledge, forming concepts, solving problems, and analyzing and/or synthesizing information). *Affective objectives* refer to outcomes that focus on emotional reactions to people, places, things, ideas, and so forth. Many of the affective objectives that are part of an educational curriculum have to do with the attitudes that students exhibit. Although these kinds of objectives are difficult to measure, they are obviously important to the full development of our students as we prepare them to become contributing citizens. The alternative assessment strategies discussed in Chapter 10 are especially useful when trying to measure affective objectives. *Psychomotor objectives* refer to outcomes that focus on physical movement and the control of muscles and muscle groups. Many school subjects require students to master psychomotor objectives. For example, penmanship requires eye–hand coordination, as do drawing, painting, and sculpture. All sports require muscle control, and playing any musical instrument requires a great deal of fine- and gross-motor coordination.

3. Clear and Understandable

The first prerequisite for a clear and understandable objective is explicitness. The objective should contain a clearly stated verb that describes a definite action or behavior and, in most cases, should refer to an object of that action. Examine the examples that follow. In each case, the verb and its object have been italicized. As you read these examples, try to see if there is more than one possible meaning for any of them. If they are well stated and explicit, only one meaning should be possible.

Examples of Clearly Stated Objectives

1. The student should be able to *label* the *parts of the heart* correctly on a diagram of the heart similar to the one on page 27 of the text.
2. When given words from the list in the back of the spelling book, the student should be able to *identify words that are incorrectly spelled*.
3. The student should be able to use a yardstick to *measure* the *length, width, and height* of any piece of furniture in the room. The measurements should be accurate to within half an inch.
4. The student should be able to *identify* correctly the *ingredients in a mixture of chemicals* prepared in advance by the teacher.
5. When given a *contemporary poem*, the student should be able to *evaluate* it according to the criteria discussed in class.
6. The student should be able to *list* all the *major parts of a friendly letter*, briefly *describing* the *function of each part*.

7. Given several occasions to listen to different types of music, the student will *select* at least *three different types of music* that he or she likes.
8. The student should be able to *list* at least *five benefits* of working on a project with students from a variety of cultures.

Only one possible meaning; observable ▶ Notice that in each of the preceding examples, not only are there a clearly defined verb and accompanying object, but there is only one possible meaning for each of the statements. It is also important to note that most people observing someone engaged in the behaviors described above, or observing the products of those behaviors, would agree in their judgments about whether the behavior had occurred as stated. In other words, the preceding objectives are not only explicitly stated but are also observable. This characteristic (observability) will be described in the next section.

A word of caution: it is easy to confuse the notion that an objective must be explicit with the idea that it must be highly specific. Objectives should be explicit, that is, unambiguous and understandable. However, being explicit does not mean they have to be highly specific, written down to the minutest of details and the lowest level of a given behavior. Below is an example[*] of an instructional objective that has been written in general terms and then rewritten several times, each time becoming a bit more specific.[8]

1. Students should be able to read with understanding.
2. When given a story to read, the student should be able to answer questions about the content of the story.
3. When given a short story, the student should be able to identify the passages that describe the traits of the main characters.
4. Students should be able to identify the passages that describe the personality traits of the main characters in *Catcher in the Rye*.
5. Students should be able to identify at least five passages from *Catcher in the Rye* that illustrates Holden's confidence in himself.
6. Students should be able to recognize five passages cited in Handout 3 that illustrates Holden's lack of confidence in himself.[9]

Not too general or too specific ▶ Notice that the most useful instructional objectives in the preceding examples are those that fall somewhere in the middle of the continuum from very general to very specific. When instructional objectives become too specific, they lose much of their value as a guide to study and become little more than test questions to be answered. Instructional objectives that are too specific might very well encourage poor study habits. Students may tend to learn just enough to meet the specific objectives but not enough to meet the more general end-of-course objectives. The value of getting students to identify the passages from *Catcher in the Rye* illustrating descriptions of personality traits is that this ability will transfer to other short stories as well. Transferability makes the objective more valuable than one asking the student to recognize those passages from *Catcher in the Rye* that had previously been discussed and identified (such as objective 6).

*Example excerpted from *Evaluation: A Practical Guide for Teachers*, by T. D. TenBrink. Copyright © 1974 by McGraw-Hill Book Company. Reprinted with the permission of The McGraw-Hill Companies.

> **YOUR TURN**   **Recognizing Clear, Unambiguous Objectives**

For each of the following objectives, determine whether it has a single meaning
(mark it with a *1*) or two or more meanings (mark it with a *2*). The first three items have
been done for you. The first is ambiguous. In fact, it could be interpreted to mean the
same thing as items 2 and 3. The problem with item 1, of course, is the fact that the
verb is not explicit. Using a more explicit verb (as in item 2 or 3) clears up the ambiguity.

_2_ 1. To know the presidents of the United States
_1_ 2. To list in writing the presidents of the United States
_1_ 3. To recognize and call by name each president of the United States on seeing his picture
___ 4. To see the connection between well-written sentences and well-written stories
___ 5. To identify the vanishing points in a three-point perspective drawing
___ 6. To establish eye contact with at least five different persons during a three-minute persuasive speech
___ 7. To develop a roll of 35-mm black-and-white film

___ 8. To run a 10-minute mile
___ 9. To appreciate music
___ 10. To mold a lump of clay into the shape of an animal that can be recognized and correctly named by the rest of the class
___ 11. Not to show favoritism to any given child in the preschool
___ 12. To understand the workings of an atomic energy plant
___ 13. To plan a miniature garden according to the criteria for such a garden as described in the article "Apartment Gardening"
___ 14. To enlarge your concept of realism

4. Observable

The evaluation of learning outcomes hinges on the observability of those outcomes. The key to an observable objective is an observable verb. Consequently, when selecting instructional objectives for use in your teaching, *watch the verbs!*

As discussed earlier, a useful objective contains an explicit verb and (usually) a well-defined object of the verb. Both these requirements help make an objective clear and unambiguous. Now we add another requirement: The verb must describe an observable action or an action that results in an observable product.

The verbs in the following box are vague and unobservable. Avoid them.

Vague, Unobservable Verbs That You Should Avoid*	
to know	to enjoy
to understand	to familiarize
to comprehend	to value
to grasp	to realize
to believe	to like
to appreciate	to cope with
to think	to love

The verbs in the following box describe observable actions or actions that yield observable products. When you write objectives, use these kinds of verbs.

*Example excerpted from *Evaluation: A Practical Guide for Teachers*, by T. D. TenBrink. Copyright © 1974 by McGraw-Hill Book Company. Reprinted with the permission of The McGraw-Hill Companies.

Verbs That You Should Use*

to identify	to analyze
to speak	to predict
to list	to locate
to select	to explain
to align	to isolate
to compute	to divide
to manipulate	to separate
to draw	to infer

There are many processes and skills that cannot be directly observed but that produce observable products. It is not possible for us to observe the thinking process of a student as he or she strives to solve an algebraic equation. However, we can examine the solution he or she arrives at and decide whether or not it is correct. We may be able to look at each of the steps taken to arrive at that solution if he or she writes them down for us (displaying his or her thinking as a product). On the other hand, a well-written prose paragraph, a poem, and an oil painting can all be observed and analyzed. These end products and others like them can serve as "observables" that may help to indicate whether or not an expected learning outcome has occurred.

When selecting or writing instructional objectives, it is helpful to distinguish between those that specify observable behaviors and those that specify end products of behaviors.

Ask what ▶ The use of strong, active verbs such as those in the second box will yield objectives that are either observable or whose end products are observable. If the object of any of these verbs does not describe an observable end product, however, the resulting objective would be vague and nonobservable. For example, examine the following objective: "To explain diversity."

What is supposed to be explained? The *value* of diversity within a society? The *reasons* why diversity in an organization is often feared? The various *strategies* that organizations can take to help individuals adapt positively in a diverse workforce? All of these and more are possible explanations. The problem is not in the verb, but in the object of the verb. Make certain that both the verb and its object are clearly defined, pointing to observable actions or observable end products.

Observation Worksheet

ANALYSIS OF OBJECTIVES

This activity is designed to give you the opportunity to examine instructional objectives, identifying their strengths and weaknesses according to the criteria set forth in this chapter.

Directions: Do not use actual names of schools, teachers, administrators, or students when using this worksheet.

Observer's Name: _____

Date: _____

*Example excerpted from *Evaluation: A Practical Guide for Teachers*, by T. D. TenBrink. Copyright © 1974 by McGraw-Hill Book Company. Reprinted with the permission of The McGraw-Hill Companies.

Grade Level: _____

Subject: _____

Class Size: _____

Source of Objectives: _____

Background Information: Give a brief general description of the school's social, economic, and ethnic makeup.

_____

_____

What to Record: Ask the teacher you are observing for copies of the objectives he/she is using to guide his/her teaching for that day or week. These objectives may be a part of the teacher's lesson plans, the course syllabus, or in the teacher's manual.

Reflections on Your Observation: Summarize your findings, indicating the major strengths and weaknesses of the objectives you reviewed. For each objective, determine if it meets the following criteria:

1. Well defined? _____

2. Student-oriented? _____

3. Sequentially appropriate? _____

4. Developmentally appropriate? _____

5. Describes a learning outcome? _____

6. Clear and unambiguous? _____

7. Observable? _____

☀ Mastery Test

> **OBJECTIVE 1   To recognize well-defined instructional objectives**

For each of the following pairs, check the objective that best meets the requirements for useful objectives.

1. _____ (a) To be able to develop a roll of black-and-white film

   _____ (b) To understand how a developing agent works

2. _____ (a) To select useful objectives

   _____ (b) To know what makes an objective useful

3. _____ (a) To select from a list of definitions the one that best defines the terms provided on Handout 10

   _____ (b) To know the meaning of the terms on Handout 10

4. _____ (a) To solve math problems requiring an understanding of the place holder

   _____ (b) To understand problem-solving techniques

5. _____ (a) To recognize the pictures of people in the news

   _____ (b) To match the names of people in the news with their pictures

6. _____ (a) To select the good poems from good and bad examples

_____ (b) To evaluate a set of poems

7. _____ (a) To remember the life cycle of the butterfly

_____ (b) To label, from memory, a diagram of the life cycle of a butterfly

8. _____ (a) To hear clearly short and long vowel sounds

_____ (b) To distinguish between short and long vowel sounds

9. _____ (a) To know the phonetic rules and their application in reading

_____ (b) To sound out nonsense words

10. _____ (a) To punctuate a prose paragraph correctly

_____ (b) To list the punctuation rules

For each of the following objectives, determine the primary fault.

11. To grasp the meaning of conservation
    (a) affectively oriented
    (b) teacher-oriented
    (c) vague and unobservable

12. To demonstrate to the students the need for cleanliness
    (a) teacher-oriented
    (b) unobservable
    (c) student-oriented

13. To paint
    (a) poorly defined product
    (b) vague
    (c) teacher-oriented

14. To do workbook pages 18–20
    (a) vague
    (b) poorly defined product
    (c) a learning activity

15. To listen to the guest speaker talk about diversity
    (a) teacher-oriented
    (b) a learning activity
    (c) vague

OBJECTIVE 2   **To write well-defined instructional objectives**

■ Three Steps for Writing Instructional Objectives

□ **INTASC Principles 1, 2, 7**

There are three simple steps for writing effective instructional objectives.[*] Although these steps should normally follow the order specified here, you may occasionally wish to go back and rework a step before moving on. This constant monitoring of your own work, always checking against the criteria

*Excerpted from *Evaluation: A Practical Guide for Teachers,* by T. D. TenBrink. Copyright © 1974 by McGraw-Hill Book Company. Reprinted with the permission of The McGraw-Hill Companies.

for well-defined objectives, will help you produce a clear list of objectives for your own use. Here are the steps:

Learning Activity 3.2

1. Specify the general goals.
2. Break down the general goals into more specific, observable objectives.
3. Check objectives for clarity and appropriateness.

Although these three steps can be applied to course planning as well as lesson planning, it is important to remember that you will not be able to write a set of objectives for an entire course in a short time. You will find it useful, therefore, to work on small units of instruction, one at a time. Eventually, you will have a set of objectives that will cover the full course you are teaching; however, your unit objectives and daily objectives should fit into the overall plan for your course. Consequently, the first step should be nearly complete before you begin working on the objectives for specific units of instruction or for daily lesson plans.

1. Specify the General Goals

In this first step, you will determine in general terms what you want your students to accomplish. At this point, don't worry too much about the wording; just get your general goal(s) written down. These goals can then be rewritten to make them more specific as well as more observable. Often a single goal will lead to several objectives, each one helping the students to attain that goal.

General goals first ▷ Look at the general end-of-course goals listed on the following page. These represent some of the possible goals for a high school psychology course. Most of these goals will each yield several specific, observable objectives.

General Goals for High School Psychology Course

I. Terminal Goals
   A. Students should understand what it means when we say that psychology is a science.
   B. Students should know the major facts about the way in which humans develop.
   C. Students should know, in general, how humans interact with their environment, including their interactions with other humans.
   D. Students should be aware of the various theories of personality, motivation, learning, mental health, and social psychology.
   E. Students should be aware of the most recent writings on diversity in our society.
   F. Students should be able to apply major findings of psychology to the solution of specific problems of human behavior and interaction.
   G. Students should be more aware of their own typical behavior and the reasons for that behavior.

> **YOUR TURN** Specifying General Goals—Parts 1 and 2

Now try writing some general end-of-course goals for the psychology course. Do not duplicate those on the list above. You should be able to write at least five more general goals for this course. Examples of such additional goals are found in the Answer Key for Part 1. Compare what you have written with those examples.

Once the end-of-course goals have been determined, intermediate goals can be written for each unit of instruction. Again, do not worry about whether or not they are observable now. First get them down in a general way; you can rewrite them later.

Below are some possible goals for Unit I: Psychology as a Science. Three cognitive and three **affective goals** have been written. Read them carefully and then try writing some yourself. **Remember:** Unit-level goals should reflect the broader end-of-course goals. Compare your work with the further examples of Unit I goals presented in the Answer Key for Part 2.

II. **The General Intermediate Goals for Unit I: Psychology as a Science**

A. Cognitive Goals
1. Students should know the major dates in the history of psychology.
2. Students should know the major avocations that have made psychology an important applied science.
3. Students should know the steps taken from the development of a theory, to the research and testing of that theory, to the final application of the research findings to practical situations.

B. Affective Goals
1. Students should appreciate the value of the science of psychology to a civilized country.
2. Students should show appreciation for the usefulness of various psychological theories.
3. Students should be sensitive to the needs and opinions of people from diverse backgrounds.

---

2. Break Down the General Goals into More Specific, Observable Objectives

In this step, each general goal is broken down into its two major parts: the subject-matter content and the expected student response to that content. Take a look at the following general cognitive goal from a high school psychology course.

Specific objectives next ▶ Students should know the major founders of psychological theory and the important points in their theories.

First of all, notice that the subject-matter content is divided into (1) the major founders of psychological theories and (2) the important points in each of these theories. When we finalize our list of objectives, these two areas should be kept separate, each serving as the basis for at least one objective. It is usually best to deal with only one area of the subject matter in a given objective.

Now we will take these descriptions of subject-matter content and answer the following questions about each.

1. Is the subject-matter content clearly defined and specific enough?

2. Precisely what response(s) do I want the students to make to that subject-matter content?

In the above goal, the subject-matter content (that is, the founders of psychological theory and points important to each theory) is fairly well defined. This goal could be made more specific, however, by listing the major founders of the theories. The most important concepts for each theory might also be listed. Of course, the real problem with the above goal lies in the use of the vague, unobservable verb "to know." What observable student response could be accepted as evidence that a student "knows"? Would "to list in writing" be acceptable?

The following three objectives were derived from the above general goal. The subject-matter content of that goal was clarified, and the expected student response to that content was more precisely specified.

1. Students should be able to list in writing all the founders of psychological theories discussed in the textbook.

2. Students should be able to match each important concept to the theory with which it is associated. (This goal is limited to the theories found in Unit I in the text.)

3. When given the name of an early psychological theorist, students should be able to identify the concept(s) that are central to the theory.

Try breaking down an **affective goal:**

> Students should become interested in finding out more about the specific aspects of human behavior that have been studied by psychologists.

Specify content + behavior ▷

Sometimes teachers fail to plan for the teaching of affective goals because these goals seem difficult to define in observable terms. It is relatively easy, however, if you clearly define the subject-matter *content* and then specify the *behavior(s)* that are likely to accompany the desired attitude toward that content. The following objective was derived from the above goal in just that way.

> In an open discussion about the value of psychology, students should ask questions that would help them discover what aspects of human behavior psychologists have studied.

In this objective, the content is "questions that would help them discover what aspects of human behavior psychologists have studied." The behavior expected is "to ask." Notice, however, that something else has been added: "In an open discussion about the value of psychology." This phrase suggests a condition or type of situation under which we expect the desired student behavior to occur.

Can include conditions ▷

Although not necessary to the formation of an effective objective, a statement describing any *conditions* of the expected performance is often helpful. Here is another such objective, derived from the above goal (the condition is italicized):

> *When given the task of formulating questions to be sent to famous living psychologists,* the student will include questions such as: "What aspects of human behavior have psychologists studied?"

Level of performance ▷

Besides a statement specifying the condition under which the student response is expected to occur, there is one other useful (though not necessary) addition that can be made to most objectives. There are times when it may be useful to specify the *level of performance* expected of the students.[10] For example, we might derive the following objective from the above goal:

> When books and pamphlets describing the aspects of human behavior studied by psychologists are placed in the class library, the students will sign out *two or more* of these resources.

This objective has the criterion for success built in: two or more resources signed out.

Not only is it possible to set a standard (level of performance expected) for each student, but this can also be done for the class as a whole. By determining the level of performance for each student, each student's performance on that objective can be evaluated. By determining how well the class as a whole should learn, you assess your performance as a teacher. Suppose, for example, the above objective is written so it reads:

> When books and pamphlets describing the aspects of human behavior studied by psychologists are placed in the class library, *at least 75 percent of the students* will sign out two or more of these resources.

If fewer than 75 percent of the students reach the expected level of performance, the goal has not been reached, even though some of your students may have signed out two or more resources.

Review: Breaking Down General Goals into Specific, Observable Objectives

1. Break the goal into two parts: (1) subject-matter content and (2) student response to that content.
2. Clarify the subject-matter content and, where necessary, make it more specific.
3. Determine the expected student response(s) to each statement of subject-matter content.
4. As needed, identify the conditions under which the student response is expected to occur and/or any useful criteria for judging the level of performance expected.

---

3. Check Objectives for Clarity and Appropriateness

To some extent, this last step may be unnecessary. If you do a good job in the first two steps, your objectives should be ready to use. A final check of your work, however, may save you the embarrassment of trying to explain to your students what it was that you "really meant to say." One way to check for the clarity of your objectives is to have a friend (preferably one teaching the subject matter under consideration) review them. If your friend can tell you in his or her own words what each objective means, you can usually

---

❯ YOUR TURN   Breaking Down a General Goal into Specific, Observable Objectives

Write observable objectives for the following goal. Make certain you:

____ 1. Identify the subject-matter content and decide whether or not it is clearly enough defined. If not, describe what is needed to clarify it.

____ 2. For each aspect of subject-matter content identified above, describe at least one ob-

servable response the students might be expected to make to it.

____ 3. If appropriate, specify the conditions under which the student response is expected to occur, and specify an acceptable level of performance.

Goal: The students should understand the major concepts, terms, and principles used in psychological research.

tell whether or not the objective is understandable. If it isn't, that objective probably needs clarification.

Not only must an objective be clearly stated in observable terms, but it must also be appropriate for your students. Use the following checklist to help you determine whether or not an objective is appropriate.

Criteria for Appropriate Objectives

_____ 1. Developmentally appropriate

_____ 2. Attainable by the students within a reasonable time limit

_____ 3. In proper sequence with other objectives (not to be accomplished prior to a prerequisite objective)

_____ 4. In harmony with the overall goals of the course and curriculum

_____ 5. In harmony with the goals and values of the institution

---

If your objectives are clearly stated in observable terms and meet the above criteria, they should be useful to both you and your students. Now, before you take the Mastery Test for Objective 2, look at the following example of a general goal from an elementary school classroom and the more specific objectives that were derived from it:

General goal ▷ Students should be able to sound out words they had not encountered before in their reading.

More specific objective ▷ When seeing words that contain two adjacent vowels, students should be able to sound out those words, using the following rule: "when two vowels go a-walking, the first one does the talking, and says its own name."

The above specific objective is useful for planning instruction but must be taught when the students have mastered at least the following objectives:

Prerequisite objectives ▷ Students should be able to correctly identify all the vowels occurring in any given word.

In words with two vowels occurring together, the students should be able to identify those vowels as "going a-walking" vowels.

Mastery Test

OBJECTIVE 2   To write well-defined instructional objectives

1. List the three steps involved in writing instructional objectives.

2. General, end-of-course goals do not need to be written in observable terms. (True or False)

3. Write at least two observable objectives for each of the following three goals:
   (a) Students should understand how people learn.
   (b) Students should know what motivates people to act.
   (c) Students should understand the value of diversity in the classroom.

4. What are the two parts needed to complete a well-written instructional objective?

5. What are the two useful (although not always needed) parts of a well-written objective?

OBJECTIVE 3   To use instructional objectives in instructional planning

For any given vowel, students should be able to make the sound of that vowel "saying its own name."

So, to review, begin with a general goal, break that goal down into more specific observable objectives and then, when necessary, specify prerequisite objectives that must first be learned. This approach will not only provide you with specific, measurable objectives, but will also help you to teach those objectives only after prerequisite objectives have been mastered.

◼ How Instructional Objectives Can Help You Plan

Learning Activity 3.3

☐ INTASC Principles 4, 7

Despite the fact that there has been considerable controversy over the usefulness of instructional objectives, it is quite clear that they serve an important function in instructional planning.[11] Well-defined instructional objectives can help you (1) focus your planning, (2) plan effective instructional events, and (3) plan valid evaluation procedures.

1. Focus Your Planning

Teachers often complain that they do not have enough time to cover the material. The process of writing instructional objectives forces you to decide, out of all the material to be covered, what you really want your students to know or be able to do. This helps to focus your planning in two ways. First, it helps you eliminate topics that are of lesser importance and highlight the more important subject matter. Second, it helps you plan for a balance of different levels of learning. By examining your final list of instructional objectives for a course (or unit within a course), you can determine whether your plans include a balance of memorization, conceptualization, problem solving, and so forth. Use taxonomies of learning such as those proposed by Bloom[12] or Gagné[13] to help determine whether you have planned for sufficient higher-order learning outcomes and whether you have included appropriate affective and psychomotor objectives. Finally, a note of caution is in order here: Once you have brought your plans into focus, check your final list of objectives to make certain they will help your students meet state and national standards.

2. Plan Effective Instructional Events

In any given instructional event, the most important thing is what is happening in the minds of the students. Everything the teacher does should be designed to get the students to do the thinking that will produce the expected learning outcome. If an instructional objective calls for the students to memorize information, the learner activities should be designed to get them to repeat that information, to form appropriate associations, and so forth. If an instructional objective calls for the students to form a new concept, the learner activities should be designed to get students to focus on the criterial attributes of the concepts to be learned, and to compare and contrast positive and negative instances. In each of these cases, the teacher activities should be designed to help the students do the thinking (memorizing, conceptualizing) required to attain the instructional objective.

It is important that you understand the concept of an instructional event. An **instructional event** is any activity or set of activities in which students are engaged (with or without the teacher) for the purpose of learning (for example, attaining an instructional objective). Listening to a teacher's explanation, watching a film, doing an assignment in history, and completing a workbook page are all examples of instructional events.

Each instructional event should be designed to optimize the learning conditions and provide appropriate activities for both the learner and the teacher. Different kinds of learning require different learning conditions.[14] Note that teachers can use carefully developed questions to help learners reach different levels of learning in Bloom's Taxonomy. Sadker, Sadker, and Zittleman, in their discussion of questioning skills (see Chapter 5), point out the fact that questions can be categorized according to the level of thinking required as defined by Bloom's Taxonomy. Objectives can also be classified according to Bloom's Taxonomy; and the various lists of words suggested by in Chapter 5 as tools to determine the level of Bloom's Taxonomy for questions can also be applied to objectives.

Once you have determined the level of learning required by an objective using any number of available educational taxonomies, you can then plan the kinds of activities that will be most effective in helping students to attain those objectives at those levels. (Watch the video case, *Preparing Students for Standardized Tests: Strategies for Success*, to see how a fourth-grade teacher uses very effective learning activities to help her reach some upper-level learning objectives.)

What type of learning? ▶ The first step in planning appropriate learner and teacher activities is to determine, for each instructional objective, the kind of learning involved. If your instructional objectives are well defined, this should be relatively easy. The secret is in the verbs. The verbs should signal the kind of learning. For example, verbs such as *list, recall,* and *describe* suggest memory learning. Verbs such as *distinguish, differentiate,* and *contrast* suggest discrimination learning. *Identify, categorize,* and *recognize* suggest concept learning. *Solve, diagnose, resolve,* and *determine* suggest problem solving. *Like, enjoy, desire,* and *prefer* suggest affective learning. *Manipulate, perform, do,* and *physically control* suggest skill learning.

What type of activity? ▶ Once you have determined the kind of learning called for by an objective, your next step is to determine the kind of activities that the students have to do to accomplish that kind of learning. There are a number of books that can help you in this task,[15] and some of the other chapters in this book will also help (see, for example, Chapters 2, 4–6, and 8). You might also wish to read some of the learning research literature to find the latest information on how humans achieve particular kinds of learning outcomes. (*Psychological Abstracts* is a particularly useful source.)

▽ **TeachSource Video Case** **Preparing Students for Standardized Tests: Stategies for Success**

Watch the video clip, noting that the teacher first determines the level of learning her students need to reach in order to effectively answer open-ended questions, and then plans effective strategies for helping them to reach that goal. To access the video, go to www.cengage.com/login. Keep in mind the following questions as you watch:

1. How does the teacher plan to help her students initially develop questioning skills while at the same time planning for year-long activities to keep their skill levels up?
2. How does the teacher deal with the fact that each of her students may be at a different level?
3. As she plans her instruction, does the teacher strive to make certain that the learning objectives are sequentially appropriate as well as developmentally appropriate?

Now you are finally ready to determine the teacher activities. The key principle to remember is that everything the teacher does should be designed to help the learners do what they need to do to learn. Therefore, you should not only be providing the students with the information they need, but you should also be helping them process that information in appropriate ways. This is why it is so important for teachers to ask the right kinds of questions at the right time (see Chapter 5).

3. Plan Valid Evaluation Procedures

Validity and reliability are the two most important considerations when evaluating learning (see Chapter 10). Instructional objectives define the expected learning outcomes and therefore are the key to developing valid tests. A test is valid if it measures what it is supposed to. Consequently, whenever teachers want to know how well their students have learned the subject material, they should measure how well those students have attained the outcomes specified in the instructional objectives. Chapter 10 tells you how to use instructional objectives to develop tests and authentic assessment tools that are both valid and reliable. For now, remember that if a test is to be a valid measure of classroom achievement, it must measure as directly as possible each of the instructional objectives taught in that classroom.

 Mastery Test

OBJECTIVE 3   To use instructional objectives in instructional planning

1. List three ways in which instructional objectives can help in instructional planning.
2. Which activities should be determined first?
   (a) Teacher activities
   (b) Learner activities
   (c) It doesn't matter which is determined first.
3. Which part of an instructional objective is most helpful when trying to determine the kind of learning required by that objective?
   (a) The verb
   (b) The description of the subject matter
   (c) The criteria for performance
   (d) The conditions of performance
4. Why is it important to determine the kind of learning required to accomplish an objective?
5. Which criterion for an effective assessment strategy is most reinforced by the use of instructional objectives in evaluation planning?
   (a) Usefulness
   (b) Reliability
   (c) Validity

OBJECTIVE 4   **To use objectives in implementing instruction**

Learning Activity 3.4

The education community has accepted the usefulness of instructional objectives in the planning process. An analysis of available instructional plans will help you appreciate more fully the value of instructional objectives in the planning process. Gather together completed copies of several different instructional plans (course syllabi, completed lesson plans, teacher's manuals, and so forth). Examine these to determine whether objectives are included and, if they are, try to decide how (if at all) the objectives influenced the student activities and/or the teacher activities. Finally, look at the objectives and try to come up with alternate student activities and/or alternate teacher activities that would also be effective in helping the students reach the objectives.

How Instructional Objectives Can Help You Teach

INTASC Principles 1, 2, 4

Well-defined instructional objectives can be a big help to you and your students during the teaching process. First, when used correctly, they can help you clarify the expectations for your students, and clarity has been shown to be a critical element in successful teaching.[16] Second, they can serve as a useful guide to the students as they listen, do assignments, and study for tests.[17] Finally, well-defined instructional objectives can help you stay on track as you teach and help you deal more effectively with sidetracks. To improve your teaching, you can use instructional objectives (1) as handouts prior to instruction, (2) to prepare students for instruction, and (3) as a guide throughout instruction.

Learning Activity 3.5

1. As Handouts Prior to Instruction

There is some evidence in the literature suggesting that students perform better on tests when they have been provided with handouts of well-defined instructional objectives.[18] There are a number of things you can do to make these handouts as effective as possible. Objectives that are clearly articulated, meeting the criteria specified earlier in this chapter, will contribute most to student achievement.[19] According to Melton,[20] however, objectives should also be of interest to the students, at the correct level of difficulty, and relevant to the content to be mastered.

Use frequent handouts and review ▶

It has been my experience that if too many objectives are given to students all at once (for example, all the objectives for a six-week period), they are not used effectively and do little to improve achievement. Try handing out a separate set of objectives for each unit of instruction for each subject. Then review those objectives daily as you work with your students. Finally, keep in mind that we must always consider the great diversity that exists in our classrooms. Adjust your teaching strategies to accommodate that diversity[21] and, where necessary, adapt to the individual needs of your students. See Chapter 6 for ways to differentiate instruction.

2. To Prepare Students for Instruction

Don't reveal answers ▶

Madeline Hunter has been a strong advocate of producing an appropriate learning set in students by telling them what they should be able to expect from any given instructional event.[22] This concept is occasionally criticized by those who advocate a discovery or inquiry approach to learning. The concern is that, if students know the outcome from the beginning, the discovery process will not work effectively. It is my contention, however, that one can adequately prepare students for learning without giving away the answers, and well-written instructional objectives can help you do that. Recall that a well-written objective should not be too specific, though it must be explicit and unambiguous. Therefore, students should be told that they will be expected to be able to solve certain types of problems or that they should be able to discover things such as relationships or causes and effects. They should not be told, however, which specific finding or answer they are expected to discover. The focus should be on the learning outcome—the skill they are expected to acquire during the discovery process—not on the specific outcome of their discovery activities.

Because each instructional activity may require something different of the learner, teachers should prepare students at the beginning of each new instructional event. There are at least four kinds of information that will help prepare students for any given instructional event: (1) learning outcome, (2) learner activities, (3) teacher activities, and (4) assessment activities.

Learning Outcome

A well-written objective is the best statement of learning outcome and is, therefore, especially useful in preparing students for an instructional event. Telling students what they will be expected to know or be able to do upon completion of the instructional event will help prepare them for the activities involved.

Learner Activities

For many students, knowing just the expected learning outcome may not be enough information to help them get the most out of an instructional event. Some students, for example, when told to study Chapter 19 (an instructional event) so that they will be able to describe the major causes of the Civil War (a learning outcome), may not know how to study for such an outcome. Consequently, when preparing students for an instructional event, it is helpful to tell them what they need to do to get the most out of the activities involved and to accomplish the expected outcome successfully. When instructional objectives are well defined, it is much easier to determine the kind of learning activities that would be most appropriate.[23]

Teacher Activities

In most instructional activities, the teacher has a definite role. The teacher activities may involve providing explanations, giving feedback, observing student performance, and so forth; however, they should always involve guiding the learner through the learner activities to the accomplishment of the learning outcome (instructional objective). It is helpful for students to know from the beginning of an instructional event exactly what the role of the teacher will be and exactly how much guidance can be expected.

Assessment Activities

How will the students know if they have accomplished an expected learning outcome? How will the teacher judge a student's performance relative to that learning outcome? Providing students with the answers to these two questions helps prepare them for an instructional event and increases the efficiency of their learning. Well-defined objectives are stated in measurable, observable terms, and the type of evaluation is easily determined. Such is not the case when objectives are poorly written.

3. As a Guide Throughout Instruction

Objectives are not only helpful in preparing students to learn, but they can also serve to keep students and teacher alike focused throughout the instructional process. By keeping instructional objectives constantly in students' minds throughout the instructional process, teachers can significantly reduce the problems of getting off track or focusing on the wrong topics during instruction. This strategy is especially effective in a constructivist approach to instruction, where the learning/discovering process is paramount. Better learning occurs when the goals to be accomplished are kept in mind throughout the discovery process. If you make it obvious that you are using instructional objectives to guide what you do as teacher, if the things you ask your students to do are designed to help them accomplish the instructional objectives, and if your tests do indeed evaluate the instructional objectives, then both you and your students will stay better focused. This is not to say that sidetracks are always bad or that something is not worth learning if an objective has not been written to cover it. But your instructional objectives should serve as a primary guide for what you teach, what your students learn, and what you assess.

Learning Activity 3.6

Here is a simple exercise that can help you understand the value of using objectives as a regular part of the instructional process. You and your classmates should divide into small groups, five to six per group. Each group will develop a handout of four or five objectives for a given unit of instruction (specify the grade level as well as the subject). Using the above guidelines, prepare a brief presentation (it may not take more than a few seconds to present) designed to prepare the students to learn. One member of your

※ Mastery Test

OBJECTIVE 4   To use objectives in implementing instruction

1. List three ways in which you can use instructional objectives to improve your teaching.
2. Which of the following schedules for handing out objectives to students is most likely to be effective?
   (a) All course objectives provided on a handout as an overview at the beginning of the course.
   (b) Unit objectives provided on a handout as an overview at the beginning of each unit.
   (c) Each objective provided as a handout at the beginning of the class when that objective will be taught.
3. List four things that should be told to students to prepare them for an instructional event.
4. Instructional objectives should guide:
   (a) Teaching.
   (b) Evaluating.
   (c) Learning.
   (d) All of the above.

group should use the handout and present an overview of the unit, preparing the students for that unit. Each of the other members of your group should make a presentation, preparing the students to begin learning a given objective from those on the handout. Make certain that you tell the students the learning outcome and describe for them the learner activities, teacher activities, and evaluation activities. Discuss each group's presentations, focusing on how well the presentations prepared you to begin to learn.

ADDITIONAL RESOURCES

Readings

Anderson, L. W., Krathwohl, D. R., eds. *A Taxonomy of Educational Objectives for Learning, Teaching, and Assessing: A Revision of Bloom's Taxonomy of Educational Objectives*, 2nd ed. Boston: Allyn and Bacon 2000.

Carver, Sharon, and David Klahr, eds. *Cognition and Instruction: 25 Years of Progress.* Mahwah, N.J.: Earlbaum, 2001.

Gagné, R. M., Wager, W. W., Golas, K., and John M. Keller. *Principles of Instructional Design,* 5th ed. Belmont, Calif.: Wadsworth, 2004.

Gallagher, Suzanne. *Educational Psychology: Disrupting the Dominant Discourse.* New York: P. Lang, 2004.

Gronlund, Norman E. and S. M. Brookhart. *Writing Instructional Objectives,* 8th ed. Upper Saddle River, N.J.: Prentice-Hall, 2008.

Krathwohl, David R., Benjamin S. Bloom, and Bertram B. Masia. *Taxonomy of Educational Objectives: Vol. 2. Affective Domain.* Reading, Mass.: Addison-Wesley, 1999.

Mager, Robert F. *Preparing Instructional Objectives: A Critical Tool in the Development of Effective Instruction*, 3rd ed. Atlanta, Ga.: Center for Effective Performance, 1997.

Marzano, Robert J., Debra Pickering, and Jane E. Pollock. *Classroom Instruction That Works: Research-Based Strategies for Increasing Student Achievement.* Alexandria, Va.: Association for Supervision and Curriculum Development, 2001.

Marzano, Robert J., and J. S. Kendall. *Designing and Assessing Educational Objectives: Applying the New Taxonomy.* Thousand Oaks, CA: Corwin Press, 2008.

Smaldino, S., Lowther, D. and J. Russell. *Instructional Media and Technologies for Learning.* 9th ed. Englewood Cliffs: Prentice Hall, Inc. 2007.

Websites

Access ERIC: http://www.eric.ed.gov
Access ERIC, the promotional and outreach arm of the U.S. Department of Education's Educational Resources Information Center (ERIC) system, keeps you informed of the wealth of information offered by the ERIC components and other education-related organizations. This site is a beginning point for access to all of the ERIC web sites and can help you in your search for the latest information on all aspects of education, including sources of information on appropriate instructional objectives for various subjects at various grade levels.

The Council of Chief State School Officers: http://www.ccsso.org
This is the web site for the Council of Chief State School Officers and includes the INTASC standards, as well as information on council projects, federal legislative positions, policy statements, and news releases of interest to educators.

Yahoo's Directory of K–12 Lesson Plans: http://dir.yahoo.com/Education/K_12/Teaching/Lesson_Plans/
This web site consists of a variety of lesson plans and resources that are already developed for a variety of subjects. It also talks about different types of media and learning activities that are helpful in teaching the subject material. On this site, click on the appropriate icon or highlighted word to bring you into the different subject areas. In addition, the "AskERIC Lesson Plans" search (http://eduref.org/Virtual/Lessons/index.shtml) will provide a listing of new lesson plans submitted to this web site for different months during the year. Each month contains many different specific lesson plans, with the subject and appropriate grade levels listed.

Teacher's Net, Lesson Bank: http://www.teachers.net/lessons/posts/posts.html
This web site contains around 200 prepared lesson plans that have been submitted by teachers around the world. The specific topic is listed, along with the grade level and subject area (for instance, *Mini Page Term Paper,* Elementary, Reading/Writing). It also provides you with the capability to submit lesson plans you have developed, search for specific lessons, and request lesson plans from certain topics.

Science Teachers' Resource Center: http://chem.lapeer.org
This web site is for science teachers to share ideas. Included are labs, demonstrations, and other information helpful in planning science instruction. Permission is granted to use and reproduce all materials at this site as long as the activities are not sold.

Mid-continent Research for Education and Learning: http://www.mcrel.org/standards-benchmarks/index.asp
This web site has an accumulation of the different subject areas in categories and lists topical areas under each subject. These sites provide national standards for benchmarking in these areas.

Educator's Reference Desk: http://www.eduref.org
This new site includes 2000 lesson plans, 3000 value-added pointers to education information and organizations, and 200 question archives that were previously accessible through askeric.org. The ERIC database can also be accessed at this site.

New York Times Learning Network: http://www.nytimes.com/learning/
"Free news and education resources for teachers, their students and parents. Includes lesson plans, vocabulary and geography builders and more."

Funbrain.com: http://www.funbrain.com
This site enables teachers to integrate games and thousands of assessment quizzes into their daily lesson plans.

Skewl Sites Online: http://www.skewlsites.com
This site features an online index of numerous helpful educational web sites.

Ed Helper: http://www.edhelper.com
This site includes thousands of lesson plans, worksheets, webquests, and teacher resources.

Education Place: http://www.eduplace.com
This web site is maintained by Houghton Mifflin Harcourt and provides Internet resources for teachers and students (K–8).

For these links and additional resources, please visit the Premium Website at **www.cengage.com/login.**

◉ NOTES

1. W. J. Popham, "Instructional Objectives 1960–1970," *Performance and Instruction* 26, no. 2 (1987): 11–14. Also see Additional Resources at the end of this chapter.

2. T. Gibbs and A. Howley, "'World-Class Standards' and Local Pedagogies: Can We Do Both?" *ERIC Digest* (December 2000). (Full text available at http://www.ael.org/eric/digests/edorc008.htm)

3. Birman, B. J.,Boyle, A., LeFloch, K. C., Elledge, A., Holtzman, D., Song, M., Thomson, K., Walters, K., and Kwang-suk Yoon, *State and Local Implementation of the "No Child Left Behind" Act.* Vol. VIII – Teacher quality under "NCLB": Final Report. Full text available at www.eric.edu.gov.

4. Jean Piaget, *Science of Education and the Psychology of the Child* (New York: Orion, 1970); Jean Piaget and Bärbel Inhelder, *The Growth of Logical Thinking from Childhood to Adolescence,* trans. A. Parsons and S. Seagrin (New York: Basic Books, 1958).

5. Lev Vgotsky, *Thought and Language* (Cambridge, Mass.: MIT Press, 1962).

6. Erik Erikson, *Identity: Youth and Crisis* (New York: Norton, 1968).

7. Lawrence Kohlberg, "The Cognitive-Developmental Approach to Moral Education," *Phi Delta Kappan* 56 (1975): 567–677.

8. For additional examples, see Chapter 4 in T. D. TenBrink, *Evaluation: A Practical Guide for Teachers* (New York: McGraw-Hill, 1974).

9. This list was adapted from T. D. TenBrink, *Evaluation: A Practical Guide for Teachers* (New York: McGraw-Hill, 1974), p. 102.

10. Some authors use the term *performance* to refer to student outcome, *condition* to refer to conditions under which the performance is expected to occur, and *criteria* to refer to the level of performance expected.

11. Lim, Cheer Ping and Ching Sing Chai, "Rethinking Classroom-Oriented Instructional Models to Mediate Instructional Planning in Technology-enhanced Learning" *Teaching and Teacher Education: An International Journal of Research and Studies,* 24, no. 8 (November 2008): 2002–2023.

12. Lorin W. Anderson and David R. Krathwohl, eds., *Taxonomy for Learning, Teaching, and Assessing: A Revision of Bloom's Taxonomy of Educational Objectives* (New York: Longman, 2000).

13. R. M. Gagné, "Learning Outcomes and Their Effects: Useful Categories of Human Performance," *American Psychologist* 39, no. 4 (1984): 377–385.

14. R. M. Gagné, *Conditions of Learning and Theory of Instruction,* 4th ed. (San Diego: Harcourt Brace Jovanovich, 1985).

15. See Additional Resources for recent books on educational psychology and teaching/learning strategies.

16. C. V. Hines, D. R. Cruickshank, and J. J. Kennedy, "Teacher Clarity and Its Relationship to Student Achievement and Satisfaction," *American Educational Research Journal* 22, no. 1 (1985): 87–99.

17. J. Hartley and I. Davies, "Preinstructional Strategies: The Role of Pretests, Behavioral Objectives, Overviews and Advance Organizers," *Review of Educational Research* 46 (1976): 239–265.

18. P. C. Duchastel and P. F. Merrill, "The Effects of Behavioral Objectives on Learning: A Review of Empirical Studies," *Review of Educational Research* 45 (1973): 53–69.

19. G. T. Dalis, "Effects of Precise Objectives upon Student Achievement in Health Education," *Journal of Experimental Education* 39 (1970): 20–23.

20. R. F. Melton, "Resolution of Conflicting Claims Concerning the Effects of Behavioral Objectives on Student Learning," *Review of Educational Research* 48 (1978): 291–302.

21. T. J. Lasley II and T. J. Matczynski, *Strategies for Teaching in a Diverse Society: Instructional Models,* 2nd ed. (Belmont, Calif.: Wadsworth, 1997).

22. Madeline Hunter, *Mastery Teaching: Increasing Instructional Effectiveness in Elementary and Secondary Schools, Colleges, and Universities (Madeline Hunter Collection Series)* Phoenix, AZ Crown Press 1994.

23. R. M. Gagné, W. W. Wager, K. Golas, and J. M. Keller. *Principles of Instructional Design,* 5th ed. (Belmont, Calif.: Wadsworth, 2004).

3 Instructional Planning

Greta Morine-Dershimer

Jonathan A. Meyers/Stock Connection Distribution/Alamy

◻ INTASC Standards

● **INTASC Principle 7:** The teacher plans instruction based upon knowledge of subject matter, students, the community, and curriculum goals.

● **INTASC Principle 3:** Understands how students differ in their approaches to learning; creates instructional opportunities adapted to diverse learners.

● **INTASC Principle 4:** Understands and uses a variety of instructional strategies.

● **INTASC Principle 5:** Creates a learning environment that encourages positive social interaction, active engagement in learning, and self-motivation.

● **INTASC Principle 8:** Understands and uses formal and informal assessment strategies.

● **INTASC Principle 9:** Reflects on teaching.

● **INTASC Principle 10:** Fosters relationships with colleagues, parents, and agencies in the larger community.

◻ OBJECTIVES

1. Given two concept maps depicting a prospective teacher's "before and after" perspectives of teacher planning, to compare these concept maps, list three features that have changed from pre to post map, and explain what these changes suggest about what the teacher learned about instructional planning

2. To identify at least four key characteristics of productive planning

3. To use an analogy to describe at least two important aspects of teacher planning

To Plan Is Human . . .

All people engage in planning on a regular basis.[1] We think in advance about things we want to do and make preparations that enable us to do them. Clearly, you have already had experience in making plans. But how effective are your plans? To what extent are they fully realized?

Do You Have a Story to Tell?

What was the most complicated event or project you ever had to plan for? Did you work alone or with a partner or team? What problem(s) did you face in planning or implementing your plan? How closely did the actual event or finished project match your original plan? Do you think your planning was successful? Why?

Talk with a partner about planning experiences you each have had. How were your experiences similar or different? What did you learn from your experiences?

Since you have probably been planning important events in your life for several years, you bring a useful experience to one of the most important tasks of teaching. In many ways, instructional planning requires the same skills as the everyday planning you already do.[2] But the planning that a teacher must do is quite complex, and this complexity necessitates some special skills and knowledge. This chapter introduces ideas related to the special skills, knowledge, dispositions, and performances that are important in planning for instruction. This book as a whole provides information about the complex variety of skills and knowledge that must be brought to bear in order for instructional plans to be carried out effectively.

OBJECTIVE 1   Given two concept maps depicting a prospective teacher's "before and after" perspectives of teacher planning, to compare these concept maps, list three features that have changed from pre to post map, and explain what these changes suggest about what the teacher learned about instructional planning

Where Do We Start? Concept Maps

Maps visually organize knowledge

A good place to start thinking about any relatively new topic is with your own ideas. What do you think is involved in teacher planning? One useful way to clarify and explicate your own ideas is to construct a concept map.[3] A **concept map** is a way of organizing your ideas about a particular topic so that the relationships you see among the various subtopics can be displayed visually.

You may already be familiar with concept mapping or know it by another name, such as *webbing* or *semantic mapping*. If not, this is a good technique for you to learn; it can be useful in organizing your ideas for a writing task, in reviewing a topic you have been studying, or in organizing information for a unit of instruction you are planning to teach.[4] Software is available to assist teachers and their students in designing and developing different types of visual maps for varied purposes.[5] Two web sites listed at the end of this chapter (PIVIT and Inspiration Software) also provide resources for developing graphic displays. These maps are useful tools for helping learners construct, organize, and communicate their knowledge.

Learning Activity 3.1

To construct a concept map of your ideas about teacher planning, follow these simple procedures. First, make a list of all the words and phrases you associate with the topic of teacher planning. Second, group the items in your list together in some way that makes sense to you, and label your groups to indicate what characteristic(s) the items in the group have in common. Third, combine your initial groups to form larger, more inclusive groups. Finally, draw a concept map or graphic display that shows how your groups and subgroups relate to each other and to the major topic of teacher planning.

Before you read any further in this chapter, you might want to construct a concept map of your ideas about teacher planning. Then you will have an opportunity to compare your ideas about teacher planning to the ideas of another prospective teacher. As you read further in this chapter and in this book, you can see how the information presented relates to the ideas about instructional planning that you already have.

Before and After

Maps show changing ideas ▶ One of the most interesting things about people is that their ideas can change. One of the most interesting things about concept maps is that they can help us trace how our ideas change as a result of education and experience. In this section, you will examine before-and-after concept maps of a secondary prospective teacher to see what changes occurred in his thinking about teacher planning as a result of planning and teaching a series of lessons.

The student whose ideas are presented was enrolled in a teacher preparation program at Syracuse University. He constructed his initial concept map at the beginning of a course on strategies of teaching. During the course, he was engaged in **peer teaching** in addition to reading and discussing information about various important aspects of planning and teaching. Each student in the course planned a series of three or four lessons on a given topic, using different instructional procedures in each lesson.[6] They taught these lessons to small groups of their peers.

At the end of the class, each student constructed a new concept map to show how his or her concepts of teacher planning had changed. Pre and post (before and after) maps for one of these students are presented in this section. If you and your classmates chose to construct concept maps, you should find it interesting to compare your own "before" map with the one presented here, as well as with those of fellow students in your own teacher preparation program. In addition, you will be asked to compare the pre and post maps presented here to determine what kinds of changes you can observe in the thinking of this prospective teacher. These changes occurred as a result of coursework and practice in planning and carrying out plans for instruction.

❯ YOUR TURN   Ted's Concept Maps

Ted was a secondary education major working on a master's degree in social studies education. He had done his undergraduate work in business administration. His pre and post maps of teacher planning are presented in Figures 3.1 and 3.2. Between constructing these two maps, he taught four lessons to a group of his peers on

(continued)

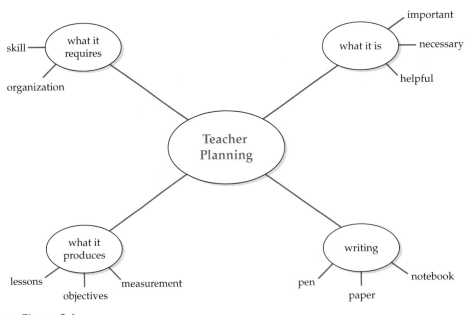

skill — what it requires
organization

what it is — important
— necessary
helpful

Teacher Planning

what it produces
lessons
objectives
measurement

writing
pen
paper
notebook

■ Figure 3.1

Ted's pre map of teacher planning

1. Do I know the content?
2. What parts should be emphasized?
3. What does the state say has to be covered?

1. How will students be evaluated?
2. Is it a fair evaluation?
3. Does it take into account different student strengths?

1. What skills will I teach?
2. Are they important skills?

methods

content

evaluation

skills

objective

1. Will the method chosen work with these students?
2. Is it the best method for the content?
3. Will the method contribute to classroom management?
4. Is it the best method for the time I have available?
5. Is it a method I can do well?
6. What variations of the method can I use?

Teacher Planning

1. Is the objective appropriate for the content?
2. Do the students have a fair opportunity to meet it?
3. How will I know when it is met? What will tell me?

style

time

classroom management

students

1. Will students respond to my style?
2. How should I act to maximize learning?
3. Can I clearly convey the ideas to the students?

1. How long will the lesson take? Is it worth the time?
2. Will the lesson fit in the time frame I have?

1. Does the lesson contribute to managing the classroom?
2. How will I manage the classroom, using this method?

1. Learning style.
2. Background knowledge.
3. Reading skills.
4. Writing skills.
5. Thinking skills.
6. Will they enjoy the lesson?

■ Figure 3.2

Ted's post map of teacher planning

(continued)

the general topic of the free-enterprise system. At the end of his peer-teaching experience, he began student teaching, teaching social studies to eighth- and ninth-graders in a suburban middle school.

Consider Ted's pre and post maps. What changes do you see? What new ideas have emerged? Do these new ideas appear to be important things to consider? How might Ted's teaching experience have contributed to the changes you observe? After studying these maps, how do you think your own concept map might change, given some practice in planning and teaching lessons in a peer-teaching or classroom setting?

How Ted's thinking changed ▶

Ted compared his own maps and noted similarities and differences. Here are some of his comments.

▢ INTASC Principle 9

Ted: Two months ago I didn't know what teacher planning was. This showed in my pre concept map with its skeletal nature. My post map focuses on what goes into teacher planning. I thought of all these things and how they are related to each other and affect each other—that any change in one component affects another. These components of teacher planning do not stand independently. Two months ago I thought they did. The peer teaching and the preparation that went into it helped open my eyes to all that is important. I was no longer watching teacher planning, but doing it. If I failed to plan for any of these components, my lesson turned out not to be as good.

A pattern of professional growth ▶

Ted's experience is not unique. It illustrates patterns of changes in thinking about teacher planning that have been identified in studies of prospective teachers like yourself. As students engage in planning and teaching lessons, they increase their awareness of the many elements to be considered in conducting a successful lesson, identify the relationships among these various elements, and reorganize their ideas to give priority to different aspects of teaching.

The pre and post concept maps presented here are evidence of **professional development.** A professional is a person who possesses some specialized knowledge and skills, can weigh alternatives, and can select from among a number of potentially productive actions one that is particularly appropriate in a given situation. The post concept map of Ted, a soon-to-be-professional teacher, shows that he has begun to develop specialized knowledge, specialized skills, an awareness of alternatives, and a sense of the situational characteristics to be considered in determining which alternative to choose. For example, the questions raised on Ted's post map ("Is the objective appropriate for the content?" "Will the method chosen work with these students?" "Is it the best method for the content?" "Will the method contribute to classroom management?" "Is it the best method for the time I have available?" "Will students respond to my style?") show that he has developed an awareness of alternatives as well as a sense of some situational characteristics to be considered in choosing from among instructional alternatives.

Changes in awareness and attention ▶

Prospective teachers at the University of Virginia's Curry School of Education have also developed pre and post concept maps of teacher planning in conjunction with classes on alternative instructional strategies and associated field experiences. The most common changes in professional thinking that they exhibited involved increased attention to students' background knowledge and characteristics, instructional materials, and evaluation processes. All of these are critical aspects of planning for instruction.[7]

These examples provide evidence that these prospective teachers are beginning to think and act like professionals. You should be able to observe similar changes in your own knowledge, skills, and awareness of alternatives as you progress through this book. Several of the terms and topics in the concept maps Ted developed are introduced and discussed in detail in other chapters: objectives (Chapter 2), classroom management (Chapter 8), and evaluation/assessment (Chapter 10). Other important considerations for planning, not mentioned as clearly by Ted, are also discussed in later chapters: questioning (Chapter 5), differentiating instruction (Chapter 6), and cooperative learning (Chapter 9). Involving students in learning (Chapter 4) and culturally responsive teaching (Chapter 7) are important in carrying out your instructional plans successfully.

When you have finished the reading and activities in this book, you might construct a final concept map of teacher planning. If you compare your own pre and post maps, you will have solid evidence of your own professional development.

OBJECTIVE 2   **To identify at least four key characteristics of productive planning**

Myths and Realities

Many people believe that planning is one of the most important skills a teacher can have and that teachers who plan better must also teach better. Some people think that planning is something teachers do in the quiet of their classrooms—before pupils arrive for the day or after they leave for the night. Others may suspect that many teachers never really plan at all, except to write down the page numbers of the textbook to be covered each day. The truth, of course, is that none of these views is completely accurate.

The myths about teacher planning are legion. Unfortunately, they are influential in determining what prospective teachers learn about the process of planning. Which of the following statements are myths, and which are probably accurate descriptions of the reality of teacher planning?

- Everybody's doing it.
- A little goes a long way.
- A plan a day keeps disaster away.
- One size fits all.
- Don't look back!
- You can do it yourself.
- We do it best in the good old U.S.

A generation ago, it would have been difficult to determine which of these statements were myths and which were realities. Little was known about how teachers went about planning in their classrooms. Since then, however, a number of researchers have observed and interviewed teachers as they were engaged in instructional planning. While there are still things to be learned, a useful base of knowledge has been established. Several of the myths discussed here were debunked by a flurry of studies conducted in the late 1970s and early 1980s. These studies have been capably summarized in some excellent reviews.[8] Only more recent studies are specifically cited in the commentary below. Since these early studies of teacher planning, instruction has changed in some important ways that affect teacher planning practices. New technology is available for use by teachers and students, so teachers must consider how to use technology as a source of content and instructional materials as well as how to help students develop skills in the use of technology. There has also been a change in thinking about how students learn and the nature of knowledge. Constructivist theories of learning suggest that our knowledge grows from our own experience and develops through interaction with others in social settings.[9]

Everybody's Doing It—In a Variety of Ways

Teachers do plan, and they plan in a variety of ways. There are four basic types of planning in which teachers regularly engage: yearly, unit, weekly, and daily planning. All are important for effective instruction.

Plans vary in form and time frame ▶

While all teachers plan, they do not all plan in exactly the same way. Some may jot down a few notes in a lesson plan book. Others may write outlines detailing lessons or units they intend to teach. Many teachers write more detailed daily plans for their substitutes than they do for themselves, wanting to ensure that established routines are understood and maintained. Teachers who have fully embraced the computer age may keep a file of lesson or unit plans stored on disks, updating or revising these each year to fit new circumstances.

Studies have shown that few experienced teachers plan precisely according to the procedures recommended by curriculum experts for many years. Rather than beginning by stating instructional objectives, and then selecting and organizing instructional activities to meet those objectives, many elementary teachers begin by considering the context in which teaching will occur (for example, the instructional materials and time available), then think about activities that will interest and involve their pupils, and finally note the purposes that these activities will serve. Secondary teachers focus almost exclusively on content and preparation of an interesting presentation. This does not mean that teachers have no real goals, but it does suggest that a basic consideration for most teachers is maintaining the interest and involvement of their pupils. Since research has shown that pupil attention and on-task behavior are associated with achievement, pupil involvement is important for teachers to keep in mind when planning for instruction.

Special education teachers focus more precisely than other teachers on individual goals for individual students as they develop an Individual Educational Plan (IEP) for the year for each student with whom they work.

Planning for every student ▶

Recent research has focused on variation in the ways teachers plan to respond to students' individual differences. Teachers in many classrooms today work with children who vary in cultural background, who have many languages other than English as their first language, and who may either have learning disabilities or be gifted and talented. As classroom diversity has increased, regular classroom teachers have had to learn to adapt their instruction to meet students' special needs and abilities. Studies indicate that elementary teachers do more planning than secondary teachers to

☐ INTASC Principle 3

meet the needs of students with learning disabilities and also collaborate more with special education teachers in developing appropriate adaptations for these students.[10] Planning with colleagues who have special expertise can improve any teacher's ability to adapt instructional plans to serve diverse pupil populations. Some useful guides are available to help teachers as well.[11]

A Little Goes a Long Way—Especially at the Beginning

The tricky thing about teacher planning is that one kind of plan is *nested* within another. This means that plans made at the beginning of the year have important effects on the weekly and daily plans that will be made throughout the year. Before the students ever enter the room, most teachers have planned the physical arrangement of the classroom: where and how students will be seated, where materials will be kept, what areas will be set up as centers for particular types of activities, and how bulletin board or wall space will be utilized. Decisions about daily and weekly scheduling of subjects are usually completed by the end of the first week of school. Within the first few weeks, student abilities are assessed and plans are made for instructional grouping. Classroom rules or management procedures are also established during these early weeks. Not all of these plans are made by individual teachers in isolation. A grade-level or subject-area team may work together to schedule classes or group pupils. General time schedules and rules for student behavior may be determined by school administrators. Wherever these plans originate, however, they will set the framework within which later plans will develop.

Many teachers identify unit planning as their most important type of planning. Weekly and daily plans are nested within unit plans. Since teachers tend to focus on activities in their planning, unit plans serve to organize a flow of activities related to a general topic for an extended period of time (two weeks to a month, typically). Experienced teachers at the secondary level may use longer-range planning and determine content and materials for a full course at the beginning of the year.[12]

A Plan a Day Keeps Disaster Away—For Novice Teachers and in Special Situations

Experienced teachers report that unit, weekly, and daily planning are the most important types of planning that they do during the year. Few of them write out complete lesson plans on a regular basis, though they will make lesson plans when they are dealing with new content or curriculum materials. They do recommend, however, that student teachers and beginning teachers write lesson plans. This suggests that lesson plans are particularly useful tools in less familiar teaching situations, such as working with new students, new subject matter, or new procedures. For novice teachers, all these aspects of teaching are new and unfamiliar, and lesson plans can be helpful.

Written plans and print materials ▶

In their daily as well as yearly planning, experienced teachers rely heavily on curriculum guides and textbook materials to determine the content and pace of their lessons. Plans for lessons may consist of selecting and adapting activities suggested in the textbook's teacher's guide so that these are particularly interesting or suitable for the instructional needs of their particular pupils. These teachers have established instructional routines over the years, and they fit these suggested activities into their routines; therefore, extensive planning of procedures does not seem as necessary. Novice teachers are in the process of developing routines, experimenting to see what procedures will work for them. More detailed planning of lessons is an essential activity at this stage of their professional development.

In certain situations more extensive planning may be especially important for experienced teachers as well. Proponents of project-based learning emphasize the need for detailed planning even though a goal of this approach is for students to develop skills in self-management and self-assessment as well as learning content. Organizing resources and grouping students for collaborative work are important planning tasks in preparing for project-based learning.[13] Using technology for instruction also requires additional planning by the teacher. Deciding when and how computers will be used cooperatively by students is one important consideration, and teachers need to try out activities in advance to test equipment and software for possible problems before students begin work.[14] As new instructional situations arise, planning skills will continue to be an essential part of every teacher's professional life.

One Size Fits All—But Not Very Well

◻ INTASC Principle 3

Most lesson plans are designed to guide instruction for a whole class of students. Thus, the typical plan aims to motivate and involve the "average" student. But of course it is a rare student who fully exemplifies the profile of the average student. Even a small group of students is made up of individuals who can exhibit a bewildering array of differences in characteristics that influence instruction, including academic performance, prior knowledge and experience, language acquisition, social skills, cultural background, physical development, intellectual ability, and home and family resources. No general lesson plan will be a perfect fit for every student in the class or group. In fact, it is the rare lesson plan that is a perfect fit for *any* individual student.

Incorporate diversity in planning ▸

Teacher beliefs can affect the ways teachers plan for diverse pupil populations. Elementary teachers with strong beliefs in the importance of student work habits reportedly plan lessons that are more responsive to student performance, and thus their students learn more.[15] Teachers who believe that all children can learn, and that all children have talents and ideas to contribute to classroom lessons, generally plan lessons that engage students more actively, thus enabling their students to become more self-directed learners.[16]

Classroom diversity compels teachers to make adaptations in their lesson plans to accommodate the instructional needs of individual students and thus promote the learning of all students. This is especially important when special education students are mainstreamed into regular classrooms. Such adaptations are more likely to be effective if they are consciously considered in advance. For example, specific activities designed to encourage student expression of personal feelings, experiences, and opinions related to the subject matter of the lesson can accommodate individual differences, celebrate diversity, and contribute to effective pupil achievement. Lesson plans that regularly include such activities enable teachers to tailor their lessons to achieve a better fit for all students.

Do Look Back—It Helps in Planning Ahead

☐ INTASC Principle 9

Experienced teachers report that soon after a lesson has been taught, they do rethink it and consider how it might be improved or varied another time.[17] This helps them in planning future lessons. Looking back can be especially helpful in long-term planning, such as unit or yearly planning. Teachers who keep records of their plans from prior years can start by considering what activities or procedures worked well and what revisions might be made in sequencing or selection of topics and activities. This is more efficient than starting from scratch every year, and it is an effective aid to teachers who want to improve by learning systematically from their own experience.

One way that prospective teachers can look back at their peer teaching or student teaching lessons is to videotape a lesson and then view it and discuss it with a small group of their peers. This process can enhance observational skills and promote dialogue and shared learning.[18]

Looking back can be useful in another way. Prospective teachers need to reflect on their own early school experiences, because their beliefs about teaching and learning have been deeply affected by their long experience as students. These beliefs have an impact on what and how teachers plan for instruction, and they make it difficult for some to use more innovative and student-centered instructional methods. Only by critically examining their past experiences and resultant beliefs can teachers be free to make informed choices about the instructional activities that will best serve their students.[19]

You Can Do It Yourself—With a Little Help from Your Friends

☐ INTASC Principle 10

Teachers rarely rely solely on their own knowledge and inspiration to design classroom instruction. For many years resources such as textbooks, teacher's manuals, and state or district curriculum guides have been available to assist them with instructional planning. Furthermore, in many schools teachers have worked with colleagues to plan lessons or instructional units, sharing ideas and materials. A recent emphasis in public school curricula has been interdisciplinary teaching. When language and methods of inquiry from more than one discipline or subject area are combined to explore a central theme or problem, students may see the topic as more relevant to real life.[20] Some state standards for new teachers require that they collaborate with their colleagues and help students make connections across subject areas.[21] Interdisciplinary instruction can be enhanced when teachers work together to plan lessons and units. This is particularly true at the secondary level, where teachers tend to see themselves as specialists in a single subject area. One prospective English teacher, after planning and teaching an interdisciplinary unit with a prospective science teacher, commented as follows:

> The fact that I was lacking in the science subject area had a positive benefit because I became dependent on [my partner] to help me understand the subject. I found this collaboration rewarding because I wasn't afraid to ask questions. Since teachers too often feel like they have to be infallible experts, being in the position of a "learner" reminded me how important it is to be constantly learning as a teacher.[22]

Finding resources on the Internet ▶

More recently, teachers have been able to draw readily on the professional knowledge of distant colleagues to enrich their instructional planning. Now, through the resources of the Internet, many opportunities exist for teachers and their students to share ideas electronically with other teachers and students in far-flung places. Because web sites are in constant flux, a published list of useful sites would soon be outdated. The George Lucas Educational Foundation has published an extensive list of electronic resources for educators[23] and has promised to update its web site (http://www.edutopia.org) regularly to provide current resources. The variety of resources available at the time of publication of this text included instructional projects, documents, visual media, and discussion networks, as well as links to resources on specific topics like integrated studies, technology integration, social and emotional learning, and assessment. An instructional module on project-based learning is also available (http://www.edutopia.org). It provides some instruction on planning for using and managing technology with learners of diverse abilities. Searches using terms such as *teacher planning* or *lesson plans* will turn up many other resources. The *New York Times* web site, listed in the Additional Resources at the end of this chapter, is particularly useful. Tomorrow's teachers need to know how to access Internet resources for use in instructional planning. They also need to know how to evaluate them to determine what will or will not be useful. Later parts of this chapter provide some helpful criteria for purposes of such evaluation.

We Do It Best in the Good Old U.S.—Except when Others Do Better

☐ INTASC Principle 10

Other cultures value collaboration ▸

Americans sometimes tend to think that our customs and ways are better than those of other countries. Not surprisingly, other countries tend to think that their ways are better than ours. It seems natural to like what is most familiar. But Americans have learned and adopted or adapted much from other cultures and used those imports to good advantage.

One import related to instructional planning is a process used in Japan for professional development, or *kenshu*, which translates as "mastery through study."[24] Japanese educators view teaching as a collaborative process and think that peer planning is a critical aspect of teaching. In many schools in Japan, teachers work together to develop a year-long theme or topic for study to improve classroom instruction. A basic part of the plan is engagement in *kenkyu jugyo*, or "study lessons." A small group of teachers plans a lesson together, and one member of the group is selected to teach the lesson to a class. The lesson is videotaped for observation by other teachers, and all observers then meet with the planning group to analyze and critique the lesson. An outside specialist is frequently invited to participate in the lesson critique as well. The observed teacher and the planning group comment on the teaching strategies selected, and student interest in and comprehension of the lesson content. The plan may be revised on the basis of this analysis, and subsequently used by other teachers. This process continues throughout the school year, with study lessons planned, taught, and critiqued by various groups of teachers, organized by grade level or subject taught. At the end of the school year, the school bulletin may publish records of the study lessons.

Japanese teachers see study lessons as an effective means for encouraging reflection on teaching for the purpose of improving instruction.[25] Some teachers and teacher educators in the United States have begun using this process, which they call "lesson study," for the same purpose. While American teachers have typically planned their lessons individually, these proponents of lesson study believe that collaborative planning, observation, and analysis of lessons has the potential to promote professional development and instructional improvement.[26] Some prospective teachers have used the lesson-study process and become more comfortable with constructive criticism by focusing on the lesson plan rather than the teacher.[27] With regard to lesson planning, we may not necessarily do it best in the good old U.S. But we do know how to learn from good practices in other countries.

Reviewing the Realities

To summarize, while we still have things to learn about teacher planning, we do know that teachers think ahead; that they consider planning to be an essential activity; and that designing lessons and units is, for many teachers, one of the most interesting parts of teaching, providing them with an opportunity to use their imagination and ingenuity. We know that a great deal of variety exists in the ways different teachers approach planning. We also know the following:

- Plans are nested, so that plans made to organize the classroom at the beginning of the year have a strong influence on later plans.
- Lesson plans of experienced teachers rely heavily on textbooks and curriculum guides, and they make use of established routines for basic instructional and managerial activities in the classroom.
- Lesson plans of effective teachers are flexible enough to allow for fine-tuning of procedures, adjusting to pupil responses to tasks.
- Teachers' beliefs about teaching and learning strongly influence the options they consider in planning for instruction.
- Effective teachers adapt instructional plans to suit the needs of diverse learners.
- Teachers' planning can be greatly enhanced by collaboration with colleagues as well as by the variety of instructional resources that are available on the Internet.

 YOUR TURN   **Observing Planning in Action**

Teachers' planning processes and beliefs are mental activities, and not directly observable. But plans and beliefs affect actions, and actions are observable. Some of teachers' planning processes can be inferred from observing their lessons, which are their plans in action. (Watch the Video Case, *Managing an Inclusive Classroom: High School Math Instruction*, to observe the six aspects of teacher planning listed above as they are revealed in action.)

▼ **TeachSource Video Case**   **Managing an Inclusive Classroom: High School Math Instruction**

To access the video, go to www.cengage.com/login. Watch the brief video clip two or three times. Observe the activities closely, and listen carefully to the teachers' comments. Select any four of the six characteristics of teacher planning and briefly describe how each is exemplified in the video through either teacher comments or teacher and student actions during the lesson.

■ Novices and Experts

Some interesting research on teaching has built on studies in cognitive psychology that compare the thinking of novices and experts in a given field. Studies of experts and novices in a variety of fields indicate that experts recall meaningful information better than novices and use different criteria to judge the relevance or utility of the information that they perceive and remember.[28]

Experts assess knowledge and lay ground rules ▶

Some studies of teacher planning suggest that expert teachers are similar to experts in other fields in their patterns of thinking. One study compared the responses of novice and expert mathematics and science teachers on a simulated task in which they had to prepare to take on a new class five weeks after school had started. One of the major differences between experts and novices had to do with how they planned to begin. Experts concentrated on learning what students already knew by planning to have them work review problems and answer questions about their understanding of the subject matter covered so far. Novices planned to ask students where they were in the textbook and then to present a review of important concepts. In other words, experts planned to gather information from students, and novices planned to give information to students. Expert teachers planned to "begin again" by explaining their expectations and classroom routines to students. Novices were more apt to ask students how the former teacher ran the classroom, with the implication that they would follow the same practices.

Expert and novice teachers differed in their judgments of the importance of different types of information. The most important information for experts was what students knew of the subject. The most important information for novices was what management system students were accustomed to following. Expert teachers planned to institute their own routines. Novices planned to adapt to someone else's routines. The expert teachers understood the nested nature of planning. They knew that the classroom management structures they adopted during the first few days of class would shape the plans they would be able to make for the rest of the year.

The Function of Routines

To some people, **routine** connotes dull, dreary, repetitive, unthinking behavior. Thus, the idea that establishing routines is important for instructional planning may be distasteful. But consider the relationship between routines and plans in your everyday life. What are your established routines as a student? Do you have a time of the day or week when you usually read assignments? Do you have a place in the library or computer lab or in your room where you typically work when you have a paper to write? If you don't have some established routines for activities like these, you are a rare person.

Routines have clear benefits ▶

Everyday routines such as these are important in relation to planning our daily activities because they free our minds to think about other things. If you had to consider a number of alternatives and choose from among them every time you performed any action, you would soon be worn out from the constant decision making.

Having established routines enables teachers to operate more efficiently for similar reasons. In planning lessons, a teacher who has a routine for collecting homework or distributing materials can concentrate on more important decisions about what information to present or what questions to ask students. In conducting lessons, a teacher who has routines for calling on students to participate can more readily concentrate on listening to what the student has to say, rather than worrying about whom to call on next. Lesson routines also help to make teacher behavior predictable to students, and when students know what to expect, they are better able to concentrate on content and are apt to learn more.

Work routines into planning ▶

Routines can operate at several different levels of teacher planning. For example, at the level of planning for a unit of instruction, routines related to evaluation may include giving a pretest to identify what students already know, scheduling weekly quizzes to assess how well students are mastering concepts presented, and preparing a unit test to determine how much new knowledge students have gained. If students learn that these evaluations are a regular part of the teacher's units of instruction, they will prepare for weekly quizzes by learning material as they go along rather than waiting and cramming for a final test.

At the level of planning for a daily lesson, routines related to a sequence of activities may include checking homework, presenting new information, conducting group practice with the new information through questioning and discussion, providing for individual supervised practice using new information in assigned seatwork, and providing for independent practice by assigning new homework. This is a pattern of lesson activities followed by many expert teachers of mathematics,[29] and it is a pattern found useful in improving student achievement in many studies of effective teaching.[30] When this sequence of activities is an established pattern for most lessons, the teacher can focus planning decisions on how best to explain and illustrate (with examples) the new information to be presented.

At the level of planning for specific activities within a lesson, management routines become important. When calling on students to participate, a teacher may regularly call only on volunteers when new information is first discussed, believing that volunteers are more apt to be able to answer questions accurately and thus move the lesson along at a lively pace. In the review portion of the lesson, however, the same teacher may use a routine of going up and down rows of students, calling on each in turn, as a way of checking whether all students clearly understand the material previously discussed. A teacher who has such established routines does not need to spend much time planning these specific details of a lesson. Students who become familiar with such routines pay more attention in initial presentations of information, knowing they can expect to be called on in a later review.

The Role of Repertoire

■ INTASC Principle 4

Routines are an important part of teacher planning for instruction, but expert teachers do not rely on routines alone. Because different actions are appropriate in different situations, expert teachers also have repertoires that they call on when necessary.

Variety of instructional procedures ▶

A **repertoire** is a set of alternate routines or procedures, all of which may serve some common, general purpose and each of which may be particularly appropriate in a different situation. For example, a teacher may have a repertoire of procedures for classroom organization that includes whole-class instruction, cooperative group work, individualized seatwork, and peer tutoring. Each of these classroom organizations can be effective in promoting student learning, but cooperative group work can be particularly effective for developing student independence, while supervised, individualized seatwork may be particularly effective for maximizing individual achievement gains. With a repertoire of procedures that are appropriate for different situations, a teacher does not need to spend hours of planning time to devise possible alternate actions. The repertoire provides a range of alternatives to be considered, and knowledge of the specific situation (including the type of students to be taught, content to be learned, and time available) enables the expert teacher to choose an alternative that fits the situation.

Alternatives to teacher-directed work ▶

Much of the early research on effective teaching produced generic principles of instruction that tended to emphasize planning for teacher-directed, whole-class lessons—beginning with review of prior knowledge, moving on to presentation of new knowledge, and ending with individual practice supervised by the teacher to consolidate the new knowledge. Much of the more recent work on subject-specific instruction has tended to emphasize planning for varied instructional processes, including inquiry or problem-solving strategies, small-group discussion, and "authentic" activities that enable students to use primary source materials and artifacts or that encourage them to apply learning to their lives outside of school.[31] This kind of planning requires the teachers of all subject areas to develop a repertoire of alternative instructional procedures.

Four-section model of activity types ▶

One useful way to think about instructional repertoire is illustrated by the grid in Figure 3.3. The vertical line denotes possible variation in the instructional process, moving from teacher-directed processes, in which the teacher selects, organizes, and presents information, to student-constructed processes, in which students share in generating, analyzing, and synthesizing information. The horizontal line denotes possible variation in the type of learning goals intended, moving from learning "accepted" knowledge (that is, understanding and using knowledge produced by

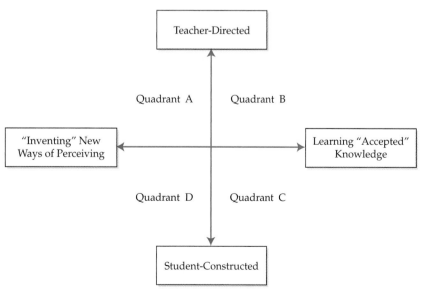

■ Figure 3.3
Repertoire Grid

☐ INTASC Principles
3, 4, 5

experts in the various academic disciplines) to "inventing" new ways of perceiving (that is, developing and communicating divergent thoughts). Different instructional strategies can be located in different quadrants on this grid.

A teacher who wants to meet the needs of a diverse group of learners will need to develop a varied instructional repertoire, using strategies from each of the four quadrants over time. For example, in planning an integrated unit of instruction on the television media, a teacher could plan a sequence of lessons, starting in Quadrant A and moving on to each of the other three quadrants, not necessarily in strict clockwise sequence. Sample lessons could include the following types of activities.

Activity 1 (Quadrant A). The teacher asks students to name the television programs that are watched most frequently in their homes, listing them on the board as they are named. When a good list has been developed, students work in pairs to determine groups of programs that have some feature or features in common. Pairs report their groups and category systems back to the class, and the teacher leads a discussion on the various types of program features students have noted. The lesson concludes with the class developing clusters of program groupings that are similar in some way (grouping the groups), thus forming their own hierarchical category system for describing types of television programs. (This activity is based on a strategy called Concept Formation.[32])

For homework, using the category system they have developed, each student interviews one family member and one neighbor to learn what category of television programs these individuals watch most frequently. The following day, the class compiles the data from their interviews and constructs a bar graph to show the viewing preferences of their families and friends. They plan to publish their category system and bar graph on the World Wide Web through a local Wikispaces project,[33] and invite other classes to collect, compile, and publish similar data.

Activity 2 (Quadrant C). Based on the class's survey data, the teacher notes that television documentaries are popular fare. She suggests that the class prepare a video documentary on an interesting historical event of local interest. The class decides together on a set of subtopics to be addressed, and students select the subtopic they will investigate. Students organize themselves into groups, with each group assigned to gather information about a particular subtopic. Groups work together over several days to access resources from a variety of locations (school library, community library, local historical museum, Internet, and so on) and prepare summary reports. When reports are ready, students share the information gathered in a new group formation. Each sharing group has one or two members from each of the original investigative groups, and students report to each other on their findings, so all students learn something about each subtopic. (This activity is based on a cooperative learning strategy called Jigsaw.[34] See Chapter 9 for more information on this strategy.)

Activity 3 (Quadrant B). The teacher introduces students to the technique of writing scripts, drawing on prior work they have done on writing essays, writing dialogue, and reading plays. She provides examples of sample segments of television scripts for documentaries, pointing out the need for attention to camera angle and background scenery, as well as to sequence of speakers and content of commentary. Students view a brief segment of a video documentary and then practice writing a script that provides necessary information for that segment. (This activity is based on a Direct Instruction strategy.[35])

Activity 4 (Quadrant D). Students work together in their original investigative groups to write television scripts providing information about their particular subtopics. Within these groups, students decide what message or perspective they want to convey to their audience and plan their script accordingly. When preliminary plans are set, the groups share their plans with their classmates and receive reactions and suggestions. Together the class decides on the overall message for the documentary and the sequence of subtopical segments that will best convey that message.

The groups finish writing their individual segments for the documentary. Each group assigns roles to students within the group (actors, commentator, camera person, and so on) and then videotapes a segment of the documentary. When all segments have been taped, the class views them in the planned sequence and makes recommendations about any needed revisions. The completed video is shown to other classes in the school and presented to parents in a special evening meeting. (This activity is based on a Group Investigation strategy.[36])

Teacher wears many hats ▶ In planning an instructional unit of this nature, teachers must draw on a repertoire of instructional strategies and play a variety of roles, from director to facilitator of student learning. Students also must draw on and practice a repertoire of academic, social, and technical skills as they engage in learning related to a variety of content areas, including language arts, mathematics, and social studies/history. Planning an integrated unit such as this requires the teacher to have a repertoire of information about all the basic elements of instructional planning (goals, curriculum content, learners and learning, instructional resources, instructional strategies, classroom management techniques, and evaluation/assessment procedures) and to view all these elements in terms of the local school and community context.

The Need for Practice

The reason that experts and novices see things differently in any field is that experts have a great deal of experience. With extensive experience in any activity, we learn what types of situations commonly arise, as well as which of our reactions to those situations work to our advantage and which do not. Experts recognize a new situation as being similar to a type of situation they have faced before and quickly call on a repertoire of routines that they have used in the past. Novices face a new situation without much prior experience to draw on. They cannot quickly identify a situation as belonging to a familiar category of situations. Even if they could, they would not have an extensive repertoire of developed routines available to use in response to the situation. Novices can become experts with time, however; all experts began as novices. To become an expert requires a great deal of practice and thought.

Novice teachers draw ▶
on classroom experience Novice teachers are different from novices in other fields in one respect: they are already quite experienced in classroom settings. Most novice teachers are expert students. They have had years of practice in recognizing certain types of classroom situations from the student's perspective. They know

which of their fellow students have ideas to contribute to class discussions, and they respond by listening carefully to those students. They quickly recognize the student who rambles on at length and says nothing, and they will tune that student out even on the first day of class. On meeting a new teacher, expert students rapidly determine whether assignments must be in on time; if this is a requirement, they adjust their schedules to ensure that the work gets completed. As expert students, most novice teachers have a ready repertoire of classroom behaviors. To become expert teachers, they must develop a new perspective and a new repertoire of behaviors, and that requires additional practice.

Planning is an unusual kind of activity because it can never really be practiced unless a plan is carried out. We learn from practice only if we can get some feedback about the effectiveness of our actions. Practice in making instructional plans that you never try out in any real or simulated setting would be useless in helping you to develop skill or expertise in planning. Unless you carry out a plan, you can never tell how effective it is. Plans must be tested in action. Japanese "study lessons," discussed earlier, are based on that important principle.

Learning through practice

◻ **INTASC Principle 9**

One study of novice teachers found that they spent a great deal of time planning lessons during their student teaching assignments and that they mentally rehearsed their lessons before presenting them by practicing what they would say and trying to anticipate what pupils might say.[37] Where possible, these student teachers also gained extra practice by using the same lesson plan to teach more than one group or class of pupils. By teaching the same lesson again within a short period of time, they were able to make revisions and improve their plans, thereby improving their lessons. The students in this study thought that both forms of practice helped to develop their skills in planning.

Ted's practice experiences

Ted, the novice teacher whose concept maps you studied earlier in this chapter, received practice in planning through peer-teaching lessons. While in one sense peer teaching is only a simulated setting for instruction, it provides an opportunity for novice teachers to practice planning skills, try out a variety of routine procedures, and develop a repertoire of routines for instruction.

Throughout this book, you will be presented with ideas about effective instructional procedures for presenting information, differentiating instruction, questioning pupils, reacting to pupil responses, managing classroom tasks, using cooperative learning, and evaluating pupil learning. These ideas can make it possible for you to learn useful routines and develop teaching repertoires, but routines and repertoires require practice. As you work through the activities in this book, be prepared to take advantage of every opportunity you have to practice thinking and acting like a teacher. You will not become an expert overnight, but you will get a head start.

> **❯ YOUR TURN**   **Practice Using the Repertoire Grid**

You can practice thinking about the options provided by the Repertoire Grid. (Watch the Video Case, *Cooperative Learning in the Elementary Grades: Jigsaw Model,* to see a lesson that would fit in Quadrant C of the Repertoire Grid. Then think about what part of the grid you might move to for a follow-up lesson.)

▼ TeachSource Video Case   **Cooperative Learning in the Elementary Grades: Jigsaw Model**

To access the video, go to www.cengage.com/login. Watch the video clip to see how the lesson exemplifies the characteristics of Quadrant C in the Repertoire Grid. Then work with a partner to identify an activity for a follow-up lesson that could fit in one of the other three quadrants of the grid. Write a brief description of the activity to share with other members of your class.

The Importance of Long-Term Goals

One defining characteristic of expert teachers is the ability to keep long-term goals in mind during both planning and interactive teaching. It is important for a teacher to be aware of the long-term goals that are most important to him or her. And it is also important to provide activities that serve a variety of long-term goals. But how do teachers choose their long-term goals?

Three types: academic, social, personal

A study of novice and experienced teachers of the sciences and humanities in grades 7 to 9 in Israel[38] found some interesting differences between their long-term goals based on the amount of teaching experience they had and also on the type of subject they taught. The three main types of goals considered were academic, social, and personal. Academic goals included improving students' knowledge mastery, facilitating student thinking, encouraging students' motivation to learn, developing students' learning skills, and improving student achievement. Social goals were expressed as developing students' interpersonal relations, helping students acquire sensitivity to others, encouraging student tolerance and adjustment to social norms, developing student acceptance of human differences, and facilitating improved student communication. Personal goals referred to developing students' unique abilities, enhancing student self-awareness, facilitating healthy self-concepts, and developing student self-confidence.

Aligning the quadrant model with goal types

To illustrate these various types of goals, consider the activities described earlier, each of which could serve a different long-term goal. Activity 1 in Quadrant A could contribute to the academic goal of facilitating student thinking (organizing and analyzing information). Activity 2 in Quadrant C could contribute to the social goals of developing students' interpersonal relations (group planning) and facilitating improved student communication (presenting information to other groups). Activity 3 in Quadrant B could contribute to the academic goal of improving students' knowledge mastery (techniques of script writing and video production). Activity 4 in Quadrant D could contribute to the personal goals of enhancing student self-awareness (choosing roles that are challenging or comfortable) and developing student self-confidence (showing a first-rate finished product to parents and peers).

Novices emphasize academic goals

In the Israeli study[39] novice teachers of both the sciences and humanities preferred academic goals more strongly than did experienced teachers. They were less strongly committed to social and personal goals than were the experienced teachers. In terms of subject matter taught, science and math teachers, both novice and experienced, emphasized academic goals more strongly, and social and personal goals less strongly than did teachers of the humanities. These subject matter differences were stronger for experienced teachers than for novice teachers.

These kinds of differences in preferred long-term goals for student learning and development can and do affect teacher planning and implementation of instruction. Understanding your own preferences may help you to plan lessons that help to accomplish your long-term goals. It may also help you to insure some balance of goals, so that your students have an opportunity to grow academically, socially, and personally.

◻ INTASC Principle 9

> **YOUR TURN**   **Prioritizing Goals**

Which goals are most important to you as a teacher? The statements listed below were made by teachers in the Israeli study.* Mark each of the fifteen statements below with a *V*, *I*, or *N* (Very Important, Important, Not So Important) according to your own preferences.

_____ 1. The most important thing is to teach the subject matter in an interesting and clear manner so that all of the children will understand.

_____ 2. I want to allow them to learn and to express themselves in different ways. I'll give them opportunities to develop additional ways of thinking.

_____ 3. I want to arouse their curiosity and instill in them a desire to learn.

_____ 4. The whole approach should be to improve learning skills, to develop independence.

_____ 5. I have to teach my very best in the discipline so that they will make maximum progress in improving their achievement.

_____ 6. I try very hard to encourage a constructive social system among the kids in the class.

_____ 7. I work to have a really positive group of children who are willing to help one another and who care about one another.

_____ 8. I want them to be willing to listen to the opinions of other children and be tolerant of each other.

_____ 9. I try to have the children decide on class norms and rules and to have them decide what's wrong with some kinds of classroom behavior.

_____ 10. The kids in my class learn to accept the exceptional children. That's really important.

_____ 11. What characterizes students in my class is the ability to listen to others, to listen carefully to one another.

_____ 12. No child is "regular." Each of the students is a unique being.

_____ 13. The most important thing is to talk about what you feel, what you want, what bothers you.

_____ 14. I try to work on awareness of the strengths they have, and to get across the message that all of us have positive traits.

_____ 15. Building self-confidence is so important. It enables my students to face challenges and to succeed.

Discuss your responses with another student in your class. How similar or different are your two sets of preferences? Are your Very Important statements mainly in academic goal areas (statements 1–5), social goal areas (statements 6–11), or personal goal areas (statements 12–15)? Does one of these three areas seem much less important to you?

Which of these goal statements are most important to you for your own learning as a student? Which of the types of goals listed above do you think might be encouraged by this exercise?

Look again at the goals you identified as Very Important to you. Indicate for each whether it is a teacher-oriented statement (*T*) or a student-oriented statement (*S*). (See Chapter 2, page 23, for a definition of these terms.) Rewrite each teacher-oriented goal statement as a student-oriented goal statement.

*Excerpts from Yisrael Rich and Malka Almozlino, "Educational Goal Preferences Among Novice and Veteran Teachers of Sciences and Humanities," *Teaching and Teacher Education* 15 (1999). Copyright © 1999 by Elsevier Science Limited. Reprinted with the permission of Yisrael Rich, School of Education, Bar Ilan University and Elsevier.

Summarizing Expert-Novice Studies

The expert-novice studies support and refine several of the major characteristics of effective teacher planning identified by the studies discussed earlier in the section on Myths and Realities. In particular, they emphasize:

- the nested nature of planning
- the importance of routines
- the value of repertoires that enable teachers to adapt lessons to the needs of diverse learners
- the influence of teacher beliefs on the options they consider in planning lessons.

These are aspects of lesson and unit planning you will need to keep in mind when you begin your own classroom teaching experiences.

OBJECTIVE 3   **To use an analogy to describe at least two important aspects of teacher planning**

The Play's the Thing

Analogies can be useful in helping us understand new ideas and processes. Researchers engaged in studying the planning and teaching of expert teachers use descriptive terms such as *scripts, scenes,* and *improvisation* to describe teacher thinking. These terms suggest that teacher planning may be thought of as being analogous to a dramatic production. This section builds on that analogy to explore important aspects of teacher planning, including lesson plans, **unit plans**, and classroom organization.

Scripts

The script is a basic feature of a dramatic production. The script provides the dialogue, which carries the message that the play is supposed to convey to the audience. It also frequently indicates specific actions that will convey nonverbal messages to the audience. Actors and actresses follow the script as they perform a play. A script has a fairly standard form, which usually includes some description of the stage arrangements and the props as well as a careful delineation of who will say what. Frequently, the first draft of a script, even one by a highly successful writer, must be revised during trial runs of the play in out-of-the-way places. This process of polishing a script after seeing the reactions of audiences is an accepted part of the tradition of the theater.

Lesson plan = act, unit plan = play

Teachers' lesson plans and unit plans are similar to scripts in many ways. A script is typically organized as a series of acts. A lesson plan is analogous to the script for one act of a play. It outlines the procedures to be carried out in a single time segment, and it may include a shift from one type of activity to another, similar to a change of scene within one act of a play. A unit plan is analogous to the full play in that it covers a larger topic and outlines a series of lessons to be carried out in relation to that topic. Like the acts of a play, the lessons in a unit plan are carefully sequenced to build to a climax. Lessons early in the unit may foreshadow information to be developed more fully at a later point. Units vary in length more than does the typical play, for they are acted out over a period of days or weeks rather than a few hours. Each of these types of plans is written with the intention of conveying an important message to an "audience." The teacher follows the plans while "performing" the lesson or the unit of instruction. Before performance of the plan, the teacher mentally rehearses the procedures to help ensure that the lesson or unit will run smoothly. When a lesson or unit is completed, the teacher frequently makes notes about possible revisions for the next time that lesson or unit is taught.

Of course, there are important differences between teachers' plans and dramatic scripts. A script that is rewritten after a trial run will be performed in its revised form almost immediately. A lesson plan or unit plan that is revised after teaching may not be taught again for a full year. A script provides the dialogue for all the roles in a play, and everyone can be counted on to play their role as scripted. Teachers can plan specific activities for students to carry out as part of a lesson or unit plan, but there is no guarantee that students will play their roles exactly as the teacher planned. Students in lessons are part of the "act" at some points and part of the "audience" at others.

Five parts of a lesson or unit plan ▶

1. Goal or Purpose

Like scripts, lesson and unit plans have a typical format. Most plans for lessons or units of instruction include five parts. A statement of the *goal or purpose of instruction* (what students are expected to learn or what message the teacher intends to convey) is an important part of a lesson or unit plan. Expert teachers have a clear goal in mind for any lesson, although they do not always write the goal out explicitly. Similarly, the author of a script hopes to engender a particular mood in the audience. Different types of plays engender different moods. Like plays, lessons can take a variety of forms. Because the goal or purpose of instruction influences the form a lesson or unit may take, novice teachers are advised to begin a lesson or unit with a clear goal statement.

The Internet can provide help with selecting goal statements. Many states and school districts have curriculum guides that are keyed to content standards. In order to keep such standards clearly in mind, it can be useful for a teacher to include a reference to an appropriate content standard as part of the goal statement of any lesson plan. (See the web site of the Mid-continent Research for Education and Learning [McREL] Laboratory for a compilation of content standards for K–12 curriculum [http://www.mcrel.org/standards-benchmarks]. The McREL web site also provides links to a variety of other sites providing lesson plans, activities, and curriculum resources that relate to these content standards.)

2. Statement of Content

A clear statement of the *central content to be addressed* in the lesson or unit is the second important piece of a lesson or unit plan. Content descriptions may identify concepts or generalizations to be developed, procedures to be implemented, controversial issues to be explored, or sets of facts to be memorized. The expert teacher is thoroughly familiar with the curriculum content and can describe it explicitly. Similarly, the author of a script must have a clear idea of the message or theme of the play. This dictates the dialogue and development of the action. Because the content drives the interaction (such as questions, answers, and explanations) of a lesson, and because novice teachers may not be fully conversant with the curriculum being taught, they need to pay particular attention to careful articulation of the content to be learned.

3. List of Materials

A statement or list of the *instructional materials* to be used in a lesson or unit is the third important part of a lesson or unit plan. A statement about needed materials is similar to a notation about props to be used in a script. It alerts the teacher to the preparations to be made before instruction begins. A stage manager cannot wait until the night of the performance to begin gathering the props for the play, and a teacher who is an effective manager does not wait until the last minute to gather or prepare materials for a lesson.

4. Set of Procedures

The fourth part of a lesson plan includes a *set of procedures* to be followed in the lesson. These procedures involve a series of activities, generally including some details about specific directions to be given or questions to be asked, in relation to each activity. The fourth part of a unit plan usually includes a series of topics to be dealt with across several lessons in the unit of instruction. Within each topic, specific plans for activities to be used may be included. This part of the lesson or unit plan is similar to the main body of a script. The set of procedures in a lesson plan and the series of topics in a unit plan both require skill in devising appropriate sequences of activities. Similarly, sequencing is important in the acts of a play, as some problem is set, developed, and carried to a conclusion.

5. Plans for Evaluating

INTASC Principle 8

The fifth part of a typical lesson or unit plan involves a statement about *evaluation procedures*. A teacher may evaluate what students have learned from a lesson or unit in a variety of ways, including tests, written homework, and observation of student responses to oral questions. While many useful means of evaluation exist, teachers need to plan their evaluation procedures in advance. Lesson and unit plans differ from scripts in this respect. Scripts are evaluated by the audiences and critics who attend the plays. Teachers' lesson and unit plans are rarely required to pass such public scrutiny, but systematic evaluation of student learning by the teacher is a critical aspect of effective teaching. If learning is not taking place, the script for the next lesson will need to be revised.

Some plans are incomplete

The five basic parts of a lesson or unit plan denote essential aspects of instruction that a teacher needs to consider in preparing for a lesson. Of course, it is possible to develop a lesson or unit plan that does not include all of these basic components, but such incomplete plans will have much less potential for successful student learning. A script that has no indication of which character is to speak which lines, or one that provides no stage directions, will be difficult to follow, and we should not be surprised if such an incomplete script results in an unsuccessful production. Similarly, a lesson or unit plan that is lacking one or more of the five basic parts will be an insufficient guide to the teacher during the performance of the lesson or unit.

The teacher who simply writes down the page numbers in the textbook that are to be covered in the next lesson has not really planned a lesson. Such a teacher has indicated the materials to be used in the lesson but has evidently not determined the procedures to be used for involving students in interacting with these materials. The teacher who writes an outline of steps to be followed in a lesson, without any indication of the particular skills or concepts that students are expected to learn as a result of engaging in the activities, has also developed an incomplete plan or script. A set of procedures that are not tied to any particular goal statement or content description provides the teacher with little or no guidance in making the frequent immediate decisions that confront every teacher during a lesson.

Figures 3.4, 3.5, and 3.6 present examples of lesson plans that include the five basic parts described above. All three of the lessons were designed to teach the general skill of writing "expanded sentences" (sentences that provide more descriptive information to the reader). The Related Standards and Related Benchmarks presented in these plans come from the www.mcrel.org web site mentioned earlier. The first two lesson plans were written for use with elementary school children and the third for secondary school students. Any of these lessons could be part of a unit plan designed to develop skill and interest in expository writing. The two elementary lessons show how a teacher might plan to teach the same content to two different groups in two different ways. The first lesson is designed for students who need more structure and direction. The second builds on student-generated ideas and encourages more independent learning.

Alternative instructional strategies are most readily recognized by examining the Procedures section of a teacher's lesson plan. The sequence of activities in the lesson will vary as a teacher moves from one quadrant to another in the repertoire grid discussed earlier and shown in Figure 3.3. To illustrate, for a lesson such as the one described for Quadrant A in the illustrative unit on the television media, the Procedures section in the lesson plan would include the following sequence of phases or major activities:

- Students identify and list data related to the topic and content area selected by the teacher (i.e., television programs they watch).
- Students group data items that have common features and label the groups to identify relevant features.
- With teacher guidance, students group the groups or categories they have developed to form a hierarchical category system.

By contrast, for a lesson such as the one described for Quadrant B in that unit, the Procedures section of the lesson plan would include a very different sequence of phases or major activities:

- The teacher orients students to the lesson topic, states the lesson objective, and reviews relevant prior learning.
- The teacher explains and demonstrates scriptwriting, the new skill to be learned.
- The teacher provides guidance as students practice using the new skill of scriptwriting.
- Students continue to practice the skill independently.

The specific format for a lesson plan can vary widely, and elements within specific segments of a lesson plan, such as descriptions of Procedures, can also vary widely, but effective lesson plans include the five basic features we

Lesson Plan A (Elementary)

Objective:

> Students will add words to a simple two-word sentence to change the meaning of the original sentence in at least two ways.

Related Standard:

> Uses the stylistic and rhetorical aspects of writing.

Related Benchmark:

> Uses a variety of sentence structures in writing (e.g., expands basic sentence patterns).

Content (Concept/Generalization/Procedure):

> A simple sentence can be expanded by adding adjectives and adverbs and by modifying phrases at the beginning or end of the sentence. Sentence expansion extends the meaning of a simple sentence.

Materials:

> 1. Wooden chart for sentence strips
> 2. Sample strips of two-word sentences with companion expanded sentences
> 3. Two-word sentence suggestions for the children in the group

Procedures:

> 1. *Beginning (set).* Place a simple two-word sentence on the chart with the first expanded sentence under it. Children will be asked to find *similarities* and *differences.*
>
>   Sample:
>   Birds fly.
>   The birds fly swiftly.
>   Have students compare each of the following expanded sentences to the base sentence, to note similarities and differences.
>   The graceful birds fly.
>   Birds fly in the sky.
>
>   Add a final expanded sentence, and ask students to compare it to the base sentence and to each of the other expanded sentences.
>   The graceful birds fly swiftly in the sky.
>
> 2. *Independent work.* Each child will be provided a two-word sentence to expand in at least two different ways. (Option for children—to originate their own if sample doesn't "appeal.") Since these will be prepared in advance, reading levels and interests of the children will be considered (see examples below).
>
> | David C. | Airplanes fly. |
> | Mike D. | Firefighters work. |
> | Larry G. | Planets rotate. |
> | Judith H. | Flowers bloom. |
> | Billy M. | Dogs bark. |
>
> 3. *Ending (closure).* Have children read their sentences aloud. Lead children to discuss which sentences "tell more" and to think about opportunities they have to use expanded sentences.

Evaluation:

> Collect written work. How complex are the sentences that the children have written? Have they added single words or phrases? Are they placed at the beginning, end, or middle of the sentence? What forms of expansion need further practice?

■ Figure 3.4

Lesson Plan B (Elementary)

Objective:

Students will add words to a simple two-word sentence to change the meaning of the original sentence in at least two ways.

Related Standard:

Uses the stylistic and rhetorical aspects of writing.

Related Benchmark:

Uses a variety of sentence structures in writing (e.g., expands basic sentence patterns).

Materials:

Chalkboard/whiteboard

Procedures:

1. *Beginning (set).* Ask students what they remember as the definition of a noun. Ask what they remember as the definition of a verb.
2. *(Guided development).* Ask for examples of plural nouns. List these on the board. Ask for examples of verbs. List these in a separate column on the board. Write a sentence frame on the board.
   The —————— ——————.
   Ask students to make up sentences, using a noun and a verb from the lists they generated to fill in the blanks in the sentence frame. Write a few of their examples on the board.
3. *(Independent work).* Have students work in pairs. Directions: Pick a sentence from the board or make a new one. Make the sentence "tell more" by adding words or phrases before the noun or after the verb. Make two or three new sentences this way.
4. *(Guided discussion).* Have each pair of students share their base sentence and one of their expanded sentences. Ask where they added words (before noun or after verb?). Which of the two sentences is more interesting? Why?
5. *(Closure).* Summarize: We can expand sentences by adding words that "tell more," that is, give a fuller description or tell where/when something happened. This can make our writing more interesting.

Evaluation:

Collect written work. How complex are the sentences that the children have written? Have they added single words or phrases? Are they placed at the beginning or end of the sentence? What forms of expansion need further practice? How well did the pairs work together? Did the two contribute equally to the task of generating new sentences?

■ Figure 3.5

have discussed here. Some school districts favor a particular format for lesson plans and ask all teachers to use the same format. Some education professors may require their students to use a particular format for lesson or unit plans. You may be introduced to new formats and terms for the various parts of a lesson or unit plan as you face new situations in your teacher preparation program and in your later teaching. Whatever the format or terms, look for the five basic parts of a plan and be sure to consider these critical aspects of instruction as you develop your own "scripts" for the lessons you teach.

Lesson Plan C (Secondary)

Objective:

> Given a set of simple sentences and a group of logical connectives, students will expand a sentence in at least four different ways while maintaining logical sense.

Related Standard:

> Uses the stylistic and rhetorical aspects of writing.

Related Benchmark:

> Uses a variety of sentence structures and lengths (e.g., complex sentences, parallel or repetitive sentence structure).

Content (Concept/Generalization/Procedure):

> A simple sentence can be expanded by adding a logical connective followed by a clause at the beginning or end of the sentence. Sentence expansion extends or modifies the meaning of the simple sentence.

Materials:

> 1. Overhead projector, transparencies, markers
> 2. Chalkboard

Procedures:

> 1. *Beginning (set).* Have each student write a simple sentence on his or her paper by completing the sentence frame, "The ——————." Have several students read their sentences aloud. Record these sentences on the chalkboard.
> 2. *Guided discussion.* On the overhead projector write "The helicopter landed *because* . . .". Have students suggest ways to end the sentence. Write these on the transparency.
>   Ask pupils to expand their own simple sentences by adding *because* and an appropriate clause. Have several examples read aloud.
>   Proceed in the same manner for *but, therefore, whenever, since, then,* and *so.*
>   On the overhead projector write "*Although* the helicopter landed, . . .". Have students suggest ways to end the sentence. Write a few on the transparency.
>   Ask students which of the logical connectives already discussed could be used at the beginning of their sentence. Have them write one or two, and have some read aloud.
> 3. *Ending (closure).* Ask each pupil to take any three of the sentences written on the board at the beginning of the lesson and to expand each sentence in four different ways, using the logical connectives listed on the transparency.

Evaluation:

> Collect written work. How accurately do students use the connectives to expand their sentences? Do they use a good variety of the connectives introduced? (Long term: Do students begin using more complex sentences with more varied connectives in later writing assignments?)

■ Figure 3.6

> **YOUR TURN** | **State Standards and the Repertoire Grid**

As the lesson plans in Figures 3.4, 3.5, and 3.6 demonstrate, a single state standard can be addressed through use of a variety of instructional processes. However, some standards may lend themselves more readily to use of a particular instructional process. An examination of standards in your own state can help you to distinguish the types of instructional processes they might promote. In Figure 3.7 some of the Virginia English Standards of Learning (SOLs) for grades 2, 4, and 7 have been placed in the four quadrants of the Repertoire Grid to illustrate the types of lessons or activities they might encourage teachers to develop. Use the Internet to locate the state standards for your own state. Choose the state standards for two different subject areas at a single grade level, or the state standards for two different grade levels in a single subject area. Using these sources, try to identify two standards that could reasonably be placed in each of the four quadrants of the Repertoire Grid. Be ready to explain your selections.

Scenes

While scripts are an important feature of play production, there are other things to be considered as well. Scenery is an important part of any dramatic production. There is a great deal of symbolic meaning in the scenery of a dramatic production—some of the message of any play is conveyed to the audience by the way the scene is set.

Similarly, when teachers plan lessons, they communicate a message by the way they set the scene for the lesson, as well as by what they say or ask students to do during the lesson. The teacher's stage is the physical classroom, and the teacher sets the scene by arranging the physical space of the classroom. In addition, the teacher sets the stage for lessons by determining the social organization of the classroom. In a well-designed classroom "scene," the physical and social organizations will complement each other.

Set the scene for the learning activity ▶

Although the three lesson plans in Figures 3.4, 3.5, and 3.6 have similar "scripts" (all include the same five basic parts of a lesson plan), the teachers who planned these lessons envisioned different classroom "scenes." In Lesson Plan A (Figure 3.4), the teacher envisions a scene (social organization) in which children will be working individually at their seats for part of the lesson, then discussing examples of expanded sentences together in a large group for another. There are several "scene changes" required for this lesson. First, students will meet in a large group to discuss sample sentences; then they will work individually at their desks. Next, they will share the sentences they have written, again in a large-group discussion. In planning for these scene changes, the teacher needs to be sure that the physical arrangement of desks in the classroom will facilitate discussion as well as independent seatwork. If children are seated in rows of single desks, they may be able to work alone without being distracted by their neighbors. But this type of seating arrangement is not conducive to a group discussion. Most children will see only the backs of other students' heads. In this type of classroom scene (physical arrangement), students talk to the teacher, not to one another. To use these two types of activities as routines in the classroom, the teacher needs to set the scene so that discussion and independent work are both facilitated. Arranging desks in a large semicircle could be one alternative.

In Lesson Plan B (Figure 3.5) children will work in a large group, then in pairs, then back in a large group. Tables may provide useful seating for both of these activities.

In Lesson Plan C (Figure 3.6), the teacher envisions a scene (physical arrangement) in which the overhead projector and screen are the focus of

Teacher-Directed

Quadrant A	Quadrant B
Grade 2. The student will make predictions about content of a story. Grade 4. The student will describe relationships between new content and previously learned concepts or skills. Grade 7. The student will compare and contrast a speaker's verbal and nonverbal messages.	Grade 2. The student will use and punctuate declarative, interrogative, and exclamatory sentences. Grade 4. The student will compare the use of fact and fantasy in historical fiction with other forms of literature. Grade 7. The student will identify persuasive techniques used in television and radio.
Grade 2. The student will create oral stories to share with others. Grade 4. The student will seek ideas and opinions of others. Grade 7. The student will ask probing questions to seek elaboration and clarification ideas.	Grade 2. The student will generate ideas before writing a story or letter. Grade 4. The student will construct questions about a topic to be investigated. Grade 7. The student will use graphic organizers to organize information.
Quadrant C	Quadrant D

"Inventing" New Ways of Perceiving (left margin)

Learning "Accepted" Knowledge (right margin)

Student-Constructed

■ Figure 3.7

Examples of State Standards in the Repertoire Gird

attention. The major activity throughout the lesson involves large-group discussion, and the teacher needs to set the scene so that students can see one another as well as the screen at the front of the room. For this activity, a large semicircle of desks might not be appropriate because students at each end of the semicircle might have difficulty seeing the screen.

In a special education classroom children may be working individually on different types of tasks, and some may be easily distracted. For this situation an appropriate scene (physical arrangement) may have desks separated and facing *away* from the center of the room, so that students can more easily concentrate on their work.

"Scene change" flexibility often needed ▶ When planning for lessons, teachers must think in advance about how the physical arrangement of the classroom will help or hinder students as they carry out the instructional activity of the lesson. If the type of activity changes frequently within lessons or from one lesson to another, the classroom arrangement must be flexible enough to support a variety of activities and social organizations (small-group work, individual work, or large-group discussion).[40] When planning units of instruction, teachers must envision a series of scenes that can encompass these various types of organization. Teachers are the stage managers and set designers as well as the scriptwriters and the actors.

Improvisation

Teachers must think on their feet ▶ While lesson and unit plans may function like scripts to cue the teacher about what to do next, no plan for instruction is detailed enough to tell a teacher exactly what to say, as a script for a play does. The teacher's guide for a textbook often provides a set of suggested questions to ask as teachers lead discussions based on readings in the text. But even if a teacher used the teacher's guide as a "script," and asked all the questions provided for a given lesson, some improvisation would still be necessary. Students never answer all questions correctly, and a teacher must react to partial or incorrect answers by asking follow-up questions or by providing additional information. Furthermore, students ask questions of their own, and neither these questions nor the answers to them are included in a teacher's guide to the textbook.

An actor or actress in a scripted play is not normally expected to improvise lines. But there is a place in the theater for improvisation. In improvisational theater, the audience may suggest characters and a situation. The actors then take on the suggested roles and, without any prior rehearsal, act out the situation.

Keys to Flexibility

Teachers are called on to improvise on a regular basis, just like improvisational actors, but their improvisations may not be as extensive. They may engage in only a brief extemporaneous dialogue with an individual student, rather than carrying out a whole skit. Expert teachers are never unprepared for these extemporaneous performances. They have studied a variety of "characters" (students) and situations through careful observation over time in their own classrooms. They also have a rich background of information about the subject they are teaching. They can call on this background of experience and knowledge when they are challenged to react on the spot to questions or suggestions from students.

Prepare for what you can't predict ▶

In one sense, a teacher can never plan ahead for the improvisational demands of the classroom. Even experienced teachers cannot predict everything that will happen in a lesson. An effective teacher needs to be flexible enough to respond to the ideas and queries of students. In another sense, it is possible for a teacher to be prepared to deal effectively with situations that are not predictable and thus require improvisation. This is one way in which routines and repertoires become invaluable. One way to improvise is to call on a familiar routine and use it in a new setting.

☐ **INTASC Principle 5**

> **YOUR TURN**   **Observing Improvisation in Action**

Some lessons involve teachers in a number of opportunities for improvisation. (Watch the Video Case, *Middle School Science Instruction: Inquiry Learning*, to see how a teacher draws on a strong subject-matter background and improvises responses to encourage student experimentation.)

▼ **TeachSource Video Case**   **Middle School Science Instruction: Inquiry Learning**

To access the video, go to www.cengage.com/login. Watch the video clip two or three times. Identify two instances of teacher improvisation in responding to a student question or suggestion, and write a brief description of each event. How do this teacher's planning processes enable him to improvise in this lesson? How do his beliefs encourage him to improvise?

Resources for Novice Teachers

Observe, discuss, develop repertoire ▶ Novice teachers do not come into the classroom armed with a set of routines and repertoires. They must develop their routines and repertoires by careful observation and practice, just as expert teachers and improvisational actors have done before them. Early field experiences that include systematic observation in classroom settings and opportunities for practice in working with small groups can be useful to novice teachers who want to become experts. The prospective teachers can observe the routines employed by experienced teachers and can practice using them. They should also discuss these routines with the teachers from whom they are borrowing them, so that they understand the purposes the routines serve and the situations in which they are most appropriately used. Eventually, they can adapt these borrowed routines and invent their own; in this way they will develop their own repertoire of routines.

■ Alternative Analogies

The analogy of teacher planning as a dramatic production is a useful one because it highlights some important features of teacher planning: the need to consider the "mood" and "message" (goal and content) that the lesson is intended to convey, the need to have the "props" (materials) prepared in advance, the need to have a "script" (sequence of planned procedures) to follow, and the importance of evaluation by "critics" (the thoughtful teacher). The analogy also emphasizes the importance of setting the "scene" (social organization and physical arrangement) for a successful lesson and indicates that an effective teacher must be skillful at improvising (responding to unpredictable events), drawing on a well-developed repertoire of routines. Like any analogy, this one does not fit completely. No teacher repeats the same script or lesson plan day after day to a series of new audiences, for example.

While the analogy of a dramatic production is a useful one for exploring the concept of instructional planning, it is not the only analogy for teacher planning. Each new analogy tends to highlight different features of a concept, so it can be helpful when clarifying a new concept to consider a variety of possible analogies.

> ❯ **YOUR TURN**   **Explaining Additional Analogies**

Some experienced educational researchers have compared teacher planning to choreography.[41] Another useful analogy for teacher planning is that of a road map. Can you think of some important characteristics of choreography or a road map that are also characteristics of teacher planning? Try listing three or four common characteristics now, and then discuss your ideas with your fellow students.

How do the analogies of choreography or a road map fail to fit the characteristics of teacher planning? List two ways in which either one is different from a teacher plan.

What new aspects of teacher planning are highlighted by these new analogies? Describe two important characteristics of teacher planning that stand out particularly in relation to the analogy of choreography or a road map.

Optional Alternative. What other analogies can you think of for the concept of teacher planning? Stretch your imagination and invent an analogy of your own. Can you think of a machine or some natural phenomenon that has some characteristics in common with a teacher's plan? Explore your analogy by listing similarities, differences, and highlighted features of teacher planning in relation to the new analogy. Share your analogy with your fellow students.

The Plan Is Only the Beginning

Since all plans are only intentions to act, a plan is only the beginning. And in the beginning, most plans are vague sketches of possible actions. These partial plans are gradually filled out with more and more definite decisions as the time for action approaches. But the phrase *only the beginning* is a deceptive one. Shakespeare wrote that "All's well that ends well," but it is equally true that things are more apt to end well if they begin well. Because a plan is the beginning, planning is one of the most critical skills that a teacher can have.

Instructional planning requires more than information about what is included in a lesson or unit plan. To plan effectively and efficiently, a teacher needs a clear understanding of the subject to be taught, as well as information about alternate goals and objectives, available instructional materials and resources, productive use of classroom questions, ways to provide for students' individual differences, procedures for classroom management, and techniques for evaluation of student learning. To carry out instructional plans, a teacher must have skills in lesson presentation and in interpersonal communication. Just as a plan is only the beginning, so is this chapter only the beginning. To develop real skill in instructional planning, you will need to absorb and apply the information in all the chapters of this book. You will also need to practice making plans for instruction, carrying them out in peer teaching or with small groups in classroom settings, and revising them on the basis of what you learn from the resulting action. Working with one or two peers in a process like "lesson study" may make your practice much more productive.

Create concept map after this course ▶

A concept map of teacher planning can serve as a record of your thoughts at this early stage of your development as a professional teacher. It can mark a point in your thinking that is "only a beginning." If you made such a map earlier, save it. When you have completed the activities in this book and have had an opportunity to practice instructional planning by putting your plans into action, construct another concept map of teacher planning. You will see that you are learning to think like a teacher. You already have a sound beginning.

Observation Worksheet

FOCUS ON TEACHER PLANNING

Teacher planning is not easy to observe, since it is mainly a mental activity. Here are three tasks you can carry out in a classroom to gather information about teacher planning.

Directions: Do not use actual names of schools, teachers, administrators, or students when using this worksheet.

Observer's Name: _____

Date: _____

Grade Level: _____

Subject: _____

Class Size: _____

Background Information: Give a brief general description of the school's social, economic, and ethnic makeup.

_____

_____

Task 1. The Plan Book and the Actual Lesson

What to Record: Before observing a classroom lesson, ask to see what the teacher has written in his/her lesson plan book as a guide for the lesson. As you observe the lesson, make a record of three things that the teacher does that were _not noted_ in the written comments in the plan book. After the lesson is over, interview the teacher briefly about these three procedures and record the answers.

Questions to Ask the Teacher:

1. When did you decide that you were going to do this in this lesson? _____

_____

_____

2. Is this a procedure that you use often with these students? _____

_____

_____

_____

3. What is your main reason for using this procedure? _____

_____

_____

_____

4. Have you ever written this procedure down as part of a lesson plan? Why or why not?

_____

_____

_____

Task 2. The Plan Book and the Substitute's Lesson Plan(s)

What to Record: Most schools require teachers to keep lesson plans for a substitute teacher on file, to be used in case of the teacher's absence. Ask to see a plan the teacher has prepared for a substitute teacher (either a plan for a single lesson, or a plan for a day's activities). Compare this plan to the plans written in the teacher's plan book. Ask the teacher to tell you the reasons for the differences you note.

Reflections on Your Observation:

1. If you were a substitute in this classroom, which set of plans would you prefer to have, and why?

_____

_____

_____

2. What would you want to know that is not included in either set of plans?

_____

_____

_____

Task 3. Teacher Planning and Student Planning

What to Record: Learning to plan and organize your own activities is an important part of becoming an independent learner. The degree to which students are encouraged to engage in the planning and organizing of instructional tasks may vary a great deal based on students' stage of development. As you observe in a classroom setting, try to identify two or three instances in which students are given opportunities to plan or structure some aspect of an activity or assignment.

Question to Ask the Teacher:

1. Ask the teacher about how and when students are given practice in planning or structuring an individual or group activity.

_____

_____

_____

☀ Mastery Test

1. Prospective teachers at the University of Virginia's Curry School of Education, at the end of an early field experience in which they planned and taught several lessons to full classes, were asked to state a maxim exemplifying an important principle they had learned as a result of their classroom experience. (A maxim is a terse or pithy statement of a rule to guide one's behavior, such as "An apple a day keeps the doctor away" or, for new teachers, "Don't smile before Christmas.")

   A number of the maxims they developed are listed below. Some, but not all, provide some useful guidelines related to instructional planning. Organize these maxims into groups or categories, based on similarities you note in the ideas they emphasize. You should develop at least four different groups, but you may form as many more than four as you like, and you may have as many items in a group as you like. Label or name each group to denote what important characteristic(s) are shared by items you place in the group. Write a brief statement for each group to explain how/whether that set of maxims is related to some important aspect of instructional planning.

Maxims

A little fun never hurt anyone.
Assume the students' mindset.
Be wise—Don't be afraid to improvise.
Clock watchers end well.

Don't be afraid to look outside yourself.
Don't do anything for students that they can do
   for themselves.
Don't stand still or you'll be a pill.

Don't underestimate your students.
Engage a student and the student will learn.
If you fail to plan, you plan to fail.
Kind but firm will help them learn.
Learning can be a team effort.
Look for written proof of students' knowledge.
Make sure students stay on task.
Never let them see you sweat.
Not knowing your students is preparing for
   trouble.
Organization is the key to elation.
Overplan—Things can blow big!
Pace the race.

Plan for the unexpected.
Prepare or beware.
Put limits on chaos, not creativity.
Students can teach, and teachers can learn.
The best discipline strategy is an engaging
   lesson.
The more you expect, the more they give.
Think before you speak.
Those who know don't always show.
Try to be wrong once a week.
Wear a poker face.
You can't win 'em all, but you can keep on
   trying.

2. Pick two lesson plans from one or two web sites of your choice—one plan that
   contains all the essential elements of a good plan and one that is lacking in two or
   more essential elements. Print out a copy of each plan.
   A. Identify each of the essential elements in the complete plan and note two
      additional positive features of the plan, explaining why you consider these
      to be valuable features.
   B. Fill in the missing elements of the incomplete plan in a way that is consistent
      with the elements already present and that improves the overall quality of
      the plan.

ADDITIONAL RESOURCES

 ### Readings

The book *Psychology and Educational Practice,* edited
by Herbert Walberg and Geneva Haertle (Berkeley,
Calif.: McCutchan, 1997), includes several chapters
with information pertinent to the planning decisions that teachers make. The following chapters are
particularly useful:

Blumenfeld, P. C., and R. W. Marx. "Motivation and
   Cognition," pp. 79–106.

Brown, A. "The Advancement of Learning," pp. 52–78.

Fraser, B. "Classroom Environments," pp. 323–341.

Kaplan, A., and M. Maehr. "School Cultures," pp. 342–355.

Wilson, S. "Teaching in the Content Areas," pp. 233–250.

 ### Websites

**Mid-continent Research for Education and
Learning (McREL): http://www.mcrel.org/
srandards-benchmarks**
This site provides a compendium of content standards
and benchmarks for K–12 education in both searchable
and browsable formats. Assessment items linked to standards are available, as well as lesson plans on a variety
of topics and subject areas.

**New York Times: http://www.nytimes.com/
learning/teachers/index.html**
Has daily lesson plans for grades 6–8 and 9–12, as well
as daily news "snapshot" activities that can be developed into lesson plans for grades 3–5. These are based on
current events and use interdisciplinary resources and
activities. Identifies academic content standards that can
be addressed by each lesson. The Learning Network at
this site includes a variety of resources for students and
parents as well as for teachers.

**The George Lucas Educational Foundation: http://
www.edutopia.org**
Provides information on resources and activities
promoting teachers' instructional use of technology and
student development of skills in the use of technology.
Instructional modules are available. Articles from the
Foundation Newsletter, *Edutopia,* can be accessed.

**Project Integration and Visualization Tool
(PIViT): http://www.umich.edu/~pbsgroup/
PIViT.html**
Provides information about a flexible design tool to help
teachers visualize and plan complex, integrated curricula like Project-Based Science. PIViT provides easy-
to-use graphical mapping tools to support teachers in
constructing project designs. Materials are distributed

through the Project Support Network (PS Net): http://www.umich.edu/~pbsgroup/psnet/.

Inspiration Software: http://www.inspiration.com/educators

Lesson and unit plans and other resource materials can be obtained from this site. Materials emphasize graphics to help students visualize problems and concepts in a variety of subject areas, for a variety of age levels.

For these links and additional resources, please visit the Premium Website at **www.cengage.com/login.**

⏺ NOTES

1. Michael E. Bratman, *Intention, Plans, and Practical Reason* (Cambridge, Mass.: Harvard University Press, 1987).

2. Margaret E. Herbert and Jean P. Dionne, "Planning Perspectives by Academic, Business, Lay, and Teacher Experts" (Paper presented at the Annual Meeting of the American Educational Research Association, New York, 1996).

3. Joseph D. Novak and D. Bob Gowin, *Learning How to Learn* (Cambridge: Cambridge University Press, 1984).

4. Charles R. Williams, "Semantic Map Planning: A Framework for Effective, Reflective Teaching, Teacher Development, and Teacher Research" (M.A. thesis, School for International Training, Brattleboro, Vt., 1994).

5. David Hyerle, *Visual Tools for Constructing Knowledge* (Alexandria, Va.: Association for Supervision and Curriculum Development, 1996).

6. Bruce R. Joyce and Marsha Weil, *Models of Teaching* (Needham Heights, Mass.: Allyn & Bacon, 1992). See also Paul D. Eggen and Donald P. Kauchak, *Strategies for Teachers: Teaching Content and Thinking Skills* (Needham Heights, Mass.: Allyn & Bacon, 1996).

7. Greta Morine-Dershimer, "Tracing Conceptual Change in Preservice Teachers," *Teaching and Teacher Education* 9, no. 1 (1993): 15–26.

8. Hilda Borko and Jerry Niles, "Descriptions of Teacher Planning: Ideas for Teachers and Researchers," in *Educator's Handbook: A Research Perspective,* ed. Virginia Richardson-Koehler (New York: Longman, 1987). See also Tracy Hogan, Mitchell Rabinowitz, and John A. Craven, III, "Representation in Teaching: Inferences From Research of Expert and Novice Teachers," in *Educational Psychologist* 38, no. 4 (2003): 235–247.

9. Gail McCutcheon and H. Richard Milner, "A Contemporary Study of Teacher Planning in a High School English Class," *Teachers and Teaching: Theory and Practice* 8, no. 1 (2002): 81–94.

10. Jeanne S. Schumm et al., "General Education Teacher Planning: What Can Students with Learning Disabilities Expect?" *Exceptional Children* 61, no. 4 (1995): 335–352.

11. Carol Ann Tomlinson, *How to Differentiate Instruction in Mixed-Ability Classrooms* (Alexandria, Va.: Association for Supervision and Curriculum Development, 1995).

12. McCutcheon and Milner, *op. cit.*

13. John R. Mergendoller, Thom Markham, Jason Ravitz, and John Larmer, "Pervasive Management of Project Based Learning: Teachers as Guides and Facilitators," in *Handbook of Classroom Management: Research, Practice, and Contemporary Issues,* eds. Carolyn M. Evertson and Carol S. Weinstein (Mahwah, New Jersey: Lawrence Erlbaum Associates, 2006).

14. Cheryl Mason Bolick and James M. Cooper, "Classroom Management and Technology," in *Handbook of Classroom Management: Research, Practice, and Contemporary Issues,* eds. Carolyn M. Evertson and Carol Weinstein (Mahwah, New Jersey: Lawrence Erlbaum, 2006).

15. Lynn S. Fuchs et al., "The Relation Between Teacher Beliefs About the Importance of Good Student Work Habits, Teacher Planning, and Student Achievement," *Elementary School Journal* 94, no. 3 (1994): 331–345.

16. Gloria Ladson-Billings, *The Dreamkeepers: Successful Teachers of African American Children* (San Francisco: Jossey-Bass, 1994).

17. McCutcheon and Milner, *op. cit.*

18. Judith Harford and Gerry MacRuairc, "Engaging Student Teachers in Meaningful Reflective Practice," *Teaching and Teacher Education,* 24, no. 7 (2008): 1884–1892.

19. Greta Morine-Dershimer and Stephanie Corrigan, "Teacher Beliefs," in *Psychology and Educational Practice,* ed. Herbert J. Walberg and Geneva Haertle (Berkeley: McCutchan, 1997).

20. Andy Hargreaves and Shawn Moore, "Curriculum Integration and Classroom Relevance: A Study of Teachers' Practices," *Journal of Curriculum and Supervision* 15, no. 2 (2000): 89–112.

21. Education Professional Standards Board, *New Teacher Standards for Preparation and Certification* (Frankfort, Ky.: Education Professional Standards Boards, 1994).

22. Elizabeth Spalding, "Of Organelles and Octagons: What Do Preservice Secondary Students Learn from Interdisciplinary Teaching?" *Teaching and Teacher Education* 18, no. 6 (2002): 699–714.

23. George Lucas Foundation, *Learn and Live* (Nicasio, Calif.: George Lucas Foundation, 1997).

24. Nobuo K. Shimahara, *Teaching in Japan: A Cultural Perspective* (New York: Routledge Palmer, 2002), p. 61.

25. Ibid.

26. Laurel D. Puchner and Ann R. Taylor, "Lesson Study, Collaboration and Teacher Efficacy: Stories From Two School-Based Math Lesson Study Groups," *Teaching and Teacher Education*, 22, no. 7 (2006): 922–934.

27. Linda Sims and Daniel Walsh, "Lesson Study With Preservice Teachers: Lessons From Lessons," *Teaching and Teacher Education,* 25, no.5 (2008): 724–733.

28. Kathy Carter, Donna Sabers, Katherine Cushing, Stefinee Pinnegar, and David Berliner, "Processing and Using Information About Students: A Study of Expert, Novice, and Postulant Teachers," *Teaching and Teacher Education* 3, no. 2 (1987): 147–157.

29. Gaea Leinhardt, "Math Lessons: A Contrast of Novice and Expert Competence" (Paper presented at the Psychology of Mathematics Education Conference, East Lansing, Mich., 1986).

30. Jere Brophy, ed., *Subject-Specific Instructional Methods and Activities (Advances in Research on Teaching,* vol. 8) (Amsterdam: JAI Press, 2001).

31. Ibid.

32. Joyce and Weil, *op. cit.*

33. Will Richardson, "World Without Walls: Learning Well With Others," *Edutopia*: http://www.glef.org/technologyintegration.

34. Robert E. Slavin, *Cooperative Learning: Theory, Research, and Practice* (Englewood Cliffs, N.J.: Prentice-Hall, 1990).

35. Eggen and Kauchak, *op. cit.*

36. Joyce and Weil, *op. cit.*

37. Hilda Borko and Carol Livingston, "Expert and Novice Teachers' Mathematics Instruction: Planning, Teaching, and Post-Lesson Reflections" (Paper presented at the Annual Meeting of the American Educational Research Association, New Orleans, 1988).

38. Yisrael Rich and Malka Almozlino, "Educational Goal Preferences Among Novice and Veteran Teachers of Sciences and Humanities," *Teaching and Teacher Education* 15, no. 6 (1999): 613–629.

39. Ibid.

40. Pam Pointon and Ruth Kershner, "Making Decisions About Organizing the Primary Classroom Environment as a Context for Learning: The Views of Three Experienced Teachers and Their Pupils," *Teaching and Teacher Education* 16, no. 1 (2000): 117–127.

41. Fritz K. Oser and Franz J. Baeriswyl, "Choreographies of Teaching: Bridging Instruction to Learning," in *Handbook of Research on Teaching,* 4th ed., ed. Virginia Richardson (Washington, D.C.: American Educational Research Association, 2001).

4

Involving Students in Learning

Robert Shostak

David Young-Wolff/PhotoEdit

INTASC Standards

● **Principle 2:** The teacher understands how children learn and develop, and can provide learning opportunities that support their intellectual, social, and personal development.

● **Principle 3:** The teacher understands how students differ in their approaches to learning and creates instructional opportunities that are adapted to diverse learners.

● **Principle 4:** The teacher understands and uses a variety of instructional strategies to encourage students' development of critical thinking, problem solving, and performance skills.

● **Principle 5:** The teacher uses an understanding of individual and group motivation and behavior to create a learning environment that encourages positive social interaction, active engagement in learning, and self-motivation.

● **Principle 6:** The teacher uses knowledge of effective verbal, nonverbal, and media communication techniques to foster active inquiry, collaboration, and supportive interaction in the classroom.

● **Principle 8:** The teacher understands and uses formal and informal assessment strategies to evaluate and ensure the continuous intellectual, social, and physical development of the learner.

OBJECTIVES

1. To define a planned beginning (set), explain its purposes, and give examples of when it is used to involve students in learning

2. To create original planned beginnings (sets) for involving students in learning

3. To define planned discussion, explain its purposes, and give examples of when it is used to involve students in learning

4. To identify student behaviors that reflect students' ability to engage in effective classroom discussion

5. To create original planned discussions for use in a given learning situation

6. To define a planned ending (closure), explain its purposes, and give examples of how it is used to involve students in learning

7. To create original planned endings (closure) for use in a given learning situation

Professionals writing and conducting research in education today continue to focus on the student as learner. They describe the classroom as a "complex social environment" in which "the characteristics of the students . . . ha[ve] implications for the way in which instruction is delivered and the effects that teachers have on student learning."[1] These researchers view learning as a social process heavily influenced by the sociolinguistic, ethnic, and cultural characteristics of the students. **Constructivist theorists** are emphasizing that students are not sponges—passive recipients of knowledge—and that effective learning occurs when students are interacting with one another and the teacher to make their own meaning and construct their own knowledge.[2]

The Council of Chief State School Officers, in its project to develop core standards for beginning teachers, has brought much of the current research and theory together to describe what they define as requisite performance standards in ten different areas necessary for demonstrating effective classroom teaching. Each of these INTASC standards is detailed in the appendix of this book.

In Chapter 1, you were introduced to Danielson's framework for teacher competencies that lead directly to the improvement of student learning. Chapter 2 introduced you to the first of the three essential steps in the instructional process: establishing the instructional objectives that provide students with informed direction and a clear notion of what is expected of them. Chapter 3 explored the second step of the instructional process: planning. In that chapter you were introduced to the notion of the lesson plan as analogous to the script of a dramatic production. Here in Chapter 4, you will have an opportunity to view the teacher as play director. Just as a play director must interpret the script and create from it an artistic production for the pleasure and edification of an audience, the teacher as decision-maker/director must choose teaching strategies that not only effectively engage students in learning, but also provide an experience they will find both enjoyable and meaningful.

☐ INTASC Principle 2

The principle focus of this chapter will be on the standards that address student learning and instructional strategies. To be able to decide which teaching strategies will prove most effective in achieving your objectives, you must be aware of the factors that most heavily influence the way students become involved in the learning process. You need to understand that your students are not all alike. They have different abilities. They learn differently, have different interests, and possess different needs. And as our society becomes more culturally diverse, teachers must be aware of and responsive to the life experiences and learning styles of these diverse students if they wish to engage them meaningfully in the learning process.

Selecting the appropriate teaching strategy to ensure that all students learn means that they must be given a variety of opportunities to understand, develop, and utilize the ideas presented in your daily lessons. Over the years, the theoretical work of researchers and the empirical efforts of classroom teachers have provided us with a number of teaching strategies that have been proven to work effectively in the classroom. For now, let's briefly review three of these strategies, and then examine three others in more detail.

☐ INTASC Principles 3–5

One useful strategy currently employed by successful teachers is **differentiated instruction**. In Chapter 6 of this text, Tomlinson defines differentiated instruction as occurring when "a teacher proactively plans varied approaches to what students need to learn, how they will learn it,

▼ **TeachSource Video Case** | **Integrating Technology to Improve Student Learning: A High School Science Simulation**

To access the video, go to www.cengage.com/login. Watch the video clip, study the artifacts in the case, and reflect upon the following questions:

1. What keys to successful inquiry-based learning did the teacher employ in his "dragon" lesson?
2. What student behaviors can you identify that clearly demonstrate that students were engaged in learning?
3. View bonus videos 1 and 3, and examine each of the artifacts used in the lesson. What evidence can you find that would support the statement that the approach used in this lesson did, in fact, help students develop new knowledge?

and/or how they can express what they have learned in order to increase the likelihood that each student will learn as much as he or she can as efficiently as possible." The author goes on to provide you with an opportunity to examine several useful strategies for using differentiated instruction in your own classroom.

□ **INTASC Principles 3–5**

Another productive strategy frequently used by teachers is **inquiry-based learning**. Although inquiry-based learning has its roots in the scientific method, its application may be extended to all subject-matter curricula. Used as an instructional strategy, this approach is based on an information-processing model that encourages students to discover their own meaning from facts and relationships; and out of this exercise develop new knowledge. The key to successful inquiry-based learning is questioning, information-gathering, discussing the findings, and obtaining some form of closure, such as a clear statement of what has been learned. The video case, *Integrating Technology to Improve Student Learning: A High School Science Simulation*, shows how high school biology teacher Ken Bateman effectively employs an inquiry-based teaching strategy while using the computer to engage his students in the learning process.

□ **INTASC Principles 2, 5, 6**

Cooperative learning probably enjoys the reputation of being the most heavily researched of all teaching strategies designed to engage students in learning. The effective use of this teaching strategy (working cooperatively in groups) can help students learn more efficiently, retain more of what they learn, and develop the attitude that learning can be intrinsically rewarding. The goal of cooperative learning is to provide outcomes that benefit both the individual and the group. Teachers who are successful using this strategy must plan carefully. Objectives must be clearly stated. All students must be involved in the group process, and each student must have a specific role to play with the opportunity to change roles when appropriate. However, simply placing students in groups and telling them to work together cooperatively does not guarantee that they will. In Chapter 9 of this text you will learn how to take the essential features of this approach and develop complex learning structures that will lead to the successful use of this teaching strategy.

The findings of motivational research clearly demonstrate that students learn by doing. Whatever teaching strategy you employ, students must be actively engaged—listening, observing, thinking, writing, speaking, touching. Three essential skills a teacher needs to involve students successfully in learning are (1) how to begin a lesson, or create a *set*; (2) how to generate a productive discussion; and (3) how to end a lesson, or make an effective *closure*.

Remember that regardless of the grade level you teach, the necessity of exposing students to new facts, ideas, and complicated relationships requires the teacher to involve students in the learning process.

OBJECTIVE 1

To define a planned beginning (set), explain its purposes, and give examples of when it is used to involve students in learning

---

What Is a Planned Beginning?

Learning Activity 4.1

INTASC Principle 3

A planned beginning, or **set**, is a combination of actions and statements designed to relate the experiences of the students to the instructional objectives of the lesson.[3] The notion of using students' knowledge to link what is known to the unknown is supported by motivational studies that show people are much more willing to "buy into" something about which they already have some interest or knowledge. Also, the requirement to directly engage students in the learning process is a reflection of another basic tenet in motivational instructional theory: **relevance**. When the educational task at hand is relevant, students are much more likely to feel a sense of accomplishment and express a desire to succeed.

Involving students in learning requires accomplishing the following critical tasks: focusing students' attention, establishing expectations for what is to be learned, motivating students to become involved, and using students' prior knowledge to make meaningful connections to new material.

A story is told about a traveler who came upon an old man beating his donkey in an effort to make the animal rise. The animal sat placidly in the middle of the road refusing to get up, and the old man continued to whip the animal until a stranger stepped up and stopped his hand. "Why don't you tell the donkey to rise?" asked the stranger. "I will," replied the old man, "but first I have to get his attention."

Focus ▶ The first purpose of a planned beginning is *to focus student attention on the lesson*. Effective teachers know that one of their primary tasks is to involve the student in the learning process. The Kelwynn Group, an educational consulting firm that developed a list of twenty criteria for effective teaching performance based on the work of Madeline Hunter, Jane Stallings, Barak Rosenshine, and others, echoes the same notion.[4]

Expectations ▶ As its second purpose, a planned beginning attempts *to establish expectations for what is to be learned*. This is done by creating a framework for the ideas, principles, or information that is to follow. Good and Brophy, in discussing how to structure presentations, speak of **advance organizers**— telling "students what they will be learning before the instruction begins. . . . Advance organizers give students a structure within which they can assimilate the specifics presented by a teacher."[5] Effective teachers frequently share their goals and objectives with students as a means of helping them establish a framework for their learning and involving them in the lesson.

Motivation ▶ The third purpose of a planned beginning is *to motivate students to become involved in the lesson*. A great deal of research has been carried on over the years on student motivation and the need to increase students' involvement in a lesson. Maria Montessori observed how deep involvement in play activities can keep a young child motivated and interested in a single game over an extended period of time. The point here is that active involvement at the beginning of a lesson can increase curiosity and stimulate student interest in the lesson.[6] A good example is the teacher who wishes to teach the concept of categorizing and brings a collection of baseball cards, CDs, or even a basket of leaves to class. Then the students, divided into groups, are asked to categorize their collections and explain how and why they did what they did.

Prior knowledge ▶ The fourth and last purpose of the planned beginning is *to relate students' prior knowledge to the new material to be learned.* Merely stating a new idea or principle does not ensure students will immediately comprehend. Moreover, many students who do understand a new idea or principle have difficulty applying their knowledge to new situations. The clever use of examples and analogies can do much to help students relate their prior knowledge to new material to be learned.

◼ When to Use a Planned Beginning

Learning Activity 4.2

Now that the planned beginning has been defined and its purposes explained, you are ready to focus on when it is used in the course of a lesson. To better understand the use of planned beginnings, think of a classroom lesson as a game. Bellack, in his research on the language used by teachers to engage students in learning, talks about "structuring moves [that] set the context for the entire classroom game."[7] Furthermore, he views the lesson as containing several "subgames," each of which is identified primarily by the type of activity taking place during a given period of "play."

Several subgames per lesson ▶ For example, you may plan to use several different activities such as reading, writing, and discussion, dealing with different subject matter. Each new activity can be seen as a subgame within the context of a larger game—the entire day's lessons. Each activity must be designed so that students are involved (play) actively in the lesson (game). Specific examples are illustrated in the sample lessons in the section discussing Objective 2.

The kinds of classroom activities (subgames) for which it is necessary to employ a planned beginning are innumerable. For help in learning when to use a planned beginning in your own lessons, carefully study the following list.

Examples of When to Use a Planned Beginning

To start a long unit of work in which the class might be studying plants, rockets, or local government

To introduce a new concept or principle

To initiate a discussion

To begin a skill-building activity such as reading comprehension or visual discrimination

To introduce a film, TV program, or video

To demonstrate a particular function of a computer

To prepare for a field trip

To present a guest speaker

To introduce a homework assignment

To begin a laboratory exercise

To redirect a presentation when you see that students do not understand the content

---

✳ Mastery Test

> **OBJECTIVE 1** **To define a planned beginning (set), explain its purposes, and give examples of when it is used to involve students in learning**

These questions are designed to determine your knowledge and comprehension level. Successful completion of these questions meets the objective of the learning activity.

1. Define the planned beginning, and explain three specific purposes it serves to involve students in learning.
2. Describe briefly three different situations in which you would use a planned beginning in your lessons.

> **OBJECTIVE 2** **To create original planned beginnings (sets) for involving students in learning**

Learning Activity 4.3

Now that you know what a planned beginning is and the general purposes for which it is used, you are ready to begin practicing how to create your own planned beginnings. Before you actually begin doing this, you should take time to familiarize yourself with some examples of how experienced teachers might use planned beginnings in their lessons.

▣ Samples of Planned Beginnings

Below is a list of specific planned beginnings used by experienced teachers. Study them carefully. Then read each of the sample lessons that follow and the accompanying analysis. You should then be ready to create your own planned beginnings for a given teaching situation.

1. To focus students' attention on the lesson by employing an activity, event, object, or person that relates directly to students' interests or previous experiences
2. To establish expectations for learning by providing a structure or framework that enables the student to visualize the objectives, content, or activities of the lesson
3. To motivate students to become involved in the lesson by employing student-centered activities or student-developed examples
4. To provide a smooth transition from known or already covered material to new or unknown material by capitalizing on students' present knowledge, past experiences, familiar examples, or analogies

Sample Lesson 1

The teacher has planned to get into the topic of percentages and is aware of student interest in the local baseball team. The teacher decides to introduce the unit with a brief discussion of the previous day's game. Talk is directed to batting averages, and the teacher demonstrates how they are calculated.

Students are encouraged to work out one or two of the averages for favorite players.

Analysis. This planned beginning is most appropriately used for introducing a unit on percentages or the concept of *percent* itself. Referring to the list of uses for planned beginnings mentioned above, note:

1. It uses an event, yesterday's baseball game, that is familiar and of interest to students to gain their attention.
2. It provides a ready frame of reference (batting averages) for the new concept to be learned, *percent.*
3. It motivates students to become involved by engaging in an activity the students enjoy—talking about a favorite sport.
4. It relates prior knowledge and experiences (previously learned math concepts and the term *batting average*) to the new concept of *percent.*

Sample Lesson 2

The students working in a science unit have already demonstrated in the first part of their lesson some basic understanding of mixtures. The teacher has planned to conduct an experiment to demonstrate visually the concept of mixtures. She brings to class several bottles of different kinds of popular salad dressings. The students are directed to experiment with the various bottles and to observe differences in their appearance before and after they are vigorously mixed.

Analysis. This planned beginning is most appropriately used to begin a laboratory exercise. Referring to the list of uses for planned beginnings mentioned above, note:

1. It uses popular salad dressings as a device to gain students' attention.
2. It establishes expectations for what is to be learned by focusing on what students are to look for while "experimenting" with the salad dressings.
3. It motivates students to become involved by engaging them in a meaningful activity.
4. It uses the students' prior knowledge of mixtures to help them discover new knowledge related to the topic they are studying.

Sample Lesson 3

The students have been learning how to type messages in their new computer e-mail program. The teacher announces that they are now ready to select a pen pal and begin to learn how to send their messages.

Analysis. This planned beginning is most appropriately used to introduce a new skill in a series of related skills. Referring to the list of uses for planned beginnings mentioned above, note:

1. It focuses students' attention on the lesson by involving them in an activity they enjoy and have been anticipating—the selection of a pen pal.
2. It establishes a framework for learning by relating what they have already accomplished to the next skill to be mastered in using e-mail.

3. It motivates students to become involved by allowing them to use what they have learned in an activity they enjoy.

4. It uses students' knowledge of language skills and the computer to create new opportunities to build meaningful relationships with others.

Learning Activity 4.4   Up until this point in the chapter, you have been engaged solely in paper-and-pencil-type activities. Now it is time to observe in real classrooms where students are actually involved in learning. Before scheduling your first observation, review the material on Observation Worksheets in the *Using This Book* section following the preface. When you are ready to observe, make a copy of the Observation Worksheet that follows to gather your data. You will be able to compare the results of your observations with others in a subsequent class activity.

Observation Worksheet

BEGINNING A LESSON

This observation activity gives you the opportunity to compare what you've learned about beginning a lesson to what you actually see in classrooms.

Directions: Do not use actual names of schools, teachers, administrators, or students when using this worksheet.

Observer's Name: _____

Date: _____

Grade Level: _____

Subject: _____

Class Size: _____

Background Information: Give a brief general description of the school's social, economic, and ethnic makeup.

_____   _____

_____

_____

What to Record: While observing teachers in action, pay attention to those times in the instructional process when the teacher introduces a new lesson. Use the following format to record what the teacher says to get students ready for that lesson.

1. How are the students made aware that the lesson is beginning? _____

_____

_____

2. How are the students motivated to become involved in the lesson? _____

_____

_____

3. What frame of reference is provided to help students organize their learning? _____

_____

_____

4. How does the teacher make use of students' prior knowledge as it relates to the new material to be learned? _____

_____

Reflections on Your Observation: Compare what you've seen the teacher do in beginning a lesson with the steps advocated by this chapter's author. In what ways are they similar and different? In your judgment, was the lesson beginning effective? Why or why not?

_____

_____

✳ Mastery Test

> OBJECTIVE 2 **To create original planned beginnings (sets) for involving students in learning**

Following these directions are five hypothetical teaching situations. Read each one carefully and create a planned beginning of your own that you feel would work effectively in that particular situation. You may refer to the list of uses for planned beginnings on page 87 and the sample lessons that follow to help you complete this task.

Situation 1.   The class has been working on a unit comparing different cultures. During the first part of the period, the students saw a short videotape that provided an overview of important cultural differences. The teacher wishes to use the remainder of the period for a new activity that will involve students more directly in the lesson.

Situation 2.   You are introducing the study of pollution and the environment to your class. It is important that you get off on the right foot.

Situation 3.   You are introducing the use of search engines on the World Wide Web.

Situation 4.   Your class has been studying the letters of the alphabet. You wish to use part of the day to take up this subject again and to determine how far your students have come in being able to place the letters in order.

Situation 5.   Your class has been working on different techniques to put life into their writing. In this lesson, you wish to present the idea of using descriptive words to paint verbal pictures.

OBJECTIVE 3   To define planned discussion, explain its purposes, and give examples of when it is used to involve students in learning

What Is Planned Discussion?

Learning Activity 4.5

Many of the changes in what has been happening in the classroom in recent years have been the result of sociolinguistic research investigating the instructional function of classroom talk. The idea that students are passive recipients of knowledge and that teachers are the transmitters of that knowledge is giving way to the notion that students learn better when they are involved in the process of creating knowledge for themselves.[8]

The educators who are bringing about these changes follow the precepts of what is known as *constructivist learning theory*. The research base for this theory stems from recent studies of the brain and how learning occurs. Although there is not widespread agreement on a definition of the constructivist theory of learning, many theorists can agree on some basic assumptions about how humans learn, or "construct knowledge."

The purpose of planned discussion ▶

Basic to constructivist theory is the notion that the individual student, not the teacher, is the focus in every **learning situation** and that classroom social interaction is critical in the learning process. Specifically, learning occurs when students interact directly with whatever materials or events encompass the learning experience and when they create their own ideas and understandings from this interaction. This means that constructivism focuses on learning, not telling. Students are encouraged to take chances, given opportunities to experiment on their own, and accept responsibility for their own learning. Moreover, great emphasis is placed on creating a classroom environment that encourages students to interact with one another.

The constructivist views the teacher, for the most part, as a facilitator. The teacher provides learning situations in which students have an opportunity to conceptualize for themselves and create their own understandings. The teacher also encourages cooperative learning and emphasizes the need for students to engage in meaningful dialogue. That is why dialogue, or classroom discussion, is being viewed as one of the most important learning situations teachers can use to help students create knowledge for themselves.[9] The video case, *Constructivist Teaching in Action: A High School Classroom Debate*, shows how high school social studies teacher *Sarabinh Levy-Brightman effectively applies basic constructivist theory in a learning situation.*

▼ **TeachSource Video Case**   **Constructivist Teaching in Action: A High School Classroom Debate**

To access the video, go to www.cengage.com/login. Watch the video clip, study the artifacts in the case, and reflect upon the following questions:

1. How does the teacher subscribe to the notion that the individual student and not the teacher is the focus of the lesson?
2. How would you describe the role played by the teacher in this lesson?
3. View each of the bonus videos. What evidence that the approach used in this lesson did, in fact, encourage students to take chances, gave opportunities to experiment on their own, and accept responsibility for their own learning?

☐ INTASC Principles
5, 6

A **planned discussion** is one that permits open interaction between student and student as well as between teacher and student. Although the teacher initiates the activity, he or she does not assume a leadership role but rather participates as a member of the group, and everyone adheres to the guidelines for acceptable discussion behavior. Discussion serves several important purposes as a vehicle for involving students in learning:

1. Students acquire new knowledge.
2. They learn to express clearly their own ideas or views.
3. They learn to evaluate their own thinking and the thinking of others.
4. They learn to reflect on ideas different from their own.
5. They learn to share personal opinions.

☐ When to Use Planned Discussion

Learning Activity 4.6

Now that planned discussion has been defined and you understand its purposes for involving students in learning, you need to know when to use discussion most effectively in a lesson. For help in completing this task, carefully study the following list.

Examples of When to Use Discussion

To compare different solutions to the same problem

To determine what can be learned from a completed laboratory experiment, an extended research project, or a meaningful field trip

To compare a novel, play, or biography to its filmed version

To examine different political ideologies

To evaluate new or proposed changes in social policy

To explore the similarities and differences of cultures

✳ Mastery Test

OBJECTIVE 3 **To define planned discussion, explain its purposes, and give examples of when it is used to involve students in learning**

The following questions are designed to determine your knowledge and comprehension level. Successful completion of these questions meets the objective of the learning activity.

1. Define in your own words the term *planned discussion*.
2. State three specific purposes for using planned discussion in a lesson.
3. Describe briefly three different situations in which you would use a planned discussion in your lessons.

▪OBJECTIVE 4 **To identify student behaviors reflecting students' ability to engage in effective classroom discussion**

■ Preparing Students for a Discussion

Learning Activity 4.7

Although learning how to plan for a successful discussion is extremely important, it is just as important to know how to prepare students to participate effectively in discussion. Most experts in group dynamics agree that one of the keys to preparing for successful classroom discussion is the ability of the teacher to create an atmosphere of trust among students and between teacher and students. Students must be made to feel that the classroom is a safe place to express their ideas and feelings without running the risk of being embarrassed or ridiculed.

Creating this kind of atmosphere in today's increasingly diverse classroom environment requires teachers to be able to recognize students' cultural and ethnic similarities and differences. These differences in language, how students learn, how they react in social situations, and how they view themselves in multicultural settings are important considerations in preparing them to use discussion in the classroom. Before beginning the next Learning Activity, you may find it helpful to review the material in Chapter 6, Differentiating Instruction for Academic Diversity.

Teach basic discussion skills ▶

Many teachers make the mistake of thinking that students are born with the ability to communicate effectively in an open discussion. This is just not true. Students must learn the basic skills required to participate effectively in a discussion. Before you implement your plan for conducting a discussion, be certain to include time for familiarizing your students with the skills needed to participate effectively in an open group discussion. The list that follows contains a set of basic skills that most experts in human communication would agree are necessary for participants to be successful in a large-group classroom discussion. Study the list carefully before initiating your first classroom discussion.

1. Listen respectfully even if you disagree with what is being said.
2. Learn to avoid interrupting others when they are speaking.
3. Learn to keep an open mind to different points of view.
4. Learn to take responsibility for getting a task done.
5. Learn to cooperate for the purpose of seeking solutions to the problem at hand.
6. Learn to listen critically.
7. Learn to stay focused on the issue and avoid irrelevant comments, questions, or stories.
8. Learn how to come to a common understanding to which all can agree.

❋ Mastery Test

OBJECTIVE 4   **To identify student behaviors reflecting their ability to engage in effective classroom discussion**

Now that you know the purposes for using planned discussion, know when to use planned discussion in a lesson, and are aware of the importance of preparing students to engage in effective discussion, you are ready to test your observational skills in a real classroom situation. Your task is to identify student behaviors that reflect their ability to engage in effective classroom discussion. Before scheduling this observation, review the material on Observation Worksheets in the *Using This Book* section following the preface. When you are ready to observe, make a copy of the Observation Worksheet that follows to gather your data. You will be able to compare the results of your observations with others in a subsequent class activity.

Observation Worksheet

PLANNED DISCUSSION

This observation activity gives you the opportunity to identify student behaviors that reflect their ability to engage in effective classroom discussion.

Directions: Do not use actual names of schools, teachers, administrators, or students when using this worksheet.

Observer's Name: _____

Date: _____

Grade Level: _____

Subject: _____

Class Size: _____

Background Information: Give a brief general description of the school's social, economic, and ethnic makeup.

_____

_____

_____

What to Record: You will be observing student behaviors reflecting their ability to engage in effective discussion. Use the following format to record what the students do during discussion.

1. How do students demonstrate their respect for others? _____

_____

_____

2. In what ways are students maintaining an open mind? _____

_____

_____

3. In what ways are students demonstrating their willingness to accept responsibility for getting the task done? _____

_____

_____

4. What evidence is there that students are trying to reach a consensus? _____

_____

_____

5. How do students demonstrate their ability to stay focused on the issues? _____

_____

_____

6. What evidence is there that students are thinking about the issues being discussed? _____

_____

_____

7. How do students demonstrate their ability to work cooperatively? _____

_____

_____

_____

Reflections on Your Observation:

1. Summarize your general impressions about the students' ability to engage in effective discussion.

_____

_____

_____

2. If you had been leading the discussion, what changes would you have made? Why?

_____

_____

_____

OBJECTIVE 5   **To create original planned discussions for use in a given learning situation**

◻ Planning a Discussion

Learning Activity 4.8

Getting yourself organized ▶

Although good discussion can evolve spontaneously, there is no guarantee this will happen on a regular basis. Ensuring meaningful discussion requires the same care you give to planning an entire lesson. This does not mean that the outcome of a discussion is something one should predict or predetermine. On the contrary, an effective plan for discussion must provide only the organizing framework to ensure meaningful and productive dialogue. This can best be accomplished by applying what you have learned in the preceding two chapters about lesson planning and writing instructional objectives. Before you begin doing this, you should take time to familiarize yourself with the kind of organizing framework an experienced teacher might use for planning a successful discussion:

1. Have a goal (objective) in mind to serve as a guideline for what students are expected to learn.
2. Develop a clear statement of the content to be covered; that is, concepts to be developed or issues to be explored.
3. Prepare the materials to be used; that is, readings, DVDs, or Web sites to be explored, list of discussion questions.
4. Formulate a set of procedures or guidelines for participation.
5. Create a means to evaluate discussion results through written homework, classroom activity, testing, or observation of student response to oral questions.

Preparing a Framework

Learning Activity 4.9

Before undertaking this task, be sure you have had the opportunity to see an experienced teacher carry on a discussion in a real classroom and to compare the data on your Observation Worksheet with the information gathered by other students in your class. Remember that planning a discussion is like planning a lesson. Assuming you have knowledge of the subject matter to be discussed and have led your students to understand how they must interact in a discussion, you now need to prepare a framework that will help to elicit meaningful and productive deliberation. First, return to Learning Activity 4.8 and study the organizing framework provided there. Then examine the model outline that follows. When you have finished this task, you should be ready to create your own planned discussions for a given teaching situation.

Planned Discussion—A Model

Goal	To develop a heightened awareness of the rhythm in oral and written language and increase students' facility in both oral and written communication.
Content	Investigate the use of rhythm as it is used in oral and written communication and discover how it helps convey and enhance meaning.
Materials	Limerick [select a limerick appropriate for the grade level you teach]
	Prose selection [select a piece of prose containing specific rhythmic devices—for example, alliteration—that are appropriate for the grade level you teach]
	Nursery rhyme [select a nursery rhyme with which you feel most of your students might be familiar]
	Prepare a set of questions to help guide students during the discussion.

Create a limerick completion sheet that requires students to fill in alternate lines of a limerick that you provide.

Procedures   **1.** One-third of the students in the class are given a copy of a limerick; a second third are given a copy of a selected prose example; and the last third are given a copy of a nursery rhyme. They are asked to take home their selections and practice reading them aloud.

2. On the day you plan to conduct your discussion, begin by distributing the discussion question sheet you prepared in advance. Then have one student from each group read that group's selection aloud. Commence the discussion using the prepared questions as a guide. At the appropriate time, have the second group read its selection and continue the discussion using the question sheet as a guide. Repeat this procedure with the next selection. Try to close by having students summarize the conclusions reached during the discussion.

Evaluation   Distribute to each student a copy of the prepared limerick completion sheet and instruct them to complete this activity according to the directions on the sheet. Finally, read orally and in a new discussion compare and contrast the results.

✴ Mastery Test

OBJECTIVE 5   **To create original planned discussions for use in a given learning situation**

Following these directions are five hypothetical teaching situations. Read each one carefully and select one for which you will develop your own planned discussion. You may refer to the preceding model for help in generating ideas for your plan.

Situation 1.   Your class has been working on different techniques used by fiction writers for developing character. Select some appropriate fictional material for your grade level and plan to conduct a discussion of some specific selections that clearly illustrate the technique you are studying.

Situation 2.   Part of your computer literacy curriculum includes material on some of the problems we face as we rely more and more on computers to accomplish everyday tasks such as shopping, banking, bill paying, and ordinary socializing. Develop a plan that will involve your students in a discussion of the problems, both real and potential, that will arise as computers increasingly become a part of our everyday lives.

Situation 3. Select a topic from current events that is appropriate for your grade level or subject area and develop a planned discussion dealing with the issue or issues pertinent to that topic.

Situation 4. Your students have been studying the Pilgrims and in particular the Thanksgiving feast. As part of their study you have introduced materials on feasts of thanksgiving held by people of other cultures. Plan a discussion in which your students can compare and contrast the thanksgiving celebration as it occurs across cultures.

Situation 5. Safety has been a major topic of study in your class, and you have visited the neighborhood fire department, where your students were able to view an excellent film on preventing fire in the home. Plan a discussion around the important ideas learned on the students' recent field trip.

> **OBJECTIVE 6**

To define a planned ending (closure), explain its purposes, and give examples of how it is used to involve students in learning

What Is a Planned Ending?

Learning Activity 4.10

Anyone familiar with weekly TV shows will find it very easy to understand the concept of planned endings (closure) when it is used to involve students in learning. TV scriptwriters use planned endings when, each week, they faithfully bring their shows to a satisfying close—that is, the audience has the comfortable feeling that all the loose ends have been tied up, the conflict has been resolved, and things are as they should be with the main characters. But the planned ending, when used by the successful teacher, is much more sophisticated than the technique used by the TV scriptwriter.

If a teacher wishes to create for students the same sense of satisfaction or completion achieved by the TV writer, then that teacher must learn how to use planned endings, or closure, skillfully. **Closure** is a term used to refer to those actions or statements by teachers that are designed to help students bring things together in their own minds, to make sense out of what has been going on during the course of the lesson. Research in the psychology of learning indicates that learning increases when teachers make a conscious effort to help students organize the information presented to them and perceive relationships based on that information.

Help students process lesson ▶

Another way to look at the planned ending is to compare it to the paper-and-pencil process of lesson planning. An effective lesson plan will usually indicate where the students will be going, how they will get there, and how they will know when they have arrived. In their discussion of the results of research on cognitive learning strategies, Rosenshine and Meister suggest that summarizing serves "a comprehension-fostering function" that leads to "deeper processing."[10] And making certain that students know *when they have arrived* is the result of the skillful teacher's use of the planned ending.

Constructivist learning theorists such as Gagnon and Collay emphasize as one of the six building blocks of their learning model the need for "reflections." Reflections come at the close of the lesson, permitting students to review what they have just experienced and connect it to what they already know in order to create new knowledge.[11]

■ INTASC Principle 8

Call attention to end ▶

The planned ending, then, has as its first purpose *to draw attention to the end of a lesson segment.* Unfortunately, many teachers have neglected the development of this important skill. Your own experience will tell you that many teachers will close the lesson something like this:

Many teachers neglect closings ▶

Teacher A: Okay. There's the bell! Get going—you'll be late for your next class!

Teacher B: Enough of this! Let's close our books and line up for recess.

Teacher C: The bell? All right, we'll stop here and pick up at the same point tomorrow.

Teacher D: Any questions? No? Good. Let's move on to the next chapter.

The students are certainly aware that something has concluded in each case, but that is about all. These rather unsophisticated attempts at closing a lesson completely ignore the fact that effective learning is a direct result of careful planning. One of the most important parts of your lesson plan is making provision for feedback and review, or what we are calling planned endings.

Planned endings alert students to the fact that they have reached an important point in the lesson and that the time has come to wrap it up. This activity must be planned just as carefully as its counterpart, the planned beginning, and its timing is critical. The teacher must be aware of the clock and must begin to initiate closure proceedings well before the lesson is due to end.

Consolidate learning ▶

Therefore, a second major purpose of the planned ending is *to help consolidate student learning.* Simply calling attention to the lesson's conclusion is not enough. A great deal of information may have been involved and a number of activities may have taken place, and it is the teacher's responsibility to tie it all together into a meaningful whole. The learner, just like the TV viewer, should not be left with a feeling of incompleteness and frustration. Like the TV detective who explains to the audience how the various pieces of the puzzle finally came together to form a complete picture, the skillful teacher needs to provide students with an opportunity to create new knowledge by consolidating what they already know with what they have just experienced.

Reinforce points ▶

The third purpose of the planned ending is *to reinforce the major points to be learned in the lesson.* Having signaled the end of the lesson and made an effort to organize what has occurred, the teacher should briefly refocus on the key ideas or processes presented in the lesson. The ultimate objective here is to help students retain the important information learned in the lesson and thus increase the probability that they will be able to recall and use the information at a later time. Gagné and Briggs, in discussing information storage and retrieval, have this to say: "When information or knowledge is to be recalled . . . *the network of relationships* in which the newly learned material has been embedded provides a number of different possibilities as cues for its retrieval."[12] The planned ending does this by calling attention to the end of the lesson, tying key points together into a coherent whole, and finally, ensuring their later use by anchoring them in the student's larger conceptual network.

◼ When to Use a Planned Ending

Learning Activity 4.11

Now that the planned ending has been defined and its purposes explained, you are ready to focus specifically on when the teacher uses it in the course of the lesson. You should be able to understand more easily when the planned ending is used if you completed the learning activity on planned beginnings. In that section, a lesson was compared to a game containing several subgames. In the classroom such subgames might involve a lesson introducing some new concept or skill or an activity with some combination of reading, writing, viewing, or discussing. Each of these activities can be viewed as a subgame within the context of the larger game—the entire class period in a particular subject or a full day of nondepartmentalized instruction.

When to use ▸
planned endings

The role of the teacher is to plan a lesson (subgame) so that it begins and ends in such a way as to involve the students in learning. This is the function of both planned beginnings and planned endings. For help in learning when to use a planned ending in a lesson, carefully study the following list of situations.

Examples of When to Use a Planned Ending

To end a long unit of work that the class might be studying, such as animals, the family, or a country

To consolidate learning of a new concept or principle

To close a discussion

To end a skill-building activity, such as locating words in the dictionary or practicing basic functions in arithmetic

To follow up a film, TV program, or video

To end a planned activity on the computer

To consolidate learning experiences on a field trip

To reinforce the presentation of a guest speaker

To follow up a homework assignment reviewed in class

To end a laboratory exercise

To organize thinking around a new concept or principle (such as "all languages are not written," or "different cultures reflect different values")

 Mastery Test

OBJECTIVE 6   **To define a planned ending (closure), explain its purposes, and give examples of how it is used to involve students in learning**

1. Define the term *planned ending (closure)* in your own words, and explain three specific purposes planned endings serve in involving students in learning.

2. Respond to the following statements by placing the letter *T* next to those that are true and the letter *F* next to those that are false.

_____ (a) A planned ending is a natural complement to a planned beginning.

_____ (b) A planned ending is less important than a planned beginning because students can tell by the clock when the class period ends.

_____ (c) A planned ending helps students know when they have achieved lesson objectives.

_____ (d) One of the purposes of a planned ending is to draw attention to the end of a presentation.

_____ (e) A planned ending provides an opportunity for students to review what they are supposed to have learned.

_____ (f) A planned ending is a natural phenomenon and does not require planning.

_____ (g) One of the purposes of the planned ending is to help organize student learning.

_____ (h) Timing is critical in using a planned ending.

_____ (i) A planned ending helps to get your lesson off on the right foot.

_____ (j) One of the purposes of a planned ending is to consolidate or reinforce the major points to be learned in a presentation.

3. Describe briefly three different situations in which you could use a planned ending to involve students in learning.

OBJECTIVE 7 **To create original planned endings (closure) for use in a given learning situation**

Learning Activity 4.12 Now that you know what a planned ending is, the general purposes for which it is used, and when it is used to involve students in learning, you are ready to begin practicing how to create your own planned endings. Before you actually begin doing this, you should take time to familiarize yourself with some examples of how experienced teachers might use planned endings in their lessons.

◼ Sample Planned Endings

A list of specific uses of the planned ending employed by experienced teachers follows. Study them carefully. Then read each of the sample lessons and the accompanying analysis. You should then be ready to create your own planned ending for a given teaching situation.

Situation 1. Attempts to draw students' attention to a closing point in the lesson

Situation 2. Reviews major points of teacher-centered presentation

Situation 3. Reviews sequence used in learning material during the presentation

Situation 4. Provides a summary of important student-oriented discussion

Situation 5. Relates lesson to original organizing principle or concept

Situation 6. Attempts to lead students to extend or develop new knowledge from previously learned concepts

Situation 7. Allows students to practice what they have learned

Sample Lesson 1

The lesson is in geography, and the teacher has planned to introduce two basic concepts: (1) humans as the active shapers of their environment and (2) environment as a limiting context within which humans must live. The teacher has reached the critical point in the lesson when it is time to call students' attention to the fact that the presentation of the first concept is ready for closure.

> *Planned Ending:* "Before moving to the next important idea, the restrictions that the environment places on humans, let's review the main points I've already covered on how humans can play a critical role in shaping the environment." The teacher then asks students to move into their small discussion groups and prepare an outline of what they believe to be the most important ideas to come out of this lesson to this point.

Analysis. This type of planned ending is appropriate to use when you wish to help students organize their thinking around a new concept before moving on to a new idea. Referring to the list of uses for planned endings, note:

1. The teacher draws attention to the end of the lesson with a verbal cue— "Before moving to the next important idea. . . ."
2. Students are asked to review by moving into small groups to identify the most important points made in the lesson.
3. The teacher helps organize student thinking around the first concept presented by having them prepare an outline of the most important ideas.

Sample Lesson 2

The lesson is in language arts, social studies, science, or some other subject, and the teacher is conducting a discussion around some specific issue that is important in the lesson plan for that particular day. The time has come to bring the discussion to a close.

> *Planned Ending:* The teacher calls on a specific student and says, "Jessica, would you please summarize what has been said thus far and point out what you felt were the major points covered?"

Analysis. This type of planned ending is appropriate to use when you wish to bring a classroom discussion to a close. Referring to the list of uses for planned endings, note:

1. The teacher draws attention to the fact that the time has come for a temporary end to discussion by requesting a student summary.
2. The teacher summarizes what students have been discussing.
3. The teacher helps students to organize or rearrange their own ideas by specifically asking students to list major points made in the discussion.

Sample Lesson 3

The lesson is on search techniques using the World Wide Web. The class has been given the homework assignment of recording the steps they used to gather specific information from the Web on vitamins. After reading student responses to the assignment and sharing some of them, the teacher believes that the students have successfully learned the first step in an effective computer search technique. She is ready to go on to new material and wishes to close.

> *Planned Ending:* "You did very well with your computer searches and turned up some interesting information. Now let's use these new techniques to help you find answers to the questions you asked about nutrition to which our textbook had no answers."

Analysis. This type of planned ending is appropriate to use when following up on a homework assignment being reviewed in class before moving on to the application of newly learned techniques. Referring to the list of uses for planned endings, note:

1. The teacher draws attention to the close of the assignment with a comment of approval: "You did very well with your computer searches and turned up some interesting information."

2. Students are encouraged to extend their knowledge of what they have already learned to a new problem through practice.

Sample Lesson 4

The lesson is in mathematics, and the teacher is presenting a general reading skills approach to problem solving: (1) preview, (2) identify details or relationships, (3) restate problem in one's own words, and (4) list computational steps to be taken. The time has come to see how well the students have understood the use of the new procedure.

> *Planned Ending:* "Before you try to use this new approach to problem solving by yourselves, help me list the steps on the chalkboard and try to apply them to the first problem in your textbooks on page 27. When you finish, I will ask some of you to share with the class your experience using this new technique."

Analysis. This type of planned ending is effective when you are ending a skill-building activity and wish to help students consolidate what they have learned. Referring to the list of uses for planned endings, note:

1. The teacher draws attention to the close of the presentation with a verbal signal, "Before you try to use this approach . . . let's list the steps . . . ."

2. Students are asked to review the sequence used in learning new reading skills during the lesson.

3. Students are encouraged to practice immediately what they have learned.

Learning Activity 4.13   Once again you have reached the point in this chapter when it is time to observe in real classrooms where students are actually involved in learning. When you are ready to observe, make a copy of the Observation Worksheet that follows to gather your data. You will be able to compare the results of your observations with others in a subsequent class activity.

Observation Worksheet

ENDING A LESSON

This observation activity gives you the opportunity to compare what you've learned about ending a lesson to what you actually see in classrooms.

Directions: Do not use actual names of schools, teachers, administrators, or students when using this worksheet.

Observer's Name: _____

Date: _____

Grade Level: _____

Subject: _____

Class Size: _____

Background Information: Give a brief general description of the school's social, economic, and ethnic makeup.

_____

_____

What to Record: While observing teachers in action, pay attention to those times in the instructional process when the teacher is ending a lesson. Use the following format to record what the teacher says and does to bring the lesson to a close.

1. How are students made aware that the lesson is ending? _____

_____

_____

2. In what ways are students helped to organize or consolidate what they have learned?

_____

_____

_____

3. In what ways is student learning reinforced? _____

_____

_____

Reflections on Your Observation:

1. In your judgment, was the lesson ending effective? Why or why not?

_____

_____

2. Think of at least one other way that the lesson could have been ended and describe that ending.

_____

_____

✳ Mastery Test

> **OBJECTIVE 7** **To create original planned endings (closure) for use in a given learning situation**

Following these directions are five hypothetical learning situations. Read each one carefully and plan a closure of your own that you feel would work effectively in that particular situation. You may refer to the list of uses for closure on page 101 for help in generating ideas for your own closures.

Situation 1. You have just completed a presentation on the steps one takes in preparing a green salad.

Situation 2. You have just completed a demonstration of how to save a file to a disk.

Situation 3. You have reached a point in a class discussion at which it would be appropriate to close.

Situation 4. You had begun a lesson on the use of theme in literature by comparing it to the threads running through a colorful tapestry. Now it is time for closure.

Situation 5. You have presented an important concept in science to the class and have asked the students how the idea might be used in other situations.

ADDITIONAL RESOURCES

📄 Readings

Bligh, Donald A. _What's the Point in Discussion._ Portland, Ore.: Intellect Book, 2000.

Campbell, L., B. Campbell, and D. Dickson. _Teaching and Learning Through Multiple Intelligences._ Boston, Mass.: Allyn & Bacon, 2004.

Gay, G. _Culturally Responsive Teaching: Theory, Research, & Practice._ New York: Teachers College Press, 2000.

Glasser, William. _The Quality School Teacher._ New York: Harper Collins Publishers, 1998.

Hudley, C., and A. E. Gottfried. _Academic Motivation and the Culture of School in Childhood and Adolescence._ New York: Oxford University Press, 2008.

Stipek, Deborah J. _Motivation to Learn: Integrating Theory and Practice._ Boston, Mass.: Allyn & Bacon, 2002.

Tomlinson, Carol A. _Fulfilling the Promise of the Differentiated Classroom: Strategies and Tools for Responsive Teaching._ Alexandria, Va.: ASCD, 2003.

 Websites

Center for Applied Special Technology: http://cast.org/ncac/index.cfm?i=2876
Helpful site for providing knowledge and materials on differentiated instruction.

Discovery School Channel: http://school.discovery.com
Teachers, parents, and students can find lesson plans, teaching tools, homework help, and online activities. The teaching tools section enables teachers to create their own classroom materials in all subjects and grade levels.

Sites for Teachers: http://www.sitesforteachers.com
Provides teachers with timely resources through pages of site links for activities, materials, and instructional aides for all grade levels.

Meeting the Needs of All Students: Success Through Differentiation & Technology: http://eduscapes.com/sessions/needs
This site focuses on differentiation and help for developing materials to meet the needs of all students.

Scholastic: http://www2.scholastic.com/browse/learn.jsp
Provides teachers with pre-K–12 online activities and interactive learning experiences.

Gateway to 21st Century Skills: http://teachers.net/
Allows teachers to connect on 150 different chat boards and includes links to lesson plans, teaching jobs, and an online gazette that accepts for publication of your own education-related articles.

For these links and additional resources, please visit the Premium Website at **www.cengage.com/login.**

NOTES

1. Thomas J. Shuell, "Teaching and Learning in a Classroom Context," in *Handbook of Educational Psychology,* eds. D. C. Berliner and R. C. Calfee (New York: Macmillan, 1996), p. 745.

2. Catherine Fosnot, *Constructivism: Theory, Perspectives, and Practice* (New York: Teachers College Press, 1996).

3. Set induction as a lesson presentation skill was developed for use in teacher training by J. C. Fortune and V. B. Rosenshine for the School of Education, Stanford University, Stanford, Calif.

4. "Criteria for Effective Teaching Performance," *Effective School Report* (February 1991): 6–7.

5. Thomas L. Good and Jere E. Brophy, *Looking in Classrooms,* 10th ed. (Boston, MA: Pearson/Allyn & Bacon, 2008), p. 309.

6. Maria Montessori, *The Montessori Method* (New York: Schocken Books, 1964), p. 170.

7. Arno A. Bellack et al., *The Language of the Classroom* (New York: Teachers College Press, 1966), p. 134.

8. George W. Gagnon, Jr., and Michelle Collay, "Constructivist Learning Design." Paper available at http://www.prainbow.com/cld/cldp.html.

9. C. T. Adger, M. Kalyanpur, D. B. Peterson, and T. L. Bridger, *Engaging Students: Thinking, Talking, Cooperating* (Thousand Oaks, Calif.: Corwin Press, 1995), p. 1.

10. Barak Rosenshine and Carla Meister, "Reciprocal Teaching: A Review of Nineteen Experimental Studies" (Paper presented at the Annual Meeting of the American Educational Research Association, Chicago, April 1991).

11. Gagnon and Collay, *op. cit.*

12. Robert M. Gagné, Leslie J. Briggs, and Walter W. Wager, *Principles of Instructional Design,* 4th ed. (Fort Worth: Harcourt Brace Jovanovich College, 1992), p. 123.

5 Questioning Skills

David Sadker • Myra Sadker • Karen R. Zittleman

Creatas/Jupiter Images

◻ INTASC Standards

● **Principle 2:** The teacher understands how children learn and develop, and can provide learning opportunities that support their intellectual, social, and personal development.

● **Principle 3:** The teacher understands how students differ in their approaches to learning and creates instructional opportunities that are adapted to diverse learners.

● **Principle 4:** The teacher understands and uses a variety of instructional strategies to encourage students' development of critical thinking, problem solving, and performance skills.

● **Principle 5:** The teacher uses an understanding of individual and group motivation and behavior to create a learning environment that encourages positive social interaction, active engagement in learning, and self-motivation.

● **Principle 6:** The teacher uses knowledge of effective verbal, nonverbal, and media communication techniques to foster active inquiry, collaboration, and supportive interaction in the classroom.

● **Principle 7:** The teacher plans instruction based upon knowledge of subject matter, students, the community, and curriculum goals.

● **Principle 8:** The teacher understands and uses formal and informal assessment strategies to evaluate and ensure the continuous intellectual, social, and physical development of the learner.

◻ OBJECTIVES

1. To explain the seven characteristics of effective classroom questions

2. To classify questions according to Bloom's *Taxonomy of Educational Objectives: Cognitive Domain*

3. To construct classroom questions on all six levels of Bloom's *Taxonomy of Educational Objectives: Cognitive Domain*

4. To write examples of questioning strategies that enhance the quality of student participation

5. To describe how the growing diversity and multicultural nature of America's students impact questioning strategies

The student teacher was composed. She quickly dispensed with the administrative details of classroom organization—attendance records and homework assignments. The classroom chatter about the Saturday-night dance and the upcoming football game subsided as the tenth-grade students settled into their seats. The students liked this teacher, for she had the knack of mixing businesslike attention to academic content with a genuine interest in her students. As the principal of Madison High walked by her room, he paused to watch the students settle into a discussion about *Hamlet.* Classroom operation appeared to be running smoothly, and he made a mental note to offer Ms. Ames a contract when her eight weeks of student teaching were over. Had he stayed a little longer to hear the discussion, and had he been somewhat sophisticated in the quality of verbal interaction, he would not have been so satisfied.

Ms. Ames: I would like to discuss your reading assignment with you. As the scene begins, two clowns are on stage. What are they doing? Brianna?

Brianna: They are digging a grave.

Ms. Ames: Right. Who is about to be buried? Jim?

Jim: Ophelia.

Ms. Ames: Yes. One of the gravediggers uncovers the skull of Yorick. What occupation did Yorick once have? Tia?

Tia: He was the king's jester.

Ms. Ames: Good. A scuffle occurs by Ophelia's graveside. Who is fighting? Bill?

Bill: Laertes and Hamlet.

Ms. Ames: That's right. In what act and scene does Ophelia's burial occur? Dontrell?

Dontrell: Act V, Scene 1.

Throughout the fifty-minute English class, Ms. Ames asked a series of factual questions, received a series of one- and two-word replies—and Shakespeare's play was transformed into a bad caricature of a television quiz show.

It is extremely important that teachers avoid ineffective questioning patterns such as the one just described because the questioning process has always been crucial to classroom instruction. The crucial role that questions play in the educational process has been stated by a number of educators.

The importance of classroom questions ▶

> To question well is to teach well. In the skillful use of the question more than anything else lies the fine art of teaching; for in it we have the guide to clear and vivid ideas, and the quick spur to imagination, the stimulus to thought, the incentive to action.[1]

> What's in a question, you ask? Everything. It is the way of evoking stimulating response or stultifying inquiry. It is, in essence, the very core of teaching.[2]

> The art of questioning is . . . the art of guiding learning.[3]

It was John Dewey who pointed out that thinking itself is questioning. Unfortunately, research indicates that most student teachers, as well as experienced teachers, do not use effective questioning techniques. Think back to your own days in elementary and secondary school. You probably read your text and your class notes, studied (or, more accurately, memorized), and then waited in class for the teacher to call on you with a quick question, usually requiring only a brief reply. It did not seem to matter much whether the subject was language arts or social studies or science; questions revealed whether or not you remembered the material. But questions need not be used only in this way, and the appropriate use of questions can create an effective and powerful learning environment. The legendary professor Mark Van Doren used questions to inspire generations of Columbia University students:

> Mark would come into the room, and, without any fuss, would start talking about whatever was to be talked about. Most of the time he asked questions. His questions were very good, and if you tried to answer them intelligently, you found yourself saying excellent things that you did not know you knew, and that you had not, in fact, known before. He had "educed" them from you by his questions. His classes were literally "education"—they brought things out of you, they made your mind produce its own explicit ideas. . . . What he did have was the gift of communicating to [students] something of his own vital interest in things, something of his manner of approach; but the results were sometimes quite unexpected—and by that I mean good in a way that he had not anticipated, casting lights that he had not himself foreseen.[4]

The need for better questions ▶ It is all too easy to describe Van Doren as a gifted teacher and to dismiss his technique of questioning as an art to which most teachers can never aspire. It is our strong belief that the teacher's effective use of questions is far too important to dismiss in this way. Unfortunately, research concerning the use of questions in the classroom suggests that most teachers do *not* use effective questioning techniques. If one were to review the research on questioning, the results would reveal both the importance of questioning in school and the need for teachers to improve their questioning technique.

◼ OBJECTIVE 1   **To explain the seven characteristics of effective classroom questions**

◼ What Do We Know About Questioning?

Learning Activity 5.1

◻ INTASC Principles 2, 4, 5, 6, 7, 8

If you are going to teach, you are not only going to ask questions, you are going to ask quite a lot of questions. Researchers have determined that during a career in the classroom, a typical teacher will ask about *one and a half million* questions. (They are still working on how many of those questions will be answered correctly.) Other educators estimate that teachers average between *30 and 120 questions an hour!* And this extraordinary reliance on questioning has not changed over time. Back in 1912, in one of the first major classroom studies, it was determined that about 80 percent of classroom discussions consisted of asking, answering, or reacting to questions. In fact, only lecturing is a more common teacher strategy. And once teachers develop their questioning pattern, this is likely to become a habit—with all its strengths and faults—for their entire career.[5]

Although teachers ask a large number of questions, they generally show little tolerance in waiting for student replies. Typically, only *one second* passes between the end of a question and the next verbal interaction! After the answer is given, only nine-tenths of a second passes before the teacher reacts to the answer. The tremendous number of questions asked and the brief amount of time provided before an answer is expected reinforce the finding that most questions do not require any substantive thought. Classroom questions simply call for the rapid recall of information.[6]

But asking a lot of questions is not the same as asking good questions. The great majority of questions that teachers ask are lower-order, memory questions. How many are lower order? While estimates vary, studies suggest that between 70 and 95 percent of all teacher questions are the kind of questions that do not require deep thinking. One of the problems is that without more higher-order, thought-provoking questions, learning becomes little more than memorization. Although the research on higher-order classroom questions is at times contradictory, there is a growing consensus that higher-order questions increase the level of student thinking and lead to an increase in student achievement.[7]

Studies also reveal that the quality and quantity of student answers increase when teachers provide students with time to think. If teachers can increase the one second of silence that usually follows a question to three seconds or more, student answers will reflect more thought and more students will actively participate in the classroom.[8]

Although learning is designed to help students receive answers for their questions, become independent citizens, and understand their world, little provision is made in schools for student questions.[9]

The significant number of research findings related to classroom questions indicates that questions play a crucial role in the classroom and that teachers need to improve their questioning strategies.[10] The activities in this chapter are designed to do just that—to increase your mastery of questioning skills.

The Seven Habits of Highly Effective Questioners

In his best-selling book *Seven Habits of Highly Effective People*,[11] Stephen Covey offers practical suggestions for personal improvement. Borrowing from the Covey approach, this chapter will translate the research findings in the previous section into seven strategies—habits if you prefer—that will improve your use of classroom questions:

1. Asking fewer questions
2. Differentiating questions
3. Questioning for depth
4. Questioning for breadth
5. Using wait time
6. Selecting students
7. Giving useful feedback

(Unlike Covey, we make no claim that this will enhance your personal life. Then again, it might.)

1. Asking Fewer Questions

It is possible to have too much of a good thing. Most teachers today ask too many questions. All of the following reasons have been given to explain the role of questions in the classroom. Any wonder why the classroom is heavy with questions?

Why teachers question ▷

- By asking questions, teachers reinforce their image as the authority figure, the person in charge, the "expert" who knows the right answers.
- Since lecturing can be seen as dogmatic, old-fashioned, and teacher-centered, perhaps questions are viewed as the opposite. If a lecturing teacher is autocratic, then it follows, as the night the day, that questioning teachers are democratic.
- The more questions teachers ask, the harder students work, and the more students learn.
- Questions help teachers stay on schedule so all critical topics are "covered."
- Questions keep the students "on their toes" and on-task, reducing or eliminating discipline problems.
- The students' role in class, their "job," is to study a subject and to answer questions. The teachers' role, their "job," is to ask questions.
- Questioning is the *only* tool some teachers have for getting students involved.
- When teachers were themselves young, their teachers might have asked lots of questions, and so they are simply modeling the teaching style they experienced as children.

2. Differentiating Questions

To reduce this torrent of questions, teachers need to **differentiate questions**. Although students in the same class may be the same chronological age, they differ in readiness, learning styles, interests, and personal backgrounds. As a teacher formulates questions, it is useful to consider individual student differences and craft quality questions based on each student's need. Teachers might ask themselves: How does this question build on this student's knowledge? Am I asking a question that is far too difficult—or far too simple—for this student's capabilities? Am I using an effective questioning technique for this particular student's learning style? What interests does this student have, and how can my questions build on those interests? Can my questions tie into this student's background and experiences?

Gauging your students ▷

Teachers who know both their students and their content area can effectively differentiate their questions. For example, if you are an English teacher and you know a student is interested in women's rights, you might fashion a question that builds on this interest: "Would the plot in *Lord of the Flies* be different if girls rather than boys were stranded on the island?" Questions based on a student's interest can transform subjects from academic tasks to personal, exciting quests. Some teachers can take this one step further, formulating questions that connect not only with student interests but also with their personal experiences. These are called **authentic questions**.[12] Authentic questions respond to the unspoken student query: "What's this have to do with me? How does this issue relate to my life and experiences?" Authentic questions that would tie students into *Lord of the Flies* might include: "What island experiences have you had?" "Have you ever felt lost and frightened like the kids on the island?"

"How do your peer conflicts compare with those in *Lord of the Flies*?" "How might your presence on the island affect this story?"

Challenging questions cause students to stretch, to risk, to grow—and sometimes to fail. Obviously, both teachers and classmates need to be part of a supportive community, one that respects the individual and encourages risk taking and experimentation. And the challenging questions that a teacher formulates must be within the student's grasp and not so challenging as to frustrate the student (and the teacher).[13]

3. Questioning for Depth

"When did Columbus come to America?" is the kind of teacher question familiar to most of us. Nothing particularly wrong with it, as far as it goes—but it doesn't go particularly far. It requires simple recall. However, questions should go beyond simple recall and *deepen a student's understanding* of a topic. A related but more demanding question could be, "How might the United States be different if Columbus had arrived a century earlier—or a century later?" Here are some additional examples of more powerful higher-order questions, questions that give meaning and substance to our learning:

Create a fictional conversation that might have occurred if Abraham Lincoln met Malcolm X.

Analyze Margaret Sanger's impact on the women's rights movement.

Contrast Picasso with Mondrian.

While the questions described above promote a deeper understanding of content, delving or **probing questions** focus less on the subject and more on individual students. In order really to understand how much a student knows or doesn't know, we may need to go beyond the student's first response and dig deeper. We call these follow-up questions *delving* and *probing*. Examples of probing or delving questions include:

What are your reasons for selecting that answer?

What characteristics of this candidate did you find most appealing?

Could you give us an example of that?

Zone of proximal development ▸

Probing puts the teacher on the frontier of a student's knowledge. On one side of the frontier is what a student knows, manifested by a correct answer. On the other side is what the student does not know or does not really understand, manifested by the wrong answer or no answer at all. In educational literature, this gap between what a student *does* know and what a student is *capable* of learning, but does not yet know, is called the **zone of proximal development**.[14] Lev Vygotsky defines this zone of proximal development as the difference between the intellectual insights a child has and the higher or deeper levels that the child could reach with the help of another. You can be that "other." Well thought-out questions, especially probing and delving questions, can move the child through the zone and to a higher level of thinking. Gauging the right level of question is the trick. If the questions are too easy and students answer them quickly and with little thought, then the child is learning little if anything. The teacher must then move to make the questions more challenging. On the other hand, if the teacher's questions are met with stony silence and a confused look, they are too difficult and must be made simpler or the student will be frustrated. So the challenge is for the teacher to learn where students are to craft questions that move them forward. Vygotsky reminds us that the teacher does not carry the burden alone: social interaction also helps students move through the zone to greater understanding. As students listen to and participate in classroom discussions, ideas are explored and insights internalized. Social interaction can unlock learning, a powerful reminder to teachers that students learn a great deal from each other.

Cues ▶ When students are unable to answer a question, teachers can also use questions to help them, to cue them to the right answer. In a sense, *cuing* is the opposite of probing and delving. In probing, for example, questions are used to explore the thinking behind the student's original answer. In cuing, we are using questions to help a student get to the right answer. By offering more information, or hints, cuing questions put the student on the road to success. Here is an example:

> We are looking for the name Europeans gave to New York City before the British took control. If you remember which European nation settled New York before the English, that will help you to recall that name.

Scaffolding ▶ Sometimes a simple cue is not enough, and a more intricate strategy is called for, a strategy educators call **scaffolding**. *Scaffolding* conjures up the image of a building under construction. A new building is barely visible at the beginning of the construction cycle, hidden behind supporting beams and platforms, a temporary support called the scaffold. But the scaffold is critical, because it gives workers the ability to slowly construct the new building from the bottom up, assisting but not obstructing others. They surround the new structure, adding to it slowly to ensure that it is solid. As the edifice takes shape, the scaffolding is reduced, and as the building nears completion, the scaffolding is finally removed. So much for buildings, but what about students?

Educators have borrowed this scaffolding imagery to describe the teacher's role in "building" a student's competencies. Educational scaffolding is substantial at the beginning of the "construction," as the teacher carefully diagnoses a student's competencies and determines where new knowledge will need to be built. Once the scaffold is planned, the teacher begins to build the student's knowledge through carefully crafted questions, well-phrased explanations, and thoughtfully designed student activities. Most of the skills described in this chapter will help teachers scaffold. As the student internalizes information, the teacher's scaffolding can be reduced. Once the student becomes fully competent, the scaffolding is removed.[15]

4. Questioning for Breadth

Convergent = closed ▶ All questions and answers fall into one of two categories: no, we are not talking about "right and wrong" but rather *convergent* and *divergent*.
Divergent = open ▶ A convergent question, also called a *closed* question, generates a single answer that is clearly right or wrong—for instance, "Who wrote this poem?" Many convergent questions are lower order and require little more than memory, But not all. A convergent question could also require higher-order thinking. For example, a complex math or science equation may have one single answer, but getting to that convergent answer could be quite challenging.

As you might have suspected by now, unlike convergent questions, divergent questions always have more than one correct answer and are usually higher order. Divergent questions are also called *open* questions— for instance, "What does this poem mean to you?" or "How would your life be different without the invention of the computer?" Teachers use divergent questions when they want to generate different ideas, infuse breadth into the classroom, and provide students with a creative springboard.

Howard Gardner's work on **multiple intelligences** has dramatically increased our ability to question for breadth.[16] Gardner believes that a serious problem with today's schools is their limited focus on only two types of intelligence, verbal-linguistic and mathematical-logical:

Draw on different intelligences ▶

1. *Verbal-linguistic:* speaking, poetic, and journalistic abilities; sensitivity to the meanings and the rhythm of words and to the function of language

2. *Mathematical-logical:* scientific and mathematical abilities, skills related to mathematical manipulations, and discerning and solving logical challenges

According to Gardner and others, much of school life, including standardized tests, emphasizes these two types of intelligence almost exclusively while ignoring others. What are the other areas of intelligence? Here are some suggested by Gardner:

3. *Bodily-kinesthetic:* physical skills related to controlling one's body movements and to handling objects skillfully, such as athletic and dancing abilities

4. *Musical:* vocal, compositional, and instrumental abilities and the ability to produce and appreciate rhythm, pitch, and timbre; appreciation of music

5. *Spatial:* abilities to perceive the physical world accurately, such as those of a sculptor, navigator, or architect

6. *Interpersonal:* the ability to analyze and respond to the moods, temperaments, desires, and needs of others, such as that shown by a salesperson, teacher, or psychologist

7. *Intrapersonal:* knowledge of one's own needs, strengths, and weaknesses and the ability to use this information to guide behavior; useful within and beyond most careers

8. *Naturalist:* ability to live wisely and respect the world's resources; associated with careers in conservation and related fields

Gardner does not view these as a definitive inventory of intelligences, for he believes that many more intelligences will be recognized in the years ahead. But his vision is instructive and useful today because his work suggests that *all* these areas of intelligence should be represented in classroom questions. Can you think of other areas of intelligence that Gardner has not yet identified?

With some planning and practice, we can move beyond questions that are limited to the traditional linguistic or logical-mathematical areas to questions such as:

Can you express what you are feeling through movement?

Can you create a physical model of your plan?

What are your personal strengths in this area?

How can you influence your classmates on that issue?

Watch the video case *Multiple Intelligences: Elementary School Instruction* to see how multiple intelligences can be integrated throughout a lesson to actively engage all learners—and make learning fun.

▼ TeachSource Video Cases   **Multiple Intelligences: Elementary School Instruction**

Watch the video clip, study the artifacts in the case, and reflect upon the following questions:

1. Describe specific examples of how this teacher used multiple intelligences to make the lesson more interesting.
2. Pick a topic for the grade level you plan to teach and create questions to ask your students using at least four multiple intelligences.
3. The teacher in the video believes that effective instruction, including good questioning, should take into account multiple intelligences and different ways of knowing. Why is this a good idea?

5. Using Wait Time

Wait times 1 and 2 ▷ In the typical classroom, the teacher waits less than a second after asking a question before calling on a student to respond. For those students who need more than a fraction of a second to formulate their answer, class participation becomes a real challenge. Not only do fewer students participate, but the quality of their responses is lowered. Less than a second is not a great deal of time to consider what to say, much less how to say it. Teachers are also victims of this brief **wait time**. With little time to think about which student to call on, teachers tend to call on the "fastest hand in the class."

There is a second wait time, less well-known but just as important, that occurs directly after a student response. This is sometimes referred to as wait time 2, and, like wait time 1, it is also less than a second in length. The brevity of wait time 2 can typically be seen in the frequent teacher interruptions of student answers, often with little more than a quick "uh-huh," "okay," or "I see." Students have little time to complete or extend their answers or their thoughts. As a result of their quick retorts and the pressure to keep moving, teachers also short-circuit themselves. After hearing the student's answer, teachers have little time to consider the student's response or to formulate their own reaction. As a result, teachers frequently react to student answers with a bland, imprecise, and ineffective comment. While less has been written about this incredibly brief second wait time, it also short-circuits effective teaching and learning.

6. Selecting Students

As you probably recall from your own elementary or secondary school days, it is not unusual for a few students to monopolize classroom interaction while the rest of the class looks on. The fast pace of classroom exchanges leads many teachers to call on the first hand that is raised. Even a fraction of a second is too long for some students to wait. Very active and animated students can sometimes eliminate even the teacher from the decision-making role by simply shouting out the answer.

Giving voice to all students ▷ But even when the teacher maintains control and selects which students to call on, there is a tendency to call on students who want to be called on. As Ted Sizer wrote in *Horace's Compromise*, this is a very comfortable situation for all concerned. Students who want to talk get to talk. Students who want to stay silent, stay silent. The teacher's lesson moves along at a good pace, and the main points are all covered. Everybody is having their needs met; everybody is happy. So what's the problem? There are several problems, including the fact that the purpose of school is not to eliminate all anxieties and make everyone comfortable (although that *sounds* awfully good!). Schools are for education, for stretching, for learning new and sometimes uncomfortable skills. Talented teachers know that if they select only students who quickly volunteer, reticent students will be relegated to the sidelines, unable or unwilling to participate, while talkative students will be reinforced for talking even more. You have probably experienced a few students dominating classroom discussion while other students are left out. Students who need a little more time to think—because they are by nature thoughtful, or because English is a new language, or because their cultural background encourages a slower response, or because they are shy—become spectators to rapid classroom exchanges. Females often lose out, as do children of color; English language learners may be left behind; and shy boys are abandoned behind a wall of silence. When teachers allow their classroom dialogue to be dominated by a few animated students, they are forgetting one of their key educational responsibilities: the responsibility to include *all* their students in active learning.

Inappropriate questions ▶

Tricks and Traps: Ways *Not* to Use Questions

Unfortunately, not all questions are wondrous, and teachers have been known to use questions inappropriately. Here are some examples of ineffective and inappropriate uses of questions. We will explain enough about these misapplications to tell you what to avoid. But we will stop there. (After all, we don't want to invest too much time in teaching you "malquestioning" strategies.)

- *To control misbehavior:* Some teachers use questions to prevent or stop misbehavior, a sort of "I see you; here's a question; can't answer it?—well, stop misbehaving and *listen!*" Rather than reducing student distractions, this "question as punishment" approach actually serves to reward misbehaving students with extra instructional attention. The problem is compounded because students who are acting appropriately are being ignored. Questions should be used to teach everyone in the class—not used to manage a few. (We might add that teachers who use effective questioning strategies that keep all students on-task *reduce* the likelihood that management problems will emerge.)
- *To "help" special needs students:* The opportunity to individualize questions exists every time a teacher formulates a question, but individualizing a question takes on even greater importance with special needs students. Questions that are too difficult can frustrate, creating embarrassing situations. If they are too easy, they are seen as patronizing. A simple rule is to shape questions that are responsive to the unique abilities and talents of each student, including special needs students. In short, know your students, and challenge them.
- *To "put down" a student:* The converse of the above occurs when teachers use questions as a tool of humiliation, a way to put down a difficult student with a really tough question, a zinger few could answer.

Or if the student somehow manages to answer the question, the teacher might respond with a sarcastic comment. Questions should not be used as weapons.

- *To manipulate answers:* Teachers have been known to take great liberties in restating student answers in order to move the lesson along a predetermined path. As a result, it is the teacher's idea rather than the student's that is heard. Such dramatic paraphrasing devalues students and should not be used as a tool for manipulating class discussions.
- *To offer the infamous "yes, but" teacher response:* Some teachers, caught between the desire to accept a student's answer and the urge to correct or disagree with that answer, fall into the trap of revealing their conflict with a "yes, but" reaction. Such teacher comments tend to discredit student contributions.
- *To promote student "involvement":* An easy way to get a number of students responding to a topic in class is to shower the students with questions. While *Jeopardy!* may be a popular show on television, "Classroom Jeopardy" is often overused. The teacher who regularly asks a torrent of nonstop questions in an attempt to involve a large number of students is far from creating an ideal learning environment.

7. Giving Useful Feedback

While educators label questions as either *higher* or *lower order*, they do not apply such labels to the reactions teachers give to student answers. If we were to label these reactions, most teacher reactions would be rated as lower order. Teacher reactions are generally imprecise and offered without the careful thought that might help student learning. Imprecise teacher feedback means that students rarely are offered a powerful reward when they have given a superb answer. When they do poorly, they are often not told what they did wrong or how best to improve their performance. Teacher feedback generally lacks specificity, with "fine" and "okay" capturing the tone of the typical feedback.

Lack of feedback opportunity ▸

Unfortunately, figuring out the reasons for the poor quality of these reactions is not surprising: simply look at what has already been described about questions. Since most questions involve only simple memory, terrific teacher reactions are hardly merited. When hundreds of questions flood the airwaves, teachers have a difficult time focusing on their reactions—or focusing at all. The incredibly short wait time afforded by teachers short-circuits their ability to thoughtfully consider what students have said, much less what their reactions should be. All these factors contribute to an environment that neither requires nor encourages quality teacher reactions. The result is a less-than-enriching educational experience for students.

Practicing these seven habits will be helpful in creating classrooms marked by meaningful learning and by the active participation of all students. The following Your Turn gives you the opportunity to review these seven characteristics of effective questioning.

> **YOUR TURN** **Characteristics of Effective Questions**

For items 1–5, mark *T* for true and *F* for false statements.

_____ 1. Typically, teachers wait three to five seconds after asking a question before calling on a student.

_____ 2. Most classroom questions can be categorized as lower order, requiring little thought to answer.

_____ 3. It is not unusual for teachers to ask several questions a minute and hundreds of questions every day.

_____ 4. Teachers wait less than a second after a student answers a question before they offer their feedback.

_____ 5. Teacher feedback to student answers could accurately be described as precise, honest, and helpful.

6. Briefly describe at least three purposes for asking questions in class, as well as one inappropriate reason for using a questioning strategy in the classroom.

✹ Mastery Test

OBJECTIVE 1 **To explain the seven characteristics of effective classroom questions**

The principal of your school has just developed a new approach to staff development. She has decided that new teachers like yourself should be responsible for some aspects of professional development. She sees it as a way to keep her faculty up-to-date with current thinking at the university, as well as offering leadership opportunities to junior faculty members. You really liked the idea—until she asked you to participate. You have been asked to prepare a ten-minute presentation on the effective uses of classroom questions. Luckily, you have just read the first part of this chapter, so you feel extremely qualified. Outline the main points of your talk. Be sure to include all seven habits of effective questioners, and, whenever possible, offer an example or illustration to help explain your point.

OBJECTIVE 2 **To classify questions according to Bloom's *Taxonomy of Educational Objectives: Cognitive Domain***

☐ The Six Levels of the *Taxonomy*

Learning Activity 5.2

☐ **INTASC Principles** 2, 4, 5, 6, 7, 8

There are many terms and classifications for describing the different kinds of questions. Most of these classification systems are useful because they provide a conceptual framework, a way of looking at questions. We have selected only one system, however, to simplify the process and eliminate repetitive terms. **Bloom's *Taxonomy***[17] is probably the best-known system for classifying educational objectives as well as classroom questions. There are six levels of Bloom's *Taxonomy*, and questions at each level require the person responding to use a different kind of thought process. Teachers should be able to formulate questions on each of these six levels to encourage their students to engage in a variety of cognitive processes. Before teachers are able to formulate questions on each of these levels, they must first understand the definitions of the six categories and be able to recognize questions written on each. The six levels are:

1. Knowledge
2. Comprehension
3. Application
4. Analysis
5. Synthesis or Creation
6. Evaluation

(Note: Some educators have recently revised Bloom's original taxonomy, putting "creation" as the highest level. They believe that creating is a more demanding intellectual activity than evaluating.[18] What do you think?)

The following definitions, examples, and exercises are designed to help you recognize and classify questions on the six cognitive levels of Bloom's *Taxonomy*. (By the way, *taxonomy* is another word for *classification*.)

Level 1. Knowledge

The first level of the *Taxonomy*, knowledge, requires the student to recognize or recall information. The student is not asked to manipulate information, but merely to remember it just as it was learned. To answer a question on the knowledge level, the student must simply remember facts, observations, and definitions that have been learned previously.

Examples of Knowledge Questions

What is the capital of Maine?

What color did the solution become when we added the second chemical?

Who is the secretary of state?

Who wrote *Hamlet?*

Useful memory questions ▸ It has become fashionable to scoff at questions that ask the student to rely only on memory. For example, a common complaint about some college exams is that they ask students to "spit back" the information they have memorized from their text and class notes. Memorization of material, however, is important for several reasons. The knowledge, or memory, category is critical to all other levels of thinking. We cannot ask students to think at higher levels if they lack fundamental information. Some memorization of information is also required to perform a variety of tasks in our society, ranging from being an effective citizen to being a good parent. Our society expects that many things be memorized. Further, use of **knowledge questions** promotes classroom participation and high success experiences for students. Students from lower socioeconomic backgrounds achieve more in classrooms characterized by a high frequency of knowledge questions. Studies show that effective teachers provide both low-ability and high-ability students with high-success opportunities and that, in these successful classrooms, students are responding correctly at least 70 to 80 percent of

Overused memory questions ▶

the time.[19] The use of knowledge questions plays a key role in establishing this high success rate.

Although important, the knowledge category does have severe drawbacks, the main one being that teachers tend to overuse it. Most questions that teachers ask both in class discussions and on tests would be classified in the knowledge category. Another drawback to questions on this level is that much of what is memorized is rapidly forgotten. A third drawback to memory questions is that they assess only a superficial and shallow understanding of an area. Parroting someone else's thoughts does not, in itself, demonstrate any real understanding. Some words frequently found in knowledge questions are listed in the following box.

Words Often Found in Knowledge Questions

define	who	list	name
recall	what	identify	reproduce
recognize	where	recite	
remember	when	review	

> **YOUR TURN** **Knowledge**

The following questions will test your understanding of knowledge-level questions and your ability to classify questions at the knowledge level of Bloom's *Taxonomy* correctly. Your answers will also provide you with a useful study guide when preparing for the Mastery Test.

In items 1–5, mark a *T* for true and an *F* for false statements.

_____ 1. The first level of Bloom's *Taxonomy* requires higher-order thinking.

_____ 2. Most classroom and test questions that teachers ask are memory questions.

_____ 3. A drawback to knowledge, or memory, questions is that they are unimportant.

_____ 4. Knowledge, or memory, questions are important because they are necessary steps on the way to more complex, higher-order questions.

_____ 5. All the questions asked so far in this activity (items 1–4) are on the first level of the *Taxonomy*—knowledge and memory.

Mark a *K* in the space in front of those questions that are at the knowledge level and a "−" for those that are not.

_____ 6. Who discovered a cure for yellow fever?

_____ 7. Can you analyze the causes of the Gulf War?

_____ 8. Where does the United States get most of its tin from?

_____ 9. What does this music mean to you?

_____ 10. Define *antediluvian.* (The class has previously been given the definition of this word.)

_____ 11. Can you think of a title for this painting?

_____ 12. What do you think might happen to teachers if a recession were to continue over several years?

Check your answers with the answers and comments included in the Answer Key. If you answered all correctly—terrific! One wrong is pretty good also. Two wrong suggests that you should check each answer and perhaps reread the section. If you got three or more wrong, reread the section, underlining key points as you read, before you proceed to the next level.

Level 2. Comprehension

Questions on the second level, comprehension, require the student to demonstrate sufficient understanding to organize and arrange material mentally. The student must select those facts that are pertinent to answering the question. To answer a comprehension-level question, the student must go beyond recall of information. The student must demonstrate a personal grasp of the material by being able to rephrase it, give a description in his or her own words, and use it in making comparisons.

Go beyond recall ▶

Use students' own words ▶

For example, suppose a teacher asks, "What is the famous quote of Hamlet's that we memorized yesterday, the quotation in which he puzzles over the meaning and worth of existence?" By asking students to recall information, in this case a quotation, the teacher is asking a question on the knowledge level. If the teacher had asked instead, "What do you think Hamlet means when he asks, 'To be or not to be: that is the question'?" the teacher's question would have been on the comprehension level. With the second question, the student is required to rephrase information in his or her own words.

Frequently, **comprehension questions** ask students to interpret and translate material that is presented in charts, graphs, tables, and cartoons. For example, the following are comprehension questions.

Examples of Comprehension Questions

What is the main idea that this chart presents?

Describe in your own words what Herblock is saying in this cartoon.

This use of the comprehension question requires the student to translate ideas from one medium to another.

It is important to remember that *the information necessary to answer comprehension questions should have been provided to the student.* For example, if a student has previously read or listened to material that discusses the causes of the Revolutionary War and then is asked to explain these causes in his or her own words, the student is being asked a comprehension question. If the student has *not* been given material explaining the causes of the Revolutionary War and is asked to explain why the war started, he or she is *not* being asked a comprehension question, but, rather, a question on a different level of the *Taxonomy*.

Words Often Found in Comprehension Questions	
describe	rephrase
compare	put in your own words
contrast	explain the main idea

❯ YOUR TURN   Comprehension

In items 1–4, mark a *T* for true and an *F* for false statements.

_____ 1. A comprehension question may require the student to use new information not previously provided.

_____ 2. Comprehension questions may require students to rephrase information.

_____ 3. It is possible to remember a definition without being able to put the definition in your own words.

_____ 4. A comprehension question asks students to recall information exactly as they have learned it.

Some of the following questions are at the knowledge level and others are at the comprehension level. Write a *C* next to those questions on the comprehension level and a *K* next to those questions on the knowledge level.

_____ 5. When did the Berlin Wall come down?

_____ 6. Use a Venn diagram to compare whales and sharks.

_____ 7. What is the meaning of this cartoon?

_____ 8. Who is the author of *The Color Purple*?

_____ 9. Describe what we saw on our visit to the planetarium.

_____ 10. Explain in your own words what the speaker suggests are the main reasons for the "Internet explosion."

Check your answers with those in the Answer Key. If you missed two or more, you should reread the description of comprehension questions and take notes. As you perhaps have already discovered, taking notes in your own words will ensure that you are comprehending the comprehension level.

Level 3. Application

It is not enough for students to be able to memorize information, or even to rephrase and interpret what they have memorized. Students must also be able to apply information. A question that asks a student to apply previously learned information to reach an answer to a problem is at the application level of the *Taxonomy*.

Application questions require students to apply a rule or process to a problem and thereby to determine the single right answer to that problem. In mathematics, application questions are quite common. For example,

$$\text{If } x = 2 \text{ and } y = 5$$
$$\text{then } x^2 + 2y = ?$$

But application questions are important in other subjects as well. For example, in social studies, a teacher can provide the definitions of *latitude* and *longitude*, and ask the student to repeat these definitions (knowledge). The teacher can then ask the student to compare the definitions of *latitude* and *longitude* (comprehension). At the application level, the teacher would ask the student to locate a point on a map by applying the definitions of *latitude* and *longitude*.

To ask a question at the application level in language arts, the following procedure might be used. After providing students with the definition of a haiku (a type of poem), a teacher would hand out a sheet with several different types of poems, then ask the students to select the poem that is a haiku—that is, the one that fits the definition of a haiku poem. To do this, the students must apply the definition to the various poems and select the poem that fits the definition.

Demonstrating what students know ▶

In all the examples given, the student must apply knowledge to determine the single correct answer. Here are some other examples of questions at the application level.

Examples of Application Questions

In each of the following cases, which of Newton's laws is being demonstrated?

According to our definition of *socialism*, which of the following nations would be considered socialist today?

Write an example of the sexual harassment policy we have just discussed.

If Brian works three hours to wash the car and it takes Alicia only two, how many hours would it take them to wash the car together?

What is the rule that is appropriate in Case Study 2?

Words Often Found in Application Questions

apply	write an example	show	demonstrate
classify	solve	translate	diagram/map
use	how many	make	record/chart
choose	which	illustrate	
employ	what is	teach	

❯ YOUR TURN   Application

Indicate the level of the *Taxonomy* that each of the following questions represents. Use a *K* for those at the knowledge level, *C* for those at the comprehension level, and *Ap* for those at the application level.

_____ 1. What does *freedom of speech* mean to you?

_____ 2. Using the Internet, locate this university's Web page.

_____ 3. Who is the author of *The Joy Luck Club*?

_____ 4. If these figures are correct, will the company make a profit or suffer a loss?

_____ 5. Categorize the plants according to the classification system we reviewed.

_____ 6. Having read about runners and swimmers, clarify the similarities shared by these athletes.

Check your answers with those provided in the Answer Key. If you missed two or more, reread this section and answer the additional questions. If you would like extra practice, the additional questions will provide you with that opportunity. When you feel ready, go on to the next level of the *Taxonomy*. At this point, you're halfway through with this learning activity.

Additional Questions

_____ 7. Solve this problem by using the procedure we enumerated in our discussion of conflict resolution.

_____ 8. Rephrase the definition of *CPR*.

_____ 9. Restate the three safety steps we have learned that should be followed on a mountain hike.

_____ 10. According to our definition of a mammal, which of the five animals in the photo would be considered a mammal?

Check your answers with those provided in the Answer Key. If you still need help, you may want to check with your instructor, with some other students who are getting the exercises correct, or the Additional Resources at the end of the chapter. If you understand the application level, move on to the analysis level.

Level 4. Analysis

Analysis questions are a higher order of questions that require students to think critically and in depth. Analysis questions ask students to identify reasons, uncover evidence, and reach conclusions.

Following are examples of three kinds of analysis questions.

1. To identify the motives, reasons, and/or causes for a specific occurrence:

What factors influenced the writings of Anne Frank?

Why did the congresswoman decide not to run for the presidency?

How do your personal finances respond to economic upswings and downturns?

In all these questions, students are asked to discover the causes or reasons for certain events through analysis.

2. To consider and analyze available information to reach a conclusion, inference, or generalization based on this information:

After reading this story, how would you characterize the author's background, attitude, and point of view?

Look at this new invention. What do you think the purpose of this invention is?

After studying about major developments in South Africa and China, what can you now conclude about the various causes of revolutionary change?

Searching for the reason why ▶ This type of analysis question calls on the learner to reach a conclusion, inference, or generalization based on evidence.

3. To analyze a conclusion, inference, or generalization to find evidence to support or refute it:

Which of the speaker's points support affirmative action?

How did the role-play promote cultural understanding?

What evidence can you cite to validate that smoking cigarettes is more harmful than drinking alcohol?

These questions require students to analyze information to support a particular conclusion, inference, or generalization.

If you tried to answer any of these questions, you probably realized that several answers are possible. Because it takes time to think and analyze, these questions cannot be answered quickly or without careful thought. The fact that several answers are possible and that sufficient time is needed to answer them is an indication that analysis questions are higher-order ones. A student cannot answer an analysis question by repeating information or by reorganizing material to put it into his or her own words or by applying a rule. Analysis questions not only help students learn what happened but also help them search for the reasons behind what happened.

Words Frequently Found in Analysis Questions

identify motives or causes	why	categorize/dissect
draw conclusions	compare/contrast	deduce
determine evidence	order/sequence	investigate
support	summarize	justify
analyze		

▶ YOUR TURN   Analysis

_____ 1. Analysis questions call for higher-order thinking. (true or false)

_____ 2. Which of the following processes is *not* required by analysis questions?
(a) identifying evidence to support a statement

(b) making a statement based on evidence
(c) explaining motives or causes
(d) making evaluations

_____ 3. "Why" questions are often on the analysis level. (true or false)

_____ 4. Analysis questions require students only to rephrase information, to state it in their own words. (true or false)

_____ 5. Analysis questions require students to use or locate evidence in formulating their answers. (true or false)

Identify the levels of the following questions (_K_ = knowledge, _C_ = comprehension, _Ap_ = application, _An_ = analysis).

_____ 6. Why didn't Hamlet act when he first learned of the treachery? (The reasons have not been discussed in the text or class.)

_____ 7. What was Hamlet's position or title in Denmark?

_____ 8. In your own words, how did we characterize Hamlet in yesterday's discussion?

_____ 9. What evidence can you now propose to support the statement that Hamlet was a coward?

_____ 10. According to our definition of _moral dilemma_, when did Hamlet confront a moral dilemma?

Check your answers with those provided in the Answer Key. Two or more wrong answers suggest you should review this section. Consider working out loud with a peer to help you analyze your thinking. If you made fewer than two errors, go directly to the fifth level of the _Taxonomy_, synthesis.

Level 5. Synthesis or Creation

Original and creative ▶ **Synthesis questions** are higher-order questions that ask students to perform original and creative thinking. These kinds of questions require students to produce original communications, to make predictions, or to solve problems. Although application questions also require students to solve problems, synthesis questions differ because they do not require a single correct answer but, instead, allow a variety of creative answers. Here are some examples of the different kinds of synthesis questions.

1. To produce original communications:

Construct a collage of pictures that represents your values and feelings.

What would be a descriptive and exciting name for this video game?

Write an e-mail to a local newspaper editor on a social issue of concern to you.

2. To make predictions:

What would the United States be like if the South had won the Civil War?

How would your life be different if school were not mandatory?

After studying about forestry on the West Coast, what do you suspect is happening in the South American rain forests?

3. To solve problems:

How would you measure the height of a building without being able to go into it?

How can we successfully raise money to fund our homeless shelter project?

Design a musical instrument (with materials found in our lab) that effectively demonstrates three principles of physics.

Teachers can use synthesis questions to help develop the creative abilities of students. Unfortunately, as in the case of analysis questions, teachers too often avoid synthesis questions in favor of lower-order questions, particularly knowledge questions. Synthesis questions rely on a thorough understanding of material. Students should not make wild guesses to answer synthesis questions. For example, one synthesis question that we suggested, "What would the United States be like if the South had won the Civil War?" requires the student to have a firm grasp of information before being able to offer a sound prediction. To review, synthesis questions require predictions, original communications, or problem solving in which a number of answers are possible.

Words Often Found in Synthesis Questions

predict	construct	create
produce	how can we improve . . . ?	imagine
write	what would happen if . . . ?	hypothesize
design	can you devise . . . ?	combine
develop	how can we solve . . . ?	estimate
synthesize		invent

> **YOUR TURN**   **Synthesis**

In items 1–10, identify the level of the question by using the code provided
(*K* = knowledge, *C* = comprehension, *Ap* = application, *An* = analysis, and *S* = synthesis).

_____ 1. What is the state capital?
_____ 2. Where is it located?
_____ 3. Point it out on the map.
_____ 4. If you could decide on a location for a new state capital, what location would you choose?
_____ 5. Why?
_____ 6. What would happen if we had two state capitals?
_____ 7. Draw a simple blueprint of your ideal state capital.
_____ 8. Quote what your textbook says about the primary function of a state capital.

_____ 9. Describe this primary function.
_____ 10. Given the categories of different kinds of state capitals, how would you classify the capital of Maine?
_____ 11. Synthesis questions require students to do all the following *except*
(a) Make predictions
(b) Solve problems
(c) Rely primarily on memory
(d) Construct original communication
_____ 12. Synthesis questions require original and creative thought from students. (true or false)

The Answer Key will provide you with feedback on your progress in this section. If you missed more than two, review the box of words often found in synthesis questions to correct your errors. If you made two or fewer errors, go directly to the final level of the *Taxonomy*, evaluation.

Level 6. Evaluation

The last level of the *Taxonomy* is evaluation. Evaluation, like synthesis and analysis, is a higher-order mental process. **Evaluation questions** do not necessarily have a single correct answer. They require the student to judge the merit of an idea, a solution to a problem, or an aesthetic work. They may also ask the student to offer an opinion on an issue. Following are some examples of different kinds of evaluation questions.

Examples of Evaluation Questions

Decide why young children should or should not be allowed to read any book they want.

How do you assess your performance at school?

Give three reasons that support why this picture is your best.

Taking the role of cultural critic for your local public radio station, offer reviews of three current movies.

Defend your choice as to whether or not busing is an appropriate remedy for desegregating schools.

Which U.S. senator is the most effective and why?

Forming sound judgments ▶ To express your opinion on an issue or to make a judgment on the merit of an idea, solution, or aesthetic work, you must use some criteria. You must use either objective standards or a personal set of values to make an evaluation. For example, if you answer the last question in the list of examples using a personal set of values, you might decide that the senator whose voting record is most congruent with your own political philosophy is the most effective senator. If you are strongly against defense spending or strongly in favor of civil rights legislation, these personal values would be reflected in your evaluation of the most effective senator.

Another way of evaluating senators would be through the use of objective criteria. Such criteria might include attendance records, campaign-financing practices, influence on other senators, number of sponsored bills that became law, and so forth. By comparing each senator to these criteria, a judgment can be made in relation to "the most effective senator."

Of course, many individuals use a combination of objective criteria and personal values when making an evaluation. The important thing to remember about evaluation questions is that they are not casual, careless, or offhand judgments: Some standard must be used and different answers are possible.

Words Often Used in Evaluation Questions

judge	give your opinion	verify
argue	which is the better picture,	rate
decide	solution, etc.	select
evaluate	do you agree	recommend
assess	would it be better	conclude

❯ YOUR TURN   Evaluation

Using all levels of the *Taxonomy*, classify the following questions (*K* = knowledge, *C* = comprehension, *Ap* = application, *An* = analysis, *S* = synthesis, and *E* = evaluation).

_____ 1. Who was the founder of the school of abstract art?

_____ 2. Describe the first attempts of the pioneers of abstract art.

_____ 3. Paint your own abstract piece.

_____ 4. What is your opinion of abstract art?

_____ 5. Which native crafts are most like these abstract oils?

_____ 6. Why have women been a central image of abstract art?

_____ 7. Which artist do you prefer, Miro or Picasso?

Observation Worksheet

FOCUS ON HIGHER-ORDER QUESTIONS

Given the rapid pace of classroom dialogue, capturing the level of a teacher's question can be quite challenging. Here is an approach that will help you analyze the teacher's use (or nonuse) of higher-order questions.

Directions: Do not use actual names of schools, teachers, administrators, or students when using this worksheet.

Observer's Name: _____

Date: _____

Grade Level: _____

Subject: _____

Class Size: _____

Background Information: Give a brief general description of the school's social, economic, and ethnic makeup.

_____

_____

What to Record: Write down each question asked in class for later analysis. After the observation, assess each question in terms of Bloom's *Taxonomy* to determine which of the six cognitive levels most appropriately describes the cognitive demand of each question. Some questions may be related to class procedures or other nonacademic areas, so you may want to create a seventh category called "Other" for these noninstructional questions.

Reflections on Your Observation:

1. How are the teacher's questions distributed across Bloom's *Taxonomy*? _____

_____

_____

2. Are some levels underutilized or not used at all? Are some categories overused?

_____

_____

_____

3. Although no one has defined an ideal distribution, as a result of this observation, what are some factors that you think are important in using the different levels of the *Taxonomy*?

_____

_____

_____

At this point, we have reviewed all levels of the *Taxonomy*, and you should know whether or not you are ready for the Mastery Test. In the Mastery Test, you will be asked to identify the levels of a number of questions; all six levels of the *Taxonomy* will be represented.

✺ Mastery Test

OBJECTIVE 2 **To classify questions according to Bloom's *Taxonomy of Educational Objectives: Cognitive Domain***

Read the paragraph below and then classify the following questions according to their appropriate level on Bloom's *Taxonomy* (*K* = knowledge, *C* = comprehension, *Ap* = application, *An* = analysis, *S* = synthesis, and *E* = evaluation).

To pass the Mastery Test, you should classify nine of the eleven questions accurately. Good luck!

Researchers Mykol Hamilton and David Anderson explored sexism in 200 distinguished children's books. These children's books tell twice as many male-centered tales than female, and illustrations depict 50 percent more males. Although female characters appear in roles such as doctors, lawyers, and scientists, they are more often passive observers, watching their active brothers at work and at play. A passage in *Johnny and Susie's Mountain Quest* highlights the rigid roles of a brave boy and a helpless girl: "'Oh, please help me, Johnny!' cried Susie. 'We're up so high! I'm afraid I'm going to fall.'" Females are not the only ones often missing from the pages of children's literature. Fathers are too, appearing in less than half of the 200 books. When present, fathers are depicted as stoic, hands-off parents, rarely seen hugging or feeding their children. Mothers are shown more often as affectionate caregivers capable of expressing a range of emotions from happiness to sadness. And surprisingly, mothers in these stories discipline children and express anger more often than do fathers.

Hamilton and Anderson also discovered that occupational stereotyping has not gone underground. In the 200 books they reviewed, women are given traditional jobs ten times as often as non-traditional ones. For example, the lead adult female character in *Alligator Tales* is a stewardess, a maid in *Mr. Willowby's Christmas Tree*, and a librarian in *Hopping Hens Here!* Boys tend to have roles as fighters, adventurers, and rescuers. They are also overwhelmingly shown to be aggressive, argumentative, and competitive.

—David Sadker, Myra Sadker, and Karen R. Zittleman, *Still Failing at Fairness* (New York: Scribners, 2009), pp. 91–92.

_____ 1. In your own words, compare the portrayal of males and females in children's books.

_____ 2. Assess how racist books might be similar and different from the sexist materials described above.

_____ 3. What do boys do in the books that were studied?

_____ 4. What is the main idea of this passage?

_____ 5. What would your ideal nonsexist book be like?

_____ 6. What is your opinion on the issue of sexism in books?

_____ 7. If all books became gender neutral, gender balanced, or gender affirming during the next five years, what do you predict would be the effects on children?

_____ 8. Why do you think that girls and boys have been historically portrayed in such a stereotyped manner in school texts?

_____ 9. How many texts were analyzed for sexism?

_____ 10. Do you think that sexist books should be banned from children's libraries?

_____ 11. Why do you think educators are concerned with the ways in which girls and boys are portrayed in children literature?

OBJECTIVE 3

To construct classroom questions on all six levels of Bloom's _Taxonomy of Educational Objectives: Cognitive Domain_

Learning Activity 5.3

☐ **INTASC Principles 2, 4, 5, 6, 7, 8**

The first, and perhaps the most difficult, step in learning to ask effective classroom questions is that of gaining a thorough understanding of Bloom's _Taxonomy_. Now that you have demonstrated your ability to classify questions, you are ready to focus on constructing them. Effective classroom questions make provision for student thinking on all levels of the _Taxonomy_. Although during a short period of time only one or two levels of the _Taxonomy_ may be reflected in a teacher's questions, over the course of an entire semester, students should have ample opportunity to answer questions phrased at all levels. The sample questions and the information in this Learning Activity provide you with useful information for constructing questions. The following review should provide you with a reference as you construct questions on the various levels of the _Taxonomy_.

■ Suggestions for Constructing Questions

In the next few pages, we will review the nature of the cognitive processes and verb prompts that are frequently associated with specific levels of the _Taxonomy_. As you go over this review, remember that it is important to analyze each question you write because inclusion of key words is not an unconditional guarantee of the taxonomic level of a particular question. After a brief review, you will get a chance to practice constructing questions that pertain to a specific reading selection.

Economy of words ▷

Before proceeding to the exercises in this Learning Activity, you may find it helpful to remember to phrase your questions carefully. You have probably been a student in more than one class where the teacher's questions were so cumbersome or wordy that you lost the meaning of the question. In fact, some studies indicate that almost half of teacher questions are ambiguous and poorly phrased. You should be explicit enough to ensure understanding of your questions, but, at the same time, you should avoid using too many words. When a question is too wordy, students become confused and unable to respond; frequently, the result is that the question has to be rephrased.

Questions worth asking ▷

Now you are ready to construct questions at each of the six levels of Bloom's _Taxonomy_. Read the paragraph in the Your Turn that follows. Then construct at least twelve questions relating to it. When you are done, you should have two questions on each of the six levels of the _Taxonomy_. As you construct your questions, keep the following in mind. What facts are in the paragraph that you might want students to recognize or recall (knowledge level)? What are the main points in the reading selection that you would want students to comprehend and be able to rephrase in their own words (comprehension level)? What information is there in the paragraph that students could apply to solving problems, classifying, or giving examples (application level)? What questions can you ask about the reading selection that require students to consider reasons and motives, examine the validity of a conclusion, or seek evidence to support a conclusion (analysis level)? Using this paragraph as a springboard, how can you stimulate original student thought—creative problem solving, the making of predictions, and the production of original communication—in writing, music, dance, art, and so forth (synthesis level)? Finally, what issues can you raise from the material in this paragraph that will cause students to judge the merit of an idea, the solution to a problem, or an aesthetic work (evaluation level)?

After you have finished writing your questions, compare them with the sample questions in the Answer Key. Obviously, a wide variety of questions could be written pertaining to this particular selection. The sample questions are simply meant to give you a basis for comparison and to indicate the kinds of questions that can be asked on each of the six levels of the *Taxonomy*.

LEVELS OF THE *TAXONOMY:* WORD PROMPTS

Knowledge	Comprehension	Application	Analysis	Synthesis or Creation	Evaluation
define	describe	apply	support	predict	judge
recall	compare	classify	analyze	produce	argue
recognize	contrast	use	why	write	decide
remember	rephrase	choose	summarize	design	evaluate
who	put in your	employ	compare/	develop	assess
what	own words	write an	contrast	synthesize	give your
where	explain the	example	order/	construct	opinion
when	main idea	solve	sequence	improve	which is
list		how many	deduce	what if	better
reproduce		which	investigate	devise	do you agree
recite		what is	categorize	solve	would it be
name		show	classify	create	better
describe		translate	draw	imagine	verify
identify		make	conclusions	hypothesize	rate
review		illustrate	identify motives	combine	select
		teach	or causes	estimate	recommend
		record/chart	determine	invent	conclude
		diagram/map	evidence		
		demonstrate	justify		

Compare your questions with the information and examples in the previous Learning Activities. Discuss the questions you develop with your instructor and with other members of your class. If eleven or twelve of your questions accurately reflect the appropriate level of the *Taxonomy*, you are doing well. If you miss two or three, you will probably want to review previous sections and study the sample questions carefully, particularly those on the levels where you did not construct the questions accurately. If you missed more than three, a careful rereading and additional practice in constructing questions may be necessary before you take the Mastery Test.

YOUR TURN   **Constructing Questions the Six Levels of Bloom's *Taxonomy***

In Des Moines, Iowa, two high school students and a junior high school student, in defiance of a ban by school authorities, wore black armbands to class as a protest against the Vietnam War. As a result, they were suspended from school. But the U.S. Supreme Court later ruled the suspensions were illegal, holding that the first amendment to the Constitution protects the rights of public school children to express their political and social views during school hours.

This case illustrates a significant new trend in American life. Young people, particularly those under twenty-one, are demanding that they be granted rights long denied them as a matter of course. And, with increasing frequency, they are winning those rights.

—Michael Dorman, *Under 21* (New York: Delacorte, 1970), pp. 3, 5.

Write two questions at each level of the *Taxonomy* based on the above material: (1) knowledge level, (2) comprehension level, (3) application level, (4) analysis level, (5) synthesis level, and (6) evaluation level.

✳ Mastery Test

OBJECTIVE 3   **To construct classroom questions on all six levels of Bloom's *Taxonomy of Educational Objectives: Cognitive Domain***

Read the following paragraphs and then construct twelve questions based on this reading selection. Two of your questions must be at the knowledge level, two at the comprehension level, two at the application level, two at the analysis level, two at the synthesis level, and two at the evaluation level. To pass this Mastery Test successfully, nine of the twelve questions should accurately reflect the level of the *Taxonomy* at which they are constructed.

Death may be an unwelcome, terrifying enemy, a skeleton with an evil grin who clutches an ugly scythe in his bony hand. Or death may be a long awaited friend who waits quietly, invisibly, beside the bed of a dying patient to ease his pain, his loneliness, his weariness, his hopelessness.

Man alone among the things that live knows that death will come. Mice and trees and microbes do not. And man, knowing that he has to die, fears death, the great unknown, as a child fears the dark. "We fear to be we know not what, we know not where," said John Dryden. But what man dreads more is the dying, the relentless process in which he passes into extinction alone and helpless and despairing. So he puts death and dying out of his mind, denying that they exist, refusing to discuss them openly, trying desperately to control them. He coins phrases like "never say die," and somehow, when he says something is "good for life," he means forever. Unable to bear the thought of ceasing to be, he comforts himself with thoughts of a pleasant afterlife in which he is rewarded for his trials on earth, or he builds monuments to himself to perpetuate at least his memory, if not his body.

—John Langone, *Death Is a Noun* (Boston: Little, Brown, 1972), pp. 3–4.

Now that you have read the paragraphs, construct twelve questions, two at each level of the *Taxonomy*. When you write the application-level questions, you may find it helpful to consider that the following information has previously been given to the class: (1) definitions of various literary images, including metaphor, simile, and personification;

(2) a list of terms and definitions that characterize various psychological states; and (3) several novels that portray death as a central or minor theme.

1. Two knowledge questions

2. Two comprehension questions

3. Two application questions

4. Two analysis questions

5. Two synthesis questions

6. Two evaluation questions

■ OBJECTIVE 4 **To write examples of questioning strategies that enhance the quality of student participation**

Learning Activity 5.4

☑ INTASC Principles 2, 4, 5, 6, 7, 8

While most of this chapter has focused on how to ask higher-order questions, this section explores several related areas that will enhance your questioning skills. Two of these areas are post-question follow-up skills: wait time and feedback. The last topic explores techniques for moving the responsibility of asking questions back to the students, where it actually all began.

■ Wait Time

If we were to stop and listen outside a classroom door, we might hear classroom interaction similar to this.

Teacher: Who wrote the poem "Stopping by Woods on a Snowy Evening"? Tomás?

Tomás: Robert Frost.

Teacher: Good. What action takes place in the poem? Sally?

Sally: A man stops his sleigh to watch the woods get filled with snow.

Teacher: Yes. Emma, what thoughts go through the man's mind?

Emma: He thinks how beautiful the woods are—*(pauses for a second)*

Teacher: What else does he think about? Joe?

Joe: He thinks how he would like to stay and watch. *(pauses for a second)*

Teacher: Yes—and what else? Rita? *(waits for half a second)* Come on, Rita, you can get the answer to this. *(waits for half a second)* Well, why does he feel he can't stay there indefinitely and watch the woods and the snow?

Rita: He knows he's too busy. He's got too many things to do to stay there for so long.

Teacher: Good. In the poem's last line, the man says that he has miles to go before he sleeps. What might sleep be a symbol for? Sarah?

Sarah: Well, I think it might be—*(pauses for a second)*

Teacher: Think, Sarah. *(waits for half a second)* All right then—Mike? *(waits again for half a second)* Marcus? *(waits for half a second)* What's the matter with everyone today? Didn't you do the reading?

There are a number of comments we could make about this slice of classroom interaction. We could note the teacher's development from primarily lower-order questions to those of a somewhat higher order. We could comment on the inability of the students to answer her later questions and on the teacher's increasing frustration. But perhaps the most devastating thing we could say about this interaction segment is that it lasts for less than a single minute.

In less than one minute of dialogue, this teacher manages to construct and ask six questions—some of them, at least, requiring a fairly high cognitive level of response. As discussed earlier, a rapid questioning rate is not at all atypical of many classrooms across the country. The mean number of questions a teacher asks averages between two and three per minute, and it is not unusual to find as many as seven to ten questions asked by a teacher during a single minute of classroom instruction.

Wait time 1: after asking a question ▷

The effect of this rapid "bombing rate" is that students have little time to think. In fact, research shows that the mean amount of time a teacher waits after asking a question (wait time 1) is approximately *one second!* If the students are not able to think quickly enough to come up with a response at this pace, the teacher repeats the question, rephrases it, asks a different question, or calls on another student. If a student manages to get a response in, the teacher reacts or asks another question within an average time of nine-tenths of a second (wait time 2). It is little wonder that high rates of teacher questioning tend to be associated with low rates of student questions and student declarations. In classrooms where questions are asked at this bombing rate, students have little time or desire to think or to express themselves in an atmosphere so charged with a sense of verbal evaluation and testing.

Wait time 2: after student response ▷

When teachers break out of the bombing-rate pattern and learn to increase wait time 1 and wait time 2 from one second to three or five seconds, many significant changes occur in their classrooms. For example:[20]

Advantages of increasing wait time ▷

1. Students give longer answers.

2. Students volunteer more appropriate answers, and failures to respond are less frequent.

3. Student comments on the analysis and synthesis levels increase. They make more evidence-inference responses and more speculative responses.

4. Students ask more questions.

5. Students exhibit more confidence in their comments, and those students whom teachers rate as relatively slow learners offer more questions and more responses.

6. Student achievement is higher.

Simply by increasing their ability to wait longer after asking a question, especially a higher-level question, teachers can effect some striking changes in the quantity and quality of student response and achievement. It is not as easy as you might think to learn to wait three to five seconds after asking a question. If a teacher does not get an immediate response to a question, the natural reaction seems to be one of panic—an assumption that the question is not an effective one and that the student does not know the answer. Indeed, teachers who have experimented with trying to increase their wait time find that they become frustrated at about the second or third week of practice. They go through a period of indecision about how long exactly they should wait after asking a question. If they receive encouragement during this difficult time, however, most teachers are able to increase wait time from one second to three or five seconds. Some teachers have found the following suggestions helpful as they try to increase their wait time.

How to increase wait time ▷

1. Avoid repeating portions of student response to a question (teacher echo).

2. Avoid the command "think" without giving the students clues to aid their thinking or sufficient time in which to get their thoughts together.

3. Avoid dependence on comments such as "uh-huh" and "okay."

4. Avoid the "yes, but" reaction to a student response. This construction signals teacher rejection of the student's idea.

Currently, too many classrooms are characterized by a rapid rate of interaction, as teachers fire one question after another at students without giving them sufficient time to think, formulate their answers, and respond. If teachers can master the skill of increasing wait time from one second to three or five seconds, particularly after questions at a higher cognitive level, they will probably find some positive changes in both classroom discussion and student achievement.

Teacher Feedback

Not too long ago, noted educator John Goodlad and his research team conducted an in-depth observation study of more than a thousand classrooms. And what were their impressions? Goodlad observed:

Bland classrooms

> [T]here is a paucity of praise and correction of students' performance as well as of teacher guidance, in how to do better next time. Teachers tend not to respond in overtly positive or negative ways to the work students do. And our impression is that classes generally tend not to be strongly positive or strongly negative places to be. Enthusiasm and joy and anger are kept under control.[21]

Goodlad concluded that the emotional tone of schools is neither punitive nor joyful. Rather, he says, the school environment can best be characterized as "flat." Part of the reason for this bland quality may lie in the way teachers deal with students' answers to questions. Trained observers visited more than a hundred classrooms along the East Coast and analyzed teacher reactions to student answers and comments. They found the following:

Ineffective feedback

- Teachers don't often praise students. Approximately 10 percent of teacher reactions praise students. In approximately 25 percent of the classrooms observed, teachers never praised students.

- Teacher criticism is even more rare. (In this study, criticism was defined as an explicit statement that a student's behavior or work was wrong.) Approximately two-thirds of the one hundred classrooms observed contained no criticism. In the approximately thirty-five classrooms where teachers did criticize students, such criticism constituted only 5 percent of teacher interaction.

- Teacher remediation of student answers was quite frequent. It occurred in all classrooms and constituted approximately 30 percent of all teacher reactions. (Teacher remediation was defined as teacher comments or questions that would help students reach a more accurate or higher-level response.)

- But neither praise, criticism, nor remediation is the most frequent teacher response. Teachers most often simply *accept* student answers. Acceptance means that they say "uh-huh," or "okay," or nothing at all. Acceptance occurred in all of the classrooms, and it constituted more than 50 percent of teacher reactions. There was more acceptance than praise, remediation, and criticism combined.[22]

Some teachers seem committed to using bland feedback, although they don't call it that. They advise new teachers to "avoid saying an answer is wrong or even inadequate" for fear of wounding a student's ego. "Find something good in all answers, and keep students happy and involved" is their advice. The following true incident illustrates the kind of problem that ensues when this advice is followed:

> A teacher in an eastern city asked students one of the most popular of all classroom questions: "When did Columbus arrive in America?"
>
> "1942" was the quick retort offered by a fifth-grade boy in the front row.
>
> "Close" replied the teacher.

Although Columbus did not arrive in the Americas in 1942, or even close to 1942, the teacher later explained that although the answer was not correct, all the digits were; just the order of the digits needed work. Rather than risk hurting the "student's ego," the teacher found something correct and accepted the answer. Teachers often avoid saying that a student is wrong, and many even find it difficult to say that an answer is wrong. The fact that thirty-five other students might be more confused as a result of this imprecise teacher reaction probably did not occur to the teacher. The teacher's good intentions led to a poor educational judgment. And, unfortunately, this is all too common.

The way the classroom question cycle most often goes is:

- Teacher asks a question.
- Student gives an answer.
- Teacher says, "Okay."

The "okay" classroom is probably a bland, flat place in which to learn. Further, the okay classroom may not be okay in terms of encouraging student achievement. Research on teaching effectiveness indicates that students need specific feedback to understand what is expected of them, correct errors, and get help in improving their performance. If a student answers or questions, and the teacher reacts by saying "uh-huh" or "okay," the student is not getting the specific feedback he or she needs. Also, these flat "acceptance" reactions to student comments are not likely to encourage high-quality student thought and discussion.

Verbal and nonverbal feedback ▶

Teachers give feedback in two ways: verbal and nonverbal. While either can be effective, sometimes messages are more powerful when they are not spoken. Nonverbal feedback refers to physical messages sent through eye contact, facial expressions, and body position. Does the teacher smile, frown, or remain impassive as a student comments in class? Is the teacher looking at or away from the student? Where is the teacher standing? Does the teacher appear relaxed or tense? All these physical messages indicate to the student whether the teacher is interested or bored, involved or passive, pleased or displeased with a student's comment.

Several studies comparing the relative effect of nonverbal and verbal feedback on students have been undertaken. One study had teachers send out conflicting messages to determine which message students accepted as the more powerful. In one group, the teacher displayed positive nonverbal rewards (smiled, maintained eye contact, indicated positive attitude to student answers with facial and body cues) but, at the same time, sent out negative verbal messages. In the second case, the process was reversed, and negative nonverbal disapproval was coupled with positive verbal praise (frowns, poor eye contact, and the like, coupled with "good," "nice job," etc.).

Although no evidence was accumulated as to whether the teacher was perceived as having multiple personalities, the results of the study were nonetheless interesting. In both cases, the nonverbal message was perceived as the stronger message by the majority of students. Whether the nonverbal message was positive or negative, most students responded to the nonverbal rather than to the verbal comments. This study provides fascinating support for the notion of "silent language," or "body language," and it emphasizes the importance of teachers' attending to what they do not say as well as to what they do say when they reinforce student participation.

Need for variety ▷ For many years educators have assumed that rewards, verbal and nonverbal, were a positive tool in promoting student learning, and certainly this is frequently the case. But reward is not always an effective teaching skill. In some cases reward is ineffectual, and, on occasion, it is detrimental to learning.[23]

When a teacher relies totally on one or two favorite types of feedback and uses these repeatedly, the eventual result may become ineffectual. The teacher, for example, who continually says "good" after each student response is not reinforcing but simply verbalizing a comment that has lost its power to reward. Overusing a word or phrase is a pattern that many teachers, both new and experienced, fall into. Continual repetition of a word such as *good* seems only to ease teacher anxiety and to provide the teacher with a second or two to conceptualize his or her next comment or question.

Short-circuiting ▷ In other cases feedback can detract from educational objectives and student learning when given too quickly and too frequently. When students are engaged in problem-solving activities, continual teacher comments can be an interruption to their thought processes—and may even terminate the problem solving altogether. Teachers who react to each student comment refocus the discussion on themselves, inhibiting the possibility of student-to-student interactions.

Differentiating feedback ▷ Finally, it should be pointed out that different individuals respond to different kinds of feedback. Teachers should learn to recognize that while some students find intensive eye contact rewarding, others find it uncomfortable; some students respond favorably to a teacher's referring to their contributions by name, but others find it embarrassing. Although it is unrealistic to expect that a teacher will be able to learn the various rewards to which each individual student responds, it is possible for teachers to try, in general, to be sensitive to the effects of different rewards on students.

Researchers who have studied teacher feedback conclude that effective feedback has the following characteristics:[24]

Effective feedback ▷ 1. Effective feedback is *contingent* on the student's answer or behavior. When someone is doing something right, praise that behavior then and there. When a student is making an error, correct it as soon as possible. Feedback that is directly related to the student's performance in both time and focus is far more effective than late, nonexistent, unfocused, or general teacher reactions.

2. Effective feedback is *specific*, communicating what precisely is praiseworthy ("Using a chronological framework made your essay clear and logically organized!") or what needs to be corrected ("Check your rules for writing footnotes; you are making several mistakes with the punctuation."). Specificity of feedback provides the student with precise direction for building on strengths or correcting errors.

3. Effective feedback is *honest* and *sincere*. Teachers who provide a constant stream of syrupy rewards are quickly dismissed by students. Effective questions and thoughtful answers merit honest feedback.

◻ Student-Initiated Questions

Natural question-askers ▷ Think back to conversations you may have had with two-, three-, or four-year-olds. Do you remember how it felt to be the center of a storm of questions, the target of a constant stream of *whats* and *hows*? With the patience of Job, you answered each question, only to be confronted by a predictable follow-up: "Why?" Before they enter school, young children are filled with questions, from "Why is the sky blue?" to "Where do babies come from?" (When given these two options, most adults make a beeline to answer the "sky" question.) In fact, children initiate more than half the questions asked in their conversations with adults.[25] Children ask questions to learn about their world, and their quest for knowledge seems insatiable—insatiable, that is, until they arrive at school. Once in school, children's natural tendency to learn by questioning mysteriously evaporates. On that first day of school, the adult becomes questioner, while the child becomes the answerer. One insightful story that captures this role transformation describes a conversation between a parent and a child.

> The parent asks his son how he liked his first day of school. "Fine," says the child, "except for the grownup who kept interrupting."

By the upper grades, students are asking fewer than 15 percent of classroom questions.[26] And even these questions are not typically about what is being taught; they are more likely to be concerned with management and organization, such as "Is this going to be on the test?" "Where do we line up?" or that ever-popular, "Can I go to the bathroom?" Real questions about learning are very rare. Why this dramatic decline when children pass through the classroom door? If you would like to take a minute and try your hand at solving this problem, this is the ideal time to do just that. What is happening at school to dampen student questions?

Barriers to student questions ▶ Did your detective work uncover time pressure as one of the critical school factors? Teachers report that they feel pressured to "cover" the curriculum and "raise student test scores." Local, state, and even national tests put schools and educators under a very intense public spotlight. Encouraging **student-initiated questions**, questions unlikely to be included on standardized tests, is certainly not the path to higher scores.

But we need not focus only on time and testing pressures, because the very organization of school inhibits student questions. Picture today's classroom (a room fundamentally unchanged in decades): the teacher's desk and chalk-board dominating a room populated by smaller desks—furniture that seems to be saying, "the teacher is the authority figure and the students are the followers; look to the teacher for direction." And unlike one child asking a parent a question, in school we have twenty or thirty students vying for the teacher's attention. This can lead to the "control" issue. Classrooms engulfed by student voices, even voices created by the excitement of questions, are classrooms some educators view as threatening, a sign that the teacher has "lost control."

Modeling ▶ Teachers can change this situation and encourage student questions through both *direct* and *indirect* techniques.[27] In fact, if your teaching reflects the skills in this chapter (you remember—"The Seven Habits of Highly Effective Questioners"), you are already using an indirect technique, one called *modeling*. Your thoughtful use of wait time, asking of both higher- and lower-order questions, and use of probing and delving questions, for example, will serve to model the kind of questioning skills that you want your students to develop. These indirect techniques create classrooms characterized by good questioning, and students, as if by osmosis, begin to model good questioning skills.

While the indirect approach is useful, more direct efforts are usually needed to develop good student questions.[28] While we do not have the space in this chapter to detail all of these direct approaches, we can offer some suggestions that will get you started in creating classrooms that encourage student inquiry.[29]

Encouraging student questions

1. *Create a classroom climate that encourages student questions.* Some teachers have found that fun questioning activities and games can be very effective in promoting student questions. The game of "Twenty Questions" is one example. In this game, a student secretly selects a person, place, or thing, and the rest of the class has to guess what it is. The class is allowed to ask twenty questions that can only be answered with a "yes" or "no." Another fun activity is to provide students with answers to topics being studied and ask them to formulate the appropriate question. Many students find this role reversal enjoyable. Even fun activities can build a climate that supports questioning and fundamental skills used to ask questions.

2. *Overtly reinforce student questioning.* Teachers can promote student questions through encouragement and praise. "What a wonderful question. Let me think about that for a moment." "Your questions are getting better and better." Questioning can be risky business, and a reward for the effort can make the risk worth taking.

3. *Support the questioner.* While "smart" questions broadcast the questioner's insight and intellect, a bad question announces a student's ignorance to all within earshot. Stupid questions can draw a groaning "duh" or other humiliating put-downs from peers. But from the teacher's side of the desk, a "stupid" question can provide a valuable insight: The student who has the courage (or even the ineptitude) to ask a "stupid" question shows that more teaching may be needed for others as well. But if students feel intimidated about the risk of asking a "stupid" question, fewer student questions of all kinds will be asked.

4. *Establish helpful guidelines.* Establishing guidelines about questioning can create a supportive class norm. Sample guidelines might include: share the floor with others, stay on the point, treat each other with respect, accept and listen to all questions, think about your question before you ask it, and everyone must write down at least one question per topic studied. You can include key questioning words as hints to help students formulate their questions at all levels of the *taxonomy*. You and your students may want to add to or modify this list together, and then display it prominently in class.

5. *Cue your students.* Teachers can get the ball rolling by focusing students on questioning opportunities. Direct teacher cues might include:

   As you read this chapter, write down questions that you might want to ask the characters.

   Write down questions to ask tomorrow's guest speaker.

   After you answer the questions at the end of the chapter, add one of your own.

6. *Have students write study guide and exam questions.* Some teachers ask students to write and submit their own questions as a study guide to help them prepare for an exam. Other teachers go one step further and ask students to create the questions that actually will be used on their exams. (This can be a real motivator for some students!)

7. *Encourage student-to-student questions.* After one student gives a report, offers an explanation, or even answers a teacher's question, other students are encouraged to direct a question to the speaker.

Courteous cross-questioning promotes open dialogue and more in-depth understanding of issues being studied.

8. *Use authentic questions.* The use of authentic questions, questions that tie into student interest and genuine curiosity, can generate not only student enthusiasm but also student questions. Teachers can ask students to list subject-related questions that interest them, and then the teacher and students can work together on finding the answers. Authentic student questions can serve as a springboard to a meaningful classroom curriculum.

9. *Teach questioning directly.* Elements of good questioning can be taught directly. For instance, different ways of phrasing questions can be discussed and practiced in class. In fact, the seven habits of highly effective questioners described in this chapter can be taught to your students. Asking effective questions is not intended to be a teacher monopoly; it is an important learning skill as well.

The purpose of this section has been to remind you that you have an invaluable partner in your teaching responsibilities: students. While this book focuses on refining your teaching skills, classrooms are not just about you. As you develop your own questioning skills on the road to being an effective teacher, remember the importance of student-initiated questions on the road to more successful learning.[30]

> YOUR TURN   Questioning Strategies

Here we will use the *Taxonomy* to strengthen your knowledge of effective questions. Using *analysis*, briefly write about the strategies that enhance student participation (wait time, effective feedback, and student-initiated questions). The correct answers are found in the previous sections. As a reminder, the italicized words ask you to analyze. (But you knew that already, right?)

1. Based on your reading, *identify* motives teachers might have for extending their wait time.
2. *Provide* one reason that supports using criticism before remediation.
3. *Why* might your understanding of multiple intelligences promote student-initiated questions?
4. *Summarize* at least one example of wait time that you observed this week (inside or outside a classroom).
5. What can you *conclude* about acceptance when it is used as the primary feedback by teachers?

In items 6–12, identify the level of the question by using the code provided (*K* = knowledge, *C* = comprehension, *Ap* = application, *An* = analysis, and *S* = synthesis). After you have identified the level, actually *do* the *synthesis*-level questions as directed. (Hint: There are three!)

_____ 6. Share your responses to questions 1–5 with a peer and discuss and improve them until you both agree that your work is correct.

_____ 7. Create a short poem or rap that embodies something you have learned about questioning skills.

_____ 8. What do you notice about this section and the previous section of Your Turn?

_____ 9. Explain the main idea of the synthesis level.

_____ 10. Which of these twelve questions is the most challenging for you?

_____ 11. Why might the pattern shift (beyond knowledge and comprehension) in these Your Turn exercises be motivating for you?

_____ 12. Write down a question that you have about this chapter. Working in a group of two or three, propose a possible answer to this question.

For items 1–5, review your comments carefully and check the Answer Key for suggestions. If further analysis and note taking aren't working for you, check with another student or with your teacher. For items 6–12, check your answers in the Answer Key. Hopefully, you are able to evaluate your own work and remediate any weaknesses!

Observation Worksheet

WAIT TIME AND TEACHER REACTIONS

Effective questioning in the classroom depends on a number of factors, including the length of the teacher's wait time and the specificity of the teacher's reactions. In this activity, you will have several opportunities to investigate these critical variables.

Directions: Do not use actual names of schools, teachers, administrators, or students when using this worksheet.

Observer's Name: _____

Date: _____

Grade Level: _____

Subject: _____

Class Size: _____

Background Information: Give a brief general description of the school's social, economic, and ethnic makeup.

_____

_____

Wait Time

What to Record: Determining a teacher's wait time requires little more than some patience, a watch that can measure seconds (or the ability to count seconds), and an ear that can hear silence. Remember, the wait time is silent time, without rephrasing of questions or any other verbal interruption. After the teacher has asked a question, simply write down the number "1" if the student receives a wait time of a second or less. If longer, write down the number that represents how many seconds long each wait time lasts.

Teacher Reactions

What to Record: Teacher reactions fall into one of four categories: praise, acceptance, remediation, or criticism. In this activity, you will determine how the teacher distributes these reactions. Write down each reaction the teacher gives to each student response or comment. You may be able to listen to the reactions and immediately record which category applies. If you need more time to classify the teacher's reactions, you could write down the reactions verbatim and classify them after the observation when you have more time. If the teacher follows a student response with a probing question, record that as well.

Reflections on Your Observation:

1. How long is this teacher's typical wait time? _____

_____

2. How many times did the teacher wait longer than three seconds? _____

_____

3. Do you believe that a longer wait time would be useful in this class? _____

_____

4. What percentage of teacher reactions went to each of the four categories? _____

_____

_____

5. What conclusions can you draw from that distribution? _____

_____

_____

6. Considering your observation data, were student-initiated questions encouraged? How?

_____

_____

_____

✳ Mastery Test

OBJECTIVE 4   To write examples of questioning strategies that enhance the quality of student participation

Create one scenario (much like the examples in this chapter) that incorporates effective questioning. You should include the following in your vignette:

   (a) *wait time* during a teacher–student interaction (*WT*)

   (b) feedback (*specific praise*) for a correct answer (*SP*)

   (c) feedback (*remediation*) of an incorrect response (*R*)

   (d) *student-initiated questioning* as created by the teacher (*SIQ*)

Indicate (with parentheses) the dialogue portions that model the four strategies and label them *WT, SP, R,* and *SIQ*.

OBJECTIVE 5   To describe how the growing diversity and multicultural nature of America's students impact questioning strategies

▢ Questioning Skills and Differentiated Learning

Learning Activity 5.5

▢ **INTASC Principles 2, 3, 4, 5, 6, 7, 8**

While diversity and multicultural issues are currently hot topics in America's schools, our national history is replete with examples of simplistic and unflattering stereotypes of Americans based on race, ethnicity, religion, and class. It is not surprising that the typical teacher wants nothing to do with such inaccurate and frequently demeaning stereotypes. It is not surprising to hear a teacher proclaim: "I don't see color; I only see children."

Such a statement suggests that the teacher is working hard to treat all students fairly. Unfortunately, pretending that group differences do not exist does not necessarily lead to either fair or effective teaching. In fact, denying group differences can make teaching in general, and questioning strategies in particular, more difficult.

Stereotypes versus generalizations ▶

Many Asian Americans excel in math, many African Americans become athletes, and Jewish Americans are known for their educational drive. Are these **stereotypes**? Or is this reality? According to educator Carlos Cortés, this is reality, and recognizing the validity of such **generalizations** is an important step in becoming a more effective teacher.[31] So what is the difference between potentially helpful generalizations and potentially destructive stereotypes? Cortés draws three fundamental distinctions between the two.

1. *Flexibility:* Generalizations are open to change, especially as new information develops or new theories emerge. On the other hand, stereotypes are inflexible, rigid, and impervious to new information.

2. *Intragroup heterogeneity:* Generalizations recognize that within a group, there are amazing differences and diversity; not all members of a group are the same. Stereotypes make the assumption that all group members are homogeneous. When an individual does not easily "fit" the group definition, a stereotypic perception would conclude that the individual is atypical, an anomaly, the exception that proves the rule.

3. *Clues:* Since we know that groups have different characteristics, when we learn that an individual belongs to a particular group, we then have a clue about that individual. Generalizations give teachers a start, an insight about group members. Stereotypes replace clues with assumptions. Because an individual belongs to a group, a stereotype assumes that certain characteristics must apply to that individual. While generalizations are subtle, stereotypes are blatant.

While each of us is a unique individual, our group memberships create certain similarities as well. Understanding the power of group membership helps teachers to understand students better and therefore to design more effective teaching strategies. How to focus eye contact when talking to a Native American, how best to approach the parents of a Mexican American, or how most effectively to use wait time with students who have limited English proficiency are all group strategies that provide teachers with a helpful direction.

Although generalizations can be beneficial, it is important to remember to use them cautiously. Boundaries can be murky, and crossing from a generalization to a stereotype is always a danger. As Carlos Cortés warns, careless generalizations can lead to damaging stereotyping and unintended bias.

When you begin teaching, one-half of schoolchildren in the United States will be nonwhite or Hispanic students. In fact, in many of our communities today, "minority" students are already the majority.[32] Teachers, on the other hand, are overwhelmingly white.[33] Educators need to learn about our diversity in order to question (and teach!) effectively. Let's look at some classroom scenarios that demonstrate questioning behaviors that we've discussed in this chapter. Only this time, let's look at these behaviors as they are played out in multicultural classrooms.

Room .25

Fastest hand in the class ▶

The teacher tends to call on students who quickly and actively raise their hands. It feels good. The pace is hot. The material is being covered, and there are always some good answers.

But . . . Many fast hand-raisers are males of the dominant culture who see themselves as achievers. They want to be called on and are comfortable in the spotlight. Many are animated learners and may even shout out answers without waiting for the teacher's okay. In a typical class like Room .25, twenty-five percent of students—usually males—capture the teacher's attention. Other students, less sure of their ability, simply choose not to raise their hand and "hide" as the teacher seeks out a volunteer. Cultural cues also influence who is heard. Asian American, Hispanic, and Native American students as well as English language learners may avoid answering questions by keeping their hands down and eyes lowered. For them, shyness is prized, while talking, especially about oneself, may not be acceptable.[34] While the class moves forward, it is with the momentum of only one-fourth of the group.

Room 911

Fast talkers

This teacher asks a question, barely waits for a student response, then quickly calls on someone else. He wouldn't want to embarrass students by pressuring them to answer. And besides, if the answer isn't on the tip of their tongue, it will probably take too long to dig it out.

But . . . A closer look reveals that the teacher is giving some students more time to formulate answers. Teachers tend to wait for students they perceive as worth waiting for. A few bright youngsters benefit and receive more "airtime" to develop and share their thoughts. They are verbal and seem to hit the points the teacher values. Ability level can dictate participation level—unless the teacher is proactive. Several other students, however, with limited or nonstandard English, could use more time to respond, but the teacher usually feels the need to move on.[35] In Room 911, we see that a small group of Hispanic females, culturally conditioned to the spectator role, are hesitant to display their academic ability in this mixed-gender setting.[36] They sit silently during the rapid verbal exchanges.

Room 411

Another teacher tends to ask many knowledge-based, factual questions. She relishes these questions because the students' correct answers build self-esteem. Unlike so many other teachers, she gets plenty of participation and is pleased with how well her students are doing.

More than factual questions

But . . . Some students thrive on factual questions, which are compatible with their learning style and their need to achieve. In Room 411, some students, including English language learners and those from lower socio-economic backgrounds, feel successful when the questions are concrete and factual. They feel the teacher is really teaching what they need to learn.[37] However, there are many other students across all ethnic and class backgrounds who want more challenging questions, drawn from real life, and would appreciate a chance to be more expressive and thoughtful.[38] They are not being engaged by the teacher's questions. In fact, a number of students find the class boring. Several of them have generated their own questions—questions they never get to ask![39]

Room 007

When to let go

This teacher takes pride in delving, probing, and scaffolding to help students deepen their understanding of the topic. High expectations are held for everybody. In this class, no one gets off the hook with a quick answer or an "I don't know." When someone answers incorrectly, the teacher firmly refocuses the student.

But . . . A few students, who are of a different race from the teacher, feel intimidated by the display of the teacher's power. The two American Indian students in classroom 007 say a great deal with very few words, but they appear uncomfortable when probed to expand an answer. Most students are comfortable with this classroom culture and are thrilled with the chance to expand their answers. They feel the teacher's guidance is supportive.[40] At one point, the teacher's critical feedback unintentionally left one student feeling humiliated.[41]

Room OK

The bland OK ▶ The teacher in this room tells students that their answers are "okay" so often that some students actually count her "okays" during the lesson (and have nicknamed her Annie Okay). A few high achievers get specific feedback for correct answers, and praise for them is quite positive. Most of the time, things are "okay."

But . . . This teacher's feedback reflects biased expectations and is probably a predictor of her students' achievement. This is even more evident among culturally diverse pupils. Most of the time, she merely accepts their answers. When she was surprised at the brilliance of an African American student, her praise was particularly enthusiastic, some would say patronizing. She didn't remediate an Asian American youngster who was working quietly, as she was grateful for the good behavior and didn't focus on the work.[42]

These scenarios show how questioning might be experienced differently by students from various ethnic or racial groups. Many teacher decisions, often instantaneous and unconscious, can have a negative impact on some students. None of these teachers intended to be biased, and some were even practicing the "Seven Habits of Highly Effective Questioners." Yet, while they were practicing them, they were *not* being responsive to cultural and individual differences. As a result, some students benefited from their skills, while others did not.

Researchers who have observed classroom interaction closely have discovered gender differences as well. Analyze the following discussion, which took place in a seventh-grade class. See if you can detect any gender biases.

Room 5050

Detecting gender bias ▶ *Teacher:* How many of you have decided, maybe you're not 100 percent sure but you have considered, what you want to be when you grow up? *(The teacher looks around; about half the students shoot their hands up.)* Justin? *(Teacher walks to the area where Justin and a few other males are seated.)*

Justin: I want to be a lawyer.

Teacher: Okay, how come? What interests you about the law?

Justin: Well, my dad is a lawyer and he works hard; he likes it a lot and is really successful. Plus, I watch TV and the lawyers really have amazing stuff going on.

Teacher: Give me an example, Justin.

Justin: Well, last week they flew my dad out to California to review some medical papers for a lawsuit they're doing on diet pills.

Teacher: Sounds intriguing, Justin, and it's good to hear you're following your dad's case. What about the TV lawyers?

Justin: Most of them are like working with criminals and the court system. It's super exciting because it's really life-and-death trials.

Teacher: Great. So, you're really up for an exciting, life-and-death work life. That's going to require plenty of academic skills. What school skills do you think Justin will need? Anyone? James?

James: Lots of reading and writing work. And probably that speech class we take next semester.

Teacher: Exactly! Would you add research to that, Marcia, like our library Internet searches last week?

Marcia: Yeah. He'd have to use the Internet to find out case histories.

Teacher: Okay. *(Teacher moves to the front of the room near the chalkboard.)* Class, the list I have put on the overhead includes some "Hot Careers" for the next twenty-five years. It's not too soon for you to realize how important your course choices are as you determine your working future. And the more you learn about different careers and build your interests and skills, the better your choices will be. *(A laptop projection screen flashes on revealing "Hot Careers.")*

Hot Careers

Biotech—Patent attorney

Geriatric—Rehabilitation therapist

Psychopharmacologist

Health lawyer

Webmaster—On-line content developer

Malcolm: What's a psychophar . . . molist?

Teacher: Psy-cho-pharm-a-col-o-gist. What do you think, Malcolm? What word parts do you see in there?

Malcolm: Well, the guy who works at a drug store—pharmacist or something.

Teacher: Great start, Malcolm. The first part—psycho—you've heard that before.

Malcolm: People who work with crazy people?

Teacher: Who can help Malcolm? Isaac?

Isaac: —It's, hmm—like a, hmm, a psychologist?

Teacher: And what's that? Someone knows—yes, Hillary?

Hillary: Someone who studies people?

Teacher: No. James?

James: Someone who studies people's minds.

Teacher: Close enough. So, put it all together. What's a psychopharmacologist? Write down in your notebook, everybody, what you think it is. Great, check with your neighbor. If you both agree and really think you got it right, put a hand up. All right. Jamal?

Jamal: (who paired with Lissa) Someone who checks out people and how they feel, mentally and stuff, but works at a drug store.

Teacher: Hey, that's one way to go and maybe not a bad idea. But, it's not quite right. Someone else? Arturo?

Arturo: Someone who gives out drugs but just for people who are feeling bad mentally.

Teacher: Absolutely! It's two jobs in one. Someone who specializes in pharmaceuticals and drugs. *And* someone who knows how the mind works. So, this single career puts the two jobs together into a new specialization. We get someone who has high expertise in understanding chemistry, drugs, the human brain, and feelings. And *that's* what I wanted you to sort out about these other hot careers. They're all double jobs. Who can figure another one out? Jennifer? You have your hand up.

Jennifer: Well, another thing is that two of the jobs have lawyer in them and four have something like in health or medicine.

Teacher: Okay. If the hot careers involve two jobs put together, I want you all to think of what you might like to be when you grow up. Settle down, Jorge, you're going to like this part. The challenge is to take two things you like to do and put them together to make a whole new and interesting profession.

Gender bias examples ▷ If you read this scenario carefully, you might have noticed that the teacher directs more questions to boys than to girls. Also, boys receive more of the questions that call for higher-order thinking and more creative responses. Several studies indicate that boys, particularly high-achieving boys, are likely to receive most of the teacher's active attention.[43] They receive more praise on the quality of their academic work,[44] and they are asked more complex and abstract questions.[45] Other research has shown that teachers in mathematics classrooms give significantly more wait time to boys than to girls. The researchers conclude that "this difference could possibly have a negative effect on girls' achievement in mathematics."[46]

When teachers realize that they are distributing their attention and their questions in an unfair manner, they can change their teaching behavior. It is important to check yourself for equity in interaction and questioning so that you actively involve all your students in classroom discussions.[47]

Watch the video case *Gender Equity in the Classroom: Girls and Science* to explore how to create a learning environment that supports girls' success in science.

▼ **TeachSource Video Case**   **Gender Equity in the Classroom: Girls and Science**

To access the video, go to www.cengage.com/login. Watch the video clip, study the artifacts in the case, and reflect upon the following questions:

1. How can wait time be used to encourage girls in math and science?
2. How did the teacher encourage student-initiated questions?
3. How can the teaching methods and questioning techniques used in the Science Club promote math and science achievement for all students in a regular classroom?

If some students are denied their fair share of the teacher's questions, then the talents of even the most effective teachers do them little good. If teachers are not responsive to the cultural, racial, gender, and ethnic differences in their classes, then a growing number of America's children will be shortchanged. The Your Turn and Mastery Test that follow will start you down the path not only of more effective teaching but also of more inclusive teaching.

❯ **YOUR TURN**   **Responding to Diversity**

Take a walk back through the school hallway and revisit Rooms .25, 911, 411, and the other classes described in these scenarios. In each room, the teacher missed at least one, and often more than one, opportunity to include all the students in the instruction. Briefly rewrite these scenarios, correcting the teacher's omission and describing how the instructional changes in your scenarios create a more responsive and effective learning environment for all students.

Observation Worksheet

EQUALITY OF DISTRIBUTION OF TEACHER'S QUESTIONS

In this activity, you will discover how teachers distribute their questions in class. Obtain a seating chart indicating the location of each student, either by asking the teacher or creating one yourself. Write down the position of each student in the class, and record student names as soon as you learn them. It may also be useful to write down student gender, race, or ethnic information, since you may want to analyze the role these factors might play in class participation. You may want to practice collecting data with a seating chart by first coding information for a small group of students before collecting observational data on a whole class.

Directions: Do not use actual names of schools, teachers, administrators, or students when using this worksheet.

Observer's Name: _____

Date: _____

Grade Level: _____

Subject: _____

Class Size: _____

Background Information: Give a brief general description of the school's social, economic, and ethnic makeup.

_____

_____

Measure Response Opportunities

What to Record: Every time a student participates, either because the teacher called on the student or because the student called out, make a mark next to that student's name on your seating chart. You may want to record "SI" for student-initiated responses and "TI" for teacher-initiated opportunities, such as calling on a student to answer a question. You will want to capture every time the teacher asks a student a question, even if the student is unable to answer. Every question the teacher asks a student, including several in a row to the same student, should get a separate mark. This will capture information about which students the teacher stays with over an extended time. If a teacher has everyone respond together to a question (a choral response), the best way to record this is to simply create a category at the bottom of the page entitled "group response" and make a mark next to that category.

Reflections on Your Observation:

1. Which students were most involved in interaction? Did they create their own opportunities by calling out or vigorously waving their hands, or did the teacher tend to call on the same students repeatedly?

_____

_____

_____

2. Do these highly participatory students fit into any special group? (For example, did they sit in a specific location or did they belong to a particular racial, ethnic, or gender group?)

_____

_____

_____

3. Were any students left out entirely? Can you suggest any reasons to explain why these students did not participate?

_____

_____

_____

4. Can you offer any suggestions for getting them involved? _____

_____

_____

5. What other conclusions can you draw from your observation data? _____

_____

_____

_____

☀ Mastery Test

OBJECTIVE 5   **To describe how the growing diversity and multicultural nature of America's students impact questioning strategies**

Review the scenario you developed for Mastery Test, Objective 4. You were asked to incorporate *effective* questioning strategies that included wait time, feedback (specific praise, remediation), and student-initiated questioning. Set your classroom in a *real* school, one that reflects the diversity of an urban center, rural community, or suburban neighborhood. As you picture the students, imagine how issues of race, ethnicity, gender, and class might impact the learning. Begin by briefly describing your classroom "culture." Develop a statement for each effective strategy (wait time, specific praise, remediation, and student-initiated questioning) that demonstrates your knowledge, high expectations, and sensitivity to groups and individuals while avoiding stereotypes!

Sample: Wait time—Many of the youngsters are refugee immigrants from Southeast Asia and are the first in their family to speak English or even attend high school. Wait time will give them the chance to shift between two languages, carefully consider content, and rehearse "in their heads" before they respond aloud. Providing five seconds of teacher silence will allow them to process information and produce answers. A side benefit will be that other students will learn to be better listeners!

ADDITIONAL RESOURCES

 Readings

Banks, James and Cherry Banks (eds.), *Multicultural Education,* 6th ed. San Francisco: Jossey Bass, 2007.

Browne, Neil M., and Stuart M. Keely. *Asking the Right Questions: A Guide to Critical Thinking*, 9th ed. Upper Saddle River, NJ: Prentice Hall, 2009.

Chuska, Kenneth R. *Improving Classroom Questions*, 2nd ed. Indianapolis, IN: Phi Delta Kappa Educational Foundation, 2003.

Delpit, Lisa. *Other People's Children: Cultural Conflict in the Classroom.* New York: New Press, 2006.

Disch, Estelle. *Reconstructing Gender: A Multicultural Anthology*, 4th ed. New York: McGraw-Hill, 2006.

Sadker, David, Myra Sadker, and Karen Zittleman. *Still Failing at Fairness: How Gender Bias Cheats Girls and Boys in School and What We Can Do About It.* New York: Scribners, 2009.

Sadker, David and Ellen S. Silber (eds). *Gender in the Classroom: Foundations, Skills, Methods, and Strategies Across the Curriculum.* Mahwah, NJ: Lawrence Erlbaum, 2007.

Simon, Katherine. *Moral Questions in the Classroom: How to Get Kids to Think Deeply About Real Life and Their Schoolwork.* New Haven, Conn: Yale University Press, 2001.

Walsh, Jackie and Beth Sattes. *Quality Questioning: Research-Based Practice to Engage Every Learner.* Thousand Oaks, CA: Corwin Press, 2004.

Websites

A Questioning Toolkit: http://www.fno.org/nov97/toolkit.html
The *Educational Technology Journal* integrates philosophy and pragmatism to assist teachers in developing effective questioning techniques.

Tips for Teachers: Asking Good Questions: http://www.edb.utexas.edu/pbl/TIPS/question.html
This Web site offers practical advice on how to make the classroom learning environment more active, student-centered, inquiry-based, and metacognitive.

Effective Classroom Questioning: http://www.cte.uiuc.edu/Did/docs/questioning.htm
From Bloom's Taxonomy to wait time to quality feedback, this Web site suggests innovative ways to engage all students in your classroom.

Classroom Questioning: http://www.nwrel.org/archive/sirs/3/cu5.html
A teacher offers practical advice on how to use effective classroom questions. Here is a realistic bridge from your textbook to your classroom.

For these links and additional resources, please visit the Premium Website at **www.cengage.com/login.**

NOTES

1. Charles DeGarmo, *Interest and Education* (New York: Macmillan, 1902), p. 179.

2. John Dewey, *How We Think*, rev. ed. (Boston: D.C. Heath, 1933), p. 266.

3. Joseph Green, "Editor's Note," *Clearing House* 40 (1966): 397.

4. Thomas Merton, *The Seven Storey Mountain* (Garden City, N.Y.: Doubleday, 1948), p. 139.

5. Romiett Stevens, "The Question as a Measure of Classroom Practice," *Teachers College Contributions to Education,* no. 48 (New York: Teachers College Press, 1912); Thomas Good and Jere Brophy, *Looking in Classrooms*, 10th ed. (Boston: Allyn & Bacon, 2007); Jackie Acree Walsh and Beth Dankert Sattes, *Quality Questioning* (Thousand Oaks, CA: Corwin Press, 2005); Jim Duffy, Kelly Warren, and Margaret Walsh, "Classroom interactions: Gender of teacher, gender of student, and classroom subject." *Sex Roles* 45, no. 9/10, (2001): 579–593; William S. Carlsen, "Questioning in Classrooms: A Sociolinguistic Perspective," *Review of Educational Research* 61 (1991): 157–178; Meredith D. Gall, "Synthesis of Research on Teacher's Questioning," *Educational Leadership* 42 (1984): 40–47.

6. Gregory P. Risner, Dorothy J. Skeel, and Janice I. Nicholson, "A Closer Look at Textbooks," *Science and Children* 30, no. 1 (1992): 42–45, 73; Kenneth Tobin, "Effects of Teacher Wait Time on Discourse Characteristics in Mathematics and Language Arts Classes," *American Educational Research Journal* 23 (1986): 191–200.

7. Thomas Good and Jere Brophy, *Looking in Classrooms,* 10th ed. (Boston: Allyn & Bacon, 2007); L. M. Barden, "Effective Questions and the Ever-Elusive Higher-Order Question," *American Biology Teacher* 57, no. 7 (1995): 423–426; Meredith D. Gall and T. Rhody, "Review of Research on Questioning Techniques," in *Questions, Questioning Techniques, and Effective Teaching,* ed. William W. Wilen (Washington, D.C.: National Education Association, 1987), pp. 23–48; William W. Wilen and Ambrose A. Clegg, "Effective Questions and Questioning: A Research Review," *Theory and Research in Social Education* 14 (1986): 153–161.

8. Mary Budd Rowe, "Science, Silence, and Sanctions," *Science and Children* 34 (September 1996): 35–37.

9. Thomas Good and Jere Brophy, *Looking in Classrooms*, 10th ed. (Boston: Allyn & Bacon, 2007); Jackie Acree Walsh and Beth Dankert Sattes, *Quality Questioning* (Thousand Oaks, CA: Corwin Press, 2005); Black, Susan, "Ask Me a Question" *American School Board Journal* 188 (5), May 2001; Angelo V. Ciardiello, "Training Students to Ask Reflective Questions," *The Clearing House* 66 (May/June 1993): 312–314; Robert J. Sternberg, "Answering Questions and Questioning Answers," *Phi Delta Kappan* 70, no. 2 (October 1994): 136–138.

10. Thomas Good and Jere Brophy, *Looking in Classrooms*, 10th ed. (Boston: Allyn & Bacon, 2007); Jackie Acree Walsh and Beth Dankert Sattes, *Quality Questioning* (Thousand Oaks, CA: Corwin Press, 2005); Black, Susan, "Ask Me a Question" *American School Board Journal* 188 (5), (May 2001); Duffy, Jim, Kelly Warren, & Margaret Walsh, "Classroom interactions: Gender of teacher, gender of student, and classroom subject." *Sex Roles* 45, no. 9/10, (2001): 579–593; Robert Marzano, Debra J. Pickering, and Jane E. Pollock, *Classroom Instruction That Works: Research-Based Strategies for Increasing Student Achievement* (Alexandria, Va.: Association for Supervision and Curriculum Development, 2001); A. C. Brualdi, *Classroom Questions. ERIC/AE Digest* (Washington, D.C.: ERIC Clearinghouse on Assessment and Evaluation, 1998), ED 422 407.

11. Stephen R. Covey, *The Seven Habits of Highly Effective People* (New York: Simon & Schuster, 1990).

12. Norah Morgan and Juliana Saxton, *Teaching, Questioning and Learning* (London and New York: Routledge, 1991), p. 76; Beverly A. Busching and Betty Ann Slexinger, "Authentic Questions: What Do They Look Like? Where Do They Lead?" *Language Arts* 72 (September 1995): 341–351.

13. Carol Ann Tomlinson "Learning to Love Assessment," *Educational Leadership* 58, no. 4 (December 2007): 8–13; Carol Ann Tomlinson, "Reconcilable Differences? Standards-Based Teaching and Differentiation," *Educational Leadership* 58, no. 1 (September 2000): 6–11; Meredith D. Gall and Margaret T. Artero-Boname, "Questioning," *International Encyclopedia of Teaching and Teacher Education*, ed. L. W. Anderson (Tarrytown, N.Y.: Elsevier Science, 1995), pp. 242–248.

14. P. Smagoinsky, "The Social Construction of Data: Methodological Problems of Investigation Learning in the Zone of Proximal Development," *Review of Educational Research* 65, no. 3 (1995): 191–212.

15. J. V. Wertsch, *Vygotsky and the Social Formation of the Mind* (Cambridge, Mass.: Harvard University Press, 1985).

16. Seana Moran, Mindy Kornhaber, and Howard Gardner, "Orchestrating Multiple Intelligences," *Educational Leadership* 64, no. 1, (September 2006); Howard Gardner, "Probing More Deeply into the Theory of Multiple Intelligences," *The National Association of Secondary Principals Bulletin* 80, no. 583 (November 1996): 1–7; Howard Gardner, "Reflections on Multiple Intelligences: Myths and Messages," *Phi Delta Kappan* 77, no. 3 (November 1995): 200–209.

17. Benjamin Bloom, ed., *Taxonomy of Educational Objectives, Handbook I: Cognitive Domain* (New York: McKay, 1956).

18. Lorin W. Anderson and David Krathwohl (eds). *A Taxonomy for Learning, Teaching, and Assessing: A Revision of Bloom's Taxonomy of Educational Objectives*. New York: Longman, 2001.

19. Lynn Fox and Janet Soller, "Gender Equity for Gifted Students," in Klein, Susan S. (ed.) *Handbook for Achieving Gender Equity through Education*, 2nd ed. (New York: Lawrence Erlbaum Associates, Taylor & Francis Group, 2007), pp. 573–582; Marjorie Montague and Christine Rinaldi, "Classroom Dynamics and Children at Risk," *Learning Disability Quarterly* 24 (2001): 75–83; Jere Brophy and Carolyn Evertson, *Learning from Teaching: A Developmental Perspective* (Boston: Allyn and Bacon, 1976).

20. The findings in this section are based on the work of Mary Budd Rowe. See also Kenneth Tobin, "The Role of Wait Time in Higher Cognitive Level Learning," *Review of Educational Research* 57, no. 1 (1987): 69–95.

21. John Goodlad, *A Place Called School* (New York: McGraw-Hill, 1984/2004), p. 124.

22. Myra Sadker, Joyce Bauchner, David Sadker, and Leslie Hergert, *Promoting Effectiveness in Classroom Instruction: Final Report* (Contract No. 400-80-0033) (Washington, D.C.: U.S. Department of Education, 1984); Susanne M. Jones and Kathryn Dindia, "A Meta-Analytic Perspective on Sex Equity in the Classroom," *Review of Educational Research* 74(4), (Winter 2004): 443–471; Renee Spencer, Michelle Porche, & Deborah Tolman, "We've come a long way—maybe. New challenges for gender equity education." *Teachers College Record* 105(9), (2003): 1774–1807.

23. Jackie Acree Walsh and Beth Dankert Sattes, *Quality Questioning*, Thousand Oaks, CA: Corwin Press, 2005; *Kohn*, Alfie. "Five Reasons to Stop Saying 'Good Job'" *Young Children* (September 2001); Jere Brophy, "Teacher Praise: A Functional Analysis," (Occasional Paper No. 2) (East Lansing: Michigan State University, Institute for Research on Teaching, 1979).

24. *Ibid.*

25. A. E. Edwards and D. G. P. Westgate, *Investigating Classroom Talk*, Social Research and Educational Studies Series: 4 (London and Philadelphia: Falmer, 1987), p. 170.

26. Jackie Acree Walsh and Beth Dankert Sattes, *Quality Questioning*, Thousand Oaks, CA: Corwin Press, 2005; D. Bridges, "A Philosophical Analysis of Discussion," in *Questioning and Discussion: A Multidisciplinary Study*, ed. J. Dillon (Norwood, N.J.: Ablex, 1988), p. 26; see also J. N. Swift, C. T. Gooding, and P. R. Swift, "Using Research to Improve the Quality of

Classroom Discussion," *Research Matters . . . to the Science Teacher* (Cincinnati: The National Association for Research in Science Teaching, 1992).

27. Morgan and Saxton, *op. cit.*, pp. 105–111; Thomas Good and Jere Brophy, *Looking in Classrooms*, 10th ed. (Boston: Allyn & Bacon, 2007); Jackie Acree Walsh and Beth Dankert Sattes, *Quality Questioning* (Thousand Oaks, CA: Corwin Press, 2005); G. W. Beamon, *Sparking the Thinking of Students, Ages 10–14: Strategies for Teachers* (Thousand Oaks, Calif.: Corwin Press, 1997).

28. Ciardiello, *op. cit.*; E. van Zee and J. Minstrell, "Using Questions to Guide Student Thinking," *Journal of the Learning Sciences* 6, no. 2 (1997): 227–269.

29. Morgan and Saxton, *op. cit.*, pp. 113–125.

30. See also Margaret A. Cintorino, "Discovering Their Voices, Valuing Their Words," *English Journal* 83, no. 6 (October 1994): 33–40; Ciardiello, *op. cit.*; Sternberg, *op. cit.*; Debby Deal and Donna Sterling, "Kids Ask the Best Questions," *Educational Leadership* 54, no. 6 (March 1997): 61–63; Christine Chinn and David E. Brown, "Student-generated Questions: A Meaningful Aspect of Learning Science," *International Journal of Science Education* 24, no. 5, (2002): 521–549.

31. Carlos E. Cortés, *The Children Are Watching: How the Media Teach About Diversity* (New York: Teachers College Press, 2000), pp. 149–150.

32. "Minority Kids Seen as Majority by 2023," *Arizona Daily Star*, March 5, 2009, p. A2; The Center for Public Education, *At a Glance: Changing Demographics* (Washington, D.C.: The Center for Public Education, December 2007); U.S. Department of Education, *The Condition of Education,* Indicator 7, 2008.

33. Tom Snyder, Sally Dillow, and Charlene Hoffman, *Digest of Education Statistics 2008* (NCES 2009-020). National Center for Education Statistics, Institute of Education Sciences, U.S. Department of Education (Washington, D.C., 2009).

34. Toni Weingarten, "When quiet kids get forgotten in class," *The Christian Science Monitor* (April 26, 2005). Available at http://www.csmonitor.com/2005/0426/p11s01-legn.html; J. C. McCroskey and V. P. Richmond, *Quiet Children and the Classroom Teacher,* 2nd ed. (Annandale, Va.: Speech Communication Association, 1991).

35. Tom Strikus and Manka Varghese, "Language Diversity and Schooling," in *Multicultural Education: Issues and Perspectives,* 6th ed., eds. James A. Banks and Cherry A. McGee Banks (Hoboken, NJ: Wiley, 2007), pp. 297–325; Ron Scollon and Suzanne B. K. Scollon, *Narrative, Literacy, and Face in Interethnic Communication: An Athabaskan Case,* Working Papers in Sociolinguistics, no. 59, 1995.

36. Lisa Delpit, *Other People's Children: Cultural Conflict in the Classroom* (New York: New Press, 2006).

37. *Ibid.*; Gary Howard, *We Can't Teach What We Don't Know: White Teachers, Multiracial Schools* (New York: Multicultural Education Series, 2006).

38. Delpit, *op cit.*; Jeanne Oakes, *Keeping Track: How Schools Structure Inequality* (New Haven, Conn.: Yale University Press, 1985/2005); Gloria Ladson Billings, "Culturally Responsive Teaching: Theory and Practice," in *Multicultural Education: Issues and Perspectives,* 6th ed., eds. James A. Banks and Cherry A. McGee Banks (Hoboken, NJ: Wiley, 2007), pp. 221–245; Jacqueline Jordan Irvine, *In Search of Wholeness: African American Teachers and Their Culturally Specific Classroom Practices* (New York: Palgrave/St. Martin's Press, 2002).

39. Jim Chesebro, Roy Berko, Carol Hopson, Pamela Cooper, and Helene Hodges, "Strategies for Increasing Achievement in Oral Communication," in Cole, *op. cit.*, p. 156.

40. Delpit, *op. cit.*

41. Chesebro et al., *op. cit.,* p. 152.

42. James A. Banks and Cherry A. McGee Banks, eds. *Multicultural Education: Issues and Perspectives*, 6th ed. (Hoboken, NJ: Wiley, 2007); Christine Bennett, *Comprehensive Multicultural Education: Theory and Practice*, 6th ed, (Upper Saddle River, NJ:Allyn & Bacon, 2006); Donna M. Gollnick and P. C. Chinn, *Multicultural Education in a Pluralistic Society*, 7th ed. (Upper Saddle River, NJ: Prentice Hall, 2005).

43. Robyn Beaman, Kevin Wheldall, and Coral Kemp, "Differential teacher attention to boys and girls in the *classroom*." *Educational Review* 58, Issue 3 (2006), 339–366; Renee Spencer, Michelle Porche, and Deborah Tolman, "We've come a long way—maybe. New challenges for gender equity education," *Teachers College Record* 105 (9), (2003): 1774–1807; Jere Brophy and Thomas Good, *Teacher–Student Relationships: Causes and Consequences* (New York: Holt, Rinehart & Winston, 1974).

44. Robyn Beaman, Kevin Wheldall, and Coral Kemp, "Differential teacher attention to boys and girls in the *classroom*," *Educational Review* 58, Issue 3 (2006): 339–366; Jackie Acree Walsh and Beth Dankert Sattes, *Quality Questioning* (Thousand Oaks, CA: Corwin Press, 2005); Renee Spencer, Michelle Porche, and Deborah Tolman, "We've come a long way—maybe. New challenges for gender equity education," *Teachers College Record*, 105 (9), (2003): 1774–1807; Sadker, Bauchner, Sadker, and Hergert, *op. cit.*

45. Ibid.

46. Delores Gore and Daniel Roumagoux, "Wait Time as a Variable in Sex Related Differences During Fourth-Grade Mathematics Instruction," *Journal of Educational Research in Education* 17 (1991): 269–334.

47. For a comprehensive review of the impact of gender in schools, see David Sadker and Myra Sadker and Karen R. Zittleman, *Still Failing at Fairness: How Gender Bias Cheats Girls and Boys in School and What We Can Do About It* (New York: Scribners, 2009); Myra Sadker, David Sadker, and Susan Klein, "The Issue of Gender in Elementary and Secondary Schools," *Review of Research in Education* 17 (1991): 269–334.

Differentiating Instruction for Academic Diversity

Carol Ann Tomlinson

Image Source/Jupiter Images

■ INTASC Standards

● **Principle 1:** The teacher understands the central concepts, tools of inquiry, and structures of the discipline(s) he or she teaches and can create learning experiences that make these aspects of subject matter meaningful for students.

● **Principle 2:** The teacher understands how children learn and develop, and can provide learning opportunities that support their intellectual, social, and personal development.

● **Principle 3:** The teacher understands how students differ in their approaches to learning and creates instructional opportunities that are adapted to diverse learners.

● **Principle 4:** The teacher understands and uses a variety of instructional strategies to encourage students' development of critical thinking, problem solving, and performance skills.

● **Principle 5:** The teacher uses an understanding of individual and group motivation and behavior to create a learning environment that encourages positive social interaction, active engagement in learning, and self-motivation.

● **Principle 7:** The teacher plans instruction based upon knowledge of subject matter, students, the community, and curriculum goals.

● **Principle 8:** The teacher understands and uses formal and informal assessment strategies to evaluate and ensure the continuous intellectual, social, and physical development of the learner.

■ OBJECTIVES

1. To develop an informed, personal definition of *differentiated instruction*

2. To construct an informed, personal rationale for teaching to address learner needs

3. To depict ways in which the learner, learning environment, and curriculum are integral to differentiated or academically responsive instruction

4. To apply specific ways to differentiate content, activities, and products in response to student readiness, interest, and learning profile

5. To analyze and understand general principles of effective differentiation

6. To propose personal first steps in becoming a responsive teacher

153

| OBJECTIVE 1 | To develop an informed, personal definition of *differentiated instruction* |

Learning Activity 6.1

Nearly 100 years ago, third-grader Betsy moved from a small town to the country and found herself—in mid-year—in a one-room schoolhouse. On Betsy's first day in her new school, the teacher asked her to read aloud to the class during a group reading session. She read at length, with ease and with feeling. The teacher told her to work later in the day with the Level 7 readers. Nine-year-old Betsy was bewildered, pleased, and worried. She was puzzled because, she thought, her teacher must surely recognize that she was too small to be a seventh-grader. Shouldn't all third-graders read third-grade books? Betsy was happy because she had always wanted to read books with interesting words and ideas, and this might be her chance. She was afraid, too, however, and the fear ultimately sent her to the teacher to explain why it would not work for her to be a part of Level 7 reading. She confessed to the teacher that she would be a dismal failure with Level 7 math. Math, she explained, was her hardest subject.

Now it was the teacher's turn to look puzzled. "I've not said anything about your math," the teacher reflected. "I haven't yet checked to see what you need in math."

By the end of the first day, Betsy (also called Elizabeth Ann) had assignments for working in all her subjects—and she was confused. This wasn't like her old classroom, where everyone did the same thing at the same time.

> Elizabeth Ann fell back on the bench with her mouth open. She felt really dizzy. What crazy things the teacher said! She felt as though she was being pulled limb from limb.
>
> "What's the matter?" asked the teacher seeing her bewildered face.
>
> "Why—why," said Elizabeth Ann, "I don't know what I am at all. If I'm second-grade arithmetic and seventh-grade reading, and third-grade spelling, what grade *am* I?"
>
> The teacher laughed. "*You* aren't any grade at all, no matter where you are in school. You're just yourself, aren't you? What difference does it make what grade you're in? And what's the use of your reading little baby things too easy for you just because you don't know your multiplication table?"[1]

Almost a century ago, Betsy's teacher understood a reality that is, if anything, more evident today than at any time in our country's past: Students in a single classroom vary in important ways. The teacher also understood a correlate truth that it's easy to lose sight of in a busy classroom: A good teacher studies and actively addresses student differences as an integral part of planning and instruction.

What Is "Differentiated Instruction"?

The term *differentiated instruction* is relatively new on the educational scene. Its practice, however, is likely as old as teachers and classrooms. A given of teaching is that as long as there's more than one student in the room, the students won't all learn what the teacher has planned in the same ways, to the same degree of sophistication, or on the same timetable. In fact, even if there *were* only one student in the room, that student would exhibit noteworthy learning differences at varied developmental stages of life, across subjects, within different parts of the same subject, and even at different times of the day.

On a simple level, differentiated instruction is teaching with student variance in mind. It means starting where the kids are rather than adopting a standardized approach to teaching that seems to presume that all learners of a given age or grade are essentially alike. Thus differentiated instruction is "responsive" teaching rather than "one-size-fits-all" teaching.

A fuller definition of **differentiated instruction** is that a teacher proactively plans varied approaches to what students need to learn, how they will learn it, and/or how they can express what they have learned in order to increase the likelihood that each student will learn as much as he or she can as efficiently as possible.

The rest of this chapter "unpacks" this latter definition by examining key underpinnings of differentiation, important components of differentiation, and some practical ways to accomplish differentiation. The overarching aim of the chapter is to help prospective teachers reflect on ways in which their early professional practice can begin with the needs of learners at its center.

This chapter has suggested several definitions of *differentiated instruction.* Differentiation is the following:

- Starting where the kids are rather than adopting a standardized approach to teaching that seems to presume that all learners of a given age or grade are essentially alike
- Teaching responsively
- Proactively planning varied approaches to what students need to learn, how they will learn it, and/or how they can express what they have learned in order to increase the likelihood that each student will learn as much as he or she can as efficiently as possible

Here are a few more definitions. Differentiation is also the following:

- Making a match between learner and material to be taught[2]
- Rising to the challenge of educating every child in the classroom[3]
- Teaching that connects with the learner[4]
- Personalizing the prescribed curriculum by offering a range of learning options and support systems, and using a range of teaching and learning strategies[5]
- Proactively planning student-centered instruction that is rooted in assessment and blends whole-class, individual, and small-group instruction to provide multiple approaches to content, process, and product with the goal of maximizing the capacity of each learner[6]

☐ INTASC Principles
2, 3, 7, 8

> **YOUR TURN**   Developing a Definition of Differentiation

1. Think about a time when a learning experience (in school or out of school) was a poor fit for you. Write or sketch your impressions of what that felt like to you. Include both cognitive (learning) and affective (feeling) descriptors.
2. Now, write a note or memo to the adult in charge of that setting explaining what he or she might have done to make the situation more appropriate for your needs. If you'd rather, make a list of dos and don'ts you would like that adult to have understood and practiced.
3. Based on the definitions here and your own reflections, develop your own preliminary definition of *differentiated instruction.*
4. Come back to your definition at the end of the chapter and after your class discussion of the chapter and revise the definition to reflect new insights you have developed.

OBJECTIVE 2   **To construct an informed, personal rationale for teaching to address learner needs**

Why Differentiate Instruction?

Learning Activity 6.2

INTASC Principles 2, 3, 5

Differentiating instruction certainly calls on teachers to develop more complex professional skills than does the more typical practice of teaching as though all students in the classroom were essentially alike. It makes sense, then, to ask the question: Is it really worth the time and effort to differentiate instruction?

There are many compelling reasons to craft classrooms that vigorously attend to student differences. A rationale for differentiated instruction comes from theory, research, and educational common sense. Consider the following:

To address classroom diversity ▶

- Today's classrooms are becoming more academically diverse in most regions of the United States (and elsewhere, for that matter). Many, if not most, classrooms contain students representing both genders and multiple cultures, frequently include students who do not speak English as a first language, and generally contain students with a range of exceptionalities and markedly different experiential backgrounds. These students almost certainly work at differing readiness levels, have varying interests, and learn in a variety of ways.[7]

To challenge each student ▶

- Psychologists tell us that a student learns only when a task is a little too hard for that student. When a student can do work with little effort and virtually independently, that student is not learning, but rather rehearsing the known. When a student finds a task beyond his or her reach, frustration, not learning, is the result. Only when a task is a bit beyond the student's comfort level, and the student finds a support system to bridge the gap, does learning occur. This optimum degree of difficulty for learning is referred to as a student's zone of proximal development.[8] Considering today's diverse classrooms, it is unlikely that a teacher will be consistently able to develop one-size-fits-all learning experiences that are in the zones of proximal development of all students in a particular class.

- Brain research suggests that when tasks are *too hard* for a learner, the brain "downshifts" to the limbic area of the brain that does not "think," but rather is designed to protect an individual from harm. Also, when tasks are *too easy* for learners, those learners do not show thoughtful brain activity, but rather display patterns that look more like the early stages of sleep. Only when tasks are moderately challenging for an individual does the brain "think" in a way that prompts learning.[9] Once again, teachers will find it difficult to consistently find single tasks that are moderately challenging for all learners in a class that includes a range of readiness and experiential levels.

To address gender differences in learning ▶

- It is likely that male and female learning patterns and preferences vary. The variance probably has biological, cultural, and environmental origins. There is also, of course, great variety among both male and female populations in regard to learning. Nonetheless, it is likely counterproductive to assume that gender is an irrelevant factor in what individuals learn and how they learn.[10]

To consider cultural issues ▶

- Culture has an important bearing on how individuals learn. While it is clearly not the case that all members of a given culture learn in similar ways, it is the case that learning environments and procedures that are comfortable for many members of one cultural group may not be so to many members of other cultural groups. Students whose classrooms are a cultural misfit often do poorly in school.[11] In classrooms where varied cultural groups are represented, a single approach to teaching and learning is unlikely to serve all students well. In fact, because students in any cultural group also vary, even classrooms that are more culturally homogeneous would benefit from multiple approaches to teaching and learning.

To draw on student's interests and learning modalities ▶

- Student motivation and task persistence increase when students can work with topics that are of personal interest. Modifying instruction to draw on student interests is likely to result in greater student engagement, higher levels of intrinsic motivation, higher student productivity, greater student autonomy, increased achievement, and an improved sense of self-competence.[12] Encouraging students to link required learning to that which is personally interesting to them seems an important modification for teachers in most classrooms.

- The opportunity to learn in ways that make learning more efficient is also likely to make learning more effective. Attention to a student's preferred mode of learning or thinking promotes improved achievement.[13]

Classroom examples ▶

Beyond information provided by theory and research, most of us can draw on both personal experience and classroom observation to understand the positive impact of instruction that fits the individual and the negative impact of instruction that is a poor fit for the individual. Consider the likely outcomes for students in the following paired statements.

A	B
Juan cannot read the text in his history class and cannot understand the teacher's lectures. No provisions are made for him to get access to the information, and he doesn't know where to begin.	Juan has a textbook in his class in which the teacher has highlighted key passages so he can focus his efforts on translating essential segments. In addition, there is always the opportunity to read with a partner or to use tape-recorded text. The teacher consistently uses small-group discussions to encourage students to summarize and make sense of notes they have taken in class.
Latisha is quite a good reader. Although a first-grader, she reads at a fourth-grade level. Her teacher makes certain every student works with the same reading materials and exercises.	Latisha's teacher is aware that she is an advanced reader. Sometimes everyone in the class reads together, but most of the time students work with a variety of peers to read books of common interest at common reading levels or to share books with classmates. The teacher also works with the students in small groups to be sure she is closely addressing their needs to continue to grow as confident readers.

A	B
David has a learning disability. He understands ideas well but has a great deal of difficulty reading quickly and writing efficiently. Nearly all assessments in David's class are written. Most tests and papers have strict time limits.	David and his teacher work together to establish timetables for his written assignments. This flexibility enables him to write with less tension and to proofread his work. The teacher also generally provides more than one way to express ideas, so that David and other students can use diagrams, sketches, oral presentations, hands-on demonstrations, and so on to show their knowledge and skill.
Linda has a special education IEP for mild mental retardation. Her reading skills are below grade level. In addition, her IEP targets specific skills to help her develop important competencies not generally taught in grade-level classes.	Linda's teacher plans instructional time for small groups in her teaching routines. One focus of small groups is reading instruction and practice. Linda is one of several students in the class who need assistance in developing reading skills. Her teacher works regularly with these students on reading skills that would otherwise not be addressed in their class. In addition, her teacher streamlines project assignments for Linda and incorporates her IEP skills in the directions. That allows Linda to work with the key ideas central to instructional units while she works on skills that are important to her development.

It does not take a great deal of thought to understand the wear and tear on Juan, Latisha, David, and Linda in the "A" scenarios. It also seems evident that student attitudes and work are likely to improve in the "B" scenarios. While it's important to have theory and research to inform our classroom practice, an observant teacher receives clear clues every day that students benefit from classrooms that address their individual needs.

We know a great many things about learners and learning that suggest the importance of attending to students' differences in the classroom. We also know, however, that few classrooms are vigorously attentive to learner variance. This is the case whether students have learning disabilities, are advanced, represent varied cultures, or are second-language learners.[14]

> **YOUR TURN** | **Developing a Rationale for Differentiation**

1. Divide a sheet of paper into two columns. In the left-hand column, list all the reasons that you think cause teachers to differentiate instruction when they do so. In the right-hand column, list all the reasons that you think cause teachers not to differentiate instruction when they do not do so.
2. Examine your two lists. What patterns do you see? What do you make of the patterns? If possible, compare your lists and patterns with those of colleagues to see whether the lists and patterns are similar in any way. Write a brief paragraph about your conclusions and thoughts resulting from this exercise. If you'd prefer, you might simply list thoughts that stem from analysis of the lists or draw an editorial-type cartoon that depicts one or more of your insights.
3. Write or tape-record a letter to yourself that provides the rationale you'd like to use in deciding whether or not to teach in ways that are responsive to learner variance in your classes. Do this with the thought that you'll read the letter or listen to the tape when you complete your teaching internship and then again when you complete your first year of teaching. You may want to add to or revise the letter or tape when you conclude your work with this chapter (and other related parts of the book).

> **OBJECTIVE 3** To depict ways in which the learner, learning environment, and curriculum are integral to differentiated or academically responsive instruction

■ The Classroom Origins of Differentiated Instruction

Learning Activity 6.3

The idea of differentiated or responsive teaching is not an isolated one. Neither is it a strategy to be used on occasion when there is extra time. Differentiation is actually a way of thinking about teaching and learning that, over time, pervades everything a teacher does. The reason for the pervasiveness is that differentiation stems from increasing awareness of a key classroom element—students. That awareness then impacts all other classroom elements and a teacher's decisions about those elements.

A helpful way of thinking about the origins and impacts of differentiation is to examine the approach in regard to four classroom elements: *who* we teach, *where* we teach, *what* we teach, and *how* we teach. A brief look at the classroom as a system in which those four elements are tightly interdependent helps us understand more about what differentiation is, where it comes from, why teachers elect to teach in a differentiated way, and even a little about how differentiation might look.

Who We Teach

□ INTASC Principles 2, 3

Howard Gardner suggests that one of the greatest mistakes we make in teaching is to assume that all learners in a given classroom are essentially the same. Once we allow ourselves to believe, for example, that all our kindergartners are basically alike, that our Spanish I learners are a homogeneous group, or that our seventh-grade social studies students are pretty much the same, we give ourselves permission to teach them the same things, to use a single method, and to allot the same amount of time for each student's learning.[15]

Consider Gardner's caution as it applies to a teacher's brief description of learners in a real classroom of twenty-five students in a very recent year. This group, the teacher noted, was fairly typical of her students in past years as well. The teacher's name is Judy Rex.[16]

Mrs. Rex's classroom ▶

- Several students appeared to work on grade level in some areas but a bit above or below grade level in other areas.
- Three students had identified learning disabilities.
- Three students were second-language learners.
- Four students were identified as gifted, one of whom consistently worked as much as five years above grade level.
- Three students were taking medication for attention and hyperactivity disorders.
- Two students had diagnosed emotional difficulties.
- Three students were working with speech and/or occupational therapists.

- Several students in the class displayed problems and needs similar to those of students who had been identified as having special needs, but they had not been formally identified as needing special assistance.

Even this listing of learning variance omits important information. The students also varied in levels of security at home, economic status, degree of parental support, experiences that affect school performance, culture, gender, talents and interests, preferences for how to learn, personality, social skills, and so on.

Mrs. Rex comes to her classroom each fall not only expecting significant academic diversity in her students but also holding several other important beliefs about the students she will teach. She believes the following:

Mrs. Rex's beliefs

- Each student is a person of worth—deserving of dignity as they are, worthy of respect by both teacher and peers, and worthy of the teacher's investment of time and attention.

- Each student is an individual—like all other humans in important ways and unlike others in important ways, bringing positives that need to be developed and negatives that need to be modified in order to help the student develop effectively.

- Each student in the room is building a life—with an evolving relationship to others and to learning, with the student's potential largely hidden from view.

Uniqueness

- Each student is uniquely shaped by a combination of culture, race, gender, experience, and biology. Understanding what shapes each learner and how the classroom can extend a learner's particular strengths and possibilities is both a responsibility and an opportunity for the teacher.

- Each student is someone the teacher must come to know and understand in order to show respect, recognize individuality, develop strengths, address weaknesses, and discover potential. While she will never know any child fully, she believes she must continually attempt to learn more about each student and to use what she learns to help students grow and develop as learners and as people.

Because of Mrs. Rex's beliefs about the students she teaches, she simply cannot disregard the obvious differences among her learners. Both their commonalities and differences become central to her instructional thinking and planning. Her mindset about teaching is significantly shaped by her beliefs about the students she teaches.

Where We Teach

☐ INTASC Principle 5

Both because of her beliefs about who she teaches and because of what she knows about the impact of environment on learning, Mrs. Rex has also developed some key beliefs about where she wants to teach and where her students can best learn:

Safety

- The classroom must be a place that feels safe to students—a place where their strengths are acknowledged and affirmed, where their weaknesses are dealt with honestly but supportively, where errors are seen as an important and acceptable part of the learning process, and where the teacher teaches for success.

Acknowledgment

- The classroom must provide ongoing opportunities for each student to be known by and know the other students—a place where every student is acknowledged in positive ways, a place where each student feels a connection or affiliation.

Expectations

- The classroom must accord dignity and respect through basic expectations for each learner—attending class regularly, meeting deadlines, demonstrating growth as a learner, displaying a commitment to learning evidenced through hard work, and being a valuable colleague for peers.

INTASC Principles 2, 3

- The classroom must be a place where each student's race and culture, gender, experiences, and strengths are not only respected but reflected and valued for their contribution to learning.

Hard work and support

- The classroom must be a place where an ethic of hard work—propelled by purpose, joy, and pride—is engendered; where there is continual support for individual growth; where growth is acknowledged and celebrated; and where clear classroom routines support efficiency, clarity about expectations, and success.

Everyone is a learner and a teacher

- Both to make time for the teacher to work with individuals and small groups and to develop learner independence and a sense of ownership in learning, the classroom must support shared teaching and learning—a place where everyone has something academically important to contribute to others, where everyone has something personally important to contribute to others, where the teacher is a learner, and where students are teachers.

These beliefs about the kind of classroom she wants to help develop stem in part from Mrs. Rex's beliefs about students. The kind of classroom she develops will also contribute to or inhibit her capacity to act upon her beliefs about students. Likewise, her beliefs about where she should teach and where her students should learn both stem from and impact her beliefs about what she should teach—in other words, the nature of curriculum.

What We Teach

INTASC Principle 1

Elsewhere in this book, authors write about key elements of curriculum. What a teacher believes about curriculum greatly affects both who the teacher teaches and where the teacher teaches. A teacher who is fascinated by his or her discipline and sees its power to make people's lives richer approaches curriculum with a curricular compass different from that of the teacher who simply sees curriculum as something to be covered.

Beliefs about curriculum

Mrs. Rex has also developed beliefs about curriculum, or what she will teach. Again, it both stems from and shapes her beliefs about her students and the learning environment she will share with them:

- Curriculum should be clear and focused—the teacher must recognize and help students master what is essential for learners to know, understand, and be able to do as a result of a learning sequence.
- Curriculum should spotlight high-quality knowledge, ideas, and skills—knowledge, ideas, and skills that lead to competence in the discipline; help students make meaning of the discipline; are valued by experts in the discipline; support retention, retrieval, and transfer of knowledge; lead students toward expertise in the discipline; and necessitate thought, reflection, application, and production on the part of students.

☐ INTASC Principle 4

- Curriculum should be invitational—important, illuminating, intriguing, purposeful, and challenging to the individual.
- Curriculum should play a role in developing a hunger for learning. It is a catalyst for developing self-awareness as a learner and for developing habits and attitudes that cause a learner to effectively pursue understanding and skill.

How We Teach

☐ INTASC Principles 2, 3, 4, 5, 7

A mission for growth and success ▶

Differentiated instruction really has to do with *how* we teach. However, *how* we teach is not an entity separate from *who* we teach, *where* we teach, or *what* we teach. Rather, how we teach is a response to the other three elements.

Mrs. Rex teaches in a differentiated way. She would say she really has no other good options. If she believes every student is worthy of respect, time, and investment, she will accept the responsibility of getting to know them. The more she knows and understands them, the more invested she is in making the learning environment a good fit for each learner. The more she knows and understands them, the more determined she is to share with each of them the power of knowledge to help them develop their capacities and build more rewarding and productive lives. It becomes her mission to help each student she genuinely cares about come to love the subject matter she finds so powerful. At that point, how she teaches is a given. She will not develop a highly responsive or differentiated classroom in a short period of time. In fact, she will spend her career working toward the goal of responsive teaching, but that journey will be propelled by her growing sense of the following four elements and their interrelationship:

- Instruction must be crafted to maximize the opportunity for the growth and success of each learner in mastering essential knowledge, understanding, and skill.
- To maximize individual growth and success, instruction must be a good fit for the readiness levels, interests, and modes of learning of individual learners.
- To maximize individual growth and success, instruction must employ varied modes of presentation, varied approaches to learning, and varied routes for expressing learning—to match both curricular goals and student needs.
- To maximize individual growth and success, instruction will involve a range of student groupings—to allow for a match between learner and what is to be learned, to allow students to work in a variety of contexts to enhance opportunities for success, to "audition" students in different settings in order to understand which approaches to learning work best for different learners, and to allow the teacher to teach in ways more targeted to the needs of individuals and small groups of learners.
- To maximize individual growth and success, instruction will build student–teacher partnerships—for determining approaches that work best, for goal-setting, for monitoring growth, and for building scaffolding for success.

The next section examines concrete strategies a teacher might use to differentiate instruction. It's important to remember, however, that differentiated teaching is most powerful when it is an outgrowth of beliefs

> **YOUR TURN**   **Examining Classroom Connections in Responsive Teaching**

It is likely that classrooms in which you teach will be academically diverse. You probably can't escape academic diversity in your teaching career. What you *can* control is your response to it. Even as you begin your career as a teacher, what you believe about your work as a professional will begin to shape how you practice that profession.

1. Draw a flowchart or some other graphic representation that shows the interrelationship among who we teach, where we teach, what we teach, and how we teach in the thinking and practice of Mrs. Rex. Annotate your graphic to make sure the connections you make are clear to colleagues who look at your work.
2. Draw a similar flowchart that reflects the thinking and practice of a teacher in a one-size-fits-all classroom. Annotate this graphic with your thoughts, too. Beneath the graphic, write a statement of comparison and contrast for the two representations.
3. Develop a list of three or four of the most important beliefs you now hold about whom you will teach, where you will teach, what you will teach, and how you will teach. Beside each of the beliefs, write how you think that belief will shape your teaching.
4. It's easy to think of grading as a process that is highly prescribed—that exists apart from a teacher's beliefs about teaching. In fact, it is often the case that because we see grading as fixed, grading shapes our beliefs about teaching rather than our beliefs about teaching shaping the way we grade. What impact would you suppose Mrs. Rex's beliefs have on her grading? How would you grade to reflect the beliefs you listed in item 3?

about teaching and learning, not when it is simply a collection of techniques applied to a classroom in which students are often taught as though they were indistinguishable from one another, or in a setting that is impersonal or intimidating, or using a curriculum that feels stale and remote to learners.

OBJECTIVE 4	**To apply specific ways to differentiate content, activities, and products in response to student readiness, interest, and learning profile**

Some Approaches to Responsive Teaching

Learning Activity 6.4

There is no formula for differentiation—no single way to respond to student variance. While that is uncomfortable in some ways, it's also positive. Teachers vary just as their students do, and it's important for teachers to be able to develop processes and procedures for addressing their learners' needs in ways that simultaneously address the personality and developing expertise of the teacher.

It is nonetheless helpful, however, for a teacher to have a way of organizing his or her thinking about and planning for academically responsive teaching. For that reason, it's useful to think in terms of differentiation in response to three student traits (readiness, interest, and learning profile) in regard to three elements of curriculum (content, process, and product) and in terms of two instructional roles (teacher role and student role).

This section presents just a few examples of how a teacher might differentiate *content* (what the student should learn or how the student gets

▼ **TeachSource Video Case**   **Academic Diversity: Differentiated Instruction**

To access the video, go to www.cengage.com/login. Watch the video clip, then reflect on the following questions:

1. Why does it matter that the teacher starts planning for differentiation thinking about common learning goals? What would change if she simply set out to "cover material" without clearly delineating essential learning outcomes?
2. In what ways might it be helpful to the teacher and to the quality of her instruction that she thinks about representative students when planning differentiated lessons, rather than simply planning a differentiated lesson without particular students in mind?
3. The teacher says she feels it's important to build on student strengths rather than emphasizing their areas of need. To what degree does this approach make sense to you, and why or why not?
4. This teacher enlists the help of specialists in this differentiated lesson. If you were not able to access that support, how might you plan the lesson and carry it out so that it would still work for the range of students in your class—and for you?
5. This video case shows a teacher planning for student readiness differences. What might you do to adapt the lesson to address student interests? To address student learning profiles (or preferred ways of learning)?

access to the information and ideas), *process* (activities, or how the student comes to make sense of and "own" the content), and/or *product* (how the student shows what he or she has come to know, understand, and be able to do) in response to student *readiness* (proximity to a learning goal), *interest* (affinity for a topic or task), and/or *learning profile* (preferred way to learn), depending on whether the focus of instruction at a given moment is *teacher as presenter* or *student as worker*.[17]

In Response to Learner Readiness

☐ **INTASC Principles 2, 3**

Readiness has to do with a student's current understandings and skills relative to a particular learning goal. A task presented at a readiness level appropriate for a student will be just a little too difficult for the student to complete independently. Often, the learning goal for a task will not change in response to student readiness, but the degree of difficulty, or degree of complexity at which the student is asked to work with the goal, should match the student's current preparedness for the work. Recall that when tasks are too difficult or too simple for a learner's readiness level, achievement is likely to be impaired. Thus the goal of readiness differentiation is to make sure a learner (1) has enough background to understand the assigned material or task, (2) has to work to link what he or she already knows to something unfamiliar introduced in the material or task, (3) has a support system in the classroom to help bridge the known and the new, and (4) generally finds that success follows effort. (Watch the video case, *Academic Diversity: Differentiated Instruction* to see how an elementary teacher thinks about addressing variance in student readiness in a writing lesson.)

☐ **INTASC Principles 2, 3, 4, 5, 7, 8**

The following table lists strategies teachers can use to make the classroom fit better for a range of learners. The list is by no means complete, but it illustrates ways in which teachers teach important content with the needs of learners forming a central part of their instructional thinking and planning.

SOME APPROACHES TO DIFFERENTIATING INSTRUCTION FOR STUDENT READINESS

Adjusting for Readiness: When the Teacher Presents

Strategy	Example
Provide organizers to help students follow the presentation sequence and focus on main ideas.	To support students who have difficulty following a lecture or other oral presentation, Mr. Jameson gives students blank graphics with spaces to record main ideas and illustrations. He also completes the graphic on the overhead as he talks.
Use concrete illustrations of complex or abstract ideas and pre-teach academic vocabulary.	To support students who have difficulty with abstract information, Ms. Higgins nearly always uses objects she's brought from home to demonstrate how principles of physics work.
List key vocabulary for student reference.	To support second-language learners and other students with reading or writing difficulties, Ms. Ahmad posts a chart of important words about a topic and discusses what students know or guess about the words before she begins a discussion on that topic. She then has her students adjust their thoughts about the words as they gain new information.
Use small-group instruction as a regular means of teaching.	Ms. Abel frequently conducts mini-workshops on skills or ideas she knows will be difficult for some of her students. She individually asks some students to attend and also invites anyone who'd like help with the topic to come to the session as well. She also regularly plans reteaching sessions for students who struggle with fundamental ideas and skills and small-group sessions to extend the thinking of students whose thinking and skills are advanced.
Stop often for student reflection and questions.	Mr. Garcia stops about every seven to ten minutes when he is explaining and demonstrating at the board or overhead. Sometimes he asks students to summarize key points or apply a skill with a partner. Sometimes he asks students individually to write a summary statement or question about what they are understanding. He walks around the room to hear or read student ideas and then concludes with questions from the class before moving ahead. He also uses what he hears to shape his teaching.
Ask questions of escalating difficulty.	To make certain everyone in the class is challenged by discussions, Ms. Rentz plans question sequences that begin by asking for fundamental information and concepts and continues by increasing the complexity of questions until everyone in the class has been both affirmed and stretched by her questioning.

Adjusting for Readiness: When the Student Is Worker

Strategy	Example
Provide materials at varied readability levels.	Ms. Glenn uses text materials, supplementary print materials, and Internet resources at a wide range of reading levels on the same topics to ensure that each student has resources that are appropriately challenging for that learner.
Bridge the language gap for second-language learners.	Ms. Hendrix finds resource materials in the native languages of students whenever she can. She also ensures that in group work, there are students who can speak both English and the language of students who are just learning English. She encourages new English learners to write first in their own language and then

(continued)

SOME APPROACHES TO DIFFERENTIATING INSTRUCTION FOR STUDENT READINESS (*CONT.*)

	Adjusting for Readiness: When the Student Is Worker
Strategy	*Example*
	translate into English so their ideas are not muted by language difficulties. In addition, she meets with these students as often as possible to coach them in their new language.
Assess often and use findings to adjust plans.	Mr. Peterson thinks of everything his students do as an assessment tool. He preassesses prior to each unit. He makes quick notes during discussions, as he spot-checks homework, as he sits with individuals and small groups, and as he grades tasks in order to be more aware of students' proficiency levels. He often uses "exit cards" on which students respond briefly to questions about a day's lesson. All these are helpful to him in knowing how to adjust instruction tomorrow or in a few days.
Provide highlighted texts.	Mr. Lupinski keeps several texts on a shelf behind his desk. In each of them, he has highlighted the most essential passages. Students with learning disabilities, who are new to English, and who have other reading problems often begin by using the highlighted books to focus their energies on important ideas. Reading seems much more manageable with the highlighted texts.
Use tape recordings of text and supplementary materials.	Ms. Ishmael nearly always has a listening station in the classroom where students can hear important materials read aloud. She records some of the materials herself but often uses student and parent volunteers to make the recordings.
Provide reading partners or reading buddies.	Ms. Feinstein uses several read-aloud strategies, including reading buddies, with similar readers paired together; interest-based read-alouds of students' own choosing; and choral reading pairs in which a more able reader reads a brief passage that is then repeated by the partner, who has more difficulty with reading. She finds that paired readings not only support her struggling readers but can also be designed to challenge and support very advanced readers.
Allow students to express what they have learned in multiple ways.	Mr. Arnold often gives students the option of writing prose to explain ideas or generating annotated diagrams or other graphics that are explanatory. He also often gives students both a hands-on product and a test on a topic. He invites students with serious reading or language problems to tell him test responses or to tape-record them so that language problems don't mask understanding of content.
Provide tasks and products at different degrees of difficulty or different levels of complexity.	Ms. Avila routinely uses tiered tasks and tiered products to ensure that all of her students are working with the same essential ideas and skills, but at challenge levels that are appropriate for them individually.
Use rubrics with clear indicators of quality at varied levels of sophistication.	Mr. Fierro uses rubrics that reflect key elements of skill and understanding, and specific descriptors of student work at varied levels of competency. He works with students to set goals for next steps in growth on the rubrics, not assuming that excellence will look the same for all students at a given time.
Vary the pacing of student work.	Ms. Askins knows that her students will need different amounts of time to work on a task. Some students may need additional time for practice, others additional time for in-depth exploration of a topic. She uses "anchor activities" that give her students directions for what to do if they finish a task early.

SOME APPROACHES TO DIFFERENTIATING INSTRUCTION FOR STUDENT READINESS (*CONT.*)

Adjusting for Readiness: When the Student Is Worker

Strategy	Example
Provide homework options.	Mr. Bandy often has students diagnose their strengths and weaknesses at a given point in a unit, then provides homework options so that students can select work most likely to help them improve.
Vary test questions.	Although Mr. Conklyn's tests cover the same core knowledge, understanding, and skill, he will often vary some questions on tests. His goal is to have at least some questions targeted to a student's current level of understanding and skill.
Coach for success.	Ms. Bellin actively moves among her students whenever they are working on a task. She monitors their progress, assesses their understanding, and coaches them individually to help them reach and extend both group and personal goals for achievement. These conversations are guided by rubrics and student samples that help students identify criteria for success and understand what quality work might look like.
Use instructional strategies such as learning centers and learning contracts to enable students to work with key content at their level of development.	Mr. Fellini routinely gives students learning contracts near the end of units of study. He designs the contracts so that all students work with the big ideas or principles of the unit, but also so that skills on a particular student's contract are a match for that student's current needs. He uses ongoing assessment information as a guide in developing varied versions of the contracts.

INTASC Principles
2, 3, 4, 5, 7, 8

Most of the time, a teacher can help virtually all students explore the same important concepts, understandings, and skills by varying the complexity of student tasks, adjusting pacing, and providing different support systems. Sometimes, however, it is necessary to change what students are studying. This is particularly true when students are working on a relatively linear sequence of skills, as is often the case in spelling, math computation, and some foreign-language acquisition. In many of these instances, a student simply cannot move to a new step of proficiency until he or she has mastered the previous step. Once a student has mastered a step, there is no growth as long as the student continues to work at the same level of mastery. In such instances, teachers do well to consider opportunities for students to work on the skills they need in order to progress, rather than force-fitting everyone into a lesson that misses the target for most learners. For example, it makes little sense for every sixth-grader always to have the same list of spelling words when some of the students are spelling at a first-grade level and others like college students. Similarly, a student who has not developed number sense will not likely succeed with addition and subtraction. Likewise, a student who is already adding and subtracting gains nothing from a continuing study of what a number is and how it is represented.

Teaching in response to students' varying readiness levels begins when a teacher asks the question: Is what I'm teaching today and how I'm teaching today likely to stretch each student a bit beyond his or her comfort level? When the answer is "no" for some students in the class, a teacher who intends to make the day work for each student in the classroom begins to ask: What adjustments can I make to ensure that each learner is challenged in a way that enhances his or her opportunity to work hard and succeed as a result of the work? Remember that "working hard" and "success" are highly individual concepts.

In Response to Learner Interest

☐ INTASC Principles
2, 3, 4, 5, 7

Interest has to do with a student's proclivity for a topic. Interests can be influenced by cultures, experiences, and a learner's particular strengths. When a student finds a topic interesting, motivation and engagement increase and achievement is likely to follow. Teachers can learn to incorporate students' interests into most facets of the curriculum. Teachers also have a great opportunity to help students develop *new* interests because of curriculum and instruction that are dynamic and relevant to students. The goal of differentiation based on learner interest is to help a student connect his or her particular talents, experiences, and preferences to required content. Given the interrelatedness of all knowledge, capturing student interest and relating it to what students "have to learn" is really not so difficult.

As is the case with differentiation in response to student readiness, there is no formula for how to modify instruction to tap into student interest. The next table suggests a few approaches to differentiation based on learner interest.

A teacher who differentiates instruction based on learner interest asks the questions: How can the content I teach become a catalyst for developing personal interests and talents, and how can personal talents and interests become a catalyst for developing students' passion about the content I teach? These teachers understand that learning is a two-way swinging door in which what students care about and what they need to learn can provide a common passageway to achievement and personal development.

☐ INTASC Principles
2, 3, 4, 5, 7, 8

SOME APPROACHES TO DIFFERENTIATING INSTRUCTION FOR STUDENT INTERESTS

Adjusting for Interest: When the Teacher Presents	
Strategy	*Example*
Link required subject matter and interests of students.	Mr. Brewster frequently uses examples from music, sports, literature, current events, and other areas of interest to his students to illustrate concepts and skills from the content he teaches.
Find out what is appealing to students about their areas of interest, and show them those elements in what you teach about.	Ms. D'Angelo looks for *why* her students like what they like. They may, for example, be drawn to humor, action, reflection, human stories, making or creating things, and so on. She then teaches in a way that brings out those elements in her presentations. She helps students come to understand why they like what they do and that those things are a part of what she teaches.
Show students how what you teach connects with and furthers your own interests.	Ms. Aiken often uses one of her interests as a metaphor for what she is teaching. For example, she recently talked about how themes in history are like themes in music. She explained to students that thinking about her content in relation to something else she liked made both things more interesting for her. Then she challenges students to reflect on how elements of her subject are related to their own interests.

SOME APPROACHES TO DIFFERENTIATING INSTRUCTION FOR STUDENT INTERESTS (*CONT.*)

Adjusting for Interest: When the Teacher Presents

Strategy	Example
Show students how the content you teach shapes people's lives.	Ms. Lightfoot makes it a point to share with her students stories about people who have shaped the discipline she teaches and about people whose lives are now centered in that discipline in one way or another. She is careful to use illustrations from various cultures, occupations, and walks of life. She finds that many of her students develop new interests in a subject when they see it as attached to life in some way.
Teach with joy in mind.	Mr. Washington always reminds himself as he plans presentations that students respond to joy, mystery, purpose, and enthusiasm. He finds that his young learners often develop ownership in ideas and skills he presents with those characteristics at the heart of his teaching.
Use student interest surveys and poll parents to understand student interests.	Early in the year, Ms. Todd gives her students general-interest surveys she has developed. As the year goes on, she seeks other ways to elicit student interests—for example, discussions, bulletin boards where students post questions of interest, and journal writing about interests. She also asks students to give her ideas about how she can draw on their interests in class.
Use interest centers and interest groups.	Mr. Leland keeps a space in the room where he and the students contribute materials related to the topic they are studying. He encourages the students to use the area to learn more about ideas and people of special interest to them as they study. He also uses interest-based discussion groups from time to time so students can discuss topics of interest in the content with peers who share the same interests. He also likes to use the cooperative strategy called Group Investigation, which teaches students skills of investigation and presentation as they learn about a student-selected aspect of the content.
Allow students to specialize in subtopics of a larger topic.	Mr. Francisco often asks his students to select one aspect of the unit they will study in which they would like to specialize. He provides time and structures for students to explore these preference areas as a way to strengthen their affinity for the subject and expand their knowledge about it.

Adjusting for Interest: When the Student Is Worker

Strategy	Example
Design tasks and products that invite students to link concepts and skills in your content to areas of interest.	Ms. Kiernan routinely asks students to show how key concepts and skills they are learning in language arts are related to student interests. For example, students have examined how the "rules" of writing vary in novels, journalism, music, science, and so on. They have also recently examined how the concept of interdependence is evidenced in athletics, the arts, science, families, governments, and literature, their primary content area.
Use WebQuests that allow students to explore facets of a larger topic that are of particular interest.	Ms. Melagros often uses WebQuests as a way of introducing units of study. She poses five or six open-ended questions about what students will soon be studying. The questions are designed to pique student curiosity and also to help students

(continued)

SOME APPROACHES TO DIFFERENTIATING INSTRUCTION FOR STUDENT INTERESTS (*CONT.*)

Adjusting for Interest: When the Student Is Worker

Strategy	Example
	forge links between their own interests and what they will study. Individuals or pairs of students select the question they want to pursue and complete a WebQuest on the question. Ms. Melagros bookmarks web sites at different reading levels to ensure that all of her students can find resources useful to them. She plans opportunities for students to share what they learned about the key questions throughout the unit as appropriate.
Provide choices.	Mr. Lin finds his students' interest enhanced almost any time he gives them choices about their work—where to sit, with whom to work, resources to use, timelines for accomplishing tasks, criteria for success, topics for investigation, and so on.
Encourage students to select modes of expressing learning.	Ms. Larsen carefully outlines for students which basic information, ideas, and skills their work must demonstrate, but she provides options for how students present their work. Among the options may be such things as monologues, editorial cartoons, video clips, museum exhibits, essays, and panel discussions.
Provide opportunities for guided independent investigations of interest areas.	Ms. Wannamaker includes independent study as a part of each year's curriculum. The lengths of the studies vary with student readiness and breadth of interest. She meets with students to work on aspects of independent learning such as posing good questions, using resources effectively, analyzing data, drawing conclusions, setting goals and timelines, and so on. Her goal is to help each student stretch in capacity to learn independently. The choice of topic is largely set by student interest.
Use Expert Groups to allow students to explore areas of interest in depth.	Mr. Lide often begins a unit by inviting students to join an "Expert Group" of their choice. Students in the Expert Groups explore guiding questions about a particular topic in the unit in order to develop a deeper understanding of the topic. Expert groups help Mr. Lide present information and design student work when their topic comes up in the unit.
Help students develop mentorships in interest areas.	Ms. Elkins uses mentorships with a variety of students to help them develop or extend interests. Mentors may be professionals or older students with developed interests in areas of interest shared by her students. She finds mentors can be particularly helpful in showing students how to apply ideas and skills in authentic ways and how to assess the quality of their work in authentic ways.

In Response to Learner Profile

☐ INTASC Principles
2, 3, 4, 5, 7

☐ INTASC Principles
2, 3, 4, 5, 7

Learning profile relates to preferences for how to learn. The goal of learning profile differentiation is to tap into a learner's best ways of learning, while perhaps also helping learners expand the number of avenues to learning that work for them. Learning profile is influenced by at least four factors: learning style, intelligence preference, gender, and culture.

Learning style refers to the environmental conditions in which a person is mostly likely to concentrate on, internalize, and retain information and skills, and it often relates to categories such as environment, physical needs, and interactions with others.[18] Used in that way, learning style might include such factors as level of noise, degree of movement, kind of seating, preference for a mode of presentation, preference for working alone or with a partner, and so on.

Intelligence preference refers to thinking style. Robert Sternberg suggests that individuals are likely to have a preference for learning analytically (in a sort of typical school-oriented fashion with an emphasis on logical arrangement of ideas, summary and repetition of information, and dealing with ideas in a text–lecture–test format), practically (in a way that encourages seeing how people use ideas and skills in the real world and learning ideas and skills in a real-world context), or creatively (in ways that tap into problem solving and imagination).[19] Howard Gardner suggests that individuals have proclivities for one of eight intelligences that he calls verbal-linguistic, mathematical-logical, bodily-kinesthetic, musical, spatial, interpersonal, intrapersonal, and naturalist. These intelligences are described briefly in Chapter 5 on page 114.[20] Gardner and Sternberg suggest that both heredity and environment affect our intelligence preferences. Both propose that attending to an individual's intelligence preferences in the learning process enhances learning. We can address intelligence preferences by presenting ideas and information in a variety of modes and by encouraging students to explore and express what they learn in a variety of ways. Often that means we have to stretch our own repertoires of teaching and learning in order to tap into the full range of intelligence preferences in our classes.

Culture and *gender* also affect our preferences for learning. While culture and gender help shape both environmental and intelligence preferences, they can also affect how we relate to others (for instance, whether we prefer to work alone or in groups; whether we focus more on groups or individuals; whether we are more responsive to messages from self, peers, adults, or a combination), how we process information (for instance, whether we learn better from whole to part or from part to whole, in a linear or nonlinear way, through collaboration or competition, orally, visually, or spatially; whether we are people-oriented or task-oriented; whether we learn best inductively or deductively; whether we relate best to facts or meanings; whether we are creative or conforming), and how we see ourselves in the world (for instance, whether we see ourselves as capable or incapable, whether we are present-oriented or future-oriented, whether we see ourselves as rule makers or rule followers, whether we see ourselves as vulnerable or powerful, whether we are self-directed or other-directed). While it is always a mistake to assume homogeneity within any culture or gender, it is the case that *patterns* of learning preference exist within a culture or gender. In general, schools serve best those whose culture is dominant in schools. There are exceptions to that trend, too, however.

The goal of a teacher who differentiates instruction in response to student learning preferences should *not* be to categorize students by gender, culture, intelligence preference, and so on and draw conclusions about the student based on those categories. The teacher should not prescribe how a student will learn or limit how that student might learn. Rather the teacher's goal is to create a classroom that is flexible enough—offers enough options—for students to investigate how they learn best and make informed choices about what approaches to learning will serve them well.

We know a great deal about learning profiles—so much, in fact, that it can be daunting to consider the options. It is likely that no teacher could address all the possible learning profile factors and options. A more

Sternberg: analytical, practical, or creative?

Gardner's eight intelligences

Culture and gender affect worldview, roles

Don't use categories

realistic goal is to begin by selecting a few learning profile options that seem both important and obtainable, talking with students about them, and establishing a classroom in which students have enough choices about learning to find an approach that seems comfortable. The following table presents a few ways of thinking about learning profile differentiation. The goal of the table, as with the two previous ones, is to be not exhaustive but illustrative.

Don't assume ▶

Understanding the variety of learning profile options takes study and time. It is particularly important in today's culturally diverse classrooms that teachers invest time in understanding the traditions, values, and perspectives of all the students they serve. It's much easier for a teacher to assume everyone sees the world (including school) as he or she does. But this is an inaccurate assumption that contributes to considerable discomfort, disenfranchisement, discouragement, and lowered achievement in large numbers of students.

Invite student input ▶

No teacher can know every student thoroughly. Every teacher can, however, learn far more about more students by setting out to do so than by assuming it is impossible to know them. In the beginning, just give students learning profile choices and have them share what they learn about themselves with you. It's also a wonderful habit to develop early in teaching to ask students often to share with you their ideas about how to make the class a better fit for all of them.

Parents deepen the picture ▶

It's also important to build bridges with parents to learn more about students. Over time, a teacher comes to know in breadth a great deal about a particular age group—for example, fourth graders or tenth graders. It will always be the case, however, that parents know their students in greater depth than teachers can. A parent can provide invaluable information about student interests, how the student learns, what has encouraged or discouraged the student in school in the past, and so on. Creating opportunities to communicate with parents and listening carefully to them also send important signals about the teacher's desire to collaborate with parents for student success. That can go a long way to helping parents feel invited into their learner's school and school experiences.

☐ INTASC Principles 2, 3, 4, 5, 7

SOME APPROACHES TO DIFFERENTIATING INSTRUCTION FOR STUDENT LEARNING PROFILE

Adjusting for Learning Profile: When the Teacher Presents	
Strategy	*Example*
Highlight past and contemporary contributions to the discipline by people from varied cultures and both genders.	Ms. Phillips talks about contributors to the field she teaches as a routine part of each unit. She includes contributors from many cultures and both genders. She also carefully relates instances of people at work in the discipline throughout the local area. She routinely provides students with web sites at varied levels of reading difficulty and sometimes in the first languages of her English-language learners where students can go to learn more about contributors to the discipline she teaches.
Present multiple perspectives on topics and issues.	Ms. Losario raises complex issues and multifaceted problems that call on students to use their knowledge and think deeply. She encourages students to look for varied viewpoints on the issues and lets them know they are thinking effectively when they do so.

SOME APPROACHES TO DIFFERENTIATING INSTRUCTION FOR STUDENT LEARNING PROFILE (*CONT.*)

Adjusting for Learning Profile: When the Teacher Presents

Strategy	Example
Present in oral, visual, and tactile modes.	Mr. Barsel always uses an overhead projector as he talks with the class. He consistently uses pictures of what he is talking about and often constructs models in front of the class. Often he provides manipulatives for students so they can work along with him. He finds that many web sites provide video clips, audio, or computer animations that make ideas clearer and more appealing to students.
Design presentations to move through a cycle of intelligence or other learning preferences.	Ms. Tepper often plans for analytical, practical, and creative illustrations and questions in her presentations. This approach ensures that each student identifies with at least one segment of the presentation and also helps students expand their learning options.
Use wait time and other approaches to reflection and student participation.	Ms. Akimba regularly uses strategies like Think–Pair–Share to ensure participation by students, including those who are less assertive in speaking before the class, those who like to reflect before they speak, those who enjoy speaking more often, and those who are reticent. She also honors the need for reflection by alerting students early in the week or marking period to tasks that will come later.
Use whole-to-part and part-to-whole approaches.	Mr. Lloyd is always certain to explain the purpose of the lesson as well as its details—to be sure students are clear on both the "what" and the "why" of what they are learning. He also routinely uses concept maps of the unit and year to help students see how parts of the curriculum connect.
Use concrete examples of abstract ideas.	Mr. Peterson shows students how the ideas he teaches look when they are used in people's daily lives, jobs, and hobbies. He also guides students in using objects (the familiar) that can serve as metaphors for what they are studying (the unfamiliar).
Use contemporary technologies to expand options for student exploration and expression of content.	Ms. Hobkin uses blogs, vlogs, wikis, and video interpretations of readings as options for students to share ideas about what they are reading and learning. She finds that for many of her students, these forms of exchange and expression feel natural. She also finds that they enhance student understanding.

Adjusting for Learner Profile: When the Student Is Worker

Strategy	Example
Develop tasks and assessments that ask students to examine multiple perspectives with empathy for various vantage points.	Mr. Malonowski uses "Think Tanks" in his class during many units. Small groups of students work together throughout the unit to develop one of several possible positions on issues. As the unit concludes, the Think Tank groups present and defend their perspectives. They also assess the effectiveness of all Think Tank presentations using a rubric developed by the students and teacher. One criterion for success is helping peers understand perspectives other than their own on an issue.
Honor student needs to work alone or with peers.	Ms. Lukin often encourages students to work alone, with one peer, or with a small group in completing activities and products. She also works with students to gain the skills they will need to succeed in whichever setting they select.

(*continued*)

SOME APPROACHES TO DIFFERENTIATING INSTRUCTION FOR STUDENT LEARNING PROFILE (*CONT.*)

Adjusting for Learner Profile: When the Student Is Worker

Strategy	*Example*
Offer multiple modes of investigation to students.	Mr. French often gives students the choice of a practical, analytical, or creative task as they work to develop new understandings and skills.
Offer multiple modes of expressing learning.	When possible, Mr. Largent develops product assignments with several modes of presenting student understanding. In a given unit, students can write a how-to piece, develop a PowerPoint presentation, or present a video or live demonstration. In each case, the same essential knowledge, understanding, and skills are requirements for whichever mode a student selects.
Offer options for competition or collaboration.	Ms. McAlister sometimes uses competitions as a mode of review for tests, sometimes uses collaborative study groups, and often gives students a choice of which way to prepare for tests.
Develop a classroom with flexible spaces.	Often Ms. Ellis's students have the option of working at a table, at an individual desk, or on the floor. She also encourages students to stand when they do paired "quick shares" of ideas during class discussions.
Develop a classroom that attends to varied needs for sound and visual stimulation.	Mr. Renfrow has some sections in his classroom that do not have things posted on walls and bulletin boards to make it easier for students who are distracted by "busy" space to work. He also uses "quiet zones," headsets, and earplugs to help students who need to screen out noise. He and his students work together to balance the needs of students whose visual and auditory needs differ.
Balance structure and openness.	Ms. Carver has learned to present task and product directions in a more structured way for some of her students and a more open-ended way for others. However, she also works with highly structured students to become more flexible and highly creative students to attend to structured requirements.
Accommodate students who need to move.	In Ms. Smith's classroom, students who need to get up and move around are free to do so as long as they don't disrupt other students. She has found that these learners are far more successful and she is far less frustrated than when she tried to keep them seated and still all the time. Sometimes she even invents jobs for them to do so that they will need to move around and use some of their energy.
Help students learn to be aware of their own learning preferences.	Ms. Gwaltney asks her students to record their experiences in varied learning modes. She guides them in analyzing what they learn about themselves and in making decisions about ways they elect to learn.
Use web sites that provide models of content.	Ms. Aaron bookmarks web sites for her students that provide explanations of important ideas at varied levels of difficulty as well as providing visual interpretation of the ideas at work. She also points students to web sites that provide analytical, practical, and creative applications of key ideas.

> **YOUR TURN** **Planning to Differentiate Instruction Based on Learner Need**

It is great practice to look at a variety of lessons through the lens of differentiation in response to students' readiness levels, interests, and learning profile. The more you think about the available options to make the classroom a better fit for more learners, the more likely you are to develop practices that allow you to do so.

1. Look at a chapter in a textbook for students of the age you might teach or in a college text you have used. Create a pre-assessment you think would be appropriate to determine student readiness to master the knowledge, understandings, and skills in the chapter. Have a colleague review the chapter and your pre-assessment to see whether there is a good match between the learning goals of the chapter and your pre-assessment.

2. Select a lesson that you have taught, that you have been taught recently, or that you have observed. Record what you think the learning goals for the lesson were. Then develop an activity for the lesson that you believe clearly addresses the learning goals. Next, develop at least two more versions of the activity—one that is more appropriately challenging for a very advanced learner and one that is more appropriately challenging for a student who has great difficulty with reading, writing, and abstract thinking. Remember that (1) the learning goals for the versions should

remain the same, (2) the activities don't need to be totally different from each other, and (3) the versions need to be more and less complex, not to provide more work or less work.

3. Think about a teacher you've had who was successful in either extending an interest you already had or developing a new interest in you. Write a letter to that teacher explaining what the teacher did to foster your interest and what that has meant to you over time.

4. Interview someone who may have a different view about school based on gender, culture, economic status, or particular life experiences. Find ways in which that person experienced school differently than you did. Note insights the conversation gives you as a teacher. If possible, share what you found out with several other peers who completed the same task.

5. Add at least one additional strategy for differentiation and an example of it to each of the three tables in this chapter.

OBJECTIVE 5 **To analyze and understand general principles of effective differentiation**

Key Principles of Differentiated Instruction

Learning Activity 6.5

There is no formula or template for developing a differentiated or academically responsive classroom. Precisely how a teacher develops processes and procedures that ensure attention to varying needs of learners will vary with the personality of the teacher, age of students, stage of professional development of the teacher, subject being taught, length of time available for teaching a given subject, and so on.

There are, however, some general principles that guide effective differentiation. They stem from the teacher's unflinching belief in the capacity of each student to succeed, the teacher's knowledge about learners and learning, and the common sense of experience in a classroom. Below are ten key principles of effective differentiation. The list is not complete, but it illustrates some important hallmarks of most effectively differentiated classrooms:

Proactive ▶

1. *The core of the differentiation is proactive rather than reactive.* The teacher comes to class with several routes to learning already planned rather than with a one-size-fits-all lesson that he or she will adjust on the spot when it becomes apparent the lesson is not working well for

☐ **INTASC Principle 7**

one or more students. On-the-spot adjustment can be very important in any classroom. However, it is unlikely that impromptu modifications to lesson plans can consistently be robust enough to address the needs of learners who are far behind in understanding, who are far ahead in understanding, who don't speak English fluently, and so on.

Clear about content ▶

☐ **INTASC Principle 1**

2. *The teacher is clear about what constitutes essential knowledge, understanding, and skills for any segment of the curriculum.* This is not only necessary to achieve sound learning in any classroom but also takes on additional importance in a differentiated classroom. It is these content essentials that must serve as the focus of instruction for students who have learning problems, should generally serve as the focus for additional challenge for advanced learners, and will give all learners a common opportunity for sharing and discussion even though their routes to the content essentials will sometimes differ.

Respectful tasks ▶

☐ **INTASC Principle 5**

3. *The teacher provides "respectful tasks"*[21] *for all learners.* When student tasks vary, the teacher works to ensure that each one is equally interesting, equally inviting, and equally powerful. The goal is for each student to find his or her work as appealing as that of any other student. This principle also reinforces the belief that virtually all students should work at a high level of thought with the essential knowledge, understanding, and skills that are key to the particular activity or product.

Continual assessment ▶

☐ **INTASC Principle 8**

4. *The teacher continually assesses student understanding and adjusts instructional plans based on what the assessment reveals.* A teacher in an effectively differentiated classroom doesn't give more tests or assignments than do teachers in most other classrooms. Rather, the teacher in a responsive classroom sees everything the student does as a source of information about how learning is progressing. Thus discussions, homework, activities, small-group conversations, and student products all become indicators of student growth. The teacher looks for clues in all these indicators, reflects on what he or she sees, and modifies instructional plans based on those reflections.

Community ▶

☐ **INTASC Principle 5**

5. *The teacher works hard to establish a sense of community.* In these classrooms, students come to understand and value the contribution of each member of the community. Students feel safe and accepted as they are, but they also feel a sense of persistent encouragement to grow and find support in doing so.

Adaptability, flexibility ▶

☐ **INTASC Principles 2, 3, 4, 5**

6. *Flexibility is a hallmark.* The teacher seems always to be asking: What's another way to do this? How else can we help students learn effectively and efficiently? Teachers work to use time, materials, and space in flexible ways. Flexible grouping is also a central goal in effective differentiation. That is, the teacher plans for individual, whole-class, and small-group work in each learning cycle. In addition, the teacher ensures that each student regularly works in a variety of student groupings—sometimes based on readiness, sometimes based on interest, and sometimes based on learning profile. Sometimes the groupings are more homogeneous in nature (with students at similar readiness levels or with similar interests) and sometimes they are more heterogeneous (such as mixed readiness groups or groups in which students bring a variety of talents to accomplish a common goal). Sometimes the teacher assigns students to groups, sometimes students decide on groupings, and sometimes groups are assigned randomly. A goal of flexible grouping is to balance a student's opportunity to experience work targeted to his or her particular needs with the opportunity to work in varied contexts and with a variety of peers.

Routines ▷

☑ **INTASC Principles 2, 5**

7. *There are clear operational routines.* Students know how to move around the room efficiently and quietly. They know how to get and return materials appropriately. They know what to do when they are assigned to a particular task or area of the room. They know how to get help when the teacher is busy. They know how to turn in work. It's safe to say that in classrooms where multiple tasks occur simultaneously and smoothly, the teacher has taught the routines for success every bit as carefully as he or she has taught math or art.

Responsibility ▷

☑ **INTASC Principles 2, 5, 7**

8. *The teacher and students share responsibility for the classroom, for teaching, and for learning.* A teacher's role is both enhanced and streamlined when the teacher comes to understand that students are teachers, too—and that teachers are learners. Teachers in student-centered classrooms ask the question: What tasks and roles am I now assuming that my students could learn to do for the class? The teacher not only enlists student help in those roles but also consistently asks student advice on how to make virtually all aspects of the class more effective. Further, a teacher in an effectively differentiated classroom works with the students to envision and bring into being a classroom in which individual differences are honored. Both philosophy and practice are shared among all members of the class.

Helps students to stretch ▷

☑ **INTASC Principles 1, 4**

9. *The teacher "teaches up."* It's likely that we underestimate the potential of nearly all students. If the goal of a differentiated classroom is to maximize the capacity of each learner, then the teacher must continually encourage each student to "stretch." Thus it is generally the case in a differentiated classroom that the teacher is looking for ways to push each student a bit beyond his or her comfort level and trying to avoid student opportunities to "coast." This can be a particular challenge for the teacher in regard to advanced learners, who are not accustomed to stretching because school often assumes students are successful when they reach a norm. No student is well served in school, however, unless that student finds his or her capacity extended by school.

Emphasis on growth ▷

10. *There is a focus on growth.* This means at least two things. First, each student is accountable for progressing or growing in important knowledge, understanding, and skills, and the teacher is accountable for guiding and supporting that growth. A student's point of entry into a subject is out of the control of the teacher and student. Both, however, can accept responsibility for growth from that point on. Second, this focus necessitates that growth (or lack of growth) be acknowledged as part of grading.

❯ YOUR TURN   Examining the Principles of Effective Differentiation

1. Divide a sheet of paper into two columns. Label the left-hand column "Proactive Differentiation" and the right-hand column "Reactive Differentiation." Now, examine the three tables in the section on Objective 4. List all the examples of proactive or preplanned differentiation from all three tables in the left-hand column and all the examples of reactive, or on-the-spot, differentiation in the right-hand column. Also include your own examples generated for Learning Activity 6.4. Finally, list as many reasons as you can that proactive differentiation is likely to be more

effective than reactive differentiation in academically diverse classrooms.

2. Earlier in the chapter, it is asserted that effective differentiation grows from a teacher's philosophy about whom we teach, where we teach, what we teach, and how we teach. Write a brief statement about how each of the ten key principles of differentiation in this section is related to beliefs about these four elements of a teacher's philosophy. If you'd prefer, create and annotate a graphic that shows the connections.

To propose personal first steps in becoming a responsive teacher

Starting the Journey Toward Responsive Teaching

Learning Activity 6.6

Beginning teachers, like the students they teach, vary in important ways. Some are younger, some older. Some have many experiences leading groups of people, some have few such experiences. For these and many other reasons, the professional development of new teachers does not follow a single timetable or a single path.

Nonetheless, it is generally the case that beginning teachers are developing the "gross-motor skills" of teaching. Differentiation is a "fine-motor skill" of teaching.[22] Creating a classroom that attends to the multiple needs of learners might then seem out of reach to someone at the beginning of a teaching career. It is the case, however, the refined skills of teaching, like refined skills in any human endeavor, are developed over time. A beginning teacher generally cannot fully differentiate instruction in the first year or two of teaching. However, there are first steps in the process of learning to be a responsive teacher—and some of these are within the reach of teachers new to the profession. Excellence in teaching is progressive—earned year by year when teachers set their own sights on the kind of continual growth we ask of students.

First steps

Here are a few possible early steps toward developing an academically responsive classroom. They reflect the early stages of practices that can become more refined in each successive year as a teacher moves along a continuum of professional knowledge, understanding, and skills from novice toward expert educator.

Study students

INTASC Principles 2, 3, 8

- *Reflect on students.* Be a student of your students. Study them. Take notes on what you see whenever you can. Try to understand how their attitudes, behaviors, and achievements change as circumstances in the classroom change. Particularly try to understand the link among classroom structures, classroom behavior, and classroom success. Be a student of your students' cultures so that you can build on their varied cultural strengths and interests in the classroom. When you can, share your thinking about the classroom with your students and ask them to help you make the classroom better. This early focus on students ultimately develops the root system of responsive teaching.

What matters?

INTASC Principle 1

- *Work for increasing clarity about the curriculum.* Continue to ask yourself: What really matters in this lesson or unit? How can I present this in a way that helps students genuinely understand what it means and why it matters? How can I share the important knowledge, understanding, and skill with my young learners in a way that makes learning inviting for them? Clarity about the essentials, meaning, and power of the curriculum will ultimately enable you to be both focused and flexible with the curriculum and to find multiple routes to inviting students to learn.

Foster routines and reflection

- *Develop and practice management routines.* In the beginning, management routines may be as simple as taking attendance without wasting time or returning papers without losing the attention of students. Take time in your planning to envision how you'd like a

▼ TeachSource Video Case · **Classroom Management: Best Practices**

To access the video, go to www.cengage.com/login. Watch the video clip and think about the following questions.

1. It's clear that the teachers in the video plan carefully for classroom management. What plans do you believe will be most important for you as a new teacher in your grade or subject to ensure that your instruction can be responsive to students with varied learning strengths and needs?

2. What do you see as the connection between student-teacher connections, building classroom community, and success with addressing varied learner needs? List as many connections as you can.

3. The seventh-grade boy in the video talks about the difference between teacher actions that attend to student concerns and ones that escalate teacher/student tensions. How do you think effective differentiation would contribute to that difference?

☐ **INTASC Principles 2, 5**

procedure to look, then plan step by step to make it work that way. After you've tried your plans, take time to reflect on what worked and what you can do to make it work even better next time. Not only does each success increase your capacity to handle more complex classroom routines, but it also clarifies your role as leader for both your students and you. (Watch the video case, *Classroom Management: Best Practices* to guide your thinking about how best-practice classroom management intersects with the principles of differentiation.)

Think beyond grades ▸

• *Think of assessment as more than grading.* Remind yourself often that what goes in the grade book is of less value to you and your students than what you can learn about student understanding from examining work, giving students feedback on it, and using what the student work shows you as you plan instruction. Become a hunter-and-gatherer of information about students from any source at your disposal. Brief assessments that you administer before a unit begins, journal entries, classroom or small-group discussion, student Individual Educational Plans, observation of students as they work, and myriad other readily available data sources can help you match what you teach to a learner's needs.

Focus on students ▸

☐ **INTASC Principles 2, 3, 4**

• *Keep an eye on the goal of student-centered teaching.* Our best understanding of learning tells us clearly that it must happen *in* students, not *to* them.[23] Continue to ask yourself what you can do to put the focus on students as workers rather than teacher as worker. Perhaps you can provide a few minutes in each lesson for students to answer a key question in pairs, or use learning logs in which students reflect their understanding of the subject matter and raise questions about what they are studying. Whatever you can do to put students on center stage as active learners takes you down the road toward differentiation.

Find many ways to teach ▸

☐ **INTASC Principles 2, 3, 5**

• *Work for flexibility.* Early on, establishing yourself as a classroom leader is critical. Even at that stage of growth, however, there are things you can do to aim for flexibility. You may be able to give students two choices of how to do a task, ask students to give you a suggestion on an index card for the best due date for a project in a week you specify, assign individual students responsibility for one or two classroom chores, provide students two options for work to do when they finish an assigned task, or examine two ways you might present tomorrow's lesson rather than only one. Once again, working toward flexibility is more likely to make you a flexible teacher than is developing early habits of "one-way" teaching.

Enlist peers and resource people

◻ INTASC Principle 4

- *Use resource staff as partners in your classroom.* Teachers of English as a second language, resource specialists in gifted education or special education, reading specialists, psychologists, counselors, media specialists, and others on a faculty have a rich store of understanding and skills they can share with you. Cultivate the habit of asking these people how they might address a particular classroom situation. Better still, ask them to come into your classroom and observe or coteach with you. Most teaching would probably be stronger if it were a team sport. This is particularly true given the range of needs and challenges in most contemporary classrooms.

- *Find and work with like-minded colleagues.* Many teachers spend their careers developing the skills of responsive teaching. Many do not. Find teachers who are willing to expend the mental and physical effort it takes to reach out to their learners on a daily basis. Cultivate these professional friendships. Work together. Share successes and failures. Celebrate your growth together.

Align practice with beliefs

- *Reflect on your beliefs about who, where, what, and how you teach, and examine the match between your beliefs and your practice.* Early on, your practices may be a bit of a mismatch for what you believe, but if you cultivate the habit of checking for match, you'll continue working toward the classroom that exists in your mind's eye.

In many sports, athletes are encouraged to see themselves as they execute a particular move. This sort of mental rehearsal is part of training for success. A similar practice in teaching may be helpful in a similar way. In day-by-day planning, it can be quite useful to "see" how you'd like it to look when you return papers, ask students to get into groups, or wrap up a class. On a longer-term basis, this sort of reflection can provide a kind of internal compass for thinking about decision making. At this point in your development as a teacher, you can only speculate on how you would like things to be in your classroom. Even now, however, you have many experiences, values, and considerable knowledge to direct your mental rehearsal.

> **YOUR TURN** **Thinking About Your Own Response to Academic Diversity**

1. Return to your notes from item 3 in the Your Turn for Learning Activity 6.3, where you listed key beliefs you now have about whom you teach, where you teach, what you teach, and how you teach. For each of those beliefs, list two or three concrete actions or steps you might take in your classroom as you begin teaching full time so that you also begin the process of developing a classroom where your practices and beliefs are a match.

2. Below are brief scenarios that give the perspectives of three students on their experiences in

school. Read the scenarios, then create advice from each of the students to their teachers based on what you read and infer from your reading. Express the advice in a list, letter, written dialogue, or oral presentation—in the student's voice.

- My name is Tia. The class seems awfully long to me. I finish my work quickly because I pretty much know the answers before class even begins. I have some other things I'd like to work on when I get through with assignments, but that seems to make my teacher unhappy, so I sit and wait a lot. I have a lot of questions

I'd like to ask about what we study, but I don't want to talk so much that my friends in class don't have a chance to talk. Besides, when I do ask the questions, I sometimes get the feeling that people are rolling their eyes. I don't know if it's because my questions seem wrong or because people don't understand them. Sometimes I wish there were time for the teacher to talk with me during class, but she always seems to need to work with kids who are having lots of trouble with what we are learning. I pretty much get A's in class, and I guess that should be satisfying, but somehow, it doesn't feel right.

- My name is Carlos. I wish I could understand what the teacher is asking us to do. I try. I really do. Sometimes I get tired of trying and I kind of drift off for a few minutes, but mostly, I really try to listen. I have a hard time writing down all the stuff the teacher says. He goes fast, and I don't always know how to spell all the words. Sometimes h   tells stories that make us laugh, but they are still hard to write down. When I try to study for tests, it's like my head gets full really fast, and when I try to cram more in my head, everything gets all mixed up. I don't get why other people can follow the directions so much better than I can

in class. But it's mostly been that way for me in school. I guess I'm just no good at school.

- My name is Sam. If I have to sit still for one more minute, I think I'll just explode. The teacher gets really crabby when I move around or tap on the desk, but I just can't stay as still as she wants me to. When I try to stay still all the time, it seems like that's all I can think about, and so I miss what she's telling us, and then that makes me get behind some more and that makes me feel worse and that makes me need to move even more. The teacher gets mad when I move around. She tells me to stay still, and I get embarrassed or mad or something and it makes me have to move more. I like it in PE when we get to do things and talk to people. I wish we could have PE twice every day. I wish I knew why we had to learn all this stuff anyhow. It seems like a lot of lists of things that people have to sit still to learn. Maybe why I don't do well in school is because I can't sit still to learn.

3. In what ways would your first steps toward responsive teaching from item 1 be helpful to each of the three students from item 2? What else would you like to be able to do to teach them even more effectively if they were part of your class in your fifth year of teaching?

☀ Mastery Test

Use the first-person descriptions of Tia, Carlos, and Sam in item 2 in the Your Turn for Learning Activity 6.6 as a basis for your work in this mastery activity.

First, reflect on the perspectives of the students in the three scenarios and make a list of specific learning needs for each of the three students.

Second, develop a lesson (or use one you have already developed) for a "typical" student in a class you might teach. Be sure that you state the goals of the lesson clearly. Then explain how you would differentiate the lesson to ensure that each of the three students finds it appropriately challenging. (In other words, differentiate the lesson based on the students' readiness needs.) Note also what you might do to make the lesson interesting for each of the three learners as well as to make the way in which students work a good fit for each of the three. (In other words, make some suggestions for differentiation based on student interest and learning profile also.) Be sure to address portions of the lesson in which you are presenting directions, examples, or information and parts of the lesson in which the student is working. For each modification you make, explain whether you are addressing readiness, interest, and/or learning profile, and why you believe your adaptation is likely to be helpful to the student.

Third, write a brief statement of ways in which your own beliefs about the nature of students, learning environments, curriculum, and instruction are reflected in your plans for differentiation.

Observation Worksheet

THINKING ABOUT RESPONSIVE INSTRUCTION

The goal of this observation is to help you reflect on the "fit" of a classroom for particular learners in that classroom and to examine ways a teacher can differentiate instruction to improve the fit for more students. Before you begin the observation, ask the teacher to point out to you one or two students who have a hard time with the content of the class, one or two who have behavior problems, and one or two who are particularly advanced. Take a few minutes as class begins to locate these students and observe them briefly. Then select three of them whom you will watch for the remainder of the observation.

Directions: Do not use actual names of schools, teachers, administrators, or students when using this worksheet.

Observer's Name: _____

Date: _____

Grade Level: _____

Subject: _____

Class Size: _____

Background Information: Give a brief general description of the school's social, economic, and ethnic makeup.

_____

_____

What to Record: First, write a very brief description of each student as a learner. Then, in the boxes that follow, take notes on the three students as the class proceeds. Do you have any evidence that they are participating actively in the class? That they are understanding the content, are confused, or are bored? What sorts of behavior do they exhibit? Why do you think they are behaving as they do? What is working well or poorly for them? Does the class seem interesting to them? In the fourth box, take notes on anything the teacher does to make the class successful for the three students you've selected. Has he or she tried to make the environment seem safe and inviting to the students? Are there materials or activities particularly appropriate for these learners? Do the students have choices about how to work? Are questions targeted to address particular learner needs? Are there opportunities to meet with the teacher to clarify or extend learning? Jot down whatever you think affects the learning of your three target students and reflects teacher attempts to actively address varied learner needs.

Student 1 Name _____ Description _____

_____

Student 2 Name _____ Description _____

_____

Student 3 Name _____ Description _____

_____

Student 1

Student 2

Student 3

Teacher

Reflections on Your Observation

1. To what degree did you feel the content and activities of the class matched the readiness level of the students you observed? On what do you base your conclusions?

_____

_____

_____

2. What ideas do you have about how a teacher might effectively address the readiness needs of the students you observed?

_____

_____

_____

3. In what ways did the teacher work to make the content and activities link to student interests?

_____

_____

_____

4. What ideas do you have about other ways in which a teacher might tap into student interests at some point during the unit that you observed briefly?

_____

_____

_____

5. In what ways did the teacher work to address varied student preferences for how to learn?

_____

_____

_____

6. What other ways can you think of to give students a range of ways to learn in this class, both when the teacher is presenting and when the student is the worker?

_____

_____

_____

7. In what ways do you think the learning environment in the classroom encourages and supports learning for the students you observed?

_____

_____

_____

8. What other ways can you think of to make the learning environment even more encouraging and supportive of the learning success of the students you observed?

_____

_____

ADDITIONAL RESOURCES

📄 Readings

Azwell, T. and E. Schmar. (1995) *Report Card on Report Cards: Alternatives to Consider.* Portsmouth, N.H.: Heinemann.

Craig, S. (2008) *Reaching and Teaching Children Who Hurt: Strategies for Your Classroom.* Baltimore: Paul H. Brookes Publishing Co.

Delpit, Lisa. (1995) *Other People's Children: Cultural Conflict in the Classroom.* New York: The New Press.

Dweck, C. (2006) *Mindset: The New Psychology of Success.* New York: Random House.

Gartin, Barbara, Nikki Murdick, Marcia Imbeau, and Darlene Perner. (2002) *How to Use Differentiated Instruction with Developmental Disabilities in the General Education Classroom.* Arlington, Va.: Council for Exceptional Children.

Greene, R. (2008) *Lost at School: Why Our Kids with Behavioral Challenges are Falling through the Cracks and How We Can Help Them.* New York: Scribner.

King-Shaver, Barbara, and Alyce Hunter. (2003) *Differentiated Instruction in the English Classroom: Content, Process, Product, and Assessment.* Portsmouth, N.H.: Heinemann.

Strachota, Bob. (1996) *On Their Side: Helping Children Take Charge of Their Learning.* Greenfield, Mass.: Northeast Foundation for Children.

Tomlinson, Carol Ann. (1999) *The Differentiated Classroom: Responding to the Needs of All Learners.* Alexandria, Va.: Association for Supervision and Curriculum Development.

Tomlinson, Carol Ann. (2003) *Fulfilling the Promise of the Differentiated Classroom: Strategies and Tools for Responsive Teaching.* Alexandria, Va.: Association for Supervision and Curriculum Development.

Tomlinson, Carol Ann. (2001) *How to Differentiate Instruction in Mixed Ability Classrooms,* 2nd ed. Alexandria, Va.: Association for Supervision and Curriculum Development.

Winebrenner, Susan. (1992) *Teaching Gifted Kids in the Regular Classroom: Strategies Every Teacher Can Use to Meet the Needs of the Gifted and Talented.* Minneapolis: Free Spirit Publishing.

Winebrenner, Susan. (1996) *Teaching Kids with Learning Difficulties in the Regular Classroom.* Minneapolis: Free Spirit Publishing.

Articles

Brimijoin, K., et. al. (2003) Using data to differentiate instruction. *Educational Leadership,* 60(5), 70–3.

Kohn, A. (1998) Hooked on learning: The role of motivation in the classroom. In Kohn, *Punished by Rewards: The Trouble with Gold Stars, Incentive Plans, A's, and Other Bribes,* Houghton Mifflin, New York.

McTighe, J. and O'Conner, K. (2005) Seven practices for effective learning. *Educational Leadership,* 63(3), 10–17.

Moon, T. R. (2005) The role of assessment in differentiation. *Theory into Practice,* 44, 226–33.

Sternberg, R. (1997) What does it mean to be smart? *Educational Leadership,* 54(6), 20–24.

Tomlinson, C. A. (1999) Mapping a route toward differentiated instruction. *Educational Leadership,* 57(1), 12–16.

Tomlinson, C. A. (2000) Reconcilable differences? Standard-based teaching and differentiation. *Educational Leadership,* 58(1), 6–11.

Tomlinson, C. A. (2002) Invitations to learn. *Educational Leadership,* 60(1), 6–10.

Tomlinson, C. A., et. al. (2003) Differentiating instruction in response to student readiness, interest, and learning profile in academically diverse classrooms: A review of literature. *Journal for the Education of the Gifted,* 27, 119–45.

Tomlinson, C. A., et. al. (2005) Reach them to teach them. *Educational Leadership,* 62(7), 8–15.

Tomlinson, C. A., et. al. (2006) Teaching beyond the book. *Educational Leadership,* 64(1), 16–21.

Sternberg, R. J. (2006) Recognizing neglected strengths. *Educational Leadership,* 64 (1), 30–5.

Tomlinson, C. A. (2007) Learning to kove assessment. *Educational Leadership,* 65(4), 8–13.

Tomlinson, C. A. (2008) The goals of differentiation. *Educational Leadership,* 66(3), 26–30.

Websites

For exceptional learners
The Council for Exceptional Children: http://www. cec.sped.org

The National Association for Gifted Children: http://www.nagc.org

For materials helpful to teachers and students with particular learning styles or needs
Inspiration Software: http://www.inspiration.com
Multiple on-line personality and learning style surveys: http://www.ldrc.ca/projects/miinventory/ miinventory.php

For professional development on curriculum development and differentiation
Association for Supervision and Curriculum Development: http://www.ascd.org/
Best Practices Institute: http://curry.edschool. virginia.edu/about-bpi-institutes-164

Summer Institute on Academic Diversity: http://curry.edschool.virginia.edu/about-siad-institutes-165
Fall Symposium on Academic Diversity: http://curry.edschool.virginia.edu/about-fall-symposium-institutes-350

For examples of differentiated lessons or ideas
The idea of differentiating instruction: http://www.differentiationcentral.com/
Getting started with differentiation: http://www.middleweb.com/MWLISTCONT/MSLamyandrick.html
The Internet TESL (Teachers of English as a Second Language) Journal: http://iteslj.org

For differentiation strategies
Differentiation strategies and applications: http://www.differentiationcentral.com/
Montgomery County Public Schools: http://www.mcps.k12.md.us/curriculum/enriched/giftedprograms/mathstations.shtm
http://www.mcps.k12.md.us/curriculum/enriched/giftedprograms/tieredinstruct.shtm

For these links and additional resources, please visit the Premium Website at **www.cengage.com/login.**

◉ NOTES

1. Dorothy Canfield Fisher, *Understood Betsy* (New York: Henry Holt and Company, 1917, 1999), pp. 89–94.

2. Tim O'Brien and Dennis Guiney, *Differentiation in Teaching and Learning: Principles and Practice* (London: Continuum, 2001).

3. Ochan Kusuma-Powell and William Powell, eds. *Count Me In!* (Washington, D.C.: Overseas School Advisory Council, 2000).

4. O'Brien and Guiney, *op. cit.*

5. Kusuma-Powell and Powell, *op. cit.*

6. Carol Ann Tomlinson, *How to Differentiate Instruction in Mixed Ability Classrooms*, 2nd ed. (Alexandria, Va.: Association for Supervision and Curriculum Development, 2001).

7. Y. Lou, P. Abrami, J. Spence, C. Poulsen, B. Chambers, and S. d'Apollonia, "Within-Class Grouping: A Meta-Analysis." *Review of Educational Research* 66 (1996): 423–458.

8. Lev Vygotsky, *Mind in Society* (Cambridge, Mass.: Harvard University Press, 1978).

9. Pierce Howard, *An Owner's Manual for the Brain* (Austin, Tex.: Leornian Press, 1994); Eric Jensen, *Teaching with the Brain in Mind* (Alexandria, Va: Association for Supervision and Curriculum Development, 1998).

10. Michael Gurian, *Boys and Girls Learn Differently: A Guide for Teachers and Parents* (San Francisco: Jossey-Bass, 2001).

11. Lisa Delpit, *Other People's Children: Cultural Conflict in the Classroom* (New York: The New Press, 1995); Shirley Brice Heath, *Ways with Words: Language, Life and Work in Communities and Classrooms* (Cambridge, England: Cambridge University Press, 1983); Thomas Lasley and Thomas Matczynski, *Strategies for Teaching in a Diverse Society: Instructional Models* (Belmont, Calif.: Wadsworth, 1997).

12. Teresa Amabile, *The Social Psychology of Creativity* (New York: Springer-Verlag, 1983); Teresa Amabile, *Creativity in Context* (Boulder, Colo.: Westview, 1996); Mihaly Csikszentmihalyi, Kevin Rathunde, and Samuel Whalen, *Talented Teenagers: The Roots of Success and Failure* (New York: Cambridge University Press, 1993); Paul Torrance, "Insights About Creativity: Questioned, Rejected, Ridiculed, Ignored," *Educational Psychology Review* 7 (1995): 313–322.

13. Robert Sternberg, "What Does It Mean to Be Smart?" *Educational Leadership* 55 (1997): 20–24; M. Sullivan, "A Meta-Analysis of Experimental Research Studies Based on the Dunn and Dunn Learning Styles Model and Its Relationship to Academic Achievement and Performance." (Unpublished doctoral dissertation, St. John's University, Jamaica, N.Y., 1993).

14. F. Archambault, K. Westberg, S. Brown, B. Hallmark, C. Emmons, and W. Zhang, *Regular Classroom Practices with Gifted Students: Results of a National Survey of Classroom Teachers* (Research Monograph 93102) (Storrs: University of Connecticut, National Research Center on the Gifted and Talented, 1993); T. Fletcher, C. Bos, and L. Johnson, "Accommodating English Language Learners with Language and Learning Disabilities in Bilingual Education Classrooms," *Learning Disabilities Research & Practice* 14 (1999): 80–91; L. Fuchs and D. Fuchs, "General Educators' Instructional Adaptation for Students with Learning Disabilities," *Learning Disability Quarterly* 21 (1998): 23–33.

15. J. Siegel and M. Shaughnessy, "Educating for Understanding: A Conversation with Howard Gardner," *Phi Delta Kappan* 75, no. 7 (1994): 563–566.

16. L. J. Kiernan, *A Visit to a Differentiated Classroom* (Alexandria, Va.: Association for Supervision and Curriculum Development, 2001), videocassette.

17. *Ibid.*; Carol Ann Tomlinson, *The Differentiated Classroom: Responding to the Needs of All Learners*

(Alexandria, Va.: Association for Supervision and Curriculum Development, 1999).

18. Rita Dunn, *How to Implement and Supervise a Learning Styles Program* (Alexandria, Va.: Association for Supervision and Curriculum Development, 1996).

19. Robert Sternberg, *The Triarchic Mind: A New Theory of Intelligence* (New York: Viking, 1988); Robert Sternberg, "What Does It Mean to Be Smart?" *Educational Leadership* 54, no. 6 (1997): 20–24.

20. Howard Gardner, *Multiple Intelligences: The Theory in Practice* (New York: Basic Books, 1993); Howard Gardner, "Reflections on Multiple Intelligences: Myths and Messages," *Phi Delta Kappan* 78, no. 5 (1997): 200–207.

21. Tomlinson, *op. cit., The Differentiated Classroom.*

22. C. Tomlinson, C. Callahan, E. Tomchin, N. Eiss, M. Imbeau, and M. Landrum, "Becoming Architects of Communities of Learning: Addressing Academic Diversity in Contemporary Classrooms," *Exceptional Children* 63 (1997): 269–282.

23. National Research Council, *How People Learn: Brain, Mind, Experience, and School* (Washington, D.C.: National Academy Press, 1999).

7

Culturally Responsive Teaching

Jason G. Irizarry

Imagestate Media Partners Limited - Impact Photos / Alamy

▣ INTASC Standards

● **Principle 1:** The teacher understands the central concepts, tools of inquiry, and structures of the discipline(s) he or she teaches and can create learning experiences that make these aspects of subject matter meaningful for students.

● **Principle 2:** The teacher understands how children learn and develop, and can provide learning opportunities that support their intellectual, social, and personal development.

● **Principle 3:** The teacher understands how students differ in their approaches to learning and creates instructional opportunities that are adapted to diverse learners.

● **Principle 4:** The teacher understands and uses a variety of instructional strategies to encourage students' development of critical thinking, problem solving, and performance skills.

● **Principle 5:** The teacher uses an understanding of individual and group motivation and behavior to create a learning environment that encourages positive social interaction, active engagement in learning, and self-motivation.

● **Principle 6:** The teacher uses knowledge of effective verbal, nonverbal, and media communication techniques to foster active inquiry, collaboration, and supportive interaction in the classroom.

● **Principle 7:** The teacher plans instruction based upon knowledge of subject matter, students, the community, and curriculum goals.

● **Principle 9:** The teacher is a reflective practitioner who continually evaluates the effects of his/her choices and actions on others and who actively seeks out opportunities to grow professionally.

● **Principle 10:** The teacher fosters relationships with school colleagues, parents, and agencies in the larger community to support students' learning and well-being.

▣ OBJECTIVES

1. To develop an understanding of the theory undergirding culturally responsive pedagogy

2. To examine critically the role of culture in culturally responsive teaching, specifically highlighting its multidimensional and fluid nature

3. To reflect on one's own identity and the various ways that it may differ from that of the students being taught

4. To identify strategies to make teaching more culturally responsive

5. To create opportunities to inform personal and professional development in relation to culturally responsive teaching

The past twenty years have been marked by unprecedented demographic changes in the United States. Students of color now constitute approximately 40 percent of all students enrolled in public schools, and this population is expected to grow considerably in the coming years.[1] Schools, generally speaking, have been slow to respond to the academic and personal needs of both newer immigrants and students of color from communities with long histories in the United States. While society at large has changed dramatically, as evidenced by the rise of electronic media and globalization, what is taught in schools and how it is taught has changed relatively little. Consequently, many students, and particularly students of color from marginalized communities, continue to be underserved by schools.

An excerpt from an essay written by a high school student participating in a research project that examined the educational experiences of Latinos speaks poignantly to the context in which many youth of color are educated. In a letter to a future teacher she crafted as part of a class assignment, Carmen, a Latina eleventh grader, wrote

> . . . just imagine how you would feel coming to school every day and never learning anything about the community that you identify with. Latinos, African Americans, and other students are invisible in the curriculum, even though we have done a lot to contribute to the development of this country. As part of this project, we examined [our] high school English curriculum, [focusing on] all of the novels assigned to students as required reading in grades 9–12. Fifty percent of all students in this school are Latino. You know how many novels either have a Latino lead character or are written by a Latino author? One! And it isn't assigned until the twelfth grade. Almost half of the Latino students in my school never get to that point. Students would do better if they connected with the content and if teachers tried harder to connect with them.[2]

Unfortunately, Carmen's experience is not that uncommon. Many students languish in classrooms where the course content and pedagogical approaches are completely disconnected from the experiences and material conditions of their lives. Consequently, these gaps in opportunities to learn have resulted in achievement gaps between students of color and white students. An array of scholars champion culturally responsive teaching as an approach to education with the potential to positively transform the experiences and outcomes of students who have been traditionally underserved by schools.[3]

■ OBJECTIVE 1   **To develop an understanding of the theory undergirding culturally responsive pedagogy**

❑ What Is Culturally Responsive Teaching?

**❑ INTASC Principles
1, 3, 4, 5, 7, 9, 10**

Culturally responsive teaching is an approach to teaching and learning that builds on the "cultural knowledge, prior experiences, frames of reference and performance styles of ethnically diverse students to make learning encounters more relevant and effective for them."[4] Also referred to as *culturally relevant*,[5] *culturally congruent*,[6] and *culturally compatible*,[7] this approach to working with students of diverse backgrounds affirms the identities of students and builds upon who students are and what they bring with them to school. It teaches to and through their experiences. In short, as Gloria Ladson-Billings notes, it is just "good teaching."[8]

Geneva Gay offered a comprehensive list of the characteristics of culturally responsive teaching.[9] Although the dimensions she describes are interrelated, taken individually, each represents a central component of this approach to teaching and learning. They include

Culturally Responsive Teaching Is Validating. It values the importance of students' cultural heritages and views them as valuable and worthy of inclusion in the curriculum. A variety of instructional strategies are implemented to address the diverse array of learning styles students bring to the classroom, thus affirming the diversity among students, even those with similar cultural identifications. Culturally responsive teaching encourages students to value their own personal cultural identities and histories as well as those of others.

Culturally Responsive Teaching Is Comprehensive. It takes a holistic approach to teaching and learning, nurturing all of the aspects of students' identities. It does not position academic success in opposition to maintaining a strong sense of cultural identity. Rather, in addition to supporting academic success, students are encouraged to remain connected to the various cultural communities of which they are members. In contrast to approaches that position the cultures of students—particularly poor students and students of color—as the "problem" within school reform efforts, culturally responsive teachers identify, value, and connect with the "funds of knowledge"[10] that are present in students' communities and utilize these information networks to support students' academic and personal growth.

Culturally Responsive Teaching Is Multidimensional. It permeates all aspects of teaching and learning, from curriculum content and the classroom climate to student–teacher relationships and assessments. Culturally responsive teaching isn't limited to one particular aspect of the curriculum or content area. The scope of this approach is far-reaching, encouraging collaboration across content areas and disciplines as well as beyond the school building, integrating students' communities and drawing on resources beyond the formal curriculum to gain a more accurate and robust understanding of course content.

Culturally Responsive Teaching Is Empowering. When students' histories and experiences are omitted or overlooked in the classroom, students can become disconnected from school and develop negative feelings about themselves and their cultural group(s). Culturally responsive teaching serves to prevent, disrupt, and dismantle this process of internalized oppression, which is detrimental to personal as well as academic success. Students are encouraged to assume responsibility for their own learning and view education as a process by which they develop the knowledge and skills necessary to become more sophisticated and active participants in democracy.

Culturally Responsive Teaching Is Transformative. For many students of color, schooling is a "subtractive experience."[11] That is, students are forced to give up or suppress particular aspects of their identities for a chance at academic success. The departure from assimilationist models of teaching that encourage students to give up their cultural identities and adopt new ones is transformative. Culturally responsive teaching requires a transformation in the approach to teaching and learning—from one that requires students to shed aspects of their identities to one that affirms them—and results in all of the participants in the classroom community being positively transformed.

Culturally Responsive Teaching Is Emancipatory. Many students have endured schooling in contexts that at best treat them as invisible and at worst treat them as if they have no history worth telling and as if their culture is pathological, responsible for a host of social ills, and needs to be replaced by a "better" one. Consequently, many students view schooling as oppressive and alienating. Centering on students' experiences and histories of their cultural communities, transforming curriculum content and pedagogical practices so that they are more closely aligned with the students' identities, represents a departure from traditional methods. Consequently, schools are transformed from oppressive spaces to liberating ones where students and teachers engage in mutually enriching relationships that support academic growth.

At its core this approach is grounded in basic learning theory. Almost all scholars agree that students learn best when teachers build upon and try to extend what they already know. Putting students and their cultural identities and histories at the center of the learning process is perfectly aligned with the tenets of learning theory advanced by Jean Piaget, John Dewey, Erick Erikson, and others.[12]

The focus of the chapter thus far has been on students of color. This makes sense, given that various academic indicators suggest that students of color have and continue to be underserved by schools, including graduation rates, performance on standardized measures of achievement, and college attendance and completion rates. However, culturally responsive teaching is not solely for ethnic and/or linguistic minority students. White students can and do benefit from culturally responsive teaching as well. In fact, since White students often share aspects of their cultural identities with their teachers, who are usually White and middle class, and since the curriculum in most schools is Eurocentric, many White students experience the benefits of an approach to teaching and learning that builds on such students' cultures and cultural knowledge.

✳ Mastery Test

OBJECTIVE 1	To develop an understanding of the theory undergirding culturally responsive pedagogy

Characteristics of Culturally Responsive Teaching

In your own words, create a list of the core characteristics of culturally responsive teaching. What, if anything, would you add to the characteristics forwarded by Geneva Gay?

OBJECTIVE 2	To examine critically the role of culture in culturally responsive teaching, specifically highlighting its multidimensional and fluid nature

◻ Culture: A Closer Look at the "C" in CRT

**◻ INTASC Principles
2, 5, 6, 7, 9**

Culturally responsive teaching helps teachers think about culture and its critical role in the teaching and learning process. To really understand how to teach in a culturally responsive way, one must think more critically about what culture really is. Much research regarding culturally responsive teaching has focused on single-group studies of African American students or Latino students. These studies have clarified a model for teachers seeking to transform their classroom into culturally responsive spaces that support the development of all students. However, more recent work in this area has encouraged teachers to think more flexibly about culture and how it is manifested in and out of the classroom. This body of literature, explored in more detail below, highlights the diversity that exists within as well as across cultural groups. We can't reduce all people or cultures to a checklist of expected traits, such as how Asian American students act or learn best, since cultural groups are not monolithic entities.

Norma González challenges the notion that "all members of a particular group share a normative, bounded, and integrated view of their own culture,"[13] asserting instead a view of culture and cultural practices as hybrid funds of knowledge. That is, while African Americans, for example, may indeed share some commonalities, they also differ in many ways. Similarly, Kris Gutierrez and Barbara Rogoff draw from a cultural-historical approach to suggest that even though individuals may share an ethnic identity, for example, they also have distinct histories and experiences that result in variations in the ways they understand and express their identities.[14] The cultural–historical approach to culturally responsive teaching foregrounds individual experiences rather than generalized group traits.

Moving beyond narrowing student identities to fit into a checklist of cultural characteristics and practices that members of a particular group are believed to employ, these more nuanced treatments of culturally responsive teaching respond to the various sites, or places, from which individuals draw to create their identities. For instance, while one might expect traditional aspects of Latino culture, such as using Spanish, to be an important source of identity for Latino/a youth, one group of Latino students told a researcher that they found their African American teacher to be practicing more culturally relevant teaching—to be connecting them to content and skills—when the teacher built on familiar aspects of "urban" culture, such as using African American Vernacular English (AAVE) and hip-hop music.[15] Students have complex identities that transcend the boundaries of ethnic affiliation as a result of their interactions with peers of diverse backgrounds in schools and communities as well as participation in hybrid cultural communities such as urban youth culture, a site from which many youth of diverse backgrounds draw to enact their identities. Notably, the students noted above were fervent in their identification of the teacher as culturally responsive, even though he, as an African American, did not necessarily share an ethnic identity with them.

Reconceptualizing the "C" within CRT requires that teachers acknowledge and value the role of race/ethnicity in the classroom, but it also encourages teachers to consider other sites from which youth (as well as adults) draw to inform their identities as well as the diversity in the various ways individuals choose to express these identities. Youth have contributed to and have been heavily influenced by popular culture, as evidenced by the pervasive impact of music, television, movies, sports, language practices, and other modes of popular culture on their lives.[16] Given the complex nature of culture and the importance of individual histories, Jeffrey Duncan-Andrade argues that overcoming "oppressive conditions requires context-specific solutions."[17] He advocates that teachers engage in what he refers to as "youth popular culture teaching and curriculum."[18] Duncan-Andrade's call for context-specific approaches underscores the nuanced approach necessary to make culturally responsive teaching more applicable and far-reaching for youth. While centering students' cultures and cultural identities is vital, students also need access to the "codes of power," norms and rules regarding the presentation of self, including but not limited to oral and written communication and patterns of social interaction. These codes are often maintained through language and literacy, contributing subtly but significantly to perpetuating systems of prejudice and inequality.[19] A culturally additive approach to schooling values students' cultural identities, connects them to these valuable information networks, and frames education as a vehicle for community empowerment.[20]

In sum, although many schools are highly segregated by race/ethnicity and class, resulting in racial/ethnic enclave communities within schools, teachers cannot treat cultural groups as a monolithic entity. Rather, if teachers are truly going to be culturally responsive in addressing the academic and personal needs of students, they have to take into account the diversity that exists within as well as across groups. In addition, teachers should try to respond to those aspects of identity that are most salient for students. While these aspects certainly may be heavily influenced by race/ethnicity, student identities are significantly more complex as a result of their participation in diverse cultural communities. Because of their experiences that cross lines of cultural difference in their personal relationships as well as through the media and participation in online digital communities, students draw from intercultural knowledge bases and therefore create and enact unique hybrid identities. A culturally responsive teacher works to become familiar with these influences and uses that knowledge to engage and work collaboratively with students.

Vignette 1

What About Kids Who Are "Half This and Half That?": The Case of Emilio Jackson

Emilio Jackson is a bright young boy, who is ten years old and currently enrolled in the fourth grade at Springfield Elementary School. He loves to read, play with his friends, and ride his bike. He lives in a predominantly Latino and Black working-class community with his mother and two younger siblings. His school district is classified as urban by the state department of education, yet it is located in a community of only 9,000 residents and feels more like a small town than a big city. However, it receives this label "urban" in part because approximately 55 percent of all students in the district are students of color and almost three-quarters of the student population is eligible for free and reduced lunch. Hence, the community is dealing with what some have referred to as the "urban condition."

Emilio's mother was born in the northeast United States to parents who immigrated from Puerto Rico. She attended schools in the community in which they currently live. Emilio's father identifies himself as an American of German, French, and Irish descent. Although he does not live with Emilio, he sees him often and remains tangibly connected to the family. Emilio has his mother's cocoa skin and his father's light eyes, and his siblings all have a unique combination of their parent's physical characteristics. He lives in a section of town that is predominantly African American and most of his closest peers identify themselves as Black. Much to his grandparent's dismay, Emilio does not speak fluent Spanish, although he understands it and at times switches between Spanish and English in conversations with them. Most often he speaks using the conventions of African American Vernacular English (AAVE[21]), the language most often utilized among youth in his neighborhood. When asked, Emilio identifies himself as half Latino and half White.

In school Emilio is extremely shy, rarely raising his hand to answer a question or share information. While he likes learning, in his teachers' and parents' estimation, he has underachieved thus far. Teachers have consistently commented that Emilio is not learning to his potential and he has struggled to achieve a passing score on the state-wide tests in reading and math. They have also noted that he is a pleasant child who often seems disconnected from school, choosing to sit quietly through most lessons. Because so many students have underperformed on the state test, last year the school introduced new math and reading curricula. Teachers are expected to follow a rigid scope and sequence schedule and their progress is monitored by the administration. Students are assessed quarterly to measure any increases in their learning. The teacher feels stifled and unable to move outside of the scripted program.

Emilio's parents, both high school graduates with some college education, check his homework, which usually consists of completing math or reading comprehension worksheets every night, and stress the importance of doing well in school. However, like many other students, Emilio often tells his parents, "School is boring." Because he is not very interested in the content he is learning or the ways in which the teacher engages the class, it is extremely difficult to get Emilio motivated to attend school and complete his assignments to the best of his ability. Both his teachers and his parents want the best for Emilio and worry that if he does not take more interest in his studies and put forth more effort in class, he will begin to lag behind other students and struggle with the transitions to middle and high school. The teacher has read a little about culturally responsive teaching and is interested in learning more about the approach and implementing it in her classroom; however, she is perplexed by how to respond to Emilio's multiracial/multiethnic identity.

The vignette above describes a scenario that is common in schools across the United States. Particularly in districts where schools have not met state-prescribed benchmarks on standardized measures of achievement, teachers are often forced to adopt scripted curricula that allow little, if any, room for teachers to be creative and apply their craft. Knowing the benefits of culturally responsive teaching in supporting the academic and personal growth of students, the teacher is committed to doing something but is not sure what to do.

> YOUR TURN

Please put yourself in the position of the teacher described in the above vignette, and work with a classmate to address the following questions:

1. What might culturally responsive teaching look like for Emilio in this setting?
2. Where is the "problem" located? That is, are Emilio and his parents completely responsible for his disconnection from school? What role does the school, and specifically the teacher, play in engaging youth in teaching and learning?

3. Based on the vignette, what are the various sites or sources from which Emilio might draw to enact his identities? How might these complicate your notions of culturally responsive teaching? What are the implications for your practice?

4. Can teachers practice culturally responsive teaching when using scripted curricula? Justify your answer.

5. As a dark-skinned Latino who actively participates in African American cultural practices, can Emilio claim to be Black or African American? What makes someone Black?

6. Is anyone really half of something (for instance, half Latino)? Should teachers seeking to be culturally responsive treat Emilio like a Latino child for half of the day and as a White student for the other half? How might conceptualizing identity in terms of percentages be problematic to culturally responsive teaching?

7. As a teacher working with Emilio, what might you do to try to make the learning experience more engaging and culturally responsive for him?

✳ Mastery Test

OBJECTIVE 2 **To examine critically the role of culture in culturally responsive teaching, specifically highlighting its multidimensional and fluid nature**

Cultural Identity Box

Before teachers can affirm the cultural identities of their students, they must be aware of and affirm their own culture(s). For teachers in the dominant group, those whose cultures are well represented in society at large, they may not spend much time thinking about how they may differ from others and the significance of these differences.

Building on what you have learned in this section, reflect on how you define your culture and how you might represent your cultural identities. Find or create items that represent these identities. For example, you might include a small flag representing your ancestral heritage or a representation of a type of food or a music CD you associate with one of your cultural identities. The possibilities are endless. Culture in this case does not have to solely entail your racial or ethnic identity. You can also choose to include any other elements that you identify as contributing to how you define yourself culturally. You do not have to share any information that might make you feel uncomfortable. As always, you are encouraged to be creative. Your box should contain at least ten items and should be decorated to reflect aspects of your cultural identity.

Share your box with at least one other member of the class. Identify any similarities and/or differences that emerged in the ways that you chose to represent your cultural identities. Use the following questions to guide your reflection:

- What was the process of creating a cultural identity box like for you?
- What, if anything, did you learn about yourself through this process?
- If you could do this again, what aspects of your box might you change? Why?
- How do you think of yourself as a cultural being after this exercise?
- What do you think some of your current or future students would put in their cultural identity boxes? How might these be similar or different from your own?

OBJECTIVE 3 **To reflect on one's own identity and the various ways that it may differ from the students being taught**

◼ "I'm Not Ethnic, I'm Just Normal": Exploring the Role of Teacher Identities in CRT

◼ INTASC Principles
2, 5, 9

Thus far, this chapter has explored the theoretical underpinnings of culturally responsive teaching, the role of culture in the process of teaching and learning, and the reality that individual students form complex, hybrid identities from multiple sources. This section explores the central role that teachers play in constructing a classroom and school climate and pedagogical practices that are culturally responsive to the needs of their students. Certainly a large part of culturally responsive teaching is about what teachers need to know. That is, to be culturally responsive and transform curricula and teaching practices, teachers need to be familiar with the histories of various groups, know literature written by and about members of these groups, and be skilled in using this "new" content to transform the curriculum. But culturally responsive teaching is also about *who* teachers are and who they need to become. This section addresses the questions: What is the role of teacher identity in the teaching and learning process? What are the intersections between teachers' personal and professional development? How do teachers become culturally responsive?

As noted earlier, schools have become increasingly diverse. Approximately 40 percent of the 50 million students in U.S. schools are students of color, and it is estimated that students now classified as "minority" will constitute the majority of school children by 2020. Approximately one in five speaks a language other than English at home,[22] and English language learners (ELLs) represent the fastest-growing group of students in public schools. Although, as demonstrated by the aforementioned demographic data, there have been significant changes in the racial/ethnic and linguistic texture of the Pre-K–12 student population in U.S. schools, the demographics of the teaching force have remained relatively unchanged. Currently approximately 85 percent of all teachers are White and the overwhelming majority are monolingual English speakers. Being White is not a problem; there are many skilled White teachers who are able to teach across lines of difference.[23] However, because neighborhoods are often segregated and schools are more segregated now than they were in 1954 when the Supreme Court ruled that legal segregation was unconstitutional, preservice teachers (and others) have fewer opportunities to develop authentic relationships across lines of racial/ethnic, linguistic, and socioeconomic difference. Consequently, the majority of teachers enter the classroom with little meaningful exposure to people of color. Research suggests that many White preservice teachers enter the teacher education programs with stereotypes and depressed expectations for poor and minority students[24] and most teacher education programs do relatively little to help preservice teachers to develop more robust and accurate understandings of poor communities and communities of color.[25]

Many teachers believe they shouldn't acknowledge differences within the classroom, or that acknowledging difference can be construed as discrimination. They hold steadfast to the color/culture-blind mantra, "I don't see color; I only see kids." On some level, viewing all students as the same may seem practical. Certainly all students should be entitled to quality educational experiences, regardless of their race, class, or other identity characteristics. However, turning a blind eye to cultural differences among students does not allow the affirmation of those aspects of identity that students may find salient. This colorblind perspective to teaching stands in contrast to culturally responsive teaching and allows for the continued exclusion of students of color and other students who have been traditionally underserved by schools from the curriculum. Moreover, it prevents the implementation of differentiated approaches to working with students that teach to and through students' cultures. (See Chapter 6 for a more detailed look at differentiated instruction.)

Most teachers have life stories and experiences that are drastically different from those of students of color. A lack of knowledge about cultural differences or ignoring those differences completely can result in cultural discontinuities in the classroom that impact student learning.[26] Moreover, many preservice teachers enact resistant stances when presented with worldviews that are incongruent with their own.[27] For example, Aja LaDuke's study reports students' tendencies to attribute disparities in resources across school districts solely to issues of class, coupled with an unwillingness to examine inherent intersections with race and ethnicity.[28] If serious attempts to bridge these potential gaps and improve the quality of education for all students are to be made, then it is imperative that teachers develop competencies for multicultural teaching. Increasing the academic achievement of students of color requires teachers to develop the skills necessary to be successful with students of diverse backgrounds. Objective 4 offers suggestions for teachers seeking to become culturally responsive educators.

 Mastery Test

> **OBJECTIVE 3**   **To reflect on one's own identity and the various ways that it may differ from the students being taught**

Identity Pie

Some aspects of our identities are more important to us than others. It is imperative for teachers to know what their students value. For this activity, create a pie chart that represents your strength of identification with the following identity categories:

Race/Ethnicity

Language

Class

Gender

Religion

One other aspect of your identity that you choose (i.e. teacher, friend, athlete, etc. . . .)

Each category should comprise a portion of the "pie" that is represented by a percentage. All of the categories should add up to 100 percent. Share your pie chart with a partner and describe your underlying reasons for constructing your chart the way that you did. Write a short reflection about any new understandings you have as a result of this exercise.

OBJECTIVE 4   **To identify strategies to make teaching more culturally responsive**

■ What Do I Need to Know to Become a Culturally Responsive Educator?

■ INTASC Principles
2, 3, 4, 5, 6, 7, 9

There is much that teachers seeking to become more culturally responsive need to know, far too much to address adequately here. In what follows, several broad concepts are addressed—including the sociopolitical context of schooling, promising practices among culturally responsive teachers, and the role of language in culturally responsive teaching—that can inform the work of teachers.

The Sociopolitical Context of Schooling in the United States

Many groups of students have been historically underserved by schools. Patterns of academic underachievement have remained consistent over time for African Americans, Latinos, and students from lower socioeconomic strata. Several scholars have suggested that these outcomes are not random but rather are the byproduct of the ways that schools are set up to reproduce racial and class-based stratification.[29] In his groundbreaking text, *Savage Inequalities,* Jonathan Kozol documented the connection between per-pupil funding and graduation rates.[30] His work, as well as that of other scholars, suggests that because schools receive a significant portion of their funding from property taxes, wealthy communities often fund their schools at a higher levels than lower-income communities.[31] He found a direct relationship between per-pupil funding and graduation rates, with higher-socioeconomic-strata districts having significantly higher high school completion and college attendance rates than districts that serve poorer communities. Given the connection between school funding, particularly per-pupil expenditure, and graduation rates, these contentions seem to have merit. While some, such as Eric Hanushek,[32] argue that there is a weak relationship between per-pupil expenditures and academic outcomes, most educators believe the two are closely related.

This may be a change from the ways that many teachers think about their work and about K–12 schooling. By and large, schools have worked well for most teachers, preparing them to pursue higher education and employment as a teacher. Conversely, schools have not worked for many of the students teachers may serve. Acknowledging and responding to the sociopolitical contexts in which students are embedded, which include their particular histories as well as experiences in schools, is a central aspect of culturally responsive teaching. To do that, teachers must become familiar with those histories and the current policies and practices that continue to marginalize some students while supporting others.

Teachers must also transform schools from sites of oppression to spaces that facilitate learning and liberation. It is not enough to identify the system as unresponsive; teachers must work with students to change it. Culturally responsive teaching has its roots in critical pedagogy, an approach to teaching and learning that uses education as a vehicle for varying degrees of liberation. That is, teachers work with students to be able to "read the words so that they can read the world."[33] Critical approaches to teaching help us think about the role of power in teaching. Students are encouraged to learn valuable literacy, numeracy, and analytical skills in the process of applying those skills to improve their lives and those of other oppressed individuals.[34] In short, culturally responsive teaching is also about power. Students are encouraged to critically analyze their own experiences and explore how their inclusion or omission from the curriculum, for example, is a reflection of power. They are urged to examine issues in their communities, like representation of elected officials or gentrification (the process through which inner-city communities are transformed by displacing poor and working class residents with more affluent ones, thus raising the property value in the neighborhood), to acquire and refine their skills and to become more critical consumers of democracy. This type of education—one that responds to the sociocultural and sociopolitical realities of students' lives by extending education beyond the walls of the school and the confines of the school calendar—can be liberating for students and teachers. This more holistic approach to working with students acknowledges the impact of power relations on the student–teacher relationship, stresses the importance of self-reflection and inner well-being as a precursor to developing positive teaching practices, and includes reflecting on teachers' own culture and the culture of the students with whom they work.

Because many teachers and/or their ancestors have gone through a process of assimilation in the United States, shedding parts of their identities in favor of becoming more "American," they often approach education through an assimilationist perspective that requires students to shed certain aspects of their identities, such as language, to experience academic success. Consequently many students who have been unable or unwilling to conform to the dominant norms have dropped out or been pushed out of schools. To become a culturally responsive educator, teachers need to look beyond standardized test scores and challenge scripted curricula and approaches to teaching that don't place value on students' identities and learning styles. Teachers must move beyond deficit perspectives, which question students' capabilities and blame cultural characteristics for student failure, to work in solidarity with students and communities to obtain a high-quality and meaningful education.

Promising Practices

One promising approach for helping students traditionally underserved by public education is Youth Participatory Action Research (YPAR). YPAR helps students learn academic skills by identifying an issue they care about, and then researching, crafting, and implementing remedies to address that issue. YPAR engages youth in learning experiences connected to their histories, their cultural identities, and the sociopolitical contexts in which they are embedded. It "is typically undertaken as critical scholarship, by multi-generational collectives, to interrogate conditions of social injustice through social theory with a dedicated commitment to social action."[35] This kind of research is deeply rooted in the struggle for social justice and educational equity. According to Shawn Ginwright, "with an emphasis on democratizing knowledge, fostering critical inquiry of daily life and developing liberatory practices, YPAR is both an art and a method to engage youth in democratic problem solving."[36] Because it is a co-constructed learning experience created by youth and teachers, YPAR represents culturally responsive teaching. As such, many of the scholars working on YPAR projects with youth have documented societal changes brought about as a result of these efforts as well as the positive impact such projects have had on students' academic trajectories.[37]

Instead of being positioned as problems to be fixed, young people engaged in YPAR are repositioned from solely consumers of knowledge to creators of knowledge. Participatory action research demonstrates the potential of culturally responsive teaching to serve as a vehicle for simultaneously facilitating the development of academic and interpersonal skills among students and engaging youth as equal partners in the struggle for social justice and educational equity.

Exploring the Role of Language in Culturally Responsive Teaching

Culturally relevant pedagogy has several components, including cultural awareness and affirmation, an examination of power relations, and curriculum reform. One aspect of culturally responsive teaching that is a fundamental part of cultural awareness and affirmation is language use in the classroom. While speaking standard English does not guarantee access to higher education, high-status professions, and opportunities to communicate effectively with elected officials to change the system, *not* having a command of standard English can definitely be a hindrance. However, the value placed on students' native languages and dialects can have an impact on their willingness to adopt a new language or language form. Moreover, it can influence their academic achievement.[38] Language policies developed by legislators, courts, and legal forums directly impact the quality of education students receive in classrooms around the country. This section will document the importance of supporting a variety of languages (particularly Ebonics/AAVE and Spanish) in culturally responsive classrooms.

In Oakland, California in 1996, there was a push to get Ebonics, a language used by many African Americans that has unique speech patterns and rules for discourse, recognized as a valid language and used in instruction as a bridge to the acquisition of standard English. The controversy transcended the borders of the state of California and became the subject of national debate. Reflecting on the debate, Delpit and Perry[39] stress that language is intricately tied to group identity and that culturally responsive teachers have a responsibility to support students in the acquisition of standard English literacy while affirming and placing value on the language that they speak at home. In her reflection, Delpit notes that a child's native language "is the language they heard when their mothers nursed them and changed their diapers and played peek-a-boo with them. It is the language through which they first encountered love, nurturance, and joy."[40] To have their speech constantly corrected and never receive support for it as an important means of communication can negatively influence children's self-esteem and consequently their motivation to learn in school.

Delpit and Perry also reveal the negative perceptions that mainstream teachers and community members have of African American communicative patterns. As a part of her research, Delpit had both African Americans and White adults comment on stories written by African American students using their native communicative patterns.[41] She found that the non-African American participants most often rated the stories as poorly constructed and had negative perceptions about the potential of the authors. Participants familiar with Ebonics rated the stories more favorably and had more positive views about the students' potential. If a teacher is not exposed to different language forms and taught to value them, it is difficult for them to practice culturally responsive instruction.

Judith Baker, a high school English teacher, concluded that there are three forms of the English language that students need to learn before they can be successful.[42] "Home" English, she contends, is learned from family members and peers and, in the case of families for whom English is a second language, it is usually a mixture of the native language and English. "Formal" English is learned in schools, and "Professional" English is learned through higher education or job training. She attempts to make students aware of the differences as a means to have them master the mechanics of all three. Like other teachers who practice culturally relevant pedagogy, essential to her work is a respect for the language of the home.[43]

In an attempt to expose the correlation between power, language, and literacy, Purcell-Gates contends

> [C]hildren come to school with different experiences. These experiences are culturally driven. Within this I see literacy use as cultural practice. It is cultural practice because reading and writing are woven into everyday experiences of people, and these everyday activities, attitudes, and beliefs help to define and distinguish among cultural groups.[44]

Purcell-Gates urges teachers not to see students from minority groups as deficient but rather as different. She suggests that it is a teacher's responsibility to expose students to what they need to know in a culturally sensitive manner, acknowledging the role that power relations play in the process.

Linda Christensen believes that language practices, in particular reading and writing, are political acts that have the potential to liberate people from the shackles of oppression.[45] She contends that the achievement gap that exists between White students and many students of color is an example of how literacy is often denied to some groups of people and used to subordinate them. According to Christensen, reading and writing have the potential to be transformative acts that can help people "rise up" and liberate themselves. Sensitive to the fact that language use is often reflective of social class and cultural background, she suggests helping students learn the standards of language use while also challenging them to evaluate who makes—and who benefits—from the rules regarding the use of standard English.

Ladson-Billings demonstrates how the status of the language that students speak can cause teachers to make judgments about the kind of education students should receive.[46] During her research she noticed that an African American speaker of Ebonics was given "permission to fail" by her teachers, and she documents examples of how such students were held to a lower standard. While White speakers of standard English in the class were held to high standards and expected to complete assignments, the African American student was not allowed to share her experiences and was not encouraged to complete her writing assignments like the rest of the class. She concludes that culturally responsive educators need to affirm the diversity of language use in the classroom while maintaining high academic standards and support for all students.

Supporting language diversity in the classroom has received considerable attention. There are significant data that underscore the importance of supporting the development of native languages of English language learners.[47] As the study of language use in the classroom evolves, it should also include study of the use of Spanish (standard and nonstandard forms) when working with Latinos in "mainstream" classrooms. For example, attempting to explain the low levels of achievement among Chicano students, Trueba found that there is a relationship between the support of students' language and culture and their school adjustment.[48] He conducted research in two low-performing districts in southern California and focused on developing culturally appropriate methodologies for teaching English. He found that the teachers in the study, the majority of whom were White, monolingual English speakers, had negative views about the potential of their students and did not think they could be successful. When the classrooms were reorganized into smaller communities within the larger class context and built on issues that were important to the students as the subjects for writing assignments, students acquired essential literacy skills and made some positive changes in their schools and communities.

In a guide for teachers, Hernandez calls for a more culturally responsive pedagogy for linguistically diverse students in multilingual classrooms and describes it as being "sensitive to cultural differences, appropriate to psychological, economic, and social realities, and characterized by the best educational practices."[49] It is her contention that teachers must understand that

- Children acquire language and culture within their communities.
- By the time children come to school, they possess some understanding of language and how it is used.
- Involvement in socially meaningful activities is conducive to development of higher-level cognitive and communicative skills.
- Language and academic development are interactive processes involving linguistic, sociocultural, and cognitive knowledge and experiences.
- Socioculturally and linguistically meaningful contexts enhance learning.

Her detailed description of culturally responsive teaching is a valuable resource for all educators who work in multilingual classrooms. As we have seen, culturally relevant pedagogy is contextual; that is, it looks different depending on the culture of the students in the classroom. While the underlying goals and themes are the same, it also *sounds* different when employed by teachers with diverse groups of students. Smith states that "teaching is, above all, a linguistic activity" and "language is at the very heart of teaching."[50] Yet the role of language is rarely addressed in the discourse on culturally responsive teaching. Affirming linguistic diversity in the classroom has become even more difficult with states across the country eliminating bilingual programs and proposing harsh penalties for teachers who do not conform to such regulations. Culturally responsive teachers have recognized the importance of language in creating relationships and practicing culturally responsive approaches in their classroom, and they have learned different languages to help them support their students and promote their academic achievement.

Creating a Culturally Responsive Classroom

One of the most exciting activities for teachers can be exhibiting students' work on the walls to celebrate their accomplishments. In addition to the physical presentation of the space, it is also important to consider the social dynamics of the classroom and treat the class, consisting of students, teachers, staff, and others, as a socially constructed community. By *socially constructed* I mean that it is created and sustained by the members of the community. Too often the culture of the classroom, including norms for behavior, curriculum content, assessment practices, and so forth, are dictated by the teacher or other adults in the building. Students, by and large, are absent from important decision-making processes and are treated as if they either have nothing to contribute or as if their potential contributions lack value. Culturally responsive teachers, in contrast, engage their students in the decision-making processes that impact the overall community. The culture of the culturally responsive classroom is negotiated and co-constructed by the various members of the community. Using this approach is more likely to create a climate that is conducive to learning. Moreover, students are more likely to conform to rules they helped create and more likely to engage in curriculum content that they influenced and/or selected.

In many districts teachers are pressured to adhere strictly to state curriculum frameworks and emphasize to students the importance of passing state standardized tests. Culturally responsive teachers find ways to take the frameworks, which often are not in and of themselves culturally responsive, and create learning experiences that affirm, engage, and educate students. This process is aided considerably when students are involved in the process and allowed to create and/or influence the curriculum. Think for a moment what it might be like to go through your entire schooling experience without ever learning anything about your cultural heritage or history or never having read a book with a protagonist or author that shares your cultural background. For many students in U.S. schools, this is a reality, particularly in schools that have placed increased emphasis and attention on raising the standardized test scores of students. Ironically, data suggest that these skill-and-drill approaches do little to support meaningful learning and may in fact do more to further alienate and marginalize students.[51]

Another practical strategy for teachers seeking to create culturally responsive learning communities involves softening the rigid dichotomy that can exist between the roles of teacher and student. Of course at times there are clear delineations in these roles that make sense. However, teachers don't have to always be the "sage on the stage," filling students with information. Culturally responsive teachers, in contrast, allow themselves to be taught by their students and others. They embody the commitment to lifelong learning that they try to instill in their students. In culturally responsive classrooms, teachers are also students while students can also be teachers. The classroom community is enriched as a whole, as all of the members are invested in each other's personal and professional development.

One of the best examples in the research literature of such a process can be found in the work of Mary Cowhey, an elementary school teacher who published a text documenting her implementation of culturally responsive teaching with early elementary school children.[52] In Mrs. Cowhey's room, dubbed by the students as the Peace Classroom, students were active participants in creating rigorous units of study, ranging from a unit on water treatment to another on the experiences of enslaved peoples enduring the Middle Passage. These units moved beyond superficial treatment of these issues "dumbed down" to be more consumable for first and second graders. Rather, the material was brought to life and connected to real-world situations. For example, as part of a unit on fractions where students learned math concepts while baking pies, students simultaneously studied poverty and the experiences of the working poor by delivering those pies to a local food pantry for Thanksgiving. Through their interaction with the pantry staff and consumers, students developed an understanding of some of the root causes of poverty while simultaneously learning fractions and other content prescribed by the state curriculum. Students in Mrs. Cowhey's

⁂ Mastery Test

OBJECTIVE 4   To identify strategies to make teaching more culturally responsive

Creating a Culturally Responsive Lesson

You are a fourth-grade teacher at a culturally and linguistically diverse elementary school. In your class of twenty-two students, you have students who identify themselves as African American, Latino, and Asian. Several of your students identify as bilingual, speaking two or more languages, and one of the Latino students in your class has recently immigrated to the United States. You are preparing a lesson designed to get students to master the following state standard: *Describe the importance of significant events in local and state history and their connections to United States history.* Identify what relevant variables should be considered in creating and delivering a culturally responsive lesson. Outline your thought process.

A Lesson Planned, Taught, and Revised

Construct and implement a lesson plan that you believe is culturally responsive to a particular class of students. Upon completion of the lesson, reflect on the process. Think about what worked, what didn't, and what new ideas you may have as a result of teaching it. Revise your original lesson plan to incorporate your reflections. Submit the original lesson plan, a revised lesson plan, and one to two pages documenting your reflections about your teaching and your students' learning.

class also created rules that governed behaviors of the students and adults as well as a system of accountability aimed at monitoring and responding to behaviors that the youth viewed as incongruent with the goals of their class. While many examples of culturally responsive teaching are focused on the secondary level,[53] Cowhey's work underscores the potential to implement critical approaches to teaching that are culturally responsive in the early grades as well.

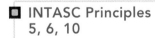

OBJECTIVE 5   **To create opportunities to inform personal and professional development in relation to culturally responsive teaching**

☐ Who Do I Need to Be(come) as a Culturally Responsive Educator?

☐ **INTASC Principles 5, 6, 10**

Creating a culturally responsive classroom is one aspect of practicing culturally responsive teaching. As emphasized in Objective 3, another important aspect of this work involves teachers reflecting on their own identities and how these identities influence teaching and learning. The "identities of the [teacher and students have] to do with the fundamental issues of the curriculum, as much as with what is hidden as what is explicit and, obviously, with questions of teaching and learning."[54] It is difficult to affirm the identities of others before acknowledging and taking inventory of your own identities.

As noted earlier, identities are complex and emerge from a variety of sources. Some identities may position an individual in the dominant group where many others, or those who are in power, share these identity categories. Other identities can result in an individual experiencing oppression and marginalization. Individuals tend to hold more fervently to identities for which they are targeted or prosecuted; dominant identities tend to receive less attention. Consequently, some identities can position youth as the "other." This process has resulted in many individuals who hold dominant identities seeing themselves as the norm and others as deviating from it. For example, I have heard teachers say things such as, "I'm not ethnic; I'm normal." This position is problematic in that it frames one particular dominant identity as the norm and other identities as deviant. Moreover, approaching youth with this lens can be alienating. Even if teachers do not have a strong sense of ethnic identity, for example, they have to allow for the possibility that students might.

The process of becoming a culturally responsive teacher is one where teachers engage in serious introspection, taking inventory of their various identities and how these can potentially shape their worldviews and their practice in the classroom. For example, if you believe that students should abandon individual ethnic identities in favor of a national one, this is certain to impact what you teach and how you teach it. It is imperative that teachers develop an understanding of themselves and of themselves in relation to others. These understandings inform the teaching and learning process. That is not to say that teachers can or should change their identities to match those of their students. However, they should be aware of their identities and how they relate to those of their students.

This process of introspection does not have to occur in isolation. It can and should also include meaningful immersion in the communities in which teachers work or with those with whom teachers want to become more familiar. This effort moves beyond the walls of the school house. It is a process whereby teachers becoming culturally connected.[55] Culturally responsive teachers don't wait for students to bring their cultures to the classroom. Rather, they go out into the community, where culture is created and expressed, to become more familiar with the "funds of knowledge"[56] that are present in those communities. This connection to the community becomes part of the culturally responsive teachers' lifestyles. They are constantly engaged in the life of the community, as learners and active participants, and use the knowledge they gain to inform their work in the classroom. Crossing these cultural boundaries can be difficult, but the benefits of connecting with youth and the promise of culturally responsive teaching are far-reaching.

Vignette 2

Ms. S. Crosses Main Street

Ms. S. is a 23-year-old, second-year teacher working in a district that is approximately 85 percent African American, Latino, and Asian. Having grown up in a predominantly White community and attending a private Christian school, Ms. S. had relatively few interactions with people of color growing up. She attended a midsize, private liberal arts college located in a city in the northeast. Although the community surrounding the college was racially/ethnically and linguistically diverse, the college looked much like the schools she attended as a child. The few students of color she encountered, in her estimation, seemed to stick together, and she never felt comfortable trying to connect with them. Her closest circle of friends was very much like her, sharing aspects of her various identities.

A child of the 90s, Ms. S. was influenced by popular music and loved television shows with diverse characters. As part of a project in one of the classes she took in her first year in college, she had an opportunity to volunteer in a local day-care facility, and this experience sparked a love of teaching. Coupled with a course on Multicultural Education she took as a junior, she developed a strong desire to work with students less fortunate than herself. Upon entering her undergraduate program, she was focused on becoming a teacher and working with students of diverse backgrounds in the settings where students would need her the most. She excelled in her coursework and student teaching experiences. Upon graduation she was quickly hired by an urban district within a 20-minute drive of her parent's house. She lived there while she was teaching to save money and eventually purchase a home of her own.

Ms. S deeply cares about her students, yet she struggles to get her fifth-grade students to complete homework assignments regularly and make progress on the quarterly assessments she administers to prepare them for the state test. She believes their struggles in the classroom must be tied to issues in their homes or communities, like poverty. Each day as she makes the commute to the school, crossing Main Street, she wonders about the people she passes along the way. She takes note of the many abandoned buildings and empty storefronts. She also admires the architecture of the local Christian church, the smells that emanate from the bakery, and the vibrant colors of the signposts advertising upcoming events in the community. While she appreciates the diversity that exists in the city in which she taught, she never seems to find time to explore the area. Besides, she is extremely nervous about how she would be received by others.

❯ YOUR TURN

1. What would you suggest that Ms. S. in the vignette above do to help her improve the experiences and academic outcomes of her students?
2. What role might culturally responsive teaching play in transforming her classroom?
3. What might Ms. S. do to learn more about her students and their community?
4. Does it make sense for Ms. S. to be nervous? Have you ever been nervous about a new experience that forced you to cross lines of difference? What was it and how did you deal with it?
5. What might Ms. S. need to know to be a more effective teacher in this setting? How should she go about learning this?

Rethinking Teacher Professional Development for CRT

There is an endless array of practices in which teachers could engage to become more culturally responsive. Because culture is fluid, dynamic, and everchanging, it would be fruitless to propose strategies for connecting to a specific group of students. Instead, what follows are several ideas that teachers may want to consider on their journey toward becoming more culturally responsive teachers. These strategies can be implemented in a wide variety of settings and can help inform the work of teachers.

- *Become a member of the community.* Throughout this chapter the intersections between professional and personal development in the process of becoming a culturally responsive teacher have been highlighted. One of the most obvious suggestions for teachers seeking to learn more about their students and connect with their students' communities would be to live in the community in which they teach. While there are benefits as well as potential drawbacks to living in the district, it does reflect a heightened level of investment in the community. In addition, teachers would have the opportunity to see students in a variety of settings outside of school, allowing them to develop extended understandings of students and their communities. Residing in the community also allows for immersion in the cultures to which culturally responsive teachers are trying to respond.

- *Asset mapping.* Teachers who choose to live outside of the districts in which they work can also make meaningful and sustained connections to the communities they serve. One way to learn more about the valuable assets that exist in students' communities is through asset mapping. Asset mapping involves developing a list of community-based organizations, resources, and other important social networks that exist in the community and utilizing them as a resource in your work with students. These spaces can also contribute significantly to teachers' personal and professional development.

- *Student-led tours.* One way to position students as teachers and engage in more equitable power relations is to allow students to take you on a journey through their communities. Ask students what aspects of the community they identify as important and which they want their teachers to know about. Engage students in conversation around what they included on the tour, what was omitted, and why.

- *Immersion experiences.* Teachers should take every opportunity to immerse themselves in the communities in which they teach. Students appreciate interacting with teachers in a variety of settings. For example, there are a lot of reasons cited to explain why so many suburban students excel in school and go on to higher education, including parents' educational level, socioeconomic status, and so forth. I assert that an additional contributing factor is the fact that many teachers either live in the suburban communities in which they teach or live in similar communities and are familiar with the sociocultural realities of these communities. Students of color are far less likely to have teachers who live in their community or communities like theirs. Particularly for teachers who are not familiar with the communities in which they teach, it is imperative that teachers take every opportunity possible to immerse themselves in the community.

◼ Conclusion: Toward a Grounded Theory of CRT

Too many students languish in classrooms where teachers overlook or completely ignore their cultural identities, resulting in a subsequent alienation from school. As teachers and other school agents search for ways to improve the educational experiences and outcomes for students traditionally underserved by schools, they often overlook the role that culture, broadly defined, plays within teaching and learning. In contrast, this chapter asserts that culturally responsive teaching, as part of a larger reform movement, has the potential to (re)engage students and promote their academic achievement. By developing a deeper understanding of culturally responsive teaching, teachers will learn the skills necessary to transform curricula and teaching practices so that they are more responsive to the cultural and educational needs of students.

This chapter has attempted to move away from overly prescriptive models for culturally responsive teaching and teacher professional development. Teachers are encouraged to develop site-specific, or grounded, approaches to culturally responsive teaching that emerge from the particular settings in which they work. There are several core aspects of this approach that were highlighted above. The recommendations for those seeking to become culturally responsive teachers include

1. Pay attention to what students already know, have experienced, and value.

2. Learn how your own students construct complex, hybrid identities from multiple sources and respond to these.

3. Value students' home languages. Put your students in a position to learn about and work on issues they care about and/or to change schooling for traditionally underserved youth.

4. Recognize your own culture and the role it plays in how you might view the experiences and values you seek to promote.

5. Integrate personal and professional development as you seek to connect to the cultural communities of which your students might be members.

While not an exhaustive list, the recommendations shared here are intended as a springboard for teachers to begin their journey into culturally responsive teaching. Taking a grounded theory approach allows teachers to respond to the complex and unique ways youth construct and enact their cultural identities. Culturally responsive teaching could look different within two classrooms in the same building serving youth from the same community. Just as each individual is diverse, the communities that diverse individuals co-construct will be equally diverse. As such, teachers need to remain open to the various ways that students will perform their identities. Implementing culturally responsive pedagogy has the potential to transform the educational experiences and outcomes for youth who have been traditionally underserved by schools.

 Mastery Test

OBJECTIVE 5   **To create opportunities to inform personal and professional development in relation to culturally responsive teaching**

You should select one cultural group with whom you currently work or have significant interaction to explore. The goal of this activity is to get you to learn about a culture other than your own, so you should select a group of which you are not a member. Learn more about this group from primary sources by engaging in any combination of the following: read history and scholarship written by members of this group; read literature, poetry, local publications or newspaper articles; the sites on the Internet that members of this group have developed; have lunch or dinner at a local restaurant; go to an art exhibit, concert, or theater performance; attend a political or cultural event in the community or a parent-teacher association meeting at a local school. Drawing from your cultural immersion experiences, develop a reflection paper about your cultural exploration and what you have learned.

Observation Worksheet

CULTURALLY RESPONSIVE TEACHING

As you have seen throughout the chapter, culturally responsive teaching is multifaceted and involves various dimensions of the teaching and learning process that include what is taught, how it is taught, to whom, and by whom. This activity offers you the opportunity to reflect critically on culturally responsive classroom practice.

Directions: Observe a classroom for a day. Use the following questions to guide your reflection.

Provide a brief description of the school, the community in which the school is located, and the class you are observing.

_____

_____

_____

_____

_____

_____

Look at walls, posters, and media centers of the school. Who is represented? Who is not represented? How does the visual representation of items displayed in the school reflect of the demographic characteristics of the school? Of the community? Of the country?

_____

_____

_____

_____

_____

_____

Examine the texts that are being used in the class. Does the content reflect the cultural backgrounds of students in the class? How are the following groups represented: people of color, women, youth, working class people?

_____

_____

_____

_____

_____

_____

Examine the interactions between teacher and students. Do these seem to be based on mutual respect? What aspects of the interactions, if any, would you classify as culturally responsive? How does the teacher connect the course content to students' prior knowledge and experiences?

_____

_____

_____

_____

_____

_____

What aspects of student identities seem to be affirmed in the process of teaching and learning? What aspects of student identities might be suppressed during the lesson?

_____

_____

_____

_____

_____

_____

What, if anything, might you do differently to make the lesson more culturally responsive?

_____

_____

_____

_____

_____

_____

ADDITIONAL RESOURCES

Readings

Racial/Ethnic Identity Development

Flores-Gonzalez, N. (2002). *School kids/street kids: Identity development in Latino students*. New York: Teachers College Press.

Tatum, B. D. (1997). *Why are all the Black kids sitting together in the cafeteria? And other conversation about race*. New York: Basic Books.

Teacher Education and Curriculum Reform

Howard, G. R. (1999). *We can't teach what we don't know: White teachers, multiracial schools.* New York: Teachers College Press.

Freire, P. (1998). *Teachers as cultural workers.* Boulder, CO: Westview Press.

Sleeter, C. (2005). *Un-standardizing curriculum: Multicultural teaching in the standards based classroom.* New York: Teachers College Press.

Gay, G. (2003). *Becoming multicultural educators: Personal journey toward professional agency.* San Francisco, CA: Jossey-Bass.

Critical Literacy

Christensen, L. (2000). *Reading, writing and rising up.* Portland, OR: Rethinking Schools.

Finn, P. J. (1999). *Literacy with an attitude: Educating working-class children in their own self-interest.* Albany: State University of New York Press.

Vasquez, V. M. (2004). *Negotiating critical literacies with young children.* Mahwah, NJ: Erlbaum.

Cowhey, M. (2006). *Black ants and Buddhists: Thinking critically and teaching differently in the primary grades.* Portland, ME: Stenhouse.

Culturally Responsive Pedagogy

Gay, G. (2000). *Culturally responsive teaching.* New York: Teachers College Press.

Ladson-Billings, G. (1994). *The dreamkeepers: Successful teachers of African American children.* San Francisco: Jossey-Bass.

Bilingual Education

Garcia, E. E. (2005). *Teaching and learning in two languages: Bilingualism and schooling in the United States.* New York: Teachers College Press.

Pérez, B., & Torres-Guzmán, M. E. (1992). *Learning in two worlds: An integrated Spanish/English biliteracy approach.* New York: Longman.

Multicultural Education

Nieto, S., & Bode, P. (2008). *Affirming diversity: The sociopolitical context of multicultural education.* Boston: Pearson.

Lee, E., Menkart, D., & Okazawa-Rey, M. (Eds.). (1998). *Beyond heroes and holidays: A practical guide to K-12 anti-racist, multicultural education and staff development.* Washington, D.C.: Network of Educators on the Americas.

Schniedewind, N., & Davidson, E. (1983). *Open minds to equality: A sourcebook of learning activities to promote race, class and age equity.* Old Tappan, NJ: Prentice-Hall.

Banks, J. A. (1993). Approaches to multicultural education reform. In J. A. Banks & A. M. Banks (Eds.), *Multicultural education: Issues and perspectives* (pp. 195–214). Boston: Allyn & Bacon.

Narratives

Rodriguez, L. J. (1993). *Always running: La vida loca, Gang days in L.A.* Willimantic, CT: Curbstone Press.

McCall, N. (1994). *Makes me wanna holler: A young Black man in America.* New York: Random House.

Thomas, P. (1997). *Down these mean streets.* New York: Vintage.

Malcolm X. (1965). *The autobiography of Malcolm X.* New York: Grove.

 Websites

Rethinking Schools: http://www.rethinkingschools.org
Rethinking Schools is an organization focused on issues pertinent to urban schools, with particular emphasis on equity across racial lines. This organization is committed to the idea of free, public, and equal education for all.

EdChange: http://www.edchange.org
EdChange is dedicated to diversity and equity in ourselves, our schools and our society. We act to shape schools and communities in which all people, regardless of race, gender, sexual orientation, class, (dis)ability, language, or religion, have equitable opportunities to achieve to their fullest.*

National Association for Multicultural Education (NAME): http://www.nameorg.org
The official website of the National Association for Multicultural Education (NAME), an organization that would bring together individuals and groups with an interest in multicultural education from all levels of education, different academic disciplines, and from diverse educational institutions and occupations.*

Native Village: http://www.nativevillage.org
The Native Village web site was created for youth, educators, families, and friends who wish to celebrate the rich, diverse cultures of the Americas' First Peoples.*

New Horizons: http://www.newhorizons.org/strategies/multicultural/front_multicultural.htm
A collection of articles and readings, by scholars and K–12 students, focused on issues of multicultural education.

Gay, Lesbian, Straight Education Network: http://www.glsen.org
The Gay, Lesbian and Straight Education Network, or GLSEN, is working to ensure safe and effective schools for all students.*

Pew Hispanic Center: http://pewhispanic.org/
The Pew Hispanic Center's mission is to improve understanding of the diverse Hispanic population in the United States and to chronicle Latinos' growing impact on the nation.*

American Indian Movement: http://www.aimovement.org/
A movement dedicated to helping the Native People regain human rights and achieve restitutions and restorations.*

National Women's History Project: http://www.nwhp.org/
An educational nonprofit organization whose mission is to recognize and celebrate the diverse and historic accomplishments of women by providing information and educational materials and programs.*

Teaching Tolerance: http://www.tolerance.org/
A principal online destination for people interested in dismantling bigotry and creating, in hate's stead, communities that value diversity.*

Understanding Prejudice: http://www.understandingprejudice.org/
A web site for students, teachers, and others interested in the causes and consequences of prejudice.*

Asian American Curriculum Project: http://www.asianamericanbooks.com/index.shtml

The Asian American Curriculum Project, Inc., an award-winning organization, has grown to offer the most complete collection of Asian American books.

Patchwork of African American Life: http://www.kn.pacbell.com/wired/BHM/index.html
A link to six web sites dedicated to African American history.

White Antiracist Community Action Network: http://www.euroamerican.org/
A multiracial organization that looks at whiteness and White American culture.*

*****Source: http://www.nameorg.org/links.html**

For these links and additional resources, please visit the Premium Website at **www.cengage.com/login**.

◉ NOTES

1. R. Fry and F. Gonzales, "One-in-Five and Growing Fast: A Profile of Hispanic Public School Students," (Washington, D.C.: Pew Hispanic Center, 2008).

2. This excerpt is taken from a student's assignment submitted as part of a class on action research in which students examined Latino education. Carmen (a pseudonym) was a junior in high school when she completed this assignment.

3. G. Ladson-Billings, "Toward a Theory of Culturally Relevant Pedagogy," *American Educational Research Journal* 32, no. 3 (1995): 465–491; C. D. Lee, "Culturally Responsive Pedagogy and Performance-Based Assessment," *The Journal of Negro Education* 67, no. 3 (Summer 1998): 268–279; T. C. Howard, "Powerful Pedagogy for African American Students: A Case of Four Teachers," *Urban Education* 36, no. 2 (2001): 179–202; A. M. Villegas and T. Lucas, "Preparing Culturally Responsive Teachers: Rethinking the Curriculum," *Journal of Teacher Education* 53, no. 1 (2002): 20–32; L. I. Bartolomé, "Beyond the Methods Fetish: Toward a Humanizing Pedagogy," in *The Critical Pedagogy Reader*, eds. A. Darder, M. Baltodano, and R. D. Torres (New York: Routledge, 2003).

4. G. Gay, *Culturally Responsive Teaching: Theory, Research, and Practice* (New York: Teachers College Press, 2000): p. 29.

5. G. Ladson-Billings, "Like Lightning in a Bottle: Attempting to Capture the Pedagogical Excellence of Successful Teachers of Black Students," *International Journal of Qualitative Studies in Education* 3, (1990): 335–344.

6. K. H. Au and A. J. Kawakami, "Cultural Congruence in Instruction," in *Teaching Diverse Populations: Formulating a Knowledge Base*, eds. E. R. Hollins, J. E. King, and W. Hayman (Albany, NY: State University of New York Press, 1994).

7. E. Jacob and C. Jordan, eds., "Explaining the School Performance of Minority Students." [theme issue], *Anthropology and Education Quarterly* 18, no. 4 (1987).

8. G. Ladson-Billings, "But That's Just Good Teaching! The Case for Culturally Relevant Pedagogy," *Theory Into Practice* 34, (Summer 1995): 159–165.

9. G. Gay, *Culturally Responsive Teaching: Theory, Research, and Practice* (New York: Teachers College Press, 2000).

10. L. Moll, "Funds of Knowledge for Teaching: Using a Qualitative Approach to Connect Homes and Classrooms," *Theory Into Practice* 31, no. 2 (1992): 132–41.

11. A. Valenzuela, *Subtractive Schooling: US-Mexican Youth and the Politics of Caring* (Albany: State University of New York Press, 1999).

12. J. Piaget, *The Origins of Intelligence in Children* (International Universities Press, 1974); J. Dewey, *Experience and Education*, (New York: Macmillan, 1959); E. Erikson, *Identity: Youth and Crisis* (New York: W.W. Norton Company, 1968).

13. N. González, "Beyond Culture: The Hybridity of Funds of Knowledge," in *Funds of Knowledge,* ed. N. González, L. C. Moll, and C. Amanti (Mahwah, NJ: Lawrence Erlbaum Associates, Inc., 2005): p. 35.

14. K. Gutiérrez and B. Rogoff, "Cultural Ways of Learning: Individual Traits or Repertoires of Practice," *Educational Researcher* 32, no. 5 (2003): 19–25.

15. J. G. Irizarry, "Ethnic and Urban Intersections in the Classroom: Latino Students, Hybrid Identities, and Culturally Responsive Pedagogy," *Multicultural Perspectives* 9, no. 3 (2007): 1–7.

16. J. M. R. Duncan-Andrade, "Your Best Friend or Your Worst Enemy: Popular Culture, Pedagogy

and Curriculum in Urban Classrooms," *Review of Education Pedagogy & Cultural Studies* 26, no. 4 (2004): 313–337.

17. J. M. R. Duncan-Andrade, "Your Best Friend or Your Worst Enemy: Popular Culture, Pedagogy and Curriculum in Urban Classrooms," *Review of Education Pedagogy & Cultural Studies* 26, no. 4 (2004): 315.

18. J. M. R. Duncan-Andrade, "Your Best Friend or Your Worst Enemy: Popular Culture, Pedagogy and Curriculum in Urban Classrooms," *Review of Education Pedagogy & Cultural Studies* 26, no. 4 (2004): 331.

19. L. Delpit, *Other People's Children: Cultural Conflict in the Classroom* (New York: New York Press, 1995).

20. A. DeJesús, "Theoretical Perspectives on the Underachievement of Latino/a Students in U.S. Schools: Toward a Framework for Culturally Additive Schooling," in *Latino/a Education: An Agenda for Community Action Research*, eds. P. Pedraza and M. Rivera (Mahwah, NJ: Lawrence Erlbaum Associates, 2005).

21. G. Smitherman, *Talkin and Testifyin: The Language of Black America* (Detroit: Wayne State University Press, 1977); H. S. Alim and J. Baugh, *Talking Black Talk: Language, Education, and Social Change* (New York: Teachers College Press, 2006).

22. U.S. Census Bureau, "School Enrollment: 2000," (Washington, D.C.: 2004).

23. G. Ladson-Billings, *The Dreamkeepers: Successful Teachers of African American Children* (San Francisco: Jossey Bass, 1994); J. G. Irizarry and R. Antrop-González, "RicanStructing the Discourse and Promoting School Success: Extending a Theory of CRP to DiaspoRicans," *Centro Journal of the Center for Puerto Rican Studies* 20, no. 2 (2007): 36–59; J. Raible and J. G. Irizarry, "Transracialized Selves and the Emergence of Post-White Teacher Identities," *Race, Ethnicity and Education* 10, no. 2 (2007): 177–198.

24. C. E. Sleeter, "Preparing Teachers for Culturally Diverse Schools: Research and the Overwhelming Presence of Whiteness," *Journal of Teacher Education* 52, no. 2 (2001): 94–106.

25. M. J. Vavrus, *Transforming the Multicultural Education of Teachers* (New York: Teachers College Press, 2002).

26. L. Delpit, *Other People's Children: Cultural Conflict in the Classroom* (New York: New York Press, 1995); R. Hernández-Sheets, "Urban Classroom Conflict: Student-teacher Perception: Ethnic Integrity, Solidarity, and Resistance," *Urban Review* 28, no. 2 (1996): 165–183; G. R. Howard, *We Can't Teach What We Don't Know: White Teachers, Multiracial Schools* (New York: Teachers College Press, 1999).

27. A. E. LaDuke, "Resistance and Renegotiation: Preservice Teacher Interactions with and Reactions to Multicultural Course Content, *Multicultural Education* (forthcoming, 2009).

28. A. E. LaDuke, "Resistance and Renegotiation: Preservice Teacher Interactions with and Reactions to Multicultural Course Content, *Multicultural Education* (forthcoming, 2009).

29. S. Bowles and H. Gintis, *Schooling in Capitalist America* (London: Routledge, 1976); J. MacLeod, *Ain't No Makin' It: Aspirations and Attainment in a Low Income Neighborhood* (Boulder, CO: Westview Press, 1987); P. Noguera, *City Schools and the American Dream: Reclaiming the Promise of Public Education* (New York: Teachers College Press, 2003).

30. J. Kozol, *Savage Inequalities* (New York: Basic Books, 1992).

31. G. Ladson-Billings, "From the Achievement Gap to the Education Debt: Understanding Achievement in US Schools," *Educational Researcher* 35, no. 7 (2006): 3–12; L. Darling-Hammond, "New Standards and Old Inequalities: School Reform and the Education of African American Students," *The Journal of Negro Education* 69, no. 4 (2000): 263–287; C. Jencks and P. Peterson, eds. *The Urban Underclass* (Washington, D.C.: Brookings, 1991).

32. Eric A. Hanushek, "School Resources and Student Performance," in Gary Burtless, ed., *Does Money Matter? The Effect of School Resources on Student Achievement and Adult Success* (Washington, D.C.: Brookings Institution Press, 1996), pp. 74–92.

33. P. Freire, *Pedagogy of the Oppressed* (New York: Seabury, 1970/2000).

34. J. M. R. Duncan-Andrade and E. Morrell, *The Art of Critical Pedagogy: Possibilities for Moving From Theory to Practice in Urban Schools* (New York: Peter Lang, 2008).

35. M. Fine, "An Epilogue, of Sorts," in *Revolutionizing Education: Youth Participatory Action Research in Motion*, eds. J. Cammarota and M. Fine (New York: Routledge, 2008).

36. S. Ginwright, "Collective Radical Imagination: Youth Participatory Action Research and the Art of Emancipatory Knowledge," in *Revolutionizing Education: Youth Participatory Action Research in Motion*, eds. J. Cammarota and M. Fine (New York: Routledge, 2008).

37. E. Morrell, *Critical Literacy and Urban Youth: Pedagogies of Access, Dissent, and Liberation* (New York: Routledge, 2008); J. Cammarota and M. Fine, eds., *Revolutionizing Education: Youth Participatory Action Research in Motion* (New York: Routledge, 2008); T. Brown, T. Bridges, and S. Clark, "Flipping the Script: Youth Teaching Teachers," (Paper presented at the annual meeting of the American Educational Research Association, New York, March 2008); M. Rivera and P. Pedraza, "The Spirit of Transformation: An Education Reform Movement in a New York City Latino/a Community," in *Puerto Rican Students in U.S. Schools,* ed. S. Nieto (Mahwah, NJ: Lawrence Erlbaum Associates, Inc., 2000).

38. T. D. Snyder and C. E. Freeman, "Look for Near-Record Elementary School Enrollments This Year, with Greater Numbers of Language Minority and Computer-Savvy Students," *Trends in Education* 83, no. 1 (2003): 50–52.

39. L. Delpit and T. Perry, eds., *The Real Ebonics Debate: Power, Language and the Education of African-American Children* (Boston: Beacon Press, 1998).

40. L. Delpit and T. Perry, eds., *The Real Ebonics Debate: Power, Language and the Education of African-American Children* (Boston: Beacon Press, 1998): p. 17.

41. L. Delpit and T. Perry, eds., *The Real Ebonics Debate: Power, Language and the Education of African-American Children* (Boston: Beacon Press, 1998).

42. J. Baker, "Trilingualism," in *The Skin That We Speak: Thoughts on Language and Culture in the Classroom*, eds. L. Delpit and J. K. Dowdy (New York: New York Press, 2002).

43. J. Baker, "Trilingualism," in *The Skin That We Speak: Thoughts on Language and Culture in the Classroom*, eds. L. Delpit and J. K. Dowdy (New York: New York Press, 2002).

44. V. Purcell-Gates, "'As Soon As She Opened Her Mouth!': Issues of Language, Literacy, and Power," in *The Skin That We Speak: Thoughts on Language and Culture in the Classroom*, eds. L. Delpit and J. K. Dowdy (New York: New York Press, 2002): p. 128.

45. L. Christensen, *Reading, Writing, and Rising Up: Teaching about Social Justice and the Power of the Written Word* (Milwaukee, WI: Rethinking Schools, 2000).

46. G. Ladson-Billings, "'I Ain't Writin' Nuttin': Permissions to Fail and Demands to Succeed in Urban Classrooms" in *The Skin That We Speak: Thoughts on Language and Culture in the Classroom*, eds. L. Delpit and J. K. Dowdy (New York: New York Press, 2002).

47. P. Gandara and F. Contreras, *The Latino Education Crisis: The Consequences of Failed Social Policies* (Cambridge, MA: Harvard University Press, 2009); J. Crawford, *Educating English Learners: Language Diversity in the Classroom* (Bilingual Education Services, 2004): M. E. Brisk, *Bilingual Education: From Compensatory to Quality Schooling* (New York:

Routledge, 2006); M. Torres-Guzmán, J. Abbate, and L. Minaya-Rowe, "Defining and Documenting Success for Bilingual Learners: A Collective Case Study," *Bilingual Research Journal* 26, no. 1 (Spring 2002): 1–21.

48. H. T. Trueba, "From Failure to Success: The Role of Culture and Cultural Conflict in the Academic Achievement of Chicano Students," in *Chicano School Failure and Success: Research and Policy Agendas for the 1990s,* ed. R. R. Valencia (London: Falmer Press, 1991).

49. H. Hernandez, *Teaching in Multilingual Classrooms: A Teacher's Guide to Context, Process, and Content* (Upper Saddle River, NJ: Merrill, 1997): p. 99.

50. B. O. Smith, "On the Anatomy of Teaching," in *Contemporary Thought on Teaching*, ed. R. T. Hyman (Englewood Cliffs, NJ: Prentice Hall, 1971).

51. D. C. Berliner, "An Analysis of Some Unintended and Negative Consequences of High-Stakes Testing" (East Lansing, MI: Great Lakes Center, 2002); A. Valenzuela, *Leaving Children Behind: How "Texas-style" Accountability Fails Latino Youth* (New York: State University of New York Press, 2005).

52. M. Cowhey, *Black Ants and Buddhists: Thinking Critically and Teaching Differently in the Primary Grades* (Portland, ME: Stenhouse, 2006).

53. T. C. Howard, "Telling Their Side of the Story: African-American Students' Perceptions of Culturally Relevant Teaching," *The Urban Review* 33, no. 2 (2001): 131–149; E. B. Moje and K. Hinchman, "Culturally Responsive Practices for Youth Literacy Learning," in *Adolescent Literacy Research and Practice* (Guilford Press, 2004).

54. P. Freire, *Teachers as Cultural Workers: Letters to Those Who Dare Teach* (Boulder, CO: Westview Press, 1998): p. 69.

55. J. G. Irizarry, "Ethnic and Urban Intersections in the Classroom: Latino Students, Hybrid Identities, and Culturally Responsive Pedagogy," *Multicultural Perspectives* 9, no. 3 (2007): 1–7.

56. L. Moll, "Funds of Knowledge for Teaching: Using a Qualitative Approach to Connect Homes and Classrooms," *Theory Into Practice* 31, no. 2 (1992): 132–41.

8

Classroom Management

Carol Weinstein • Wilford A. Weber

INTASC Standards

● **Principle 3:**   The teacher understands how students differ in their approaches to learning and creates instructional opportunities that are adapted to diverse learners.

● **Principle 5:**   The teacher uses an understanding of individual and group motivation and behavior to create a learning environment that encourages positive social interaction, active engagement in learning, and self-motivation.

● **Principle 6:**   The teacher uses knowledge of effective verbal, nonverbal, and media communication techniques to foster active inquiry, collaboration, and supportive interaction in the classroom.

● **Principle 9:**   The teacher is a reflective practitioner who continually evaluates the effects of her/his choices and actions on others and who actively seeks out opportunities to grow professionally.

● **Principle 10:**   The teacher fosters relationships with school colleagues, parents, and agencies in the larger community to support students' learning and well-being

Stretch Photography/Jupiter Images

OBJECTIVES

1. To define classroom management, explain the relationship between classroom management and discipline, and describe the concept of "culturally responsive classroom management"

2. To contrast the characteristics of authoritative, authoritarian, and permissive teachers

3. To identify the ongoing tasks involved in classroom management and to explain how each contributes to a well-functioning learning environment

▣ Rationale

Beginning teachers consistently perceive classroom management as their biggest challenge. They despair over students who constantly talk or text message in the back of the room, who repeatedly come late to class, who bully and harass their peers, and who are disengaged, disruptive, or openly defiant. At the very least, management problems cause stress, anxiety, and a loss of instructional time; they can also lead teachers to feel burned out and to leave teaching.

Beginning teachers also contend that their teacher preparation programs inadequately prepared them for the challenges of classroom management. They call for more preparation in areas such as communicating with parents and responding to inappropriate behavior. They want "real life stories on how to resolve classroom management issues"[1] and decry courses that are too theoretical. One new teacher put it this way:

> I felt bewildered and more than a bit betrayed by my own teacher education program: all the learning theories and stages of development that I studied helped little when I was faced with managing a classroom of real third grade children with unique needs, wants, and personalities. . . . On the few occasions when my courses did deal with management issues, the lessons were so far removed from the actual classroom situations that benefits proved minimal.[2]

This complaint has validity: Numerous studies indicate that the study of classroom management is frequently neglected in teacher preparation programs.[3] For example, one recent study of 26 programs in New York City found that only 11 (42 percent) required a course in classroom management, a figure that is actually higher than many of the percentages reported in similar research.[4] Furthermore, while some programs require a separate course in classroom management, many others offer classroom management as an elective or embed management content in educational psychology, child development, or a student-teaching seminar. Even when classroom management issues *are* addressed, the approach may not be grounded in the realities of managing a classroom.

This chapter begins by defining *classroom management* and distinguishing it from *discipline*. The chapter then discusses three styles of classroom management, borrowing from the literature on effective parenting. Next, the chapter examines six ongoing management tasks that teachers face and provides readers with research-based suggestions for creating respectful, orderly environments for learning. Underlying the chapter is the conviction that most problems of disorder can be avoided (or at least minimized) if teachers use good preventive management strategies.

OBJECTIVE 1	To define classroom management, explain the relationship between classroom management and discipline, and describe the concept of "culturally responsive classroom management"

◼ What Is Classroom Management and Why Is It Such a Problem?

Learning Activity 8.1

Concern about student behavior is not new. During the colonial period, schoolmasters were frequently selected because they were "big enough and tough enough" to deal with their teenage male students, who "took pleasure in beating their masters."[5] Student "mutinies" were also common, with "students chasing the teachers out of school houses and locking them out."[6] After the Revolutionary War, chaos and disruption continued to be common. One observer commented, "There is as little disposition on the part of American children to obey the uncontrovertible will of their masters as on the part of their fathers to submit to the mandates of kings."[7]

What *is* new is our perspective on such acts of disorder. Instead of focusing solely on *discipline*—what to do to individuals *after* misbehavior occurs—we now emphasize how to *prevent misbehavior in the first place*. Discipline is still important since prevention sometimes fails, but educators now talk about the much broader concept of *classroom management* (of which discipline is only one part). The term *classroom management* refers to the actions teachers take to create an environment that is respectful, caring, orderly, and productive. Classroom management supports and facilitates both academic and social-emotional learning. In other words, effective classroom managers not only create an environment to foster *academic achievement*, they work hard to enhance students' *social skills* (including empathy, communication skills, anger management, and conflict resolution) and their capacity for *self-regulation*.

In order to appreciate the need for effective classroom management, consider this not uncommon scene: Twenty-eight students are packed into a relatively small space. They come from diverse ethnic/racial backgrounds and have widely varying levels of achievement. Four are learning English, three have been diagnosed with learning disabilities, and one student with autism has a full-time aide. One has just became homeless when her parents were laid off and they lost their home to foreclosure. The specter of high-stakes standardized tests looms over the class, and it's hard to find time for instructional activities that would be engaging and relevant to students' lives. In fact, many of the students are completely disinterested in the subject matter, and they are frequently off-task. In order to help teachers cope, the school has just provided an in-service workshop entitled "10 Surefire Ways to Improve Student Behavior."

This scene illuminates some of the challenges facing today's teachers and highlights the difficulties that beginning (and even experienced) teachers face with respect to classroom management. First, *classrooms are crowded, complex environments*. It's hard to think of another setting (except prison) in which so many people are packed so tightly together for so many hours. Within this environment, teachers must attend to the needs of individuals with different levels of achievement, different interests, and different attitudes toward the content. At the same time, teachers must often adhere to a set curriculum and implement instructional activities designed to prepare students for standardized tests (rather than connecting with their lives and interests).

Second, *classes are more culturally diverse than ever*, with students from varying racial, ethnic, linguistic, and social class backgrounds. Although teachers sometimes try to be "color-blind," ignoring students' background means ignoring an essential part of their identity. Furthermore, definitions and expectations of appropriate behavior are culturally influenced, and conflicts inevitably occur if we are insensitive to legitimate differences in assumptions, values, and communication patterns. For example, Geneva Gay[8] points out that African Americans often use "evocative vocabulary" and "inject high energy, exuberance, and passion" into their verbal communication. If European American teachers perceive such speech as rude or vulgar, this interpretation can lead to a cultural conflict, resulting in unnecessary disciplinary interventions and student resentment.

In order to avoid such conflicts, teachers must become *culturally responsive classroom managers*.[9] This means developing the knowledge, skills, and dispositions to work with students from diverse backgrounds. Culturally responsive classroom managers recognize that we are all cultural beings, with our own beliefs, values, and assumptions about human behavior. We must bring these cultural biases to a conscious level, reflect on how they affect our interactions with students, and learn about the cultural norms and values of those from diverse backgrounds. For example, a White middle-class worldview emphasizes individual achievement, independence, competition, and efficiency. This is in stark contrast to the worldview of more collectivist cultures (for instance, Asian, Latino, and Native American), which avoid displays of individual accomplishment and, instead, stress cooperation, harmony, and working for the good of the group. One worldview is not necessarily better than the other—but they are certainly different. Failing to appreciate and respect these differences can lead to misunderstanding and miscommunication.

A third challenge stems from the fact that about *half of the nation's children with disabilities are now educated in general education classrooms* with their nondisabled peers.[10] Successful inclusion requires more than simply putting disabled and nondisabled students in the same classroom. It requires teachers to create an atmosphere of acceptance, promote interaction and cooperation, and modify instruction and norms for behavior when necessary. Inclusion may also require general education teachers to coordinate and collaborate with special services personnel who are providing in-class support (such as special education teachers and paraprofessionals). These additional responsibilities may seem overwhelming to regular classroom teachers, who frequently feel that they lack the professional preparation necessary to help children with special needs.

Fourth, many children are growing up in *circumstances that create physical, emotional, and psychological problems*. Family and societal factors like divorce and family instability, substance abuse, and abuse and neglect can negatively affect students' academic achievement and behavior. In addition, the economic crisis of 2008–2009 has certainly exacerbated the incidence of poverty and homelessness, causing severe stress in families. When children coping with these problems come to school, their problems come with them. More than ever, teachers need the skills to create a warm, supportive, consistent environment for students whose lives are stressful and precarious.

Finally, as mentioned earlier, beginning teachers frequently report that their *teacher education programs did not prepare them for the challenges of today's classrooms*. Given this lack of preparation, many teachers have to rely on in-service workshops that emphasize a cookbook approach to classroom management, consisting of lists of things a teacher should or should not do (for example, always reprimand a student in private; never raise your voice when admonishing a student; always be fair; never play favorites).

Although these suggestions seem sensible, they are far too simplistic to be helpful in dealing with complex challenges. "Recipes" like these are not derived from a well-conceptualized set of principles that can guide teachers' thinking and behavior. Thus, if a specific recipe fails to achieve its objective, or if the specific recipe is impossible to implement in a particular situation, the teacher cannot posit alternatives. Moreover, a cookbook approach deals in absolutes—and classroom incidents usually come in subtle shades of gray. For example, it is hard to argue with the importance of being fair, but it's not always easy to figure out exactly what this means in the messy world of the classroom. On one hand, being fair suggests that rules apply to everyone, no matter what. On the other hand, being fair also implies that people need different, personalized treatment. From this perspective treating everyone the same is *unfair*. So what's a teacher to do?

INTASC Principle 5

Fortunately, today's teachers do not have to rely on a cookbook approach. Research conducted in the last 30 years has provided us a good deal of information on effective classroom management and a set of principles that can help us to think through the complexities of the classroom and guide our actions. This chapter reflects this knowledge base and provides research-based suggestions for creating caring, supportive, orderly classroom environments.

✳ Mastery Test

OBJECTIVE 1 **To define classroom management, explain the relationship between classroom management and discipline, and describe the concept of "culturally responsive classroom management"**

Answer the following questions. When you have responded, compare your answers to those presented in the Answer Key at the end of the book.

1. In your own words, how would you define the term *classroom management*?
2. What is the difference between classroom management and discipline? Which is the broader concept?
3. What is meant by *culturally responsive classroom management*?
4. How do the values of White middle-class culture contrast with those of more collectivist cultures (such as Native American)?

OBJECTIVE 2 **To contrast the characteristics of authoritative, authoritarian, and permissive teachers**

Three Styles of Classroom Management

Learning Activity 8.2

Mr. A runs a tight ship. He is a no-nonsense teacher who stresses high expectations and consistency. He believes strongly that students need to know exactly what they're supposed to do when they walk in the door, and he readily uses punishment when students "mess up." He knows they often complain that he is a "really mean teacher," but he feels that his reputation of being strict helps him to stay in control. He says, "I want students to respect me and my rules so that we can have a well-functioning classroom. I'm not here to be their friend; I'm here to teach." Mr. A shows little affection for students. He frequently admonishes them in front of their peers, assigns frequent detention, and expresses irritation at their lack of cooperation.

In contrast, Ms. B wants students to enjoy school. She makes few academic or behavioral demands on them, believing strongly in the importance of giving students autonomy. In her interactions with students, she tries hard to be a good listener, to empathize, and to show warmth and affection. She knows that students sometimes take advantage of her, but believes that students will eventually develop a sense of responsibility for their own learning and behavior. She says, "I don't want students to comply just because they're afraid of punishment, and I hate using things like popcorn parties and star charts to get students to do what I want. Instead, I want them to develop a sense of self-discipline and personal responsibility." Ms. B wants to create a comfortable atmosphere in which students feel free to ask for help and to admit when they don't know something.

Mrs. C has yet another style of classroom management. Like Mr. A., she believes in holding students to high expectations, both in terms of academic achievement and behavior; however, like Ms. B, she also thinks it's important to create a warm, supportive classroom environment that is sensitive to students' needs. She is firm, but she takes the time to provide rationales for various classroom rules. She believes there must be consequences when students violate the rules, but she tries to invoke penalties that are fair and that don't humiliate students. As she puts it, "Students have to understand that their behavior has consequences, but it's important to not get into power struggles with them and to allow them to 'save face.'"

Borrowing terminology from the literature on parenting style,[11] we can describe Mr. A as *authoritarian*, Ms. B as *permissive*, and Mrs. C as *authoritative*.[12] A teacher with an authoritarian style establishes and maintains order through the use of controlling strategies. The teacher uses force, pressure, competition, punishment, and the threat of punishment to control student behavior. The teacher is high in demandingness, but low in responsiveness to students' needs and desires. The teacher makes no effort to promote students' autonomy.

A permissive teacher encourages the freedom of students and interferes as little as possible. The teacher provides a great deal of affection and warmth, but little if any leadership, and makes few demands on students. In other words, the teacher is low in demandingness, but high in responsiveness.

An authoritative style combines the best of the two other orientations—high demandingness with high responsiveness. The teacher makes developmentally appropriate demands, but is also responsive to students' needs and interests. The teacher shares responsibility with students, who are treated as responsible, worthwhile individuals capable of decision making. The teacher exhibits leadership but promotes students' autonomy. An authoritative teacher can be characterized as a "warm demander,"[13] combining warmth and respect with an insistence that students work hard, comply with classroom norms, and treat one another with consideration. The current chapter advocates an authoritative approach to classroom management.

Research has confirmed the fact that students respond well to teachers who are both demanding and responsive. Theo Wubbels and his colleagues, for example, have demonstrated that high school students prefer teachers who are strong authority figures, but are also caring and respectful.[14] It is clear that students don't like having teachers who "let kids run all over them." At the same time, students consistently talk about the importance of having teachers who "don't put students down" and who work hard to promote positive teacher-student relationships.

✳ Mastery Test

> **OBJECTIVE 2** **To contrast the characteristics of authoritative, authoritarian, and permissive teachers**

Each of the following statements reflects an authoritative, authoritarian, and/or permissive style of classroom management. Your task is to identify the style(s) that each statement represents, using the following code letters:

AN authoritarian approach

P permissive approach

AV authoritative approach

Compare your responses to those presented in the Answer Key at the end of the book.

_____ 1. The teacher believes that maintaining order in the classroom requires the use of forceful external strategies to control students' behavior.

_____ 2. The teacher believes that teachers should not impose limits on students because this will keep them from developing self-discipline.

_____ 3. The teacher tries to respond to problem behavior in a way that minimizes the potential for negative side effects (like resentment and humiliation).

_____ 4. The teacher believes that effective management requires teachers to have high expectations for students' behavior and achievement and to also be warm and supportive.

_____ 5. The teacher believes in being consistent when dealing with students' problem behavior.

_____ 6. The teacher believes that being perceived as strict and mean makes it easier to manage the classroom.

_____ 7. The teacher believes in helping students understand, accept, and follow established rules and regulations.

_____ 8. The teacher tries to be tolerant of all forms of student behavior.

_____ 9. The teacher believes that a central role of the teacher is the establishment and maintenance of positive teacher-student relationships.

_____ 10. The teacher recognizes the importance of treating students with respect and helping them develop self-responsibility and feelings of self-worth.

> **OBJECTIVE 3** **To identify the ongoing tasks involved in classroom management and to explain how each contributes to a well-functioning learning environment**

◻ The Tasks of Classroom Management

Learning Activity 8.3   Classroom management is a multifaceted concept that encompasses a whole array of distinct tasks, from designing an appropriate physical setting and building an atmosphere of caring and respect to teaching standards for behavior and responding to violations of classroom norms. The following sections of this chapter elaborate on six of these tasks.

Designing the Physical Environment

☐ INTASC Principle 6

The physical setting of the classroom can affect the way teachers and students feel, think, and behave. These effects can be both *direct* and *indirect*.[15] For example, imagine that an elementary teacher has put some enticing science equipment (such as microscopes) on a set of shelves mounted high on a wall. Because the shelves are so high, students cannot reach the materials—a direct effect. In addition, the very height of the shelves communicates the message that students are not *supposed* to use these materials—an indirect or symbolic effect. This message may be accurate: The teacher may have deliberately placed the materials on high shelves to minimize the likelihood that students will use them without permission. On the other hand, the message may be inaccurate: The teacher may want students to use the materials, but just hasn't thought about their being too high for young children to reach comfortably. As you think about designing your classroom, be sensitive to both the direct and indirect or symbolic effects of the physical environment.

Although teachers don't have control over the "fixed features" of the classroom (such as the location of electrical outlets, bulletin boards, or doors), they are usually able to decide on the arrangement of chairs, desks, and tables; computers and printers; and content-related materials and equipment. Careful planning of the physical environment should begin before the school year starts and should *support the type of instruction you will carry out*. For example, if you plan to emphasize small-group work and cooperative learning, it makes sense for students' desks to be placed in clusters. On the other hand, if you plan to emphasize teacher-directed, whole-class instruction, it's more appropriate for students' desks to be placed in rows facing the front of the room. Still another option is a horseshoe arrangement (with perhaps an additional row in the middle of the horseshoe). This configuration allows students to have some face-to-face interaction during whole-class discussions and to work easily with the individuals sitting on either side, but it is also appropriate for teacher presentations and whole-group instruction.

Keep in mind that the physical design of the classroom also *affects the atmosphere of the classroom*. Too often classrooms are barren and unappealing (especially at the secondary level). The addition of some warm colors, plants, and attractive bulletin board displays can make the room much more welcoming and aesthetically pleasing. These amenities also communicate the message that you care enough about students to make the space appealing and comfortable.

Some specific suggestions for designing classroom space are:

- Make sure that frequently used classroom materials are accessible to students.
- Organize shelves and storage areas so that it is clear where materials and equipment belong. Using labels can help students find materials when they need them and put materials back when they're finished.
- Plan pathways through the room to avoid congestion and distraction.
- Design a seating arrangement that allows students to have a clear view of instructional presentations. Students shouldn't have to turn around in their chairs to get a view of the chalkboard.
- Think about how much interaction you want among students and then design an appropriate seating arrangement. For example, don't put students in four-person clusters if you don't want them to engage

in collaborative learning activities. Don't put students in rows if you want to encourage collaboration and cooperation.

- Decide where to store your own personal teaching aids and supplies.
- Think about ways to personalize classroom space (for instance, posting displays that reflect students' cultural backgrounds). The classroom should reflect students' interests, activities, backgrounds, and accomplishments, as well as your own interests, goals, and values.
- Consider whether environmental modifications are needed for students with special needs. For example, if you have students in wheelchairs, are aisles wide enough for them to navigate the classroom?
- If you are working with paraprofessionals or co-teaching, think about the spatial needs of other adults in the room. For example, do they need a desk? A place to sit? A place to store materials?

> YOUR TURN

1. Think about the grade level or subject area you are planning to teach. What kinds of amenities (plants, animals, furniture, rugs, and so on) would you want to incorporate into your classroom in order to make a more attractive space?
2. Reflect on your own cultural background, interests, and values. In an attempt to personalize the classroom space, what kinds of artifacts could you bring in to reflect these? (For obvious reasons, it's not a good idea to bring in items that are fragile or valuable!)
3. Draw a map of your ideal classroom showing the arrangement of classroom furniture. Write a brief commentary explaining your design decisions.

Building Positive Student-Teacher Relationships

☐ INTASC Principle 3

Common sense tells us that students are more likely to cooperate with teachers they perceive as caring and respectful, and research has confirmed this idea.[16] Indeed, a review of more than 100 studies has shown that positive teacher-student relationships are the key to effective classroom management and that such relationships can actually reduce behavior problems by 31 percent.[17] When students feel supported and cared for, they are more willing to accept the authority of others and to regulate their own behavior consistent with classroom norms. As a teacher in one study commented, "If you have a relationship with your students, they're gonna trust you more and they're gonna respect you more and then they'll be nicer to you."[18] It appears that caring, respectful teachers are especially important to African American and Hispanic students, who often feel that their teachers (generally European American) stereotype them and fail to honor their cultural backgrounds or understand their perspectives.[19]

Like motherhood and apple pie, caring and respect are easy to endorse. But how do you really *show* students that you want to establish positive teacher-student relationships? The following suggestions address this question.

Be welcoming. Standing by the classroom door and smiling as students enter the room is an easy way to show students you're glad to see them. This gives you an opportunity to say hello to individual students (by name), inquire how they're doing, and comment on a new hairstyle. In just a few minutes, you can reach out and build a connection. You can also use this time to notice if someone looks unusually morose or angry. A brief inquiry at the beginning of class (such as "You okay? You look a little down") can ward off problems and show students you are concerned about their feelings and well-being. You can follow that up with an invitation to talk privately at a mutually convenient time.

Learn about your students' lives. Another way of showing care and respect is to learn about students' lives. You might have your students complete a questionnaire about favorite school subjects, hobbies, pets, or after-school jobs, along with anything else they want you to know about them. Attending their concerts, plays, and sporting events also allows you to see your students in a different context and conveys that you are interested in learning about them as individuals. Chatting informally before and after class can provide you with important information about what's going on in their lives outside of school.

The following vignettes[20] illustrate how an elementary and a secondary teacher learn about their students' lives:

> *"I notice that whenever you doodle, it always has something to do with horses. I loved horses when I was a girl, too. Bring in some of your pictures, because I would love to see them, and they might help you with topics in your writing." Devon blushed with pleasure and surprise that her teacher actually noticed how passionate she was about horses. . . . She couldn't wait to bring in her horse pictures to show her teacher. She also noticed that she was actually excited about her next writing assignment—a story about a horse.*

> *When each issue of the school newspaper was released, Ms. Jackson read through every article. This was just one of the many techniques she used for discovering something about the interests of her students, especially those who were so quiet they almost became invisible. More than once she stared into stunned eyes when she asked students about their times in the track meet, their attendance at a debate, or their volunteer work at the animal clinic.*

Another suggestion comes from JoBeth Allen,[21] who was part of a teacher study group in Georgia that used photography to learn about students' families. With a small grant, the study group teachers bought three cameras for each classroom and invited students to photograph what was important to them in their homes and neighborhoods. Students took the cameras home on a rotating basis, and students and family members wrote personal stories, memories, poetry, and letters about the photos.

☐ INTASC Principle 6

Develop cultural literacy. This chapter has already touched on the critical need to develop the knowledge, skills, and dispositions to work effectively with students from diverse cultural backgrounds ("culturally responsive classroom management"). In particular, acquiring cultural content knowledge or *cultural literacy* is essential for building positive teacher-student relationships. (Chapter 7 in this book addresses culturally responsive teaching in depth.) As we mentioned earlier, different cultures have different values and beliefs. They also have different ways of communicating, different rules of etiquette, and different social taboos. Obviously, these cultural characteristics are not exhibited by all group members, and certainly not in the same way or to the same extent; nonetheless, acquiring knowledge about core cultural characteristics can provide teachers with valuable information.

Teachers can gain cultural literacy by asking questions like the following:[22]

- *Family background and structure*: Where did the students come from? How long have the students been in this country? What is the hierarchy of authority? What responsibilities do students have at home? Is learning English a high priority?

- *Education*: How much previous schooling have the students had? What kinds of instructional strategies are they accustomed to? In their former schools, was there an emphasis on large-group instruction, memorization, and recitation? What were the expectations for appropriate behavior? Were students expected to be active or passive? Independent or dependent? Peer-oriented or teacher-oriented? Cooperative or competitive?

- *Interpersonal relationship styles*: Do cultural norms emphasize working for the good of the group or for individual achievement? What are the norms with respect to interaction between males and females? What constitutes a comfortable personal space? Do students obey or question authority figures? Are expressions of emotion and feelings emphasized or hidden?

- *Discipline*: Do adults act in permissive, authoritative, or authoritarian ways? What kinds of praise, reward, criticism, and punishment are customary? Are they administered publicly or privately? To the group or the individual?

- *Time and space*: How do students think about time? Is punctuality expected or is time considered flexible? How important is speed in completing a task?

- *Religion*: What restrictions are there concerning topics that should not be discussed in school?

- *Food*: What is eaten? What is not eaten?

- *Health and hygiene*: How are illnesses treated and by whom? What is considered to be the cause? What are the norms with respect to seeking professional help for emotional and psychological problems?

- *History, traditions, holidays*: Which events and people are a source of pride for the group? To what extent does the group in the United States identify with the history and traditions of the country of origin? What holidays and celebrations are considered appropriate for observing in school?

Communicate high expectations. An important part of showing that you care is pushing students to do their best academic work and to behave appropriately. This is well illustrated in interviews with inner-city middle schoolers about "good" teachers.[23] Students repeatedly talked about the importance of "strict" teachers who push students to do their school work and refuse to let them fail. One student commented:

> *I like the ones that don't allow excuses. It's my turn to get an education. I need to have someone to tell me when I'm tired and don't feel like doing the work that I should do it anyway.*

According to these middle schoolers, good teachers "nag" them about doing homework, offer reminders about assignments, give rewards, and call parents. They keep pressing students to do their best work. At the same time, they provide the support necessary for success. They offer multiple, repeated explanations until everyone understands, they vary classroom activities, and they are willing to help students who are having difficulty. Mrs. Franklin, an African American sixth-grade teacher, is a good example of this kind of teacher.[24] Mrs. Franklin didn't give her students an excuse not to do well. Her grading policy required any student work earning a grade lower than a C to be done over. Interestingly, students appreciated this strict grading policy rather than resenting it. As one student commented: "My teacher never let people settle for D or E; she don't let people get away with it. She give us an education. Other teachers don't care what you do."

Develop good communication skills. In order to develop positive teacher-student relationships, teachers must be good listeners. A high school chemistry teacher comments:

> *How come there are only certain teachers in the school that kids will go to when they have a problem? It's all about listening. When you're a high school teacher, you have to listen seriously to problems that might not be problems to you, but they are to them. And that's a way of gaining their trust. A kid is not going to come to you and say I want to commit suicide if three weeks earlier you said, "Oh grow up, you'll get over her."[25]*

Good listening begins with being attentive and acknowledging the student's feelings. By orienting your body toward the student, leaning forward, making eye contact, and nodding, you nonverbally communicate that you are paying close attention to what the student is saying. You can also use verbal cues like "uh-huh" and "I see," and invite students to talk more by using "door openers" such as "Go on" or "Would you like to tell me more about this?"[26]

In addition to being attentive, you can use *active listening*. This is a process in which you listen carefully to the student and then reflect or "feed back" the message in your own words. This allows students to verify the accuracy of your understanding or to correct the message. Active listening creates a situation in which students' feelings are validated, and they are more likely to feel understood and valued. Consider the following examples:

Student: I hate this stupid assignment.

Teacher: You don't think this work has any value.

Student: It's not that it's not valuable. It's just so boring.

Teacher: So the assignment doesn't interest you.

Student: And I really don't understand what we're supposed to do.

Teacher: The work is boring *and* confusing.

Student: I guess so.

Teacher: Maybe we could get together at lunch time and I could go over it with you. I'd really like to make sure you understand it, and I don't want it to be boring.

Student: Wait till my dad sees this test grade. He's gonna kill me.

Teacher: Your dad's going to be really mad.

Student: Yeah. If I come home with anything less than an A, he freaks out.

Teacher: Sounds like you're under a lot of pressure to get all As.

Student: That's for sure. My dad acts like getting a B is failing. But this stuff is really hard for me.

Teacher: You think a B is a pretty good grade in a tough course like this, but your dad thinks you can do better.

Watch the video case, *Classroom Management: Handling a Student with Behavior Problems*, to see a Student Support Coach advising teachers about the use of active listening.

▽ TeachSource Video Case — Classroom Management: Handling a Student with Behavior Problems

To access the video, go to www.cengage.com/login. Watch the video clip and think about the following questions:

1. Ellen Henry, the Student Support Coach, can have a sustained, private interaction with Peter that helps to calm him down. In contrast, the male teacher admits that his attempt at active listening was unsuccessful—perhaps because it was in full view of the rest of the class. How might a teacher enhance the effectiveness of an active listening interaction given the public nature of the classroom?
2. Why do you think Peter began to cry?
3. What do you see as the advantages and disadvantages of active listening for children who are experiencing emotional problems?

> YOUR TURN

1. You want to learn about your students' out-of-school lives. Think of five questions that you could include in a questionnaire at the beginning of the school year.
2. In the following conversations, students have confided in their teachers about problems they are experiencing, and the teachers have responded in ways that do *not* show empathy and caring. Provide a new teacher response for each case, using active listening.

    a. *Student:* Joshua is spreading rumors about me. He's telling everyone that I'm in love with Steven!

       Teacher: Oh, just ignore him.

    b. *Student:* I hate my math class. It's just so stupid.

       Teacher: Math is not stupid. You really need to do well in math if you're going to go to college.

Fostering an Atmosphere of Community

☐ INTASC Principle 5

In addition to building positive teacher-student relationships, teachers need to think about ways to create supportive, respectful student-student relationships and an atmosphere of community. This is not a one-shot deal. Building community takes time and effort, especially in middle school and high school, where periods may be only 45 or 50 minutes. As Mara Sapon-Shevin[27] observes:

> *Communities don't just happen. No teacher, no matter how skilled or well intentioned, can enter a new classroom and announce, "We are a community." Communities are built over time, through shared experience, and by providing multiple opportunities for students to know themselves, know one another, and interact in positive and supportive ways.*

The following suggestions can be helpful ways of building a feeling of community.

Provide opportunities for students to learn about each other. Don't assume that students already know one another and have nothing more to learn. It's important for students to discover the ways they are different and similar, especially if they are a racially and ethnically diverse group. At the beginning of the school year, for example, you can do a get-acquainted activity that requires students to "Find Someone Who." Armed with a list of short descriptive statements (such as, "someone who works at a fast-food restaurant after school," "someone who plays the violin," "someone whose favorite color is yellow"), students have to find one person in the class who fits each description. When they find someone, that person signs his or her name next to the appropriate statement, but students can sign their names only once, even if more than one statement applies.

As the school year progresses, you need to continue activities like this if you want students to be relaxed and to interact comfortably. Some additional getting-to-know-you activities are listed here:

- *Guess Who?* Students write a brief autobiographical statement (family background, hobbies, extracurricular activities, and so on), which they do not sign. Collect the statements, read each description, and ask students to write the name of the individual they believe wrote the description. (You can participate too.) After all the descriptions have been read, reread them and ask the authors to identify themselves. Ask students how many classmates they correctly identified.[28]

- *Two Truths and a Lie (or Two Facts and a Fiction).* Students write down and then share three statements about themselves, two of which are true and one of which is a lie. The activity can be done as a whole class or in small groups. In either case, since the activity allows students to select what to disclose about themselves, there is little chance of embarrassment. It also provides opportunities for students to discover common interests and experiences and to test assumptions and stereotypes.[29]

- *Little-Known Facts about Me.* This is a variation of the previous activity. Students write a statement about themselves that they think others won't know. The papers are folded, collected, put in a box, and shaken. Students take turns drawing a paper and reading the statement aloud. Everyone guesses who wrote the little-known fact.[30]

- *Lifelines.* Each student draws a line on a piece of paper and then marks six to ten points representing important events in their lives that they are willing to share (such as the birth of a sibling, the death of a close family member, the time they starred in the school play, when they moved to this school). Students then get into pairs and share their life stories. Members of each pair could also introduce each other to the rest of the class, referring to points on the lifeline.[31]

- *Your Inspiration.* Students bring in photographs of people or things that inspire them, along with an accompanying quotation. Post them on a bulletin board.[32]

- *What About Yourself Makes You Most Proud?* Students write their individual responses to this question on paper footprints. On a bulletin board, post the footprints so that they form a path labeled "success."[33]

Use small-group work and cooperative learning. By providing opportunities for students to work together in pairs and small groups, teachers can promote a sense of community in which students serve as resources for one another. Research demonstrates that cooperative learning facilitates interaction and friendship among students who differ in terms of achievement, gender, cultural and linguistic background, and race. It can also promote acceptance of students with disabilities, increase positive attitudes toward the class, and promote empathy.[34]

It's important to recognize that simply putting students into groups and telling them to work together may not yield these positive results. David and Roger Johnson,[35] two experts on cooperative learning, warn teachers not to assume that students know how to interact effectively. Rather, students must be taught social skills such as listening, explaining, encouraging, and sharing. Without such training, students may put one another down, rather than providing encouragement; monopolize the conversation rather than making sure everyone has a chance to participate; and withdraw or socialize rather than contributing constructively. (See Chapter 9 of this book for a comprehensive discussion of cooperative learning.)

Hold group meetings to encourage open communication and group problem-solving. There are many different kinds of group meeting formats, but all of them are designed to encourage communication among students and to increase the feeling of community. For example, *Morning Meeting*, used in elementary schools, is comprised of four sequential components:[36] (1) a greeting, in which students greet one another by name; (2) sharing, when a few students share some news of interest to the class and others ask questions and comment in a positive manner; (3) a group activity, in which the whole class does a short activity to build cohesiveness; and (4) news and announcements, during which students learn about the day's events and discuss a daily message posted for them. The middle school version of Morning Meeting is called *Circle of Power and Respect* (CPR) and contains the same four components.

Nelsen, Lott, and Glenn[37] recommend another type of class meeting to enhance students' social skills (such as listening, taking turns, and appreciating different points of view) and solve classroom problems. The prescribed agenda, fully discussed in *Positive Discipline in the Classroom*, begins by students expressing compliments and appreciation. Next, the class follows up on earlier solutions applied to problems and discusses ways to solve new problems that have been identified. Finally, students make plans for future class activities.

Still another type of meeting is Thomas Gordon's "no-lose" problem-solving method of conflict resolution.[38] This consists of six steps: (1) defining the problem, (2) brainstorming possible solutions (without evaluation); (3) evaluating alternative solutions; (4) selecting a solution; (5) deciding how to implement the solution (for instance, who will do what by when?); and (6) obtaining feedback and evaluating the solution. The basic premise underlying this strategy is that students, given the opportunity, skills, and necessary guidance, can and will make responsible decisions regarding their classroom behavior.

☐ INTASC Principle 3

Be alert for bullying and peer harassment. Every day, students suffer teasing, ridicule, name calling, exclusion, and even physical injury at the hands of their peers. To curb bullying and peer harassment, you need to be alert to hateful comments about race and ethnicity, body size, disabilities, sexual orientation, unfashionable dress, use of languages other than English, and socioeconomic status. You also need to make it clear that disrespectful speech is absolutely unacceptable. This means intervening when you hear students say hurtful things (for example, "Words like that are never acceptable in this class!"). Too often, teachers ignore the disrespectful speech they hear, but if you stay silent, students are likely to think that you don't care or even that you condone the degrading language. Furthermore, you're serving as a poor model for students who need to develop the courage and skills to speak up when they witness bullying.

With the advent of email, cell phone text messaging, instant messaging, blogs, and social networking sites such as Facebook, bullying has expanded to cyberspace, and victims cannot even find refuge at home. Online bullying can be vastly more humiliating than off-line bullying. Rumors, venomous comments, and embarrassing photographs can be spread among a huge number of people with just a few keystrokes. Furthermore, youngsters may say things online they would never say in person, mainly because of the feeling of anonymity and the distance from the victim. As one student comments, "Over the Internet you don't really see their face or they don't see yours, and you don't have to look in their eyes and see they're hurt."[39]

Schools need to develop explicit policies to deal with this new method of harassment, and teachers need to make sure students understand that cyber-bullying will lead to serious consequences. Furthermore, students should not only be taught to speak out against cyber-bullying, they should learn what to do if they become a victim (for instance, do not delete messages; show them to a trustworthy adult; never reply to the message; show the message to the police if it contains physical threats).

> YOUR TURN

1. Think about your years in elementary school or high school. What were some of the ways that teachers worked to foster positive student-student relationships and create a cohesive community?
2. As a student in elementary school or high school, did you witness and/or experience incidents of bullying? Did your teachers intervene, and if so, were their interventions effective? Why or why not?

Teaching the Norms for Behavior

☐ INTASC Principle 5

Research on effective classroom management at the beginning of the school year has confirmed the importance of establishing and teaching *norms for behavior*.[40] Norms are shared expectations about how group members should behave. They help students understand what is expected of them and what they should expect from others.

To function smoothly, classrooms must have two different kinds of norms. First, *norms for general conduct* (often called rules) describe how students are to behave at all times. Some examples of common rules are "Be respectful," "Come prepared," "Listen when other people are speaking," and (in elementary school) "Keep your hands and feet to yourself." Rules should be realistic, reasonable, well defined, limited in number, and clearly understood. No group can work together successfully without established standards of behavior.

Some teachers believe that students should have a central role in making rules because they are more likely to follow rules they have had a hand in developing. Others believe that the teacher alone should make the rules because it is the teacher who clearly understands which student behaviors are acceptable and which are not. As a beginning teacher, you may feel more comfortable presenting rules you have developed yourself, or you might decide to specify a limited number of rules and then work with students to add any that seem necessary. In any case, it is essential that teachers discuss the rationales for rules they have established and solicit examples from students. For example, one fourth-grade teacher has only one basic, nonnegotiable rule: "Be courteous," which she presents to students. She spends considerable

▼ TeachSource Video Case   **Cardinal Rules of Classroom Management: Perspectives from an Urban Elementary School**

To access the video, go to www.cengage.com/login. Watch the video clip, examine the artifact "Class Rules," and reflect upon the following questions:

1. Give two examples in which teacher, Benvinda Timas, demonstrates a positive, caring approach to students, even as she is telling them that her behavioral expectations are not being met.
2. Which class rules might you use in your own classroom?
3. Note that except for #8, all the class rules are stated in positive terms ("Do this," rather than "Do not do that"). This is consistent with the recommendations of many educators. What do you think about this recommendation?

time, however, asking students for examples of what that actually means (for instance, listen when other people are talking; clean up any messes you make; don't call people "stupid"; use indoor voices when working in groups). She also explains that the rule applies to her too and that being courteous will help to make the classroom a good place to be.

Once classroom rules have been presented to or developed with students, some teachers post them on a bulletin board, distribute them on a handout to students, or send a copy to parents (perhaps to be signed and returned). Whatever you decide to do, it is critical to spend as much time as needed to make sure that students understand exactly what is expected. Landmark studies by Ed Emmer, Carolyn Evertson, and their colleagues[41] found that effective classroom managers spent considerable time during the first few days of school teaching behavioral expectations. They then reviewed and reinforced the rules frequently during the first three weeks. At the secondary level, this process can probably be shortened; even so, it is essential to make sure that students are well aware of the ways you expect them to behave.

Watch the video case, *Cardinal Rules of Classroom Management: Perspectives from an Urban Elementary School,* to see how a teacher explains and enforces her rules while still maintaining a positive relationship with students.

In addition to norms for general conduct, teachers need to establish *norms for specific situations*. These are often called routines or procedures. They help students understand what it is they are to do with regard to typical daily activities. For example, how are students expected to behave when they enter or leave the classroom? How do they hand in homework? What do they do if they have to use the restroom? With clear routines, precious instructional time is not wasted because of confusion and interruptions.

Some of the classroom situations that need routines are:

- Administrative tasks
    - Taking attendance
    - Recording lunch orders
    - Distributing school notices
- Student movement
    - Entering and leaving the room
    - Going to the restroom
    - Going to the nurse
    - Fire drills
    - Sharpening pencils

- Housekeeping
    - Cleaning chalkboards or whiteboards
    - Watering plants
    - Maintaining common storage areas
- Tasks related to instructional activities
    - Collecting and returning homework
    - Keeping track of homework for students who are absent
    - Collecting in-class assignments
    - Distributing and collecting learning materials
    - Preparing paper for assignments (for example, headings, margins, pen or pencil)
    - What to do when assignments have been completed
- Interaction (when and how talking is permitted)
    - Talk between teacher and students during whole class lessons (for instance, do students have to raise hands?)
    - Talk among students during independent work
    - Talk among students during cooperative learning activities
    - Talk among students during transitions

If classrooms are to function smoothly and efficiently, teachers must explicitly teach students how to carry out procedures for typical daily activities like those listed above. Effective classroom managers *explain and demonstrate procedures*, allow students to *practice* them, *provide feedback* to students about their performance, and then *reteach* the procedures if necessary. Once again, such thoroughness is particularly important at lower grade levels when children have had little experience with the routines of school. Even in middle school and high school, however, it's important to make your routines explicit, since students move from teacher to teacher, and routines will surely vary. For example, one teacher may direct students to drop their homework in a box on the teacher's desk, while another may want homework placed in the front-right corner of the student's desk. It's only fair to students to make these expectations absolutely clear.

> ### YOUR TURN

1. Develop a set of possible rules for your classroom. (About three to five should be enough.) Would you create the rules yourself and then present them to students, or would you develop the rules jointly? Why?
2. Think about the different ways your elementary or high school teachers collected homework. Which seemed most effective? Least effective? What kind of routine do you think you would establish to collect homework?

Working with Families

☐ INTASC Principle 10

Establishing a good working relationship with students' families can yield numerous benefits. First, learning about students' out-of-school life provides insights into their in-school behavior, and these insights can help you work sensitively and effectively with your students. Second, families can provide valuable support and assistance when they understand what you are trying to achieve and how you expect students to behave in your classroom. Third, families can help to develop and implement behavior management efforts. In the following anecdotes, an elementary teacher and a secondary teacher relate how each worked with families to help change students' problem behavior.

> *I had this boy in my class who was extremely disruptive. He wouldn't work, kept "forgetting" his homework, distracted other children, wandered around the room. You name it; he did it. The three of us—the mother, the boy, and I—talked about what we could do, and we decided to try a system of home rewards. We agreed that I would send a note home each day, reporting on the boy's behavior. For every week with at least three good notes, his mother let him rent a video game. In this way, the child's access to video games was directly dependent on his behavior. This system really made a difference!*[42]

> *I had this kid in my U. S. History II class who wasn't doing any work at all. It was his senior year, and I think he just decided he didn't have to do anything anymore. His parents didn't have a clue about what to do. We all sat down and worked out a plan. They were to call me at 10:30 every Friday morning. If the report on their son was good, he got the car keys, [and] got to go out with friends. . . . If the report was bad, the weekend did not exist. We told him, "We really care about you and if this is what we have to do to get you through senior year, then so be it." The kid tested the plan once, and there was no weekend for him. After that, he really started to perform and ended up with a B for the year. Plus, there was an additional payoff. His parents were able to give him all kinds of good strokes because he started taking responsibility.*[43]

Changes in American society have made communication and collaboration with families more difficult than ever. There are fewer stay-at-home mothers. About half of all marriages end in divorce,[44] and about one-half of today's children will spend some portion of childhood in a single-parent family[45] without the human or economic resources available to those growing up in two-parent families. In some cases, the significant adults in children's lives are not their parents at all, but grandparents, aunts, uncles, brothers, sisters, or neighbors. With a surge in immigration, many students come from homes where a language other than English is spoken, and their families are unfamiliar with schools in the United States.

Despite these challenges, it is teachers' attitudes and practices—not parents' educational level, marital status, or workplace—that determine whether families become productively involved in their children's schooling.[46] In other words, if parents are to be productively involved, teachers need to reach out, communicate about children's progress and school programs, and invite participation of all kinds. The next few sections of this chapter provide some suggestions for enhancing communication with parents. (Note that in this chapter, references to "parents" actually refer to all the various types of caregivers that students may have in their lives.)

Deciding on the goals of communication. The first step in the process of communicating with parents is to decide on the goal or purpose of the communication. Examples of goals include introducing yourself, building a positive relationship, notifying parents about the best way to contact you, providing them with information about classroom norms, informing them about students' problem behaviors, requesting assistance in dealing with those behaviors, keeping parents informed about positive or negative changes, and explaining when an administrator must become involved in behavioral issues. Keep in mind that it is far better to establish communication *before* a problem arises.

Deciding on the timing and means of communication. Having decided on the goal of the communication, the next step is to select the timing of the contact and the means of communication. The teacher has an array of options from which to choose; these include telephone calls, parent-teacher conferences, home visits, open houses and back-to-school nights, personal notes and letters, notices, class newsletters, a class Web site, individual email messages, and group email messages. If your goal is to introduce yourself to parents and to foster positive interaction, an introductory letter or phone call at the beginning of the school year can set the right tone. If your goal is to provide a list of classroom rules and consequences, a class newsletter sent home with students on the first day of school and a posting on a class Web site are good alternatives. If your goal is to make parents aware of their child's misbehavior and to enlist their assistance, a parent-teacher conference is an effective way to proceed. A major consideration in selecting the means of communication is the amount of time involved. A secondary teacher with 120 students who spends only five minutes a week communicating with the parents of each student would spend a total of ten hours a week! Obviously, you need to select a means of communication that is not only effective but is also a wise use of your time.

Preparing for parent-teacher conferences. Conferences have a much greater likelihood of being successful if all parties are prepared.[47] Both parents and students should be made aware of the purpose of the conference and the agenda. It is very helpful to provide students with an opportunity to fill out a "report card" on themselves and the class, to be shared with parents at the conference. This can be a simple rating form that asks students about their attitudes toward the class and has them evaluate their academic work and behavior, noting successes as well as areas needing improvement. The self-evaluation can also include goals for the coming grading period (both academic and behavioral).

When preparing for a parent-teacher conference, be sure to write down the points you wish to make and the questions you want to ask parents. Try to anticipate the questions that parents might bring up, and reflect on how to best respond to those questions. Well-organized data are especially important when a conference focuses on students' problem behavior or poor academic work.[48] It's also a good idea to create a neat, welcoming physical environment in which everyone can be comfortable. (If you're teaching in a primary grade, try to get some adult-sized chairs for parents!)

Conducting a parent-teacher conference. Ten or fifteen minutes doesn't allow a lot of time for something as important as a parent-teacher conference. Nonetheless, this may be your only opportunity to have face-to-face interaction with members of a student's family, so you want to make best use of the available time. Conferences should be sequenced to develop rapport, obtain and provide information about the student, and summarize. Some suggestions for conducting the conference follow:

- Begin the conference by introducing yourself in a friendly manner and mentioning something positive about the student's behavior.

- Focus on the student's appropriate behaviors before describing the behaviors needing improvement.
- Be sure to provide data to document problems.
- Focus on the student's behavior and not his or her character or personality. For example, "Simon has failed to turn in his homework three out of the past five days," rather than "Simon is lazy about doing his homework."
- Attempt to establish a partnership with the parent by inviting them to help you understand what might be contributing to the student's challenging behavior and plan a course of action cooperatively.
- Seek and encourage parental backup and support at home in ways that recognize that the parent is an important resource.
- Make a list of follow-up actions.
- End the conference with a positive comment.
- Use good communication skills—active listening, paraphrasing, empathy, and acceptance—during the conference.
- Follow up as proposed during the conference.
- Stress the fact that you both share a common goal; namely, to help the student be as successful as possible.

To see how an elementary teacher conducts a parent-teacher conference, watch the video case, *Home-School Communication: The Parent-Teacher Conference*.

▼ TeachSource Video Case — Home-School Communication: The Parent-Teacher Conference

To access the video, go to www.cengage.com/login. Watch the video clip and the bonus video, *Making a Recommendation for Specialized Testing*. Also study the artifacts in the case and reflect upon the following questions:

1. Earlier in the year, Julia had "social issues" such as temper tantrums. Although the teacher, Jim St. Claire, alludes to these, what does he do to set a positive tone for the parent conference?
2. How does the teacher use classroom artifacts to document his reporting?
3. What do you think about his explanations for the recommendation to have specialized testing? If you were the parent, how would you react to his explanations?

Communicating with diverse families. It is absolutely critical that teachers not assume that uneducated parents, poor parents, or parents with limited English proficiency have nothing of value to offer. During parent-teacher conferences, encourage families whose first language is not English to help you understand their children's educational and cultural background. Avoid jargon and explain educational terms that immigrant parents may not know (for instance, *cum file, grade equivalence, student-centered*). Be sensitive to cultural differences in communication styles. For example, different cultures have different norms for who can initiate conversation, whether it's all right to interrupt, and how long to pause between a question and its answer.

In addition, you need to recognize what constitutes appropriate classroom behavior may vary from culture to culture. A European American teacher may want students to participate actively in class discussions, voice their opinions, and ask questions. But some Latino and Asian American parents may have different expectations; they may want their children to be quiet and obedient and not to contradict the teacher or ask questions. At parent conferences, Latino immigrant parents may show more interest in their children's social and moral development than their academic achievement, asking *"Como se porta mi hijo/a?"* (How is my son/daughter behaving?).[49]

> ## YOUR TURN

1. Before the beginning of school, you want to send a letter to the family of every student you will be teaching. The purpose of the letter is to introduce yourself, describe some of the things students will be studying, and reassure everyone that this will be a good year. Select a grade level or subject area and write such a letter.
2. Consider the following scenario: Joshua frequently "forgets" his homework. He has received numerous zeros and often stays for detention to make up work. You have called home to report on his behavior and ask for help, but his mother says she cannot get involved. She tells you that she's overwhelmed by having to work two jobs. She says, "This is a school issue; *you* deal with it!" If possible, interview two experienced teachers about what they would do in a case like this. Then formulate your own course of action.

Responding to Inappropriate Behavior

Despite a teacher's best efforts to prevent inappropriate behavior, some problems are bound to occur. It is important to respond in ways that preserve a positive teacher-student relationship and to keep the instructional program going with a minimum of disruption. It is also essential to make sure that the severity of the disciplinary intervention is matched to the severity of the problem behavior. The following discussion provides suggestions for responding effectively to minor behavior problems, more serious problems, and chronic problems that don't respond to routine interventions.

Dealing with minor misbehavior. When problems are minor, it's best to use the most unobtrusive strategy possible. This way you won't create an even bigger distraction than the misbehavior itself.

Nonverbal strategies such as a disapproving stare (the "teacher look"), making eye contact, and using hand signals can be very effective. Teachers can also use proximity by moving closer to a student who is misbehaving or who seems on the verge of misbehaving. Many times the physical presence of the teacher will be sufficient to get the student back on task. Proximity lets the student know—by the teacher's presence—that the teacher is aware of the student's behavior.

If a nonverbal strategy is impossible or ineffective, you can try a *mild, nondirective verbal strategy* that prompts the appropriate behavior while leaving the responsibility for figuring out what to do with the misbehaving student. Sometimes just saying the student's name is sufficient. You can also incorporate the student's name into the ongoing instruction, or call on the student to participate in some way.

An "I" message is another nondirective verbal strategy that can be very useful in prompting appropriate behavior.[50] Here, the teacher describes

(1) the student's behavior (in nonjudgmental terms), (2) the effects of that behavior, and (3) how the teacher feels about that effect. For example, "If you talk while I'm giving directions, you won't know what to do, and other people get distracted. Then I have to repeat everything, and I find that very frustrating." Here are some other examples of I-messages:

"When you leave your backpack in the middle of the aisle, people can trip over it, and I'm afraid someone will get hurt."

"You left the room a mess after that activity, and I had to clean it up before I went home. That made me really annoyed."

Note that I-messages ideally contain all three parts in the recommended sequence. However, I-messages in any order, or even with one part missing, can still be effective—for example, "When you guys call out instead of raising your hands, it drives me nuts!"

Finally, there are times when it is necessary and appropriate for the teacher to tell students directly what they are supposed to be doing. In fact, *commands* and *directives* (such as "Sit down and get to work," "Pick up that pencil and begin the assignment") may be particularly appropriate for African American students who are accustomed to authorities "taking charge." Lisa Delpit, African American author of *Other People's Children: Cultural Conflict in the Classroom*,[51] observes that framing directives as questions (for instance, Will you please open your books to page 46?) is a particularly mainstream, middle-class (and female) way of speaking.

Dealing with more serious misbehavior. Sometimes nonverbal cues or verbal strategies (nondirective and directive) are ineffective in bringing about the appropriate behavior. Other times, the misbehavior is just too serious to use these kinds of unobtrusive responses. In these cases, you may have to impose a penalty or a consequence. Some possible penalties include the following:

- Holding a mandatory private conference with the student to discuss the behavior and decide what is to be done
- Withholding a privilege (for instance, choosing one's seat, free time, chewing gum, joining in a class party)
- Isolating the individual from other students (in an isolated or secluded area of the room)
- Contacting parents
- Assigning detention
- Excluding the student from class (for example, having the student sit in another teacher's classroom for the remainder of the period)
- Referring the student to the office.

Note that these last two consequences should be used only as a last resort. As one high school teacher comments: "Some students want to get out; they'll provoke a teacher just so they can leave the room. I know teachers who throw kids out all the time, but what's the point? Kids can't learn if they're in the office."[52]

Whenever possible, it's also preferable to use a *consequence that is logically related to the misbehavior*, rather than an arbitrary or generic punishment. For example, consider the following situations:

- A student carelessly breaks a test tube. A logical consequence would be requiring the student to pay the cost of replacing it. Punishment would be having the student write "I will be more careful" one hundred times.

- A student creates a mess at the pencil sharpener. A logical consequence would be cleaning it up. Punishment would be having the student stay for detention.
- A student constantly whispers to the person sitting nearby. A logical consequence would be isolating the student; a punishment would be making the student do an additional homework assignment.

Note that in order for a logical consequence to be effective, the student must see the relationship between the inappropriate behavior and the consequence; otherwise, the positive effect is lost.

Despite the temptation to yell and scream when you are frustrated by a student's behavior, consequences are best imposed calmly, quietly, and privately. It's important to avoid power struggles and help students save face in front of their peers. It is also critical to talk to the situation, not to the personality and character of the student.[53] In other words, teachers should make it clear that they accept the *student*, but not the student's *behavior*. In addition, you should avoid the use of sarcasm, be brief, avoid preaching and nagging, and monitor the impact your words and actions are having on students.

Dealing with chronic misbehavior: **Using reality therapy.** Some students with persistent behavior problems fail to respond to the routine strategies described thus far. In this case, it's necessary to design a more extensive intervention. One possible approach is offered by William Glasser, who proposes an eight-step, one-to-one counseling process to help students change problematic behavior.[54] The eight steps are briefly described here.

1. Become personally involved with the student. Accept the student, but not the student's misbehavior. Indicate a willingness to help the student solve the behavior problem.

2. Ask the student to describe his or her present behavior.

3. Assist the student in making a value judgment about the problem behavior. Ask, "Is it helping?" Focus on what the student is doing to contribute to the problem.

4. Help the student plan a better course of action. If necessary, suggest alternatives; help the student reach his or her own decision, thereby fostering self-responsibility.

5. Get a commitment from the student to the course of action he or she has selected.

6. Reinforce the student as he or she follows the plan and keeps the commitment. Be sure to let the student know that you are aware that progress is being made.

7. Accept no excuses if the student fails to follow through on the commitment. Acceptance of an excuse communicates a lack of caring. Alert the student to the need for a better plan.

8. Allow the student to suffer the natural and realistic consequences of misbehavior, but do not punish the student; help the student try again to develop a better plan and expect the student to make a commitment to it.

Glasser views the above process—"reality therapy"—as effective for the teacher who wishes to help the misbehaving student develop more productive behavior. In addition, Glasser proposes a similar process for helping a whole class deal with group behavior problems—the social-problem-solving classroom meeting.

Dealing with chronic misbehavior: Using strategies based on behavioral learning principles. Behavior modification (or applied behavior analysis) is based on the principle that changes in behavior are the result of external events rather than thinking or knowledge. When a student behaves, that behavior is followed by a consequence, either positive or negative. Behaviorists assume that the frequency of a particular behavior is contingent or dependent on the nature of the consequence that follows the behavior.

Two possible consequences of behavior are the *introduction of a reward* ("positive reinforcement") and the *introduction of an aversive or undesirable consequence* ("punishment"). Positive reinforcement causes the behavior to *increase* in frequency. Rewarded behavior is thus strengthened, and it is repeated in the future. Consider the following scenario:

> Brad prepares a neatly written paper, which he submits to the teacher (student behavior). The teacher praises Brad's work and comments that neatly written papers are more easily read than those that are sloppy (positive reinforcement). In subsequent papers, Brad takes great care to write neatly (the frequency of the reinforced behavior is increased).

In contrast, punishment causes the behavior to decrease in frequency. Punished behavior tends to be discontinued:

> Jim prepares a rather sloppily written paper, which he submits to the teacher (student behavior). The teacher rebukes Jim for failing to be neat, informs him that sloppily written papers are difficult to read, and tells him to rewrite and resubmit the paper (punishment). In subsequent papers, Jim writes less sloppily (the frequency of the punished behavior is decreased).

The teacher can *encourage* appropriate student behavior by using positive reinforcement (the introduction of a reward). The teacher can *discourage* inappropriate student behavior by using punishment (the introduction of an undesirable stimulus). These consequences influence student behavior in accordance with established behavioral principles. However, if the teacher rewards misbehavior, it is likely to be continued; if the teacher punishes appropriate behavior, it is likely to be discontinued.

When considering the use of positive reinforcement, keep in mind several important points. *First, a reward is defined in terms of its ability to increase the frequency of the rewarded behavior.* Thus, reward (and punishment) can be understood only in terms of an individual student. A response that the teacher intended to be rewarding may actually be punishing. For example, individual public praise may be upsetting and embarrassing to students whose cultures emphasize the good of the group over individual achievement.[55] Similarly, a response intended to be punishing may actually be rewarding. A common example is when a student misbehaves to get attention. The teacher's subsequent scolding rewards rather than punishes the attention-hungry student and, consequently, the student continues to misbehave in order to get attention.

Second, rewards can be divided into three categories: social rewards, such as a pat on the back, a thumbs-up, and verbal praise; *activity rewards*, such as being first in line or having five minutes of free time at the end of class; and *tangible or material rewards*, such as popcorn or an award certificate. Although you must take care in selecting a reinforcer that is appropriate to a particular student, the selection process need not be difficult. A straightforward method is to simply ask students what they would like to work for. You can also observe what they do during free time: Do they use the computer? Read a magazine? Chat with friends? If so, then these activities can be used as a reward for behaving appropriately.

Third, some educators argue that the use of positive reinforcement is counterproductive because it produces students who are compliant rather than self-disciplined. In *Punished by Rewards: The Trouble with Gold Stars, Incentive Plans, A's, Praise, and Other Bribes*,[56] Alfie Kohn argues that rewards are "every bit as controlling as punishments, even if they control by seduction." Extensive use of external controls may undermine the development of students' autonomy, responsibility, and self-regulation. There is also the fear that teachers will use positive reinforcement to manipulate students into complying with boring, irrelevant curriculum, rather than examining ways to make lessons more engaging to students.

The use of punishment has its own set of caveats. The judicious use of punishment can have desirable, immediate effects on student misbehavior, but punishment also carries the risk of negative side effects. It's important to be aware of both the benefits and disadvantages of using punishment.[57] On the positive side,

- punishment does stop the punished student behavior immediately, and it can reduce the occurrence of that behavior for a long period of time.
- punishment is informative to students because it helps them discriminate rapidly between acceptable and unacceptable behaviors.
- punishment is instructive to other students because it may reduce the probability that other class members will imitate the punished behaviors.

On the negative side,

- punishment may be misinterpreted (sometimes a specific, punished behavior is generalized to other behaviors; for example, the student who is punished for talking out of turn may stop responding, even when it is appropriate to do so).
- punishment may cause the punished student to withdraw altogether.
- punishment may cause the punished student to become aggressive.
- punishment may produce negative peer reactions; for example, students may exhibit undesirable behaviors (ridicule or sympathy) toward the punished student.
- punishment may cause punished students to become negative about themselves or about the situation; for example, punishment may diminish feelings of self-worth or produce a negative attitude toward school.

Because of the disadvantages of using punishment, teachers should always consider alternative procedures for reducing problem behaviors. Furthermore, once a punishment procedure is selected, it should be employed with the utmost caution and its effects should be carefully monitored. Teachers should also find desirable behaviors to reinforce at the same time they are punishing undesirable behavior.

The principles of behavioral learning offer a number of specific managerial strategies:

- A *cue* is a verbal or nonverbal prompt or signal given by the teacher when the student needs to be reminded to behave in a certain way or to refrain from behaving in a certain way. Thus, a cue can be used to encourage or discourage a given behavior. Unlike a reinforcer, a cue precedes a response; it "triggers" a behavior.

- *Shaping* is a strategy used to encourage the development of new behaviors by reinforcing progress toward the desired goal. Each time the student performs a behavior that is one step closer to the desired behavior (*successive approximations*), the teacher reinforces the student. Eventually, the student is consistently able to perform the desired behavior.

- A *token economy system* usually consists of three elements intended to change the behavior of students: (1) a set of carefully written instructions that describe the student behaviors the teacher will reinforce, (2) a well-developed system for awarding tokens to students who exhibit the behaviors that have been specified as appropriate, and (3) a set of procedures that allows students to exchange tokens they have earned for prizes or opportunities to engage in special activities. The implementation and operation of a token economy requires a great investment of time and energy on the part of the teacher. Consequently, its most typical—and efficient—use is in situations where a large number of students are misbehaving and the teacher seeks to rapidly change the behavior of those students.

- A *contingency contract* is a written agreement negotiated between the teacher and a misbehaving student. It specifies the behaviors the student has agreed to exhibit and indicates what the consequences—the payoff—will be if the student exhibits those behaviors. As in all contracts, both parties obligate themselves. The student is committed to behave in certain ways deemed appropriate, and the teacher is committed to reward the student for doing so. Contracting tends to be a somewhat time-consuming process. Therefore, it is usually reserved for those instances in which a student is exhibiting serious misbehaviors on a rather routine basis.

- *Self-monitoring* is a strategy in which students record some aspect of their behavior in order to modify that behavior. Self-monitoring systematically increases awareness through self-observation. For example, students can record how many times they call out during a discussion, or how many times they get out of their seats during one class period.

Keeping anecdotal records. It is very helpful to keep anecdotal records describing serious incidents of problematic behavior and your own interventions. Such written documentation serves a number of purposes: (1) it organizes information in a way that allows you to gain better insights into a student's patterns of behavior; (2) it provides a written record that can be shared with others—the student, a counselor, an administrator, or a parent—in an effort to help that person better understand the nature and scope of the student's misbehavior; and (3) it provides a written record to which you can refer should you be called on to provide information concerning the misbehavior of the student and/or your handling of that misbehavior.

An anecdotal record can be rather simple and informal or more complex and formal. It can range from notes jotted down on an index card to a carefully constructed form completed by the teacher and retained in a file established for a particular student. In any event, the record should contain (1) the name of the student, (2) the date and time on which the incident occurred, (3) the location of the incident, (4) the names of any others who might have been involved in or witnessed the incident, (5) a complete and accurate description of the student's misbehavior, (6) a complete and accurate description of the teacher's actions, (7) the signature of the teacher, and (8) the date on which the record was written. If you provide the student with the opportunity to read what you have written, the form might also provide a space for the student's signature. You might also invite the student to write a response to what you have written. Finally, the record can also include a description of any follow-up actions, any improvement in the student's conduct, or any additional occurrences of similar misbehaviors.

Three additional recommendations regarding anecdotal records are worth mentioning. First, it is critically important to describe the behavior without making judgments or inferences. Second, complete the anecdotal record as quickly as possible after the occurrence of the incident, when the memory of what happened is freshest. Should you be called upon to share your documentation of the incident with the administration or with legal authorities, your records will have most credibility if they are contemporaneous accounts. Third, if there is a question as to whether or not an incident of student misbehavior is serious enough to warrant the writing of an anecdotal record, the prudent course is to document. To have documentation and not need to refer to it is far better than needing documentation and not having it.

❯ YOUR TURN

1. Suggest two strategies for dealing with each of the following instances of problematic behavior.

   a. You're reviewing math homework with your second-grade class. You notice that one child is playing with a toy car instead of paying attention.

   b. You have just returned test papers to your junior chemistry students. Michael takes his paper, crumples it up, and throws it on the floor.

   c. Your fifth-grade students are working in cooperative groups. You overhear Joseph say to Melissa, "You're so stupid!"

   d. Tanya repeatedly calls out during class discussions. You have repeatedly reminded her to raise her hand if she wants to speak, and she's okay for about five minutes. Then she starts to call out again.

   e. Your sophomore English class is discussing *Moby Dick*. Brittany is slouching down in her seat and appears inattentive.

2. Consider the two following anecdotal records. Which of the two is the better anecdotal record? Why?

   a. While Joseph, Adam, and other members of the class were walking to the cafeteria, I saw Joseph shove Adam in the back with no apparent warning. The shove knocked Adam to the floor. When confronted, Joseph claimed he had been provoked by Adam. Adam stated that he was not hurt but claimed that he had not provoked what he called an "attack." I saw no behavior on the part of Adam that I felt was provocation for Joseph's actions.

   b. Joseph knocked Adam to the floor because he doesn't like Adam. Because of long-standing animosity between the boys, it is possible that Adam provoked Joseph.

Mastery Test

OBJECTIVE 3   **To identify the ongoing tasks involved in classroom management and to explain how each contributes to a well-functioning learning environment**

List the six major tasks of classroom management that are discussed in this chapter.

1. For each task, explain how it contributes to effective classroom management. For example, consider the task "building positive student-teacher relationships." Then think of an example of how this contributes to an orderly, respectful environment. You might say, "Students are more likely to cooperate with teachers whom they perceive as caring and respectful." Or, "If teachers use good communication skills like active listening, students are more likely to feel understood and valued."

2. Reflecting on these six tasks, make a list of at least two important things to remember for each task. These "important things" can guide your management planning for the school year. For example, consider the physical environment. If you plan to be a kindergarten teacher, you might want to remember to put picture labels on the shelves so that children will know where materials are stored. If you hope to teach Spanish, you might want to collect and post art and artifacts from Spain and Mexico.

Since responses will vary depending on the individual, no Answer Key is provided at the end of the book.

Final Comments

Prospective teachers often talk about how much they "love kids." They believe that good teachers are caring teachers who treat students with respect. They imagine themselves working with students who are intellectually curious and academically engaged, in classrooms that are orderly, productive, and warm.

Unfortunately, these prospective teachers often possess only vague notions of how to achieve this kind of classroom. Moreover, in an effort to be seen as respectful, they may be reluctant to establish norms for behavior, enforce expectations, or make any demands on students. Ironically, this may lead to a classroom environment characterized by inappropriate behavior and disorder—hardly an environment in which caring relationships can flourish. Then, perceiving students as disrespectful, teachers may go to the other extreme, becoming dictatorial and imposing harsh, punitive consequences for misbehavior. "I want to be nice, but I have to be mean" is a common lament of beginning teachers. In fact, some beginning teachers may conclude that caring for students and maintaining control are mutually exclusive.[58]

Hopefully, the concepts and suggestions provided in this chapter will help to avert this scenario. Teachers who understand the distinctions among authoritative, authoritarian, and permissive styles of management are able to appreciate the need for both leadership *and* warmth. Authoritative teachers know how to make demands on students while still being respectful and supportive. They recognize the fact that holding high standards for behavior and achievement is actually one way of showing caring. They grasp the difference between being "mean" and being firm and assertive.

☐ INTASC Principle 9

As you think about the goals and challenges of classroom management, also keep in mind the distinction between classroom management and discipline. Classroom management is far more than responding to students' misbehavior. It encompasses a wide range of tasks, some of which have been described here: designing an appropriate physical setting, planning ways to establish positive teacher-student and student-student relationships, establishing norms for behavior, enforcing those norms, and reaching out to families. Clearly, learning to be an effective classroom manager is a multifaceted, complex endeavor. It involves knowledge, reflection, hard work and time. And like skiing or swimming, it requires on-site learning. Reading this chapter is just the first step.

✳ Mastery Test

When you have responded to the following items, compare your answers to those presented in the Answer Key at the end of the book.

1. For each of the following design decisions, think of a possible direct effect, as well as a possible indirect or symbolic effect. In other words, how is the physical design likely to affect students' behavior, and what message is the design likely to communicate to students?

   a. Putting student desks in rows

   b. Putting student desks in four-person clusters

   c. Labeling shelves in Spanish and English in your elementary classroom

   d. Placing several wastebaskets around the room

   e. Locating the pencil sharpener behind the teacher's desk

2. You are teaching in a school with a great many students from an ethnic background you have never encountered before. You need to acquire cultural content knowledge. What are four questions you might ask students and/or their families to help you develop some knowledge of their norms, values, and experiences?

3. You notice a lot of name-calling and put-downs occurring in your class. When you confront the students who are doing the harassment, they say, "But we're just teasing." What do you say to them?

4. What is the difference between rules and procedures?

5. What are five suggestions for conducting a successful parent-teacher conference?

6. What are some strategies you can use for dealing with minor misbehaviors?

7. What are some penalties or consequences you can use for more serious misbehavior, or misbehavior that does not respond to your unobtrusive strategies?

8. What is the difference between traditional punishment and a logical consequence? A student in your class writes his name on his desk. What would be a traditional punishment for this incident? What would be a logical consequence?

9. Why is it useful to keep anecdotal records? What are five items you should include in an anecdotal record?

10. Five problems are briefly described in the exercise below. Your task is to describe what you would do in each case and to justify the course of action you select. Your justifications ought to describe the reasoning behind your decisions. You may also find it helpful to describe the assumptions you made about the nature of the problem, other alternatives you considered, and the condition you would be attempting to establish or reestablish.

Obviously, there are no right or wrong answers. For this reason, no Answer Key is provided for this exercise. If possible, share your responses with a partner or a small group of peers.

a. When Linda's mother brought Linda to your kindergarten class on the first day of school, she warned you that Linda was "a very sensitive child." After only two weeks of school, you have some idea of the reason she felt the need to warn you. If she can't be first in line—temper tantrum. If she is not allowed to do what she wants—temper tantrum. And Linda's temper tantrums are complete with kicking, crying, screaming, and rolling on the floor. You have tried to ignore her outbursts, but now you find that the other children are making fun of Linda. Typical comments include: "There she goes again!" "What a baby she is!" "Grow up, crybaby!" What do you do?

b. Jim is one of the brightest students in your third-grade class, but he constantly misbehaves. He does nothing really serious, just a continuous series of minor incidents—talking out, laughing loudly, slamming his desktop, throwing wads of paper, and teasing fellow classmates, for example. Although these are not major misbehaviors, they are annoying and disruptive. In addition, the other students think these things are funny. They laugh and treat Jim's behavior as a joke. What do you do?

c. You are not sure of the problem, but the symptoms are obvious. Your middle school math class is not working well. Assignments are generally late. The students are constantly complaining about your assignments, the fairness of tests, and everything in general. During class discussions, no one participates. No one volunteers to answer questions you believe many can answer. Little accidents such as pencils breaking, books falling on the floor, and an overturned wastebasket seem frequent. What do you do?

d. Tom has been a member of your Spanish I class for nearly three weeks now, having transferred to Wilson High School after the Christmas break. Although he seems to be a nice young man, it is obvious that he has not been accepted by his classmates. Small-group projects designed to involve Tom have not helped. Tom remains outside an otherwise cohesive group. The other students seem to ignore him, and he seems to ignore them; however, you have not seen any signs of hostility on anyone's part. What do you do?

e. Your fourth-period social studies class has always been a bit more of a problem than your other tenth-grade classes. After six months, however, the students in that class work quite well, with one bothersome exception. Despite your telling them on numerous occasions that they are to wait until you dismiss them when the bell rings for them to go to fifth-period lunch, they invariably get out of their seats and rush to the door, pushing and shoving into the hallway. As luck would have it, today Mr. Blake, the principal, was almost run over by your stampeding students. What do you do?

Observation Worksheet

CLASSROOM MANAGEMENT: GOALS AND STRATEGIES

This observation focuses on the managerial strategies the teacher uses in the classroom to prevent and respond effectively to students' problem behavior.

Directions: Do not use actual names of schools, teachers, administrators, or students when using this worksheet.

Observer's Name: _____

Date: _____

Grade Level: _____

Subject: _____

Class Size: _____

Background Information: Give a brief general description of the school's social, economic, and racial/ethnic makeup.

_____

_____

Observation:

1. Draw a map of the classroom and evaluate the physical layout. Consider the following questions:

    Does the classroom feel like a safe, comfortable place to be?

    Does the desk arrangement seem to match the teacher's instructional goals?

    Are there displays of student work around the room?

    Are frequently used classroom materials accessible?

2. Does the teacher seem to promote positive teacher-student interaction? For example, does he or she:

    Stand by the door and greet students when they come in?

    Show an interest in students' out-of-school lives?

    Communicate high expectations yet convey warmth and caring?

3. Does the teacher try to create positive student-student interactions? For example, does he or she:

    Use cooperative learning activities?

    Encourage students to be respectful to one another?

    Intervene if instances of teasing or name-calling occur?

4. Does the teacher make expectations for behavior clear to the students? For example:

> Are classroom rules posted?

> Do students seem to know the routines for going to the restroom, sharpening pencils, and so forth?

5. How does the teacher deal with problem behaviors? Does he or she:

> Use unobtrusive, nonverbal strategies (such as proximity) whenever appropriate?

> Use nondirective verbal strategies (such as calling the student's name or using an I-message) whenever appropriate?

> Impose penalties quietly, calmly, and privately?

Teacher Interview

Try to arrange to speak with the teacher for a few minutes about his or her approach to classroom management. Ask questions such as the following:

1. How would you describe your general approach to classroom management?

_____

_____

_____

2. What are your goals for classroom management?

_____

_____

_____

3. Do you do anything in particular to build a sense of community and caring in your classroom?

_____

_____

_____

4. How do approach classroom rules? Do you give students a handout with the rules? Do you post them? How much time do you spend teaching and talking about the rules? Do you involve students in generating the rules?

_____

_____

_____

5. What kinds of disciplinary interventions do you find most effective?

_____

_____

_____

Reflections on Your Observation and Interview

1. What is the tone of the classroom? Do students and teacher seem to have a positive, warm relationship? Do students interact with one another in a respectful, supportive way?

_____

_____

_____

2. What, if any, managerial strategies did you observe the teacher use to prevent managerial problems? In your view, was the use of these strategies effective in preventing behavior problems?

_____

_____

3. What, if any, managerial strategies did you observe the teacher use to deal with problem behaviors? In your view, was the use of these strategies effective?

_____

_____

_____

4. What student behaviors did you observe that indicated the teacher was successful or unsuccessful in achieving his or her managerial goals?

_____

_____

_____

5. Would you describe the teacher's managerial style as authoritarian, authoritative, or permissive? Explain.

_____

_____

_____

ADDITIONAL RESOURCES

Readings

Bear, G., with Cavalier, A. R., & Manning, M. A. (2004). *Developing self-discipline and preventing and correcting misbehavior.* Boston: Pearson/Allyn & Bacon.

Brady, K., Forton, M. B., Porter, D., & Wood, C. (2003). *Rules in school.* Greenfield, MA: Northeast Foundation for Children.

Cartledge, G., & Lo, Y. (2006). *Teaching urban learners: Culturally responsive strategies for developing academic and behavioral competence.* Champaign, IL: Research Press.

Charles, C. M. (2008). *Building classroom discipline* (9th edition). Boston: Pearson/Allyn & Bacon.

Emmer, E. T., & Evertson, C. M. (2009). *Classroom management for middle and high school teachers* (8th edition). Upper Saddle River, NJ: Pearson.

Evertson, C. M., & Emmert, E. T. (2009). *Classroom management for elementary teachers* (8th edition). Upper Saddle River, NJ: Pearson.

Gordon, T. (2003). *Teacher effectiveness training* (revised edition). New York: Three Rivers Press.

Jones, V., & Jones, L. (2007). *Comprehensive classroom management: Creating communities of support and solving problems* (8th edition). Boston: Pearson/Allyn & Bacon.

Marzano, R. J., with Marzano, J. S., & Pickering, D. J. (2003). *Classroom management that works: Research-based strategies for every teacher*. Alexandria, VA: Association for Supervision and Curriculum Development.

Mendler, A. N., & Curwin, R. L. (1999). *Discipline with dignity for challenging youth*. Bloomington, IN: National Educational Service.

Weinstein, C. S. (2007). *Secondary classroom management: Lessons from research and practice*. New York: McGraw-Hill.

Weinstein, C. S., & Mignano, A. J. (2003). *Elementary classroom management: Lessons from research and practice*. New York: McGraw-Hill.

 Websites

The Southern Poverty Law Center: http://www.teachingtolerance.org
The Teaching Tolerance project provides teachers at all levels with ideas and free resources for building community, fighting bias, and celebrating diversity.

Collaborative for Academic, Social, and Emotional Learning (CASEL): http://www.casel.org
Dedicated to the development of children's social and emotional competencies and the capacity of schools, parents, and communities to support that development. CASEL's mission is to establish integrated, evidence-based social and emotional learning (SEL) from preschool through high school.

The Family Involvement Network of Educators (FINE): Harvard Family Research Project, http://www.hfrp.org.
FINE brings together thousands of stakeholders committed to promoting strong partnerships among schools, families, and communities. FINE provides information about family involvement, including teaching tools, training materials, and research reports. Members can receive a free subscription to the FINE email newsletter, which regularly highlights new resources for strengthening, family, school, and community partnerships.

The National Network of Partnership Schools: http://www.partnershipschools.org.
NPPS provides information on implementing comprehensive, goal-oriented programs of school, family, and community partnerships. Check out the interactive homework assignments (TIPS) and the collections of "Promising Partnership Practices" on their web site.

For these links and additional resources, please visit the Premium Website at **www.cengage.com/login.**

NOTES

1. V. Jones, "How Do Teachers Learn to Be Effective Classroom Managers?" in *Handbook of Classroom Management: Research, Practice, and Contemporary Issues*, ed. C. M. Evertson and C. S. Weinstein (Mahwah, NJ: Lawrence Erlbaum Associates, 2006), 889.

2. M. Pilarski, "Student teachers: Underprepared for classroom management?" *Teaching Education* 6 (1994): 78–79.

3. L. Stough, "The Place of Classroom Management and Standards in Teacher Education" in *Handbook of Classroom Management: Research, Practice, and Contemporary Issues*, ed. C. M. Evertson and C. S. Weinstein (Mahwah, NJ: Lawrence Erlbaum Associates, 2006).

4. K. Hammerness, "Classroom Management in New York City," *Teaching Education* (in press).

5. E. Midlarsky and H. M. Klain, "A History of Violence in the Schools" in *Violence in Schools: Cross-National and Cross-Cultural Perspectives*, ed. F. Denmark, H. H. Krauss, R. W. Wesner, E. Midlarsky, & U. P. Gielen (New York: Springer, 2005), 41.

6. Ibid.

7. H. Mann, 1934, p. 288. Cited in E. Midlarsky and H. M. Klain, "A History of Violence in the Schools" in *Violence in Schools: Cross-National and Cross-Cultural Perspectives*, ed. F. Denmark, H. H. Krauss, R. W. Wesner, E. Midlarsky, & U. P. Gielen (New York: Springer, 2005), 41–42.

8. G. Gay, "Connections between Classroom Management and Culturally Responsive Teaching" in *Handbook of Classroom Management: Research, Practice, and Contemporary Issues*, ed. C. M. Evertson and C. S. Weinstein (Mahwah, NJ: Lawrence Erlbaum Associates, 2006), 355.

9. C. S. Weinstein, M. Curran, and S. Tomlinson-Clarke, "Culturally Responsive Classroom Management: Awareness into Action," *Theory Into Practice* 42, no. 4 (2003): 269–276; C. S. Weinstein, S. Tomlinson-Clarke, and M. Curran, "Toward a Conception of Culturally Responsive Classroom Management," *Journal of Teacher Education* 55, no. 1 (2004): 25–38.

10. L. C. Soodak and M. R. McCarthy, "Classroom Management in Inclusive Settings" in *Handbook of Classroom Management: Research, Practice,*

and Contemporary Issues, ed. C. M. Evertson and C. S. Weinstein (Mahwah, NJ: Lawrence Erlbaum Associates, 2006).

11. D. Baumrind, "Parental Disciplinary Patterns and Social Competence in Children," *Youth and Society* 9 (1978): 239–276.

12. J. M. T. Walker, "Looking at Teacher Practices Through the Lens of Parenting Style," *The Journal of Experimental Education* 76, no. 2 (2008): 218–240; J. M. T. Walker, "Authoritative Classroom Management: How Control and Nurturance Work Together," *Theory Into Practice* 48, no. 2 (2009): 122–129.

13. E. Bondy, E. and D. Ross, "The Teacher as a Warm Demander," *Educational Leadership* 66, no. 1 (2008): 54–58; J. J. Irvine, "'Warm Demanders,'" *Education Week* 17, no. 35 (May 13, 1998): 56; J. Kleinfeld, "Effective Teachers of Eskimo and Indian Students," *The School Review*, 83 (1975): 301–344.

14. T. Wubbels, M. Brekelmans, P. den Brok, and J. van Artwijk, "An Interpersonal Perspective on Classroom Management in Secondary Classrooms in the Netherlands" in *Handbook of Classroom Management: Research, Practice, and Contemporary Issues*, ed. C. M. Evertson and C. S. Weinstein (Mahwah, NJ: Lawrence Erlbaum Associates, 2006).

15. E. Proshansky and M. Wolfe, "The Physical Setting and Open Education," *School Review* 82 (1974): 557–574.

16. K. F. Osterman, "Students' need for belonging in the school community," *Review of Educational Research* 70 (2000): 323–367; A. Woolfolk Hoy and C. S. Weinstein, "Student and Teacher Perspectives on Classroom Management" in *Handbook of Classroom Management: Research, Practice, and Contemporary Issues*, ed. C. M. Evertson and C. S. Weinstein (Mahwah, NJ: Lawrence Erlbaum Associates, 2006).

17. R. J. Marzano, with J. S. Marzano and D. J. Pickering, *Classroom Management that Works: Research-Based Strategies for Every Teacher* (Alexandria, VA: Association for Supervision and Curriculum Development, 2003).

18. D. J. Cothran, P. H. Kulinna, and D. A. Garahy, "'This is kind of giving a secret away . . .': Students' perspectives on effective class management," *Teaching and Teacher Education*, 19 (2003): 439.

19. S. R. Katz, "Teaching in tensions: Latino immigrant youth, their teachers, and the structures of schooling," *Teachers College Record*, 100, no. 4 (1999): 809–840.

20. Marzano, Marzano, and Pickering, *op cit.*: 53.

21. J. Allen, "Family Partnerships that Count," *Educational Leadership* 66, no. 1 (2008): 22–27.

22. Weinstein, Tomlinson-Clarke, and Curran, *op cit.*

23. D. Corbett and B. Wilson, "What Urban Students Say About Good Teaching," *Educational Leadership* 60, no. 1 (2002): 19.

24. D. Corbett, B. Wilson, and B. Williams, "No Choice but Success," *Educational Leadership* 62, no. 6 (2005): 10.

25. C. S. Weinstein, *Middle and Secondary Classroom Management: Lessons from Research and Practice*, 3rd ed. (Boston: McGraw-Hill, 2003), 73.

26. T. Gordon with N. Burch, *Teacher Effectiveness Training* (New York: Three Rivers Press, 2003).

27. M. Sapon-Shevin, "Building a safe community for learning," in *To Become a Teacher: Making a Difference in Children's Lives*, ed. W. Ayers (New York: Teachers College Press, 1995), 111.

28. V. Jones and L. Jones, *Comprehensive Classroom Management: Creating Communities of Support and Solving Problems*, 8th ed. (Boston: Pearson/Allyn & Bacon, 2007).

29. M. Sapon-Shevin, *Because We Can Change the World: Practical Guide to Building Cooperative, Inclusive Classroom Communities*. (Boston: Allyn & Bacon, 1999).

30. Ibid.

31. Ibid.

32. C. S. Schmollinger, K. A. Opaleski, M. L. Chapman, R. Jocius, and S. Bell, "How Do You Make Your Classroom an Inviting Place for Students to Come Back to Each Year?" *English Journal* 91, no. 6 (2002): 20–22.

33. Ibid.

34. N. A. Madden and R. E. Slavin, "Cooperative learning and social acceptance of mainstreamed academically handicapped students." *Journal of Special Education* 17 (1983): 171–182; R. E. Slavin, *Student Team Learning: A Practical Guide to Cooperative Learning*, 3rd ed. (Washington DC: National Education Association, 1991).

35. D. W. Johnson and R. T. Johnson, "Social Skills for Successful Groupwork," *Educational Leadership* 47, no. 4 (1989/90): 29–33.

36. R. Kriete, *The Morning Meeting Book*, 2nd ed. (Greenfield, MA: Northeast Foundation for Children, 2002).

37. J. L. Nelsen, L. Lott, and H. S. Glenn, *Positive Discipline in the Classroom*, 3rd ed. (Roseville, CA: Prima, 2000).

38. Gordon with Burch, *op cit.*

39. J. Leishman, "Cyberbullying: The Internet Is the Latest Weapon in a Bully's Arsenal," (2002). http://cbc/ca/news/national/news/cyberbullying/index.html.

40. E. T. Emmer, C. M. Evertson, and L. M. Anderson, "Effective Classroom Management at the Beginning of the School Year," *The Elementary School Journal* 80, no. 5 (1980): 219–231; C. M. Evertson and E. T. Emmer, "Effective Management at the Beginning of the School Year in Junior High Classes," *Journal of Educational Psychology* 74, no. 4 (1982): 485–498.

41. Ibid.

42. C. S. Weinstein and A. J. Mignano, *Elementary Classroom Management: Lessons from Research and Practice,* 4th ed. (Boston: McGraw-Hill, 2003), 127.

43. C. S. Weinstein, *Middle and Secondary Classroom Management: Lessons from Research and Practice*, 3rd ed. (Boston: McGraw-Hill, 2003): 120.

44. P. Heuveline, "Estimating the proportion of marriages that end in divorce," research brief prepared for the Council on Contemporary Families (2005). http://www.contemporaryfamilies.org.

45. E. Heilman, "Hegemonies and 'Transgressions' of Family: Tales of Pride and Prejudice," in *Other Kinds of Families: Embracing Diversity in Schools*, ed. T. Turner-Vorbeck and M. Miller Marsh (New York: Teachers College Press, 2008).

46. J. Epstein, *School, family, and community partnerships: Preparing educators and improving schools* (Boulder, CO: Westview Press, 2001); J. Griffith, "The relation of school structure and social environment to parent involvement in elementary schools." *The Elementary School Journal* 99, no. 1 (1998): 53–80.

47. Jones and Jones, *op cit*.

48. Ibid.

49. E. Trumbull, C. Rothstein-Fisch, P. M. Greenfield, and B. Quiroz, *Bridging Cultures Between Home and School: A Guide for Teachers* (Mahwah, NJ: Lawrence Erlbaum Associates, 2001).

50. Gordon with Burch, *op cit*.

51. L. Delpit, *Other People's Children: Cultural Conflict in the Classroom* (New York: The New Press, 1995).

52. Weinstein, *op cit*., 325.

53. H. G. Ginott, *Between Parent and Child* (New York: Macmillan, 1965); Haim G. Ginott, *Between Parent and Teenager* (New York: Macmillan, 1969); Haim G. Ginott, *Teacher and Child* (New York: Macmillan, 1972).

54. W. Glasser, *Schools Without Failure* (New York: Harper & Row, 1969).

55. Trumbull, Rothstein-Fiksch, Greenfield, and Quiroz, *op cit*.

56. A. Kohn, *Punished by Rewards: The Trouble with Gold Stars, Incentive Plans, A's, Praise, and Other Bribes* (Boston: Houghton Mifflin Company, 1993): 51.

57. B. Sulzer and G. R. Mayer, *Behavior Modification Procedures for School Personnel* (Hinsdale, IL: Dryden, 1972).

58. C. S. Weinstein, "'I Want To Be Nice, But I Have To Be Mean': Exploring prospective teachers' conceptions of caring and order," *Teaching and Teacher Education* 14, no. 2 (1998): 153–163.

9 Cooperative Learning

Mary S. Leighton

JHDT Stock Image/Shutterstock.Com

◘ INTASC Standards

● **Principle 2:** The teacher understands how children learn and develop and provides learning opportunities that support their development.

● **Principle 3:** The teacher understands how students differ in their approaches to learning and creates instructional opportunities adapted to diverse learners.

● **Principle 4:** The teacher understands and uses a variety of instructional strategies.

● **Principle 5:** The teacher creates a learning environment that encourages positive social interaction, active engagement in learning, and self-motivation.

● **Principle 6:** The teachers uses knowledge of communication techniques to foster active inquiry, collaboration, and supportive interaction.

● **Principle 8:** The teacher understands and uses formal and informal assessment strategies.

● **Principle 10:** The teacher fosters relationships with colleagues, parents, and agencies in the larger community.

◘ OBJECTIVES

1. To identify the functions of teachers, students, and content in effective lessons

2. To describe the attributes of cooperative learning that contribute to student achievement in social and academic arenas and to discriminate academically productive cooperative learning strategies from less structured group activities that may not improve achievement

3. To integrate simple cooperative learning structures into more complex or extended lessons

4. To implement complex cooperative learning strategies, including Student Teams Achievement Divisions (STAD), Jigsaw, and Academic Controversy

5. To integrate instruction in process skills into cooperative learning activities

6. To build support from the physical, organizational, and instructional environments for effective use of cooperative learning strategies

7. To describe how schoolwide implementation of cooperative learning can increase student achievement and professional collaboration and reduce violence

T he sixth-grade reading and language arts class is working on vocabulary. On Monday, the class members created a list of new and interesting words drawn from the novel they are studying. The teacher, Ms. Harriman, helped the class trim the original list to twenty words and then find sentences in the novel that show what each word means. On Tuesday, she suggested that as a journal-writing exercise they try using the words in sentences about their own lives. Today students are working in learning teams to prepare for a quiz on the spelling and meaning of the words.

Example from language arts ▶

As usual, each team has its own lesson packet, which Ms. Harriman uses to distribute and collect materials. The packet for this lesson includes an alphabetized word list with a text sentence for each word; a guide with definitions and some examples of common usage of the words; and four cards, numbered 1 to 4. The Cougars—Isaac, Kate, José, and May—are old hands at team practice. May, assigned the role of materials manager for the week, fetches the team packet from the materials shelf and brings it to the team table. Each member draws a numbered card and glances at the chalkboard, where Ms. Harriman has written starting roles for each number. Isaac has drawn number 1, designated for this practice session as the starting questioner. He reaches for the word list, while Kate—as number 3, the starting checker—takes the answer key. Isaac reads the opening question to May, number 2, the first answerer: "'[Muna] got no closer to those exalted figures than their horses' feed troughs.' What does 'exalted' mean?"[1] May responds promptly, "High class, important, rich." Kate checks May's explanation against the study guide and decides that the definition is acceptable. José looks puzzled, though. Isaac pops up from his chair and mimes kingly stature, pulling Kate into the act to curtsey deeply. "I am the exalted one," claims Isaac grandly. "My subjects all bow down to me." José nods, smiling, and the session continues. May then spells the word correctly, and the action moves on: May becomes the questioner; Kate, the answerer; and José—as number 4, a listener during round one—becomes the checker. Isaac becomes the listener.

Today's Practice Session Starting Roles

1. Questioner
2. Answerer
3. Checker
4. Listener

Supporting English learners ▶

Because this is José's first year in an English-language reading group, he asks for and gets extra help from his teammates, who have become adept at illustrating word meanings with lots of examples from their daily routines. Occasionally, they recruit the help of Raphael on the Pumas, because as a Spanish speaker like José he can offer examples in Spanish, too. Kate, whose extensive recreational reading makes her a star in this class, is another good resource for José, a peer with whom she previously had limited acquaintance. The Cougars finish their work early and use the extra time to try a practice test. Each is eager to make this week's individual quiz score higher than usual and contribute to the team's improvement points.

Ms. Harriman has been circulating around the room monitoring work, and she stops near the Cougars to check their progress. She has had a private coaching session with Isaac, who is very assertive, to teach him how to exercise his irrepressible initiative (a mixed blessing, in her view!) in drawing out

Measuring growth ▶ May, who is shy. Ms. Harriman sees that Isaac is making progress in this skill and that everyone is participating appropriately in the practice activity.

The class expects a quiz tomorrow. Each group member's score will be compared to his or her **base score**, calculated by averaging the student's three previous quiz scores in vocabulary. The team earns points when the comparison shows individual progress. All the teams that reach the Super Team standard of growth will be able to display their teams' pennants on the library bulletin board next week. Those that meet the slightly lower Great Team standard will display pennants on the classroom bulletin board. Since Ms. Harriman has been using this strategy, Isaac's quiz scores have risen from 70s to 80s and his interest in reading has visibly increased. José's scores have improved dramatically, and by the end of the semester Ms. Harriman expects to see him reading on grade level in English, as he already does in Spanish. May smiles and participates more often in class discussions now, and her grades have risen to a solid B. Kate, always an A student but sometimes careless in her work, now often makes perfect scores on quizzes. For Kate's 100s and José's dramatic improvement, the team earns a lot of team points and is frequently included among the celebrated Super Teams of the week. Equally important—at least from Kate and José's point of view—they are much more often recruited for playground games and lunchtime socializing than they used to be. Team points do not change students' individual grades, which reflect individual accomplishments, but they lead to public recognition and token rewards, which the children enjoy.

Skills for living ▶ The Cougars are active participants in a learning activity that promotes development on multiple levels and takes advantage of students' diverse resources to meet their diverse needs. In the long run, this activity can help them become valued and productive members of their community. Success in all dimensions of life increasingly depends on the ability to solve problems using the right combination of knowledge, skill, and creativity. Every day, modern life poses new challenges arising out of new social arrangements, technology, political and economic systems, and uses of space (on earth, around it, beyond its orbit). Long after the Cougars leave sixth grade, they will remember how to find answers by using available expertise, to view differences in talent as opportunities to compare and enrich thinking, and to engage in forms of peer leadership and negotiation that sustain collective progress. The care that Ms. Harriman takes to structure the academic tasks leads to sustained, cooperative engagement to meet worthwhile cognitive challenges. The quality and quantity of student work make a significant and measurable contribution to their learning. The way they interact as they work also enhances their social relations.

Higher achievement ▶ Cooperative learning strategies, properly structured, have proven to be efficient and effective in promoting mastery of knowledge and skills among students of all abilities and ages. To improve learning in the novel study, the Cougars' teacher is using a form of Student Team Learning,[2] one of several complex configurations of cooperative learning elements that work effectively. In reviews of hundreds of studies conducted in the first ninety years of the 20th century, Johnson and Johnson found consistent evidence of the effectiveness of cooperative learning strategies.[3] Improved achievement was found in a broad array of subjects, from math and physical education to second-language learning. Such studies often focus on elementary and secondary teaching. However, experimental studies in economics education,[4] mental health training,[5] and chemistry,[6] among other subjects, showed positive results with postsecondary students as well. These studies extend the earlier work of Cooper and his colleagues at California State University, who have documented the success of cooperative learning strategies across the college curriculum.[7] In short, properly structured cooperative learning activities are a reliable way to improve academic achievement.

Social cohesion

☐ **INTASC Principles 5, 6**

Furthermore, cooperative learning strategies can enhance creativity by harnessing the power of many kinds of human intelligence and providing task structures that facilitate shared work and responsibility. Considerable evidence suggests that schools where teachers and students are frequently engaged in cooperative activities provide the social and cultural foundations necessary to cultivate general civility and support peaceful and productive conflict resolution. One summary of a major research review reported the regular finding that cooperative learning led to measurable improvement in group cohesion, positive relationships, ability to provide peer support, and appreciation of diversity.[8] In addition, the review noted evidence of the positive impact of cooperative learning on self-esteem, social skills, and stress management. These indicators of good social and psychological health serve as a nurturing context for collective openness and innovation, which in turn stimulate and sustain creativity. When it engages diverse students in productive activity focused on achieving a shared goal, cooperative learning produces positive intergroup relations.

Research and practice in cooperative learning since the 1960s have built on the work of Kurt Lewin and Morton Deutsch. They studied the ways that conditions of cooperation and competition affected human interactions.[9] In the 1960s education researchers were interested in the challenges posed by changing laws and social expectations affecting schools. Students who used to attend separate and unequal schools were brought together on one campus. At first, the segregation that had been the norm between buildings prevailed as the norm within buildings. Early work in developing cooperative learning models arose in part from the desire to weave together these frayed edges of the social fabric and at the same time improve achievement.[10] The thoughtful assignment of different kinds of students to the same team and design of academic tasks to require cooperation for individual as well as team success showed reliable benefits to social cohesion, across social, ethnic, and racial divides.

In this chapter, we will explore forms of cooperative learning that teachers all over the world have found useful and identify the key elements that define them. For the sake of clarity, the term *cooperative learning* will be used here exclusively to refer to lesson activities of a particular type, elaborated in the next section of the chapter. The term *group work* will be used for other lesson activities that may involve two or more students but that do not possess the defining traits of cooperative learning.

☐ **OBJECTIVE 1** — **To identify the functions of teachers, students, and content in effective lessons**

☐ The General Context of Cooperative Learning

Learning Activity 9.1

Teachers, students, and content all play vital roles in good lessons; the fundamental nature and importance of those roles is the same in effective cooperative learning as in other lesson formats. Teachers control the lesson elements that students do not have the knowledge or skill to control. Students work hard to construct and transform lesson content for their own use. Lesson content is substantively adequate and worthy of students' time and effort.

Expert instruction ▶

☐ INTASC Principle 3

Teachers present the content. That is, they stage an encounter from which students can learn the new material, the structure of relevant knowledge, and the processes of knowing. They may, for example, demonstrate, explain, provide media events (a movie, an interactive computer activity), tell a story, or take the class on a trip. Whatever the format, they ensure a representation of content and process that is just beyond but within reach of the learners' current knowledge. For example, to introduce primary students to the concepts of municipal governance, a teacher might first lead a discussion that explores the roles, relationships, and responsibilities of members of families and the school community. Only then would the teacher launch the class into a study of civic authority. Metaphors from family and school life might serve as organizers and illuminators of the general structure; observed discrepancies could illustrate the nature of differences and extensions with respect to familiar social systems.

If students have appropriate print materials, Internet resources, hypertext, opportunities to interview, videotapes, or other sources of data that they can review independently, the teacher may shift from presenter to coach. As coach, the teacher guides students through the lesson content as they become familiar with details of the new information. Teachers must know the general terrain of the curriculum and the present level of student understanding in order to determine what lesson content represents a reasonable, stimulating stretch for students and what presentation mode offers them the richest, most supportive opportunity to learn.

☐ INTASC Principle 6

There is a widespread and worrisome misconception that in cooperative learning students are each other's main teachers. A related concern is that the resulting absence of real expertise limits learning—how can a student learn from someone just as uninformed? Such conditions may occur in some forms of group work, but not in cooperative learning. In effective cooperative learning, the teacher uses presentation strategies that ensure that accurate, complete information is available to all students. Lesson activities stimulate students' mediation of each other's learning through sharing insights and examples, collaborating over solutions, and coaching each other's practice of skills. The teacher may rely on good media or well-developed learning centers for content presentation, rather than a traditional lecture and demonstration. However, the teacher's expertise is at work in selecting and organizing the presentation of content. Students' learning is not limited by reliance on peers who may not initially know any more than they about the lesson content; rather, learning is enriched by peers' active involvement in explaining, showing, and motivating as part of their own work.

Student work ▶

Expression during the process of learning, in the company of other students, performs the important function of revealing both to the learners and to their audience the nature and extent of their mastery. Whether adults or children, novices frequently think they know something until they try to explain it. As they hear their own words, even before the other listeners can comment, the speakers can assess their own knowledge. If the speakers do not pick up their own inaccuracies, the other listeners generally do. Learners need to express their knowledge as it is developing, both to confirm and to correct its adequacy. Good cooperative learning strategies engage students in sharing how they think, examining it themselves, gaining insight from the reactions of their peers, and enlarging their conceptual understanding by hearing how others understand the same content.

Solid content ▶

As in other lessons, those using cooperative learning strategies to engage students depend ultimately on the adequacy of the content itself—both the knowledge and the processes of developing it—to promote growth. If the initial presentation of new content is muddled or shallow, if the practice exercise offers too fragmented a view of substance, or if meaningful interaction with content is sacrificed for rote learning, then the lesson is doomed no matter how deftly the cooperative learning incentive system is implemented.

The concepts and activities explained in this chapter show how to motivate students to work hard together so that each one makes the most of his or her ability. To lead to measurable gains in achieving mastery of targeted skills and content, however, cooperative learning must operate in a context in which teachers provide accessible and engaging opportunities to learn and the content is substantively compelling.

✳ Mastery Test

OBJECTIVE 1 **To identify the functions of teachers, students, and content in effective lessons**

Read the statements below and determine whether they are true or false, based on the information in Learning Activity 9.1.

_____ 1. Use of cooperative learning usually improves achievement in reading, but not in math.

_____ 2. The achievement outcomes for cooperative learning have been documented in elementary, secondary, and postsecondary classrooms.

_____ 3. Cooperative learning takes advantage of students' diverse talents and resources.

_____ 4. Although cooperative learning may produce achievement effects, it does not significantly change social skills or group cohesion.

_____ 5. In cooperative learning lessons, students are each other's main teachers.

_____ 6. Teachers seldom use multimedia in cooperative learning, because it is a text-based strategy.

_____ 7. Most students learn from observing their own performance, as well as from observing others or hearing others' feedback.

_____ 8. The quality of lesson content is not as important in cooperative learning as the structure of the task.

OBJECTIVE 2 **To describe the attributes of cooperative learning that contribute to student achievement in social and academic arenas and to discriminate academically productive cooperative learning strategies from less structured group activities that may not improve achievement**

▣ Essential Features of Cooperative Learning

Learning Activity 9.2

▢ **INTASC Principle 4**

Cooperative learning is an instructional task design that engages students actively in achieving a lesson objective through their own efforts and the efforts of the members of their small learning team. What distinguishes cooperative learning from other activities that involve working in small groups is a combination of features that weave through an academic task.

Different schools of thought propose different ways to name and number these features, but they converge on the basic idea that the structure of the learning task engages students in productive and mutually supportive ways so that all achieve mastery of the lesson objective. In a good cooperative learning lesson, completing the assignment successfully is easier and more engaging to do as a team and more difficult to do any other way.

Positive interdependence ▶

Four features have been regularly shown to be central to the success of any cooperative learning lesson. These features increase students' "efforts to achieve"—they positively affect such factors as productivity, retention of learning, time on task, higher-level thinking, transfer of learning, and positive feelings about school.[11] First and foremost is *positive interdependence*, a spirit of "all for one and one for all."[12] Having *goal interdependence* means that if any member is to succeed, all must succeed. With *reward interdependence* the prize or recognition is available to all members of the team when they all achieve a certain standard. For example, each will earn five bonus points if all earn a passing score on the test. *Resource interdependence* means that each group member has a share of the materials needed to complete the group task, which requires the shares held by all. *Role interdependence* is what characterized the Cougars' practice session: Each student's role interlocked with the others' roles.

Playing jump rope is a good example of positive interdependence: Two people must coordinate hand and arm motions while the third jumps in a pattern. The game goes smoothly only when all three do their jobs properly.

Furthermore, the nature of the reward should make it equally available to high- and low-ability students who work hard and make progress.[13] Interdependence is intrinsically unrewarding if the group is denied access to rewards because the members have unequal resources for a given task. Recognizing achievement of a standard of growth—rather than absolute achievement—is one way to support interdependence within a team.

Some models of cooperative learning have highly elaborated roles, while others are fairly simple. All the models that produce improved achievement have built-in positive interdependence.

Individual progress ▶

The second key feature is *accountability at the group and the individual level*. That is, the group cannot succeed unless each member demonstrates success or significant progress. The task structure rewards the group for cooperation and at the same time rewards individuals for achieving lesson objectives. In the opening scenario, for example, the Cougars gain recognition as a team for supporting each other's measurable learning, while each member of the team gains recognition for progress and absolute achievement. Whatever form team recognition takes, teams cannot earn it unless they work together and prove their effectiveness by means of individual growth. Slavin has conducted extensive research in this area and consistently comes up with the same evidence: Grading strategies must be based on individual achievement and team rewards must be based on individual growth if cooperative learning is to work well.[14] Every person who has worked on a team without **individual accountability** has stories to tell about "hitchhikers" who let the hard workers do what needed to be done and coasted along on others' efforts. Hitchhikers don't learn; workers learn. If they are to succeed, lesson activities must promote every student's work at learning.

Promoting peer learning ▶

The third essential feature is what the Johnsons call "face-to-face promotive interaction"—*the acts of helping each other learn*.[15] Fine-tuned studies of what exactly goes on in successful cooperative groups have found that explaining what one knows is positively associated with mastery. Now, one might normally assume that the smart students who know more also get to explain more and, of course, eventually show higher achievement on tests. But it is not as simple as that. Among students of equal ability, those who demonstrate mastery by explaining actually reinforce and extend mastery. When students of modest ability in a given academic task explain their answers and thinking to their peers, they learn better. In addition, the opportunity of high-achieving students to explain their knowledge or demonstrate their skills adds materially to their own learning.[16] For this reason, studies of the contribution of cooperative learning strategies to the achievement of academically gifted students usually show benefits to them. The insights gained from translating new knowledge into different terms or modeling new skills for another substantially enhance learning across ability groups.[17]

Mastering process skills ▸

The fourth essential feature is the *focus on interpersonal and small-group skills* that students use in completing cooperative learning lessons. Working successfully in a team demands particular social skills, which are best learned and practiced in the context of real tasks. Included in this arena is the students' ability to review their own skills critically with a view to improving group effectiveness.

Using multiple intelligences ▸

When done properly, cooperative learning not only stimulates cognition but also gives play to the multiple forms of intelligence that students bring to any shared task.[18] In the context of their small learning team, students

☐ INTASC Principle 3

MULTIPLE INTELLIGENCES AND COOPERATIVE LEARNING

Gardner[19] has identified at least eight forms of human intelligence that are "rooted in biology" and "valued in one or more cultural settings." He views intelligence as "the ability to solve problems or fashion products that are of consequence in a particular cultural setting or community." Listed below are the types of intelligence, brief descriptions, and a sketch of the contributions each might make to a simple team-learning task, such as the vocabulary and spelling lesson engaging the Cougars. See also Nicholson-Nelson, 1998.[20]

Intelligence	Description	Contribution to Word Study
Linguistic	Uses words and learns languages easily and well	Offers alternative definitions
Logical/mathematical	Thinks scientifically, processes data spontaneously and quickly	Connects ideas logically, shows how the meaning links to other familiar meanings
Spatial	Uses visual cues well to design, navigate, draw, etc.	Draws or creates visual models of meanings
Musical	Uses songs, tunes, sounds, and rhythms	Recalls songs that help fix new words in memory
Bodily/kinesthetic	Controls physical movement with special grace or precision	Acts out meanings
Interpersonal	Perceives the feelings and needs of others accurately and uses that information to approach them	Can see when a struggling teammate is frustrated, offers extra support
Intrapersonal	Knows own feelings and needs well and uses that to make sense of the world	Empathizes, listens, observes
Naturalist	Recognizes the elements and systems of the natural world	Uses images from nature to illustrate meaning

have a chance to identify and take advantage of each other's strengths and expand their own notions of how to approach a challenge. For instance, think back to the Cougars. José is an English-language learner. His teammates cannot speak Spanish, his first language, but they want him to learn the lesson. Kate's gift for language enables her to provide several alternative English explanations of *exalted*. Isaac, a natural actor, brings the team to giggles demonstrating the meaning of that term. Successful people—adults and children—not only draw on their own innate talents; through practice and observing others, they also build up competence in areas where their native gifts may be initially quite modest. The academic task structure and social skill-building emphasis of cooperative learning ensure opportunities for students to use their special gifts and expand their repertoires. Implicitly and often explicitly, cooperative learning promotes metacognition—knowing how one knows, how one learns, and how to enhance others' learning. The challenge of representing knowledge and skill in different ways for the purpose of helping teammates learn takes advantage of students' different learning styles and forms of intelligence.

◼ Three Popular Families of Models

◻ INTASC Principle 4

There are three popular families of models of cooperative learning, each with an advocate who is prominent among others. The models overlap significantly in their research base and to some extent in their practice. But they nevertheless have their own distinctive qualities.

Student Team Learning ▸   The **Student Team Learning** model promoted by Slavin focuses on task structure, team composition, and reward systems.[21] In most forms of Student Team Learning, task structure ensures that every team member participates. Teachers compose learning groups that are microcosms of the class with respect to diversity. Reward systems for teamwork recognize progress of individual members. Grades for individual achievement are completely determined by individual performance. Student Team Learning models—such as Student Teams Achievement Divisions (STAD), discussed later in this chapter—often have the most detailed scoring systems for team recognition. The skills of teamwork are taught and nurtured as needed to support the academic work, but academic success is the goal of teamwork; social coherence is more an intended side effect. Among the widely used programmatic versions of this model are Team Accelerated Instruction (TAI) in math, Cooperative Integrated Reading and Composition (CIRC), and Success for All (SFA).

Learning Together ▸   Johnson and Johnson are more directly concerned with group process and interpersonal skills.[22] While group skills are taught in the context of learning activities, social coherence is viewed as an important goal in itself. Achievement in academic and social arenas is highly valued. Students study, practice, and critique their teamwork skills with a view to improving academic outcomes. Through their models of **Learning Together**, Johnson and Johnson hope to lay the foundations of a society whose members are adept at collaborating and negotiating, who know how to find peaceful and satisfying solutions to social problems. While using the Student Team Learning model has proved to have significant, beneficial effects on social relations, its explicit goal is usually described as academic.[23] Learning Together engages students in both academic and social skill acquisition, and is more often promoted as a community-building strategy.

Structural Approach ▷ Kagan espouses a kind of molecular model, in which complex lessons may include one or more cooperative elements among other kinds of learning activities.[24] Like the others, Kagan aims for improved efficiency in academic learning and improved social skills. However, his **Structural Approach** views lessons as compositions of interlocking parts, some of which may demand cooperation while others do not. The cooperative structures he uses serve different purposes, which he classifies as team building, class building, mastery, thinking skills, information sharing, and communication skills.

These three schools of thought converge on the principle that an effective cooperative task structure has embedded in it features that elicit and support certain kinds and levels of collaborative effort directed toward achieving a lesson objective. Both carefully controlled studies and the somewhat larger body of less rigorous professional reports consistently indicate that effective strategies include some combination of the key elements. In practice, teachers adapt the characteristics of all three models to fit particular teaching situations. As the models have evolved in the last decade, they have all produced evidence of increased achievement and have focused more directly on social relations.

■ When Is Group Work Not Cooperative Learning?

Informal small-group tasks ▷ Teachers often put students in small groups to move through some part of a lesson or achieve a goal. For example, in a science or computer lab, a teacher might assign two or three students to the same station to complete a series of tasks. Although they may indeed help each other if they feel like it, there are usually no structures in place to focus and enhance their exchanges, no particular reason to invest in each other's learning. The reason for doubling up may be lack of enough stations to serve each student otherwise.

Socializing during a lesson ▷ In a given lesson, any class of students represents a range of interests and abilities. Putting students in small groups with others may encourage them to work or may make it easier for them to coast along. The relatively gifted students may resent the distraction; the students who find the material too challenging may continue to suffer in silence. Nothing about the assignment to a small group under these conditions ensures their engagement. Nothing in such an ad hoc arrangement requires on-task conversation or rewards individual success as a product of group work. No part of the setup instructs students in how to get past interpersonal hurdles or motivates interest in another's achievement. Of course, people are sometimes inspired simply by the opportunity to promote each other's good and to concentrate on the learning at hand, but such opportunities often go unheeded. Group work does little to offset human distractibility; cooperative learning activities use predictable human inclinations to improve conditions for learning.

Low structure = low learning ▷ If a group can earn recognition despite ignoring the needs of a relatively low-performing student or because some gifted members are carrying along the others, the group work is not cooperative learning. If a group's product earns a grade awarded to all students without regard to individual growth or participation, the group work is not cooperative learning. If the reward structure penalizes groups whose members include low achievers by failing to recognize improvement as an important contributor to team success, the group work is not cooperative learning. If a group activity does not involve members in promotion of each other's achievement, it is not cooperative learning. If in the context of group work no instruction is offered on how to work together effectively and how to evaluate effectiveness, the group work is unlikely to generate cooperative learning. Group work may be engaging and lively, but without the key features of cooperative learning, it has not been reliably demonstrated to improve student achievement or promote development of social skills or social cohesion.

The next part of this chapter describes some simple cooperative learning strategies that can be integrated into different kinds of lessons. These strategies embed some of the key features described above, adding effectiveness to group work or whole-class work. They have the merit of being fairly easy to launch and demanding few unfamiliar social skills. While they are not as powerful as complex strategies, they are useful and can be incorporated with little preparation.

☀ Mastery Test

OBJECTIVE 2   **To describe the attributes of cooperative learning that contribute to student achievement in social and academic arenas and to discriminate academically productive cooperative learning strategies from less structured group activities that may not improve achievement**

A. Write short answers to the questions below:
  1. List and describe the four essential features of cooperative learning.
  2. For each of the three families of models of cooperative learning listed below, name a well-known advocate and describe the approach:
     a. Student Team Learning
     b. Learning Together
     c. Structural Approach

B. Scenarios: Now that you have read something about the factors that generate improved achievement in cooperative learning strategies, see if you can distinguish between strategies that have those critical factors and other group strategies. Indicate your opinion by writing next to each scenario either *CL* (for cooperative learning) or *Other*.

_____ 1. During Multicultural Month, Señor Gomez visits each class in the primary grades to read aloud children's stories set in Mexico. The story he reads to the third-graders is about Elida, an eight-year-old girl who lives on a farm in a remote area of the country. When he finishes the story, he has the students sit in their regular, heterogeneous learning teams and write words and phrases describing the life of a rural Mexican child. He reviews their work and tests them individually, rewarding teams that reach preset standards of average individual growth.

_____ 2. Ms. Cheung has assigned each of her three reading groups (advanced, on-grade, and remedial) to choose a single book from her list and make a class presentation about it. Each group will receive a collective grade for its report.

_____ 3. Mr. Klein's American History class has been investigating the contributions of men and women to the development of the first thirteen American colonies. On Friday, he will give a test on where and when the men and women lived and what each contributed. He has assigned students to heterogeneous, four-member teams to review the material they have covered. After grading the tests, Mr. Klein will post on the

"Notable Historians" bulletin board the names of teams (and members) whose average gain scores are ten or more points.

_____ 4. Ms. Juniper taught a lesson on dividing decimal numbers. She assigned students to work on practice problems in heterogeneous, four-member teams. At the end of the lesson, Ms. Juniper administered the test. She rewarded teams on the basis of the team test grade average; Great Teams averaged in the 80s and Super Teams averaged in the 90s.

_____ 5. Mr. Jefferson has been lecturing and showing films about the structure of DNA, a major component of genes. Before he started the unit, he calculated base scores representing each student's usual achievement in his course. After he finished presenting the material, he assigned students to study together in self-selected learning teams, using a study guide. After administering the unit test in the regular way, he calculated gain scores for each student by comparing the unit test score with the base score. On a special awards bulletin board, he posted the names of the individual students who made exceptional progress.

C. True/False Statements: Indicate whether the following conditions are essential for academic productivity in cooperative learning strategies (*T* = True) or not (*F* = False). If a statement is false, revise it to make it true.

_____ 1. In the first stage of the lesson, students usually conduct independent research on the topic of study.

_____ 2. Productive learning teams are made up of members who have a lot in common, such as gender or membership in a voluntary social group.

_____ 3. Students' participation on learning teams in the classroom usually translates to more cooperative social interactions elsewhere.

_____ 4. Academic progress in cooperative learning activities is measured by having the team take a test together, to build team spirit.

_____ 5. If a student does exceptionally well on a test after working with a learning team, the teacher may recognize the team in public.

_____ 6. Team rewards are usually based on earning high grades on a test; for example, teams earn rewards by scoring an average of 90 percent.

| OBJECTIVE 3 | To integrate simple cooperative learning structures into more complex or extended lessons |

Simple Cooperative Learning Structures

Learning Activity 9.3

☐ INTASC Principles 4, 6

Although most teachers are implementing a variety of new instructional formats made possible by advances in technology and training, many find that well-balanced programs still regularly include occasions when students are all attending to the same instructional event at once—a lecture, demonstration, or film, for example. Several very simple tactics can ensure that students maintain engagement and integrate lesson content with their prior knowledge. Three are described below; Kagan and others have collected and tested ideas for many more that promote active learning, even in lesson formats that are otherwise relatively passive in nature.[25]

Think–Pair–Share (TPS) and Story Buddies

During lessons in which teachers are lecturing or demonstrating, they often ask questions to check comprehension. Addressed to a single person, such a question provides only the respondent with the opportunity to demonstrate learning. Using **Think–Pair–Share (TPS)**, teachers offer every student a practice opportunity and get a broader picture of mastery.[26] Here is how it works.

1. *Plan.* Identify places in the lesson where pausing for reflection and exchange of ideas will be helpful to students.

2. *Explain strategy to students.* Before beginning the lesson, explain the Think–Pair–Share strategy: Students will have partners with whom they will exchange ideas during the lesson, whenever the teacher signals them to do so.

3. *Form pairs.* Form pairs, using a simple scheme such as having students count off in duplicate—1, 1; 2, 2; 3, 3; 4, 4; and so on. If necessary, the last group may be a threesome or the teacher may take a partner.

4. *Pose question; signal "think."* At appropriate points during the lesson, pose a question and call for a short "think-time," perhaps ten seconds or more, depending on the nature of the question. During this think-time, students must remain silent, forming their own answers.

5. *Signal "share."* At a signal, usually just a word—"share"—or the sounding of a timer's bell, have students turn to their partners and exchange answers, spending a minute to explain their thinking and resolve differences, if there are any.

6. *(Optional) Have two pairs share.* After individual silent thinking and partner sharing, have two partnerships compare and discuss responses together before reconvening the whole class for discussion.

7. *Have pairs report.* At the end of share-time, ask a pair (or a pair of pairs) to report. Depending on the lesson and the time available, discuss the item further, invite other pairs to comment, or simply move along to the next lesson segment.

8. *Continue lesson.* Cycle through steps 4–7 as necessary.

One variation that can enrich storytime is called Story Buddies.[27] Before the teacher begins reading or telling a story, students are assigned a partner or asked to choose someone sitting nearby. As the story unfolds, the teacher

---

Think–Pair–Share (TPS)

1. Plan TPS breaks.
2. Explain strategy to students.
3. Form pairs.
4. Pose question and signal "think."
5. Signal "share."
6. (Optional) Have two pairs share.
7. Have pairs report to class.
8. Continue lesson.

pauses briefly at points of special interest and invites buddies to engage in a responsive activity. For example, students might be asked to show their buddies the meaning of a word by assuming a certain facial expression (angry, anxious, delighted), silently imagine what is coming next and quietly share their predictions with their buddies, or jointly to create an ordered list of story events.

These activities have little structure and no assurance of accountability, but they attach students' inclination to interact socially to the academic agenda. They also multiply by a large factor the participation rate in comprehension checking. Students are encouraged to internalize the words and images, to follow the action, and to construct meaning.

3 by 3 by 3

"3 by 3 by 3,"* a slightly simpler and more flexible version of Think–Pair–Share, works especially well with older students—including adults—during otherwise conventional large-group lessons, such as lectures. It requires no prior planning or special instruction for students and has been used successfully even in college lecture classes with hundreds in attendance.

1. *Present.* Present a lesson segment—for instance, the first ten or fifteen minutes of a lecture or film—and then pause.

2. *Assign task to trios.* Have students form groups of three with those sitting nearby and brainstorm at least three ideas, facts, or issues that have been raised during the previous segment of the lesson. Ask them to write down questions they wish the teacher to answer. Give them three minutes to complete this activity.

3. *Ask for questions or continue.* After three minutes, ask for questions or simply continue the lesson, stopping again for a "3 by 3 by 3" whenever necessary or desirable.

As in TPS, the teacher may direct the group's discussion by posing a question. If time does not permit dealing with the questions raised by students in their mini-discussions, the teacher collects written questions at the end of the period and deals with them later. In the normal course of events, many questions raised early in the period are answered either by peers during the three-minute discussions or later in the lecture as the topic unfolds. Students hand in only those questions that remain unanswered at the end of the period.

By means of strategies such as TPS, Story Buddies, and 3 by 3 by 3, teachers enhance students' time on task and encourage the expectation that talking about academic work can be fun. They nurture students' continuous alertness and involvement in situations where whole-group instruction is the method of choice.

3 by 3 by 3
1. Present content.
2. Assign task to trios.
3. Ask for questions.

***"3 by 3 by 3" stands for *three students, three ideas, three minutes.*

Numbered Heads Together

Numbered Heads Together makes drills and quick reviews of facts engaging and productive for the whole class.[28] It may add depth to students' participation in more complex academic work as well. Numbered Heads is easy to use when the class has existing learning teams, but it also adapts readily to situations in which teams are formed on an ad hoc basis for a single lesson. It has six components.

1. *Plan.* Identify appropriate practice material.

2. *Form teams.* Assign students to four-member teams, using five-member teams only as needed. In general, it is best to make teams approximately equal in the range of student ability.

3. *Assign numbers to students.* Give each student on the team a number. In classes where learning teams are already in place, a set of numbered cards may be kept in each team's materials packet; students each draw a number when playing this game. Numbers 4 and 5 on the team may trade off answering when the number 4 is drawn (as described below). After students play this game once or twice, they establish routines for numbering off. In the example at the beginning of this chapter, Isaac, José, Kate, and May use the numbers in their team packet for a variety of tasks.

4. *Pose the question.* When the teams are settled and students numbered, pose a question. This activity is best suited for low-inference, high-convergence questions, such as "How do you find the answer to 25 times 31?" or "What are the main industries of Kansas?" or "What is the shape of a DNA molecule?" or "What is the meaning of the word *exalted*?"

5. *Call for "heads together."* After the question is posed, have the teams put their heads together and talk very quietly to keep other teams from overhearing. Team members must figure out what the answer is and then make sure that each person knows it, whether it is a fact or a process, because they do not know which member's number will be called. The team point will be available only if the person whose number is called can answer accurately on the team's behalf.

6. *Call the number of respondents.* Signal for the teams to stop conferring and call a number at random. Some use a spinner to assure randomness. Have the student on each team with that number raise a hand or stand up. During this stage of the game, enforce absolute silence among teammates in order to maintain conditions that support effective coaching during the assigned "heads together" time. Depending on the circumstances and the nature of the questions, one of two respondent selection tactics can be used at this point. Either call on one of the identified team representatives at random, taking care to give approximately equal numbers of response opportunities to all teams over the course of the lesson, or have all of the identified representatives—one from each team—respond simultaneously by writing the answer on a piece of scrap paper or the chalkboard, joining in choral response, or signaling in some predetermined way. The team receives a point for each correct response made by its randomly selected representative.

Some enterprising student teachers worked out a *Jeopardy*-like variation on Numbered Heads Together, using items from study guides developed for secondary students in various subjects. They created "answer grids" with columns of categories related to unit topics and rows of items of increasing difficulty with increasing point value. They reproduced these grids on either large chart paper or overhead projector transparencies, obscuring

> ### Numbered Heads Together
>
> 1. Plan.
> 2. Form teams.
> 3. Assign numbers.
> 4. Pose questions.
> 5. Call for "heads together."
> 6. Call on numbered respondent.

Numbered Heads variation ▶

the answers with removable covers. In the class sessions scheduled for unit review, they assigned numbers to members of existing learning teams and provided each team with a supply of scrap paper and a marker.

In this version, the order of play goes like this: (1) At the beginning of the game, the teacher gives the answer to the first easy item in the first column and signals for "heads together." (2) After teams confer, the teacher uses a spinner to choose a number. Strict silence is enforced while the team member with that number writes the answer in the form of a question in marker on scrap paper. (If a team member breaks the silence, the team loses the opportunity to answer.) (3) At a signal, all respondents put markers down and reveal to the teacher what they have written. Those who offer the correct question earn the designated number of points for their teams. (4) The teacher allows one of the winners to choose the next category. Winning teams earn one "late homework" pass for each member.

Like more elaborate cooperative learning strategies that are used over a longer period, Numbered Heads Together provides an incentive for students to harness their interest in socializing to an academic agenda, to invest in the learning of their teammates, and to work hard themselves. Furthermore, most students really enjoy playing. However, it does not address some of the underlying problems that erode the motivation of less able students. If one team's Number 2 student happens to be very bright academically and another team's Number 2 has a learning disability, neither the teams nor the individuals experience equal opportunities for success in competition with each other when Number 2 is the respondent and the question is complex or the pace rapid. In addition, the quick pace of the game and necessarily short "heads together" time make it practical for students to give answers rather than explanations to each other. For these reasons, Numbered Heads Together is best used as a small part of an incentive system generally driven by rewards for making progress and achieving "personal bests."

OBJECTIVE 4

To implement complex cooperative learning strategies, including Student Teams Achievement Divisions (STAD), Jigsaw, and Academic Controversy

■ Complex Cooperative Learning Structures

Student Teams Achievement Divisions (STAD)

Learning Activity 9.4

Student Teams Achievement Divisions (STAD), one of the Student Team Learning models developed by Slavin, has five basic components: forming heterogeneous learning teams; presenting content; engaging teams

✳ Mastery Test

OBJECTIVE 3   To integrate simple cooperative learning structures into more complex or extended lessons

Listed below are ten brief descriptions of lessons that teachers have chosen to offer as whole-class, teacher-centered activities. Most of them would benefit from investing part of the lesson time in simple cooperative structures such as TPS, Story Buddies, Numbered Heads Together, or 3 by 3 by 3. For each lesson, indicate which simple structure could be used effectively or whether the whole-class format should be dropped altogether in favor of a different strategy.

1. The second-grade teacher is reading aloud *The Story of Ping* to her class of twenty-five during their regular half-hour storytime.

2. During a one-hour period, the American history class is watching a forty-five-minute segment of a film series on the Civil War to learn more about how the lives of ordinary soldiers were affected by their participation.

3. The Spanish-language teacher has introduced and explained the new vocabulary in the chapter, and today, after a quick review, he will give students practice in comprehension and use by telling them a story using the words and asking occasionally for responses to questions about content.

4. After spending several days in hands-on experiences with manipulatives, the fifth-grade teacher plans to spend a period demonstrating how to add and subtract fractions.

5. The computer specialist plans to spend one class session in the lab giving students an overview of new software, a practice that experience has taught her works most efficiently. In the next class session, they will try it out for themselves, with her help.

6. The students have worked on a variety of team and whole-class activities in their study of the mid-Atlantic states. In preparation for the district's standardized test for this unit, the teacher wants to spend a period reviewing the basic facts that everyone needs to know.

7. The fourth-grade math class will spend today working all together on computation problems with mixed operations, as a prerequisite for beginning a problem-solving unit tomorrow. The teacher wants to be able to check everyone's understanding and provide additional instruction if it seems necessary.

8. The sixth-grade class is working on essays based on family stories, and in the process of discussing drafts, the teacher has discovered that almost everyone is confused about the placement of quotation marks. He plans to spend twenty minutes of today's class giving the whole class an explanation of quotation marks and using examples paraphrased from their stories for guided practice.

9. Students have asked many questions about the history of settlement in North America, especially about the precolonial era, but the syllabus for this course does not allow much time for exploration of the topic. The teacher has decided to devote one class to aspects of the historiography of the pre-Columbian period, responding to students' evident interest in knowing how the stories that make up history texts are put together.

Student Teams Achievement Divisions (STAD)

1. Form heterogeneous learning teams.
2. Present content.
3. Have teams discuss and practice.
4. Assess individual mastery.
5. Calculate improvement scores and recognize team accomplishments.

in practice or concept development activities; assessing individual student mastery; and calculating team improvement scores and recognizing team accomplishments.[29] Each segment involves some planning.

■ INTASC Principle 5

Balance by achievement ▸

Balance by demographics ▸

Balance by social group ▸

Be a little flexible ▸

■ INTASC Principle 3

Form Heterogeneous Learning Teams. To form learning teams, the teacher first computes the current achievement level of each student in the whole class and ranks students by achievement. A simple way to do this is to average the last three performance scores in the content area in which the team will work. This average is called the *base score*. For example, to form learning teams for math, one creates a base score by averaging the last three math test scores. It is important to use achievement measures that give a reliable indication of typical end-of-lesson performance. (Teachers are sometimes tempted to use pretest scores, but they are not suited for this purpose because they are intended to reflect entering ability, not final achievement.) The teacher then sorts students into the top 25 percent, the bottom 25 percent, and the middle 50 percent by achievement. Other characteristics that may affect group participation—such as race, gender, handicapping condition, or language-minority status—are then noted for each student.

Using this information, the teacher forms groups of four or five by choosing one or two students from each ability group, attending to the array of other characteristics. For example, in a class of twenty-eight, with seventeen boys and eleven girls, eight minority students, two students with physical handicaps, and one student with a learning disability, every team should have one high, one low, and two average achievers. Every team should have at least one girl, and no team should have more than two. Every team should have at least one minority student, and three teams should include a student with a disability. If the class had thirty students, an additional student of average ability should be added to each of two groups of four. For students in the intermediate grades and above, groups of four are ideal, adding a fifth only when necessary. For younger students, groups of two or three may work a little better; a foursome can be created for some projects by pairing pairs. For adults, groups as large as six may be productive.

Teams composed of members of preexisting social groups may tend to slide off-task or interact over the nonacademic issues that form the basis of their voluntary association. Teams formed for the purpose of academic work and composed of members with different perspectives and abilities are more likely to pursue the academic goals. Evidence suggests that their success in this pursuit creates new, enduring, and positive social ties outside of class.[30]

Four predictable possibilities require teachers to adapt this team formation formula. First, a class conducted in one language may include several students who share a different home language and vary in proficiency in the language of the class. It may be useful to place two of these second-language learners on a team—one with better skills in the class language to provide support for a second with more limited skills in that language.

Second, where relations between two individuals or members of different social groups are actively hostile, discretion is the better part of valor. They should not initially be assigned to the same teams. Ultimately, they will acquire the group-process skills to work together, but it is not wise to force the issue in early days.

Third, under certain conditions, the success of some students may be put at risk by isolating them as singles in heterogeneous groups. For example, students whose gender or ethnic type is usually underrepresented in particular courses may get more peer support in groups that include at least two students like them. As all students gain expertise in using structures that maximize participation and achievement for all group members, teachers can move to greater heterogeneity.[31]

Finally, occasionally a student will simply refuse to work in a group at all. This initial resistance is not rare, and Kagan[32] offers some good ideas for coping. He suggests, for example, starting with tasks that can be done more quickly in a group than alone, and giving the reluctant joiner the choice. He also recommends coaching teams in recruitment through persuasive gambits, such as "we need your help." Most reluctant students can be persuaded to try out teamwork by the judicious application of modest incentives. Some students need a few days or even weeks to see how well the system works with their classmates before they will join a team. Very few students hold out for long. Most teachers find that permitting a student to work alone poses no real problems. In that case, the student would *not* be entitled to rewards offered for group work but should receive the report card grade and other recognition that might otherwise be earned by solitary effort. Such students should be offered regular invitations to join teams, and if they do, the scoring formula should reflect concern with fairness to those already on the team.

Learning teams usually choose names based on positive images. They stay together for several weeks (about four to six), long enough to complete a project or a related series of tasks. They are reformed when work or conditions change. For example, the class may finish a unit of study, providing an opportunity for reorganization. Or a student who has been functioning as a low achiever may gain sufficient strength to be reclassified as average or even a high achiever. Periodic changes in team membership give students

> ## YOUR TURN   Forming Learning Teams

Use the grades from the class list below to calculate base scores and form a master list of students ranked by achievement. Then form three learning teams balanced according to achievement, gender, and ethnicity.

Name	Quiz 1	Quiz 2	Quiz 3	Gender	Ethnicity
Ali	70	73	75	M	Lebanese
Andy	76	79	70	F	African American
Carol	62	64	65	F	Other
Danielle	74	85	80	F	White
Eddy	98	94	100	M	Latino
Edgar	79	82	85	M	White
Jack	40	49	50	M	White
Mary	91	100	85	F	African American
Sarah	100	97	100	F	Latino
Senri	82	73	80	M	Japanese
Tammy	91	94	85	F	White
Travis	67	64	75	M	African American

ongoing practice in using social skills to create productive work groups and further experience in forging alliances with new, formerly unfamiliar classmates. The balance to be struck is between the benefits of such change and the benefits of remaining on a team long enough to develop insights about teammates that enable teams to make best use of diverse talents.

☐ INTASC Principles 3, 4

Present Content. Using any format that ensures adequate quantity and quality, the teacher presents the content of the lesson. In a straightforward lesson about a math computation skill, for example, the teacher might explain and demonstrate the skill and lead students through whole-class guided practice. In analyzing the characters of a novel, the teacher might brainstorm with students some of the questions they will use to guide group research. In developing a learning center where groups will explore a topic, the teacher uses materials and tasks that represent the topic effectively. Usually in STAD, the presentation includes three parts: (1) the introduction, including a simple statement of lesson goal, set induction, and a brief review of prerequisite skills; (2) lesson development, which emphasizes meaning and focuses on demonstration, explanation, and informal, ongoing assessment; and (3) guided practice, requiring all students to attempt responses and calling on a random selection of students to sustain attention.[33]

STAD is *not* a self-instruction model but a model in which students help each other learn content that has been presented effectively and clearly. Whether the teacher chooses the role of lecturer, guide, critic, or coach, he or she takes responsibility for the adequacy of lesson content. The teacher provides the resources, materials, and experiences that students need to understand lesson content and begin the process of making it their own.

☐ INTASC Principle 6

Have Teams Discuss and Practice. Two factors contribute to the productivity of learning teams. The first factor is the *academic task structure.* The academic tasks and the procedures for completing them are designed to involve each member actively in learning. In many forms of successful cooperative learning, team members engage in group practice, discussion of material, individual practice, and peer coaching. Students attempt practice problems together and, individually, explain their solutions, comment on each other's problem solving, and share insights about the nature of the problem and its relation to familiar issues. The second factor responsible for the productivity of learning teams is *heterogeneity.* Productive teams are microcosms of the larger class. Students with different kinds of intelligence should be represented, if possible, to enrich the discussion of content.

☐ INTASC Principle 8

Assess Individual Student Mastery. Each student must demonstrate mastery of the lesson content in an individual assessment, without assistance from team members during testing. While some engaging practice task structures include filling out worksheets together or creating collective products, the team's goal is for each student to perform well independently. Asking for and giving coaching help to teammates as they learn is the norm; asking for and giving answers for a test is a shortcut to individual failure. Teachers' decisions about whether to reteach or move on to the next lesson, how to assign course grades, and how to interpret each student's academic achievement are based on individual test scores, performances, or portfolio items—that is, evidence of individual mastery.

The final test is based on the same material as the study questions or practice items and may take any valid and reliable form. Individual grades reflect whatever system the teacher normally uses—numbers, letters, mastery checklists, or other indicators of achievement.

Calculate Team Improvement Scores and Recognize Team Accomplishments. Team points are based on **improvement scores** that are calculated according to a special formula designed to motivate students at all levels and reward teams for attention to the success of all members. A formula often used in STAD is:

Posttest Score (expressed as percentage)	Improvement Points
10 or more below base score	0
Within 10 points (+ or −) of base score	10
11–20 points above base score	20
>20 points above base score or a perfect score	30

Improvement points are calculated for each member of the team and then averaged for the team. Teams whose average improvement scores reach a predetermined level are eligible for **team rewards**.

Good Team: Average team improvement score 5–10

Great Team: Average team improvement score 11–20

Super Team: Average team improvement score higher than 20

In STAD, public recognition goes to all teams that reach a preset standard of individual gain, such as earning an average individual gain score of 10. Terms such as *Super Team, Great Team,* and *Good Team* are used to convey the concept of collective achievement. The recognition is mostly ceremonial, accompanied by appropriate fanfare. Some teachers offer elaborate (photocopied) certificates, sometimes with small additional prizes—for example, Super Teams may be given a "no homework" pass, extra recess, or some other token. For the most part, however, praise and honor serve as the coin of this academic realm. Occasionally, recognition comes from the team's public display of expertise—for example, in a presentation. Outstanding individual progress may be recognized as evidence of effective teamwork as well as of individual effort. If José makes a spectacular showing in the weekly vocabulary test, his team will be honored for its contribution to his learning.

> **YOUR TURN** **Student Team Learning**

Imagine that the students in the following teams earned these scores. Use the improvement point formula above to determine which team(s) qualified for Good Team, Great Team, and Super Team awards.

	Team A			Team B			Team C	
	Base (Percent)	Posttest (Percent)		Base (Percent)	Posttest (Percent)		Base (Percent)	Posttest (Percent)
Alice	90	92	Auggie	95	85	Bernard	90	100
Eliz.	80	95	Ed	85	90	Gertrude	85	94
Keith	70	69	Neera	65	70	Irene	65	76
Padma	40	49	Olivia	50	55	Ned	55	85

Team D	Base (Percent)	Posttest (Percent)	Team E	Base (Percent)	Posttest (Percent)
Collette	95	84	Imad	95	90
Fred	80	70	Kim	70	81
Zelda	70	60	Issac	60	73
Mike	50	59	Carl	60	72
Xan	40	48	Danny	45	52

Jigsaw

Learning Activity 9.5

☐ INTASC Principle 4

Jigsaw is designed to promote interdependence. Students participate in expert groups and learning teams. In **expert groups**, students gather information about one aspect of complex content and become experts in this aspect of content. Then they return to their learning teams and share their expertise with their teammates, each of whom has likewise become expert in a different aspect of the content. Teammates coach each other toward mastery of the complex body of information by sharing expertise. All class members are then tested on all aspects of the content. The elements of developing expertise and sharing it with teammates may involve different planning than is otherwise used.

Jigsaw has six elements:

1. *Form learning teams.* Learning teams are formed in the same way for Jigsaw as for STAD. (See above.)

2. *Form expert teams.* One member of each learning team is assigned to each heterogeneous expert group with a focus on a particular area of study within the broader lesson focus. Expert groups may have six to eight members. Because each learning team needs to have an expert in each area of study, normally there will be only four or five expert groups for any lesson.

3. *Develop expertise.* For each expert group, provide a study guide that directs attention to one aspect of the material to be covered. Then direct the group to discover the answers to the questions or problems in its own area. Two variations of Jigsaw have been developed for different work contexts. In Jigsaw I, each expert group receives only the resources that address its particular problem or issue. For example, in an instructional unit about the country of Chile, the expert group assigned to learn about Chile's waterways might be given all of the reference books, web site addresses, and audiovisual materials that focus primarily on

---

Jigsaw

1. Form learning teams.
2. Form expert teams with representatives from each learning team.
3. Develop expertise.
4. Share expertise in learning teams.
5. Assess individual achievement.
6. Calculate improvement scores and recognize teams.

that topic. The expert group investigating the people of Chile would use different resources to pursue its objective. This variation is most appropriate when the learning materials with the right focus are readily available or the teams have the skills and opportunities to conduct research independently. In Jigsaw II, all expert groups use the same resources but concentrate their learning on finding the information of particular interest to them. For example, the groups might all use the appropriate chapters of their geography texts, online resources, and other common materials, but each group would gather only data related to its own focus of study. This variation is easier to plan and can involve fewer resources. It can work especially well in the absence of whole-class sets of materials—students can go on a kind of "treasure hunt" to find answers to questions and later compare notes. Furthermore, although the experts are responsible for presenting only the specific information about their topic, their research involves reading through materials that cover the other topics, which provides a sound backdrop for understanding the other experts. Whichever form of Jigsaw is used, the point of the expert team discussion is to pool learning to create the best data set in response to questions posed on the study guide. Experts can also brainstorm interesting ways to present the material to their home teams.

4. *Share expertise in learning teams.* Once the expert teams have cultivated their knowledge, they return to learning teams. Part of the preparation for this activity should include having students learn a few simple strategies for active teaching, appropriate for their age. Using their expert study guides and teaching tips, they present the information developed in expert team discussions. When the experts finish reporting, the learning team turns to discussing the comprehensive study guide, which calls for analysis and evaluation based on the whole data collection activity.

5. *Assess individual achievement.* As in STAD, students take individual tests on the whole unit of study and earn individual grades, which form the basis of individual and team improvement scores.

6. *Calculate team improvement scores and recognize team accomplishments.* Using a system of scoring such as the one for STAD, the teacher determines the level of team improvement and celebrates accordingly.

▼ **TeachSource Video Case**   **Cooperative Learning at the Elementary Level: Jigsaw Model**

To access the video, go to www.cengage.com/login. Watch the video clips, study the artifacts in the case, and reflect upon these questions:

1. What is the general topic of study and what subtopics did the teacher use as areas for developing expertise?
2. As sources of information about each subtopics, the teacher gave expert groups the fact sheets shown as artifacts. What other sources of more context-rich information might be readily available in a classroom or school?
3. What specific strategies did students and teacher list as (a) ways to teach and (b) ways to assess? Why did the teacher take time to review these strategies?
4. In the bonus video of an expert teaching his home group, you can see and hear the teacher coaching the expert. Which aspects of her coaching do you think were effective? What, if anything, would you do differently?

> YOUR TURN   Jigsaw

Several general topics are listed below. For each topic, write at least four subtopics that might be suitable for study by expert groups in a Jigsaw format.

1. Comparison of formats for displaying survey data
2. Analysis of "The Legend of Sleepy Hollow" or some other story
3. Explanation of the elements of a desert community
4. Economic development in Botswana

Do It Yourself

Use this Jigsaw activity to review for sections A through D of the Mastery Test for Objective 4 on pages 278–279. (Note: Sections E, F, and G can be taken as a separate test.)

1. Create four- or five-person learning teams that represent the visible heterogeneity of your class.
2. Delegate one person from each group to each of four expert groups:
   a. STAD: Forming learning teams
   b. STAD: Presenting content; team discussion and practice
   c. STAD: Assessing and calculating team scores
   d. Jigsaw
3. Members of each expert group study the text pages that explain the details of their topic and prepare explanations and exercises that will help them teach those details to the others on their learning teams.

4. When expert groups have completed their work, reform as learning teams with experts on each topic. The team experts teach their teammates the content, altogether covering the whole of Objective 4.
5. Take sections A, B, C, and D of the Mastery Test for this objective individually.
6. Each team member reports to the team the difference between his or her last Mastery Test score and the score for Objective 4, A–D.
7. Using the formula given in this section, calculate the team points and average team gain, and report the team's status (Good, Great, or Super).
8. Debrief the activity as a class.

Academic Controversy

Learning Activity 9.6

☐ INTASC Principles 4, 5, 6

Present opposing positions ▶

Academic Controversy is a cooperative learning strategy developed and researched extensively by Johnson and Johnson.[34] It is based on the observation that people are often most engaged when they are contesting a point warmly and on the certainty that nurturing civility in society requires skill in negotiating differences. Academic Controversy involves students in (1) constructing a well-reasoned defense of a position about which thoughtful people may disagree, (2) presenting their case to others who argue the other side, and (3) developing sensible common ground. The goal of Academic Controversy is not to rush to agreement (seek concurrence) or to defeat those holding another position (debate); it is to explore the evidence thoroughly and expand and adjust frames of reference in order to resolve disagreements creatively. Through engagement in Academic Controversy, students may increase familiarity with the structure and nature of knowledge and the rules of evidence in various disciplines. This strategy also provides an opportunity for interdisciplinary instruction that weaves language arts and critical thinking into the study of other core subjects.

In Academic Controversy, students are placed in teams of four, and each pair on a team is assigned one of two opposing positions regarding a key point in content. Examples include whether homeland security laws are consistent with constitutional rights, whether an animal should be put on the endangered species list, and whether a character in a novel did the right thing, to name a few. Each pair builds an argument in favor of its position, using the evidence available. Pairs who are advocating the same position on different teams may meet to share ideas and strengthen their case. Then within the team, each pair presents its case to the opposition, which listens carefully and takes notes. After the presentation, the pairs within a team critique each other's arguments and evidence, using guidelines developed by the teacher and avoiding personal attacks. Following the critique, the pairs reverse sides and argue the counterposition, in order to ensure mastery of its content and shape. Then the team begins the process of synthesizing evidence to create a position more defensible than either of the original ones. The teams present their syntheses to the whole class and discuss the merits of each. For purposes of individual accountability, all students take a test on the content to be mastered. Teams whose members individually reach a preset standard of growth or achievement earn team recognition.

Long-term gains

The Johnsons' studies showed that Academic Controversy led to higher achievement and more extended retention of information than debate, individual study, or activities intended to produce immediate consensus.[35] In addition, they found that students were able to generalize the skills to new subjects and situations.

Because it deliberately lights the spark of intellectual conflict to heat up engagement, Academic Controversy depends more than other cooperative learning strategies on students' having the requisite interpersonal skills. Opportunities to teach these skills in direct aid to the success of the activity at hand abound in this strategy. Setting a few essential ground rules and practicing some special skills of discourse at the outset will be helpful. (See Learning Activity 9.7.)

Academic Controversy involves two major sets of tasks: teacher planning and student implementation of the project.

Planning a Project. Planning a project usually involves four steps:

1. *Design the content and structure of the task.* The teacher selects the content of the project, choosing a topic that is central to the course focus and that lends itself to lively discussion. It must be a topic about which at least two contrasting opinions are frequently advocated and for which there is ample documentation of each position. The teacher then identifies the cooperative goals and resources to be shared. Finally, the teacher develops a scoring system to reward effective teamwork and a final test, to be taken individually, that addresses the learning goals to be achieved by all students participating in the project.

2. *Prepare materials.* For each position, the teacher must produce a clear description, a useful set of resources, and guides to further information (for example, web sites or videos). In addition, team materials should include a simple set of directions for planning and conducting the controversy, for reference as the work progresses.

3. *Form teams and assign positions.* The teacher creates heterogeneous, four-member teams and, within each, designates pairs. Teams should be roughly equal to each other in student abilities, and pairs should include a proportionate share of team talent. The teacher assigns each pair to a position and makes the appropriate study materials available to them.

4. *Teach/review cooperative skills and procedures.* The teacher presents an overview of the tasks and briefly reviews the academic and interpersonal skills necessary for success. For example, the research may

be conducted by dividing the resources between partners; drafting and revising statements may require editing and feedback skills; presenting and listening to positions may demand skill in paraphrasing and asking clarifying questions. Coaching in these areas will be embedded in the process of implementation (described below), but the issues should be raised early.

Synthesis of information ▷ *Implementing a Project.*[36] Academic Controversy projects usually unfold in five steps, each of which takes about an hour.[36] Each step is carefully choreographed to ensure productive participation and useful, comprehensive exchange of ideas and information. The culminating group activity is the presentation of a new synthesis of information, but the individual grades are based on individual testing, administered after the project is finished.

1. *Pairs develop positions.* Each pair of each team has an assigned position and access to materials to develop supporting arguments. Beginning with a thesis statement (which the teacher may provide with the position assignment or the pair may develop), the pair gathers information related to its thesis and organizes it into a persuasive and logical presentation. Pairs from different teams who are representing the same position may consult at this stage to trade advice and insights for developing better arguments. During this stage, the teacher provides individual, pair, and team coaching, as needed, in the skills required to divide tasks and pull results together.

2. *Pairs present positions.* Within the team, each pair presents its position clearly. The work of presentation is divided between partners. As one pair presents, the other pair takes notes and asks clarifying questions to ensure that it fully understands what is being said. At this stage, the teacher coaches teams on the development of good arguments and the ways to elicit information that was not clear as first presented.

3. *Pairs compare and contrast positions.* Within the team, each pair evaluates the evidence supporting both positions. Members raise critical questions, advance contradictory evidence, and challenge each other's reasoning and documentation, with a view to creating a complete case with all the relevant evidence and argument. Here the teacher monitors carefully and offers coaching in strategies for criticizing and challenging ideas without making their advocates feel defensive.

4. *Pairs reverse sides and teams build new position.* Each pair attempts to present the opposing argument in order to get a firm grip on its merits (and weaknesses) and accurately restate what the other pair communicated. Then the team builds a synthesis of information designed to support a new position and better accommodate the full range of facts. At this point, the teacher remains alert to opportunities to coach on negotiation and attention to the goal of making the best case rather than securing "peace at any cost."

5. *Teams present synthesis positions to the class.* Sharing responsibility for developing, writing, and articulating the new position, the team presents its work. The teacher grades the team on the quality of the contribution of each member as well as on the overall quality of the content and presentation.

After the team presentations, the teacher administers a final test, which is taken individually. Students' grades are based on performance on this test.

❯ YOUR TURN   Academic Controversy

A. Identify a content area and grade level of interest to you. List two opposite positions with respect to this content. For each position, describe the materials that would be easily available at that grade level to develop support. (The web site of Educators for Social Responsibility, listed at the end of this chapter, provides topics that are timely and useful for this purpose.)

B. For each of the statements below, indicate whether it is true (*T*) of a well-designed Academic Controversy project or false (*F*). If false, rewrite the statement so that it is true.

_____ 1. Academic Controversy is like a debate, in that its goal is to identify winning and losing positions.

_____ 2. The goal of Academic Controversy is to produce quick but heartfelt concurrence.

_____ 3. In Academic Controversy, teams are heterogeneous with respect to student traits.

_____ 4. Academic Controversy, like other effective cooperative learning strategies, leads to improved achievement and retention of learning, even when compared with apparently similar strategies such as debate.

_____ 5. Assignment to pairs and positions on teams is random in Academic Controversy.

_____ 6. The point of developing a strong position in Academic Controversy is so that one pair can beat the other in its internal debate.

_____ 7. Pairs trade sides in Academic Controversy so that each can better learn the merits of the other's position.

_____ 8. Individual grades in Academic Controversy are based on team presentation of the synthesis position.

Mastery Test

OBJECTIVE 4   **To implement complex cooperative learning strategies, including Student Teams Achievement Divisions (STAD), Jigsaw, and Academic Controversy**

A. The following are activities or characteristics of student work groups. Some are typical of groups participating in effective cooperative learning; others are irrelevant or perhaps even inimical to learning. Circle the number in front of those that support cooperative learning.

1. High achievers tell everyone how to fill in the blanks.
2. Team members ask for and get explanations.
3. Everyone in a group belongs to the same social crowd.
4. Group members talk to each other about academic tasks.
5. Group members discuss nonacademic issues of common interest during work time.
6. Minority students are usually grouped together.
7. Two students with hearing impairments are put in the same group to simplify communication.
8. Team scores are based on the improvement points earned by each member.
9. Average achievers are all put together.
10. Low achievers are put in a remedial-level team.
11. The grade earned on a worksheet or project completed collectively is the grade recorded for each member.
12. Students are tested individually, and individual scores form the basis for team recognition.

B. The following class list includes the average of the last three test scores (given as a percentage) in one subject for each student and information about student characteristics. Form teams whose composition will stimulate positive social interdependence and academic success.

Name	Average (Percent)	Gender	Ethnicity
Ann	87	F	White
Bud	67	M	White
Marvin	86	M	American Indian
Doris	81	F	Other
Frank	96	M	African American
George	56	M	White
Hattie	75	F	White
Joy	88	F	White
LaTanya	72	F	African American
Melissa	45	F	White
Nan	65	F	African American
Paul	85	M	Latino
Ross	90	M	White
Sam	18	M	White
William	77	M	African American
Yu	97	M	Chinese American

C. List and describe the five elements of STAD. Illustrate briefly how each would be implemented in the subject and grade of interest to you.

D. List and describe the six elements of Jigsaw. Illustrate briefly how each would be implemented in the subject and grade of interest to you.

E. For a subject of your choice, explain how these aspects of planning an Academic Controversy project would be carried out: design of task content and structure; preparation of materials; team formation and assignment; and review of requisite process skills.

F. For the lesson described in part E, list the five parts of an Academic Controversy project and explain briefly how they would be implemented.

G. Explain how individual grades are determined in an Academic Controversy project.

OBJECTIVE 5

To integrate instruction in process skills into cooperative learning activities

---

Developing Students' Social Skills

Learning Activity 9.7

INTASC Principles 5, 6

Cooperative learning strategies are strengthened by their reliance on the social aspect of learning.[37] Students like to socialize. Acquiring academic competence often involves skills better nurtured in groups, where modeling and feedback occur more frequently than in independent work. In other strategies, students are asked to sacrifice highly desired interaction with peers. In cooperative learning strategies, they are given a structure in which they can and do interact with each other productively. Lessons are organized to use the impulse to chat for developing new interaction patterns and directions and improving learning opportunities for students at all achievement levels through peer coaching. Conversation about content under these circumstances becomes a social event. Participation in the social event is, by virtue of the assigned group task, academic.

Fostering productive teamwork involves teaching prerequisite group-process skills and, in some cases, adopting new classroom management strategies. Many teachers begin by posting guidelines developed jointly with students. Such guidelines might include:

Rules for cooperating

1. Work *quietly* together on team assignments.
2. Ask for and give *explanations*, not answers.
3. Listen carefully to teammates' questions.
4. Ask teammates for help if you need it.
5. Work at the pace that is right for your team.
6. Help each other stay on-task; don't talk about or work on other things.
7. Remember that the team's work is finished only when every member knows the material.
8. Ask the teacher for help only if you have asked everyone on your own team and discovered they cannot help.

In classrooms of diverse students, teachers cannot assume that everyone knows how to follow such rules. In some situations, working "quietly" may mean total silence—which is seldom useful in this group-based learning activity. In others, asking for help from peers may be construed as cheating. Many students will initially feel that the teacher is the only acceptable authority in the class, and they will consequently deluge the teacher with questions about both process and content that peers could answer with equal accuracy and greater speed. Concepts of good manners and respectful behavior vary greatly among different American subgroups, and their importance relative to other social values also varies in interesting ways. Assuming that all students have the prerequisite skills and similar rules about social interactions will be counterproductive and lead to frustration and embarrassment.

GOOD TEAM WORK

Looks like this:	Sounds like this:
Team members are facing each other; desks or chairs are close to each other.	Team members are using twelve-inch voices
Team members have all material ready.	Team members are asking, "Will you please explain?"
Team members are taking turns.	Team members are saying, "It's your turn now."
Every team member is working hard and team members are listening to each other.	Team members are saying, "Let's see if each of us knows this."

Acquiring social skills necessary for successful group work also contributes to competence in adulthood. Recent analyses of the learning demands that adults face at work reveal that the skills recommended for productive participation in cooperative learning activities continue to be useful outside of school.[38] Therefore, during a lesson, time invested in teaching students how to work together may pay great dividends in both the near- and long-term future.

Mastering process skills ▶ For these reasons, teachers will find it useful to demonstrate how to work in groups and to engage students in rehearsal, practicing to the point of mastery in the same way and with the same patient persistence they would use to teach any new, difficult content. Such practice will contribute to the creation of a classroom culture accessible to all students, not mistakenly assumed to be familiar to students whose experience has not, in fact, prepared them. Once the skills have been demonstrated and practiced, teachers nurture them by circulating among learning teams and shaping behaviors in unobtrusive ways. When they can do so without interrupting ongoing work, teachers can reinforce effective group process by publicly praising good examples. Some post charts on which they list instances of cooperative student behavior observed during a lesson.

Teamwork skills might be sorted into four categories: forming skills, functioning skills, formulating skills, and fermenting skills.[39] Kagan organizes skill categories differently, but his strategies also directly target development of useful group processes.[40]

Teamwork Skills

Forming skills make routines flow smoothly.
Functioning skills build group cohesion and participation.
Formulating skills promote solid mastery.
Fermenting skills nurture critical thinking.

Forming skills are essentially procedural. They involve, for example, moving quickly and quietly into team workplaces or positions and staying there, speaking softly in "twelve-inch" voices (voices audible from no more than twelve inches away), taking turns, using each other's names, and avoiding put-downs. Once these skills have been mastered, the logistical aspects of teamwork become simple and manageable. Conversely, as long as students are not skilled in this area, teamwork will not go smoothly, and time will be lost in transition.

Facilitating transitions ▶ To teach turn-taking in conversation, Kagan suggests Talking Chips.[41] In this simple tactic, each member of the group uses one object (such as a pen or a text) as a marker. When a member takes a turn answering or contributing to the group task, he or she puts the marker in the center of the team table and may not contribute again until all the teammates' markers are in the center. Then they all retrieve their markers and continue. This practice may be intrusive, but it can heighten students' consciousness of the importance of give-and-take in a group activity. Because a response opportunity is a learning opportunity, fair distribution of participation is essential for the success of all students. This process helps promote fairness.

Functioning skills address the routines of working, often on the affective level. Once teams are positioned to work, they use generic functioning skills to move their work forward. Restating directions, paraphrasing each other's contributions, and asking for or offering clarification are all functioning skills that build group cohesion and reinforce the need for full participation. Regular critical assessment of the team's group process in these areas is a key feature of learning together.

Moving work forward ▶ A variation of Talking Chips, called Colored Chips, promotes discussion of group process.[42] Each team member is given a set of colored chips or markers, one color per person. As the discussion continues, members put a chip in for each contribution. When the time for discussion ends, teammates count the chips in the center and evaluate whether the discussion involved each fairly. If students decide participation was inequitable, they discuss how to improve it in future discussions. Several other Kagan "chip games" promote improvement in the quality of interpersonal content in task-related discourse. For instance, Affirmation Chips are distributed to all students before a team discussion. Participants deposit one in the center pile each time they make a statement that recognizes how hard a teammate is trying. Gambit Chips remind students how to start statements that have particular purposes. For example, to begin a statement intended to paraphrase a teammate, a student might use the phrase, "Tell me if I have it right . . ."—which is printed on the paraphrase Gambit Chip. The Gambit Chip for practicing feedback might have written on it: "What I like about your idea is . . ." Having the physical object with words written on it can help ensure that every student feels called on to exercise the skill during a particular activity. The need for chips and gambits fades as functioning skills become parts of students' daily repertoires.

Assessing peer learning ▶ *Formulating skills* help students probe each other's mastery of lesson content. They are often cultivated by assigning roles to students. For example, one student might be the summarizer, another the checker, a third the explainer. Alternatively, skills can be practiced by all participants, after appropriate instruction. The purpose of formulating skills is to ensure that students dig deeply into the content of their lesson and engage in different kinds of mental processing to assist comprehension, application, and retention of learning. Using a strategy such as Kagan's Pairs Check is one way to stimulate growth in formulating skills. In Pairs Check, students on teams divide into pairs to complete a practice exercise. They begin by doing one item each, with the first student working while the second student watches. The first student finishes and explains to his or her partner what has been done. If they agree that the answer is correct, the partner does the next item while the first student watches, listens, and discusses. At this point, they consult with the other pair on their team to see if they agree on the process and the answer. If not, they discuss the differences until they find a solution. Then they continue. A version of Pairs Check can also be used in computer-based learning. One partner serves as Navigator, directing the movement of the Mouse Captain, who executes decisions. Switching roles periodically allows both students to gain skills.[43] During this process, students also practice praising each other's progress.

Fermenting skills challenge students to extend and elaborate their thinking, to analyze and synthesize, and to evaluate. These skills include providing critical or challenging feedback in ways that do not offend the originator of a plan, product, or idea; probing for further information; generalizing to new settings or applications; and synthesizing different elements of information.

Thinking critically ▶ The purpose of activities such as these is to ensure that every student has familiarity with and inclination to use appropriate group-process skills during team learning periods. However, from the first time teachers use cooperative learning strategies, they must balance attention to lesson content with attention to group-process skills. In properly functioning team-learning activities, students learn how shared norms of civility can contribute to attaining a worthy end; in school, the worthy end is academic. If cooperative learning activities focus too much on group process, students may benefit in the social skills arena but forfeit the academic gains they have a right to demand from schoolwork. On the other hand, if they do not receive instruction in how to work cooperatively, their squabbling may itself impede access to substantive learning opportunities.

Interdependence

Teaching students how to function effectively in groups is a key factor in cooperative learning, but teachers must also cultivate their own supportive behaviors. In some cases teaching skills useful in cooperative learning are quite different from the behaviors that work well in more directed lesson activities. For example, after students have been dispatched to work on teams, teachers should respect their need for concentration and keep whole-class communications to an absolute minimum. When conferring with individual teams, teachers should speak in voices audible only to the team. When responding to questions, teachers should model coaching and explaining whenever appropriate.

For many teachers, the hardest new skill to practice when students are engaged in team activities is turning individual student questions back to the team instead of answering them immediately. Once the initial presentation of new material in a lesson is complete, answering questions posed by other students is one way that students can improve understanding and retention. Furthermore, once directions have been given, students are usually capable of repeating them for peers. It is amazing how many teachers reinforce student inattention during directions by their willingness to repeat directions over and over, despite having given them quite clearly the first time. When students are required to ask their peers for replays of directions, the peers are quick to note whether the query stems from poor attention and, if so, to comment on the need for improvement.

By creating lesson structures that rely on students to manage independent practice and engage them in meaningful, substantively valuable interactions with each other about lesson content, teachers promote productive effort among students at every ability level. When students work hard and skillfully in the socially appealing task structures of cooperative learning, they improve achievement in basic skills, content, and critical thinking. This positive outcome reinforces a principle underlying most human enterprises: Hard work on relevant tasks produces better outcomes.

✹ Mastery Test

OBJECTIVE 5   **To integrate instruction in process skills into cooperative learning activities**

A. Students' Social Skills:

1. List and describe four kinds of process skills that can be taught directly in the context of cooperative learning lessons and give an example of how to teach one of each.
2. Explain why interpersonal and process skills must be taught directly.

B. Teacher Types: Each of the imaginary teachers below has a habit that seems helpful when he or she is using teacher-centered instructional methods. Explain how each teacher should adjust his or her behavior to make a cooperative learning lesson format more effective.

1. Ms. Butler, having trained as an opera singer before becoming a teacher, can project her voice so well that she can get the whole class's attention no matter how noisily engaged they are in a project.
2. Mr. Rais prides himself on his patience. He willingly answers questions about task directions until every student in the room is able to get to work. Although his directions are always clear from the beginning, he sometimes spends half of the period repeating himself.

3. Ms. Jackson understands that Joey's reticence makes it hard for him to answer a question in front of the class, so she seldom calls on him for answers or comments.

4. Mr. Rogers is famous in his school for having the quietest, most orderly classroom. During language arts, you can hear a pin drop while his students are working on their essays or writing answers to questions about a novel they have just read.

| OBJECTIVE 6 | To build support from the physical, organizational, and instructional environments for effective use of cooperative learning strategies |

◼ Managing Effectively to Support Cooperative Learning

Learning Activity 9.8

☐ **INTASC Principles 4, 5**

Some typical teaching activities look easy from the outside. For instance, giving a lecture and administering a test appear deceptively simple—the hard parts happen in private, as preparation. Cooperative learning, however, is a complex activity that looks daunting from the start. One learns eventually that developing the perfect lecture or test is also quite a complex undertaking, but one sees at the very beginning that cooperative learning strategies require careful planning. Those who use cooperative learning routinely discover in the long term that their early investment of time pays off—the students soon become active learners, applying their own energy to lessons and moving forward with their own momentum. On the other hand, in teacher-centered strategies, the teacher is often doing the lion's share of the work, pulling the class along; students only have to listen, take notes, and fill in blanks. To be successful in adding cooperative learning strategies to their professional repertoires, teachers must address the physical, organizational, and instructional aspects of environment that affect implementation.

Physical Environment

Desk arrangements ▶

A classroom's physical arrangements can either support easy use of learning teams or get in the way. The ideal arrangement includes several elements. First, desks, chairs, or tables organize students into groups of four or five. Students are always sitting in teams, whether or not a given lesson calls for teamwork. In most cases, desks or chairs can be adjusted to face the front when the activity requires it, and individual work can be completed as easily with students seated in clusters as otherwise. Teachers often place movable desks in rows facing front to reduce distractions, but as a practical matter, in the history of education, this tactic has by itself never been able to extinguish all student chatter. Furthermore, seeing students sitting in rows encourages teachers to overuse methods that limit students to an audience role. Seeing the students arranged in teams will spontaneously prompt teachers more often to use strategies like TPS, Numbered Heads Together, or less formal discussion options to promote students' reflection on and application of new ideas, as the content and pace of a lesson permit.

Second, the room should have areas designated for displays and supplies. An awards display site suitable for the grade level of the students should be prominent. If it is a room used by more than one class, there should be enough space for each. Team supplies—team packets, pennants, work-in-progress—and other materials should be easily available. If the room has general-use areas, such as a library corner, policies should establish how they may be used during team time.

Third, the arrangements for desks, supplies, and teamwork should minimize the class's impact on others sharing open-space areas or in immediately adjacent rooms. With thoughtfully designed physical arrangements, cooperative learning strategies have been used successfully even in schools where large open spaces serve several classes. The trick is to use area rugs, furniture, floor space, and tightly clustered workgroups to keep noise levels low.

Managing mess

Finally, if the new ways of using furniture, space, or supplies result in different demands on custodial staff, teachers should alert them to the change and find out how to facilitate reasonable maintenance. For instance, diligent custodians might routinely straighten the desks back into rows each night, thinking it their responsibility, if they are not advised of the change. New learning tasks might at first cause undue messiness, which students must learn to manage. Awarding team bonus points for neatness at the end of the day is one useful approach. Teachers often report that more student activity results in more mess—and that sometimes results in active resistance from those who share or clean the space used for teamwork. It is important to keep in mind that cooperative learning pays off generously in student achievement, so solving the problem of more mess should not involve decreasing the use of cooperative learning.

Organizational Environment

☐ INTASC Principle 10

Trial and error have shown teachers many ways to gain the support of coworkers as they begin implementing cooperative learning strategies. Starting to learn and apply these methods with a colleague has been a real asset to adoption. Peers can plan together, share resources, critique new ideas, observe each other, and generally provide the moral support to help each other through the first tentative steps.

Supervisory help

Teachers report that principals and other supervisors can offer important assistance. Supervisors who have participated in cooperative learning training can, of course, provide insightful feedback on new plans and practices. Those who have little background in this area will need a briefing so they will know what to expect if they drop in to visit. They can be offered a small observation assignment for their next planned visit. For example, they can take verbatim data on a team discussion or document the participation of mainstreamed special-education or language-minority students in teamwork. Such data are difficult for a teacher to collect, and they are very useful for reflecting on a lesson. Supervisors who have not been alerted to the new practices may mistake the lively buzz of conversation in a properly functioning team activity for off-task chatting. Taking a proactive stance in explaining how the lesson is supposed to work and soliciting supervisors' input can promote their productive participation in implementation.

Collegial negotiation

In a similar fashion, colleagues who are unfamiliar with cooperative learning strategies may be curious about what is happening in a newly cooperative classroom. Definitions of acceptable noise levels may have to be renegotiated. Explanations of the incentive value of team scoring may need to be offered. Some teachers will have the misconception that team points are substitutes for individual achievement; qualms of those who have such misconceptions can often be relieved by giving them the right information. Field experience has already taught every first-year teacher that good practicing teachers do not all agree on what belongs in a complete professional repertoire. Some features of cooperative learning—the hum of teamwork is the most notorious—raise questions that are usually resolved in early conversations with colleagues. Converts are most often won by the evidence of the effectiveness of cooperative learning strategies in achieving academic and social goals with every student.

Parental reassurance ▸ Teachers often inform parents when they begin using cooperative learning to enlist their support and understanding. Parents of the highest and lowest achievers may have questions. Bright students' parents worry that cooperative learning strategies will make their children the workhorses of teams and that working with a group of less able students will hold their children back. Teachers need to explain how the scoring system requires every child to work hard to earn team points and to review the data that show how much the brightest students gain in real achievement in such settings. Less able students' parents worry that their children will not be able to keep up. While limited ability may indeed result in more modest achievement, the record is clear that in cooperative learning groups less able students gain significantly. Their individual achievement rises because they are working harder. They are unlikely to become the academic stars of the class, but they will learn more than they learned before. Furthermore, they gain in popularity and acceptance because their progress (not their ultimate achievement level) contributes to the team score. Some of the structures of cooperative learning are unfamiliar to parents, and they will appreciate an explanation. Because positive outcomes are evident very soon after implementation begins and so many students eventually earn higher grades based on better performance, parents can become champions of the new strategy. Parent volunteers, appropriately oriented to the principles of cooperative learning, can be of great help in managing materials and supporting productive teamwork during lessons.

Instructional Environment

☑ INTASC Principle 6 Whatever complex or simple cooperative learning strategy a teacher is using in a particular lesson, productivity will be increased if students share common expectations about how to proceed. The environment created by general social and behavioral expectations influences instruction. As discussed earlier, teaching prerequisite skills is an important step in successful use of cooperative activities. In addition to teaching such things as how to talk in an "inside" voice that only one's group can hear or how to give an explanation instead of an answer, preparation may include team-building exercises, such as those recommended by Kagan.[44]

Nurturing teamwork ▸ To sustain and nurture a productive instructional environment, teachers must help students remain aware of how their civility contributes to their academic progress, creating social and academic achievements that are intrinsically satisfying. A good assignment to launch cooperative learning is choosing a team name. Even high school and adult students enjoy this task. Teams who will work together for several weeks may want to create a team poster or pennant that "flies" at their workplace whenever they are working together. Some teachers use part of the poster for ad hoc rewards such as stickers earned for winning a game of Numbered Heads Together or for demonstrating exemplary skill in group process. Team posters can also serve as displays for weekly team scores. (The actual student grades should not be displayed, but the improvement points, based on gains, could be.)

Managing materials   Teachers have found that two management practices are particularly helpful in implementing cooperative learning strategies. The first is using what this chapter has called **team packets**, which could be large envelopes, boxes, or file folders. The team packet serves many purposes: teachers can collect and return homework papers by means of the packet, which is handled by the team's materials manager. Packets can hold teams' works-in-progress, practice exercises, score sheet, pennant, number cards for Numbered Heads Together, and any other handouts or supplies that the teacher can place in the packet before class; this makes for easy distribution by team members.

Practicing zero noise   The second is adopting a **zero-noise signal**, which is any signal that can be perceived by the whole class. Teachers use this signal on the very rare occasions when they must interrupt teams' deliberations to make an announcement of general interest, restore more reasonable noise levels, or for some other reason have everyone's attention. The signal may be as simple as raising one hand while catching the eye of the nearest team, each member of which then silently raises a hand until the whole class has noticed and is waiting in silence. Some teachers find that flicking the lights or ringing a small bell works. The most important aspect of this signal is that it must work almost instantly in order to reduce teams' downtime. Rehearsing purposefully with a stopwatch and setting class goals for speedy compliance help most classes learn to respond to the signal effectively. However, teachers should not overuse the signal; working teams ought not be disturbed. Students will not be inclined to take their own teamwork seriously if the teacher is continuously interrupting them.

✹ Mastery Test

OBJECTIVE 6	To build support from the physical, organizational, and instructional environments for effective use of cooperative learning strategies

In the interest of refreshing his professional repertoire, Mr. Wilt attended a three-day workshop on cooperative learning strategies at the staff development center. He is now eager to put his new knowledge into practice in his second-grade class. He is working with Ms. Deyo, his school's master teacher, to plan for the first lessons and reflect on his practice in the first few months. He has prepared a list of problems that require some action and will discuss them with Ms. Deyo after school today. Read the list below and propose solutions consistent with the recommendations in Learning Activity 9.8.

1. The individual student tables in his classroom have been arranged in rows since time immemorial.

2. Ms. Jones, the custodian, has been tidying the desks into rows after school since time immemorial.

3. Neither the principal nor the grade-level lead teacher have ever used (or apparently heard of) cooperative learning. The principal often comes in for informal visits.

4. Mr. Zack, across the hall, runs a very orderly and silent classroom and already thinks Mr. Wilt is an easy grader.

5. Alison's mother and father, successful attorneys with a civil law practice, are grooming her for a fast-track Ph.D. program in an Ivy League school. They fret constantly about perceived slights to her considerable intellectual gifts.

6. Mr. Wilt's students are sometimes uneasy about taking leadership roles in academic work; some appear unable to participate productively in group work.

OBJECTIVE 7

To describe how schoolwide implementation of cooperative learning can increase student achievement and professional collaboration and reduce violence

---

■ Schoolwide Dimensions of Using Cooperative Learning

Learning Activity 9.9

■ **INTASC Principle 10**

As educational research expands its view of the impacts of new programs and practices, new ways of characterizing and measuring progress are being discovered. Recent studies have shown improvements in student achievement and other indicators of schools' success as learning communities. The evidence of improvement is promising in three important dimensions of schooling. First, schoolwide programs that apply cooperative learning strategies across the curriculum have begun to document substantial gains in student achievement.[45] Second, greater use of cooperative learning is being perceived as a sturdy and empowering context for peer mediation and conflict resolution among students.[46] Third, adoption of cooperative learning strategies in the classroom is providing a nurturing and stimulating context for the professional collaboration that underlies successful school reform.[47]

Cooperative Schools

After a continuous stream of research on cooperative learning, adding incrementally over the years to the initial elements of Student Team Learning, the team at the Johns Hopkins University Research Center has developed Success for All (SFA).[48] It is a schoolwide instructional model most often adopted by schools with a high percentage of students at risk of school failure. Success for All focuses on reading, writing, and language arts from kindergarten through grade 6. During an extended reading and language arts block scheduled every day, the whole school devotes itself to this instruction. Children are assigned to small reading groups, homogeneous in reading achievement, with enriched curriculum opportunities from storytelling and decoding to writing workshops and novel studies.

Students use teamwork and partner reading from the very earliest stages of literacy development to make their lessons productive. In addition, carrying out the cooperative theme, the most challenged students receive individual tutoring from a teacher whose goal is to help them succeed in the regular reading program. Students with nonacademic problems are the focus of the work of a family support team, composed of teachers and specialists who provide extra help to families to ensure student success. In Success for All,

all teachers embrace the same approach, spend extra time in professional development, and evaluate student growth with a view to continuous improvement. As a result, even the students most at risk gain from one-quarter to one full grade equivalent more than their peers in control groups each year they participate. The results are equally impressive for students in the Spanish/English bilingual and the English as a Second Language groups.

The Turnaround version of SFA extends the original program to integrate cooperative learning and conflict resolution strategies across the learning environment. Teacher learning groups work with coaches to solve problems. Leadership skills are developed across the faculty. Tutoring, nurturing positive connections with parents, and helping with problems outside of academics contribute to the well being of the whole school community.[49]

These two programs address academic learning with strong and aggressive strategies based on cooperative learning. Their comprehensive and ambitious agenda appears to be generating significantly improved learning for the participating students and changing the way whole faculties approach teaching.

Cooperative Learning as a Context for Violence Prevention

Among the traits regularly characterized as essential to school effectiveness is maintenance of a safe and orderly environment. Recent reviews indicate that despite a proliferation of violence-prevention programs, the incidence of violence has gone up in schools.[50] This finding seems to arise from two causes. First, most programs define *prevention* narrowly—as squashing the event—and therefore focus on a narrow range of strategies. Second, programs target a broad segment of the population for training, thus having little impact on the fairly small segment whose behavior is most threatening. Johnson and Johnson's alternative prescription is to create a schoolwide cooperative context in which peer mediation and conflict resolution are natural extensions of the usual ways of working together.[51] Then special strategies could be used with the few students whose misbehavior accounts for the most problems.

Six-part approach to safety ▶

Building on the skills students learn in cooperative lessons, schools aiming to improve safety should take a six-part approach that extends and enriches the usual violence-prevention curriculum.

1. They should take the role of community service center, doing what they can to help students and their families get the support they need.

2. They should create a cooperative environment that includes widespread use of cooperative learning across the curriculum.

3. They should nurture longer-term relationships between teachers and students. For example, they should extend the time teachers and students spend together by creating schools-within-schools, keeping students with the same teacher for more than one grade, and/or using block schedules that reduce the number of different students teachers see in a day.

4. They should offer an array of extracurricular activities and host community-sponsored clubs and events to reduce the amount of out-of-school time in situations where such time is seldom spent productively or safely.

5. They should establish partnerships with members of the community who can help promote peaceful life choices through such things as mentoring and internships.

6. They should offer mediation and violence-prevention lessons to all students, in a curriculum of increasing complexity.

If a student experiences school as a place where only the "best" person wins—and it's never oneself—and the social valuing that comes with success is routinely awarded to others whose gifts make it easier for them to shine, then the self-respect and discipline required to resist the temptation to violence may be in short supply. Furthermore, the willingness to search for a solution to conflict that all participants can appreciate and the creativity to invent such a solution may not be cultivated in a competitive academic arena. If daily learning routines support the habit of cooperation and the confidence that gives rise to creativity, students are arguably in a better position to view themselves as problem solvers and peacemakers.

Collaborating in School Reform

Finally, cooperation seems to be the key concept in most current approaches to school reform. The movements toward total quality management (TQM) and facilitative leadership rely on developing a collegial approach to reach high levels of proficiency in achieving an organization's mission. Improved training, shared leadership, lowered tolerance for failure, and a commitment to excellence are among the elements that produce powerful collaboration. Continuous improvement is the basis of team rewards—in the classroom and on the faculty. Helping each other adopt and adapt ideas presented in shared professional development activities strengthens the professional culture that is the foundation for faculty growth. Learning together is how the modern school faculty meets the demands of society and the needs of the students. Learning together is not just for kids.

Observation Worksheet

COOPERATIVE LEARNING

This observation focuses on (1) how the teacher uses cooperative learning strategies to promote student engagement with and mastery of lesson goals and (2) how the organization of the room supports such activities.

Directions: Do not use actual names of schools, teachers, administrators, or students when using this worksheet.

Observer's Name: _____

Date: _____

Grade Level: _____

Subject: _____

Class Size: _____

Background Information: Give a brief general description of the school's social, economic, and ethnic makeup.

_____

_____

What to Record: Select a classroom from grades K–12, preferably one in which the teacher frequently uses some form of cooperative learning. Be certain you have discussed your objective with the teacher in advance and have confirmed that the class will be engaged in activities that relate to your assignment.

Orientation to the Lesson

In the preliminary conference with the teacher, find out:

- Which cooperative learning strategies or complex structures are used

- How (if at all) social and procedural skills are taught and reinforced

- How the teacher forms learning teams

- How long learning teams stay together

- What forms of recognition are used (for instance, points, tokens, or certificates)

- What the teacher views as the benefits and costs of cooperative learning

Lesson Observation

As you watch the lesson, describe the following:

- The apparent (or stated) lesson objective

- The teacher's role in presenting lesson content

- The academic task—What exactly are students supposed to do? How are they to help each other?

- The things students say to each other about their work (such as prompts and corrections)

- The social skills required to perform the work together

- The things the teacher does during team learning time

- How the arrangement of furniture and materials supports or detracts from the lesson format

- How this kind of student activity seems likely to impact on nearby classes

Postlesson Discussion

As soon as possible after the observation, ask the teacher to explain any part of the lesson that did not occur as usual or as planned.

Reflections on Your Observation:

1. To what extent was what you observed consistent with the models for cooperative learning recommended in this chapter?

_____

_____

_____

2. On the day that you visited, did the classroom environment and activities appear to be "normal" or were they modified to accommodate your visit?

_____

_____

_____

3. Identify and discuss any discrepancies between what you observed the teacher doing and the suggestions for strategies and activities advocated in the chapter.

_____

_____

_____

4. If other students had the same assignment, organize in small groups and compare notes with fellow students to evaluate what you observed.

_____

_____

_____

✳ Mastery Test

OBJECTIVE 7 **To describe how schoolwide implementation of cooperative learning can increase student achievement and professional collaboration and reduce violence**

Indicate whether the following statements are true (*T*) or false (*F*). Rewrite the false statements to make them true.

_____ 1. Success for All is too new to have demonstrated achievement outcomes for participating students.

_____ 2. Having a safe and orderly environment is essential to school effectiveness.

_____ 3. Violence-prevention programs work best if they target their efforts narrowly.

_____ 4. Supporting a wide range of family services is one way to reduce violence in schools.

_____ 5. Extracurricular activities help keep students safe.

_____ 6. Students used to cooperative learning have a harder time than others in conflict resolution.

_____ 7. Cooperative learning in particular and collaboration in general are not just for kids.

ADDITIONAL RESOURCES

Readings

Anderson, R., and K. Humphrey. *61 Cooperative Learning Activities for Computer Classrooms.* Portland, Maine: J. Weston Walch, 1996.

Gillies, R. M. *Cooperative Learning: Integrating Theory and Practice.* Los Angeles: SAGE Publications, 2007.

Gillies, R. M., A. Ashman, and J. Terwel (eds.). *The Teacher's Role in Implementing Cooperative Learning in the Classroom.* New York: Springer, 2008.

Jacobs, G. M., M. A. Power, and L. W. Inn. *The Teacher's Sourcebook for Cooperative Learning.* Thousand Oaks, CA: Corwin Press, 2002.

Johnson, D. W., R. Johnson, and E. Holubec. *Cooperative Learning in the Classroom.* Alexandria, Va.: Association for Supervision and Curriculum Development, 1994.

Johnson, D. W., R. Johnson, and E. Holubec. *The New Circles of Learning: Cooperation in the Classroom and School.* Alexandria, Va.: Association for Supervision and Curriculum Development, 1994.

Kagan, S. and M. Kagan. *Kagan Cooperative Learning.* San Clemente, Calif.: Kagan Publishing, 2009.

Oczkus, L. D. *Reciprocal Teaching at Work.* Newark, Del.: International Reading Association, 2003.

Slavin, R. E. *Cooperative Learning: Theory, Research, and Practice,* 2nd ed. Boston: Allyn & Bacon, 1995.

Slavin, R. E., and O. S. Fashola. *Show Me the Evidence: Proven and Promising Programs for America's Schools.* Newbury Park, Calif.: Corwin, 1998.

Websites

The Jigsaw Classroom: http://www.jigsaw.org
Developed by Elliot Aronson and the Social Psychology Network, this site contains "how-to" explanations, research summaries, implementation tips, and related links.

The Cooperative Learning Center (CLC) at the University of Minnesota: http://www.co-operation.org
Provided by the CLC, this site contains descriptions of center work, essays and research reports by Johnson and Johnson and others, and book and supply catalogues.

Educators for Social Responsibility: http://www.esrnational.org
This site includes lesson plans and resource materials that can be easily adapted for cooperative learning lessons on current events. Some plans are especially well suited to Academic Controversy lessons.

International Association for the Study of Cooperation in Education: http://www.iasce.net
This site includes resources for teaching and networking.

Success for All: http://www.successforall.net
This site describes many features of the schoolwide cooperative learning curriculum and includes links to the full text of journal articles and research reports on cooperative learning.

George Jacobs Web site: http://www.georgejacobs.net

Richard Felder's Homepage: http://ncsu.edu/felder-public/
These web sites are treasure troves of online articles, links to other sites, and other items of interest to those who want to implement cooperative learning strategies from pre-K through graduate school.

For these links and additional resources, please visit the Premium Website at **www.cengage.com/login**

 NOTES

1. K. Paterson, *The Sign of the Chrysanthemum* (New York: Harper & Row, 1973).

2. R. E. Slavin, *Cooperative Learning: Theory, Research, and Practice,* 2nd ed. (Boston: Allyn & Bacon, 1995).

3. D. W. Johnson, R. Johnson, and M. Stanne, "Cooperative Learning Methods: A Meta-Analysis," http://www.clcrc.com (accessed May 2000); D. W. Johnson and R. T. Johnson, "Social Interdependence Theory and Cooperative Learning: The Teacher's Role," in *The Teacher's Role in Implementing Cooperative Learning in the Classroom* (New York: Springer, 2008).

4. S. Yamarik, "Does Cooperative Learning Improve Student Learning Outcomes?" *Journal of Economic Education* (Summer 2007).

5. S. Bahar-Ozvaris et al., "Cooperative Learning: A New Application of Problem-based Learning in Mental Health Training," *Medical Teacher* 28, no. 6 (2006): 553–557.

6. K. Doymas, "Teaching Chemical Equilibrium with the Jigsaw Technique," *Research in Science Education* 38 (2008): 249–260.

7. J. Cooper et al., *Cooperative Learning and College Instruction: Effective Use of Student Learning Teams* (Carson, CA: California State University Foundation on Behalf of the California State University Institute for Teaching and Learning, 1990).

8. D. W. Johnson, R. Johnson, and E. Holubec, *The New Circles of Learning: Cooperation in the Classroom and School* (Alexandria, VA: Association for Supervision and Curriculum Development, 1994); R. M. Gillies, *Cooperative Learning: Integrating Theory and Practice* (Los Angeles: SAGE Publications, 2007).

9. D. W. Johnson and R. T. Johnson, *Cooperation and Competition: Theory and Research* (Edina, MN: Interaction Book Company, 1989).

10. E. Aronson, http://www.jigsaw.org/history.htm

11. D. W. Johnson and R. T. Johnson, "Social Interdependence Theory and Cooperative Learning: The Teacher's Role," in *The Teacher's Role in Implementing Cooperative Learning in the Classroom* (New York: Springer, 2008).

12. D. W. Johnson, R. Johnson, and E. Holubec, *The New Circles of Learning: Cooperation in the Classroom and School* (Alexandria, VA: Association for Supervision and Curriculum Development, 1994).

13. Slavin, *op. cit.*; R. E. Slavin, "Cooperative Learning," in *The Routledge International Encyclopedia of Education*, ed. G. McCulloch and D. Crooks (Abingdon, UK: Routledge, 2009).

14. *Ibid.*

15. Johnson, Johnson, and Holubec, *op. cit.*

16. N. Webb, "Small Group Problem-Solving: Peer Interaction and Learning" (paper presented at the annual meeting of the American Educational Research Association, New Orleans, April 1988); N. Webb, "The Teacher's Role in Promoting Collaborative Dialogue in the Classroom," *British Journal of Educational Psychology* 79 (2009): 1–28.

17. R. E. Slavin, "Research on Cooperative Learning and Achievement: What We Know, What We Need to Know," (1995), http://www.successforall.com/resource/research/coolearn.htm

18. H. Gardner, *Multiple Intelligences: The Theory in Practice* (New York: Basic Books, 1993); K. Nicholson-Nelson, *Developing Students' Multiple Intelligences* (New York: Scholastic Professional Books, 1998).

19. H. Gardner, *Multiple Intelligences: The Theory in Practice* (New York: Basic Books, 1993), 15–16.

20. K. Nicholson-Nelson, *Developing Students' Multiple Intelligences* (New York: Scholastic Professional Books, 1998), 10–12.

21. R. E. Slavin, *Cooperative Learning: Theory, Research, and Practice,* 2nd ed. (Boston: Allyn & Bacon, 1995).

22. D. W. Johnson, R. Johnson, and E. Holubec, *Cooperative Learning in the Classroom* (Alexandria, VA: Association for Supervision and Curriculum Development, 1994).

23. Slavin, *op. cit. Cooperative Learning: Theory, Research, and Practice,* (1995).

24. S. Kagan and M. Kagan, *Cooperative Learning* (San Clemente, CA: Kagan Publishing, 2009).

25. *Ibid.*

26. F. Lyman, "Think–Pair–Share, Thinktrix, Thinklinks, and Weird Facts: An Interactive System for Cooperative Learning," in *Enhancing Thinking Through Cooperative Learning,* ed. N. Davidson and T. Worsham (New York: Teachers College Press, 1992).

27. L. Baloche and T. Platt, "Sprouting Magic Beans: Exploring Literature Through Creative Questioning and Cooperative Learning," *Language Arts* 70, no. 4 (1993): 264–271.

28. Kagan, *op. cit.* (Numbered Heads Together is credited by the author to Russ Frank, a teacher in Diamond Bar, CA.)

29. Slavin, *op. cit.* (1995).

30. R. E. Slavin, "Effects of Biracial Learning Teams on Cross-Racial Friendships," *Journal of Educational Psychology* 71 (1979): 381–387; D. W. Johnson and R. T. Johnson, "Social Interdependence Theory and Cooperative Learning: The Teacher's Role," in *The Teacher's Role in Implementing Cooperative Learning in the Classroom* (New York: Springer, 2008).

31. R. M. Felder and R. Brent, "Effective Strategies for Cooperative Learning," *Journal of Cooperation and Collaboration in College Teaching* 10, no. 2 (2001): 69–75.

32. Kagan, *op. cit.*

33. Slavin, *op. cit.,* (*Cooperative Learning*).

34. D. W. Johnson and R. Johnson, *Reducing School Violence Through Conflict Resolution Training* (Alexandria, VA: Association for Supervision and Curriculum Development, 1995).

35. Johnson and Johnson, *op. cit.,* (*Cooperation and Competition*).

36. Johnson and Johnson, *op. cit.,* (*Reducing School Violence*).

37. L. Corno, "Teaching and Self-Regulated Learning," in *Talks to Teachers,* ed. D. C. Berliner and B. V. Rosenshine (New York: Random House, 1987); J. Trimbur, "Collaborative Learning and Teaching Writing," in *Perspectives on Research on Scholarship in Composition,* ed. B. W. McClelland and T. R. Donovan (New York: Modern Languages Association, 1985).

38. L. Resnick, "Learning in School and Out," *Educational Researcher* 16, no. 9 (1987): 14–20.

39. Johnson, Johnson, and Holubec, *op. cit.,* (*New Circles of Learning*).

40. S. Kagan and M. Kagan, *op. cit.*

41. *Ibid.*

42. *Ibid.*

43. G. M. Jacobs, C. Ward, and P. Gallo, "The Dynamics of Digital Groups: Cooperative Learning in IT-based Language Instruction," *Teaching of English Language and Literature* 13, no. 2 (1997): 5–8.

44. S. Kagan and M. Kagan, *op. cit.*

45. R. E. Slavin and O. S. Fashola, *Show Me the Evidence: Proven and Promising Programs for America's Schools* (Newbury Park, CA: Corwin, 1998); G. D. Borman, R. E. Slavin et al., "Final Reading Outcomes of the National Randomized Field Trial of Success for All," *American Educational Research Journal* 44, no. 3 (2007): 701–731.

46. D. W. Johnson and R. Johnson, *Reducing School Violence Through Conflict Resolution Training* (Alexandria, VA: Association for Supervision and Curriculum Development, 1995); *op. cit., (Reducing School Violence)*; D. W. Johnson and R. Johnson, "Why Violence Prevention Programs Don't Work—And What Does," *Educational Leadership* 52, no. 5 (1995): 63–68; D. W. Johnson and R. Johnson, "Reducing School Violence Through Conflict Resolution Training," *Bulletin of the NASSP* 80, no. 579 (1996): 11–18.

47. J. Bonstingl, *Schools of Quality* (Alexandria, VA: Association for Supervision and Curriculum Development, 1992); *How We Are Changing Schools Collaboratively* (New York: Impact II, The Teachers' Network, 1995); L. Lezotte, *Total Quality Effective School* (Okemos, MI: Effective Schools Products, 1992); A. Lieberman, ed., *Building a Professional Culture in Schools* (New York: Teachers College Press, 1988).

48. Slavin and Fashola, *op. cit.*

49. Success for All Foundation, http://www.successforall.net/elementary/turn.htm

50. Johnson and Johnson, *op. cit., (Reducing School Violence)*.

51. Johnson and Johnson, *op. cit., (Reducing School Violence)*.

10 Assessment

Terry D. Tenbrink

David Young-Wolff/PhotoEdit

■ INTASC Standards

● **Principle 8:** Understands and uses formal and informal assessment strategies.

● **Principle 9:** Reflects on teaching.

● **Principle 10:** Fosters relationships with colleagues, parents, and agencies in the larger community.

■ OBJECTIVES

1. To define *evaluation* and to describe each of the four stages in the assessment process

2. To select appropriate information-gathering strategies when seeking to make classroom assessments

3. To write effective test items for assessing achievement

4. To develop rubrics (including checklists and rating scales) for evaluating student products and performances

5. To use portfolios to assess ongoing performance and progress

6. To describe how to use information to evaluate; that is, to grade, to judge student progress, and to judge changes in student attitudes

7. To describe how to use assessment data to help students learn more effectively

8. To select and use standardized instruments

9. To describe the role of technology in classroom assessment

E ducational evaluation is useful only if it helps the educator (administrator or teacher) and student make sound educational judgments and decisions. In this chapter, you will learn about some of the basic principles of evaluation as applied to classroom problems. I would encourage you, however, to go beyond this introductory level of understanding. Purchase a basic text on classroom evaluation techniques. Practice your test-writing skills whenever possible. Learn from your mistakes as you begin to evaluate your own students, and learn to use evaluation as a necessary and important teacher tool. Use evaluation to help you teach better and to help your students learn better.

OBJECTIVE 1

To define *evaluation* and to describe each of the four stages in the assessment process

Evaluation or Assessment?

Learning Activity 10.1

INTASC Principle 8

In recent years, educators have begun replacing the word **evaluation** with the word **assessment**. Although the two terms basically refer to the same process, the newer term is being used in an attempt to expand our thinking about the role of evaluation. Assessment strategies include far more than formal testing, which has historically been the emphasis in textbooks on measurement and evaluation. Such procedures are finally being recognized as an integral part of the teaching process. Generally, assessment techniques that are authentic provide us with information about behaviors, skills, ideas, attitudes, and so on that are "real world." What we try to measure with authentic assessments are those things that represent skills and information that are useful in everyday living and important in helping students reach t̶ ̶ ̶ ̶ ̶f ̶ ̶ill in a given subject. Furthermore, authentic assessme ̶ ̶ ̶ ̶ ̶ ation under conditions that are as close a ̶ ̶ ̶ ̶ ̶se of the information or skills being asse ̶ ̶ ̶ ̶ most likely to provide authentic assessme ̶ ̶ ̶ ̶checklists, rating scales, and portfolios. In t ̶ ̶ ̶ ̶se authentic assessment tools as well as mo ̶ ̶ ̶ ̶s such as tests and questionnaires. Nevert ̶ ̶ ̶ ̶ ̶ent procedures is the act of evaluating.

[handwritten note: Do this with math example aquarium]

To evaluate is to judge

Stated most simply, to evaluate is to place a value upon—to judge. Forming a judgment is not an independent action. To judge, one must have information. The act of judging depends on this prerequisite act of obtaining information. The act of forming a judgment is itself prerequisite to an action one step further along: decision making. So *evaluation*, the process of forming judgments, depends on information gathering and leads to decision making. Picture it this way:

| obtaining information | → | forming judgments | → | making decisions |

Or this way:

| *Evaluation* is the process of obtaining information and using it to form judgments that, in turn, are used in decision making. |

This definition clearly specifies the interrelationships among the various stages in the evaluation process, yet it also clearly indicates the centrality of forming judgments. If you have not formed a judgment, you have not evaluated.

■ The Evaluation Process

It is important for you to understand the *total* evaluation process. So let's expand this definition. So far, it is obvious that evaluation involves at least three stages: obtaining information, forming judgments, and using those judgments in decision making. By adding a preparation stage and enlarging a bit on the last stage, we come up with the following four stages:

The Evaluation Process

Stage 1: Preparing for assessment
Stage 2: Obtaining needed information
Stage 3: Forming judgments
Stage 4: Using judgments in making decisions and preparing reports

---

☐ INTASC Principle 9

Let's look at a rather typical teaching/learning situation. Notice how this teacher goes through these four stages as she attempts to make her instruction more effective.

Stage 1. Preparing for Assessment

Bonnie, a third-grade teacher, has become concerned about Billy. He seems to be having trouble keeping up in reading. Bonnie wonders how long he will be able to function within his current reading group. She wonders whether or not she should move him to a slower group. Perhaps there is something she can do to help—some extra work, for example, or some extra attention. She decides she needs more information before she can accurately judge Billy's level of achievement in reading. After determining the kind of information she needs (for example, information about the kind of errors made when reading orally, Billy's use of various word attack skills, Billy's interests), Bonnie determines when and how to obtain that information.

Stage 2. Obtaining Needed Information

Over a period of several days Bonnie obtains a great deal of information about Billy. She gives him a standardized reading test, listens to him read orally, carefully records the errors he makes, and observes him throughout the day, watching for patterns of behavior that might indicate particular attitudes toward various subjects.

Stage 3. Forming Judgments

After analyzing all the information she has obtained, Bonnie comes to the following conclusions:

- Billy is not capable of reading material written at a third-grade level.

- Billy reads comfortably only that material written on a second-grade level or lower.
- Billy's primary weakness lies in the area of word attack skills.
- Billy does not have a comprehension problem. He understands what is read to him.
- Billy likes the children in his reading group.
- Billy enjoys the stories in the third-grade reader.

Stage 4. Using Judgments in Making Decisions and Preparing Reports

On the basis of her judgments, Bonnie decides that she should keep Billy in his present reading group. She also decides to take the following action:

- Prepare a checklist of word attack skills.
- Systematically teach Billy those skills on a one-to-one basis.
- Continue to have the stories read to Billy so that he will not fall behind on his comprehension skills.
- Have Billy check off each word attack skill as he demonstrates competence in using it.

Having made these decisions, Bonnie writes a brief summary of her judgments, noting the actions she anticipates taking. She files this in her own files for future reference. She also calls in Billy's parents and shares her findings with them. She asks them to cooperate, give Billy lots of encouragement and praise, and support him as he struggles to make up the deficiencies she has discovered.

Note the key features of each of the stages:

1. *Stage 1: Preparation.* Determine the kind of information needed and decide how and when to obtain it.
2. *Stage 2: Information gathering.* Obtain a variety of information as accurately as possible.
3. *Stage 3: Forming judgments.* Judgments are made by comparing the information to selected criteria.
4. *Stage 4: Decision making and reporting.* Record significant findings and determine appropriate courses of action.

▼ TeachSource Video Case | **Assessment in the Elementary Grades: Formal and Informal Literacy Assessment**

To access the video, go to www.cengage.com/login. Watch this video to see how Chris Quinn, a second-grade teacher, uses a variety of assessment strategies to help her gauge her student's progress and plan her instruction. As you watch this video, consider the following questions:

1. Why does Chris Quinn think it is important to use a variety of assessment strategies? Do you agree?
2. What techniques does Chris find especially helpful for tracking student growth?
3. How does Chris involve students in the various assessment strategies?

Mastery Test

OBJECTIVE 1   **To define *evaluation* and to describe each of the four stages in the assessment process**

1. Give a brief definition of *evaluation*.
2. List the four stages in the assessment process. Describe briefly what goes on in each stage. Use examples from the classroom to clarify your descriptions.

OBJECTIVE 2   **To select appropriate information-gathering strategies when seeking to make classroom assessments**

Selecting Strategies

Learning Activity 10.2

INTASC Principles 8, 9

The first step in preparing to evaluate is determining what you will be evaluating and what kind of information you will need to make your assessments.[1] Once that has been determined, you are ready to choose a strategy for obtaining that information. There are two steps involved: (1) determine the information-gathering technique you want to use and (2) select the type of instrument that should be used.

Step 1. Choose an Appropriate Technique

Information-gathering techniques

There are four different techniques classroom teachers use to obtain information about themselves and their students: **inquiry**, observation, analysis, and testing. To inquire is to ask. Whenever you wish to know someone's opinions, feelings, interests, likes and dislikes, and so forth, ask that person. Effective teachers always ask their students how they feel about what is going on. They know the value of information gained through inquiry. **Observations** are made by teachers whenever they look, listen, feel, or use any other senses to find out what is going on in the classroom. Observations of student performances, habit patterns, and interpersonal interactions all provide the teacher with helpful information. Analysis is the process of breaking something down into its component parts. For example, a teacher might analyze a math assignment to discover the kinds of errors students are making, or a vocational education teacher might analyze a coffee table made by a woodworking student to evaluate the project according to the design, overall construction, and finish of the table. Testing is being used whenever there is a common situation to which all students respond (for example, a test question), a common set of instructions governing the students' responses, a set of rules for scoring the responses, and a description (usually numerical) of each student's performance—a score.

The following table compares these four techniques. Study the chart and then complete the worksheet that follows.

SUMMARY OF THE MAJOR CHARACTERISTICS OF THE FOUR INFORMATION-GATHERING TECHNIQUES*

	Inquiry	Observation	Analysis	Testing
Kind of information obtainable	Opinions Self-perceptions Subjective judgments Affects (especially attitudes) Social perceptions	Performance or the end product of some performance Affects (especially emotional reactions) Social interactions Psychomotor skills Typical behavior	Learning outcomes during the learning process (intermediate goals) Cognitive and psychomotor skills Some affective outcomes	Attitude and achievement Terminal goals Cognitive outcomes Maximum performance
Objectivity	Least objective Highly subject to bias and error	Subjective, but can be objective if care is taken in the construction and use of the instruments	Objective but not stable over time	Most objective and reliable but subjectivity can play a part in formation of the questions
Cost	Inexpensive but can be time-consuming	Inexpensive but time-consuming	Fairly inexpensive Preparation time is somewhat lengthy but crucial	Most expensive, but most information gained per unit of time

* Excerpted from *Evaluation: A Practical Guide for Teachers*, by T. D. TenBrink, pp. 276–277. Copyright © 1974 by McGraw-Hill Book Company. Reprinted with the permission of The McGraw-Hill Companies.

Observation Worksheet

ASSESSMENT ACTIVITIES

Talk to a teacher about how he or she decides what to teach, when to teach, and how to teach. Probe for specific answers. Try to identify the various stages in the assessment process as that teacher explains his or her decision making to you. How could you use the terminology of this chapter to explain what the teacher has done?

Directions: Do not use actual names of schools, teachers, administrators, or students when using this worksheet.

Observer's Name: _____

Date: _____

Grade Level: _____

Subject: _____

Class Size: _____

Background Information: Give a brief general description of the school's social, economic, and ethnic makeup.

_____

_____

_____

What to Record: Observe the teacher in action. Note how assessment is an integral part of his or her teaching. Use the following format to keep track of the information being gathered, the information-gathering techniques being used, and the judgments being made.

Time	Information Obtained	Assessment & Technique	Judgment(s) Made
9:15–9:45	Students' ability to sound words during reading class	Observation	Most did well. George and Mary had trouble with some words.

Reflections on Your Observation:

1. What variety of assessment techniques did the teacher use?

_____

_____

_____

2. In what ways did the teacher use the results of the assessment? Did he or she adjust instruction or learning activities based on assessment results?

_____

_____

_____

3. If so, in what ways? _____

_____

_____

4. What questions would you want to ask the teacher regarding his or her use of assessment?

_____

_____

_____

Step 2. Select the Best Instrument to Obtain the Information You Need

Once you have selected an appropriate information-gathering technique, you should choose the type of information-gathering instrument to be used. An information-gathering technique is a *procedure* for obtaining information. An information-gathering instrument is a *tool* we use to help us gather information. We will briefly examine three basic types of instruments: tests, rubrics, and questionnaires.

Tests measure aptitude, achievement ▷

A **test** is an instrument that presents a common situation to which all students respond, a common set of instructions, and a common set of rules for scoring the students' responses. Tests are used primarily for determining aptitude and achievement. When we want to know how much a student knows, or how well he or she can perform certain skills, a test is an appropriate instrument to use. Most classroom tests are constructed by the teacher and are referred to as *teacher-made tests* or *classroom tests* to distinguish them from *standardized tests*. The instructions on standardized tests have been carefully standardized so that everyone taking the test does so under similar conditions. Most standardized tests are developed and sold by test publishers and have been carefully developed, tried out, revised, standardized, and evaluated for reliability and validity.

A **rubric** is a set of rules for scoring student products or student performance. Rubrics typically take the form of a checklist or a rating scale, but they can also take other forms. They are especially helpful when you are trying to assess learning outcomes and processes that closely match the kind of performances that are useful in daily living and in real-life vocational settings. Such assessment is sometimes called *authentic assessment*. For example, assessing a student's ability to present a cogent and logical argument for a given political stance is most directly measured by assessing position papers written by the student. A less direct method would be to present students with several statements and ask them to choose the one that best supports a specified position.

Checklists note presence or absence ▷

A **checklist** is basically a list of criteria (or "things to look for") for evaluating some performance or end product. One uses a checklist by simply checking off those criteria that are met. For example, one could use a checklist to be certain that a student goes through all the routines in an exercise program, or a list of criteria for an effective speech could be checked as an indication of what a student did correctly when making a speech to inform. Whenever it is helpful to know whether an important characteristic is present in a performance (or is found in some end product), a checklist would be an appropriate instrument to use.

Rating scales note quality ▷

If we wish to rate the quality of a performance or end product, a **rating scale** would be the instrument to use. We might judge a speech, for example, by whether or not gestures were used. But if we want to determine the quality of those gestures (whether they were good, fair, poor, and so on), a rating scale should be used. A rating scale provides a scale of values that describe someone or something being evaluated.

Questionnaires seek opinions ▷

Questionnaires are instruments designed to obtain information about opinions, feelings, and interests. They can be used when we are not certain about the type of responses we might get.

The advantages and disadvantages of each type of instrument are highlighted for you in the following table. Again, study the table carefully, and then take Your Turn at selecting an appropriate instrument.

ADVANTAGES AND DISADVANTAGES OF EACH TYPE OF INFORMATION-GATHERING INSTRUMENT

Type of Instrument	Advantages	Disadvantages
Standardized tests: Used when accurate information is needed.	Usually well developed and reliable. Include norms for comparing the performance of a class or an individual.	Often do not measure exactly what has been taught. Expensive. Limited in what is measured.
Teacher-made tests: Used routinely as a way to obtain achievement information.	Usually measure exactly what has been taught. Inexpensive. Can be constructed as need arises.	No norms beyond the class are available. Often unreliable. Require quite a bit of time to construct.
Rubrics: Used to assess the quality of student performance.	**Helpful for assessing typical performance as well as maximum performance.**	Not easy to construct well and are sometimes subject to observer bias.
Checklists: Used to determine the presence or absence of specific characteristics of performance.	Helpful in keeping observations focused on key points or critical behaviors.	Measure only presence or absence of a trait or behavior.
Rating scales: Used to judge quality of performance.	Allow observational data to be used in making qualitative as well as quantitative judgments.	Take time and effort to construct. Can be clumsy to use if too complex.
Questionnaires: Used to inquire about feelings, opinions, and interests.	Keep inquiry focused and help teacher obtain the same information from each student.	Take time and effort to construct. Difficult to score. No right or wrong answers. Data difficult to summarize.

❯ YOUR TURN   Selecting an Information-Gathering Instrument

Read each of the following classroom situations. First decide what technique is being called for (inquiry, observation, analysis, or testing), and then write down which instrument you would use and why. Compare your answers with those of your peers and those found in the Answer Key.

1. A second-grade teacher wants to find out if her pupils now understand how to form the vowels in cursive writing.
2. A high school social studies teacher wants to know how his students feel about the outcome of the latest elections.
3. A fourth-grade teacher wants to know how well his class compares to other fourth-grade classes in their achievement of the basics: reading, writing, and arithmetic.

4. An eighth-grade teacher just finished teaching her students how to compute the volume of a cube, and she wants to know how well her students learned this skill.
5. A music teacher wants to rank-order her clarinet players so that she can assign them chairs in the band.
6. A shop teacher wants to make sure that all his students follow the safety precautions when operating a radial arm saw.

Mastery Test

OBJECTIVE 2 **To select appropriate information-gathering strategies when seeking to make classroom assessments**

For each of the situations described in the following questions, determine the best technique and/or instrument to be used.

1. A fifth-grade teacher wants to ask all her students how they feel about each of the subjects they are studying.
   a. Testing—classroom test
   b. Observation—questionnaire
   c. Inquiry—rating scale
   d. Inquiry—questionnaire

2. A fifth-grade teacher wants to know if her students are including the new girl from Mexico in their games during recess.
   a. Observation
   b. Inquiry
   c. Testing
   d. Analysis

3. The school superintendent wants an overall picture of the level of achievement for each class in the school system.
   a. Checklist
   b. Classroom test
   c. Standardized test
   d. Rating scale

4. A speech teacher is trying to improve her ability to judge impromptu speeches.
   a. Analysis
   b. Observation
   c. Testing
   d. Inquiry

5. An English teacher examines each student's theme carefully so she can get an idea about each person's particular strengths and weaknesses in writing.
   a. Analysis—checklist
   b. Analysis—test
   c. Inquiry—checklist
   d. Inquiry—test

6. To determine academic aptitude for placement in special programs, one should use which of the following?
   a. Rating scale
   b. Checklist
   c. Classroom test
   d. Standardized test

OBJECTIVE 3   To write effective test items for assessing achievement

Learning Activity 10.3

The first step in test construction is to determine what it is you are trying to test and what kind of item would be best suited to testing that type of information. Most classroom tests are used to measure learning outcomes. The best statements of learning outcomes are instructional objectives. As you may recall from the discussion in Chapter 2, instructional objectives define clearly, in observable terms, the achievement we expect of our students; the importance of well-chosen verbs in writing instructional objectives was emphasized. The verb should describe precisely the kind of response you expect the student to make to particular subject-matter content. If the verb used in an instructional objective does that, it is a relatively simple matter to determine the type of test item you should use. For example, suppose you are trying to find out if your students have mastered the following objectives:

To list the names of the first ten presidents of the United States

To describe the major contributions of Washington and Lincoln

To explain the changes that occur when a different political party takes control of Congress

The first objective obviously calls for a short-answer question in which the student is asked to list names. The other two objectives would best be tested with an essay question because students would have to describe or explain—not the kind of thing they could do on an objective test such as true/false or multiple choice. What kinds of learning outcomes are best measured with objective-test items (true/false, matching, or multiple choice)? These types of items are best suited for measuring learning outcomes for which the student must be able to choose among alternatives. For example:

To choose the word that best describes the author's feelings

To select the sentence that best represents the democratic position

To identify the emotive language in a paragraph

To determine which of several experiments would most likely provide the information needed by a particular researcher

Note that each of these objectives could readily be measured with an objective test; however, it is possible to measure some of them with another type of item. For example, the third objective in the list (to identify emotive language) could be measured with a variety of test items:

1. *True/false:* The statement underlined in the paragraph above uses emotive language.

2. *Multiple choice:* Which of the following sentences (as numbered in the paragraph above) represents emotive language?

   a. Sentence 2

   b. Sentence 3

   c. Sentence 6

   d. Sentence 9

3. *Short answer:* Pick out three emotive statements from the paragraph above and write them on your paper.

ADVANTAGES AND DISADVANTAGES OF DIFFERENT TYPES OF TEST ITEMS

Type	Advantages	Disadvantages
Short answer	Can test many facts in a short time. Fairly easy to score. Excellent format for math. Tests recall.	Difficult to measure complex learning. Often ambiguous.
Essay	Can test complex learning. Can assess thinking process and creativity.	Difficult to score objectively. Uses a great deal of testing time. Subjective.
True/False	Tests the most facts in the shortest time. Easy to score. Tests recognition. Objective.	Difficult to measure complex learning. Difficult to write reliable items. Subject to guessing.
Matching	Excellent for testing associations and recognition of facts. Although terse, can test complex learning (especially concepts). Objective.	Difficult to write effective items. Subject to process of elimination.
Multiple choice	Can assess learning at all levels of complexity. Can be highly reliable. Objective. Tests fairly large knowledge base in short time. Easy to score.	Difficult to write. Somewhat subject to guessing.

Examine the objectives ▶ You can readily see that the first step in selecting the type of item to use is to examine the instructional objectives. There is often still room for choice, however; some objectives can be measured by more than one type of item. Consequently, other things must be taken into account. The table on page 306 highlights the advantages and disadvantages of the major types of test items.

> ❯ **YOUR TURN**   **Selecting the Type of Item**

For each learning outcome, determine the type of test item you would use and briefly state your reason.

1. To explain the value of using strong, active verbs in writing paragraphs
2. To list the steps to take when processing a film
3. To select, from among alternatives, the best way to introduce a new topic
4. To discuss the implications of the new world order
5. To write down the names of at least five generals from World War II
6. To choose the most likely cause of a given kind of engine malfunction
7. To determine the key of a given musical score

◻ Writing Test Items

The secret to effective item writing is to be as clear and concise as possible. Don't try to trick the students. Test each learning outcome (instructional objective) in as straightforward a manner as possible. When reading a test question, a student should understand exactly what is being asked. If the student knows the material, he or she should be able to answer the question correctly.

Writing Essay Questions

Objectivity is especially difficult to attain when writing and grading essay questions. By following the simple guidelines listed, however, you should be able to produce well-written essay questions.

Guidelines for writing essay questions

1. Make certain that your question really tests the learning outcome of interest.
2. Each essay item should include:
   a. A clear statement of the problem
   b. Any restrictions on the answer
3. For each item, construct a model answer. It should include:
   a. The content of an ideal answer
   b. Any important organizational features one might expect in an ideal answer

Once you are certain that an essay is the type of item you wish to use, you need to formulate the question so that every student reading it will have the same understanding about what is expected in the answer. Every student need *not* be able to answer the question; however, every student should know what the question is asking. That criterion for a well-written essay question will be easier to meet if you:

Be clear and concise ▶

1. Use clear, concise language
2. Are precise about any restrictions you want to place on the answer

Examine the following sets of questions. Note that the questions that are easiest to understand are shorter, contain simpler language, involve simple sentence structures, and do not include extraneous verbiage.

Set A

Clear: Describe a wedge, and list three or four of its uses.

Not so clear: Explain what a wedge is and its function with a few examples.

Downright confusing: Produce a descriptive paragraph concerning the wedge and its functional utility.

Set B

Clear: Explain why certain chemicals should always be mixed in a certain order.

Ambiguous: Exploding chemicals can be dangerous, which should not happen. How do you avoid this?

Impossible: Sometimes reactions occur that are potentially volatile when the proper order of mixing certain chemicals is not maintained. Can you explain this?

Using clear, concise language is not enough. An effective essay question must also indicate the level of specificity you expect in the answer. It must let the student know whether opinions are acceptable, whether or not arguments must be substantiated, and, if so, whether or not references are needed. It should provide the student with an indication of just how much freedom he or she has in responding. Take, for example, the following essay item:

Discuss the various properties of water.

The language of this item is certainly clear and concise. But what kind of response would be acceptable? Would "water tastes good and gets you wet when you fall in it" be an acceptable answer? Maybe. Only the author of the question knows. Look at the following alternative ways of writing this item. Each one imposes slightly different restrictions on the student's answers, and each one is better than our original item because of those added restrictions.

Describe what happens to water when it is exposed to extreme temperatures.

List the chemical properties of water.

List the nutritional properties of drinking water.

Why does the taste of water vary so greatly from one location to another?

List and briefly describe five ways that water helps to sustain life.

Restrict student responses ▶

Note that each of these items clearly calls for a different kind of response. Note, too, the variety of ways one can restrict or shape a student's response. Now try your hand at writing essay items by doing the following Your Turn exercise.

> YOUR TURN Writing Essay Items

Write two essay questions. One should be an open-ended question. The second should place restrictions on the response the student is asked to make.

1. Write an open-ended question with few restrictions.
2. Write an essay question that somehow restricts or limits the student's response in one or more of the following ways.
   a. Limit the amount of time to answer or the number of words that can be used in the answer.
   b. Limit the topic to certain, specified subtopics.
   c. Ask the student to focus on one aspect of the topic.
   d. Restrict the response to only one point of view.

Well-written essay items will help make it easier for the students to respond *and* easier for the teacher to grade. The biggest problem with essay tests is that they are difficult to grade objectively. That problem can be greatly reduced if a model answer is developed and used as a guide when the students' answers are graded. There are two major considerations when writing a model answer.

1. All important content should be included in a model answer.
2. Any important organizational features that would be expected in a comprehensive answer should be specified.

> YOUR TURN Constructing a Model Answer

Write two or three essay questions with various degrees of freedom. Then write a model answer for each question.

First, a model answer should contain any content you hope to find in the students' answers. When comparing a student's answer to the model answer, you should only have to check through the student's answer to see whether or not it includes the items listed as important content in the model answer. Facts, concepts, principles, and acceptable problem solutions are the kinds of things one should list in a model answer. Two examples of model answers follow. The first is for an essay question calling primarily for factual material; the second calls for a specific type of answer but allows the student some freedom in the particular content to be discussed.

Example of a Model Answer for a Factual Essay Question

Question: Describe the steps to take when developing black-and-white film.

Model answer: Student answers should include the following information.

Step 1: In darkened room (red light only), load film onto developing reel, grasp film by edges, check to see that film surfaces are not touching each other.

Step 2: Place reel in developing tank and cover with light-tight lid.

Step 3: Wet down the film, and so forth.

> ### Example of a Model Answer for an Essay Question Allowing Some Freedom of Content
>
> *Question:* Defend *or* refute the following statement: Civil wars are necessary to the growth of a developing country. Cite reasons for your argument, and use examples from history to help substantiate your claim.
>
> *Model answer:* All answers, regardless of the position taken, should include (1) a clear statement of the position, (2) at least five logical reasons, (3) at least four examples from history that *clearly* substantiate the reasons given.

Construct a model answer ▶

Note that in the second example, the student has great freedom to choose what to discuss, but restrictions are placed instead on the *type* of information to be included in the answer. For some essay questions, the order in which topics are included in the answer may be important. Other questions may call for a carefully developed logic, and the specific content is less important. Just remember this basic rule: A model answer should highlight the features that best reflect the learning outcome being measured by the essay question.

Writing Multiple-Choice Questions

Multiple-choice questions are perhaps the most frequently used type of test item. To make it easier to talk about these items, labels have been developed for each part of such an item:

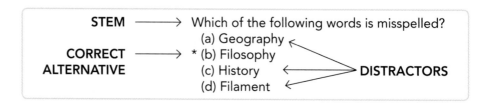

The multiple-choice item is the most versatile of all item types. You can ask questions at almost all levels of understanding with a high degree of reliability. To be both a reliable and a valid measure of a learning outcome, however, a multiple-choice item should meet the following criteria:

1. Present a single problem or question.
2. Measure a learning outcome that can be tested by selecting a right or best answer from among several alternatives.
3. Include alternatives that are terse—most of the item's information occurs in the stem.
4. Include alternatives that are similar in wording, writing style, length, and so forth.
5. Include alternatives that follow logically and grammatically from the stem.
6. Include distractors that are plausible but not correct.

Let's examine a few multiple-choice items to see if they meet the criteria listed. Then you will have an opportunity to evaluate items and try writing some of your own.

Examples of Multiple-Choice Items

Poor item: Alternatives too lengthy, question unclear.
1. Frozen foods
   a. Can be quick-frozen and then stored at zero degrees and then only for specified periods of time.
   b. Are tastier than any other kind of processed foods.
   c. Should always be washed and blanched before being packed for freezing.
   d. Can be stored at 28° or less if they are properly packaged and sealed.

Improved: Question clarified, alternatives shortened.
1. What is most important to a long shelf life for frozen foods?
   a. 0° temperature
   b. Air-tight packages
   c. Blanching foods before freezing
   d. Selection of food for freezing

Poor item: Alternatives do not follow grammatically from stem.
1. The constituents of air that are essential to plant life are
   a. Oxygen and nitrogen.
   b. Carbon monoxide.
   c. Nitrogen and iodine.
   d. Water.

Improved: All alternatives are plural, stem shortened.
1. Which of the following pairs is essential to plant life?
   a. Oxygen and nitrogen
   b. Carbon oxide and iodine
   c. Polyethyl and water
   d. Water and carbon monoxide

Improved: All alternatives are singular.
1. Which of the following is essential to plant life?
   a. Nitrogen
   b. Carbon monoxide
   c. Polyethylene
   d. Iodine

 YOUR TURN   **Evaluating and Writing Multiple-Choice Questions**

Choose a subject with which you are familiar and write five multiple-choice questions.
Write at least two of them at a level of learning higher than just the memorization of facts.

Writing True/False Items

True/false items are often criticized because they are so susceptible to guessing on the student's part. Certain kinds of learning outcomes, however, lend themselves naturally to a true/false format. If the items are carefully written to make them as reliable as possible, it seems reasonable to include a few true/false items in a test.

Clearly true or clearly false ▶ The most important rule to remember when writing true/false items is that each item must be clearly true or clearly false. Look at the following examples.

1. Squares have only three sides and two right angles.
2. Liquids always flow in the direction of gravitational pull.
3. Complete sentences include both a subject and predicate.
4. Cities are built on major traffic routes.
5. Our moon reflects the light of the sun.
6. Extroverts are outgoing and always popular.

Note that items 3 and 5 are clearly true and that only item 1 is clearly false. Item 2 is basically true, but "always" is extremely strong language. Might there be some exceptions? And what about item 4? It is a reasonable generalization, to be sure, but not true in every case. Finally, item 6 is partially true (outgoing, yes, but not always popular). Does the part that is false make the whole statement false? The problem with item 6 can often be avoided by remembering a second rule: Each true/false statement must present one and only one fact. For example, we could improve item 1 by making two items from it:

1. Squares have a total of three sides.
2. Squares have only two right angles.

A final rule to remember when constructing a true/false item is do not try to trick the students. Don't take a perfectly true statement, for example, and insert a "not" or other qualifying word that would make the statement false.

Good item: The sun is closer to the earth at the equator.

Good item: The sun is farther from the earth at the equator.

Bad item: The sun is not closer to the earth at the equator.

Don't lift a statement out of context, hoping that the student will remember reading it and think it true because it is familiar.

Poor: Nouns modify nouns.

Improved: Although they do not normally do so, in some situations nouns can modify nouns; for example, "baseball bat."

There are many other ways to trick students. You'll know it when you are doing it. Avoid the temptation. Always ask yourself, "Am I measuring an important learning outcome in a straightforward manner?"

Writing Matching Items

Matching items are written as a group of items divided into two lists. The students' task is to match each item from one list with an item from the other list. A well-written set of matching items will illustrate some particular relationship between pairs of items from the two lists. A common use of the matching exercise, for example, is to test the relationship between a term and its definition. Other relationships that might be tested with a matching exercise are:

1. Historical events and dates
2. Novels and their authors
3. Tools and their uses

4. Problems and their solutions
5. Elements and their symbols
6. Causes and their effects
7. Drawings and their interpretations

Test relationships Relationships like these are relatively easy to test with a matching exercise. Simply make two lists and write a clear set of instructions, telling the student the kind of relationship you are testing (the rationale, or basis, for matching). When writing a matching exercise, make sure that you keep the following points in mind.

Points to Remember When Writing a Matching Exercise

1. An obvious, natural relationship must exist between the items in the two lists.
2. The basis for matching must be made clear to the student.
3. One of the lists should be approximately 50 percent longer than the other list (which makes it difficult to obtain correct matches by the process of elimination).
4. The shorter list should not contain more than seven or eight items.

Learning Activity 10.4 As an optional learning exercise, you may find it helpful to examine a variety of test items, judging them in light of the criteria set down in the last few pages. Ask your instructor to help you locate both standardized and teacher-made tests to examine. For each item, ask yourself what makes the item effective or ineffective. Also ask: "What is the writer of this item really trying to measure?" This activity can be done individually or in small groups, but any findings should be shared with others in a general class discussion.

✳ Mastery Test

OBJECTIVE 3 **To write effective test items for assessing achievement**

Write a set of objectives for a unit of instruction. (Choose the subject matter and grade level.) Next, develop a test designed to find out whether students have mastered the objectives. You may wish to put your items on index cards to file for future use.

OBJECTIVE 4 **To develop rubrics (including checklists and rating scales) for evaluating student products and performances**

Learning Activity 10.5 There are many times when tests will not give you the information you need: You want to rate a student's musical performance, judge a speech contest, or grade an art project, or you are on a committee evaluating textbooks for possible adoption. These and similar situations represent the kind of evaluation problems best solved through the use of checklists or rating scales.

 INTASC Principle 8

▼ TeachSource Video Case **Performance Assessment: Student Presentations in a High School English Class**

To access the video, go to www.cengage.com/login. Watch this video to see how Laura Mossman assesses student presentations and how she involves her students in the process. As you watch, consider the following:

1. Do you think it is a good idea for the students to help develop the scoring rubric for the literature project? Why or why not?
2. Students in Laura's class also critiqued each other's performance. What are the pros and cons of this strategy?
3. How does student involvement in assessing these performances improve the assessment process as well as student learning?

☐ Developing Rubrics

Rubrics provide a recording and/or scoring system for assessing performance (or products of a performance) and generally take the form of a checklist or a rating scale. We will discuss the development of both of these kinds of rubrics and briefly discuss other types of rubrics. Rubrics not only provide for a scoring system that allows you to quantify your assessment of a student's performance; they also help you to focus on the critical elements of student performance. This focusing of your attention can reduce errors due to the "halo effect" and other biases.

Checklists

Checklists provide a systematic way of checking whether or not important characteristics are present in someone's performance (or in a product that someone has produced). Note the key consideration: Are some characteristics of this performance or product so important that it is valuable simply to know whether or not they are present? When the answer to that question is yes, a checklist is what you are looking for. The kinds of performances and products that might be evaluated through the use of checklists are:

Performances	**Products**
Playing a musical instrument	Drawings and paintings
Singing	Sculptures
Speaking	Maps
Participating in a discussion	Wood products
Leading a discussion	Handicrafts
Conducting an experiment	Outlines
Working through a math problem	
Conducting a library search	
Painting in oils	
Sculpturing	

When developing a checklist for evaluating a performance, your focus will be on behaviors; in developing one for use with products, it will be on observable features or characteristics. Note this difference by comparing the following two checklists. The first has been designed to evaluate a student while he is doing an oil painting (performance). The second has been designed to evaluate an oil painting after a student has completed it (product). How are these lists similar? How are they different?

EXAMPLE: EVALUATING A STUDENT'S OIL PAINTING

PERFORMANCE	PRODUCT
_____ General layout sketched out first	_____ Paints "worked" little, to keep them crisp
_____ Overall layout pleasing	_____ Sufficient details, but not overdone
_____ Background wash painted over the large areas	_____ Brushes and painting knives selected carefully to produce the desired textures
_____ Colors crisp and clean	
_____ Colors mixed on canvas	
_____ Composition appropriate to subject	

The process of developing a checklist is relatively simple. First, list the important behaviors or characteristics. Second, add any common errors to the list. Finally, arrange the list so that it is easy to use.

Listing the important behaviors of a performance is not as easy as listing the important characteristics of a product. That is because when we are good performers, we are often unaware of the things we do that make our performance good. It is especially difficult for a motor-skill performer to verbalize what he or she does when performing. Try to list, for example, the steps you take to balance a bicycle and move it forward. One way to deal with this problem is to watch a good performer and list all the things you observe that person doing. Later, pick out the most important behaviors and include them in your final checklist.

The common errors are most easily listed after you have had an opportunity to watch a beginning performer or to examine a beginner's early products. Note that a checklist is especially useful as a diagnostic tool when it includes common errors. If you anticipate using a checklist only as a final check on performance, there is no need to include common errors.

A well-designed checklist should meet the following criteria:

1. The list should be relatively short.
2. Each item should be clear.
3. Each item should focus on an observable characteristic or behavior.
4. Only important characteristics or behaviors should be included.
5. The items should be arranged so that the total list is easy to use.

Rating Scales

Checklists help us determine the presence or absence of a list of behaviors or characteristics. Rating scales help us determine the quality of a behavior or characteristic. It is helpful to know, for example, that a speaker uses gestures. It is even more helpful to be able to judge the quality of those gestures. A rating scale is used to evaluate that quality of performance. It helps you answer the question: How well does the speaker gesture?

Rating scales judge quality ▶

A rating scale is developed by taking a list of behaviors or characteristics (as one might use in a checklist) and constructing a qualitative scale for evaluating each behavior or characteristic.

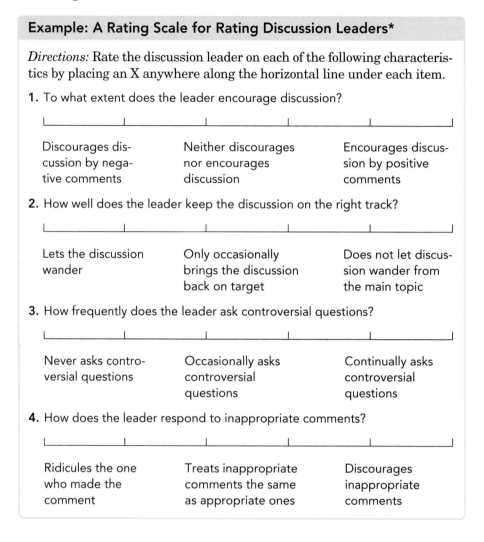

Example: A Rating Scale for Rating Discussion Leaders*

Directions: Rate the discussion leader on each of the following characteristics by placing an X anywhere along the horizontal line under each item.

1. To what extent does the leader encourage discussion?

| Discourages discussion by negative comments | Neither discourages nor encourages discussion | Encourages discussion by positive comments |

2. How well does the leader keep the discussion on the right track?

| Lets the discussion wander | Only occasionally brings the discussion back on target | Does not let discussion wander from the main topic |

3. How frequently does the leader ask controversial questions?

| Never asks controversial questions | Occasionally asks controversial questions | Continually asks controversial questions |

4. How does the leader respond to inappropriate comments?

| Ridicules the one who made the comment | Treats inappropriate comments the same as appropriate ones | Discourages inappropriate comments |

This rating scale would help an observer focus on specific, observable aspects of each behavior. Each time the scale was used, the same things would be examined. This would help improve the reliability of evaluating a performance and would reduce the errors due to observer bias.

Developing a rating scale involves the same steps used to develop a checklist, plus the step of defining a scale for each characteristic. This added step is sometimes difficult, but it will be easier if you first define the extreme ends of each scale and then describe the midpoints. Defining the extremes is easiest if you can think of some real-life examples. Suppose, for example, that you are developing a rating scale for evaluating the social development of third-graders. Among the many characteristics you feel are important is that of sharing with friends. To define the extreme ends, think first of a child you know who exemplifies this characteristic. This child shares readily with all her friends in an unselfish manner. Imagine this child as she shares with others. See her in your mind. Write down what you

* Excerpted from *Evaluation: A Practical Guide for Teachers*, by T. D. TenBrink, pp. 276–277. Copyright © 1974 by McGraw-Hill Book Company. Reprinted with the permission of The McGraw-Hill Companies.

see her do; describe her sharing. That description defines the positive end of your scale. To define the extreme negative or low end of the scale, think of a child who is poor at sharing and describe that child's behavior. Now you have the basis for the description at the low end of the scale. By examining these two extremes, you will be able to imagine fairly easily what someone would be like who falls in the middle, and the midpoints of the scale should be easy to define. A completed scale for the characteristic of sharing might look something like:

Sharing with Friends

| L_____|_____|_____|_____|_____L |

| Complains when a friend has other friends. Won't let others borrow possessions. | Shares occasionally, but is somewhat possessive of friends and possessions. | Encourages others to share friends and possessions. |

Note that at this point we have placed no numbers on the scale. For purposes of scoring, one might number the points along the scale. The lowest point could be assigned 1; the highest, 5. A scale without the numbers is *descriptive*; one with numbers is a *numerical–descriptive* scale. Removing the description and simply using numbers would produce a *numerical* scale. Numerical scales are usually not helpful unless the characteristic can be easily quantified (for example, number of times the child shares toys in one day: 0, 1–2, 3–4, 5–6, 6 or more).

Following these suggestions should help you produce some reasonably effective rating scales. There are many techniques for producing scales that are much more sophisticated, however, and these are discussed in some of the works listed in the Additional Resources at the end of this chapter.

Space does not allow a complete treatment of the topic of rating-scale development and use. However, several of the questions teachers ask most often about rating scales follow, along with brief answers. Read these carefully, and ask your instructor for more detailed explanations of any that interest you.

Questions teachers often ask about rating scales

Question: What advantage is there to using a rating scale? Isn't it easier to construct a checklist that is effective?

Answer: Whenever you simply need to know whether a characteristic is present or absent, the checklist is a better tool. Checklists simply record quantitative information, however, and are not helpful for judging the quality of a performance or product.

Question: Do I have to have a rating scale in front of me when I evaluate performances? Can't I keep the information that I think is important in my head?

Answer: After you have used a particular rating scale many times, you may be able to evaluate effectively without having the scale in front of you. Even in that situation, however, the scale offers you a convenient way to record the information you have observed. Having an

---

Students can use rating scales ▶

instrument in front of you while you are observing helps you to focus on the important characteristics and greatly reduces observer bias.

Question: How many points should a rating scale have? Is a five-point scale best? Is a three-point scale okay?

Answer: Generally speaking, you will get your most reliable results if you use a five- to seven-point scale. Also, scales with an odd number of points (five or seven) are usually better than those with an even number of points (four or six).

Question: Can students use rating scales to help evaluate each other?

Answer: Definitely. If the scale is well designed and if there are clear instructions for the observer, students can rate each other. Student evaluations can be used quite successfully in the performing arts. Well-designed scales can also be used by students to evaluate their own take-home projects, art projects, and so forth.

Other Rubrics

Although the majority of rubrics being used as assessment tools take the form of a rating scale or a checklist, any clearly defined system (or set of rules) for recording or scoring performances could be considered a rubric. For example, a model answer developed for scoring an essay question is essentially a rubric. So is a set of guidelines for assessing student behavior over time or in different situations. In fact, whenever a teacher wishes to assess typical performance (as compared to maximum performance), a number of situations arise where a rubric would be helpful. For example, a fifth-grade teacher wants a better picture of how well his students behave in school. A rubric could be developed that would specify when to observe his students (for instance, when a new lesson is being introduced) and in what settings (math class, social studies, art class, and so on). It could also clarify exactly what kinds of observations to make (for instance, interactions with other students, attentive behaviors, note taking, disruptive behaviors). Or suppose a middle school science teacher wants to find out how well her students stay on task during lab sessions. She could develop a rubric that lists specific times during the hour (for example, 1:10, 1:19, 1:27, and 1:41) when she would make her observations. The rubric could direct her to focus on well-defined on-task and off-task behaviors. Her rubric might also take the form of a diagram of the room, divided into sections. Certain sections would be marked for observation at certain times. This strategy would help her get a sampling of behavior patterns from different parts of the room and might help her identify trouble spots.

Most rubrics use verbal descriptions to define various levels of performance. However, samples of work representing different levels of performance or degrees of quality can also be used. For example, a rubric for scoring a report on the basis of how well it is organized could be developed using examples of reports arranged in groups representing different levels of organization from poorly organized to exceptionally well organized. A rubric designed for scoring perspective drawings could be made by arranging sample drawings (or photos of sample drawings) in order from those having no perspective to those showing very good perspective. A rubric for assessing the use of gestures in a speech class could be made by producing short video clips representing poorly- to well-executed gestures. These clips could be placed on a CD and viewed on a computer monitor.

It should be obvious that rubrics of this type would be helpful to students for learning what a good performance "looks" like as well as to teachers for assessing performances.

 Mastery Test

OBJECTIVE 4   **To develop rubrics (including checklists and rating scales) for evaluating student products and performances**

1. Select one of the following (or similar) student products and develop a checklist that lists the most important criteria for evaluating that product.
   a. Soap sculpture
   b. Relief map
   c. Pencil sketch
   d. Book report
   e. Model of a village
   f. Educational game
   g. Cursive handwriting
   h. Health poster

2. Use the following format as a guide to develop a rating scale that you might find useful in your own teaching.

   a. Name the performance or social-personal trait to be evaluated.
   b. List the major steps to take, or important characteristics to be considered, in the evaluation.
   c. Select four or five items from the list in item 1 and produce a scale for each item, describing the extremes first and then the midpoints. (You may decide to have more than four or five items in your full scale, but do at least four or five for purposes of this exercise.)

OBJECTIVE 5   **To use portfolios to assess ongoing performance and progress**

Student Portfolios

Learning Activity 10.6

A **portfolio** is a carefully selected collection of a student's work designed to provide the opportunity to make very specific kinds of assessments. The two most common types of portfolios used for assessment purposes are best-work portfolios and growth and learning-progress portfolios.

Best-work portfolios are a collection of a student's best products (such as art projects, math papers, or writing assignments); they provide a sample of student work over time, across media, and for a variety of problem types. *Growth and learning-progress portfolios* are used to collect samples of a student's typical work over time. These portfolios allow one to assess such things as the type and quantity of errors as learning progresses, the type of thinking and problem-solving strategies used by students as they learn, and the ability of students to catch and fix their own mistakes as they progress.

Portfolios: an integral part of teaching ▶

For portfolios to be most effective, they should be an integral part of the classroom activities on an ongoing basis throughout the year. To find out some of the things the Kentucky State Educational System did to bring this about, look at the works found in the Additional Resources at the end of this chapter.

▼ **TeachSource Video Case**   **Portfolio Assessment: Elementary Classroom**

To access the video, go to www.cengage.com/login. Watch this video to see how Fred Park uses portfolios as an integral part of his classroom activities and then answer the following questions:

1. Why does Fred think that portfolios are such a valuable assessment tool in the elementary classroom?
2. Describe ways in which portfolios are a teaching/learning tool and not just an assessment tool.
3. Reflect on the idea that all assessment techniques have the potential to help teachers improve their teaching and learners to improve their learning.
4. What are some of the drawbacks to using portfolio assessment?

Steps for Using Portfolios for Assessment

Using portfolios as an assessment tool requires at least the following six steps.

1. *Decide on the portfolio's purpose.* The key here is to determine why you want to collect a portfolio of student work. Answering the following questions should help: Which learning objectives could be assessed? What could you and your students learn about the progress being made? Would a portfolio help determine areas of misunderstanding? Do you want to evaluate a sample of a student's best work or are you interested in assessing growth or progress? Do you wish to evaluate a process or a product? Is a portfolio the best way to obtain the assessment information you need?

2. *Decide who will determine the portfolio's content.* To collect everything a student does is inefficient and makes a portfolio difficult to interpret. A carefully selected sample of work makes a portfolio manageable and easier to evaluate. Usually the teacher determines which work samples will be placed in the portfolio, but sometimes you may prefer to have the students choose. A great deal can be learned about students' ability to evaluate their own work if you ask them to select the work to be included. In either case, it is helpful to establish the criteria for determining what should be included.

3. *Establish the criteria for determining what to include in the portfolio.* Which learning objectives are to be evaluated, and what work would best represent progress toward, or accomplishment of, those objectives?

   Do you want a student's best work? Do you want early drafts as well as subsequent revisions, or only the final product? Do you want to see materials related to preliminary work, such as references (perhaps including those identified but not used, as well as those used in the work), note cards, outlines, and so forth? Perhaps an audiotape of interviews conducted in preparation for a report would be useful in determining how a student selects information to report.

4. *Determine how the portfolio will be organized and how the entries will be presented.* How should the entries be labeled? Should there be a "container" for all entries and, if so, how will it be labeled? Would a table of contents be helpful? Besides the student's name and the date of completion, what

other information about an entry might be helpful? Would the student's own evaluation of each entry provide useful information? Should the entries be organized chronologically or grouped to represent different learning outcomes or different kinds of problems? If there are several categories of entries, how many entries should be placed in each category? When are entries to be placed in the portfolio? These questions, and others that will be dictated by the type of portfolio being developed, must be addressed *before* students begin the work that will eventually end up in a portfolio.

5. *Determine when and how the portfolio will be evaluated.* Will you be evaluating entries at several points in time as the portfolio takes shape (formative evaluation), or will the evaluation only occur once the entire portfolio is complete (summative evaluation)? Will the teacher or the student evaluate the portfolio, or will the teacher and the student do the evaluation together? Have criteria for evaluating been developed, or has a scoring rubric been designed? Will a single score (or grade) be given, or will a more analytical assessment be made? How much and what kind of feedback will be given to the student? Would written comments be more helpful than a score or grade?

6. *Decide how the evaluations of the portfolio and its contents will be used.* Will the evaluations be used to determine a grade that will be a part of the report card grade? Will the evaluation results be used primarily to assess final achievement, or will they be used to determine progress? Will the findings be used to help students learn from their efforts? Will your teaching strategies change as a result of how effectively and/or efficiently students are learning? What information should be given to the parents that would help them better understand the portfolio and its contents? Will the contents be judged on the basis of established criteria or by comparing a student's work to the work of other students? Will comparisons be made across time, comparing a student's early work with his or her later work? These and similar questions should help you to determine the kind of judgments and decisions that will be made on the basis of the information obtained from portfolio assessment.

Electronic Portfolios

Electronic portfolios (e-portfolios) are gradually gaining in popularity. They offer a number of advantages over the traditional file folders and "scrap books." As computers are becoming more accessible (at home, in the school, and in libraries), it is becoming easier for students and teachers to develop e-portfolios. Most significantly, e-portfolios virtually eliminate storage and retrieval problems. Teachers can put numerous portfolios on a single CD and take them home to evaluate. E-portfolios can be e-mailed between home and school—a great help to the home-bound student. File folders and notebooks get tattered over time and are easily lost (e-portfolios should always be backed up, however!).

There are a number of things to consider when deciding whether to develop portfolios in an electronic format:

1. Availability of computers for students and teachers
2. Availability of appropriate software (word processor that will track changes, software to manipulate and organize photos, and software for creating scrapbooks, posters, and so on)

3. Availability of scanners and/or digital cameras for recording student products and performances

4. The level of skill in the use of technology of both teachers and students (and the availability of training for those not skilled in the use of technology)

5. Whether it is more or less difficult to use e-portfolios versus traditional portfolios

E-portfolios may make the storage, retrieval, sharing, and evaluation of student work easier. However, unless the technology is available to everyone and everyone is well trained to use it, it may be easier to simply file samples of student work in file folders.

Portfolios: a powerful tool ▷ Portfolios can be a very powerful tool if they are fully integrated into the total instructional process and not just a "tag-on" at the end of instruction. Read the works about portfolios listed in the Additional Resources at the end of this chapter, and search the Internet for examples of portfolios and discussions of how they can be used to enhance instruction. Remember, too, that all kinds of materials can be organized into portfolios. Besides the obvious paper-and-pencil entries, one can collect samples of art objects, 3-D models, audiotapes and/or videotapes of performances (music, speeches, interviews), and samples of a student's thinking process (written or recorded). Be creative, but always ask these very important questions: How would samples of students' work help to assess student performance or progress? How would such an assessment help improve my teaching and my students' learning?

 ## Mastery Test

OBJECTIVE 5   **To use portfolios to assess ongoing performance and progress**

1. In your own words, define the term *portfolio*.
2. List three things about student learning that portfolios can be used to assess.
3. Students should not be allowed to evaluate their own portfolios. True or false?
4. It is best to wait until a few samples of work have come in before you decide how to organize a portfolio. True or false?

OBJECTIVE 6

To describe how to use information to evaluate; that is, to grade, to judge student progress, and to judge changes in student attitudes

Learning Activity 10.7

To evaluate is to judge ▷ To evaluate is to judge, to place a value on. When we assign grades, determine that a child is functioning below grade level, evaluate a child's progress, or evaluate a teacher's effectiveness, we are judging. The basic question we will answer in this section of the chapter is: How can one use information that has been obtained (through observation, tests, and so on) to evaluate and to form judgments? Let's take a look at the process of forming **judgments** in general and then examine more carefully several specific kinds of classroom judgments (for example, grading, judging student progress, judging changes in student attitudes, and judging the effectiveness of teaching).

Forming Judgments

To judge is to compare ▶ The process of forming judgments is well known to all of us because we use it many times each day. We judge the value of a car we want to buy, the quality of a restaurant, the value of a television show, the neatness of our classroom, the warmth of our home, the friendliness of our neighbors, and so forth. Each time we make these judgments, we use the same basic process. We compare information we have about what we are judging to some **referent**. For example, we say that a restaurant is bad because the food is not nearly as good as Mom's. We decide that it's cold in the house because the thermometer reads below 65°. We may determine that a car is too expensive because other, similar cars are selling for less, or we may feel that it's too expensive because it's $500 more than we can afford to spend. In each case, we compare information we have to some referent. The following table, which illustrates this process for a variety of judgments, breaks each judgment down into two parts: (1) information used and (2) the referent to which the information is compared.

COMMON JUDGMENTS

Judgment	Information Compared to Referent	
Peter is my best speller.	Peter's spelling test scores	The spelling scores of his classmates
Sally reads above grade level.	Sally's reading achievement score	The average reading score of students at her grade level
This book is the best one I've seen on teaching math.	My perusal of the book	My perusal of other math books
Bobby has an above-average IQ.	Bobby's IQ score	The average IQ test score of students Bobby's age
The class is ready to move to the next unit in the math book.	The math achievement scores	The level of math achievement deemed necessary to do the work in the next unit
George is too tall for the Navy.	George's height	Navy's maximum height limit
Elaine has made a great deal of progress in learning to study in her seat.	The number of times Elaine left her seat today	The number of times Elaine left her seat one day last week

Note that different kinds of referents are used in the examples in the table. We frequently compare information we have with some referent or norm (for example, the food in the restaurant compared to food in most other restaurants we have dined in, or the number of problems George got correct compared to the average number answered correctly by the class as a whole). This kind of judgment is based on a **norm-referenced approach**.

Whenever we want to determine whether the persons or things we are judging meet some minimal criterion or standard, we specify that criterion carefully and use it as our basis for comparison. For example, a car is judged to be too expensive when we compare its price to the amount we can afford to spend. The amount we can afford to spend is our criterion, and the kind of judgment we make using such a standard is called a **criterion-referenced judgment**. Criterion-referenced judgments allow us to judge a student's work independently of how well or how poorly the other students have done. It is an important type of judgment when using a mastery learning approach to classroom teaching.

A third type of judgment that is quite useful is called a **self-referenced judgment**. When making this type of judgment, the individual (or thing) being judged serves as his or her own (self) referent. For example, we judge Sam's performance to be very good. Compared to what he was doing yesterday, today's performance was very good. Whenever we are concerned about student progress, we should make self-referenced judgments. Self-referenced judgments should also be used for diagnosing a student's strengths and weaknesses. To answer the question "How are Sarah's math skills compared to her reading skills?" is to make a self-referenced judgment.

Whenever you need to select a few students from among a larger group, you will need to make norm-referenced judgments. Comparing a student to a norm group such as other classmates is helpful whenever you need to make comparisons among several individuals to judge their relative merit (for example, who is the best math student). To select one student and not another (as in choosing a class leader) requires you to be able to compare those two students on certain characteristics. That requires norm-referenced judgments. These types of judgments should always be used when you need to compare students.

Criterion-referenced judgments, on the other hand, are most helpful when making decisions about the kind of assignment to give a student or the level of achievement at which to begin a student. In other words, whenever a certain specified standard of performance or achievement is necessary before an action can be taken, criterion-referenced judgments are most useful. When making decisions that rely on information about a student's progress or about his or her relative aptitude in different subjects, self-referenced judgments are in order.

❯ YOUR TURN   Types of Judgments

Answer the following questions to see how well you understand the basic process of forming judgments of different types.

1. What is the heart of the process of forming judgments?
   a. Information
   b. Comparisons
   c. People
   d. Statistics

2. To make a judgment is to place a _____ on something.
   a. mark
   b. number
   c. value

For each of the situations in items 3–6, determine the kind of judgment being made. Use the following key: *A*, norm-referenced; *B*, criterion-referenced; *C*, self-referenced.

_____ 3. A third-grade teacher discovers that her class scored above the national average on a math achievement test.

_____ 4. A high school biology teacher selected his best students to help him set up the experiments for the next day.

_____ 5. Misty's teacher was really pleased because of her progress in reading. Her gains since last year are obvious.

_____ 6. Four of the students who took the algebra aptitude test failed to get a high enough score, and they were not allowed to take beginning algebra.

Types of Judgments

Grading

To grade is to judge ▶

Assigning grades has forever been a task teachers dislike. There seems to be no fair way to do it, and any grading system seems subject to all kinds of interpretation problems. (See the articles on grading listed under Additional Resources at the end of this chapter.) The next few paragraphs will not resolve the problems of grading, but they should help you understand better the alternatives available to you.

One of the most common questions teachers get from students concerning grading policy is: Are you going to grade on the curve? Whether grades are fitted to a normal curve or just curved to make a reasonable distribution, the basic idea behind grading on a curve is the same: making norm-referenced judgments, a common form of assigning grades. The class as a whole is used as a norm group, and the class average usually serves as the referent against which all other grades are judged. Usually the average score is assigned a grade of C, and some proportion of scores on either side of that average are also assigned grades of C (the C range usually includes 30 percent to 50 percent of the class). After that, grades are assigned by selecting some cutoff points so that a certain (usually smaller) percentage of students fall into the B and D ranges. Finally, those left fall into the A and F ranges, as their scores deviate above or below C. What do you think are the advantages and disadvantages of this form of grading? List them on a sheet of paper, and then compare your answers later on with the information in the table on page 326. Remember that whenever you grade someone's work by comparing it to someone else's (or to the average of some group), you are using a norm-referenced approach, and all the disadvantages of that type of approach apply.

Another way to assign grades is to establish certain cutoff points for each grade. These cutoff points serve as criteria against which a given student's performance is judged. A common way in which this approach is used is for a teacher to assign points for every assignment and every test. Next, the teacher determines how many total points a student must get to get an A, a B, and so forth. Each assignment or test can be graded that way. The total number of points for the marking period can be added together and compared to cutoff totals in the same way to assign report card grades. This could be called criterion-referenced grading. True criterion-referenced evaluation is a bit more complex, however, than what we have just described because the cutoff scores should be determined on the basis of some meaningful external criterion. What do you think are the advantages and disadvantages of this kind of criterion-referenced grading?

Teachers often find themselves wanting to give a student a high grade for having made so much improvement. Grading on the basis of improvement is a popular kind of self-referenced grading. Comparing a student to himself or herself is a desirable, humane way to grade; however, this kind of grading has many disadvantages. Can you think of some of them? After writing down your ideas, study the table on page 326.

Using an appropriate referent (norm, criterion, or self) is a first, and important, step toward making sure that grades given are appropriate and meaningful. However, there are a number of other very important factors to consider when assigning grades. Concerns over grading practices have brought several of these considerations to the forefront.[2] (See Additional

ADVANTAGES AND DISADVANTAGES OF DIFFERENT TYPES OF GRADING

Type of Grading	Advantages	Disadvantages
Norm-referenced	1. Allows for comparisons among students. 2. Classes can be compared to other classes. 3. Allows teacher to spot students who are dropping behind the class.	1. If the whole class does well, some students still get poor grades. 2. If the class as a whole does poorly, a good grade could be misleading. 3. Does not allow individual progress or individual circumstances to be considered. 4. The whole class (or large portions of it) must be evaluated in the same way. 5. Everyone in the class (or norm group) must be evaluated with the same instrument under the same conditions.
Criterion-referenced	1. Helps teacher decide if students are ready to move on. 2. Criteria are independent of group performance. 3. Works well in a mastery learning setting. 4. Each individual can be evaluated on different material, depending on his or her level of achievement.	1. It is difficult to develop meaningful criteria (therefore arbitrary cutoff scores are often used). 2. Presents unique problems in computing the reliability of criterion-referenced tests. 3. Makes it difficult to make comparisons among students.
Self-referenced	1. Allows you to check student progress. 2. Makes it possible to compare achievement across different subjects for the same individual.	1. All measures taken on an individual must be taken with similar instruments under similar circumstances. 2. Does not help you to compare an individual with his or her peers.

Resources at the end of this chapter for other articles describing various grading practices.)

In the next few paragraphs, several of the common grading practices currently being questioned by parents, educators, and evaluation experts will be discussed. The issues raised here are very important, but solutions to the problems are not always simple. In some cases experts disagree about the best way to handle a given problem. Therefore, this chapter will familiarize you with the problems and indicate which grading practices you should avoid where possible. You should study these problems further on your own, talk further with your instructor about them, or enroll in a test and measurement course that will provide you with some of the measurement and statistics concepts needed to understand the various solutions to these problems.

Inconsistency in the use of grading scales is a problem that plagues virtually every school district in the country and affects education at all levels, kindergarten through graduate school. A student in one class might receive a grade of B for a score of 80 percent, while in another class that 80 percent might merit an A or a C! Grading scales differ from class to class, from school to school, from school district to school district, and may even differ from test to test within the same classroom by the same teacher.

A second, very troubling problem is the practice of averaging grades. Averaging scores can produce inaccurate results because the procedure for obtaining those averages does not consider the difficulty level of the tests or assignments that make up each individual score. This problem can be overcome by converting test scores to standard scores and then averaging the standard scores.

Another problem, not so easily solved, occurs when an extreme score is averaged along with other scores. Suppose, for example, a student has all scores in the A range except one, which he failed (perhaps he was ill, misunderstood a major concept, or studied the wrong material). That one low score could bring his average to a B or a C depending on how many scores were being averaged. Here is a student who probably knows the material as well (and maybe better) than the other students receiving a grade of A. However, because of one test or one assignment, that student receives a much lower grade at report card time.

Assigning zeros for unfinished work or as a disciplinary measure ("You talked out of turn—zero for today!") is another very unfair practice. A zero, when averaged with other grades, is given tremendous weight. A zero, when averaged in with several grades in the A range, could easily drop the average to a D or F range. In such a case, a student whose tested knowledge is at the A level is given a failing, or close to failing, grade because he missed a test or was being disciplined (in most cases for a behavior that had nothing to do with academic ability).

Pop quizzes, testing obscure facts, and other strategies for catching students off guard are other practices that produce grades that reflect something other than academic achievement. Furthermore, these kinds of testing practices usually produce short, unreliable, and invalid measures. Although teachers rarely pay any attention to the reliability or validity of their tests, the impact of measurement error on final grades must be accounted for. A teacher may carefully add up and average a large number of scores, only to end up with an inaccurate grade because of the inaccuracies in the individual scores being averaged. The author has personally analyzed hundreds of teacher-made tests of such low reliability (and, consequently, such high measurement error) that the distribution of grades would have been just as accurate had they been assigned randomly!

Be aware of measurement error ▶ **Measurement error** should be clearly understood by every classroom teacher and every school administrator. Unfortunately, courses teaching these concepts are not always a mandatory part of the teacher preparation curriculum. The tests and measurement and assessment books listed under Additional Resources at the end of the chapter discuss the concept of measurement error. You are encouraged to read those discussions carefully.

One final grading practice that you need to avoid is the practice of averaging every piece of a student's work into the final grade. Students are given assignments so that they can learn new knowledge or gain a new skill. These assignments frequently represent practice exercises. They offer the students an opportunity to try out a skill, to make some errors, and then, with appropriate feedback from the teacher, learn from those errors. Is it really fair to average those grades in with tests given *after* the students have had sufficient time and practice to reach a reasonable level of proficiency?

When the author taught writing skills to junior and senior high school students, he encouraged them to experiment with different sentence structures, different styles of prose, and so forth. Early attempts were often a disaster, but soon students would learn from their mistakes and become very good at using their new skills in subsequent writing assignments. Surely any risk-taking behavior and any exploring of new ideas would have been penalized had those early attempts been graded and the scores averaged in with those of their later, well-written essays.

Strive to be fair ▶ Assigning grades is more complex than we would like it to be. However, it is important that we do everything we can to make the process fair and the results as meaningful as possible.

Judging Student Progress

Teachers have an ongoing concern about the amount of progress their students are making. If students are making a reasonable amount of progress, the methods, materials, and so forth are probably working. If no progress or too little progress is being made, some changes may need to be made somewhere in the instructional program.

A judgment of student progress is, of course, a self-referenced judgment, and thus all the disadvantages of that type of judgment will hold. It is especially important that progress in achievement be measured the same way each time progress is checked. Suppose that you were trying to check a student's progress in reading. It would be best if you could use the same type of test each time progress was checked (alternate forms of the same standardized tests, observations of oral reading, using the same type of checklist or rating scale, and so forth).

The following suggestions should help you assess student progress. Study them carefully, and then discuss with your classmates ways in which these suggestions could be carried out at various grade levels for different subjects.

Suggestions for assessing student progress.

1. Determine ahead of time what student characteristics or skills you are going to track. (Don't suddenly ask, halfway through the semester, "Has any progress been made?")

2. Establish a baseline (achievement level, behavior patterns, and so on) early in the semester.

3. Choose and/or develop instruments (such as tests and rubrics) in advance that you can use throughout a student's progress (portfolios are particularly helpful here).

4. Describe the changes you expect will occur as your students progress. This description will help you focus your assessment on appropriate behaviors and achievements.

5. Obtain information often enough so that you can see any progression that might be occurring and so that a single bad sample of information won't throw your evaluation off.

Assessing Changes in Attitude

Most psychologists would define *attitude* as a predisposition to act in a negative or positive way toward some object or person. Note that the attitude is a *predisposition*, which is not observable or measurable; however, it is a predisposition to *act*, and that is observable. This means that to measure attitudes, one must focus on the actions or behaviors of students. Of course, the difficult part is discerning what any given action or pattern of actions means (which attitude is producing the actions).

Focus on behavior ▶ Usually a teacher becomes concerned about attitude change when he or she discovers that one or more students have a bad attitude. Common among these are negative attitudes toward a given subject, a negative attitude toward the teacher, or feelings of prejudice toward minority students or special students in the class. The important thing to remember when you first become aware of a negative attitude is that there must have been some behaviors that led you to discover that attitude. The student(s) must have said something (speech is an observable behavior), done something, or refused to do something that made you aware of the attitude. Your first step, therefore, is to try to determine what specific behaviors led you to believe that there was an attitude that needed changing.

Once you have determined what behaviors associated with an attitude you think should change, your next step is systematically to obtain information about the frequency of occurrence of those behaviors. These data will serve as the baseline (the referent) against which you will judge any future changes in attitude.

Establish a baseline ▷ When you are sure that the behaviors you observed are frequent and do indeed represent an inappropriate attitude, you are ready to set down a plan for observing any possible changes in attitude (as they would be reflected in changes in behaviors). There are two important things to consider at this point. First, be certain that you make frequent observations so that you can feel confident that the behavior you are observing is representative, not isolated. Second, look for the behaviors when the student is in the presence of or thinking about the object of his or her inappropriate attitude (for example, look for disruptive behaviors during math if the student dislikes math).

Finally, when the information is obtained, you must judge whether or not the attitude has changed. Remember the disadvantage of making self-referenced judgments: Differences between any two sets of observations may not mean too much. If you find over a period of time (and attitudes usually take considerable time to change) that the undesirable behaviors are decreasing and the desirable ones increasing, an attitude change is probably occurring.

Watch for changes ▷ You can use a rating scale to help you summarize the data from your observations. Suppose that you were trying to see if a student's attitude toward math was improving. You might develop a rating scale that would look something like this.

Hates math 1	2	*Tolerates math* 3	4	*Loves math* 5
Complains about math, puts off doing assignments, turns in sloppy math papers		Says, "Don't care about math grade"; does assignment but delays some; never chooses math over other subjects		Says, "I like math"; gets right at assignments; does extra-credit work; chooses math over other subjects

Note that the behaviors characteristic of different attitudes have been placed under the two endpoints and the midpoint of the scale. Each time we observed our student react to math, we could determine which set of behaviors his or her actions were most like and mark an X on the scale accordingly. Several scales each marked in turn over a semester would give us a picture of any progress the student was making.

The basic steps ▷ In summary, the basic steps involved in assessing a student's change in attitude are the following:

1. Determine the behaviors associated with the attitude you think should change.

2. Systematically obtain information about the frequency of occurrence of these behaviors.

3. Decide if the behaviors occur frequently enough and consistently enough to represent an inappropriate attitude.

4. Set down a plan for observing any possible changes in attitude over time.

5. Decide whether the attitude has changed by comparing the information obtained at two or more different times.

6. Record your findings, possibly using a rating scale or other rubric.

Assessing Instructional Effectiveness

☐ INTASC Principle 9

Most teachers have a genuine desire to know whether or not their instruction is effective. They also fear that they, or their principal, will find out that it is not effective. Principals, fellow teachers, students, and parents are all going to judge the quality of instruction. Therefore, it is advantageous for the teacher to have well-documented evidence of his or her teaching effectiveness.

Besides accountability, of course, teachers are concerned about improvement. They always want information to help them upgrade their courses. So let's explore briefly some of the options available to teachers who wish to evaluate their own teaching. The information provided here will help you start thinking about assessing instruction, but it in no way pretends to make you an excellent evaluator. Several books on program evaluation are cited in the Additional Resources at the end of this chapter. Later, you may have an opportunity to enroll in a program-evaluation course. In the meantime, here are a few basic suggestions.

There are two primary considerations in assessing your own instruction. First, you must determine the kind of information you will obtain about the effectiveness of your instruction. Second, you must determine an appropriate referent for judging the effectiveness of your instruction.

There are at least three kinds of information that can be used to determine the effectiveness of your instruction. The first is information about your own behaviors as a teacher. If you feel, for example, that effective instruction occurs when teachers do certain things (for example, provide behavioral objectives for their students, interact a great deal with their students, or ask certain types of questions during instruction), obtaining

▼ **TeachSource Video Case** — **Assessment in the Middle Grades: Measurement of Student Learning**

To access the video, go to www.cengage.com/login. Watch this video to see how Martin Somers, a middle school math teacher, assesses his students' mastery of a unit of instruction. Note, too, that he also uses assessment to evaluate his own teaching effectiveness. As you watch consider the following questions:

1. If Martin's assessment strategies show that his students have not done well, how does he then go on to assess his teaching?
2. What do you think of the idea that the students should be taught to keep track of their own progress?
3. What are some ways that students can provide meaningful information about their teacher's effectiveness?

information about whether or not you do these things is a place to begin in the assessment of your teaching. Many teacher-effectiveness rating scales do focus on such teacher behaviors. Although this kind of information can be helpful to you as you check your own progress as a teacher, it may be misleading about the *effectiveness* of instruction. A teacher's doing certain things doesn't necessarily ensure either effective teaching or improved learning.

A more popular (and slightly better measure) of teaching effectiveness comes from student ratings of teacher effectiveness. There are a number of fairly well-developed instruments that allow students to evaluate their teachers. If you decide to design one of your own, focus on those characteristics of effective teachers that seem to make a difference. Even open-ended questions ("What did you like best about this class?" or "What could be done to make this class more effective?") can sometimes give the teacher useful information.

Assess the components of instruction ▶

Of course, the ultimate test of teaching effectiveness is how well the students learn. There are several problems, however, with using learner achievement as a measure of teaching effectiveness. First, students may learn well despite the teacher. Second, it is difficult to know what would have happened had a teacher used a different approach. Even though the students learned well, could they have learned better? Suppose that a class does poorly. Were there extenuating circumstances? Were the textbooks poorly written? Would the students have done that poorly had another teacher taught the lesson? These last questions are not easy to answer, but they do suggest an important solution to the many problems of assessing instructional effectiveness. That solution is to assess the various *components* of the instructional process separately, rather than trying to obtain an overall measure. Suppose, for example, that we were developing a rating scale for students to assess the instruction in a high school English class. Instead of focusing all our questions on the teacher, we would also ask questions about some of the other components of instruction in that classroom. We might ask the students for their opinions about the textbook, workbook, library assignments, small-group discussions, tests, and so forth.

A second major consideration when assessing instruction is the choice of an appropriate referent. You must decide to what you are going to compare your teaching. Will you compare it to that of other teachers (for example, by comparing your students' standardized achievement scores to the scores of other classes in your school district)? Will you judge your teaching effectiveness by some predetermined criterion (such as "At least 80 percent of my students should score at or above grade level on the Iowa Test of Basic Skills")? Will you use a self-referenced approach (such as comparing the student ratings from this semester with those of the previous two semesters)? All three types of referents are legitimate. You simply need to decide which would be most useful in improving your teaching. A discussion of this issue with your peers may help to clarify your own thinking.

Learning Activity 10.8

1. Take a poll among your peers, and ask them to list all the things they dislike about the way they have been graded throughout their educational careers. Find out what they think would be the most equitable way to grade. Share these findings with your classmates, and discuss the implications for your own teaching.

2. Ask as many parents as you can what kind of information they would like to have about their children's progress in school. Get them to be as specific as possible.

3. Once you have written effective test questions, you still need to put some of them together in a test format. Ask a teacher you know to tell you some of the important things to consider when putting a test together (for example, make sure the copy machine produces clear copy).

✳ Mastery Test

OBJECTIVE 6 **To describe how to use information to evaluate; that is, to grade, to judge student progress, and to judge changes in student attitudes**

1. What is the major advantage of grading on a curve?

   a. Allows comparisons among students

   b. Produces more accurate judgments

   c. Allows for differences in individuals

For items 2–5, determine the kind of grading that is involved. Use the following key: *A*, norm-referenced; *B*, criterion-referenced; *C*, self-referenced.

2. A teacher gives George a D because his scores were far below the class average.

3. A high school biology teacher promises an A to anyone scoring above 90 percent on the test.

4. Ms. Kelly tells Maria's parents that she reads well above grade level, as judged by her scores on a standardized test.

5. "I think your language arts grade will soon be up to the same high level as your math grade."

6. What is the biggest problem in judging student progress?

   a. Deciding when to measure progress

   b. Getting similar measurements from one time to the next

7. What type of judgment is being made when a teacher evaluates a student's progress?

   a. Norm-referenced

   b. Criterion-referenced

   c. Self-referenced

8. What is being measured or observed in the evaluation of attitude changes?

   a. Feelings

   b. Ideas

   c. Predispositions

   d. Behaviors

OBJECTIVE 7 **To describe how to use assessment data to help students learn more effectively**

▢ Assessment and Standards

Learning Activity 10.9   Two very important movements in education are having a major impact on how we assess our students and how we *use* our assessment results. The first is the emphasis on state and national standards and the accompanying accountability. The second is the movement toward ever-increasing reliance on authentic assessment techniques. These two movements have made us much more aware of the need to use assessment strategies to help us do a better job of teaching and to help our students do a better job of learning.

Authentic assessment procedures such as portfolios, rubrics, and checklists are especially helpful when trying to determine what students are doing *as they are involved in the learning process*. For example, to find out what students are doing as they learn to write a position paper, one might have them contribute the various drafts of the paper to a portfolio (beginning with a list of potential topics from which the final topic was chosen and continuing with an outline, a list of arguments and supporting evidence to be used, a list of resources used, the initial draft, subsequent drafts showing changes made, and ending with the final draft).

Note, too, that many of the local, state, and national standards call for goals that emphasize the process, not just the final product of learning. For example, Mid-continent Research for Education and Learning lists the following as one of its standards for mathematics: "Uses a variety of strategies in the problem solving process."[3]

Product or Process?

Assess during learning ▷

Historically, classroom evaluation has focused on assessing the products of learning. So we test to see what information has been retained, we check student work for right or wrong answers, and we carefully plan for unit exams and final exams. These final product evaluations can tell us a great deal about how well our students have learned and how successful our teaching has been. However, if we can learn to assess our students *while* they are learning as well as *after* they have learned, we will be able to adjust our teaching and help the students to make changes in the way they are processing information. We can catch misconceptions earlier, move ahead more quickly when appropriate, and suggest more effective learning strategies to students who are struggling. Observation of students engaged in the learning process becomes an especially helpful tool in this regard. Also, asking students to keep a portfolio of their work as it develops can be very revealing. A great deal can be learned, for example, by having students keep each draft of a given writing assignment in a portfolio. The portfolio could contain a list of all the topics they considered writing about, the outline (or outlines) they developed prior to writing, the references they looked up (including those they chose not to use), and their first through their final drafts.

To help students learn more effectively, then, you need to determine what they do (and how they think) as they strive to learn. Often, the strategies of effective learners can be discovered through this process, and those strategies can then be taught to the learners who were less effective.

Involving Parents in Assessment

☐ INTASC Principles
1, 7, 4

Although teachers can do a great deal to help students become better learners, there is no substitute for parental involvement in that process. However, parents seem to be less and less involved in what goes on in the school. Parent-teacher conferences seem to be poorly attended and frequently ineffective. Today's busy families make it difficult for such conferences to work. Consequently, teachers need to use a variety of ways to communicate with parents. Notes sent home (or mailed to the home), weekly newsletters, e-mails, phone calls, and impromptu visits at school events can all be used to stay in touch with parents.

More important than how you communicate is why you communicate and what you communicate. Your primary reason for communicating with parents is to get them involved in their children's education. Do you want the parents to help their children and be supportive of you and the school? If so, your goal should not simply be to complain about the student and tell

▼ TeachSource Video Case — Home-School Communication: The Parent-Teacher Conference

To access the video, go to www.cengage.com/login. Watch as Jim St. Clair puts a parent at ease and then effectively communicates with that parent, informing her of her child's progress while at the same time gaining valuable insights about the child from the parent. Having watched the entire video, answer the following questions:

1. How do you feel about Jim's positive approach and relaxed demeanor during the parent-teacher conference? Does this approach allow Jim to be honest and complete in sharing his assessment of this student?
2. How does Jim use this parent-teacher conference to obtain additional assessment data about the child being discussed?
3. Can you identify several different assessment strategies that Jim uses? How does he share his findings with the parent?

how "bad" he or she is. When you communicate with parents, you should show genuine interest in them and their child. You should show them respect, listen well, and convey your thoughts clearly. Tell parents what your goals are for their child, how you plan to help the child reach those goals, what the child is expected to do to reach those goals, what progress has been made to date, and how the parents can help. Listen carefully to the parents' perspective; they likely know their child better than you do. Don't put them on the defensive with accusations and only negative comments.

✳ Mastery Test

OBJECTIVE 7 To describe how to use assessment data to help students learn more effectively

1. Why is it important to assess students while they are learning, not just at the completion of learning?
2. What do you need to find out about students as they learn?

OBJECTIVE 8 To select and use standardized instruments

☐ What Are Standardized Tests?

Learning Activity 10.10

Standardized tests are helpful when you need highly reliable information to make a wide variety of educational decisions. Although standardized instruments are usually commercially prepared, their most important characteristic is their standardization. A standardized test has a standard set of procedures that must be followed each time the test is used. There is a fixed set of questions that must be administered according to a carefully specified set of directions, within certain time limitations. Standardized tests have usually been administered to a norm group, and the performance of that group is summarized in a manual so that you can compare the performance of your group to that of the norms. There are three major types of standardized instruments.

1. Aptitude tests
2. Achievement tests
3. Interest, personality, and attitude inventories

Aptitude tests attempt to predict how well someone might do in an area of human endeavor: intelligence tests measure general academic ability, creativity tests measure the ability to be creative, and so forth. Besides these general aptitude measures, there are numerous academic subject aptitude tests that measure ability to learn those subjects (math aptitude, writing aptitude, and so forth).

Achievement tests measure how well an individual has achieved in some specific area. There are general achievement tests with subtests covering several different subjects (for example, the Iowa Tests of Basic Skills) and those that measure achievement more in-depth in a given subject (for example, Gates-MacGinitie Reading Tests). Most achievement tests are graded by grade levels, and scores are often reported as grade equivalency scores.

Interest, personality, and attitude inventories are not technically tests because there is usually no single right answer to any given question. These instruments seek to measure typical rather than maximum performance. Inventories that measure interest, study habits, learning style, and attitudes toward academic pursuits are very helpful to school counselors and teachers.

◻ Selecting Standardized Tests

Selecting standardized tests can be a daunting task but you can make the task much more manageable if you ask the following four questions about each test you are considering.

Key Questions

There are four major considerations when selecting a standardized test:

1. Will it give me the information I need?
2. Will the information be reasonably reliable?
3. Is the test easy to administer, score, and interpret?
4. Is the cost within our budget?

Consider validity ▶ **Will it give me the information I need?** To ask this question is to ask if the test is valid for your purpose(s). The **validity** of a test is an estimate of how well it measures what it is supposed to measure. Obviously, if a test is not valid—if it does not provide you with the information you need—then look for another test.

There are many ways to determine the validity of a test. Perhaps the most important of these is **content validity**, which is simply a judgment about how well the items in a test measure what the test has been designed to measure. If you obtain a specimen set of a test you are considering, you can examine the items and compare what they measure with your perception of what you want to measure. If you are examining an achievement test, for example, you could compare the test items to your classroom objectives. By comparing several achievement tests, you could select the one that most closely measures the learning outcomes specified by those objectives.

Predictive validity is an estimate of how well a test predicts scores on some future test or performance. **Concurrent validity** estimates how well a test approximates a score on another test that was designed to measure the same variables. Both tests are given at the same time and their scores are correlated. Predictive validity estimates are generally lower than concurrent validity estimates, so always compare the same kind of validity estimates.

The manuals that accompany a standardized test will usually also provide validity estimates in the form of coefficients of validity. These coefficients will be reported as a number from 0 to 1 (1 being the highest). By comparing tests measuring the same thing, you can get a feel for what size number might represent a reasonable validity coefficient for that type of test. It is important, however, that you compare tests on the same type of validity.

Consider reliability ▶ ***Will the information be reasonably reliable?*** A test is reliable when it measures consistently. **Reliability** is computed several different ways, and the resulting coefficients, like validity coefficients, will be numbers ranging from 0 to 1. Reliability coefficients are generally higher than validity coefficients. Perhaps the most useful reliability estimates are *internal consistency measures*—they estimate how consistently the test measures from item to item. These are usually reported using one or more Kuder Richardson formulas: KR20, KR21. *Test–retest reliability* estimates how consistently a test measures from one time to the next. *Alternate form reliability* is an estimate of how closely two forms of the same test measure the same thing. Always compare tests by comparing similar reliability coefficients.

Is the test easy to administer, score, and interpret? These factors are not as easy to assess when selecting a test, but there are a number of things you should look for. Are the directions for administering the test easy to follow? Are the examples used appropriate, and would they make sense to your students? Are the guidelines for timing clear? Is there an adequate explanation of how to handle student questions? Are the answer sheets easy to use? Is hand scoring a reasonable option? Is machine scoring available, and if so, how much does it cost? What other information (summary statistics, local norms data, response patterns, score interpretation) would be available through the scoring service? Are there adequate charts and/or explanations to help you interpret the data? The answers to these questions can be found by examining specimen sets, or by reading critiques of the test published in journals or in the *Mental Measurements Yearbooks*.

Is the cost within our budget? When determining the cost of a test, make certain you consider the cost of each of the following: test booklets, manuals, answer sheets, scoring services, training time (for teachers who will administer the test, if such training seems necessary), report forms (for reporting results to parents), and cost/time involved in interpreting the results.

Sources of Information About Tests

There are valuable sources of information that can help you answer your questions about selecting a standardized test. Read the following descriptions carefully so you will know where to turn for the information you need.

Mental Measurements Yearbooks. There is probably no better single source of information about specific standardized tests than the *Mental Measurements Yearbooks.*[4] Besides basic descriptive information (author, publication date, forms available, types of scores reported, administration time, prices, scoring services available, and so forth), these yearbooks provide critical reviews by measurement experts. A bibliography of journal articles that review a given test is also included.

Tests in Print. *Tests in Print*[5] summarizes information that has appeared in previous *Mental Measurements Yearbooks.* It allows one to make a quick check of pertinent information when narrowing down choices among several tests. A more detailed analysis can be done using the *Mental Measurements Yearbooks.*

Professional Journals. There are numerous journals that contain reviews of tests. To locate those articles not referenced in the *Mental Measurements Yearbooks*, refer to references such as *Psychological Abstracts* or *Education Index.*

Specimen Sets. There is no substitute for a careful examination of the tests themselves. Read the administration and technical manual, try taking the test, get a feel for its ease of use, look at the answer sheets, and so forth. You can order specimen sets from most test publishers at a nominal cost, or you can often find them at the testing center or library on a college or university campus.

Using Standardized Tests

Administration

Follow the directions ▶

The most important thing to remember when administering a standardized test is that the scores will be difficult, if not impossible, to interpret unless the directions for administering the test are followed exactly. Read those directions carefully ahead of time. For most standardized tests, timing is critical. Be certain that you time the test carefully and that there is a way to hand out and collect the tests so that all students have the same amount of time. For example, ask students to leave their booklets closed until you say open them, and then to close them when you call time and leave them closed on their desk until you pick them up.

Students will have questions during the explanation of the directions and during the test. Handle these questions carefully. Each student must understand the directions, and clarification should be made. If there seems to be ambiguity in the questions themselves, or students don't seem to understand what is being asked, you should help them understand what is being asked of them, but you should do nothing that would give away the answer.

Questions can often be minimized if students are prepared in advance for the test. Respond honestly to their questions about how the test is to be used. Reassure them that standardized tests are designed so that almost no one gets all the answers correct. Tell them to do their best, but not to worry if there are some questions they cannot answer.

Scoring

Most standardized tests are objective and are not too difficult to score manually. A scoring template is usually provided. There are several advantages, however, to using the publisher's scoring service when it is available. The scoring will be accurate. You will often get charts and graphs showing the distribution of the scores for your class. Summary statistics are usually made available, and you can ask for summary data for several classes within your school (or school district). Finally, some services will help you develop local norms.

✳ Mastery Test

OBJECTIVE 8   **To select and use standardized instruments**

1. What is the most important characteristic of standardized tests?

2. Write down, in your own words, the four questions you need to answer when trying to select a standardized test.

3. Which statistical estimate would be important if you were trying to determine if a test measures what it says it does?

   a. Reliability   c. Usability

   b. Validity   d. None of the above

4. Which one of the following sources will give you the most information about a specific standardized test?

   a. *Mental Measurements Yearbooks*

   b. *Tests in Print*

5. What is the most important thing to remember about administering a standardized test?

6. Briefly explain how a teacher should handle questions that students ask about a standardized test they are taking.

◾ OBJECTIVE 9   **To describe the role of technology in classroom assessment**

◼ The Role of Technology

Learning Activity 10.11

☐ INTASC Principle 9

Technology is getting faster, cheaper, more sophisticated, and more readily available. Most students and teachers have access to computers, scanners, printers, and the overwhelming amount of information (good and bad) available on the Internet. Computerized testing is becoming more commonplace, but it is only one way technology can be used to assess student knowledge and performance. The role of technology is to help make our assessment activities easier, more secure, and often faster (because we can gather, store, and analyze information more efficiently). Students can develop e-portfolios, complete assignments using a wide variety of educational web sites, post their work to a web site on the school's local area network, and use digital cameras and videos to complete assignments or record performances. A big advantage of computerized testing is that visual and/or auditory information can be presented to which the student can respond (identify, answer a question about, analyze, critique). Internet access also brings to students lots of opportunities to plagiarize, and that kind of cheating has become quite widespread. Teachers can combat this problem by submitting student work to an Internet-based program that will scan the work and determine how much, if any, of the work has been plagiarized. To learn more about this program go to http://www.turnitin.com.

Technology-aided assessment strategies should only be utilized after carefully considering the following:

1. Is there a simpler, easier way to assess students?
2. What are the costs involved (in time and money)?
3. What are the privacy/security risks involved?
4. Will lack of understanding of the technology contribute to measurement error?

When and if you choose to use technology to aid you in your assessment strategies, remember that using high-tech methods does not make up for poorly constructed assessment instruments or strategies. Always adhere to good, sound evaluation principles and in everything you do, strive to be clear, concise, and consistent.

✳ Mastery Test

OBJECTIVE 9   **To describe the role of technology in classroom assessment**

1. Describe, in your own words, why you might choose to use technology to help you assess student progress.

2. List at least three things that need to be considered when deciding whether or not to use technology to help you assess your students.

ADDITIONAL RESOURCES

Readings

Airasian, Peter W., and Mark Russell. *Classroom Assessment: Concepts and Applications,* 6th ed. New York: McGraw-Hill Higher Education, 2008.

Atkin, Myron J., Paul Black, and Janet Coffey, eds. *Classroom Assessment and the National Science Education Standards: A Guide for Teaching and Learning.* Washington, D.C.: National Academy Press, 2001.

Atkin, M. J., J. E. Coffey, S. Moorthy, M. Thiveault, and M. Sato. *Designing Everyday Assessment in the Science Classroom.* New York: Teachers College Press, 2005.

Barton, James, and Angelo Colins, eds. *Portfolio Assessment.* West Plains, N.Y.: Dale Seymour Publications, 1997.

Cohen, Ronald J., and Mark E. Swerdlik. *Psychological Testing and Assessment,* 7th ed. New York: McGraw-Hill, 2009.

Evans, E. D., and R. A. Engelbert. (1988). "Student Perceptions of School Grading." *Journal of Research and Development in Education* 21 (Winter): 45–54.

Gipps, Caroline V. *Beyond Testing.* Philadelphia, Pa.: Taylor and Francis, 2007.

Gribbin, A. (1992). "Making Exceptions When Grading and the Perils It Poses." *Journalism Educator* 46 (Winter): 73–76.

Gronlund, N. E., and C. Keith Waugh. *Assessment of Student Achievement,* 9th ed. Boston: Allyn and Bacon, 2009.

Kentucky Department of Education. *Portfolios and You.* Frankfort, Ky.: Office of Assessment and Accountability, 1993.

Kentucky Department of Education. *Teacher's Guide: Kentucky Mathematics Portfolio.* Frankfort, Ky.: Office of Assessment and Accountability, 1993.

Koretz, D., et al. (1994). "The Vermont Portfolio Assessment Program: Findings and Implications." *Educational Measurement: Issues and Practice* 13, no. 3: 5–16.

Kuhs, Therese, ed. *Put to the Test: Tools and Techniques for Classroom Assessment*. Westport, Conn.: Heinemann, 2001.

Lyman, H. B. *Test Scores and What They Mean*, 6th ed. New York: Allyn & Bacon, 1998.

McMillan, James H. *Classroom Assessment: Principles and Practice for Effective Standard-based Instruction*, 4th ed. New York: Allyn & Bacon, 2006.

Mehrens, W. A., and Irvin J. Lehmann. *Measurement and Evaluation in Education and Psychology*, 4th ed. Belmont, Calif.: Wadsworth, 1991.

Miller, David, Robert L. Linn, and Norman E. Gronlund. *Measurement and Assessment in Teaching*, 10th ed. Upper Saddle River, N.J.: Prentice-Hall, 2008.

Nitko, Anthony J. *Educational Assessment of Students*, 5th ed. Upper Saddle River, N.J.: Prentice-Hall, 2006.

Paulson, F. L., P. R. Paulson, and C. A. Meyer. (1991). "What Makes a Portfolio a Portfolio?" *Educational Leadership* 49, no. 5: 60–63.

Payne, David Allen. *Applied Educational Assessment*, 2nd ed. Belmont, Calif.: Wadsworth, 2002.

Popham, W. James. *Classroom Assessment: What Teachers Need to Know*, 5th ed. New York: Allyn & Bacon, 2007.

Salvia, John, James E. Ysseldyke, and Sara Bolt. *Assessment: In Special and Inclusive Education*, 10th ed. Boston: Cengage Learning, 2010.

Sunstein, Bonnie S., and Jonathan H. Lovell, eds. *The Portfolio Standard: How Students Can Show Us What They Know and Are Able to Do*. Portsmouth, N.H.: Heinemann, 2000.

Tanner, David Earl. *Assessing Academic Achievement*. New York: Allyn & Bacon, 2001.

Zubizarreta, J. *The Learning Portfolio: Reflective Practice for Improving Student Learning*, 2nd ed. San Francisco, Calif.: Jossey-Bass, 2009.

Websites

Buros Institute of Mental Measurements: http://www.unl.edu/buros
This site provides professional assistance and information to users of commercially published tests.

Buros Institute: Standards for Teacher Competence in Educational Assessment of Students: http://unl.edu/buros/bimm/hrtml/article3.html
This site contains information regarding the approach used to develop standards, the scope of a teacher's professional role and responsibilities for student assessment, and standards for teacher competence in the educational assessment of students.

Central New York Regional Information Center: http://www.nysed.gov
Go to this site and search on "authentic assessment" for interesting articles discussing the value of authentic assessment procedures.

Access ERIC: http://www.eric.ed.gov
Access ERIC, the promotional and outreach arm of the U.S. Department of Education's Educational Resources Information Center (ERIC) system, keeps you informed of the wealth of information offered by the ERIC components and other education-related organizations. This site is a beginning point for access to all of the ERIC web sites and can help you in your search for the latest information on all aspects of education, including sources of information on assessment and evaluation issues.

The National Center for Research on Evaluation Standards and Student Testing: http://www.cse.ucla.edu
This site contains numerous articles and reports that discuss current assessment and evaluation issues. It also references past conference proceedings of the National Center for Research on Evaluation Standards and Student Testing.

Yahoo!'s Directory of K–12 Lesson Plans: http://dir.yahoo.com/Education/Standards_and_Testing
This site contains a large variety of resources for testing, assessment, measurement, and benchmarking.

For these links and additional resources, please visit the Premium Website at **www.cengage.com/login.**

NOTES

1. For more details, see T. D. TenBrink, *Evaluation: A Practical Guide for Teachers* (New York: McGraw-Hill, 1974).

2. Canady, R. L., and P. R. Hotchkiss, "It's a Good Score: It's Just a Bad Grade," *Phi Delta Kappan* (September 1989): 68–71.

3. Go to their web site (http://www.mcrel.org/standards-benchmarks/) for a comprehensive listing of standards in multiple subjects for grades K–12.

4. Geisinger, K. F., R. M. Spies, J. F. Carlson, and B. S. Plake, eds., *The Seventeenth Mental Measurements Yearbook* (Lincoln: University of Nebraska Press, Buros Institute of Mental Measurements, 2007).

5. Murphy, L. L., R. A. Spies, and B. S. Plake, eds., *Tests in Print VII* (Lincoln: University of Nebraska Press, Buros, 2006).

Answer Keys

Chapter 1
MASTERY TEST

Mastery Test, Objective 1

1. Answers will vary, but could include such characteristics as:
   - *knowledge of subject matter*
   - *repertoire of teaching skills* (including planning, questioning and discussion techniques, use of technology, differentiating instruction, etc.)
   - *attitudes that foster learning and positive human interaction*
   - *command of theoretical knowledge about learning and human behavior*
   - *personal practical knowledge*
   - *knowledge of students' interests and cultural heritage*
   - *knowledge of students' varied approaches to learning*
   - *management of classroom procedures and student behavior*
   - *habit of reflecting on teaching*
   - *working well with colleagues*

Mastery Test, Objective 2

2. Reflective decision making is critical to effective teaching because it is only through the process of reflection on one's teaching that one can grow, learn as a professional, and improve his or her teaching. By reflecting on their practice, teachers learn to question the assumptions that undergird their actions. Through reflection on their actions, teachers can bring to the surface some of these assumptions that often go unrecognized and, in doing so, can criticize, examine, and improve these tacit understandings. The process of reflection enables teachers to understand better their values and beliefs.

Mastery Test, Objective 3

3. Some techniques or processes that teachers can use to promote reflective teaching include:
   - keeping a journal to record thoughts and reactions to each day's events.
   - video record teaching lessons, which can then be examined to capture the events of the lesson and to reveal patterns of behavior.
   - create teaching portfolios to provide a record of growth and development for both teachers and students.
   - work with fellow teachers to observe and critique one another's teaching.

Mastery Test, Objective 4

4. The reflective decision-making model consists of the following parts: *planning, implementation, evaluation, feedback,* and *reflection.* The teacher makes *planning decisions* taking into consideration such factors as content standards, students' needs, time allotted, and instructional strategies and methods to attain goals and objectives. The teacher then *implements* the lesson and or unit of instruction, making interactive decisions as the lesson unfolds, based on student questions or responses to questions. The teacher decides to move on or repeat instruction based on whether the students seems to be learning the objectives of the lesson. The *evaluation* function requires decisions about the suitability of chosen objectives as well as the teaching strategies keyed to those objectives and, ultimately, whether or not the students are achieving what the teacher intended.

The **feedback and reflection** dimension of the decision-making model simply means that you examine the results of your teaching, consider their meaning, and then decide how adequately you handled each of these three teaching functions. On the basis of this examination, you determine whether you have succeeded in attaining your objectives or whether you need to make new plans or try different implementation strategies. Feedback and your reflection on the feedback, then, is the new information you process into your decision making to adjust your planning, implementation, or evaluation functions—or to continue as before. It is the decision-making system's way of correcting itself.

5. Many factors influence the teacher's decision-making process, including:
   - cultural, racial, and ethnic background of the students
   - gender
   - socio-economic status of the students
   - needs for belonging, safety, and self-esteem
   - differing abilities and motivation levels
   - teacher's personal practical knowledge and knowledge of self

Teachers need to take these and other factors into consideration when making instructional decisions. The diversity of these factors presents a challenge to teachers to differentiate instruction to meet student needs.

Examples of each factor and how a teacher's decision making might be affected will vary according to choice, grade level, and subject matter.

Chapter 2
YOUR TURN EXERCISES

Your Turn: Recognizing Student-Oriented Objectives

1. *S.* A desirable learning outcome.

2. *T.* The IEP will help the teacher decide what student objectives to present later in the year.

3. *T.* Probably helpful to students, but not an expected student outcome.

4. *S.* A student who can do this has learned well.

5. *T.* How would a teacher do this?

6. *T.* Lecturing is important only if it helps the students reach a desirable learning outcome.

7. *S.* A learning outcome requiring several prerequisite skills.

8. *T.* Of course, maintaining self-discipline may be an important student-oriented objective.

9. *S.* A goal most art teachers hope their students will eventually attain.

10. *S.* A student-oriented objective. The teacher might work through such an evaluation with the students, however, as one activity designed to help them reach this goal.

Your Turn: Recognizing Clear and Unambiguous Objectives

1. *2*
2. *1*
3. *1*
4. *2*
5. *1*
6. *1*
7. *1*
8. *1*
9. *2*
10. *1*
11. *2*
12. *2*
13. *1*
14. *2*

Your Turn: Specifying General Goals—Parts 1 and 2

Part 1

Here are additional general goals for a high school psychology course. Your goals may not be identical to these, but there should be some similarity between these and the ones you have written. If there is not, have your instructor check your work.

1. Students should be aware of their major personality traits, usual learning strategies, the intrinsic and extrinsic motivating factors that influence their decisions and behavior, and the ways in which they respond under social pressure.

2. Students should have an appreciation for the value of psychological research.

3. Students should have an understanding of the importance of specialists in the area of psychology.

4. Students should have an appreciation for the intricacies of personality development.

5. Students should have developed better study habits based on the principles of learning.

6. Students should have a better understanding of why people act the way they do.

7. Students should have developed attitudes of concern and understanding toward the mentally ill.

8. Students should have developed an attitude toward mental illness that is positive.

Part 2

Here are some additional goals for Unit I: Psychology as a Science. Many other goals could be written. They need not be written in observable terms, but they should be compatible with the end-of-course goals that have been specified.

Cognitive Goals

1. Students should know the major founders of psychological theory and the important points in their theories.

2. Students should be able to describe those aspects of psychology that make it a science.

3. Students should be able to list the methodological steps in psychological research.

4. Students should be able to define the major concepts and terms found in psychological science and research.

Affective Goals

1. Students should be able to accept differences that exist among the ideas of famous psychologists.

2. Students should enjoy doing simple psychological research.

3. Students should become interested in finding out more about the specific aspects of human behavior that have been studied by psychologists.

Your Turn: Breaking Down a General Goal into Specific, Observable Objectives

Below are three objectives that could have been derived from the goal you were given. Compare your objectives to these. Do your objectives contain the necessary elements to make them understandable and observable? Also, compare your objectives with those written by your classmates.

1. When given a major concept or term used in psychological research, the student should be able to select from among a number of alternatives the one definition or example that best illustrates that concept or term.

2. When asked to write a short paper explaining the methodologies of psychological research, the student should be able to use correctly ten out of fifteen major concepts that were presented in class lecture.

3. When given a description of a psychological research problem, the student should be able to select from among a number of alternatives the principle(s) that would be most appropriate to the solution of the problem.

MASTERY TEST

Mastery Test, Objective 1

1. (a)
2. (a)
3. (a)
4. (a)
5. (b)
6. (a)
7. (b)
8. (b)
9. (b)
10. (a)
11. (c)
12. (a)
13. (a)
14. (c)
15. (b)

Mastery Test, Objective 2

1. Specify the general goals. Break down the general goals into more specific, observable objectives. Check objectives for clarity and appropriateness.

2. True. When broken down into more specific objectives, the end-of-course goals should be observable; however, the general goals are just a step along the way toward the development of usable, observable objectives.

3. (a) Given a description of a learning task, students should be able to describe the process utilized by the learner to accomplish that task.

   Students should be able to describe the major variables affecting the learning process—tell what makes a learning task easier and what makes it more difficult.

   (b) Given several possible motivators and a description of a particular human behavior, students should be able to select the motivator(s) that would most likely stimulate the behavior.

   Students should be able to list the major motivators of human behavior.

   (c) Students should be able to list at least six benefits of having children from many different backgrounds and cultures in the class.

   Students should be able to explain how having children from different backgrounds and cultures makes the class more interesting.

4. (a) A description of subject-matter content.

   (b) An observable, expected response to that content.

5. (a) The conditions under which the student response is expected to occur.

   (b) The level of performance expected, or level of performance that would be acceptable, as evidence that the objective was met satisfactorily.

Mastery Test, Objective 3

1. (a) Focus your planning

   (b) Plan for effective instructional events

   (c) Plan valid evaluation procedure

2. (b)
3. (a)
4. Because different kinds of learning require different kinds of thinking and/or different learning conditions

5. (c)

Mastery Test, Objective 4

1. (a) As handouts prior to instruction

   (b) To prepare students for instruction

   (c) As a guide throughout instruction

2. (b)
3. (a) Learning outcome

   (b) Learner activities

(c) Teacher activities

(d) Assessment activities

4. (d)

Chapter 3
YOUR TURN EXERCISES

Your Turn: Ted's Concept Maps

In examining Ted's pre and post maps, make note of changes such as the following:

1. Ted's pre map is limited and reflects his lack of experience in thinking about teaching when he began his teacher preparation program.

2. The two most striking features of Ted's post map are his use of questions and the way his questions emphasize relationships among the various aspects of teacher planning he has identified. His questions show that he has learned to think of teacher planning as a series of decisions. His focus on relationships shows he has learned that these decisions are interrelated, not isolated.

3. Ted's map refers to lessons, but the concepts related to teacher planning that he has identified, and the questions he raises, are equally applicable to long-range planning, for example, unit planning or yearly planning.

In comparing your own map to Ted's and to those of your fellow students, you should consider:

1. What terms have I used that others have omitted, and vice versa?

2. In what ways is the structure of my map similar to or different from the maps of others? For example, how many subconcepts have I included? How have I shown relationships among the terms?

Your Turn: Observing Planning in Action

The following teacher comments, in the videos or on the interview transcripts, relate to the six characteristics of teacher planning.

1. Plans are nested.

   Kari Abdal-Khallaq: I think we established from the beginning of the year clear norms in the classroom, clear rituals, clear roles for students, that help students become really clear about their expectations, but also give students the opportunity to own the classroom. . . . (Students learn certain roles to play in groups early in the year, and these are available to use in lessons throughout the year.)

2. Teachers make use of established routines.

   Ellie Goldberg: I like to use a lot of different roles when students are working in groups. Today, I chose the roles that I wanted them to use. I gave them an envelope with four different roles. I used four roles with my students to help them, guide them through their group work. There was a facilitator, a gatekeeper, a clarifier, and a reader. I really find that assigning students roles helps to keep them focused. (Playing roles in a group is an established and familiar routine to students, so little time is required to assign roles in this lesson.)

   Teacher actions: EG refers students to the rubrics posted above the chalkboard to remind them about established group procedures. EG raises hand to get attention and reminds students about group norms regarding noise level when working in groups.

3. Plans are flexible, allow for adjusting to student responses.

   Ellie Goldberg: If I notice that a group is beginning to be distracted or talking about non-math related content, by moving over to sit with that group, it just does a lot . . .

   . . . asking questions to refocus them on the math that they're doing . . . asking "How can I help you? How can I help you get started on this problem? Which problem are you on?" I try to ask questions that will redirect them to the task that they're supposed to be working on.

4. Teacher beliefs influence the options they consider in planning.

   Ellie Goldberg: We tend to do a lot of group work in my classroom so I try to think about the group dynamics, how the students might interact, how they might interact with potential materials; so how they might interact with manipulatives . . . with the technology we may be using that day.

   Teacher actions: EG explains that students will have one minute to play with the manipulatives being distributed before they begin using them for math.

5. Teachers adapt plans to suit needs of diverse learners.

   Ellie Goldberg: . . . as far as accommodations, there are extended time, extended deadlines for individual students . . .

   I think we really have to accommodate more for their skill level and their prior knowledge in the content area.

   . . . maybe students with IEPs do less problems or maybe they're still being asked to master the same content in a slightly different way.

6. Teacher plans can be enhanced by collaboration with colleagues.

   Ellie Goldberg: Kari and I work together regularly. . . . We check in about the lessons . . .

what's going on in class, how can I help you in class support certain students. We'll debrief after class, talk about what we saw in the class, next steps in supporting our students.

Kari Abdal-Khallaq: Ellie and I work in multiple ways together. . . . We do curriculum mapping, we share a lot of lesson plans and ideas for specific lessons, and we debrief lessons constantly and check in about individual kids on a weekly basis, share resources.

Your Turn: Practice Using the Repertoire Grid

Here are some sample activities that could be used as follow-up lessons to the Jigsaw lesson on the ancient Greek Olympic games, in a unit on ancient Greece. These are only suggestions. Other activities could fit in the quadrants of the Repertoire Grid as well.

Quadrant B (Teacher-Directed, Learning "Accepted" Knowledge)

The teacher (T) tells students that many of the Greek Olympic sports have counterparts in modern sports, including horse races, foot races, wrestling, boxing, and the pentathlon. T. then provides some information about other aspects of Greek culture that have carried over to modern Western culture in some form: the Greek alphabet is used to name fraternities and sororities; the Hippocratic oath is used in medical training; senates are used to make laws in many democracies; and many common words in modern vocabularies have roots in Greek words. Following the presentation students choose one of two related exercises to complete individually: practice learning and writing the letters of the Greek alphabet, including writing their own name with Greek letters; or taking a list of common vocabulary words prepared by the teacher, using a dictionary to determine which words in the list have a Greek word as the root, and writing sentences using each of those (Greek-based) vocabulary words.

Quadrant D (Student-Constructed, "Inventing" New Ways of Perceiving)

The teacher (T) asks students what they think about safety for athletes engaging in Greek Olympic sports. Student comments are recorded on the chalkboard or an overhead projector. T. then divides the class into 10 small groups to prepare for a mock Greek senate debate. Each small group is to develop arguments for improving the safety of one of the five Olympic events covered in the Jigsaw lesson (their choice of event) by changing the rules of the event. They are also asked to develop arguments for maintaining the traditional rules in a *different* one of the five Olympic events. Students in each small group practice making brief speeches presenting their arguments. The mock debate will be held the following day.

Quadrant A (Teacher-Directed, "Inventing" New Ways of Perceiving)

The teacher (T) does an Internet search to identify a series of varied facts about ancient Greece. T. lists these in random order on a paper, and provides a copy to each student. (See sample page in Figure 3.1.) Students work in small self-selected groups to categorize the facts, putting together items that they think have characteristics in common. T. explains that there are no right or wrong answers, the facts can be grouped in a variety of ways, and groups can be composed of different numbers of items (2, 3, 8, etc.). Each group of students prepares a chart to display the categories they have formed, listing the items in each, and naming each category based on the common element(s). They report back to the class on their categories and discuss similarities and differences in the ways the student groups have categorized the items. T. asks how/whether the categories they have formed might be useful in guiding their further study of ancient Greece.

Your Turn: Prioritizing Goals

Coding of the fifteen goal statements will vary. The exercise in general could promote accomplishment of personal goals for prospective teachers (enhancing self-awareness). If responses are shared with classmates, some social goals could also be promoted (developing interpersonal relationships and acceptance of human differences).

The goals stated by the Israeli teachers do not use the kind of format presented in Chapter 2. However, statements 1–9, 13, and 14 are all framed as teacher-oriented goal statements, while statements 10, 11, and 15 appear to be more like student-oriented goal statements. Statement 12 is neither, for it states a belief about a common student characteristic, rather than a goal to be attained.

Sample restatements of the teacher-oriented goals as student-oriented goals are listed below. (Note that these are general rather than specific goals, in keeping with the long-term goals stated by the Israeli teachers.)

1. Students will understand the subject matter taught.

2. Students will express themselves in different ways and develop new ways of thinking.

3. Students will exhibit creativity and a desire to learn.

4. Students will demonstrate improved learning skills and independence.

5. Students will show improved achievement.

6. Students will socialize with classmates in a constructive manner.

7. Students will help each other and show that they care about each other.

Random Facts About Ancient Greece

1. Ancient Greeks believed that their gods liked to see strong, fit bodies on men and boys.
2. A vase from ancient Greece shows Achilles and Ajax playing checkers.
3. In ancient Greece a slave could become a free person, and a free person could become a slave.
4. Greek musicians played the lyre, a stringed instrument, and the pipes, a wind instrument.
5. The Greek word for house was *oikos*.
6. Ancient Greek men and boys enjoyed competitive games.
7. Ancient Greeks thought men were rational and stable but women were irrational and dangerous.
8. A vase made in ancient Greece shows a young girl juggling balls in the air.
9. The Greek god Dionysos was associated with drinking wine.
10. Sappho was a Greek woman who wrote short poems around 600 BC.
11. In the late Bronze Age Greek city-states were monarchies, ruled by kings.
12. Greeks used the word *agape* to mean brotherly love.
13. Greece has a lot of coastline and beaches, so many ancient Greeks were good sailors.
14. Ancient Greeks believed in oracles, which were the gods sending messages to people.
15. A Greek named Homer wrote two epic (long) poems called the Iliad and the Odyssey around 700 BC.
16. Ancient Greeks believed that it was wrong to kill and eat a tame, domesticated animal without first sacrificing it to the gods.
17. Greek city-states like Athens, Sparta, Corinth, and Thebes often fought against each other.
18. Ancient Greeks believed that men were more like gods and women were more like animals.
19. Greek houses in the Bronze Age had paintings painted on the walls of the rooms for decoration.
20. *Agon* was the Greek word for competition.
21. Some Greek soldiers were paid to fight for other countries as mercenaries.
22. A Greek structure called a *stoa* was a place where men could meet and talk.
23. In 510 BC the city-state of Athens created the first democratic government.
24. Greek traders sailed on ships, buying things at one port and selling them at another port.
25. Demosthenes was a famous Greek writer of speeches.
26. The Parthenon was a Greek temple to the gods, built in the 440s BC.
27. Shields were an important part of the armor worn by ancient Greek warriors.
28. In ancient Greece, boys went to school and girls stayed at home with their families.
29. Greek men who worked as fishermen sold their fish in markets.
30. A Greek marketplace or public square was called an *agora*.
31. Women, slaves, and children were not allowed to vote in Athens.

(Source: www.historyforkids.org)

■ Figure 3.1

8. Students will listen to the opinions of their classmates and be considerate of different opinions.

9. Students will decide the class norms and rules, and determine what behaviors are inappropriate.

13. Students will express their feelings and indicate the things that bother them.

14. Students will acknowledge their own strengths and be aware of the positive traits of their classmates.

Your Turn: State Standards and the Repertoire Grid

Answers will vary from student to student, depending on the subject area and grade level selected. Use Figure 3.7 in the textbook as a guide for the types of statements that might fit within each quadrant of the Repertoire Grid. It can be helpful for students to compare their answers to one or more of their peers.

Your Turn: Observing Improvisation in Action

Sample instances of teacher improvisation, responding to student questions or suggestions:

Some students say that sand came first, before sandstone. Rob Cho asks all students, whether or not they agree with this idea, to consider, if sand came first, where did it come from. A student suggests using paper to collect the "sand" they might produce by rubbing rocks together. Mr. Cho asks the student to elaborate—why use the paper? He then repeats the idea to the class, reinforcing the student suggestion.

Another student suggests using a bucket to "act like an ocean" and splash water on rocks to see what comes off. Rob Cho asks if the jar could be used as a bucket. When student agrees, Mr. Cho recommends keeping the lid on the jar so water doesn't spill around the classroom.

How teacher's planning processes enable him to improvise:

Rob Cho: [Inquiry learning] can be more intensive in terms of time, in terms of my own mental energy, the preparation needed to get ready for this type of class, and also in terms of materials. . . . I need to have microscopes. I need to have hand lenses. I need to have rocks. I need to have hydrochloric acid. I need to have containers and so on for them to actually do the science. All of that requires preparation beforehand. . . . I need to think long term. (By providing a variety of materials, the teacher enables students to generate a variety of ideas or procedures, so that he can encourage them to test those ideas/procedures, even though he may not know in advance what students will propose.)

How the teacher's beliefs encourage him to improvise:

Rob Cho: I use the Inquiry approach in my classroom to model the way scientists approach science, because . . . it allows the students to actually approach a problem to see and to think like a scientist. . . . Inquiry learning . . . engages the students, it grabs their attention, it addresses different modes of learning for them. . . . It's very tactile. . . . Like today's lesson, they were taking rocks and they were actually holding them, shaking them, rubbing them together. They were also discussing it together. They are problem solving as a group. I'm not spoon-feeding the way to do it. Rather, they're coming up with different ways to approach the problem. And I'm, to the best that I can, I'm letting them run with it.

Your Turn: Explaining Additional Analogies

There are many ideas you could mention in exploring these two analogies. Here are some possible ideas for the analogy, "Teacher planning is like a road map."

Similarities

1. You use a road map to figure out the best way to reach a certain destination, and teacher planning helps to identify the best way to achieve an instructional goal.

2. A road map shows that there is more than one way to arrive at your destination, and teacher planning helps you to consider alternatives before deciding how to proceed.

3. A road map shows points of interest along the way that you may want to stop and see, and teacher planning can identify special materials that may add interest to a lesson or unit.

4. When you have a routine way to get to a familiar place, you don't use a road map, and when you have a routine procedure that you commonly use in a lesson, you don't need to write it down in your plan.

5. There may be detours along a highway because of road repairs, and road maps don't show these detours. Similarly, there may be interruptions in lessons that are not anticipated in lesson plans.

6. Road maps can show a variety of areas, such as a city, state, or region. Teacher planning can address a variety of time periods, such as a lesson, week, or unit.

7. It is hard to read a road map and drive at the same time, and it is not effective to read your lesson plan while you are in the middle of teaching a lesson.

Differences

1. Road maps are prepared by someone else to be used by a motorist, but teachers prepare their own plans.

2. Road maps are printed in a variety of colors, but most teacher plans are written in black and white.

3. A road map is kept in the glove compartment of the car, to be used again and again, but a lesson plan is usually changed or improved before it is used again.

Key Features

1. The road map analogy emphasizes the idea of trying to reach a goal or destination, and this is an important aspect of teacher planning.

2. The road map emphasizes the idea of alternative routes to the same destination, and this is another important aspect of teacher planning.

Here are some possible ideas for the analogy, "Teacher planning is like choreography."

Similarities

1. Choreography provides a design for a sequence of steps to be used in a dance, and teacher planning provides a design for a sequence of activities to be used in a lesson or unit.

2. Choreography uses a variety of different types of movement to make a dance more interesting, and teacher planning uses a variety of types of activities to make a lesson or unit more interesting.

3. Choreography may involve different steps for different dancers, depending on their levels of skill or ability, and teacher planning may result in different tasks for different learners, depending on their levels of skill or ability.

Differences

1. Choreography is a plan to be followed by a group of dancers in order to entertain a separate group, the audience. Teacher planning is focused on instructing the group of learners who will follow the steps in the plan.

2. Choreography often highlights the work of a star, with supportive roles played by the larger group. Teacher planning aims at highlighting the accomplishments of all the members of the class.

3. Choreography is a design for physical activity. Teacher planning is typically a design for mental activity.

Key Features

1. The choreography analogy emphasizes the importance of sequence and variety to create interest, and these are important in teacher planning.

2. The choreography analogy emphasizes the importance of attention to group interaction in designing a dance, and teacher planning needs to consider group interaction to insure successful learning.

MASTERY TEST

1. There are a variety of ways to organize the maxims listed in the mastery test in relation to concepts of importance for instructional planning.

The examples provided here do not exhaust the possibilities, but they do provide some suggestions that can be useful for you in evaluating your own categories and explanations.

Maxims Related to the Content Discussed in the Restated Myths About Planning

Everybody's Doing It—In a Variety of Ways

Engage a student and the student will learn.

The best discipline strategy is an engaging lesson.

[A basic consideration for most teachers is maintaining the interest and involvement of their pupils.]

A Little Goes a Long Way—Especially at the Beginning

Organization is the key to elation.

[Plans made about classroom organization at the beginning of the year have important effects on plans and activities throughout the year.]

A Plan a Day Keeps Disaster Away—For Novice Teachers

If you fail to plan, you plan to fail.

Overplan—Things can blow big!

Prepare or beware.

[Detailed planning of lessons is an essential activity for novice teachers, who are still developing routines and experimenting to see what procedures work best for them.]

Plans Are Not Made to Be Broken—Just Bent

Be wise—Don't be afraid to improvise.

Plan for the unexpected.

[Effective teachers are flexible enough to note pupil reactions and adjust their plans when necessary.]

One Size Fits All—But Not Very Well

Assume the students' mindset.

Don't underestimate your students.

Not knowing your students is preparing for trouble.

[Classroom diversity compels teachers to make adaptations in their plans to accommodate the instructional needs of different students.]

Time Is of the Essence—And Planning Gets Easier with Time

Clock watchers end well.

Pace the race.

[Effective teachers use management procedures that save time, so that teacher and students can concentrate on content to be learned.]

Do Look Back—It Helps in Planning Ahead

You can't win 'em all, but you can keep on trying.

[Rethinking lessons recently taught is an effective aid to teachers who want to improve by learning systematically from their own experience.]

You Can Do It Yourself—With a Little Help from Your Friends

Don't be afraid to look outside yourself.

Students can teach, and teachers can learn.

[Teachers rarely rely solely on their own knowledge and inspiration to design classroom instruction.]

Try It, You May Like It—And You Can Learn from the Process

We Do It Best in the Good Old U.S.—Except When Others Do It Better

[These two restated myths refer primarily to the ways that teachers themselves can derive long-term benefits from particular types of planning and evaluation activities. Prospective teachers who stated the maxims presented in this exercise were more focused on the short-term benefits or problems they experienced during their fieldwork, so their maxims do not easily relate to these two restated myths.]

Maxims Related to the Basic Parts of a Lesson Plan

Goal/Purpose of Instruction

The more you expect, the more they give.

[Teacher expectations for student performance and learning are explicated in a clear goal statement.]

Content to Be Addressed

Try to be wrong once a week.

[This tongue-in-cheek maxim refers to the fact that novice teachers may not be very familiar with the curriculum being taught and thus need to pay particular attention to careful delineation of content.]

Procedures

Don't do anything for students that they can do for themselves.

Learning can be a team effort.

Put limits on chaos, not creativity.

[Alternative beliefs about appropriate or effective instructional activities are revealed most clearly in the Procedures section of a lesson plan.]

Evaluation

Look for written proof of students' knowledge.

Those who know don't always show.

[While many useful means of evaluation exist, systematic evaluation of student learning is a critical aspect of effective teaching and should be planned for in advance.]

Maxims More Related to Classroom Interaction Than to Prior Planning

A little fun never hurt anyone.

Don't stand still or you'll be a pill.

Kind but firm will help them learn.

Make sure students stay on task.

Never let them see you sweat.

Think before you speak.

Wear a poker face.

[Instructional plans are an important beginning, but teachers need many additional skills to carry out their instructional plans effectively.]

2. Responses will vary according to the lesson plans selected. Here are some things to keep in mind as you evaluate your response. The five essential elements of a complete lesson plan are: (1) stated goal or purpose of instruction, (2) central content to be addressed, (3) list of instructional materials required, (4) set of procedures to be followed, and (5) statement of evaluation process to be used. Additional positive features could be specific aspects of any of the five essential elements, for example, a goal statement with related standard of learning or benchmark, instructional materials with web sites as sources for follow-up investigation, or procedures with alternatives for students with differing abilities.

Chapter 4
MASTERY TEST

Mastery Test, Objective 1

1. *General definition:* Should include the idea that a planned beginning is something a teacher does or says to relate the experiences of students to the objectives of the lesson.

   Any three of the following four purposes could be listed: (1) to focus student attention on the lesson, (2) to establish expectations for what is to be learned, (3) to motivate students to become involved in the lesson, and (4) to relate students' prior knowledge to the new material to be learned.

2. You may use any of the situations described in the examples or include situations of your own.

Mastery Test, Objective 2

Of course, responses to any of the five situations will not be the same. If you have carefully read each of the situations, however, each suggests a general direction that you might follow.

Situation 1. A planned beginning to determine how well the students understood the videotape or how they could apply what they learned to some new activity seems appropriate here.

Situation 2. A planned beginning to orient students or focus their attention on the significance of pollution and its effect on the environment would be helpful in this case.

Situation 3. In this instance student attention needs to be focused on the search skills they have already acquired in other areas, for example, a table of contents, dictionary, or encyclopedia.

Situation 4. The planned beginning in this situation should incorporate some kind of evaluation activity so that students are actively engaged in using previously learned information and the teacher has an opportunity to see how much students have learned.

Situation 5. This planned beginning should be transitional so that students have an opportunity to integrate previously learned material with new techniques.

Mastery Test, Objective 3

1. *General definition:* Should include the idea that planned discussion permits open interaction between student and student as well as student and teacher. It is student centered and requires all participants to adhere to guidelines for acceptable discussion behavior.

2. Any three of the following five purposes could be listed: (1) Students acquire new knowledge; (2) students learn to express clearly their own ideas; (3) students learn to evaluate their own thinking and the thinking of others; (4) students learn to reflect on ideas different from their own; (5) students learn to share personal feelings.

3. You may use any of the examples described in Learning Activity 4.6 or include examples of your own.

Mastery Test, Objective 4

Compare your observations with those of other students and prepare a written or oral report on the results of your discussion.

Mastery Test, Objective 5

Of course, responses to this question will not be the same. Your answer should include, however, each of the steps included in the guidelines provided on page 96.

Mastery Test, Objective 6

1. *General definition:* Should include the idea that a planned ending is something a teacher says or does to bring a presentation to an appropriate close.

   Purposes: Your explanation should include the following purposes: (1) To draw attention to the end of a lesson; (2) to help organize student learning; and (3) to consolidate or reinforce major points to be learned.

2. (a) *T.* Whereas the planned beginning initiates instruction, the planned ending terminates it.

(b) *F.* Clocks tell time, but only teachers can close a lesson.

(c) *T.* Appropriate use of the planned ending enables students to evaluate their own understanding of a lesson.

(d) *T.* The planned ending signals the natural conclusion of a presentation sequence.

(e) *T.* One purpose of the planned ending is to recapitulate the important points in a lesson presentation.

(f) *F.* An effective planned ending does not occur naturally but requires conscious control by the teacher.

(g) *T.* An effective planned ending helps provide coherence to learning through review.

(h) *T.* Since the planned ending is part of an ordered sequence of instructional events, it requires careful timing.

(i) *F.* The planned ending terminates a lesson, whereas the planned beginning initiates it.

(j) *T.* The planned ending helps students organize and retain learning through review.

3. You may use any of the situations described in the examples or include situations of your own.

Mastery Test, Objective 7

Of course, responses to any of the five situations will not be the same. If you have carefully read each of the situations, however, each suggests a general direction you might follow.

Situation 1. A planned ending that reviewed the sequence demonstrated in the presentation would seem most appropriate in this lesson.

Situation 2. A planned ending that would give students an opportunity to practice what they have observed seems appropriate in this instance.

Situation 3. A review of the points, ideas, or concepts developed in the discussion would seem to be the most appropriate planned ending at this point in the lesson.

Situation 4. As in the previous situation, a planned ending that reviews what has gone on and relates to the organizing principle introduced at the beginning of class seems most appropriate.

Situation 5. A planned ending in which students can apply what they have learned in the lesson to a new situation seems most appropriate in this instance.

Chapter 5
YOUR TURN EXERCISES

Your Turn: **Characteristics of Effective Questions**

1. *F*
2. *T*

3. *T*. Amazing and true.

4. *T*

5. *F*. Sorry.

6. Purposes for asking questions in class: they provoke thoughts, play crucial role in learning, are intellectually demanding, deepen understanding, promote convergent or divergent thinking, and expand multiple intelligences; in addition, students learn lower- and higher-order content.

    Inappropriate reasons for questioning: habit, to maintain authority, it's not lecturing, students work harder, to cover the subject, to keep students on the edge, it's my job, it gets students involved, it's what was done to me.

Your Turn: **Knowledge**

1. *F*. Knowledge, or memory, requires recall, a lower-level activity.

2. *T*. Unfortunately.

3. *F*. Memory, or knowledge, questions are important. Learners must have mastery of a wide variety of information. Other levels of thought are not possible without such a base.

4. *T*

5. *T*

6. *K*

7. *–*. Unless the student has just learned this material and is remembering it, this is *not* a knowledge-level question. It calls for analysis, a higher-level thought process.

8. *K*

9. *–*. Calls for higher-order thinking.

10. *K*

11. *–*. Calls for a more creative thought process than recall or recognition.

12. *–*. Unless students have been told what will happen if a recession continues, they must use a thought process at a higher level than memory to answer this question.

Your Turn: **Comprehension**

1. *F*. Although the student would use original phrasing, only previously provided information could be used.

2. *T*

3. *T*. That's one reason why comprehension questions are important.

4. *F*. A comprehension question asks students to reorganize information and to phrase it in their own words.

5. *K*. Calls for recall of a fact.

6. *C*. Calls for a comparison.

7. *C*. Asks the student to translate from one medium to another.

8. *K*. Asks for the recall of a fact.

9. *C*. Asks the students to describe something in their own words.

10. *C*. Again, placing information in one's own words is the key.

Your Turn: **Application**

1. *C*. Must interpret in your own words.

2. *Ap*. Learner must apply the skills to solve a problem.

3. *K*. Recall of a name is needed.

4. *Ap*. Must apply information about profit and loss to determine if there will be a profit or loss.

5. *Ap*. To classify the plants, the definitions of the categories must be applied to each case.

6. *C*. Calls for a comparison.

7. *Ap*. To solve the problem, the rules of the definition must be applied.

8. *C*. Rephrasing implies that you use your own words.

9. *K*. Requires recalling previous information.

10. *Ap*. To choose the correct answer, the rules of the definition must be applied.

Your Turn: **Analysis**

1. True

2. (d) Making evaluations belongs at another level of the *Taxonomy*.

3. True. "Why" questions usually require the analysis of data to locate evidence or to determine causes, reasons, or motives.

4. False. Rephrasing information is required when a student answers a comprehension question.

5. True

6. *An*. The student must analyze Hamlet's actions to identify a motivation.

7. *K*. Only memory is required.

8. *C*. Requires rephrasing of a previous discussion.

9. *An*. Evidence to support a statement is sought.

10. *Ap*. Requires applying a definition to Hamlet to determine an answer.

Your Turn: **Synthesis**

1. *K*

2. *K, C,* or *Ap*. Depending on the student response, it could be at any of these levels. Pure repetition would be the knowledge level. Rephrasing the description of the location would place the answer at the comprehension level. Going to a map to point it out would place the response on the application level.

3. *Ap.* Calls for the student to demonstrate or apply the information.

4. *S.* Calls for problem solving, with more than one answer possible.

5. *An.* Calls for evidence to support decision.

6. *S.* Calls for a prediction.

7. *S.* Original communication required.

8. *K.* Memorization of author's comments is required.

9. *C.* Rephrasing and description needed.

10. *Ap.* The student needs to apply rules to solve a problem.

11. (c). Synthesis is a higher-order activity that calls for much more than memorizing.

12. True

Your Turn: Evaluation

1. *K.* Recall required.

2. *C.* Description in one's own words needed.

3. *S.* Original communication required.

4. *E.* Calls for judgment.

5. *Ap.* Calls for classifying the characteristics of one style with regard to another.

6. *An.* Calls for considering evidence and making a generalization.

7. *E.* Calls for a judgment.

Your Turn: Constructing Questions on the Six Levels of Bloom's *Taxonomy*

Here are some questions on the six levels of the *Taxonomy* that you might have asked about the paragraphs. They are *not* the only questions that could have been asked but are simply meant to provide examples.

1. *Knowledge-level questions*

    (a) What action did the three students in Des Moines, Iowa, take that caused their suspension?

    (b) What was the ruling of the Supreme Court on their case?

    (c) What part of the Constitution did the Supreme Court refer to as a basis for its decision?

2. *Comprehension-level questions*

    (a) What is the main idea in this paragraph?

    (b) In your own words, explain why the Supreme Court declared the suspensions illegal.

3. *Application-level questions*

    (a) Considering the ruling in the Des Moines case, what would the legal ruling be on a student who, despite a ban by school authorities, wore a yellow cloth star sewn on her jacket as a protest against the United Nations policy toward Israel?

    (b) Considering the Supreme Court ruling in the Des Moines case, what do you think the legal ruling would be on a group of students who blockaded the entrance to a classroom as a protest against race discrimination?

4. *Analysis-level questions*

    (a) Why did the Supreme Court support the rights of students to express their political and social beliefs during school hours?

    (b) What evidence, other than the specific case described in this paragraph, can you cite to support the conclusion that young people are now gaining long-denied rights?

5. *Synthesis-level questions*

    (a) Develop a short story that portrays a young person seeking to attain a legal right denied to those under 21.

    (b) If children gained the full legal rights enjoyed by adults in America, what implications would it have for family life?

6. *Evaluation-level questions*

    (a) What is your opinion on the issue of minors enjoying the full legal rights of adults?

    (b) If you had been a judge on the Court in the case of the Des Moines students who protested the Vietnam War with black armbands despite a school ban, how would you have ruled?

Your Turn: Questioning Strategies

Note the key points that are included in this section. They should serve as the framework of your analysis.

1. Motives for extending wait time: increase the number of students responding; increase the participation rate of students who typically do not take part in class interaction; increase the length, accuracy, creativity, and quality of student answers; provide the opportunity for adequate consideration of higher-order questions.

2. Reasons for criticism before remediation: it's okay for a student to know an answer is incorrect, especially when it is followed by accurate teacher assistance; criticism need not be sarcastic, threatening, or personal but can encourage students to tune in for remediation; it is a message that they can improve, that you hold high expectations of them, and that they are worthy of correction rather than neutral acceptance.

3. Using multiple intelligences promotes student-initiated questions for the following reasons: students whose talents and interests are in art or music, for example, are more likely to have their curiosities awakened when the teacher works in these nontraditional intellectual areas; variety

in class will also develop and nurture nascent interests in some students, opening up the possibility of still more student-initiated questions; finally, the teacher's openness to new areas and intelligences will contribute to a supportive climate for inquiry and questions.

4. Wait-time summary (here is just one example of a possible, and all-too-common, wait-time summary that students might write): A teacher asked at the end of a lecture, just before we were excused, if anyone had any questions. We had already stacked our books, there was zero wait time, and we all dashed out the door. Sure, there were certainly questions, but no one is going to ask at that point. It was a setup for a quick exit, not thinking.

5. Acceptance as feedback: teachers don't know how often they use acceptance feedback; it doesn't encourage achievement; it's easy and requires little thought; it is inoffensive. Acceptance *can* be valuable when opening up questions and encouraging opinions or dialogue.

6. *S*. We hope your work becomes even better through the reciprocal review. If you and your partner agree, that's a good start.

7. *S*. Limerick. Here goes (hopefully, you'll do better):

There once was a teacher who pondered 'bout questions and answers that wandered, yet when a scaffold was built the form came without guilt, and the students were ever much fonder!

8. *K/C*. (Often a tough line to draw.)

9. *C*

10. *E*

11. *An*

12. *S*. We *did* the poem. You can't expect us to guess what your question might be. Now it's really . . . Your Turn!

Your Turn: Responding to Diversity

Here's one example to get you started.

Room .25

The teacher is drawn to the active learners. The stereotypic behaviors (by gender and ethnicity) are reinforced. The teacher needs to use an instructional strategy to get everyone participating. One idea is to give every student two "response tickets." They must use them up by the end of class. Some students will have to push themselves to turn in even one ticket. Others will have to filter and select the right answer for the right time. This procedure will remind everyone to "share airtime."

These selected points are to guide you as you rewrite the scenarios.

Room 911

Lack of wait time, especially for students with limited English; low expectations for Hispanic females; teacher avoids embarrassing students by avoiding them altogether, which also suggests low expectations.

Room 411

Factual questions work well for some learners, but many others feel it is boring or the teacher is "dumbing down" to them. The teacher, in search of success, gets stuck at the lowest learning levels. The students too often get stuck there as well.

Room 007

An interesting aspect of this scenario is that this is a generally skillful teacher in an effective class climate. Yet even here, a few quieter students with a different cultural background can become invisible.

Room OK

Ho-hum. The minimal interest in student answers suggests that the questions and the content were neither interesting nor challenging. The exceptional praise given the African American student may be an indicator of low expectations or unconscious bias.

Room 5050

The paragraph that follows the scene uncovers the research disparities, from males getting more questions to females getting less wait time. So, what would you do differently?

MASTERY TEST

Mastery Test, Objective 1

Faculty Presentation
Effective Questioning and Examples
A. What we know about questioning

1. Highlight the research on questioning

   Key points: too many questions, no wait time, too many lower-order questions, most questions come from the teacher

2. Identify the traps that trick students

   Key points: control overhelping, put-downs, manipulation, discrediting, "showering"

B. Seven questioning habits that improve teacher effectiveness plus examples

1. Asking fewer questions

   Example:

   (This is where all those unnecessary questions are not being asked.)

2. Asking better questions

   Example: How could we create class rules we will respect?

3. Questioning for depth

Example: Consider how are our class rules are like those in your barrio. Design a set that will work in both places.

4. Questioning for breadth

Example: Create a skit, poster, or poem that incorporates our class rules.

5. Using wait time

Example: Yes, that's right, and what other points might you add? (5-4-3-2-1 . . . seconds of silence)

6. Selecting students

Example: I will wait until at least half of the students have their hands up.

7. Giving useful feedback

Example: Your class rules skit was totally entertaining because you showed what might happen on a day without rules. We now see their benefit!

Mastery Test, Objective 2

1. *C*
2. *E*
3. *K*
4. *C*
5. *S*
6. *E*
7. *S*
8. *An*
9. *K*
10. *E*
11. *An*

Mastery Test, Objective 3

To pass this Mastery Test, you must have constructed twelve questions relating to the given reading selection. There should be two questions on each level of the Taxonomy; at least nine of the twelve questions you develop should be well constructed and should accurately reflect the appropriate taxonomic level.

Obviously a wide variety of questions could be constructed on the given paragraphs. Below are three sample questions for each of the six levels of the Taxonomy.

1. *Knowledge questions*

(a) What are two somewhat contradictory images that man holds of death?

(b) Who alone, among all things that live, realizes the eventual coming of death?

(c) Who was the author who said, "We fear to be we know not what, we know not where"?

2. *Comprehension questions*

(a) In your own words, what did Dryden mean by his sentence "We fear to be we know not what, we know not where"?

(b) People often hold different images of death. Compare two different conceptions of death that people hold.

(c) What is the main idea of the second paragraph?

3. *Application questions*

(a) Considering our previous study of metaphor and simile, which of these two literary devices applies to the statement in the first paragraph: "Death may be an unwelcome, terrifying enemy, a skeleton with an evil grin who clutches an ugly scythe in his bony hand"?

(b) You have previously been given a list of terms and definitions that characterize various psychological states. Which of these terms best applies to people's tendency to push the reality of death and dying out of their minds?

(c) Give an example of a character from one of the novels we have read this semester who clearly exhibits this tendency to deny the reality of death.

4. *Analysis questions*

(a) Why do you think people push the reality of death and dying out of their minds?

(b) The author suggests that people are unable to face the notion of death. What evidence can you find to support this contention?

(c) Considering the information you have in these paragraphs, how do you think the author feels people should react to death?

5. *Synthesis questions*

(a) Write a poem or short story in which the main character must face his or her own death or another's impending death.

(b) What do you predict life would be like if there were no death?

(c) What ideas can you propose to help people become more accepting of their own mortality?

6. *Evaluation questions*

(a) Do you think it would be better for people to ignore death, as many do now, or to be more aware and accepting of death in their daily living patterns?

(b) What do you judge to be the finest literary or artistic expression that has the inevitability of death as its central theme?

(c) In your opinion, is it a good idea for children to read books about death?

Mastery Test, Objective 4

To pass this Mastery Test, you must have designed a scenario that incorporated four effective questioning strategies and labeled them correctly. Since there are many possibilities, here is a sample excerpt.

Scenario

Teacher: Let's do a brief review of lungs for life information so that you're ready for the test next week. What are some of the issues we have studied about the lungs? Take some time to jot down at least four ideas on your organizer sheet. (*Time passes, students write.*)

Who has at least six ideas? Okay, wow, almost everybody. Sarita?

Sarita: Smoking is bad for your lungs.

(Four seconds pass. *WT*)

Teacher: Please be more specific. (*R*)

Sarita: I know this because I have seen photographs of the lungs of smokers. They are terrible to see, black and diseased.

Teacher: Do you remember what we call that disease?

Sarita: Emphysema. I remember from the video.

Teacher: Absolutely correct on the name (*SP*). Now, you all read a brief description and watched the video about emphysema. Who has a question about this disease and how it affects the lungs that will help us to review? (*SIQ*) Take some time to think. (Five seconds pass. *WT*)

Mastery Test, Objective 5

To complete this Mastery Test, you needed to begin by reviewing the scenario that you developed for Mastery Test, Objective 4. Then, you had to intersect some of the information on student diversity with questioning strategies. You had to provide an example of how your questioning would model knowledge, high expectations, and sensitivity to groups and individuals for each strategy. As in other cases, your answer is very individualized, so only a portion of a response is included below.

Classroom description: An urban elementary school with predominantly African American students. I am the music specialist (African American female) who visits once every other week. Most of the students love listening to and singing "their" songs, but many are tentative when I introduce music theory and notation. Today I am having them make the connection between rest notes (pauses), rhythm, and syncopation.

One African American male (Jerod) is very musical but doesn't like talking in class. He'll rap and step with friends all the time, but he takes his academic detachment behaviors into music class. He doesn't like participating and really doesn't like being complimented by teachers. Toward the end of the lesson I had the students marking out measures with very complicated rest notes. They were doing this with counting and movement combined and had to demonstrate for four measures.

Specific praise: Jerod took his beat sequence to the front of the room, counted and moved perfectly, and demonstrated the correct rest notes and time signature. My specific praise? "Jerod, way to go! You got it all and you got it right. Somebody help me here. Given all the parts of today's lesson, what was something he did that was really right? There could be at least four or five separate parts that were correct. Who's got one?" The praise will be specific and positive, and it will reinforce the learning objectives. Hopefully, Jerod will be more accepting of the feedback because it comes from his peers.

Chapter 6
YOUR TURN EXERCISES

Your Turn: Developing a Definition of Differentiation

1. Be sure to include how the situation struck you mentally (for instance, were you confused because you were uncertain of what the content was good for—why you needed to learn it, uncomfortable because the language of the classroom wasn't your primary language and explanations went too fast for you to absorb, restless because you kept hearing explanations of things you already knew how to do, frustrated because you finished tasks early and weren't allowed to work on other things that were interesting to you, or resentful of homework because you had to do what you had already mastered?) and affectively (did you feel rejected by the group because you dressed differently than others in the room, believe the teacher didn't approve of you for some reason, feel torn because many of your peers disapproved of your interest in school?).

2. Be specific about what the adult might have done to modify the learning experience or learning environment to make it work better for you. For example, did he or she do any of the following?

   - Make opportunities for students to ask questions individually

   - Have students work in pairs to summarize ideas and clarify uncertain areas

   - Use hands-on examples or models of student work to illustrate ideas

- Allow students who were still learning English to write in their primary language and then translate their work into English
- Give students tasks that demonstrate how the ideas and skills are used
- Give homework alternatives when students already knew how to do the basic assignment
- Find time to build a relationship with each student
- Help students see one another's strengths

3. Your definition might include references to differentiation as
   - Being actively planned by the teacher (rather than impromptu).
   - Being based on a teacher's assessment of a student's learning needs.
   - Being a teacher's attempt to make sure learning works for each child in the classroom.
   - Involving flexible use of time, materials, human resources, and space to help students learn better.
   - Providing varied activities, products, ways of learning, and support systems for students with varied needs.
   - Being student-centered instruction.
   - Involving multiple ways of teaching and multiple ways of learning.

     If you left some of these elements out, why do they seem less significant to you than the ones you included? What else did you include that you feel must be a part of a good definition, and why do you feel strongly about those elements?

     Another way of analyzing your definition is to see whether it contains references to what changes in a differentiated classroom (versus a nondifferentiated one), how those things change, and why they change.

4. Think about ways in which your view may be changing in regard to the varied needs of students, the teacher's role in addressing those needs, the role of curriculum and instruction in the classroom, and/or the role of the learning environment in helping each learner succeed.

Your Turn: Developing a Rationale for Differentiation

1. Lists generated by teachers who are asked why they and their colleagues do or do not modify or differentiate instruction often include the following items.

Why

Students learn more.

Behavior is better.

Students like school better.

Students develop their strengths.

Fewer students feel frustrated.

Fewer students feel bored.

Students understand and remember better.

The classroom is livelier.

The teacher feels more creative.

Students learn at different rates.

Why Not

It takes time to plan.

Parents might not understand.

There are not enough materials.

There is not enough planning time.

Rooms are too small.

There is too much material to cover.

It wouldn't be fair.

I don't know how.

Colleagues would resent me.

Room would be noisy.

The students can't work independently.

2. Think about ways in which your lists (and the lists of colleagues) are similar to or dissimilar from these lists. Why do you think similarities exist? Dissimilarities? One common pattern in lists such as these is that the majority of reasons for differentiating instruction focus on student needs and benefits, whereas the majority of reasons for not differentiating instruction focus on teacher needs and concerns. What do you make of that pattern? Does it mean teachers put students in second place? Or might it mean something different (for instance, teachers must be comfortable with the ways they teach before they can serve students well)? What implications do you see in your list for yourself as a beginning teacher?

3. Think about what you wrote or said as it relates both to your needs as a developing professional and your students' needs for challenge and success. For example, you may have said you want to help students maintain motivation to learn and will therefore have to discover what motivates different learners. In that case, what will you need to do to understand what motivates your students and to become comfortable using the information you gather?

Your Turn: Examining Classroom Connections in Responsive Teaching

1. In thinking about a graphic representation of how Mrs. Rex links "who we teach," "what we teach," "where we teach," and "how we teach," there are two key considerations. First, her thinking about her students shapes everything else she thinks about. Second, each of the four elements forms a "feedback loop" for all of the other elements. For example, thinking about what the classroom needs to be like (*where* she teaches) so that all students find challenge and success shapes *how* Mrs. Rex teaches at a given point in time. Likewise, thinking about *how* she needs to teach an idea or skill so that each student grows as a result of the lesson helps Mrs. Rex reflect on *what* is truly essential and compelling in her content.

2. In this graphic, it is likely that the four elements either remain distinct from one another and disconnected, or they connect in some way that does not place the student at the apex of thinking. For example, "what we teach" may be at the apex of thinking, and the graphic might suggest the importance of everyone (*who* we teach) covering the same material in the same way (*how* we teach), in an environment that maintains tight control (*where* we teach) to allow for the coverage.

   The important thing in analyzing your graphics for questions 1 and 2 is to be aware of how teacher thinking shifts when planning begins with a focus on student growth and success compared to when that is not central in the teacher's thinking.

3. This answer will vary depending on the beliefs you select. If, for example, you believe that students of a particular age or grade should learn the same content in the same way and over the same time period, that will affect who you teach because you will not feel a need to address their particular learning differences; it will affect where you teach because it will enable you to be comfortable with a more teacher-centered classroom; it will affect what you teach because it will give you permission to use the same materials and goals for everyone without variance; and it will affect how you teach because you will feel comfortable with the same instructional approaches for all learners at a given time. On the other hand, if you believe strongly that students must feel safe and secure in classrooms in order to progress effectively as learners, that will influence who you teach because you will be looking for what each student needs in order to feel safe and secure; it will influence where you teach because you will continually look at students' responses to the learning environment and will make adaptations based on what you see; it will influence what you teach because you will see in the content ways to make connections with varied student interest and affect; and it will have an impact on how you teach because you will be seeking instructional strategies and approaches that maximize success for each learner.

4. Grading in most classrooms assumes that a fundamental role of grades is to "separate the sheep from the goats," or to compare everyone to a norm. In a differentiated classroom, an assumption is that individual growth must be at least one important aspect of grading. Does your response to the question about grading recognize connections between Mrs. Rex's beliefs about students and her likely beliefs about grading? Does your response recognize connections between Mrs. Rex's beliefs about learning environment and her beliefs about grading? Does your response recognize that grades in Mrs. Rex's classroom probably wouldn't continually punish someone for having learning difficulties or reward someone who happens to be more able just for coming to school as they are?

   In thinking about your own beliefs about teaching and grading, did you look for matches between your beliefs about each of the four elements—who you teach, where you teach, what you teach, and how you teach—and your beliefs about grading?

Your Turn: Planning to Differentiate Instruction Based on Learner Need

1. A pre-assessment should ask students to explain and/or demonstrate the knowledge, understandings, and skills that are central to whatever you are pre-assessing. In other words, you have a match between your pre-assessment and a textbook chapter if your pre-assessment contains questions about the most important knowledge, understandings, and skills in the chapter.

2. First, check to make sure your original activity clearly addresses the learning goals you specified for the lesson. In other words, is it highly likely that by completing the task, a learner would accomplish the learning goals?

   When you complete a version of the original learning task for a student who is struggling with the content, be sure you (a) provide support necessary for the student to learn from the task and complete it successfully, (b) develop the task at a level of complexity that seems appropriate for the student, and (c) continue to address the essential learning goals in the task. Among the ways you can make a task more accessible for a struggling learner are making what the student needs very familiar to the student, making the task more structured, reducing the number of steps required, using resources that are simpler to read, or modeling what the student needs to do. For example, if your lesson contained a graphic organizer, you might complete a portion of the organizer on the graphic the student receives. That helps illustrate for the student the kind of information called for. If a student needs to do research, you might provide a template to guide collecting and analyzing information. That additional structure may be more helpful to the student than open-ended direction to gather information and figure out what it means.

When you complete a version of the original learning task for a student who is advanced with the content, be sure you (a) provide a catalyst for extending the student's thought about ideas central to the task and/or application of skills through the task and (b) continue to address the essential learning goals in the task. Among the ways you can make a task more appropriately challenging for an advanced learner are making the ideas and/or applications more complex or abstract, making the task more open-ended, making the application or format less familiar, developing a task that requires more stages of thinking for successful completion, asking students to work toward criteria that are more expert-like, and providing resources that are more advanced.

3. You might want to reflect on how the teacher extended your interest in the subject or topic as well as how he or she changed your image of yourself as a person and/or a learner. Was there any sort of signal from the teacher to let you know the teacher was aware of your talents? Did it require any extra thought or effort on the teacher's part to extend or develop an interest in you? Did you ever see any evidence that the teacher did similar things for other students? Why do you think the teacher did what he or she did to develop or extend your interests?

4. To what degree did your interviewee talk about how he or she felt in school versus what he or she learned there? In what ways was that person's impression of teachers, homework, students, life goals, friendships, grades, and classroom routines similar to or different from yours? At this point in your development as a teacher, in what ways do you think you would have been an effective or less-than-effective teacher for your interviewee? Think about why that might be the case.

5. There are many strategies you could add to the tables in the chapter. Here are just a few.

Adjusting for Readiness: When the Teacher Presents

Having students choral read key passages of print and important directions is a means of supporting struggling students.

Asking students to listen and respond to your presentation in the role of a person who might have a different viewpoint on the topic (for instance, listening to a story you are reading as though the student were a character in the story, or listening to a lecture on the Westward Movement as though the student were a Native American) can extend the thinking of advanced learners about a topic.

Adjusting for Readiness: When the Student Is Worker

Ask students to work in formats that are quite familiar to support students who are having difficulty with the content of a task, and asking students to work in formats that are quite unfamiliar for students who are advanced with the content (for example, writing a story is far more familiar to most students than is writing a letter to the editor).

Requiring students to consult with peers who can push their thinking forward as they complete assigned tasks or products can enable everyone to get useful ideas about how to improve their work.

Adjusting for Interest: When the Teacher Presents

Read selections from famous people who talk about their passions and interests—for example, in a middle school history class, read some of Maya Angelou's thoughts about civil rights; in an art class, read some of John Lennon's thoughts about connections between art and music; in a science class, read Murray Gell-Mann's thoughts about literature or Lewis Thomas's thoughts about music. There are always people noted in one area whose interests link to other areas, and they provide wonderful bridges between the interests of students and a particular subject.

Make analogies as you present: How is working this math problem like building with blocks? How is the evolution of the U.S. Constitution like working in a darkroom? After students begin to see what you're doing, ask them to make analogies between things they are interested in and ideas you are teaching.

Adjusting for Interest: When the Student Is Worker

Have students develop products that compare experts' ways of working and contributions in the field you are teaching and experts' ways of working and contributions they make in fields of particular interest to students.

Provide time for students to generate their own questions about topics they are studying both as a unit begins and as it progresses. Adjust student tasks to address as many of the questions as possible. Also help students cultivate the habit of looking for unanswered questions at the end of a study to help them understand and engage in the ongoing quest for knowledge.

Adjusting for Learning Profile: When the Teacher Presents

Ask students to suggest to you ways they have learned best in past settings, and incorporating those into your modes of presentation.

Help students develop an awareness of your intentional use of varied presentation styles and having them analyze which approaches are working best for them.

Adjusting for Learning Profile: When the Student Is Worker

Have students approach tasks or products in varied ways, keeping a record of how they have worked, analyzing results of the various approaches over time, and generating conclusions about their own work and study preferences.

Challenge students to examine a topic, complete a task, or develop a product in more than one mode. Then have them think about what happened when they learned through two lenses rather than one, as well as which route was most instructive for them.

Your Turn: Examining the Principles of Effective Differentiation

1. Most of the strategies in the three tables would require planning in advance of a lesson. Some, of course, require more planning than others. Among strategies that could be applied "on the spot" with relatively little preplanning (reactive differentiation) might be:

   - Using concrete illustrations of complex or abstract ideas

   - Stopping often during presentations to prompt student reflection and questions

   - Asking questions of escalating difficulty in class discussions

   - Coaching for success

   - Using wait time

   Even these strategies, however, take a certain amount of thought and planning to be effective—especially in the early stages of teaching when nearly all routines require careful thought. For example, it is not nearly as easy as it seems to ask in a coherent sequence a series of questions that begins with fundamental understandings and becomes more and more complex. Be sure to analyze your own additions to the tables to determine whether they would require preplanning.

2. There are multiple ways to see the key principles of differentiation as they relate to the elements of who, where, what, and how we teach. Here are a few ways to think about those connections with three of the principles.

(a) Effective differentiation is more likely to be proactive rather than reactive.

Who we teach: Careful attention to student differences draws to the teacher's attention the fact that on-the-spot differentiation is not likely to be robust enough to address learning gaps, provide meaningful challenge, attend to language needs, address a range of interests, and so on.

Where we teach: The teacher is likely to have to plan consistently for flexible and effective use of space and to help students build a positive learning community.

What we teach: It takes careful examination of standards, text materials, and a teacher's own knowledge of a subject to determine what constitutes the essential knowledge, understanding, and skill necessary for each learner to progress in the subject.

How we teach: The teacher will have to carefully plan tasks that are both differentiated and that ensure that each student has the opportunity and support to develop key knowledge, understanding, and skill.

(b) The teacher continually assesses student understanding and adjusts instructional plans based on what the assessment reveals.

Who we teach: If I value a student, I will use many different resources to find out what that student knows, what he or she is interested in, and what makes learning most effective for that student.

Where we teach: Everyone in the classroom will have to be respectful of student similarities and differences, understand why the teacher takes time to address particular learning needs, and contribute to the routines of a differentiated classroom.

What we teach: Ongoing assessment helps the teacher develop logical sequences of teaching, know when to reteach or extend teaching related to learning goals, and how to make content more interesting to learners.

How we teach: Using tasks and products at differing levels of readiness or focused on differing interests allows more students to learn more effectively and with greater intrinsic motivation.

(c) An effectively differentiated classroom focuses on growth.

Who we teach: Students cannot generally control the readiness levels and background experiences they bring to class. The teacher is most likely to play a role in maximizing student potential by expecting growth of each learner, supporting each learner in growth, and acknowledging growth when it happens.

Where we teach: The teacher cannot make the classroom a safe learning place if it seems punitive when errors are made or when a student cannot reach a norm on a prescriptive timetable. The teacher cannot make it a challenging place if he or she rewards students for "excellence" that is not earned.

What we teach: As a teacher comes to understand what he or she teaches, there is a sequence of ideas and skills through which the teacher needs to guide students in order to assess and support growth.

How we teach: The teacher will need to teach in a variety of ways and help students learn in a variety of ways to support the maximum growth of each individual.

Your Turn: Thinking About Your Own Response to Academic Diversity

1. The actions you state here will need to stem from your particular beliefs. Here are some examples of how that might look.

   Belief: My students will learn at different rates.

   Action: I will have some time in class where students who need to can continue to work on a task and students who finish have important work to move on to.

   Belief: Making errors in a classroom is part of the learning process and students need to feel safe as they learn.

   Action: On very important assignments, I will make sure students get feedback on how to improve their work before the assignments are turned in.

   Belief: Students learn better when the subject matter interests them.

   Action: I will look for ways to raise student curiosity and to show them how the subject is at work in their own lives.

2. There are many things a teacher could do to help Tia, Carlos, and Sam have a more productive school experience. Here are a few thoughts about each of the students.

   Tia: She is more advanced in this subject than many members of the class, and the pace and sophistication level of the content are frustrating to her because she sits and waits for others to learn far more often than she has a chance to grow herself. In addition, the learning environment is not one where she feels free to express questions and ideas because they make her appear not to "fit in" with her peers.

Suggestions

- Provide materials or activities focused on the same learning goals but requiring a more advanced level of thought and understanding.

- Develop with Tia an ongoing product assignment related to the learning goals that she can work on when she has mastered the key information and skills in the unit.

- Provide Tia with complex journal prompts on the topic so she can extend her thinking about the topic as she responds in her journal.

- Make time in class to work with all students (including those who are advanced) in small groups that allow the teacher to push students beyond their current comfort levels with ideas and skills.

- Make sure Tia often works with peers who are also advanced so they can bounce ideas off of one another at an advanced level.

Carlos: This student is clearly overwhelmed by the amount of content, level of content, and pace in the class. This might be the case because he has a learning disability. It could be the case because he is a second-language learner. He may just be missing background knowledge and experiences other students have that enable them to "play the school game" better. He might have an undiagnosed learning problem. Whatever the case, he feels swamped by the class and is discouraged by the repeated sense that he can't keep up.

Suggestions

- Pre-assess student knowledge and skill as a unit begins and plan to use small, teacher-led groups to help students master knowledge and skills needed to close gaps in their thinking.

- Use graphic organizers, including lists of key vocabulary, when students have to take notes in class.

- Help students learn how to determine what the key points are in a lecture and what is illustrative or less important.

- Make sure the teacher completes the organizer on the board or overhead projector as students take notes.

- Use "summary groups" after presentations so students can compare what they heard in a presentation to what peers heard. Then follow up with student questions.

- Be sure students get a chance to use skills and knowledge with which they are comfortable as a vehicle for working toward things that are harder for them.

- If a student does not speak English well, help that student build a support system for translating, reteaching, checking ideas, getting feedback on work, developing a study group, and so on.

- If a student does not speak English well, help peers understand the immense task of learning a new language and a new subject at the same time. Enlist their help in figuring out ways to support the student and to celebrate his or her growth.

Sam: For whatever reason, Sam cannot sit still very well. Maybe he is hyperactive. Maybe he's just a wiggler, or someone who learns best when he's moving rather than sitting and listening. He also seems to need a reason for what he's learning—perhaps to see how the information looks when it's used. He seems to need a classroom that is more tolerant of movement and perhaps more practical than informational in nature.

Suggestions

- Allow students to move around in the classroom as long as they do so without disturbing others.

- Help Sam understand his need to move and help him learn to move around when he's studying and reading in order to boost concentration.

- Shift from one activity to another, or from teacher-talk to student-work, often.

- Use brief peer discussion groups often to ensure ongoing engagement of students and to give everyone a chance to participate actively.

- Consistently include illustrations of the content at work in people's lives.

- Call on Sam to make practical applications of what he's learning and/or give him class and home tasks that call for practical application.

3. These responses will vary greatly depending on what your own goals for early responsive teaching are. It's likely that almost any steps toward responsive teaching would be helpful in some way to Tia, Carlos, and Sam. Check to see if it's the case that each of your goals would, in fact, be of help to all three of the students, compared to a classroom in which a teacher does not have those goals.

MASTERY TEST

1. Use the following information to help you think about your answers to the first two parts of the Mastery Test. There are many ways you could adapt lesson plans and classroom instruction to make the class a good fit for Tia, Carlos, and Sam. The information provides samples of learning needs of the three students and possible teacher responses. Answers to the third part of the Mastery Test will be highly individual.

Tia

Student Needs

- Work at a fast pace

- Greater level of challenge

- Meaningful tasks when assignments are completed

- Opportunity to answer her own questions

- Chance to work with like-readiness peers

- Time with the teacher

- A sense that excellence stems from effort and growth

- Self-efficacy as a learner

- A classroom in which individual differences are valued and in which growth is required, supported, and acknowledged

Sample Teacher Responses to the Needs

- Provide advanced books and other resources on the topic.

- Develop tiered tasks with more complex directions, steps, and requirements.

- Use interest centers, specializations on subtopics, and/or independent studies to allow pursuit of student questions and interests.

- Use flexible grouping that includes similar-readiness groups.

- Ensure that you meet with advanced students to coach for continuing growth.

- Encourage students to develop some of their own criteria for success in tasks and products.

- Provide rubrics with very advanced indicators of success.

- Ensure that individual growth is an important factor in feedback and grading.

- Talk with students about the need for valuing one another's ideas, and model acceptance in your work with students.

- Call on gifted-education resource teachers for suggestions.

Carlos

Student Needs

- Support with writing
- Support with note taking
- Support with understanding and following directions
- Guidance in seeing the "big picture" of ideas in a topic or unit
- Structure and feedback while working in order to promote success
- A chance for extra teaching on a topic or skill
- A sense that excellence stems from effort and growth
- Self-efficacy as a learner
- A classroom in which individual differences are valued and in which growth is required, supported, and acknowledged

Sample Teacher Responses to the Needs

- Use some task options that call for demonstration of understanding with minimal writing.
- Use guided note taking in which you model effective note taking on the board or overhead projector.
- Provide note-taking templates or guides.
- Ensure small-group peer debriefing about ideas in a lecture or presentation as it proceeds.
- Use concept maps or similar organizers to help students see how ideas and information connect and make sense.
- Put directions on a tape recorder.
- Use reteaching sessions or mini-workshops to reach students who need additional instruction.
- Use flexible grouping, including opportunities to work in mixed-readiness groups in which all students have an important contribution to make to the group.
- Use high-interest products or assessments that call on students to use what they have learned in a meaningful way.
- Provide rubrics with clear guidelines for success.
- Provide your own and peer feedback as tasks and products evolve.
- Encourage students to develop some of their own criteria for success in tasks and products.

- Ensure that individual growth is an important factor in feedback and grading.
- Talk with students about the need for valuing one another's ideas, and model acceptance in your work with students.
- Call on special education resource teachers or reading specialists for suggestions.

Sam

Student Needs

- Opportunity to be an active learner
- Hands-on learning
- Frequent breaks in intense work
- Understanding of the relevance of particular knowledge and work
- Practical tasks
- Understanding of his own learning style
- A sense that excellence stems from effort and growth
- Self-efficacy as a learner
- A classroom in which individual differences are valued and in which growth is required, supported, and acknowledged

Sample Teacher Responses to the Needs

- Provide many hands-on learning opportunities.
- Use multiple resources and flexible groups to provide variety.
- Use tasks and options that connect knowledge and skills with people's lives, work, and interests.
- Use interest centers, interest groups, and high-interest tasks.
- Use problem-based tasks, products, and assessments.
- Encourage multiple modes of expressing learning.
- Use concept maps or similar organizers to help students see how ideas and information connect and make sense.
- Help students identify, understand, and respond to their own learning styles.
- Provide rubrics with clear guidelines for success.
- Ensure your own and peer feedback as tasks and products evolve.
- Encourage students to develop some of their own criteria for success in tasks and products.

- Ensure that individual growth is an important factor in feedback and grading.
- Talk with students about the need for valuing one another's approaches to learning, and model acceptance in your work with students.
- Call on special education resource teachers or gifted education resource teachers for suggestions.

2. Sample Responses

(a) Students differ as learners in readiness, interest, and learning profile. Those differences impact how they learn, and if teachers address the differences appropriately, students will learn more effectively.

Learner needs are shaped by experiences in and out of school, opportunities, culture, gender, and individual strengths and weaknesses.

Addressing varied needs of learners requires teachers to believe in the possibilities of each learner; study their students to understand them well enough to teach them effectively; have clearly articulated curriculum goals; use ongoing assessment to understand student progress toward the goals and to shape instruction based on what they learn; and to plan instruction with student readiness, interest, and learning profiles in mind.

Teachers learn to address student needs more and more effectively over time.

I really care about students and I think that caring will serve me well. I want to make my classroom work for them and I am willing to work hard to make that happen.

I don't mind making mistakes and want to learn from them. I think that's important in learning to differentiate instruction because it takes patience and persistence to get good at it.

(b) I think studying my students will come naturally to me because I like to learn about people. I know the teachers who made a difference to me knew me as a person and I want to do that for my students.

I think having clear curriculum goals will be natural for me because I have always been very good with science. I understand how it makes sense and want my students to see its meaning rather than just memorizing information. I am already careful to state learning goals before I plan to check my lessons to make sure they match the goals before I teach them. I also try hard to make sure my students know what the goals of lessons are and to reflect on how comfortable they are with the goals at the end of lessons and units.

I think I will be good with using ongoing assessment to let me know how my students are learning. I can't imagine teaching without finding out who has learned what I taught—and doing something about it when they don't know what they need to know.

(c) I think it will be challenging for me to manage a differentiated classroom. It's hard to be confident about managing any classroom right now, and managing one in which students are doing different things at the same time seems really difficult to me.

I think it will be hard to really get to know my students. I will be teaching in high school and will teach nearly 150 students. I don't see how I can get to know them all. In addition, there is so much curriculum to cover that I don't see how I'd make time in a class period to talk with the students about anything but what they have to learn for the tests at the end of the year.

I think it will be hard to understand how school looks from the perspective of students whose lives are so different from the one I had at their age. I came from a home where we had what we needed. I spoke the language of the school I went to. My parents were understanding and supportive. I knew I was expected to do well in school. These are things not all my students will have and I can't afford to assume they'll look at school like I did.

(d) I know it will take a long time to get really good at knowing how to teach so that it works for each of my students. I'm willing to start slowly and to work at it year after year. I don't expect myself to be perfect in a hurry. I am willing to be in it for the long haul—just like I want my students to stick with learning in our class.

I am willing to watch my students and learn from them. I am willing to ask them what is working for them in my class and what isn't. I'm willing to ask their advice on how to make the classroom a better fit for them.

I want to be an active student myself throughout my career as a teacher. To do that, I want to keep reading and studying about teaching. I hope my school will support me in that, and if they do, I will chose opportunities that help me be a better teacher. If they don't I can learn independently. I want to study from a variety of areas to learn how to teach students who are very advanced, students with learning problems, students from different cultures and races, and students who have problems at home. I know I have a lot to learn in all these areas. I am an eager learner and an eager reader. I want to persist in that for myself. I also want my students to know I am learning like they are.

Chapter 7

Your Turn Questions

Answers to Your Turn questions will vary with the individual.

MASTERY TEST

Mastery Test, Objective 1

Characteristics of Culturally Responsive Teaching

You will have your own interpretation of Gay's taxonomy, however, your answers should address the key components of culturally responsive teaching, which include:

- An affirmation of students' identities.
- A holistic approach to teaching that does not force students to shed aspects of their cultural identities to achieve academic success.
- An understanding of the far-reaching nature of culturally responsive teaching, encompassing what is taught (the curriculum), how it is taught, and the climate and culture of the classroom.
- Utilizing teaching and learning as a vehicle for students to become empowered.
- Allowing students to imagine and realize expanded possibilities for their lives.
- Addressing power relations in the school and in society at large, with special attention on the impact on students who have been traditionally underserved by schools.

Mastery Test, Objective 2

Cultural Identity Box

It may be difficult to recognize and represent all of your personal and cultural identities with this activity, but here are four areas to consider when creating and reflecting on your cultural identity box:

1. *Content:* Did you demonstrate complex thinking about your identities through the creation of your culture boxes? Does your box represent various aspects of your identity? Did you include a diverse array of items to represent yourself? Can you articulate the meaning of the items you included?

2. *Presentation:* Did you put forth sufficient effort in the creation of the box? Is the box reflective of the level of workmanship you would expect from your own students?

3. *Creativity:* Is your box original? Did you utilize or create a box that reflects your identities? Were you creative in selecting or creating items to include inside the box?

4. *Reflection:* How do you make meaning of your identities, particularly in relation to others who may or may not share aspects of your identities?

Mastery Test, Objective 3

Identity Pie

Your reflections should demonstrate a depth of thinking. They should explore what you have learned about yourself through this process as well as what you have learned about others in the classroom. You should address the identities you feel especially proud of and any aspects of your identities for which you have been singled out or treated negatively. Finally, consider discussing the implications of your new or enhanced understandings of yourself—and yourself in relation to others—for their work in the classroom. How might being more self-aware improve your ability to work with students who may be culturally different from yourself?

Mastery Test, Objective 4

Creating a Culturally Responsive Lesson

Your lesson plan should include (but is not limited to) the following:

Rationale

You should provide an insightful rationale to support the main ideas of your lesson. The rationale should also directly reference your attempts to make the lesson culturally responsive.

Objectives

The lesson plan should contain clearly stated, concise objectives that are relevant to the topic(s) you have chosen to address. You should consider utilizing Bloom's *Taxonomy* in the construction of your objectives.

State or District Learning Standards

You should reference the appropriate state learning standard(s) you are attempting to address in your lesson. Make sure to include a brief description of how the learning standard is met by the proposed lesson.

Accommodations

When applicable, you should reference any accommodations that might need to be made to more appropriately address the learning needs of all students in the class.

Procedures

The lesson plan should include an outline of the anticipated progression of the lesson. For example, it may begin with an anticipatory set, move on to the presentation of the new material, and conclude with an experiential activity and discussion.

Assessment

The lesson plan should reference how the teacher is going to assess the extent to which students learned the material.

Materials

Where appropriate, the lesson plan should include a list of and briefly explain the materials you are going to need to make the lesson successful. Any relevant handouts or other materials should be submitted with the lesson plan.

Mastery Test, Objective 5
Cultural Immersion

	Exceptional	Accomplished	Novice	Unsatisfactory
Scholarship Sources / Developing Understanding	Uses a breadth of diverse written sources; explains findings in great depth and with great understanding; uses several nontraditional sources.	Uses several diverse written sources; sufficient explanation of findings and a good understanding; uses a few nontraditional sources.	Uses several written sources; explains findings satisfactorily and with some understanding; uses one, if any, nontraditional sources.	Uses few written sources with little or no diversity; pedestrian explanation of sources with little understanding; no nontraditional sources.
Personal Experience Sources	Outstanding effort to physically immerse into community using many genres (performances, restaurants, radio, TV, Internet, etc.); clear evidence of long-term immersion	Above-average immersion effort, using several genres; evidence of lengthy immersion	Some effort at immersion, with little difference in genre; evidence of a short immersion	Little or no effort at immersion, little diversity of sources; little if any time spent attempting to become immersed
Personal Reflection How does this group preserve its culture in the United States?	Connection of experiences in new culture smoothly and aptly with own culture and general American culture; discusses personal feelings while immersed; makes several in-depth, personal conclusions about cultural differences.	Above-average connection of experiences in the new culture with own culture and American culture; discusses some personal feelings from immersion; makes some personal conclusions about cultural differences.	Adequate connection of experiences in the new culture with own culture and/or American culture; little discussion of personal feelings from immersion; few personal conclusions about cultural differences.	Little or no connection of new experiences with own culture or American culture; little or no discussion of personal feelings from immersion; few, if any, conclusions about cultural differences.

Chapter 8

Your Turn Questions

Answers to Your Turn questions will vary with the individual.

MASTERY TEST

Mastery Test, Objective 1

1. Classroom management is defined as the actions teachers take to create an environment that is respectful, caring, orderly, and productive.

2. The term *discipline* refers to the actions teachers take in response to misbehavior (for instance, the use of a verbal command or a penalty such as the loss of a privilege). Discipline is only one facet of *classroom management*, which is a much broader concept, encompassing strategies designed to both *prevent* and *respond to* problem behaviors. Classroom management is intended to support and facilitate both academic learning and social-emotional learning.

3. *Culturally responsive classroom management* refers to the knowledge, skills, and dispositions

needed to work with students from diverse racial, ethnic, language, and social class backgrounds. Culturally responsive classroom managers recognize that different cultures have different beliefs, values, and assumptions about human behavior. We must bring these cultural biases to a conscious level, reflect on how they affect our interactions with students, and acquire "cultural content knowledge"—an understanding of the values and norms of diverse cultures (including White middle-class culture).

4. White middle-class culture (which is reflected in schools) values individual achievement, independence, competition, and efficiency. In contrast, collectivist cultures emphasize cooperation, harmony, and working for the good of the group. Individuals from collectivist cultures generally avoid displays of individual accomplishment.

Mastery Test, Objective 2

1. AN
2. P
3. AV
4. AV
5. AN and AV
6. AN
7. AV
8. P
9. AV and P
10. AV and P

Your Turn, **page 242**

1. The answers to question 1 will vary with the individual.
2. (a) is the better anecdotal record because it is more objective, detailed, and comprehensive.

Mastery Test, Objective 3

1.

	Direct Effect	Indirect (Symbolic) Effect
a.	Students cannot have face-to-face contact during whole-class discussions; students in the back of the room have difficulty hearing those in the front.	The teacher does not want to have whole-class discussions; the teacher does not value whole-class discussions.
b.	Students will interact. They may socialize and help one another with academic tasks.	The teacher wants students to interact and to collaborate on academic tasks.
c.	Both Spanish-speakers and English-speakers will know where to put things and will learn some terms in the other language.	The teacher values both Spanish and English.
d.	Students will be able to throw things away more easily and will be less prone to throw things on the floor or stuff them in their desks.	The teacher values neatness; the teacher wants students to keep the room clean; the teacher is considerate and doesn't make students walk all the way to the front of the room to throw something away.
e.	It is difficult to sharpen a pencil.	The teacher doesn't want students to sharpen pencils; the pencil sharpener is for the teacher's use.

2. For possible questions you might ask students and/or their families to acquire "cultural content knowledge," see the list of bulleted items in the section "Develop cultural literacy."

3. "This is more than friendly, gentle teasing"; "Put-downs and name-calling can hurt"; "This kind of behavior is unacceptable in this classroom"; "We want this classroom to be a safe, respectful place, where we are careful about others' feelings."

4. Rules are norms for general conduct. Procedures or routines are ways of carrying out specific tasks (like sharpening pencils or lining up).

5. See the list of bulleted items under the headings "Preparing for parent-teacher conferences" and "Conducting the conference."

6. For minor misbehavior, teachers can use nonverbal strategies (such as the "teacher look," gestures, proximity); mild, nondirective verbal strategies

(calling the student's name, incorporating the student's name into instruction, using an I-message); or more directive strategies (including commands).

7. For more serious misbehavior, teachers can use penalties or consequences such as private conferences, withholding a privilege, isolating the student from other students, contacting parents, and assigning detention. If necessary, the teacher can exclude the student from class or refer the student to the office.

8. A traditional punishment seems arbitrary and unrelated to the offense. A logical consequence is related to the misbehavior; the student sees the relationship. If a student writes his name on his desk, a traditional punishment would be making him stay in from recess or staying for detention. A logical consequence would be having the student clean the writing off the desk.

9. Anecdotal records are useful because they (a) allow you to gain insight into a student's behavior patterns; (b) provide a written record that can be shared with others; and (c) provide a written record that you can refer to if you are called on to provide information. Anecdotal records should contain the name of the student; the date and time of the incident; the location of the incident; the names of others who might have been involved or been witnesses; an objective description of the student's behavior; a description of the teacher's responses; the signature of the teacher; the date of the record; and (if the student reads the record) the student's signature.

10. Answers to question 10 will vary with the individual. No answer key is provided.

Chapter 9
YOUR TURN EXERCISES

Your Turn: Forming Learning Teams

Name	Base/Rank	Team*
Ali	73/9	C
Andy	75/8	B
Carol	64/11	A
Danielle	80/6	B
Eddy	97/2	B
Edgar	82/5	A
Jack	46/12	B
Mary	92/3	C
Sarah	99/1	A
Senri	78/7	A
Tammy	90/4	C
Travis	69/10	C
*Answers may vary.		

Your Turn: Student Team Learning

Team A
Great Team $\bar{x} = 12.5$

Team B
Good Team $\bar{x} = 7.5$

Team C
Super Team $\bar{x} = 22.5$

Team D
(No recognition) $\bar{x} = 4$

Team E
Great Team $\bar{x} = 16$
$\bar{x}$ = improvement point average

Your Turn: Jigsaw

Answers will vary. The following are examples:
1. Scattergram, number table, pie chart, bar graph
2. Plot, characters, setting, historical context
3. Flora, fauna, geology, weather
4. Education, transportation, industry, social roles

Your Turn: Academic Controversy

A. Answers will vary.
B. *True/False*
1. *F.* Academic Controversy is designed to familiarize students with the facts of an issue and several points of view about it.
2. *F.* The goal is to integrate all information and relevant values into a new, well-supported synthesis position.
3. *T*
4. *T*
5. *F.* Assignment to pairs and teams in Academic Controversy should produce heterogeneous teams.
6. *F.* The point of developing a strong position is to learn the content of the lesson well.
7. *T*
8. *F.* Individual grades are based on individual achievement.

MASTERY TEST

Mastery Test, Objective 1
1. *F*
2. *T*
3. *T*
4. *F*
5. *F*
6. *F*
7. *T*
8. *F*

Mastery Test, Objective 2

A. *Short answers*

1. (a) Positive interdependence—all for one, one for all

   (b) Accountability at the individual and team levels—team success is predicated on the growth of all members

   (c) Face-to-face promotive interaction—helping each other learn

   (d) Interpersonal and small-group skills—social skills are taught directly and explicitly in the context of the academic task

2. (a) Slavin; primarily academic, detailed team scoring

   (b) Johnsons; equally social and academic, emphasis on teaching social skills

   (c) Kagan; every lesson has elements, some of which are cooperative, that are assembled into a complex event

B. *Scenarios*

1. *CL*
2. *Other*
3. *CL*
4. *Other*
5. *Other*

C. *True/False*

1. *F.* In the first stage of the lesson, the teacher presents information or arranges the presentation of information.
2. *F.* Productive learning teams are made up of members who are a microcosm of the diversity in class.
3. *T*
4. *F.* Academic progress in cooperative learning activities is measured by individual improvement.
5. *T*
6. *F.* Team rewards are usually based on achieving preset standards of progress. For example, teams earn rewards when members improve individual test scores by 1–10 points.

Mastery Test, Objective 3

1. Story Buddies
2. 3 by 3 by 3
3. TPS—it offers more practice opportunities
4. Different strategy—too long a time for demonstration
5. 3 by 3 by 3 or different strategy—too long a time for demonstration

6. Numbered Heads Together
7. Numbered Heads Together
8. TPS
9. 3 by 3 by 3 or TPS

Mastery Test, Objective 4

A. Items 2, 4, 8, and 12 support cooperative learning.

B. Answers will vary. However, only one team should have three white students; only one team should have one female; three teams should have two minority students. Each team should have one of the four highest-scoring and one of the lowest-scoring students. Example: Team A—LaTanya, Melissa, Paul, Victor; Team B—Doris, Frank, George, Sam; Team C—Ann, Nan, Ross, William; Team D—Bud, Charles, Hattie, Joy.

C. The five elements of STAD are: (1) form heterogeneous learning teams, (2) present content, (3) have teams practice, (4) assess individual learning, and (5) recognize team accomplishments. The applications will vary.

D. The six elements of Jigsaw are: (1) form learning teams, (2) form expert teams, (3) develop expertise, (4) share expertise, (5) assess individual achievement, and (6) recognize team accomplishments. The applications will vary.

E. Answers will vary.

F. (1) Pairs develop positions; (2) pairs present positions to each other; (3) pairs compare and contrast positions; (4) pairs reverse sides and teams build new positions; (5) teams present new positions to class.

G. Grades are based on individual performance on assessments of content.

Mastery Test, Objective 5

A. *Students' Social Skills*

1. *Forming*—procedural, use Talking Chips to teach turn-taking; *functioning*—affective routines, restating, paraphrasing, clarifying, use Gambit Chips; *formulating*—mastering lesson content, Pairs Check; *fermenting*—expanding on lesson content, probing, critiquing, challenging.

2. Different cultural groups in any country will have different norms and expectations. Children do not come to school with shared definitions of good manners.

B. *Teacher Types*

1. She should address only individuals or teams during group time.

2. He should let teams take care of their own process questions.

3. She should encourage his team to engage him.

4. Students can and should be talking quietly about their work from time to time; it would deepen their learning.

Mastery Test, Objective 6

1. He should move the desks and let folks know why.

2. He should have a special meeting with Ms. Jones to explain what he is doing and ask for her cooperation. Perhaps he can get her to give him daily feedback on the state of the room when she gets to it or give the class such feedback in the form of stickers she places on the posters of teams that are doing a good job of cleaning up.

3. He should do a quick review of the workshop for the principal and lead teacher. He should ask the principal for specific help with data collection. Verbatim data are useful and easier for an observer than for the teacher to get.

4. He should explain the cooperative learning approach to Mr. Zack, with special attention to the continued reliance on individual performance for individual grades.

5. He should gather and share data on the benefits to gifted students and describe other opportunities Alison has during the day to stretch her thinking.

6. He should routinely rotate roles and teach leadership skills directly. All students should know how to exercise leadership, even if some have greater natural skill and inclination than others.

Mastery Test, Objective 7

1. *F.* They have both shown achievement effects.
2. *T*
3. *F.* They work best if they target their efforts broadly.
4. *T*
5. *T*
6. *F.* They have learned many requisite skills in the classroom.
7. *T.* Cooperative learning is NOT just for kids!

Chapter 10
YOUR TURN EXERCISES

Your Turn: **Selecting an Information-Gathering Instrument**

1. Observation is the best choice because to find out *how* the pupils form their letters, you must watch them forming them.

2. Feelings are best discovered by inquiry. This teacher should ask his students how they feel.

3. Achievement is best measured through testing.

4. Whenever you want a measure of maximum performance of a cognitive skill, test.

5. Observing their performance and perhaps analyzing what she hears—that's the answer to this music teacher's evaluation problem.

6. Observation is best, preferably without the students' knowing that they are being watched.

Your Turn: **Selecting the Type of Item**

1. *Essay:* To explain, the student needs considerable freedom to respond.

2. *Short answer:* No freedom here, just the steps.

3. *Multiple choice:* Selection from among alternatives is being called for.

4. *Essay:* To discuss requires freedom to respond.

5. *Short answer:* This objective calls for just a list, no explanation.

6. *Multiple choice:* This requires choosing among alternatives; or *matching,* with types of malfunctions in one column and the possible causes in another.

7. *Multiple choice:* A musical score followed by several choices representing the correct key and other incorrect keys. This could also be tested with a short answer format: "In which key is the above musical score written?"

Your Turn: **Writing Essay Items**

1. *An open-ended question:* This question should allow the student a great deal of freedom to respond, but it should be quite clear about what is being asked. You can see from the following samples that open-ended questions can be difficult to grade because each student may choose to restrict his or her own answer in a different way.

   Sample Questions
   (a) Discuss ways you might reduce your anxiety when preparing to make an extemporaneous speech.
   (b) What could you do to reduce the number of germs on medical instruments if you have no sterilization equipment?
   (c) Discuss the pros and cons of draft registration.
   (d) Convince me that it is important to understand the history of the English language.

2. *A restricted essay question:* Again, make certain that your question has been clearly written. Check to see that your question limits the answers in a way that will help the student to respond (the student will know how to answer *if* he or she knows the information being asked for).

Sample Questions

(a) In no more than ten lines, describe a typical Eskimo village from the early 1900s.

(b) List and explain each of the steps we discussed for setting up an experiment.

(c) Cite five reasons for having a 55-mph speed limit. Defend one of your reasons with supporting evidence.

Your Turn: Constructing a Model Answer

Check your model answer against the criteria for model answers. Compare your model answers with those of your peers. If you are uncertain about your answers, ask your instructor to check them.

Your Turn: Evaluating and Writing Multiple-Choice Questions

Check your items against the criteria for effective multiple-choice items. In addition, exchange your items with a classmate and evaluate each other's items.

Your Turn: Types of Judgments

1. b.
2. c.
3. *A*
4. *A*
5. *C*
6. *B*

MASTERY TEST

Mastery Test, Objective 1

1. Evaluation is the process of obtaining information and forming judgments to be used in decision making.

2. (a) *Preparing for assessment.* In this stage, you need to determine the judgments and decisions you anticipate making (for example, when to begin Unit 2, what assignments to give, where to place Johnny). Next, you must decide what information you will need to make those judgments and decisions (for example, how quickly the students are moving through Unit 1, what the students' interests are, how well Johnny reads). Finally, you will decide when and how to obtain the information needed (for example, weekly, through quizzes; first week of class, using an interest inventory; second week of class, using a standardized test of reading and observing students during oral reading).

(b) *Obtaining needed information.* Involves asking students (inquiry), observing students (watching students setting up an experiment), or testing students (giving a multiple-choice test of history facts).

(c) *Forming judgments.* In this stage, you compare the information with some referent and make a value judgment. Grades reflecting achievement and predictions about how well a student might be expected to do are both common examples of classroom judgments.

(d) *Using judgments in decisions and preparing reports.* Deciding what action to take (for example, move Johnny to a slower reading group) and reporting the evaluation results that led to that decision compose the major tasks of the final stage of assessment. Note that the emphasis is on the *use* of judgments.

Mastery Test, Objective 2

1. d.
2. a.
3. c.
4. b.
5. a.
6. d.

Mastery Test, Objective 3

Evaluate your test against these criteria:

1. The test clearly measures the objectives.
2. The items are clear and concise (unambiguous).
3. The type of items used represents the most direct way to measure the objectives.
4. The readability of the items is appropriate for the grade level you selected.
5. Any necessary instructions to the students are clearly stated.

Mastery Test, Objective 4

1. *Developing checklists:* Your checklist should be clear, concise, and easy to use. If possible, try using it. Ask someone who is an expert at the performance to check your list to see if you have included only the important behaviors.

2. *Constructing rating scales:* Check your scale against the criteria for an effective rating scale. Share your scale with classmates, and ask them if they feel that they would be able to use it successfully.

Mastery Test, Objective 5

1. A portfolio is a carefully selected collection of students' work.

2. Portfolios can be used to assess type and quantity of errors, type of thinking or problem-solving strategies, and the ability of students to catch and fix their own mistakes.

3. *F*

4. *F*

Mastery Test, Objective 6

1. a.

2. *A*

3. *B*

4. *A*

5. *C*

6. b.

7. c.

8. d.

Mastery Test, Objective 7

1. The answer should include at least: to adjust our teaching as needed, to catch misconceptions early, to determine more effective learning strategies.

2. What they do and how they think during the learning process?

Mastery Test, Objective 8

1. Validity. If a test does not measure what you need measured, it is not valid for your use. It is of no use to you, even if it is extremely reliable.

2. (a) Will it give me the information I need?

   (b) Will the information be reasonably reliable?

   (c) Is the test easy to administer, score, and interpret?

   (d) Is the cost within our budget?

3. b.

4. a.

5. To follow exactly the instructions for administering the test.

6. The teacher should try to clarify and help students understand what is being asked of them but should do nothing that would give away the answer.

Mastery Test, Objective 9

1. The main role of technology is to make assessment easier, more secure, and possibly more efficient.

2. Is there a simpler, easier way to assess students? What are the costs involved (in time and money)? What are the privacy/security risks involved? Will lack of understanding of the technology contribute to measurement error?

INTASC Model Standards for Beginning Teacher Licensing and Development

● **Principle 1** The teacher understands the central concepts, tools of inquiry, and structures of the discipline(s) he or she teaches and can create learning experiences that make these aspects of subject matter meaningful for students.

Knowledge

The teacher understands major concepts, assumptions, debates, processes of inquiry, and ways of knowing that are central to the discipline(s) s/he teaches.

The teacher understands how students' conceptual frameworks and their misconceptions for an area of knowledge can influence their learning.

The teacher can relate his/her disciplinary knowledge to other subject areas.

Dispositions

The teacher realizes that subject matter knowledge is not a fixed body of facts but is complex and ever-evolving. S/he seeks to keep abreast of new ideas and understandings in the field.

The teacher appreciates multiple perspectives and conveys to learners how knowledge is developed from the vantage point of the knower.

The teacher has enthusiasm for the discipline(s) s/he teaches and sees connections to everyday life.

The teacher is committed to continuous learning and engages in professional discourse about subject matter knowledge and children's learning of the discipline.

Performances

The teacher effectively uses multiple representations and explanations of disciplinary concepts that capture key ideas and link them to students' prior understandings.

The teacher can represent and use differing viewpoints, theories, "ways of knowing," and methods of inquiry in his/her teaching of subject matter concepts.

The teacher can evaluate teaching resources and curriculum materials for their comprehensiveness, accuracy, and usefulness for representing particular ideas and concepts.

The teacher engages students in generating knowledge and testing hypotheses according to the methods of inquiry and standards of evidence used in the discipline.

The teacher develops and uses curricula that encourage students to see, question, and interpret ideas from diverse perspectives.

The teacher can create interdisciplinary learning experiences that allow students to integrate knowledge, skills, and methods of inquiry from several subject areas.

● **Principle 2** The teacher understands how children learn and develop, and can provide learning opportunities that support their intellectual, social, and personal development.

Knowledge

The teacher understands how learning occurs—how students construct knowledge, acquire skills, and develop habits of mind—and knows how to use instructional strategies that promote student learning.

The teacher understands that students' physical, social, emotional, moral, and cognitive development influence learning and knows how to address these factors when making instructional decisions.

The teacher is aware of expected developmental progressions and ranges of individual variation within each domain (physical, social, emotional, moral, and cognitive), can identify levels of readiness in learning, and understands how development in any one domain may affect performance in others.

Dispositions

The teacher appreciates individual variation within each area of development, shows respect for the diverse talents of all learners, and is committed to help them develop self-confidence and competence.

The teacher is disposed to use students' strengths as a basis for growth, and their errors as an opportunity for learning.

Performances

The teacher assesses individual and group performance in order to design instruction that meets learners' current needs in each domain (cognitive, social, emotional, moral, and physical) and that leads to the next level of development.

The teacher stimulates student reflection on prior knowledge and links new ideas to already familiar ideas, making connections to students' experiences, providing opportunities for active engagement, manipulation, and testing of ideas and materials, and encouraging students to assume responsibility for shaping their learning tasks.

The teacher accesses students' thinking and experiences as a basis for instructional activities by, for example, encouraging discussion, listening and responding to group interaction, and eliciting samples of student thinking orally and in writing.

● **Principle 3** The teacher understands how students differ in their approaches to learning and creates instructional opportunities that are adapted to diverse learners.

Knowledge

The teacher understands and can identify differences in approaches to learning and performance, including different learning styles, multiple intelligences, and performance modes, and can design instruction that helps use students' strengths as the basis for growth.

The teacher knows about areas of exceptionality in learning—including learning disabilities, visual and perceptual difficulties, and special physical or mental challenges.

The teacher knows about the process of second language acquisition and about strategies to support the learning of students whose first language is not English.

The teacher understands how students' learning is influenced by individual experiences, talents, and prior learning, as well as language, culture, family, and community values.

The teacher has a well-grounded framework for understanding cultural and community diversity and knows how to learn about and incorporate students' experiences, cultures, and community resources into instruction.

Dispositions

The teacher believes that all children can learn at high levels and persists in helping all children achieve success.

The teacher appreciates and values human diversity, shows respect for students' varied talents and perspectives, and is committed to the pursuit of "individually configured excellence."

The teacher respects students as individuals with differing personal and family backgrounds and various skills, talents, and interests.

The teacher is sensitive to community and cultural norms.

The teacher makes students feel valued for their potential as people, and helps them learn to value each other.

Performances

The teacher identifies and designs instruction appropriate to students' stages of development, learning styles, strengths, and needs.

The teacher uses teaching approaches that are sensitive to the multiple experiences of learners and that address different learning and performance modes.

The teacher makes appropriate provisions (in terms of time and circumstances for work, tasks assigned, communication, and response modes) for individual students who have particular learning differences or needs.

The teacher can identify when and how to access appropriate services or resources to meet exceptional learning needs.

The teacher seeks to understand students' families, cultures, and communities, and uses this information as a basis for connecting instruction to students' experiences (e.g. drawing explicit connections between subject matter and community matters, making assignments that can be related to students' experiences and cultures).

The teacher brings multiple perspectives to the discussion of subject matter, including attention to students' personal, family, and community experiences and cultural norms.

The teacher creates a learning community in which individual differences are respected.

● **Principle 4** The teacher understands and uses a variety of instructional strategies to encourage students' development of critical thinking, problem solving, and performance skills.

Knowledge

The teacher understands the cognitive processes associated with various kinds of learning (e.g. critical and creative thinking, problem structuring and problem solving, invention, memorization and recall) and how these processes can be stimulated.

The teacher understands principles and techniques, along with advantages and limitations, associated with various instructional strategies (e.g. cooperative learning, direct instruction, discovery learning, whole group discussion, independent study, interdisciplinary instruction).

The teacher knows how to enhance learning through the use of a wide variety of materials as well as human and technological resources (e.g. computers, audiovisual technologies, videotapes and discs, local experts, primary documents and artifacts, texts, reference books, literature, and other print resources).

Dispositions

The teacher values the development of students' critical thinking, independent problem solving, and performance capabilities.

The teacher values flexibility and reciprocity in the teaching process as necessary for adapting instruction to student responses, ideas, and needs.

Performances

The teacher carefully evaluates how to achieve learning goals, choosing alternative teaching strategies and materials to achieve different instructional purposes and to meet student needs (e.g. developmental stages, prior knowledge, learning styles, and interests).

The teacher uses multiple teaching and learning strategies to engage students in active learning opportunities that promote the development of critical thinking, problem solving, and performance capabilities and that help students assume responsibility for identifying and using learning resources.

The teacher constantly monitors and adjusts strategies in response to learner feedback.

The teacher varies his or her role in the instructional process (e.g. instructor, facilitator, coach, audience) in relation to the content and purposes of instruction and the needs of students.

The teacher develops a variety of clear, accurate presentations and representations of concepts, using alternative explanations to assist students' understanding and presenting diverse perspectives to encourage critical thinking.

● **Principle 5** The teacher uses an understanding of individual and group motivation and behavior to create a learning environment that encourages positive social interaction, active engagement in learning, and self-motivation.

Knowledge

The teacher can use knowledge about human motivation and behavior drawn from the foundational sciences of psychology, anthropology, and sociology to develop strategies for organizing and supporting individual and group work.

The teacher understands how social groups function and influence people, and how people influence groups.

The teacher knows how to help people work productively and cooperatively with each other in complex social settings.

The teacher understands the principles of effective classroom management and can use a range of strategies to promote positive relationships, cooperation, and purposeful learning in the classroom.

The teacher recognizes factors and situations that are likely to promote or diminish intrinsic motivation, and knows how to help students become self-motivated.

Dispositions

The teacher takes responsibility for establishing a positive climate in the classroom and participates in maintaining such a climate in the school as a whole.

The teacher understands how participation supports commitment, and is committed to the expression and use of democratic values in the classroom.

The teacher values the role of students in promoting each other's learning and recognizes the importance of peer relationships in establishing a climate of learning.

The teacher recognizes the value of intrinsic motivation to students' life-long growth and learning.

The teacher is committed to the continuous development of individual students' abilities and considers how different motivational strategies are likely to encourage this development for each student.

Performances

The teacher creates a smoothly functioning learning community in which students assume responsibility for themselves and one another, participate in decision making, work collaboratively and independently, and engage in purposeful learning activities.

The teacher engages students in individual and cooperative learning activities that help them develop the motivation to achieve, by, for example, relating lessons to students' personal interests, allowing students to have choices in their learning, and leading students to ask questions and pursue problems that are meaningful to them.

The teacher organizes, allocates, and manages the resources of time, space, activities, and attention to provide active and equitable engagement of students in productive tasks.

The teacher maximizes the amount of class time spent in learning by creating expectations and processes for communication and behavior along with a physical setting conducive to classroom goals.

The teacher helps the group to develop shared values and expectations for student interactions, academic discussions, and individual and group responsibility that create a positive classroom climate of openness, mutual respect, support, and inquiry.

The teacher analyzes the classroom environment and makes decisions and adjustments to enhance social relationships, student motivation and engagement, and productive work.

The teacher organizes, prepares students for, and monitors independent and group work that allows for full and varied participation of all individuals.

● **Principle 6** The teacher uses knowledge of effective verbal, nonverbal, and media communication techniques to foster active inquiry, collaboration, and supportive interaction in the classroom.

Knowledge

The teacher understands communication theory, language development, and the role of language in learning.

The teacher understands how cultural and gender differences can affect communication in the classroom.

The teacher recognizes the importance of nonverbal as well as verbal communication.

The teacher knows about and can use effective verbal, nonverbal, and media communication techniques.

Dispositions

The teacher recognizes the power of language for fostering self-expression, identity development, and learning.

The teacher values many ways in which people seek to communicate and encourages many modes of communication in the classroom.

The teacher is a thoughtful and responsive listener.

The teacher appreciates the cultural dimensions of communication, responds appropriately, and seeks to foster culturally sensitive communication by and among all students in the class.

Performances

The teacher models effective communication strategies in conveying ideas and information and in asking questions (e.g. monitoring the effects of messages; restating ideas and drawing connections; using visual, aural, and kinesthetic cues; being sensitive to nonverbal cues given and received).

The teacher supports and expands learner expression in speaking, writing, and other media.

The teacher knows how to ask questions and stimulate discussion in different ways for particular purposes, for example, probing for learner understanding, helping students articulate their ideas and thinking processes, promoting risk taking and problem solving, facilitating factual recall, encouraging convergent and divergent thinking, stimulating curiosity, helping students to question.

The teacher communicates in ways that demonstrate a sensitivity to cultural and gender differences (e.g. appropriate use of eye contact, interpretation of body language and verbal statements, acknowledgment of and responsiveness to different modes of communication and participation).

The teacher knows how to use a variety of media communication tools, including audiovisual aids and computers, to enrich learning opportunities.

● **Principle 7**   The teacher plans instruction based upon knowledge of subject matter, students, the community, and curriculum goals.

Knowledge

The teacher understands learning theory, subject matter, curriculum development, and student development and knows how to use this knowledge in planning instruction to meet curriculum goals.

The teacher knows how to take contextual considerations (instructional materials, individual student interests, needs, and aptitudes, and community resources) into account in planning instruction that creates an effective bridge between curriculum goals and students' experiences.

The teacher knows when and how to adjust plans based on student responses and other contingencies.

Dispositions

The teacher values both long-term and short-term planning.

The teacher believes that plans must always be open to adjustment and revision based on student needs and changing circumstances.

The teacher values planning as a collegial activity.

Performances

As an individual and a member of a team, the teacher selects and creates learning experiences that are appropriate for curriculum goals, relevant to learners, and based upon principles of effective instruction (e.g. that activate students' prior knowledge, anticipate preconceptions, encourage exploration and problem-solving, and build new skills on those previously acquired).

The teacher plans for learning opportunities that recognize and address variation in learning styles and performance modes.

The teacher creates lessons and activities that operate at multiple levels to meet the developmental and individual needs of diverse learners and help each progress.

The teacher creates short-range and long-term plans that are linked to student needs and performance, and adapts the plans to ensure and capitalize on student progress and motivation.

The teacher responds to unanticipated sources of input, evaluates plans in relation to short- and long-range goals, and systematically adjusts plans to meet student needs and enhance learning.

● **Principle 8**   The teacher understands and uses formal and informal assessment strategies to evaluate and ensure the continuous intellectual, social, and physical development of the learner.

Knowledge

The teacher understands the characteristics, uses, advantages, and limitations of different types of assessments (e.g. criterion-referenced and norm-referenced instruments, traditional standardized and performance-based tests, observation systems, and assessments of student work) for evaluating how students learn, what they know and are able to do, and what kinds of experiences will support their further growth and development.

The teacher knows how to select, construct, and use assessment strategies and instruments appropriate to the learning outcomes being evaluated and to other diagnostic purposes.

The teacher understands measurement theory and assessment-related issues, such as validity, reliability, bias, and scoring concerns.

Dispositions

The teacher values ongoing assessment as essential to the instructional process and recognizes that many different assessment strategies, accurately and systematically used, are necessary for monitoring and promoting student learning.

The teacher is committed to using assessment to identify student strengths and promote student growth rather than to deny students access to learning opportunities.

Performances

The teacher appropriately uses a variety of formal and informal assessment techniques (e.g. observation, portfolios of student work, teacher-made tests, performance tasks, projects, student self-assessments, peer assessment, and standardized tests) to enhance her or his knowledge of learners, evaluate students' progress and performances, and modify teaching and learning strategies.

The teacher solicits and uses information about students' experiences, learning behavior, needs, and progress from parents, other colleagues, and the students themselves.

The teacher uses assessment strategies to involve learners in self-assessment activities, to help them become aware of their strengths and needs, and to encourage them to set personal goals for learning.

The teacher evaluates the effect of class activities on both individuals and the class as a whole, collecting information through observation of classroom interactions, questioning, and analysis of student work.

The teacher monitors his or her own teaching strategies and behavior in relation to student success, modifying plans and instructional approaches accordingly.

The teacher maintains useful records of student work and performance and can communicate student progress knowledgeably and responsibly, based on appropriate indicators, to students, parents, and other colleagues.

● **Principle 9** The teacher is a reflective practitioner who continually evaluates the effects of his/her choices and actions on others (students, parents, and other professionals in the learning community) and who actively seeks out opportunities to grow professionally.

Knowledge

The teacher understands methods of inquiry that provide him/her with a variety of self-assessment and problem-solving strategies for reflecting on his/her practice, its influences on students' growth and learning, and the complex interactions between them.

The teacher is aware of major areas of research on teaching and of resources available for professional learning (e.g. professional literature, colleagues, professional associations, professional development activities).

Dispositions

The teacher values critical thinking and self-directed learning as habits of mind.

The teacher is committed to reflection, assessment, and learning as an ongoing process.

The teacher is willing to give and receive help.

The teacher is committed to seeking out, developing, and continually refining practices that address the individual needs of students.

The teacher recognizes his/her professional responsibility for engaging in and supporting appropriate professional practices for self and colleagues.

Performances

The teacher uses classroom observation, information about students, and research as sources for evaluating the outcomes of teaching and learning and as a basis for experimenting with, reflecting on, and revising practice.

The teacher seeks out professional literature, colleagues, and other resources to support his/her own development as a learner and a teacher.

The teacher draws upon professional colleagues within the school and other professional arenas as supports for reflection, problem-solving, and new ideas, actively sharing experiences and seeking and giving feedback.

● **Principle 10** The teacher fosters relationships with school colleagues, parents, and agencies in the larger community to support students' learning and well-being.

Knowledge

The teacher understands schools as organizations within the larger community context and understands the operations of the relevant aspects of the system(s) within which s/he works.

The teacher understands how factors in the students' environment outside of school (e.g. family circumstances, community environments, health and economic conditions) may influence students' life and learning.

The teacher understands and implements laws related to students' rights and teacher responsibilities (e.g. for equal education, appropriate education for handicapped students, confidentiality, privacy, appropriate treatment of students, reporting in situations related to possible child abuse).

Dispositions

The teacher values and appreciates the importance of all aspects of a child's experience.

The teacher is concerned about all aspects of a child's well-being (cognitive, emotional, social, and physical), and is alert to signs of difficulties.

The teacher is willing to consult with other adults regarding the education and well-being of his/her students.

The teacher respects the privacy of students and confidentiality of information.

The teacher is willing to work with other professionals to improve the overall learning environment for students.

Performances

The teacher participates in collegial activities designed to make the entire school a productive learning environment.

The teacher makes links with the learners' other environments on behalf of students, by consulting with parents, counselors, teachers of other classes and activities within the schools, and professionals in other community agencies.

The teacher can identify and use community resources to foster student learning.

The teacher establishes respectful and productive relationships with parents and guardians from diverse home and community situations, and seeks to develop cooperative partnerships in support of student learning and well-being.

The teacher talks with and listens to the student, is sensitive and responsive to clues of distress, investigates situations, and seeks outside help as needed and appropriate to remedy problems.

The teacher acts as an advocate for students.

Source: Interstate New Teacher Assessment and Support Consortium. (1992). *Model Standards for Beginning Teacher Licensing and Development: A Resource for State Dialogue.* Washington, D.C.: Council of Chief State School Officers. Reprinted with the permission of Interstate New Teacher Assessment and Support Consortium.

Glossary

Academic Controversy. A cooperative learning strategy in which pairs of partners on four-person teams each develop the case for opposite sides of an issue, present their cases to each other, trade sides and present the opponents' case, develop together a position that synthesizes the information presented by both sides, and present the synthesis position as a team to the class.

Achievement Gaps. A term referring to discrepancies between the academic performances of students of color and their White counterparts, most commonly measured by standardized testing.

Active listening. A process in which one person listens carefully to another and then reflects or "feeds back" the message in his/her own words.

Activity rewards. Allowing students to engage in desired activities (such as being first in line or having five minutes of free time) as a positive consequence for appropriate behavior.

Advance organizers. A means of informing students of the way new information that they are about to learn is organized.

Affective goals. Goals that deal primarily with emotion and feeling.

African Americans. Term used to refer to people of African heritage living in the United States; some individuals may prefer the term *Black*, which is more inclusive of people of African descent from around the world, such as Jamaicans, Haitians, and so on.

African American Vernacular English (AAVE). A form of English with a distinctive structure and special lexicon reflecting African origins, commonly used by African Americans and Black Americans in the United States; sometimes referred to as *Ebonics*.

Analysis questions. Questions that require the student to break down a communication into its constituent parts, such that the relative hierarchy of ideas is made clear and/or the relations between the ideas expressed are made explicit.

Application questions. Questions requiring the student to apply a rule or process to a problem to determine the correct answer.

Assessment. Used interchangeably with *evaluation*, the term *assessment* is being used to expand our thinking to include practical and more authentic evaluation procedures and informal as well as formal evaluation tools.

Assimilation. The process by which an individual or group adopts the attitudes, customs, and values of another group or population.

Attitude. A predisposition to act in a positive or negative way toward persons, ideas, or events.

Attraction. Friendship patterns in the classroom group.

Authentic assessment. Assessment that seeks to assess tasks that most directly measure learning outcomes.

Authentic questions. Questions that are motivational and meaningful because they connect with real-life student curiosity, interests, needs, and experiences.

Authoritative teachers. Teachers who are strong leaders, but who are also caring and respectful. Authoritative teachers make developmentally appropriate demands on students, but are also responsive to students' needs and interests; they are high in demandingness as well as in responsiveness to students' needs and desires.

Authoritarian teachers. Teachers who establish and maintain order through the use of controlling strategies (including force, pressure, competition, punishment, and the threat of punishment); they are high in demandingness but low in responsiveness to students' needs and desires.

Base score. A percentage score calculated for each student by averaging scores of three recent tests of equal weight to show the student's relative achievement standing in a class and to serve as the point of comparison with later test scores. Base scores are designed to provide a relatively stable indicator of a student's typical performance in a content area.

Behavior modification. A set of strategies based on the principle that changes in behavior are the result of external events rather than thinking or knowledge. Behaviorists assume that the frequency of a particular behavior is contingent or dependent on the nature of the consequence that follows the behavior.

Checklist. A list of criteria for evaluating a performance or end product.

Chicano/Chicana. A term popular that grew out of the Brown Power movement of the 1960s and 1970s referring to individuals in the United States of Mexican origin; meant to emphasize the culture and realities of urban Mexican Americans.

Classroom management. The actions teachers take to create an environment that is respectful, caring, orderly, and productive. Classroom management supports and facilitates academic learning as well as social-emotional learning (i.e., the development of social skills and self-regulation).

Closure. Ending actions and statements by the teacher designed to help students organize their thinking around the major points of a presentation or discussion.

Cohesiveness. The collective feeling that the class members have about the classroom group; the sum of the individual members' feelings about the group.

Comprehension questions. Questions requiring the student to select, organize, and mentally arrange the materials pertinent to answering the question.

Concept mapping. A way of organizing and graphically displaying ideas relevant to a given topic so that relationships among the ideas are clarified.

Concurrent validity. An estimate of how well a test approximates a score on another test that was designed to measure the same variables.

Conditioned reinforcers. Reinforcers that are learned.

Constructivist theorist. An educator who believes that learners acquire meaning or knowledge by interacting directly with their environment.

Content knowledge. Concepts, facts, and propositions that make up much of the content of the disciplines.

Content validity. A judgment about how well the items in a test measure what the test has been designed to measure.

Contingency contract. A written agreement negotiated between the teacher and a misbehaving student, specifying the positive behaviors the student will exhibit and the rewards that will be earned.

Convergent thinking. Thinking that occurs when the task or question is so structured that several people will arrive at similar conclusions or answers, and the number of possible appropriate conclusions is limited (usually to one conclusion).

Cooperative learning. An instructional task design that engages students actively in achieving a lesson objective through their own efforts and the efforts of the members of their small, heterogeneous learning team.

Criterion-referenced judgments. Judgments made by comparing the information you have about an individual with some performance criterion; that is, some description of expected behavior.

Critical pedagogy. An instructional practice based on critical theory that examines the relationships among knowledge, authority, and power. Critical pedagogy involves the construction of particular relations between teachers and students, institutions and society, and classrooms and communities.

Cue. A verbal or nonverbal prompt given by a teacher to remind a student to behave in a certain way.

Cultural literacy. Knowledge about the core characteristics of a culture (including its values, beliefs, rules of etiquette, and communication patterns).

Culturally responsive classroom management. The knowledge, skills, and dispositions to work effectively with students from diverse cultural backgrounds.

Culturally responsive teaching. A term describing an approach to teaching and learning that builds on the cultural knowledge, prior experiences, frames of reference, and performance styles of ethnically diverse students to make learning encounters more relevant and effective for them.

Culture. The values, traditions, worldview, and social and political relationships created, shared, and transformed by a group of people bound together by a common history, geographic location, language, social class, age group, religion, or other shared identity; these manifestations are both tangible and intangible and are constantly in flux or dynamic.

Deficit perspectives. Deficit perspectives and theories claim that low-achieving students and dropouts inherently lack the attributes needed for school success. Deficit views propose a causal relationship between characteristics such as language, culture, and socioeconomic standing and low academic achievement.

Desist behaviors. Behaviors the teacher uses in an effort to stop student misbehavior.

Differentiated instruction. Varied approaches to what students need to learn, how they will learn it, and/or how they can express what they have learned, intended to increase the likelihood that each student will learn as much and as efficiently as possible.

Differentiating questions. Teacher questions that respond to and build on student differences, including skill levels, learning styles, and individual interests.

Directives. Telling students directly what they are supposed to be doing.

Discipline. The actions teachers take in response to problem behavior. Discipline is one component of classroom management.

Divergent thinking. Thinking that occurs when the task or question is so open that several people will arrive at different conclusions or answers, and the number of possible appropriate conclusions is fairly large.

Domain. A field of study, for example, physics or mathematics.

Effective teacher. One who is able to bring about intended learning outcomes.

Ethnicity. A socially-constructed term that refers to membership in a particular cultural group (see *culture*); defined by shared cultural practices, not citizenship to a particular country. For example, citizens of the United States are of many different ethnic backgrounds.

Evaluation. The process of obtaining information and using it to form judgments that, in turn, are to be used in decision making.

Evaluation questions. Questions requiring students to use criteria or standards to form judgments about the value of the topic or phenomena being considered.

Expectations. Those perceptions that the teacher and the students hold regarding their relationships to one another.

Expert group. In the cooperative learning strategy Jigsaw, a small group of students whose task is to learn very well certain parts of a complex lesson, in order to effectively coach the members of the (home) learning team.

Extinction. Withholding of an anticipated reward in an instance where that behavior was previously rewarded; results in the decreased frequency of the previously rewarded behavior.

Feedback. Information about the effects or consequences of actions taken.

Funds of knowledge. A term referring to an alternative to the deficit perspective model that recognizes the rich resources and prior knowledge that people and communities of color hold, which may be harnessed for effective classroom teaching and home-school relationships.

Generalization. A broad and potentially useful observation about racial, ethnic, class, and gender groups. Such statements are flexible, responsive to individual differences, and can assist teachers in planning for instruction.

Goals. General statements of purpose.

Group-focus behaviors. Those behaviors teachers use to maintain a focus on the group, rather than on an individual student, during individual recitations.

Heterogeneous learning teams. In cooperative learning, working groups made up of four or five students whose differences in entering achievement levels, gender, and ethnicity reflect the variety in the whole class.

"I" message. A nondirective verbal response to problem behavior in which the teacher describes the student's behavior, the effect of that behavior, and how the teacher feels about that effect.

Improvement scores. In cooperative learning, team scores are calculated by comparing the entering achievement levels (see *base score*) with the test scores of each individual. Differences of a given amount translate into improvement points and are added to create a team improvement score according to a predetermined formula. Improvement scores are the basis of team rewards.

Individual accountability. In cooperative learning, the design of outcome measures to assure that the achievement of each student is measured independently and that individual achievement provides the basis for earning team rewards.

INTASC. An acronym standing for "Interstate New Teachers Assessment and Support Consortium." INTASC, a project of the Council of Chief State School Officers, is developing both general and subject-specific teaching standards for beginning teachers.

Inquiry. Obtaining information by asking.

Inquiry-based learning. An approach to teaching and learning in which students deepen their understanding of the underlying principles of a domain by conducting investigations. These investigations typically include asking questions, making predictions, gathering evidence, and constructing explanations.

Instructional event. Any activity or set of activities in which students are engaged (with or without the teacher) for the purpose of learning.

Instructional grouping. Dividing a class of pupils into small subunits for purposes of teaching. Groups can be formed according to achievement, learning profiles, or interest, depending on instructional purpose.

Instructional objectives. Statements of desired changes in student's thoughts, actions, or feelings that a particular course or educational program should bring about.

Interdisciplinary teaching. Integrating the subject matter from two or more disciplines, such as English and history, often using themes such as inventions, discoveries, or health as overlays to the study of different subjects.

Interval schedule. A type of intermittent reinforcement in which the teacher reinforces the student after a specified period of time.

Jigsaw. A cooperative learning strategy in which students participate first in expert groups, where they learn about a particular aspect of a subject, and then return to learning teams (each having one or more experts of each kind), where the experts in turn teach teammates, who eventually share the knowledge mastered by each expert group.

Judgment. Estimate of present conditions or prediction of future conditions. Involves comparing information to some referent.

Just-in-time learning. A problem-based approach to teaching and learning in which knowledge is acquired just as it is needed to solve a problem.

Knowledge questions. Questions requiring the student to recognize or recall information.

Latinos/Latinas. Term used to refer to people of Latin American and Caribbean Spanish-speaking heritage, for example, Mexicans, Puerto Ricans, Cubans, Dominicans, Central Americans, and so forth; also referred to as *Hispanics*.

Leadership. Those behaviors that help the group move toward the accomplishment of its objectives.

Learning situation. Any classroom activity in which students are actively engaged in learning.

Learning Together. The general term for cooperative learning activities of a certain type, developed and advocated by David and Roger Johnson, with a joint emphasis on academic learning and group-process skills.

Logical consequences. Consequences that have a logical, understandable relationship to the misbehavior, rather than being arbitrary or generic punishments.

Measurement error. The error that occurs when any measurement is made. Theoretically, it is the difference between the "true" score and any given obtained score.

Metacognition. An awareness of and control over one's own thinking and problem-solving processes, for example, knowing what one knows and what still needs to be learned or discovered.

Movement management.   Those behaviors that the teacher uses to initiate, sustain, or terminate a classroom activity.

Multiple intelligences.   Distinct forms of human talent that have biological roots and are valued in one or more cultures, identified by Howard Gardner; among those currently identified are linguistic, mathematical-logical, bodily-kinesthetic, musical, spatial, interpersonal, intrapersonal, and naturalistic.

Negative reinforcement.   The withholding or withdrawal of punishment; the withholding or withdrawal of a negative consequence.

No-lose problem solving.   A method of conflict resolution proposed by Thomas Gordon, consisting of six steps: defining the problem, brainstorming possible solutions, evaluating alternatives, selecting a solution, deciding how to implement the solution, and evaluating the solution.

Nondirective verbal strategies.   A mild response to a problem behavior that prompts the student to behave appropriately, but does not specify exactly what the student should be doing (such as just saying the student's name).

Nonverbal disciplinary strategies.   Unobtrusive ways of responding to student misbehavior without speaking, such as the use of facial expressions, gestures, and proximity to convey "I am aware of your behavior, and I don't approve."

Norm-referenced judgments.   Judgments made by comparing the information you have about an individual with information you have about a group of similar individuals.

Norms.   Shared expectations of how group members should think, feel, and behave.

Numbered Heads Together.   A gamelike cooperative learning strategy in which four- or five-student teams first make sure all members know the answer to a question and then earn points if their randomly selected teammate can respond correctly.

Observation.   The process of looking and listening, noticing the important elements of a performance or a product.

On-task behavior.   Student behavior that is appropriate to the task.

Overlapping behaviors.   Those behaviors by which the teacher indicates that he or she is attending to more than one issue when there is more than one issue to deal with at a particular time.

Pedagogical content knowledge.   The blending of content and pedagogy into an understanding of how particular topics, problems, or issues are organized, represented, and adapted to the diverse interests and abilities of learners and presented for instruction.

Peer teaching.   A procedure that provides teachers an opportunity to practice new instructional techniques in a simplified setting by teaching lessons to small groups of their peers (other prospective or experienced teachers).

Permissive teachers.   Teachers who encourage students' freedom, interfere as little as possible, and provide a great deal of affection and warmth; permissive teachers are high in responsiveness but low in demandingness.

People of color/youth of color.   Term used to describe those of minority groups, such as American Indians, Latinos/as, African Americans, and Asian Americans. This term is preferred because it is more accurate and helps to illustrate important connections and common experiences between groups.

Per-pupil expenditure.   Total expenditures for a school or district, with some exceptions (facilities costs, for instance) divided by total student enrollment.

Personal practical knowledge.   The understanding that teachers have of the practical circumstances in which they work, which include the beliefs, insights, and habits that enable them to do their jobs in schools.

Planned discussion.   A discussion that permits open interaction between student and student as well as between teacher and student.

Portfolio.   A collection of work assembled over time to demonstrate the meeting of a learning standard or the acquisition of a skill. Portfolios can be developed by both students and teachers.

Positive reinforcement.   The introduction of a positive consequence (a reward) after a behavior, thereby increasing the frequency of the rewarded behavior.

Predictive validity.   An estimate of how well a test predicts scores on some future test or performance.

Primary reinforcers.   Reinforcers that are unlearned and necessary to sustain life.

Probing (delving) questions.   Questions following a response that require the respondent to provide more support, be clearer or more accurate, or offer greater specificity or originality.

Problem solving.   A way to organize and interrelate existing knowledge as well as to acquire new information. It combines knowledge already acquired and adds new elements, such as facts, concepts, and generalizations.

Professional development.   The process of acquiring specialized knowledge and skills, as well as an awareness of the alternative actions that might be appropriate in particular situations.

Punishment.   The introduction of an undesirable, aversive consequence to eliminate an undesired behavior.

Questionnaire.   A list of written questions that can be read and responded to by the student or other respondent.

Rating scales.   Instruments that provide a scale of values describing someone or something being evaluated.

Ratio schedule.   A type of intermittent reinforcement in which the teacher reinforces the student after the behavior has occurred a certain number of times.

Reality Therapy.   An approach developed by William Glasser, consisting of an eight-step, one-to-one counseling process to help students change problematic behavior.

Referent. That to which you compare the information you have about an individual to form a judgment.

Reflection. The process by which teachers inquire into their own teaching and think critically about their work.

Reflective decision maker. A model of the teacher that emphasizes the use of reflection as teachers make planning, implementation, and evaluation decisions.

Reinforcement. The process of using reinforcers; in general, any event that increases the strength of a response. A reward for the purpose of maintaining an already acquired behavior is called *positive reinforcement*. Strengthening a behavior through the removal of an unpleasant stimulus is called *negative reinforcement*.

Relevance. The perception by students of whether instruction meets their personal needs or goals.

Reliability. A characteristic of a test that measures its consistency. Several kinds of reliability exist, including *internal consistency* (estimates how consistently the test measures from item to item); *test-retest* (estimates how consistently a test measures from one time to the next); and *alternative form* (estimates how closely two forms of the same test measure the same thing).

Repertoire. A set of alternative routines or procedures, all of which serve some common, general purpose and each of which serves some additional, unique purpose. A person who has a repertoire of procedures available is recognized as being practiced and skillful in use of these procedures, as well as sensitive in selecting the appropriate procedure to use in any given situation.

Routines. Norms specifying how students are to carry out typical daily activities like sharpening pencils or handing in homework. Also called *procedures*.

Rubric. A set of rules for scoring student products or student performance. Typically takes the form of a checklist or a rating scale.

Rules. Norms for general conduct, describing how students are to behave at all times (such as "be respectful").

Scaffolding (scaffolds). Instructional assistance—through questions, explanations, and activities—that bridges the gap between what a student knows and what a student needs to learn.

Self-monitoring. A strategy in which students record some aspect of their behavior (such as calling out) in order to modify that behavior. Self-monitoring increases awareness through self-observation.

Self-referenced judgments. Judgments made by comparing information you have about an individual to some other information you have about that same individual.

Set. Actions and statements by the teacher that are designed to relate the experiences of the students to the objectives of the lesson.

Shaping. A behavioral strategy used to encourage the development of new behaviors. Each time the student performs a behavior that is one step closer to the desired behavior, the teacher provides a positive consequence.

Social rewards. A positive consequence such as a pat on the back, a thumbs-up, or verbal praise.

Standardized test. A test that has a fixed set of questions that must be administered according to a specified set of directions and within time limitations.

Stereotype. A broad and potentially damaging conception about racial, ethnic, class, and gender groups. Such statements are inflexible, ignore individual differences, and can create an obstacle for effective instruction.

Structural Approach. Kagan's framework for cooperative learning, in which complex lessons are assembled from one or more elements, some of which involve cooperative learning activities that address team building, class building, mastery, thinking skills, information sharing, and communication skills.

Student-initiated questions. An often neglected aspect of an effective questioning strategy that emphasizes the importance of students, as well as the teacher, asking productive questions.

Student Team Learning. The general term for cooperative learning activities modeled according to the guidelines established by Robert Slavin and associates at Johns Hopkins University. See also *Student Teams Achievement Divisions*.

Student Teams Achievement Divisions (STAD). A cooperative learning strategy in which teacher presentation is followed by team practice and individual testing, with individual improvement scores contributing to team scores and rewards.

Synthesis questions. Questions requiring the student to put together elements and parts to form a whole. These include producing original communications, making predictions, and solving problems for which a variety of answers are possible.

Tangible rewards. A positive consequence that is material, such as popcorn or an award certificate.

Taxonomy. A classification system; used here in reference to a classification system of educational objectives or skills.

Teaching skill. A distinct set of identifiable behaviors needed to perform teaching functions.

Team packet. In cooperative learning, an envelope, box, or file used to expedite distribution and collection of lesson materials.

Team rewards. In cooperative learning, four- or five-member learning teams win certificates and other forms of public recognition on the basis of individual improvement scores.

Teamwork skills. Group-process skills having particular value in cooperative learning activities; they include forming skills that make routines flow smoothly, functioning skills that build group cohesion and participation, formulating skills that promote solid mastery, and fermenting skills that nurture critical thinking.

Test. An instrument that presents a common situation to which all students respond, a common set of instructions, and a common set of rules for scoring the students' responses. Used primarily for determining aptitude and achievement.

Token economy system. A managerial system based on the principles of behavioral learning, in which the teacher describes the positive student behaviors that will be reinforced; awards tokens to students for exhibiting those behaviors; and allows students to exchange tokens they have earned for prizes or rewards.

Theoretical knowledge. A body of scientifically derived educational concepts that help teachers interpret the complex reality of their classrooms.

Think–Pair–Share (TPS). A cooperative learning strategy in which preformed pairs of students discuss questions or complete short assignments together in the course of a lesson at the direction of the teacher or on an ad hoc basis.

3 by 3 by 3. A cooperative learning strategy in which students break at points in a lesson to process information and develop questions in groups of three.

Tiered lessons. An approach to having all students work with essentially the same key information, ideas, and skills, but at different levels of difficulty or sophistication in order to be a match for each student's particular readiness level.

Time out. The removal of a student from a rewarding situation.

Unit plan. A plan for a sequence of several lessons dealing with the same general topic.

Validity. The extent to which the results of an evaluation procedure serve the particular uses for which they are intended. There are several kinds of validity, including content validity, predictive validity, and concurrent validity.

Wait time. The amount of time the teacher waits after asking a question before calling for the answer.

Withitness behaviors. Behaviors by which the teacher communicates to students that he or she knows what is going on.

Youth Participatory Action Research (YPAR). Youth Participatory Action Research (YPAR) is a form of action research that provides young people with opportunities to study social problems affecting their lives, and then determine actions to rectify these problems.

Zero-noise signal. In cooperative learning, an action that communicates a need for silence and immediate attention, to permit the teacher to provide additional whole-group directions during a team activity.

Index

Heritage University Library
3240 Fort Road
Toppenish, WA 98948